An Introduction to Payment Systems

An Introduction to Payment Systems

Lary Lawrence
Harriet L. Bradley Professor of Contract Law
Loyola Law School, Los Angeles

ASPEN LAW & BUSINESS
A Division of Aspen Publishers, Inc.

To the three loves of my life, my wife, Konjit, and my daughters, Deleyla and Simone.

I would like to express my gratitude to the following persons without whose help this book would not have been possible: my research assistants Kelly Dunlap, Christopher Petit, Jay Bettinger, Natalie Ryan, and David Brown; my secretary Denai Burbank; and our research librarian, Lawrence Liebert.

Summary of Contents

Table of Contents

CHAPTER 2

Holder-in-Due-Course Status: Right of Purchaser to Take Free of Claims and Defenses to Instrument

53

Table of Contents

CHAPTER 4

Forgery, Alteration, and Other Fraudulent Activity   225

CHAPTER 5

The Bank Collection Process   **301**

CHAPTER 6

Payor Bank/Customer Relationship 373

CHAPTER 7

WHOLESALE FUNDS TRANSFERS 405

CHAPTER 8

Consumer Electronic Fund Transfers   **469**

CHAPTER 9

LENDER CREDIT CARDS — 513

Table of Contents

To the Student

This book was written to show students that the law of payment systems does not have to be difficult. It is intended to be used alongside a payment systems casebook and UCC code book and can be used for class preparation, study, and/or examination review. It can be read in its entirety to get an overview of the course or can be used as needed to understand particular terms, concepts, or rules.

My aim has been to write neither a highly detailed treatise nor a "bare bones" account of course topics. Rather, I have written an accessible book that will help the student learn the subject of payment systems *and* understand why the law is as it is. For this reason, I emphasize the legal rules governing payment systems and the policy and practical rationales that underpin the rules.

To aid understanding, I have presented various negotiable instruments in familiar settings and emphasize how ubiquitous they are in everyday life. I have also defined unfamiliar terms and used many examples, diagrams, and facsimiles of actual instruments.

I hope you will find this book a help as you study the law of payment systems.

Lary Lawrence

November 1996

An Introduction to Payment Systems

Introduction to Payment Systems

Whether you realize it or not, you are already intimately familiar with the highly technical world of payment systems. You have written checks. You have used a credit card. You have probably transferred funds electronically. You have most likely withdrawn funds from an ATM (Automated Teller Machine), made payment at a supermarket through a point of sale terminal, and may have had your paycheck automatically deposited in your bank account. No problem, right?

Right. In the vast majority of cases, problems do not arise. Yet, when they do arise, whether in a consumer or business setting, the law of payment systems comes into play. This is a somewhat difficult but highly important field, touching virtually every aspect of personal and business transactions. For example, when Federated Department Stores (Bloomingdale's parent corporation) purchased Bullock's Department Stores, Federated had to pay for the acquired company. When Bloomingdale's purchased property in Beverly Hills to build a new department store, Bloomingdale's had to find a way to pay for the land. When U.S. Steel later sold steel to the contractor who constructed the new Bloomingdale's store, the contractor had to pay for the steel. When a consumer purchased a coat from Bloomingdale's, she had to choose among various ways of paying for it.

Suppose that something goes wrong with one of these transactions. What happens if the funds wired by Federated—supposedly to the account of the seller—are by accident wired to the account of a third person who subsequently withdraws the funds? Who suffers the loss—Federated, the seller, Federated's bank, or the seller's bank? What if the bank that issued the cashier's check that Bloomingdale's used to pay for the property goes insolvent; does Bloomingdale's suffer the loss or does the seller? What happens if the steel shipped by U.S. Steel does not meet the contract specifications; does the contractor's bank that accepted the draft drawn by the contractor to pay for the steel have to pay the draft? Or can the consumer refuse to pay her MasterCard bill if the new coat proves to be defective? Each of these questions can be answered only by understanding the law of payment systems.

COVERAGE OF BOOK

This book covers the three types of payment systems that do not include the use of cash, that is, negotiable instruments, electronic funds transfers, and credit cards. We will examine all types of negotiable instruments, not just those functioning as a means of payment. For example, although promissory notes are primarily a means of promising to repay a debt rather than a means of payment, they are covered here. The basic law governing negotiable instruments is contained in Articles 3 and 4 of the Uniform Commercial Code (the "Code"). There is also a substantial amount of federal law that affects the rules found in the Code. In fact, the bank collection aspects of Article 4 have been largely preempted by Congress' enactment of the Expedited Funds Availability Act ("EFAA")[1] and by the Federal Reserve Board's promulgation of Regulation CC[2] and Regulation J.[3] This book covers Articles 3 and 4 as well as the EFAA and Regulations CC and J.

The basic law governing consumer electronic funds transfers is found in the Electronic Funds Transfer Act (EFTA)[4] and in Regulation E, which implements EFTA and clarifies some of its provisions.[5] The law governing commercial electronic funds transfers is, for the most part, contained in Article 4A of the Code. This book covers the EFTA, Regulation E, and Article 4A.

The law regulating credit card transactions is not as developed as the law of negotiable instruments or the law governing electronic funds transactions. However, many of the issues arising in consumer credit card transactions are covered by the federal Truth in Lending Act and its accompanying Regulation Z.[6] Some of the Truth in Lending Act's rules also apply to business credit

---

1. 12 U.S.C. §4001 et seq., U.C.C. § 4-102, Official Comment 1.

2. 12 C.F.R. Pt. 229. Specifically, the check return collection aspects of Article 4 have been substantially preempted by Regulation CC. The forward collection aspects of Article 4 are, to a far lesser degree, preempted by Regulation CC.

3. 12 C.F.R. § 210(b).

4. 15 U.S.C. §1693 et seq.

5. 12 C.F.R. Pt. 205.

6. 15 U.S.C. §§1602, 1603; 12 C.F.R. Pt. 226.

cards.[7] We will cover the important provisions of the Truth in Lending Act as well as those of Regulation Z.

OVERVIEW OF TYPES OF PAYMENT SYSTEMS

Let us get an overview of the different types of payment systems. A payment system is a means of satisfying obligations. A modern economy could not exist without some sort of payment system. Otherwise, how would you purchase food, pay your rent, or buy a new car?

The four basic types of payment systems currently in use are cash, negotiable instruments, electronic funds transfers, and credit cards. Let us examine each of these payment systems in the context of a simple purchase transaction in which you go to Radio Shack to buy a clock radio. Obviously, you have to pay for the clock radio in some fashion.

To make matters simple, you could just hand the cashier the purchase price in cash. To be on the safe side, the cashier may examine the cash to make sure that it is not counterfeit. Assuming that none of the cash is counterfeit, the transaction is complete. You own the clock radio and Radio Shack has the money.

However, for any number of reasons that we will explore in this book, you may not want to pay in cash. As a second method of payment, you might choose to pay by a check drawn upon your account with Bank of America. A check is a type of negotiable instrument. In Chapter 1 we will discuss the numerous types and uses of negotiable instruments. As we will see, some instruments like checks are primarily means of payment. Other negotiable instruments, like notes and certificates of deposits, are primarily ways of promising to repay an extension of credit.

You may wonder what happens after you have filled in the check and handed it to the cashier. In simple terms, you have made a demand upon Bank of America to pay Radio Shack the specified amount of money. Radio Shack will deposit the check in its bank account at Wells Bank. Wells Bank will then send the check to Bank of America. Bank of America will pay Wells Bank the funds represented by the check. Bank of America will, at the same time, debit your account for the amount of the check. This entire process, from the writing of your check to Radio Shack's receipt of the funds, may take several days or, in some cases, weeks depending on how quickly Radio Shack deposits your

---

7. 15 U.S.C. §1645.

check and the method by which Wells Bank sends the check to Bank of America.

Third, rather than paying by check, you might purchase the clock radio by using an electronic funds transfer. During the past two decades, great advances in computer and electronic communication systems have spawned electronic funds transfers—a far faster and simpler means of transferring funds than the use of checks. There are many ways in which funds can be transferred electronically. Electronic funds transfers range from multimillion dollar computer transfers of funds between corporations to a $20 withdrawal of cash at an automated teller machine. We will examine the range of these transactions in Chapters 7 and 8.

If you were going to use an electronic funds transfer to pay for your purchase at Radio Shack, you would probably use a point of sale ("POS") terminal. By using a POS terminal, you can electronically initiate a transaction by which your bank account is immediately debited for the amount of the purchase and Radio Shack's bank account is immediately credited in the same amount. To initiate a POS transaction, you pass your debit card through the POS terminal. The terminal reads the information on your bank and your bank account number contained on the debit card. You enter your personal identification number ("PIN"), which enables the computer to verify whether you are the person who has the right to use the debit card. You then enter the amount of the purchase. Assuming that the POS system is an on-line system, the debit goes through an Automated Clearing House, which immediately debits your bank account at Bank of America and credits Radio Shack's account at Wells Bank. The transaction is now complete. The funds have been transferred from your bank account to Radio Shack's.

The fourth way that you might choose to pay for the radio is by credit card. You might prefer to pay in this way if you do not have sufficient funds in your bank account. To pay by credit card, you hand the cashier the MasterCard issued to you by Bank of America ("card issuer"). The cashier runs a blank sales slip form and your MasterCard through an imprinting machine. The machine imprints upon the form not only your name, a number identifying Bank of America as the issuing bank, and your credit card account number, but also Radio Shack's name, address, and its merchant number at Wells Bank, the bank at which Radio Shack maintains its account. The clerk completes the sales slip by adding the date, description, and amount of the transaction.

Before accepting payment by MasterCard, Radio Shack, for its own protection, can seek authority from Bank of America for the charge. To do so, Radio Shack will probably use an electronic terminal connected to a computer that will determine whether your account is still active, whether the purchase amount is within your credit limit, and whether your card has been lost or stolen. By authorizing the charge, Bank of America is obligated to pay the amount of the charge; otherwise, it might not be liable. The clerk now hands you the sales slip for your signature.

Radio Shack will then send the sales slip to Wells Bank. Wells Bank and Radio Shack have an agreement under which Radio Shack agrees to honor MasterCard in payment for purchases and Wells Bank agrees to reimburse Radio Shack, minus a small discount, for any purchases made by the use of a MasterCard. Wells Bank, while retaining the original slip, electronically transmits to Bank of America the information contained on your sales slip. Bank of America then pays Wells Bank and charges your account for the amount of the purchase. Bank of America thereafter will bill you periodically (for example, every 30 days) for the total charges made on your card during the preceding month.

Credit cards are both a payment system and a means of obtaining credit. As between you and Radio Shack, a credit card is a method of payment, for Bank of America becomes liable for the amount of your purchase. However, as between you and Bank of America, the transaction is a credit transaction in which Bank of America loans you the money to make the purchase.

DIFFERENCES IN USE OF THE VARIOUS PAYMENT SYSTEMS

Which particular payment system you choose to use can have significant consequences for both you and Radio Shack. Radio Shack would always prefer payment in cash, thus immediately obtaining payment for the clock radio and completing the transaction.

You, on the other hand, may have reasons why you do not want to pay in cash. Because of your fear of theft, you may not want to carry much cash around with you. Or, because you need to make the purchase before payday, you may not have sufficient cash available. Or you may want to reserve the right to prevent Radio Shack from receiving payment in the event that you are dissatisfied with your purchase.

Despite the fact that there are many reasons why Radio Shack would prefer payment in cash, Radio Shack is willing to take other means of payment. If Radio Shack required payment in cash, it might lose many customers. Radio Shack has determined that the risks involved in taking payment by other means are outweighed by the additional sales that are generated thereby.

Although payment by check is not as desirable from Radio Shack's point of view as payment in cash, it is still happy to receive a check in payment. There are, however, some disadvantages from Radio Shack's point of view. It must assume the risk that there are not sufficient funds in your account to cover the check. However, this risk is greatly reduced by the fact that most states now have laws making it a criminal offense to write a check without sufficient funds; in addition, state laws provide civil remedies to the recipient of the "bounced" check in such a case.

Radio Shack also takes the risk that you may exercise your right to stop payment on the check. This risk is not as great as it may first appear because banks have established an efficient system for collecting checks. Immediately upon the bank opening in the morning, Radio Shack will deposit all of the checks received the day before. Upon depositing these checks, Radio Shack's bank, Wells Bank, will give Radio Shack the immediate right to use the funds represented by the checks deposited. If your bank, Bank of America, is in the same city as Wells Bank, Wells Bank will present the check to Bank of America for payment on the next day. So unless you stop payment on the check immediately, the check will be paid before Bank of America has had time to process your stop payment order.

When you pay by check, Radio Shack also incurs the risk that you are not the person authorized to write the check. You may have stolen someone else's checkbook and forged their signature. However, there are some protections against this risk. With Radio Shack's ability to use a computerized service that verifies whether your driver's license number correlates with your checking account number, forgery is no longer a substantial risk. Furthermore, as we will see, the law of negotiable instruments protects Radio Shack to some extent against forgeries.

From your point of view, there are advantages in making payment by check. Since it will usually take at least two days for the check to be paid by your bank, you can make your purchase the day before payday knowing that there will be adequate funds in your account by the time the check is presented for payment. And although you may not have a substantial amount of time within which to stop payment on a check, you will be able to prevent Radio Shack from obtaining payment if you are dissatisfied with the clock radio within a day or two of the purchase. Finally, there is little risk in carrying checks with you, for even if your checkbook is lost or stolen, your account usually cannot be debited unless you personally sign the check.

Due to the risks associated with payment by check, Radio Shack would prefer that you pay by electronic funds transfer. If you make payment through a POS terminal, your account is immediately debited while Radio Shack's account is immediately credited. The transaction, like payment in cash, is complete. In all but a few states, you have no right to reverse the transfer in the event that you are dissatisfied with your purchase. Thus, from your point of view, payment by electronic funds transfer has many of the disadvantages of cash. However, because payment by electronic funds transfer requires only that you carry with you a debit card, you do not need to worry about theft or loss as in the case of cash. Even if you lose your debit card, the thief or finder cannot use the card unless he has your PIN. As we will discuss in Chapter 8, as long as you do not voluntarily give the PIN to the user, you are not liable for a purchase even if you had written your PIN on your debit card.

The form of payment that Radio Shack likes the least is payment by credit card. Issuers of credit cards, such as MasterCard, Visa, and American Express, charge merchants a certain percentage of the purchase price as a fee for the credit card company's services. For this reason, some retailers charge a higher price for credit card purchases.

A major reason why you should prefer to pay by credit card (and why Radio Shack would prefer not to be paid by this means) is that as long as certain conditions are met, you may refuse to pay the charge for the clock radio. Upon your refusal, the credit card issuer will in turn refuse to pay Radio Shack. Radio Shack will then have to commence legal action to recover from you. During this time, you will have use of the funds.

You may also like the fact that in the event that your card is lost or stolen, you are subject to only limited liability. In Chapter 9 we will see that your risk of loss from someone else using your credit card is minimal because of federal limits on consumer liability for such charges. If someone else used your card to make purchases from Radio Shack, Radio Shack will likewise probably not suffer the loss. The agreement between the credit card issuer and Radio Shack will more than likely obligate the credit card issuer to pay Radio Shack as long as Radio Shack verifies your identity and obtains authorization from the credit card issuer for the purchase.

CHAPTER 1

What Is a Negotiable Instrument?

A. INTRODUCTION

We are exposed to negotiable instruments such as checks and promissory notes all the time, but until we take a course in commercial law, few of us know the legal consequences attaching to the issuance of a check or note. Checks and notes serve very different purposes. Checks are payment instruments. They developed as a substitute for cash. As we will see, checks serve the same payment function as cash without the accompanying danger and awkwardness associated with carrying around large amounts of cash. Notes, on the other hand, serve the credit purpose of promising to repay a debt. As we will also see, notes are preferable to other ways of promising to repay a debt because of their negotiability.

A "negotiable instrument" is a cross between a contract and money. On the one hand, a negotiable instrument is a simple contract by which you either promise to make payment or order someone to make payment on your behalf. On the other hand, a negotiable instrument gives to the holder (for our purposes now, treat the holder as the person who has the right to collect on the instrument) certain rights and protections that equate a negotiable instrument to cash. These cash-like features are what make a negotiable instrument acceptable to a creditor as payment for an obligation.

A negotiable instrument differs from an ordinary contract in that the holder of a negotiable instrument is freed from many of the risks and burdens associated with the assignment of an ordinary contract right. Let us look at these potential risks and burdens and the effect that negotiability has on them.

Assume that Buyer wants to purchase equipment from Equipment Dealer for $5,000 but cannot at present pay for the equipment in full. At the same time, Equipment Dealer, needing to purchase new inventory, cannot itself finance Buyer's purchase. Equipment Dealer talks to Finance Company about the possibility of financing the transaction. Equipment Dealer wants to net $4,500 from the sale. Although Equipment Dealer convinces Finance Company that Buyer is a safe credit risk, Finance Company expresses certain other concerns to Equipment Dealer that prevent it from paying Equipment Dealer $4,500 for the right to collect $5,000 from Buyer. Finance Company tells Equipment Dealer that if these concerns are relieved, it will pay Equipment Dealer the $4,500.

Finance Company's primary concern is that Buyer may refuse to pay Finance Company if something goes wrong with the equipment. If Buyer purchases the equipment under an ordinary sales contract and Equipment Dealer assigns the right to payment under the contract to Finance Company, Buyer has the right to refuse payment to Finance Company in the event that Equipment Dealer breaches any warranty given to Buyer or in any other manner breaches the sales contract.

The lawyer for Equipment Dealer proposes to Finance Company that Buyer sign a document called a "note," which is simply a promise by Buyer to pay Equipment Dealer the purchase price of the equipment. If this note meets the requirements for negotiability spelled out in Article 3 of the Uniform Commercial Code ("Code"), the note can qualify as a negotiable instrument. Equipment Dealer will sell the note to Finance Company. If Buyer evidences his debt by a negotiable instrument, Finance Company is shielded from virtually any dispute that may arise from the underlying equipment sale. This protects Finance Company from the risk that Buyer may refuse to make payment because it has a defense arising from the transaction in which he purchased the equipment from Equipment Dealer. To qualify for this protection, Finance Company must, however, qualify as a holder in due course.[1] In contrast, if Equipment Dealer merely assigns Finance Company the right to payment under the equipment sales contract, Finance Company would take subject to virtually any defense that Buyer may have against Equipment Dealer arising under the sales contract.[2]

In addition, there are other advantages to Finance Company in taking a negotiable instrument rather than in receiving an assignment of the underlying sales contract. If an ordinary contract right has been assigned, Finance Company takes the risk that Buyer will have already made payment to Equipment Dealer before Buyer receives notice of the assignment to Finance Com-

---

1. U.C.C. §3-305(b).
2. See Restatement (Second) of Contracts §336(1) (1979).

pany. In this event, Buyer's payment to Equipment Dealer will discharge its obligation and Finance Company will have no recourse against Buyer. On the other hand, if Buyer evidences its obligation by a note, once the note has been negotiated to Finance Company by Equipment Dealer, payment to Equipment Dealer does not provide a discharge to Buyer.[3] Buyer pays Equipment Dealer at its own risk unless Buyer gets the note back from Equipment Dealer upon payment.

In many jurisdictions pleading a cause of action on a negotiable instrument is simpler than on an ordinary contract right. The holder is merely required to attach the original negotiable instrument or a copy thereof to the complaint and allege that he is the holder. When signatures on an instrument have been admitted or established, the holder is entitled to recover on the instrument simply by producing it unless the defendant establishes a defense.[4] Thus, for example, the holder does not have to plead or prove consideration. Instead, the burden of proving want, or failure, of consideration rests on the obligor. This makes it easier for the holder to obtain summary judgment on a negotiable instrument.

Due to these advantages, Finance Company has far less hesitation in purchasing the note. Furthermore, it will pay a higher price for the note than for a debt evidenced by an ordinary contract of purchase because use of the note reduces both the risk of nonpayment and the costs of collection. Because Equipment Dealer receives a higher price for the note, it may be willing to pass on part of this profit to Buyer in the form of a lower price for the equipment. Of course, Finance Company still faces the risk of Buyer's insolvency, but this is a risk that Finance Company can guard against, to some extent, by thoroughly investigating Buyer's credit, by taking a security interest in the equipment to secure the note, or by having Equipment Dealer guarantee the obligation.

For similar reasons, a check is often freely taken as the full equivalent of payment in cash since checks are easily convertible into cash. Because of the sophisticated and efficient system for check collection, the "payee" (the person to whom the check is payable) need only deposit the check into his own bank account and within a few days payment of the check is collected from the payor bank. In addition, the depositary bank will often allow the payee immediately to use the funds represented by the check even before the bank has collected the check from the payor bank. One of the reasons why the depositary bank will allow the payee immediate use of the funds is the negotiability of the check. Because of the check's negotiability, the depositary bank (assuming the

3. U.C.C. §3-602(a).
4. U.C.C. §3-308(b).

bank qualifies as a holder in due course) may recover in full from the drawer (the person who wrote the check) despite any defense that the drawer may have against the payee.

B.   SCOPE OF ARTICLES 3 AND 4

The basic law governing negotiable instruments is contained in Articles 3 and 4 of the Code. As we will see, Article 3 governs writings meeting the requirements of section 3-104 (a). However, Article 3 does not cover all writings meeting these requirements. Section 3-102 specifically excludes from the scope of Article 3 some writings which otherwise qualify as negotiable instruments. For example, even though some investment securities may qualify as negotiable instruments, section 3-102 expressly excludes them from the scope of Article 3; instead, such securities are governed by Article 8.[5] Money is likewise excluded from the scope of Article 3 because of its inherent differences from negotiable instruments.[6] Payment orders, as defined in section 4A-103(a)(1)(iii) and governed by Article 4A, are also excluded from the coverage of Article 3.[7] As a consequence, Article 4A and Article 3 are mutually exclusive.

Article 4 governs the bank collection process. Curiously, you will find no statement contained in Article 4 as to its scope. Rather, the scope of Article 4 is implied in the definition of the term "item."[8] An "item" is defined as "an instrument or other written promise or order to pay money handled by a bank for collection or payment."[9] Through this definition, only instruments or writings handled by a bank for collection or payment are items. "Item" covers more than just Article 3 negotiable instruments.[10] *Any* promise or order to pay money handled by a bank for collection or payment is an item. Both "promise" and "order" retain their Article 3 definitions, but the requirements for negotiability under Article 3, including the requirement that the order or promise be unconditional, are not found in the definition of item under Article 4.

5. U.C.C. §3-102(a); U.C.C. §3-102, Official Comment 2; U.C.C. §8-102(1).
6. U.C.C. §3-102(a).
7. U.C.C. §3-102(a); U.C.C. §3-102, Official Comment 2.
8. U.C.C. §4-102, Official Comment 1.
9. U.C.C. §4-104(a)(9).
10. See U.C.C. §4-104(a)(9); U.C.C. §4-104(c); U.C.C. §4-104, Official Comment 8 for further explanation.

Thus, a conditional promise or order if handled by a bank for collection is an item. A savings account withdrawal slip that contains an order to the bank is also an item. Bonds and other investment securities that qualify as instruments or promises are items even though governed by Article 8.

Because "instrument," "promise," and "order" are all defined as requiring a writing, only a writing may qualify as an item. For this reason, an electronic funds transfer is not an item. Even if the transfer is effectuated by means of a writing, the definition of "item" specifically excludes payment orders governed by Article 4A and debit and credit cards slips.[11]

When an instrument governed by Article 3 is handled by a bank for collection or payment, Article 3 and Article 4 both apply. Because Article 4 was specifically drafted to govern problems arising in the bank collection process, when the results reached under an applicable provision of Article 4 conflict with the results reached under a provision of Article 3, Article 4 controls.[12] When Article 4 is silent on the issue presented, Article 3 controls. However, Articles 3 and 4 have been so well coordinated and cross-referenced that few, if any, conflicts will arise.

C.   TYPES OF NEGOTIABLE INSTRUMENTS

Article 3 negotiable instruments are classified into two basic categories: drafts and notes.[13] A "draft" is any instrument that contains an order (a written instruction by one person to another to pay a third person).[14] A "note" is any instrument that contains a promise (a written undertaking to pay money).[15]

1. Notes

A note is a promise by one party (called the "maker") to pay to another party (called the "payee") a sum of money. A note may be simple or complex. A note can be as simple as a writing that states in full, "I promise to pay to the order

11. U.C.C. §4-104(a)(9).
12. U.C.C. §3-102(b); U.C.C. §4-102(a).
13. U.C.C. §3-104, Official Comment 4.
14. U.C.C. §3-104(e); U.C.C. §3-103(a)(6).
15. U.C.C. §3-104(e); U.C.C. §3-103(a)(9).

of Carol McGeehan the sum of $100. (s) Lary Lawrence." Notes can, however, be several pages long and contain, among other things, provisions for collateral securing the loan, conditions under which the note may be accelerated, attorney's fees in the event of default, and different rates of interest before and after default.[16] Look at the sample note in Figure 1.1. Notice that the maker typically signs the note in the bottom right-hand corner at the place identified "1" and that the payee is identified often in the beginning of the note at the place designated "2."

FIGURE 1.1

October 1, 1996

_____90 Days_____after Date, the undersigned promises to pay to

the order of_____Paul Payee_____②_____

the sum of _____40,000_____Dollars, with interest thereon at the rate of

_____7_____percent per annum after maturity.

The undersigned further promises to pay any expenses, including reasonable attorney's fees, incurred in the collection of this note. Each person who signs this note waives demand of payment, presentment, and notice of dishonor.

_____①_____
Michael Maker

2.   Certificates of Deposit

A "certificate of deposit" is a note issued by a bank. It is defined as an acknowledgment by a bank of the receipt of money together with an engagement by the bank to repay the money.[17] Look at the sample certificate of deposit in Figure 1.2.

Notice that it is in the same basic form as a note with the issuing bank typically signing the certificate in the bottom right-hand corner at the place identified "1" and the payee being identified in the body of the certificate in the

16. There are also notes payable through a bank and notes payable at a bank. These notes are more like drafts and are discussed in connection therewith at the end of this section.

17. U.C.C. §3-104(j).

C. Types of Negotiable Instruments

FIGURE 1.2

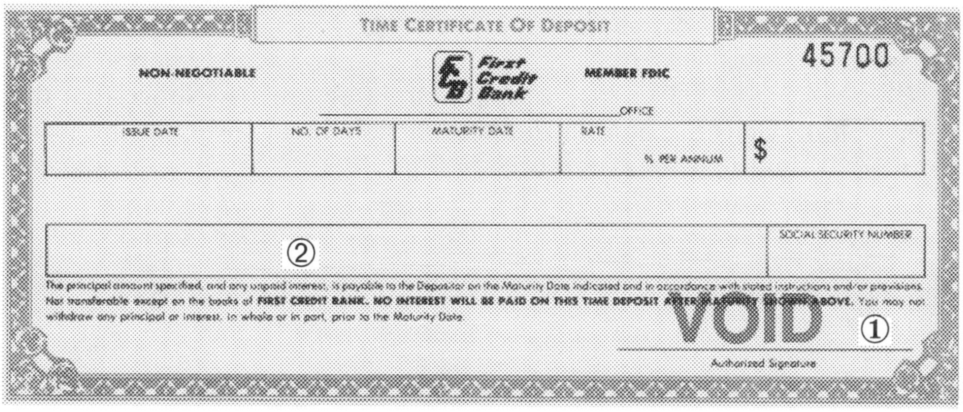

place designated "2." Certificates of deposit are the means by which banks raise money and depositors assure themselves of a good return on their money. Certificates of deposit often provide a substantial forfeiture of interest where the depositor attempts to withdraw the funds or call the loan prior to maturity. Article 3, in fact, does not cover most certificates of deposit. Some certificates of deposit are not negotiable and therefore are not governed by Article 3.[18] Other certificates of deposit qualify as investment securities under Article 8[19] and thus are excluded from the coverage of Article 3.

3. Drafts

A "draft," sometimes known as a bill of exchange, is a three-party instrument by which a "drawer" (the person who typically signs the draft in the lower right-hand corner) orders a "drawee" (the person named in the draft to whom the order is directed) to pay the payee. Look at the sample sight draft in Figure 1.3.

---

18. A bank may ensure that a certificate of deposit is not negotiable simply by omitting words of negotiability, i.e., "order" or "bearer." We discuss in section 1D, infra, what constitutes words of negotiability.

19. See Abraham Lincoln Ins. Co. v. Franklin Sav. & Loan Assn., 302 F. Supp. 54 (E.D. Mo. 1969) (investment certificates issued by a savings and loan).

FIGURE 1.3

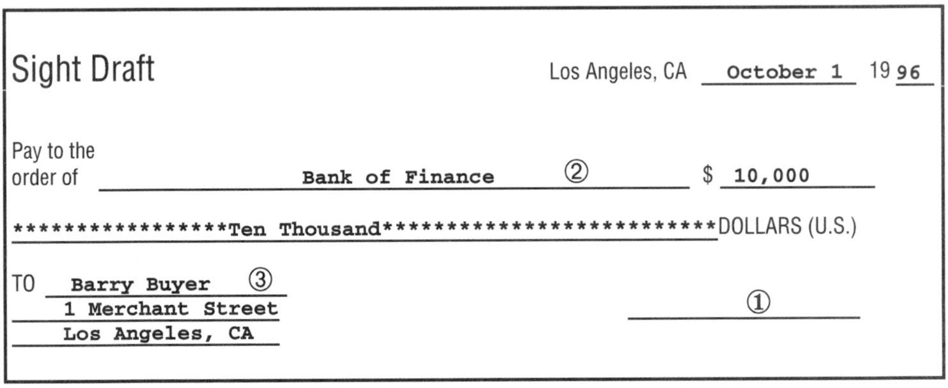

```
┌─────────────────────────────────────────────────────────────────────┐
│                                                                       │
│  Sight Draft                        Los Angeles, CA  October 1  19 96 │
│                                                                       │
│  Pay to the                                                           │
│  order of _____ Bank of Finance    ②    $  10,000 _____  │
│                                                                       │
│  ****************Ten Thousand**********************DOLLARS (U.S.)      │
│                                                                       │
│  TO  Barry Buyer   ③                                                  │
│      1 Merchant Street                              ① _____    │
│      Los Angeles, CA                                                  │
│                                                                       │
└─────────────────────────────────────────────────────────────────────┘
```

Notice that the drawer signs the draft in the bottom right-hand corner at the place designated "1" and that the payee is typically identified in the beginning of the draft at the place designated "2." Particularly notice that the drawee, in this case "Barry Buyer," is identified in the lower left-hand corner in the place designated "3." The drawee could also be identified in the upper left-hand corner. Notice also that there is no language specifically telling the drawee that it is the one that is being ordered to pay the payee. In some drafts, the word "to" precedes the drawee's name in order to make it clear to whom the order is addressed.

4. Checks

The most common type of draft is a check. A "check" is a draft drawn upon a bank and payable on demand.[20] A draft is a check only if it is drawn upon a bank. A "bank" is "a person engaged in the business of banking, including a savings bank, savings and loan association, credit union and trust company."[21] Look at the check in Figure 1.4.

Notice that it is in the same form as a draft with the drawer, drawee, and payee being identified in the same positions as on a draft. The drawee bank is also identified by the routing fraction in the place identified by "1" and on the MICR encoded line in the place identified by "2." The name in the upper left-hand corner of the illustration is the drawer's name.

20. U.C.C. §3-104(f).
21. U.C.C. §4-105(1).

C. Types of Negotiable Instruments

FIGURE 1.4

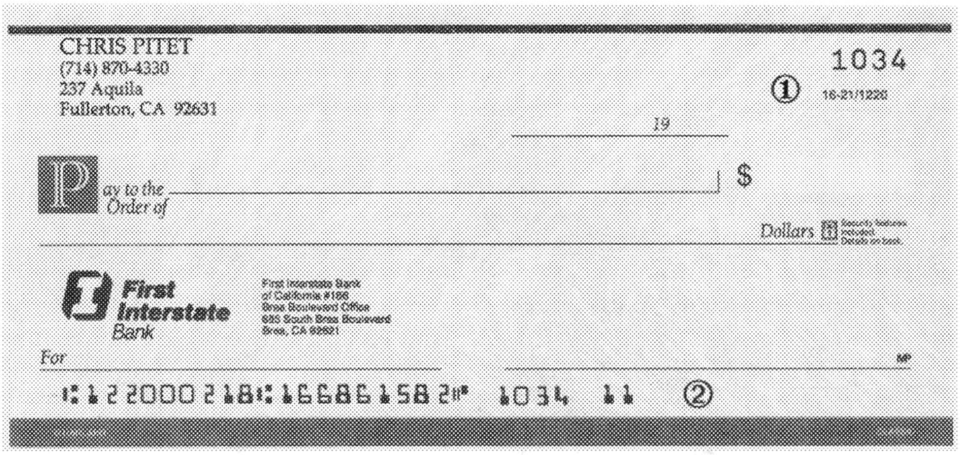

All checks are drafts. Thus, unless the Code specifically provides otherwise, checks are governed by the same rules that govern drafts. The drawer of the check is the customer of the drawee bank (also called the "payor bank"). The drawer will usually maintain an account at that bank. The relationship between the customer and the payor bank is governed by a depositor's contract, subject to certain limitations imposed by Article 4 and Regulation CC (we discuss Regulation CC in Chapter 5). The depositor's contract determines under what situations the bank must honor the customer's checks. By issuing the check, the drawer promises to pay the amount of the check to the payee in the event of its dishonor,[22] but until certification or payment by the payor bank, the holder acquires no rights against the payor bank.[23] The payor bank's only liability for failing to pay a check is to its customer for wrongful dishonor; the holder cannot sue the payor bank either for wrongful dishonor or to compel payment of the check itself.[24]

5. *Time Drafts, Banker's Acceptances, and Trade Acceptances*

Many other types of drafts and checks are used in various kinds of situations. Assume that, for example, Grain Broker agrees to purchase grain from Farmer

22. U.C.C. §3-414(b).
23. U.C.C. §3-408.
24. U.C.C. §4-402.

to be delivered on February 1st, but that payment for the grain is not due until March 1st. Grain Broker may draw a draft upon its bank, Omaha State Bank, payable to Farmer on March 1st. Being payable at a definite time rather than on demand, this is a "time draft". Look at the time draft in Figure 1.5.

FIGURE 1.5

```
No.   013                                        January 1    19 97
_____                                       _____      ___

                        On March 1st,    1997
_____

Pay to the
order of  _____Farmer_____  $  10,000
                                                                     ___

********************Ten Thousand****************************DOLLARS


TO  ____Omaha State Bank____
        Omaha, Nebraska              _____
                                          Grain Broker
```

Being drawn upon a bank, this draft would also be a check if it were payable on demand. By issuing the draft, Grain Broker, the drawer, promises to make payment if Omaha State Bank, the drawee, refuses to make payment.[25] As in the case of a check, Omaha State Bank is not liable to Farmer solely by Grain Broker's issuance of the draft to Farmer. Omaha State Bank may, however, become liable on the draft if it "accepts" the draft[26] by signing its name to the draft. By so doing, Omaha State Bank promises to pay the draft when due.[27] When the draft is drawn upon and accepted by a bank, the draft becomes a "banker's acceptance." Look at the banker's acceptance in Figure 1.6.

Notice that the bank usually signifies its acceptance by its signature across the face of the draft in the place designated "1." Had the draft been drawn by Farmer upon Grain Broker and thereafter accepted by Grain Broker, the accepted draft would be called a "trade acceptance." Examine the trade acceptance in Figure 1.7.

25. U.C.C. §3-414(b).
26. U.C.C. §3-409(a).
27. U.C.C. §3-413(a).

C. Types of Negotiable Instruments

FIGURE 1.6

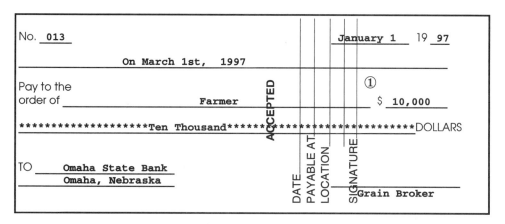

FIGURE 1.7

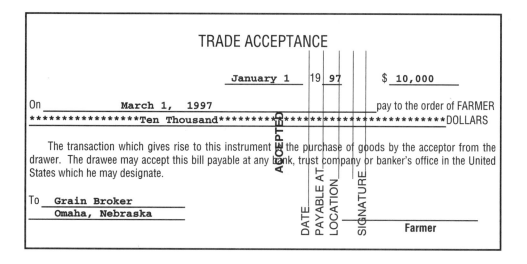

Returning to our example, if Farmer presents Grain Broker's draft to Omaha State Bank for payment, Omaha State Bank will not be liable to Farmer for payment unless and until Omaha State Bank accepts the draft. However, even absent acceptance by Omaha State Bank, if Grain Broker has a contract with Omaha State Bank under which Omaha State Bank promises to pay drafts drawn by Grain Broker, Omaha State Bank will be liable to Grain Broker for wrongful dishonor if it refuses to pay a properly drawn draft. In the absence of such a contract, Omaha State Bank will not be liable to either party for refusal to pay the draft when presented.

6.   Documentary Drafts

A variation on the above transaction involves use of a "documentary draft," which is often used as a method of financing a sale of goods. Continue with our example above involving Grain Broker. Assume that Grain Broker does not entirely trust Farmer. Grain Broker does not want to make payment until it is virtually assured that it will obtain possession of the grain. Grain Broker issues to Farmer a documentary draft. The draft accompanies a letter containing instructions to Omaha State Bank that it should only pay the draft if Farmer delivers to Omaha State Bank a negotiable warehouse receipt for the requisite number of bushels of grain. A "negotiable warehouse receipt" is a statement by the owner of an independent warehouse indicating that it has in its possession the required number of bushels of grain together with the warehouse's promise to deliver the grain to the person who has proper possession of the warehouse receipt. By requiring delivery of a negotiable warehouse receipt before payment, Grain Broker is thereby guaranteed that it will be entitled to possession of the grain upon the draft's payment. If the draft is payable on presentment (called a "sight draft"), Omaha State Bank must either pay or dishonor the draft within a few days of the time the draft is presented for payment. Look at the sample sight draft in Figure 1.3. After payment of the draft, Omaha State Bank retains the warehouse receipt representing the goods, turning the receipt over to Grain Broker only when Grain Broker has reimbursed the bank for the payment. If the draft is not paid by Omaha State Bank, Farmer has the right to proceed against Grain Broker both on the draft and on the underlying sales contract.[28] Look at the documentary draft in Figure 1.8.

Notice the reference to the enclosed warehouse receipt at the place designated "4."

Because Grain Broker's draft is payable at a later date, Omaha State Bank (the drawee) must, upon presentment, either accept or dishonor the draft. Upon acceptance, Omaha State Bank will retain the documents of title until the bank is reimbursed by Grain Broker or suitable credit arrangements are made. A banker's acceptance is usually payable a fixed period after sight ("after sight" means after acceptance), generally 90 to 120 days after acceptance. Documentary drafts are often drawn under a letter of credit. By issuing a letter of credit, Omaha State Bank promises Farmer that it will accept or pay the draft if Farmer complies with the terms of the letter of credit. Most international sales of goods are financed by documentary drafts issued under letters of credit. Look at the letter of credit in Figure 1.9.

---

28. U.C.C. §3-310(c); U.C.C. §3-310(b)(3).

C. Types of Negotiable Instruments

```
┌─────────────────────────────────────────────────────────────────────────────┐
│                                                                               │
│    Payable at Sight              Omaha, Nebraska        October 1    19  97   │
│        (WHEN PAYABLE)                                                          │
│                                                                               │
│  PAY TO THE                                                                    │
│      ORDER OF                    Farmer                           $  10,000   │
│                                                                               │
│  *********************Ten Thousand***************************DOLLARS          │
│                                                             ④                  │
│            Enclosed is Warehouse Receipt                                       │
│                                                                               │
│  CHARGE TO ACCOUNT OF GRAIN BROKER                                            │
│                                                                               │
│  TO     Omaha State Bank                                                       │
│         Omaha, Nebraska                                                        │
│                                                                               │
└─────────────────────────────────────────────────────────────────────────────┘
```

Notice that the signature of the bank appears at the place designated "1." Farmer would be named as the "beneficiary" in the place designated "2" and the section designated "3" would contain the conditions that must be met in order for the issuing bank to be obligated to pay the draft.

7. *Negotiable Order of Withdrawal*

A "negotiable order of withdrawal" ("NOW") is a draft that permits the depositor of an interest-bearing account, usually a savings account, to transfer money from the account to a third person. NOWs can be drawn on any of the following institutions:[29] (1) an insured bank, (2) a state bank, (3) a mutual savings bank, (4) a savings bank,[30] (5) an insured institution, (6) a building and loan association, or (7) a savings and loan association. A NOW, if payable on demand, is a check because these institutions are banks.[31]

---

29. 12 U.S.C.A. §1832.
30. See 12 U.S.C.A. §1813 for definitions of these first four institutions.
31. U.C.C. §4-105(1). If a NOW account explicitly requires that notice be given a prescribed period prior to withdrawal, not being payable on demand, it would not be a check.

FIGURE 1.9

Irrevocable Letter of Credit

IRREVOCABLE LETTER OF CREDIT   *Date of Letter of Credit:* October 1, 1997
CUSTOMER   ISSUING FINANCIAL INSTITUTION   *Number of Letter of Credit:* 1468
                                        Amount (U.S. Dollars): 10,000
Grain Broker   Omaha State Bank   *Expiration Date:* October 28, 1997
Omaha, Nebraska   Omaha, Nebraska   *To be available by Drafts:* Payable 90 days
                                                      after sight

BENEFICIARY   ADVISING FINANCIAL INSTITUTION

Farmer   ②
Topeka, Kansas

GENTLEMEN:

We hereby issue this Irrevocable Letter of Credit and authorize you as Beneficiary to draw on ourselves for the account of Customer for any sum or sums not exceeding in the aggregate the amount of this credit as indicated above.

Drafts must be accompanied by the following document:

    1.   Warehouse receipt made out to order of grain broker.

    2.   Commercial invoice   ③

    Covering: 600 Bushels of grain.

Drafts drawn under this credit must be marked that they are drawn under this Financial Institution's Letter of Credit and must show the Date and Number of the Letter of Credit.

We hereby agree to honor each draft drawn under and in compliance with the terms of this credit, if duly presented (together with the documents specified) to us on or before the close of business on the Expiration Date shown above.

Unless otherwise expressly stated, this Credit is subject to the Uniform Customs and Practice for Documentary Credits (1993 Revision), International Chamber of Commerce Brochure No 500, and, where not inconsistent therewith, to Article Five of the Uniform Commercial Code of the state of the principal office of the Issuing Financial Institution. Unless otherwise expressly stated above, only original documents will be accepted. No reproductions or carbon copies may be substituted for originals.

Very Truly Yours,

①
Authorized Signature - Issuing Financial Institution

8. *Personal Money Order*

A variant of an ordinary check is a "personal money order," which is a draft sold by a usually financially solid company acting as the drawee to the purchaser who becomes the drawer. The drawee, not having signed the order,

C. Types of Negotiable Instruments

incurs no liability to the payee.[32] The drawee's only obligation is to the drawer to pay the order upon proper presentment. Look at the personal money order in Figure 1.10.

FIGURE 1.10

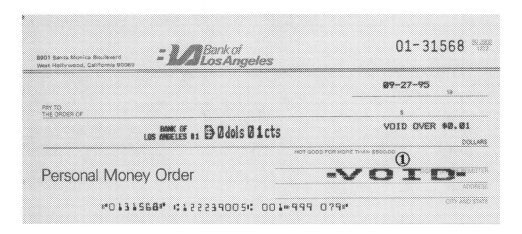

Notice that it is in the same basic form as a check. The purchaser of the personal money order signs in the lower right-hand corner in the place designated "1." Notice that there is no place for the bank or other drawee to sign the order. Personal money orders are primarily used by drawers who do not have a checking account. The drawee may be a bank, in which case the personal money order is a check; or a nonbank, in which case the personal money order is a draft.[33] For example, a postal money order is a draft, not a check, because the post office is not a bank. Most postal office money orders are written in a way so as not to be negotiable.[34] Furthermore, because postal money orders are issued by a branch of the federal government, disputes involving postal money orders are governed by federal law.[35] Examine the postal money order in Figure 1.11.

---

32. U.C.C. §3-401(a).

33. U.C.C. §3-104, Official Comment 4. A money order may be a check even though it is labelled "money order." U.C.C. §3-104(f).

34. Post office money orders often limit transferability to the first transferee and as a result any such money order would not be negotiable. See United States v. First Natl. Bank, 263 F. Supp. 298, 4 U.C.C. Rep. Serv. 89 (D. Mass. 1967).

35. U.C.C. §3-104, Official Comment 4.

FIGURE 1.11

9. Bank Checks—Cashier's, Teller's, and Certified Checks

Slightly different from ordinary checks are bank checks. There are three types of bank checks. The first type, "cashier's check," is a check with respect to which the drawer and the drawee are the same bank or branches of the same bank.[36] For example, Bank of America may draw a cashier's check upon itself. Look at the cashier's check in Figure 1.12.

Notice that the check is signed in the lower right-hand corner in the place designated "1" by a representative of the issuing bank, which is identified in the upper left-hand corner in the place designated "2." Notice that in the place designated "3" there is a line for the name of the purchaser, called a remitter, who does not sign the check.

The second type of bank check is a teller's check (sometimes also called an "official check"). A "teller's check" is a check drawn by one bank on another bank or "payable at" or "payable through" the other bank.[37] Historically, teller's checks were drawn by savings and loan associations upon commercial banks. A check drawn by Home Savings of America (the drawer)

---

36. U.C.C. §3-104(g); see Lawrence, Making Cashier's Checks and Other Bank Checks Cost-Effective: A Plea for Revision of Articles 3 and 4 of the Uniform Commercial Code, 64 Minn. L. Rev. 275, 285 (1980).

37. U.C.C. §3-104(h). "Payable at" and "payable through" drafts are discussed subsequently.

C. Types of Negotiable Instruments

FIGURE 1.12

upon Wells Fargo Bank (the drawee) would be a teller's check. Traditionally, because savings and loan associations were not permitted to provide checking services, they used teller's checks drawn upon commercial banks in situations where commercial banks would simply issue their own cashier's checks.[38] Now that savings and loan associations are permitted to issue checks, they can issue cashier's checks. Look at the teller's check in Figure 1.13.

FIGURE 1.13

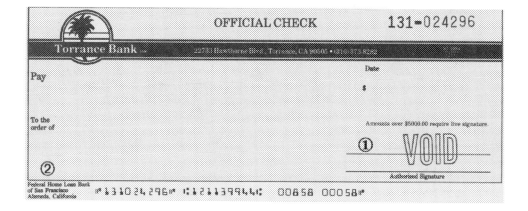

38. Prior to 1980, both federal and state law prohibited savings and loan associations from engaging in checking accounts. See, e.g., 12 U.S.C. §1464(b)(1); Cal. Fin. Code §5003; N.Y. Banking Law §§378-383. Under 12 U.S.C. §1832, savings and loan associations may now offer NOW accounts.

It is signed in the lower right-hand corner in the place designated "1" by a representative of Torrance Bank and is drawn upon Federal Home Loan Bank of San Francisco designated in the lower left-hand corner in the place designated "2." Notice that Federal Home Loan Bank does not sign the check. By not signing the check, Federal Home Loan Bank does not incur liability on the check.

The third type of bank check is a "certified check," which is a check drawn by the bank's customer and accepted by the bank. Upon acceptance, the customer is discharged from liability and the bank is liable for payment of the check. For example, Chris may request that First Interstate Bank certify his personal check drawn upon First Interstate Bank. By certifying the check (the equivalent of "accepting" a draft), First Interstate Bank promises to pay the check upon presentment. First Interstate Bank immediately debits Chris' account in the amount of the check and Chris, upon certification, is discharged from liability on the check. Look at the certified check in Figure 1.14.

Figure 1.14

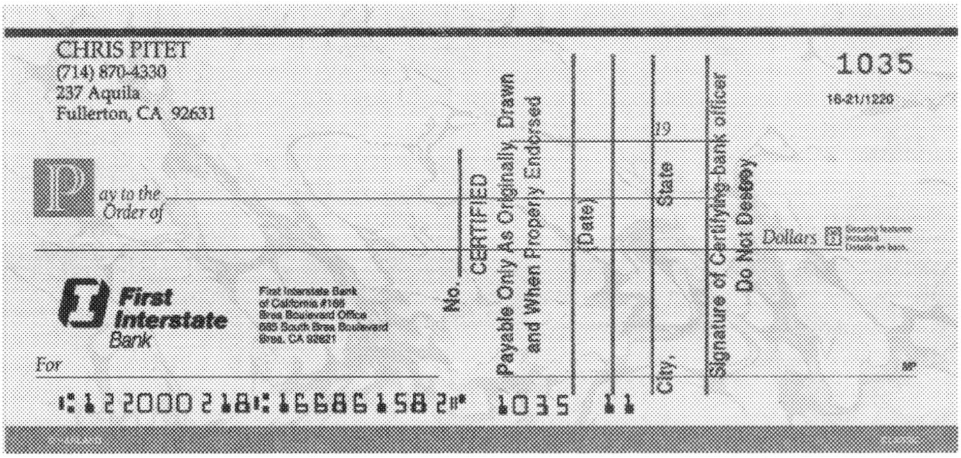

Notice that its form is that of an ordinary check signed by Chris as drawer and that the only difference is that First Interstate Bank has stamped "Certified" across the face of the check together with its accompanying signature. Banks rarely certify checks anymore. Because certified checks cannot easily be processed through computerized check processing systems, banks instead issue cashier's checks, which can be easily processed, whenever possible.

Bank checks are treated differently than ordinary checks for several purposes including the ability of the issuing bank to refuse payment,[39] the loss or destruction of the check,[40] the effect of taking a bank check on the underlying obligation,[41] and the statute of limitations on bringing an action against the issuing bank.[42]

10. Traveler's Checks

A traveler's check is similar to a bank check. Traveler's checks are used by persons desiring to have a cash equivalent that is accepted by people all over the world. Because the drawer is usually a company of substantial financial responsibility, traveler's checks are treated as the equivalent of cash.

A "traveler's check" is "an instrument that (i) is payable on demand, (ii) is drawn on or payable at or through a bank, (iii) is designated by the term traveler's check or by a substantially similar term, and (iv) requires, as a condition to payment, a countersignature by a person whose specimen signature appears on the instrument."[43] Look at the traveler's check in Figure 1.15.

FIGURE 1.15

---

39. U.C.C. §3-411.
40. U.C.C. §3-312.
41. U.C.C. §3-310(a).
42. U.C.C. §3-118(d).
43. U.C.C. §3-104(i).

Notice that it is signed by a representative of Interpayment Services (the issuer) in the lower right-hand corner in the place designated "1" and that Lary Lawrence (the purchaser) signs the check in the place designated "2" upon its purchase. When Lary wants to use the check, he countersigns the check in the place designated "3" and fills in the name of the payee in the place designated "4."

Traveler's checks are issued by both banks and nonbanks, and although traveler's checks are called "checks," they may be in the form of a note or draft.[44] If the traveler's check is drawn upon a bank, it is a check. If the traveler's check is payable through or at a bank, it is a draft. Unlike an ordinary check or draft, a traveler's check has two lines for the signature of the purchaser. Although the purchaser is neither the drawer nor the payee, a countersignature must be present before the check can be negotiated. However, as long as the check is taken by a holder in due course, the countersignature need not be made by the same person who had originally purchased the check or who had signed as purchaser in order for the person whose name is inserted as payee to become the holder of the check and collect payment.[45] A holder in due course, as a result, does not take subject to the risk that the traveler's check was stolen and the countersignature forged.

11. Payable Through Items

An interesting instrument that is used often in lieu of a check is an item payable through a bank. A "payable through item" may be used in the same situations in which a check is used but with advantages not present in the case of a check. Let us take as an example State Farm Insurance Company settling a claim with Bob Marley. State Farm Insurance Company wants to ensure that the settlement draft will not be paid until Bob Marley signs the release agreement. Because Marley may not agree to the settlement, the draft may never be presented for payment. In fact, many of State Farm's settlement drafts will never be cashed because State Farm Insurance Company tries to settle claims by mailing a settlement draft along with a release agreement. If the insured does not accept the settlement, he will not sign the release agreement and has no right to cash the settlement draft. Because the total of outstanding drafts is in a far greater aggregate amount than the amount that State Farm will ulti-

44. U.C.C. §3-104, Official Comment 4. The instrument need not name the bank as the drawee or paying agent as long as the instrument bears an appropriate routing number that identifies the bank as the paying agent. U.C.C. §3-104, Official Comment 4.

45. U.C.C. §3-106(c); U.C.C. §3-106, Official Comment 2.

mately pay, State Farm does not maintain a sufficient balance in its account to cover all of the outstanding drafts. For reasons to be explained shortly, State Farm Insurance Company, instead of a check, issues a draft payable through Bank of America, the bank at which State Farm keeps its accounts. The draft is mailed to Bob Marley together with an agreement releasing State Farm Insurance Company from any further liability. The accompanying letter states that the agreement must be signed prior to Marley's cashing of the draft. Look at the payable through draft in Figure 1.16.

FIGURE 1.16

State Farm Insurance Company Los Angeles, CA

October 1, 1996	Q 1111	SF 1234
(Date)	(Claim Number)	(Policy Number)
Bob Marley	State Farm Insurance Co.	
(By)	(Against)	
	Santa Monica, CA	July 4, 1996
	(Arising out of an accident or loss occuring at or near)	(Date)
Two Thousand Four Hundred Twelve and 90/100		Dollars $ 2412.90

UPON ACCEPTANCE, PAY TO ORDER OF: State Farm Insurance Co.- Claim Account

Payable Through
BANK OF AMERICA
Los Angeles, CA

Bob Marley ②

3472:;:4210 00579::; By ①

A representative of State Farm Insurance Company signs the draft in the lower right-hand corner in the place designated as "1" payable to Bob Marley identified in the lower left-hand corner at the place designated as "2." The draft is drawn upon State Farm Insurance Company itself.

Notice that in the lower right-hand corner the draft states that it is "payable through Bank of America." By being "payable through" Bank of America, Bank of America has no right to pay the draft.[46] State Farm Insurance Company is the drawee and is the only person authorized to pay the draft. Being the only person authorized to pay the draft, the drawer/drawee is the party to whom presentment must be made. Being the person to whom presentment is to be made, State Farm does not have to maintain adequate funds in its account to cover the draft. It can deposit funds immediately prior to the

46. U.C.C. §4-106(a); U.C.C. §4-106, Official Comment 1.

time it decides to pay the draft. This allows State Farm use of the funds during the delay between issuance and presentment of the draft. In addition, State Farm can verify that Bob Marley has signed the release agreement before telling Bank of America to debit State Farm's account in the amount of the draft. Had a check been used instead, these advantages would be lost because the check would be paid automatically by Bank of America. However, the advantages to State Farm of having used a check are retained in that the draft must be presented through Bank of America[47] and therefore payment may be accomplished by a simple directive from State Farm to Bank of America to remit funds in payment of the draft.

Because State Farm is the person who makes payment, a draft cannot qualify as a check if it is payable through a bank unless the drawer itself is a bank. For example, a draft drawn by an insurance company payable through a bank is *not* a check because the insurance company, the person upon whom it is drawn, is not a bank.[48]

12. Payable at Items

An instrument similar to a payable through item is a note or acceptance payable at a bank. To be a "payable at" a bank, the note or acceptance must explicitly state that it is payable at a bank, for example, "Payable at Continental Bank." Look at the sample "payable at" draft in Figure 1.17.

FIGURE 1.17

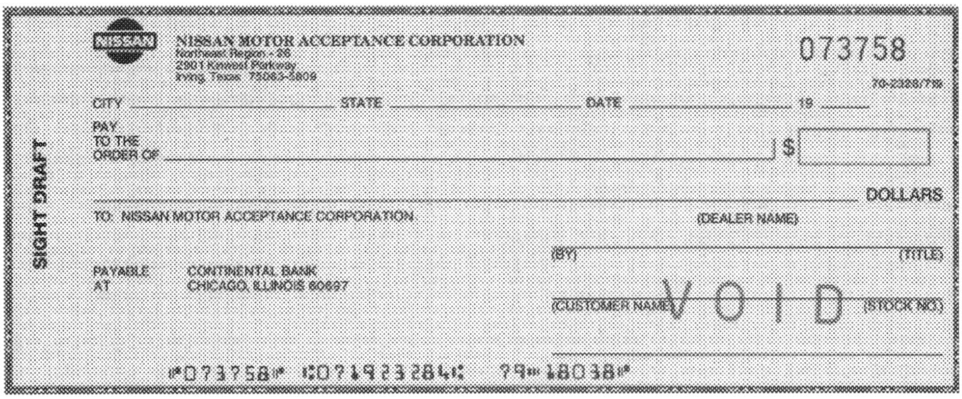
NISSAN MOTOR ACCEPTANCE CORPORATION
073758
CITY ______ STATE ______ DATE ______ 19 ____
PAY TO THE ORDER OF ______ $
______ DOLLARS
SIGHT DRAFT
TO: NISSAN MOTOR ACCEPTANCE CORPORATION
(DEALER NAME)
(BY) (TITLE)
PAYABLE AT CONTINENTAL BANK
(CUSTOMER NAME) (STOCK NO.)
VOID

47. U.C.C. §4-106(a); U.C.C. §4-106, Official Comment 1.
48. U.C.C. §3-104, Official Comment 4.

D. Requirements for Negotiability

What effect does this language have? Historically, banks in different states treated payable at items differently. To accommodate this difference in treatment, Article 4 provides two alternative provisions that a state may adopt as to the manner in which instruments payable at a bank are to be treated. The first alternative provision treats a note or acceptance payable at a bank as a draft drawn upon that bank.[49] The maker of the note (or the acceptor of the draft) is treated as the drawer of a draft and the bank at which the instrument is payable is treated as the drawee. Therefore, a note or acceptance payable on demand is a check. Under the second alternative, a note or acceptance payable at a bank is treated as though it is "payable through" the bank.[50] The maker of the note (or acceptor of the draft) is treated as both the drawer and the drawee of a draft while the bank at which the instrument is payable is the only person who may present the instrument to the maker or acceptor for payment.

D. REQUIREMENTS FOR NEGOTIABILITY

1. Introduction

Because the legal consequences of the use of a negotiable instrument are quite different from those attending the use of a simple contract to pay money, negotiable instruments law has had to devise a clear means by which a person can distinguish a negotiable instrument from a simple contract. A person purchasing an instrument has to know with ease and certainty whether the instrument is negotiable or not. Similarly, a person signing an instrument has to know that she is thereby giving up certain very important rights. If the person does not want to give up these rights, she must be able to know that the instrument she is signing is not negotiable. Negotiable instruments law chose to have the form of the writing be the distinguishing mark between negotiable writings and writings that are not negotiable. There is no middle ground; with rare exception, all writings that comply with the required form are negotiable, whereas all writings that do not comply are not negotiable.

Because Article 3 sets out a comprehensive set of rules governing the rights and duties of parties to a negotiable instrument, parties often want to ensure that their instrument is governed by Article 3. In order to be governed by Article 3, a writing must comply with the requirements of section

49. U.C.C. §4-106 (b), Alternative A; U.C.C. §4-106, Official Comment 2.
50. U.C.C. §4-106 (b), Alternative B; U.C.C. §4-106, Official Comment 2.

3-104(a).[51] A writing not meeting these requirements is not a negotiable instrument under Article 3. The writing can still be an enforceable obligation. The only consequence of its noncompliance with the negotiability requirements is that the writing is not governed by Article 3. For example, typical assignments, sales agreements, guaranty agreements, and letters of credit often either include provisions not authorized by Article 3 or omit provisions required thereby and so do not qualify as negotiable instruments under Article 3.

However, an Article 3 negotiable instrument is not the only type of negotiable instrument: There may be negotiable instruments outside of the coverage of Article 3.[52] These instruments may be created by other Articles of the Code, for example, investment securities are made negotiable by Article 8, by other statutes, or by judicial opinion. Even absent formal compliance with section 3-104, a writing of the parties may be treated as having the characteristics of a negotiable instrument. For example, if a writing contains a provision denying the obligor a right to raise defenses against a subsequent assignee, a court could, by applying the doctrine of estoppel or ordinary principles of contract law, deny the obligor the right to raise any of her defenses against the assignee. Similarly, as provided in section 1-102(2)(b), the parties may, by agreement, provide that one or more provisions of Article 3 determines their rights under the writing.[53]

A writing to be negotiable under Article 3 must conform to all of the requirements of section 3-104(a) and contain no unauthorized terms.[54] Section 3-104(a) sets forth the requirements for negotiability:

1. a signed writing;
2. containing an unconditional promise or order;
3. payable in a fixed amount of money, with or without interest or other charges described in the promise or order;
4. payable to bearer or to order at the time it is issued or first comes into possession of a holder;
5. payable on demand or at a definite time; and
6. containing no other undertaking or instruction by the person promising or ordering payment to do any act in addition to the payment of money, except (i) an undertaking or power to give, maintain, or protect collateral to secure payment, (ii) an authorization or power to the holder to confess judgment or realize on or dispose of collateral, or

---

51. U.C.C. §3-104, Official Comment 1.
52. U.C.C. §3-104, Official Comment 2.
53. U.C.C. §3-104, Official Comment 2.
54. U.C.C. §3-104(a)(3); U.C.C. §3-104, Official Comment 1.

(iii) a waiver of the benefit of any law intended for the advantage or protection of an obligor.[55]

Negotiability is determined solely by reference to the four corners of the instrument. A separate agreement cannot affect the negotiability of an instrument. Missing terms cannot be supplied by reference to another writing. But if an instrument is incomplete solely because spaces for essential terms have been left blank, once the spaces are filled in, the instrument is negotiable.[56]

A writing that fails to otherwise conform to the requirements of section 3-104(a) does not become negotiable simply because the parties have agreed that it should be negotiable. An instrument is not made negotiable merely by inclusion of phrases like "This instrument is negotiable" or "I will not raise any claim or defense."[57] As mentioned above, a court may, however, give the writing certain characteristics of negotiability. By contrast, a legend such as "Not Negotiable" defeats an instrument's negotiability even though the instrument otherwise complies with section 3-104(a). Note, however, that this latter rule does not apply to checks.[58] Because of the cash-like nature of checks and the swiftness of their negotiation and payment, there is no justification for allowing a drawer to deny negotiability to a check.

2.   *A Signed Writing*

A negotiable instrument must take the form of a writing signed by the maker or drawer.[59] The requirement of a signed writing is not explicitly contained in section 3-104(a). Rather, it is incorporated through the requirement that a negotiable instrument contain a promise or an order.[60] "Promise" is then defined as a *written* undertaking to pay money *signed* by the person undertaking to pay.[61] "Order" is similarly defined as a *written* instruction to pay money *signed* by the person giving the instruction.[62] Since an instrument must contain a promise or an order to be negotiable and both a promise and an order require a signed writing, an instrument cannot be negotiable if it is not a signed writing.

---

55. See U.C.C. §3-104 (a)(1)–(3) for definitions.
56. U.C.C. §3-115(b).
57. U.C.C. §3-104, Official Comment 2.
58. U.C.C. §3-104(d); U.C.C. §3-104, Official Comment 3.
59. U.C.C. §3-104, Official Comment 1.
60. U.C.C. §3-104(a).
61. U.C.C. §3-103(a)(9); U.C.C. §3-104, Official Comment 1.
62. U.C.C. §3-103(6); U.C.C. §3-104, Official Comment 1.

A writing is a "printing, typewriting or any other intentional reduction to tangible form." [63] Any form of marking on paper or similar material qualifies as a writing. Although a phonograph record or a tape recording is an "intentional reduction to tangible form," words contained on neither of these media should be held to qualify as a negotiable instrument. Electronic fund transfers that might take the form of impulses on tapes or computer disks also should not qualify as negotiable instruments. The rules of Article 3, especially those for allocating losses for forgery and alteration, were formulated for more traditional "written" instruments and were not intended to be applied to recorded or computerized "instruments."

A "signature" is "[a]ny symbol executed or adopted by a party with the present intention to authenticate a writing."[64] As long as the signer intends that the name, words, or mark be her signature, she may use any name, words, or mark as her signature. A fictitious name, a trade name, or the signer's first name may be used as long as the signer intends to use the name as a means of indicating that she is the drawer or maker of the instrument. A signature may be in the form of printing, handwriting, typing, or even the imprinting of a thumbprint.[65]

The mark or symbol need not appear at the bottom of the instrument. An instrument in handwriting stating "I, John Doe, promise to pay..." has been signed if no signature line is found on the bottom of the instrument.[66] Because no signature line appeared on the instrument, it could be presumed that John Doe intended the written words "John Doe" appearing in the body to be his signature. In contrast, although a signature may be typed, neither the name of the drawer (or maker) contained in a letterhead nor her typed name under the signature line should be regarded as a signature. In the latter case, leaving blank a line for the drawer's or maker's signature makes it clear that her typed name was not intended to be her signature.

3. Unconditional Promise or Order

An instrument to be negotiable must contain an unconditional promise or order.[67] A promise is an undertaking to pay money.[68] Although the word

---

63. U.C.C. §1-201(46).

64. U.C.C. §1-201(39).

65. U.C.C. §1-201, Official Comment 39; U.C.C. §3-401(b); U.C.C. §3-401, Official Comment 2.

66. U.C.C. §3-401, Official Comment 2.

67. U.C.C. §3-104(a).

68. U.C.C. §3-103(a)(9).

D. Requirements for Negotiability

"promise" need not be used, the language must be promissory in nature. A mere acknowledgment of a debt is not sufficient to constitute a promise. For example, the words "I owe you $500, which I hope to repay within a month" is not a promise. An order is an instruction to pay money.[69] Although the word "order" does not have to be used, the language must demand that the drawee make payment and not merely authorize or request him to make payment.

Negotiable instruments are meant to be substitutes for cash. If a negotiable instrument is to be accepted as a medium of payment in substitution for cash, the order or promise to pay must be unconditional and absolute. A creditor will not accept a writing in lieu of cash if there are conditions attached to its payment. Similarly, a purchaser of a note will require a substantial discount from the note's face value if payment of the note is subject to a contingency. The goal of negotiable instruments law is to make it simple and safe for a person to purchase such instruments.

For these reasons the order or promise contained in the instrument must be unconditional.[70] An instrument is not negotiable where it contains a promise or order that is expressly conditioned upon the happening of a specified event.[71] For example, a check is not negotiable where the drawer has written that payment is conditioned upon the performance of a specified agreement.[72] Even if, in fact, the agreement is performed and therefore the condition is fulfilled, the instrument is still denied negotiability. The purchaser should not be required to refer to extrinsic facts to determine whether the condition has been fulfilled.

In contrast, where the promise or order is subject only to an implied or constructive condition, the promise or order is treated as being unconditional.[73] A promise is subject to only an implied or constructive condition whenever the condition itself is not expressed. Thus, a recitation that the drawer's order is made in payment of a "car to be delivered" is unconditional because no condition is expressed. Although, under contract law, a court may imply that payment is constructively conditioned upon delivery of the car, such a constructive condition will not defeat the draft's negotiability. Similarly, a promise or order that is subject to a parol, or oral, condition is also deemed to be unconditional. Despite the fact that the implied, parol, or oral condition is ignored in determining whether the instrument is negotiable, the maker or drawer is not necessarily deprived of the benefit of the condition. In our example above, the drawer may have the right to raise the failure of the payee to

69. U.C.C. §3-103(a)(6).
70. U.C.C. §3-104(a) ; U.C.C. §3-104, Official Comment 1.
71. U.C.C. §3-106(a).
72. U.C.C. §3-106, Official Comment 1.
73. U.C.C. §3-106, Official Comment 1.

deliver the car as a defense. The drawer's right to raise this defense depends upon whether the plaintiff has the rights of a holder in due course. We discuss in a subsequent chapter the status of holder in due course. For our purposes now, you may treat a holder in due course as the rough equivalent of a good faith purchaser for value.

a.   Payment Out of Particular Fund

A promise or order is not made conditional merely because payment is to be made solely out of a particular fund or source.[74] For example, payment may be limited to the proceeds of a particular mortgage. The rationale for permitting such a limitation is that there is no good reason to require an obligor to pledge his general credit behind a negotiable instrument. If the purchaser does not like the source or fund out of which payment is to be made, he does not have to purchase the instrument. Although this rule makes sense in theory, problems may arise in determining whether an instrument is subject to a condition (in which case it is not negotiable) or is payable out of a particular source or fund (in which case it is negotiable). For example, an instrument payable "from profits" would appear to be negotiable because it is payable out of a particular source. In contrast, an instrument payable "only if there are profits" would appear not to be negotiable because the promise is conditioned on the presence of profits. Skilled drafting can result in making almost any conditional promise negotiable by phrasing it as the source out of which payment is to be made and not as a condition. It remains to be seen whether courts will allow skilled drafting to convert a truly conditional promise or order into an unconditional one.

b.   Impermissible Reference to Separate Agreements

Early on in the history of negotiable instruments law, a decision was made that a prospective purchaser of a negotiable instrument should be able to determine from the face of the instrument itself all of his rights. This would theoretically enable him to decide how much to pay for the instrument by looking solely at the instrument itself. A reference to other documents contained in an instrument would require that a potential purchaser of the instrument locate and examine these documents. This would cause negotiable instruments to lose a lot of their appeal because it would complicate the procedures required to make a safe purchase. As to payment instruments, such a

---

74. U.C.C. §3-106(b)(ii); U.C.C. §3-106, Official Comment 1.

limitation makes sense. Because a payment instrument is meant to be a substitute for cash, payment by instrument should be as simple and expedient as possible. In contrast, there is little reason for such a requirement in the case of a note. A note is generally a instrument representing an extension of credit rather than payment of an obligation. A potential purchaser of a note will often be basing its decision as to whether to make the purchase upon the likelihood of the maker being able to repay the note. Making this determination requires that the purchaser examine information outside of the note itself to determine the financial stability of the maker. For this reason, simplicity and speed are of far less importance especially when a person is contemplating the purchase of note, which may represent a substantial, long term investment, as contrasted to a draft, which is usually intended for immediate payment. The maker's insolvency is usually a greater risk of nonpayment than would be any condition to the payment of the note.

Despite the questionable nature of the rationale behind the requirement that the purchaser be able to determine his rights from the face of the instrument itself when applied to a note, this requirement long ago became well entrenched in negotiable instruments law. As a result, subject to certain exceptions discussed below, an instrument is not negotiable if reference must be made to a separate agreement in order to determine the holder's right to payment.[75] The promise or order contained in the writing is deemed to be conditional, and therefore not negotiable, if it states that the promise or order contained therein is subject to or governed by or stated in another writing. For example, a note stating that "payment of this note is subject to the terms of the Master Finance Agreement dated February 1, 1993," is not negotiable. In order for the holder to determine his right to repayment of the note, he would have to consult the Master Finance Agreement. The mere existence of the requirement that another writing be consulted is sufficient to destroy negotiability; it is irrelevant that examination of the other writing does not reveal a condition precedent to payment.[76]

While an instrument expressly made subject to another writing is not negotiable, an instrument that merely refers to the existence of another writing may be negotiable.[77] Thus, a reference in a writing stating that the promise or order arises out of a particular transaction or agreement, or is drawn under a letter of credit does not defeat the writing's negotiability. For example, a note which states that it is made "pursuant to" the Master Franchise Agreement dated February 1, 1993, is considered to contain an unconditional

75. U.C.C. §3-106(a)(ii) and (iii).
76. U.C.C. §3-106, Official Comment 1.
77. U.C.C. §3-106(a).

promise.[78] In contrast to use of the term "subject to," use of the term "pursuant to" does not indicate that the note is controlled in any manner by the Master Franchise Agreement. Rather, the reference indicates merely the source out of which the note arose. Needless to say, there will be situations in which it may be very difficult to determine whether the particular phrase used makes the instrument "subject to" the separate writing or whether the phrase simply indicates the instrument's origin. In making this determination, the question that must be answered is whether the parties intended to make their rights and duties under the instrument conditional upon terms found in the separate writing. If the parties have no such intent, then the instrument is negotiable because it is not "subject to" the separate writing.

c. Permissible Reference to Separate Agreement

At times a conflict arises between the desire to keep negotiable instruments as simple and unencumbered as possible and the desire to permit the purchaser to be able to determine all of his rights from the instrument itself. Three exceptions developed in an attempt to accommodate these conflicting interests. Reference may be made to another writing for rights as to (1) collateral, (2) acceleration or (3) prepayment.[79]

Provisions governing the collateral that secures the note or other instrument may be very detailed. If the instrument had to restate every duty and right of the parties regarding the collateral given by the maker to secure repayment of the note, the note would be needlessly long. Allowing reference to the security agreement dispenses with the need to restate in its entirety. Little additional burden is placed upon a potential purchaser in allowing reference to the security agreement in that any person contemplating the purchase of a secured note would surely demand to see the security agreement before purchasing the note.

Likewise, a provision requiring reference to another agreement as to the holder's right to accelerate payment of the instrument should cause little concern to a potential purchaser of the instrument. The purchaser knows by reading the instrument itself when it is due. If he also wants to know what right he has to demand payment prior to the due date, he may refer to the other writ-

78. See Third Natl. Bank in Nashville v. Hardi-Gardens Supply of Illinois, Inc., 380 F. Supp. 930, 15 U.C.C. Rep. Serv. 853 (M.D. Tenn. 1974). The result would be the same if the note was made "as per" another agreement. See D'Andrea v. Feinberg, 45 Misc. 2d 270, 256 N.Y.S.2d 504, 2 U.C.C. Rep. Serv. 410 (1965).
79. U.C.C. §3-106(b)(i).

ing. If he chooses not to, he still at least knows the latest date by which he will receive payment.

Allowing reference to another writing as to the obligor's right to prepay an instrument is more disturbing. A holder may desire to purchase an instrument because of the favorable interest rate that he is receiving. If the obligor has the right to prepay the instrument at will, he has the option of depriving the holder of the favorable return on his investment if the rate of interest drops significantly. The potential purchaser will need, therefore, to see the writing allowing for prepayment.

4. Fixed Amount

Unless a purchaser can determine how much he will be paid under the instrument, he will be unable to determine a fair price to pay for it, thus defeating the basic purpose of negotiable instruments as a money substitute (in the case of drafts) or as a freely transferable promise of repayment (in the case of notes). Even provisions for the payment of attorney's fees or for the payment of increased interest upon default make it impossible for the purchaser to know precisely how much he will ultimately be paid under the instrument since the interest rate and attorney's fees cannot be determined until default has occurred. However, these and other similar provisions must, at times, be included because otherwise the holder may be unwilling to purchase the instrument. In many situations a holder would not have purchased the note unless the note provided for the payment of attorney's fees upon default and yet remained negotiable. Provisions allowing for a discount upon early payment, although rendering the sum payable uncertain, are sometimes necessary in order to encourage the maker to issue the note.

Section 3-104(a) attempts to reach an accommodation between the need for certainty and commercial reality. It does so by providing that the principal sum must be payable in a fixed amount.[80] An instrument is not payable in a fixed amount if the terms used in the instrument to express the sum payable or any component thereof are ambiguous or if reference must be made to an outside source or writing to determine the principal amount. For example, a writing is not negotiable where it guarantees "all indebtedness" or a "sum not to exceed."

Note, however, that certain ambiguities are eliminated by rules of construction found in Article 3 itself: (1) when the words and numbers conflict, the amount designated by the words controls and (2) when handwritten terms

---

80. U.C.C. §3-104(a); U.C.C. §3-112, Official Comment 1.

conflict with printed terms, the handwritten terms control.[81] Thus, for example, if a check provides that it is payable both in the sum of "$100" and "One dollar," the check is payable in the sum of one dollar. Absent this rule of construction, the check, being ambiguous as to the amount payable, would not be payable in a fixed amount.

a.   Provisions for Interest

An instrument may provide for payment with or without interest or other charges as described in the order or promise.[82] Note that only the principal amount of the note needs to be in a fixed amount. Interest or other charges do not have to be payable in a fixed amount.[83] Virtually any type of provision for payment of interest is permissible. An instrument may state the obligation to pay interest as a fixed or variable amount of money or as a fixed or variable rate or rates. The amount or rate of interest may be stated or described in the instrument in any manner and may require reference to information not contained in the instrument.[84] For example, a note payable with interest at the rate of "2% over the Bank of America prime rate" is negotiable. It would even seem that interest can be stated as a described percentage of the profits of a specified business. Since the primary purpose of allowing the interest rate to be described in any manner is to permit variable interest rates, an argument can be made that tying the interest rate to the profits of a company would not be acceptable. However, the fact that the Code clearly states that the rate of interest may be described in any manner would probably compel a court to find such a note to be negotiable.

Instruments do not always make clear the rate at which interest is to be payable or the time from which interest is to be paid. For example, a note may merely state that it is payable "with interest." In these cases, it is clear that the parties intended that interest be paid on the instrument. In order to honor the parties' intentions, Article 3 contains certain rules of construction intended to resolve these uncertainties. When no date is stated from which interest is to be payable, interest on an interest-bearing instrument is payable from the date of the instrument,[85] which is that stated as its date of execu-

81. U.C.C. §3-114.
82. U.C.C. §3-104(a).
83. U.C.C. §3-112, Official Comment 1.
84. U.C.C. §3-112(b); U.C.C. §3-112, Official Comment 1.
85. U.C.C. §3-112(a).

tion.[86] Interest runs on an undated instrument from the date that the instrument was issued.[87]

An obligor need not pay interest on an instrument lacking a provision for the payment of interest. However, when an instrument provides that it is payable "with interest" but the description in the instrument does not allow for its calculation, interest is payable at the judgment rate applicable at the place of payment and at the time interest first accrues.[88] Thus, in our example of an instrument "payable with interest," interest is payable at the judgment rate applicable at the place of payment and at the time interest first accrues. In contrast, an instrument that describes the rate of interest as "the highest rate permitted by law" is payable at the highest rate allowed under the usury laws of the state. Because the "highest rate of interest permitted by law" can be determined, the instrument is payable at such a rate and not at the judgment rate of interest.

b. Provisions for Other Charges

Nothing in section 3-104 or its comments indicates what constitutes "other charges." It is clear, however, that "other charges" include attorney's fees and costs of collection. As a result, an instrument is payable in a fixed amount even though it provides for the payment of costs of collection or attorney's fees, or both, upon any default. The provision for attorney's fees need not specify a particular sum. It may provide for a percentage of the principal balance due, "reasonable attorney's fees," or "attorney's fees." The provision for the payment of attorney's fees or costs of collection must be limited to costs of collection or attorney's fees incurred in the collection of the instrument alone. However, the fees or costs provided for may include those incurred without the institution of legal action.

"Other charges" should also include prepayment penalties, late payment penalties, or other penalties. In addition, inclusion of provisions for discounts or rebates should not defeat an instrument's negotiability.

A more difficult question arises as to the extent that the drafters intended to expand the permissible types of charges that an instrument could contain and remain negotiable. For instance, an argument can be made that a duty to pay taxes or to pay to insure collateral constitutes permissible "other charges."

---

86. U.C.C. §3-113(a). This is true even if the instrument has been dated later than its actual date of execution (called "postdated") or dated prior to its actual date of execution (called "antedated").

87. U.C.C. §3-113(b).

88. U.C.C. §3-112(a); U.C.C. §3-112(b); U.C.C. §3-112, Official Comment 1.

This argument may succeed if the drawer or maker is promising to pay to the holder the costs the holder incurred for taxes or insurance. However, if the drawer or maker is promising to directly pay taxes on collateral or to insure the collateral, these promises may fall under the heading of "other promises" (thus defeating an instrument's negotiability as discussed in subsection D(8), infra) rather than "other charges" since the money will not be paid to the holder.

5. *Payable in Money*

An instrument is not negotiable unless it is payable in money. An instrument providing that the maker shall pay "$50," "50 dollars in currency," or the like is payable in money.[89]

"Money" is defined as "a medium of exchange authorized or adopted by a domestic or foreign government and includes a monetary unit of account established by an intergovernmental organization or by agreement between two or more nations."[90] A monetary unit of account established by an intergovernmental organization would be, for example, European Community Units ("ECU"), which are issued by the European Community, an organization consisting of several nations.

Instruments need not be payable in United States dollars.[91] Any medium of exchange authorized or adopted by any domestic or foreign government is money.[92] The instrument does not have to be payable in the country in whose currency the instrument is payable. For example, an instrument payable in the United States in Swiss francs and an instrument payable in Canada in United States dollars are both payable in money.

Unless it otherwise provides, an instrument that states the amount payable in foreign currency may be paid either in that foreign currency or in an equivalent amount of U.S. dollars. Only if the instrument requires that the medium of payment shall be the foreign currency must payment be made in that currency.[93]

---

89. U.C.C. §3-104(a); U.C.C. §3-104, Official Comment 1.

90. U.C.C. §1-201(24); U.C.C. §1-201, Official Comment 24; U.C.C. §3-104, Official Comment 1.

91. U.C.C. §3-107, Official Comment.

92. U.C.C. §1-201(24).

93. U.C.C. §3-107; U.C.C. §3-107, Official Comment.

6. Payable to Order or to Bearer

The goal of negotiable instruments law is served only if the purchaser can readily determine whether a writing qualifies as a negotiable instrument. Unless a prospective purchaser can quickly and with certainty determine whether an instrument is negotiable, the prospective purchaser will not purchase the instrument. Likewise, the obligor needs to know with certainty whether by signing the writing the obligor is forfeiting the right to raise defenses that arise from the underlying transaction. For these reasons Article 3 requires that certain magical words be used in order for a writing to qualify as a negotiable instrument. A negotiable instrument must either be payable to order or payable to bearer.[94] With the exception of checks, an instrument that is not payable to order or bearer is not governed by Article 3.[95] As a result, there is supposedly a simple line between those writings covered by Article 3 and those that are not. Unfortunately, with the exception of bankers, a few lawyers, and students studying the law of negotiable instruments, most people do not realize that the inclusion or omission of words like "order," "bearer," or "cash" determine whether the writing is a negotiable instrument or not. Many makers therefore execute notes without realizing the rights they are thereby giving up.

There is a significant exception to the requirement that an instrument to be negotiable must be payable to "order" or to "bearer." A check that meets all of the requirements of section 3-104(a) except for not being made payable to "order" or "bearer" is a negotiable instrument governed by Article 3.[96] This means that such a check may be acquired by a holder in due course who could cut off the drawer's defenses or claims to the instrument. The rationale for this rule is twofold. First, most people look at checks as a substitute for cash. The transaction in which a check is taken is usually fairly quick. A taker of a check would probably not even notice if the check omitted the words "to the order of."[97] In contrast, in a transaction involving a note or other draft, the taker will usually spend more time examining the instrument to determine all of her rights. She will therefore, it is assumed, likely notice the absence of words of negotiability. Second, depositary banks process checks by computer. If the omission of the words "order" or "bearer" could defeat the depositary bank's status as a holder in due course, a depositary bank may be required to visually inspect checks simply to determine whether words of negotiability are present.

94. U.C.C. §3-104(a)(1).
95. U.C.C. §3-104, Official Comment 2.
96. U.C.C. §3-104(c).
97. U.C.C. §3-104, Official Comment 2.

Little is gained by having banks incur these expenses, which, of course, will be passed on to their customers in the form of increased costs of maintaining a checking account.

The manner in which an instrument payable to bearer may be negotiated is significantly different from the manner in which an instrument payable to order may be negotiated. An instrument payable to bearer may be negotiated by delivery alone while an instrument payable to the order of an identified person also requires, in addition to delivery, indorsement by that person. As a result, it is crucial that a purchaser know whether the instrument is payable to order or payable to bearer.

An instrument *payable to bearer* may take one of several forms. The instrument may simply state that it is payable "to bearer." Or the instrument may use language indicating that the person in possession of it is entitled to payment.[98] For example, instruments payable to "holder," to "cash," or to the "order of cash" are payable to bearer.[99] Similarly, an instrument that does not name a payee, for example, "pay to order of _____," is payable to bearer.[100] The instrument, although negotiable, is also an incomplete instrument until the name of the payee is inserted.[101]

In contrast, an instrument is *payable to order* if it is payable (1) to the order of an identified person, for example, "order of John Jones" or (2) to an identified person or order, for example, "John Jones or order."[102] It appears necessary that the instrument include the word "order." There is no indication that synonyms for "order of" such as "assigns of" are sufficient. Any deviation from the word "order" makes it unclear to a potential purchaser whether or not the instrument is negotiable.

Only when an instrument is not payable to bearer may it be payable to order.[103] When an instrument is payable both to order and to bearer, the instrument is payable to bearer.[104] Instruments containing the following designations are payable to bearer: (1) "bearer or order," (2) "order of bearer," (3) "John Doe or bearer," or (4) "order of cash."[105] The rationale for treating these instruments as payable to bearer is that use of bearer words like "cash" or "bearer" more likely evidence the issuer's intention than does the word "order." This is especially likely where the drawer of a check clearly desired to

98. U.C.C. §3-109(a)(1).
99. U.C.C. §3-109(a)(3).
100. U.C.C. §3-109(a)(2).
101. U.C.C. §3-109, Official Comment 2.
102. U.C.C. §3-109(b).
103. U.C.C. §3-109(b); U.C.C. §3-109, Official Comment 2.
104. U.C.C. §3-109(b); U.C.C. §3-109, Official Comment 2.
105. U.C.C. §3-109(a)(1); U.C.C. §3-109(a)(3); U.C.C. §3-109, Official Comment 2.

make the check payable to cash but simply neglected to cross out the words "order of" on the check form. By treating these instruments as payable to bearer, subsequent transferees, who in believing that the instrument is payable to bearer fail to obtain their transferor's indorsement, are protected.[106]

7. Payable on Demand or at a Definite Time

We have already discussed how a potential purchaser of an instrument needs to know how much she will be paid under the instrument in order to determine the amount she will pay for it. For the same reasons, a potential purchaser needs to know when payment will be made. Therefore an instrument is not negotiable unless it is payable either at a definite time or on demand.[107]

a. Payable on Demand

A promise or order is "payable on demand" if it states that it is payable on demand or at sight or otherwise indicates that it is payable at the will of the holder.[108] The distinguishing characteristic of an instrument payable on demand is that the time payment is due is determined in the sole discretion of the holder. Thus, an instrument is not payable on demand where it is payable upon a contingency limiting the discretion of the holder to determine the time of payment; for example, instruments payable "upon an acceptable permanent loan being secured" or "at the earliest convenience of the maker" are not payable on demand. Certain instruments expressly state that they are payable on demand. Obviously where an item states that it is payable "on demand," the instrument is payable on demand. When the instrument states that it is payable "on presentation" and "at sight," it is likewise payable on demand since these terms are synonyms for the phrase "on demand."[109] An instrument otherwise payable on demand remains payable on demand even though it is postdated or antedated.[110] However, with one exception, a postdated instrument payable on demand is not payable before its date. As subsequently discussed in Chapter 6, a payor bank that is not given proper notice of the postdating may pay a check even before its date.

---

106. U.C.C. §3-109, Official Comment 2.
107. U.C.C. §3-104(a)(2).
108. U.C.C. §3-108(a).
109. Do not confuse the phrase "after sight" with the phrase "at sight." "After sight" means after acceptance of the draft by the drawee. Thus, an instrument payable, for example, "30 days after sight" is payable 30 days after its acceptance and not on demand.
110. U.C.C. §3-113(a).

An instrument that fails to state when payment is due is deemed to be payable on demand.[111] Thus, a note that states "I promise to pay to the order of Jill the sum of $200" is payable on demand. It is presumed that the failure of the parties to state the date at which payment is due means that the parties intended that the instrument be payable on demand. Where an instrument is payable both at a fixed date and also on demand before the fixed date, the instrument is payable on demand. For example, a note may be payable "on June 1, 1997, or earlier upon demand of the holder." However, if demand for payment has not been made before that date, the instrument becomes payable at a definite time on the fixed date.[112] The only significance of this transformation is as to the time when the statute of limitations begins to run.

b.   Payable at a Definite Time

A promise or order is "payable at a definite time" if it is payable at a time or times readily ascertainable when the promise or order is issued.[113] An instrument is payable at a definite time as long as the date is readily ascertainable at the time the promise or order is issued even though the date is not specified in the instrument. As a result, an instrument payable on "the day that the 2000 Summer Olympic Games commence" is payable at a definite time only if the date the 2000 Summer Olympic Games begin has been set at the time that the instrument is issued.

An instrument that is payable (1) at a fixed date, for example, "on February 1, 1997," (2) a definite period after a stated date, for example, "30 days after date" or (3) on "elapse of a definite period of time after sight or acceptance," for example, "45 days after acceptance," is payable at a definite time.[114]

A note or draft payable a fixed period "after date," for example, "30 days after date," which does not state a date, is an incomplete instrument. Once the note or draft is completed by the addition of a date, the instrument becomes payable at a definite time. Whether the addition of the date is binding upon the obligor depends upon the rules as to the completion of incomplete instruments discussed subsequently in Chapter 4. In contrast, a draft payable a fixed period after sight or after acceptance is a complete and negotiable instrument. For example, a draft may be payable "30 days after sight," which means 30 days after the drawee has accepted the draft. A draft payable a fixed period after sight or acceptance is payable at a definite time.[115] Even though no time for

111. U.C.C. §3-108(a)(ii).
112. U.C.C. §3-108(c).
113. U.C.C. §3-108(b); U.C.C. §3-108, Official Comment.
114. U.C.C. §3-108(b); U.C.C. §3-108, Official Comment.
115. U.C.C. §3-108(b).

payment can be determined at the time of the instrument's issuance, the holder has it within his ability to set the date of payment by presenting the draft for acceptance.

c. Subject to Acceleration or Prepayment

An instrument that is otherwise payable at a definite time remains so even though the time of payment is subject to acceleration.[116] The time of payment is said to be subject to acceleration where a clause, either in the instrument or in another writing referred to in the instrument, allows the holder to demand, under specified conditions, payment prior to the time set in the instrument for payment. Allowing the holder this right does not make the time of payment uncertain because it is usually within the holder's discretion to decide whether to accelerate the time of payment.

The type of acceleration clause is irrelevant. Great leeway is given for acceleration clauses because of the importance of these clauses to lenders. A lender, especially a bank, needs to have the ability to accelerate the time payment is due upon any number of possible risks materializing. The clause may provide for acceleration at the unrestricted option of the holder. It may limit acceleration to circumstances where an installment has not been paid or where the holder "deems himself insecure." The Code attempts to limit the potential abuse of the latter type of acceleration clauses by giving a holder the right to activate such clauses only when he believes in good faith that the prospect of payment or performance is impaired.[117] To protect the lender, the burden of establishing lack of good faith is upon the borrower.[118]

Even where the lender is not worried about the possibility of repayment, an acceleration clause may come in handy. For example, the lender may want to protect against an unexpected rise in the rate of interest. Although this could be accomplished by use of a variable rate of interest, the borrower may not want to risk a dramatic increase in the rate of interest. As an accommodation to the interests of both the lender and the borrower, the instrument may provide for automatic acceleration when, for instance, there is a designated rise in the prime rate of interest of a particular bank. By use of this type of clause, the lender will not be saddled with an unprofitable loan while the borrower will not have to pay a burdensome rate of interest.

The liberality in the type of permissible acceleration clauses allows for the conversion of an instrument that otherwise would not be negotiable to one

116. U.C.C. §3-108(b)(ii).
117. U.C.C. §1-208.
118. U.C.C. §1-208.

that is negotiable. For example, a note "due on the death of the maker" is not payable at a definite time because it is not reasonably ascertainable when death will occur. Not being payable at the holder's discretion, it is also not payable on demand. As a result, the note is not negotiable. However, a note payable "on January 1, 2300, but subject to acceleration in the event of the maker's death" is technically negotiable even though the maker's death will certainly occur before the year 2300. It would not be surprising if a court looked through this charade and found such a note not to be negotiable.

Similarly, an instrument that is subject to *prepayment* by the obligor also remains payable at a definite time.[119] Despite the fact that the obligor reserves the right to make early payment of the instrument, the holder knows the latest date by which the instrument will be paid.

d.   Subject to Extension

An instrument is also payable at a definite time even though it is subject to *extension* at the option of the holder, maker or acceptor or automatically upon or after a specified act or event.[120] Even if the holder has the right to extend the time of payment indefinitely, the instrument remains negotiable.[121] In contrast, when the maker or the acceptor has the right to extend the time for payment or where the time for payment is automatically extended upon the occurrence of a specified event, the instrument is payable at a definite time only if the right to extend is limited to extension to a further definite time.[122] For example, a clause allowing the maker to "extend payment until the maker has sufficient cash to make payment" defeats the instrument's negotiability. In contrast, a clause providing that the maker may "extend the time of payment for a period of two additional years" will not destroy negotiability because the holder knows that he will receive payment no later than two years after the original due date. When the maker or acceptor has the option to extend the time of payment or when the time is extended automatically upon a specified act or event, the holder has no power to determine when payment will be made. Thus, unless the option to extend is limited to an extension to a definite time, the holder will not know when he can expect payment.

---

119. U.C.C. §3-108(b)(i).
120. U.C.C. §3-108(b)(iii) and (iv).
121. U.C.C. §3-108(b)(iii); U.C.C. §3-108, Official Comment.
122. U.C.C. §3-108(b) (iv); U.C.C. §3-108, Official Comment.

D. Requirements for Negotiability

8. *No Other Promises or Orders*

Negotiable instruments law has evolved over several centuries often advancing seemingly strange requirements for the negotiability of writings. Early on, the law viewed negotiable instruments as "couriers without luggage";[123] in other words, naked promises or orders unencumbered by any excess baggage. Frankly, it is unclear why this view gained such acceptance. However, as commerce grew more complex, instruments containing naked promises became less and less saleable. Creditors wanted the means to coerce obligors to pay instruments thereby limiting the creditor's exposure to the risk of nonpayment. As the law evolved, the logic behind the creditor's position began gradually to win out.

Thus, although the general rule is that an instrument to be negotiable can contain "no other undertaking or instruction by the person promising or ordering payment to do any act in addition to the payment of money," this general rule is subject to some important exceptions. These exceptions are that an instrument may contain any of the following promises or instructions and retain its negotiability:[124] (1) an undertaking or power to give, maintain, or protect collateral to secure payment, (2) an authorization or power to the holder to confess judgment[125] or realize on or dispose of collateral, or (3) a waiver of the benefit of any law intended for the advantage or protection of an obligor.[126]

Inclusion in an instrument of a promise, obligation, order, or power not authorized by Article 3 defeats the instrument's negotiability. A negotiable instrument may not contain a promise to pay taxes or to maintain a minimum working capital. An instrument cannot be negotiable if the holder has the right to require the obligor to do something in lieu of the payment of money.

The prohibition against additional terms is limited to undertakings and instructions given by the person promising or ordering payment. A promise by

---

123. Overton v. Tyler, 3 Pa. 346 (1846).

124. U.C.C. §3-104(a)(3); U.C.C. §3-104, Official Comment 1.

125. The holder may be given the power to confess judgment at "any time." However, section 3-104(a)(3)(ii) does not validate the use of confession of judgment clauses in the great majority of states where such provisions are illegal.

126. The waiver may be made by the drawer, maker, acceptor, or indorser regardless of whether the party is the principal obligor or a surety. The term may waive a condition precedent like presentment or notice of dishonor, or it may waive a suretyship defense. The term may also waive rights like homestead rights, other exemptions, and statute of limitations protections. U.C.C. §3-104(a)(3)(iii).

Section 3-104(a)(3)(iii) does not validate the inclusion of a waiver that is otherwise illegal. For instance, the right to raise real defenses cannot be waived. See Geiger Fin. Co. v. Graham, 123 Ga. App. 771, 182 S.E.2d 521, 9 U.C.C. Rep. Serv. 598 (1971).

the holder does not violate this prohibition.[127] However, if the maker's or drawer's obligation to pay is conditioned upon the holder's performance of his promise, the promise or order contained in the instrument is conditional and the instrument is not negotiable. For example, if the holder of a note is concerned that the death of the maker may leave her estate with insufficient funds to pay off the note, the holder may want to eliminate this risk by having the right to purchase, at the holder's own cost, a life insurance policy on the maker's life. Obtaining such a policy would establish a fund to pay off the note in the event of the maker's death. The fact that the holder is given this right does not destroy the negotiability of the note.[128] However, if the promise of the maker is made expressly conditional upon the holder's purchase of the life insurance policy, the maker's promise is thereby made conditional.

An instrument may contain a statement that collateral has been given to secure the obligation evidenced by the instrument.[129] Because of the risks to subsequent holders of the maker's insolvency, a note unsecured by collateral is usually not readily marketable except at a substantial discount. Rather than having the note refer to a separate agreement granting the payee a security interest in the collateral, it may be simpler to allow the note to contain provisions dealing with the collateral.

For this reason, an instrument may include a provision granting the holder a security interest in the collateral. The collateral may secure both the obligation evidenced by the instrument itself and any other obligation of the obligor. An instrument may also require that the obligor furnish additional collateral.[130] The obligation to furnish additional collateral may arise automatically upon the occurrence of a specified condition, at the will of the holder, or at the option of the holder whenever he feels insecure. The obligation to give additional collateral may be accompanied by a provision that in the event of the obligor's failure to furnish the additional collateral, the holder may accelerate the balance of the principal due. If the right to require additional collateral is at the will of the holder or at the option of the holder whenever he deems himself insecure, the holder may not exercise the right unless he believes in good faith that the prospect of payment or performance is impaired.[131]

Although the phrase "maintain, or protect collateral" is broad and can be read to include a promise to pay taxes on or insure the collateral, inclusion of such promises risks destroying an instrument's negotiability. Comment 1 to

127. U.C.C. §3-104 (a)(3).
128. See Universal C.I.T. Credit Corp. v. Ingel, 347 Mass. 119, 196 N.E.2d 847, 2 U.C.C. Rep. Serv. 82, 3 U.C.C. Rep. Serv. 303 (1964).
129. U.C.C. §3-104(a)(3)(i).
130. U.C.C. §3-112(1)(c) (1989).
131. U.C.C. §1-208.

D. Requirements for Negotiability

section 3-104 states "The three exceptions stated in Section 3-104(a)(3) are based on and are intended to have the same meaning as former Section 3-112(1)(b),(c), (d), and (e). . . ." Under former Article 3, a promise to pay taxes[132] or insure the collateral destroyed an instrument's negotiability.[133] We will have to wait to see if courts will now read the exception for maintaining and protecting collateral broadly enough to permit inclusion in a note of promises to pay taxes on or insure collateral.

A similar problem arises as to whether a conditional sales contract can qualify as a negotiable instrument. Under a conditional sales contract, the buyer usually agrees to pay for goods in installments with the seller retaining title to the goods until payment in full has been made. During the drafting of Revised Article 3, it was generally agreed that conditional sales contracts, being much more like Article 2 contracts for the sale of goods rather than negotiable instruments, were not the type of writing that should be governed by Article 3. However, despite substantial discussion concerning how they could be effectively excluded, the drafters were unable to devise a suitable standard that effectively excluded conditional sales contracts while including writings that were properly regarded as negotiable instruments. Official Comment 2 to section 3-104 states in part:

> Words making a promise or order payable to bearer or to order are the most distinguishing feature of a negotiable instrument and such words are frequently referred to as "words of negotiability." Article 3 is not meant to apply to contracts for the sale of goods or services or the sale or lease of real property or similar writings that may contain a promise to pay money. The use of words of negotiability in such contracts would be an aberration. Absence of the words precludes any argument that such contracts might be negotiable instruments.

Although it is possible to argue that a conditional sales contract that is payable to order or to bearer is a negotiable instrument, it is clear that the drafters intended otherwise. A similar problem existed under former Article 3. Courts under former Article 3 generally held that such contracts did not fall under former Article 3.[134] The result should be the same under Revised Article 3.

---

132. See Hinckley v. Eggers, 587 S.W.2d 448, 27 U.C.C. Rep. Serv. 1024 (Tex. App. 1979).

133. See P & K Marble, Inc. v. La Paglia, 147 A.D.2d 804, 537 N.Y.S.2d 682, 9 U.C.C. Rep. Serv. 2d 966 (1989) (note not negotiable where it contains promise to keep property insured); Massey Ferguson Credit Corp. v. Bice, 450 N.W.2d 435, 11 U.C.C. Rep. Serv. 2d 116 (SD 1990) (promises to purchase property damage insurance and credit life insurance make note not negotiable).

134. See Jefferson v. Mitchell Select Furniture Co., 56 Ala. App. 269, 321 So. 2d 216, 18 U.C.C. Rep. Serv. 431 (1975); Discount Purchasing Co. v. Porch, 12 U.C.C. Rep. Serv. 600 (Tenn. App. 1973); Geiger Finance Co. v. Graham, 123 Ga. App. 771, 182 S.E.2d 521, 9 U.C.C. Rep. Serv. 598(1971).

CHAPTER 2

Holder-in-Due-Course Status: Right of Purchaser to Take Free of Claims and Defenses to Instrument

As we discussed in Chapter 1, one of the reasons negotiable instruments were created was to be a cash substitute without the burdens accompanying the use of cash. To serve this purpose, the owner of a negotiable instrument had to be able either to convert the instrument into cash or use the instrument as she would cash with little risk, cost, or difficulty. At the same time, the owner had to be freed from the problems associated with the use of cash: the minor problem of the cumbersomeness of carrying around large amounts of cash and the significant problem of its potential loss or theft. Lost or stolen cash is almost never returned to its original owner.

Negotiable instruments law greatly reduces the risks of theft or loss by creating the status of "holder" which ensures the owner of the instrument that payment cannot be obtained without his signature (called an "indorsement"). The risk of nonpayment is greatly reduced by the creation of "holder-in-due-course status," the negotiable instrument's version of good faith purchaser for value. A holder in due course takes the instrument free from virtually any ground of nonpayment, including all possessory claims to the instrument, and virtually all defenses and claims in recoupment of any party.[1] A holder in due course is protected from other risks as well.[2] The only real risk to which a holder in due course is exposed is the possible insolvency of the parties obligated to pay the instrument, and the holder can greatly reduce this risk by knowing the party with whom he has dealt.

However, these very protections given to a holder in due course are at the expense of another, usually innocent, party. Allowing a holder in due course

---

1. U.C.C. §3-305(b).
2. See, e.g., U.C.C. §3-601(b).

to take free of a prior party's claim of ownership to the instrument means that the prior owner suffers the loss. For example, assume that Abe, the original holder of a note payable to bearer, loses the note. The note is found by Bill who negotiates the note to Carl who, paying value for the note in good faith and without notice of Bill's lack of title, qualifies as a holder in due course. (See Figure 2.1.)

FIGURE 2.1

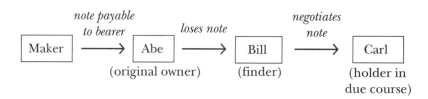

By protecting Carl, Abe (the innocent original owner of the note) loses the value of the note. Although Abe has an action for conversion against Bill, it is unlikely that Bill will be around to atone for his sin. Similarly, if the maker of the note had a defense, allowing Carl to take free of the maker's defense would result in the innocent maker suffering the loss.

Because the protection accorded to a holder in due course is at the expense of other, often innocent, parties, the qualifications for holder-in-due-course status had to be crafted to balance the need to encourage worthy persons to purchase instruments with the need to protect innocent parties. The rules also had to take into account the burden imposed upon the aspiring purchaser in proving his holder-in-due-course status. If a potential purchaser must face a complex lawsuit in order to prove his holder-in-due-course status, he will be leery of purchasing the instrument even if he is likely to prevail in the lawsuit.

Keeping in mind the need to balance the foregoing interests, let us look at the requirements for holder-in-due-course status. To obtain holder-in-due-course status, a purchaser of an instrument must: (1) be a holder, (2) take for value, (3) take in good faith, and (4) take without notice of numerous proscribed facts.[3] Each of these requirements serves its own purpose. Section A discusses how a person becomes a holder. Section B discusses the taking of an instrument for value and section C discusses when a holder takes an instrument in good faith and without notice of any proscribed fact.

3. See U.C.C. §3-302(a); U.C.C. §3-302(a)(2)(i); U.C.C.§3-302(a)(2)(ii) for definitions of these first three terms.

A. HOLDER STATUS

1. *Requirements for Obtaining Holder Status*

Even though most holders of an instrument are probably also the owners of the instrument, a "holder" does not have to be the "owner";[4] holder status is acquired by meeting certain formalistic requirements apparent from the instrument itself, not by having any legal or equitable right to the instrument. The reason for this is simple. A person paying or buying an instrument does not have the time to determine whether the person who has the power to negotiate or discharge the instrument owns the instrument. The payor or purchaser must be able to immediately determine from the face of the instrument itself, together with identification of the purported holder, whether that person is the "holder."

The primary advantage of using a negotiable instrument—that is, the ease by which it can be sold or converted into cash—would be defeated if a person could not safely pay or purchase the instrument without investigating whether the person with whom he is dealing is truly the owner of the instrument. To make the burden on the payor or purchaser as minimal as possible, only two conditions must be satisfied in order for a person to qualify as a holder of an instrument: (1) the person must have possession of the instrument; and (2) the obligation evidenced by the instrument must run to him.[5]

a. Possession of Instrument

A person cannot be a holder of an instrument unless that person has possession of the instrument. The requirement of possession is a necessary one. It is necessary that at any given time only one person can be the holder of the instrument. An example will make this point clear. John makes a check payable to "cash." When a check is payable to cash, it is payable to bearer, which means that the person in possession of the check is its holder. If John negotiates this check to Bill for value, Bill can become a holder in due course of the check. Assume, though, that Bill loses the check. The finder sells the check to Mira who, having no idea that the check was lost, takes the check for value and becomes its holder in due course. (See Figure 2.2.)

---

4. See Chapter 2E(2)(d) for a discussion of ownership.
5. This is subject to an exception for collecting banks. U.C.C.§4-205(1).

FIGURE 2.2

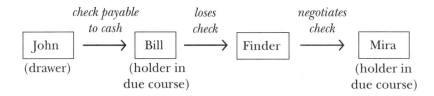

If possession were not necessary for holder-in-due-course status, both Bill and Mira would have claims to holder-in-due-course status. Because a holder in due course takes free of all claims of ownership to the instrument,[6] both would claim to take free of the other person's claim to the check. Would Bill or Mira prevail? Who knows? However, because a person cannot become a holder unless the person is in possession of the check, only Mira is a holder, and therefore Mira, not Bill, is the only holder in due course of the check.

Mira, therefore, takes free of Bill's claim of ownership to the check.

A person can acquire possession of an instrument, and holder status, in one of two ways:[7] (1) by having the instrument issued to him; or (2) by the post-issuance act of negotiation.

b.   Issuance of Instrument

An instrument is *issued* when it is first delivered by the maker or drawer to either a (1) holder or (2) nonholder for the purpose of giving rights on the instrument to any person.[8] For example, the drawer issues a check when he delivers the check to the payee. The payee is a holder because the payee is in possession of an instrument payable to himself. The drawer has issued the instrument in that he has delivered it to the holder (the payee) for the purpose of giving rights on the instrument to the holder (the payee). For that matter, when a drawer delivers a check to a remitter, he also issues the check. For example, if Jim buys a cashier's check from Bank of America in order to purchase a car from Southwest Auto, he may request Bank of America make the check payable to Southwest Auto. When Bank of America gives the check to Jim, it issues the check even though Jim is not the payee of the check. Bank of America delivered the check to Jim, a nonholder, for the purpose of giving rights on the check to Southwest Auto. Bank of America would likewise have issued the check to Jim if he were the payee of the check.

6. U.C.C. §3-306.
7. U.C.C. §3-201, Official Comment 1; U.C.C. §3-105(a); U.C.C. §1-201(20).
8. U.C.C. §3-105(a).

c. Negotiation of Instrument

"Negotiation" is a transfer of possession of an instrument, whether voluntary or involuntary, by a person other than the issuer (maker or drawer) to another person who thereby becomes its holder.[9] In our example of a cashier's check made payable to Southwest Auto, Jim's delivery of the check is a negotiation of the check because Southwest Auto, now having possession of the check made payable to itself, thereby becomes the holder of the check. If the check is payable to Jim himself, he would, in addition to delivering the check, have to indorse the check to Southwest Auto in order for his transfer of possession to be a negotiation.

d. Delivery of Instrument

With an exception to be mentioned shortly, both issuance and negotiation require delivery of the instrument to the aspiring holder. "Delivery" is defined as the voluntary transfer of possession.[10] Two elements are required for delivery of an instrument. First, the deliverer must intend to transfer possession of the instrument, and second, the deliverer must actually transfer possession of the instrument. Neither issuance nor negotiation occurs until possession has been transferred.[11] Until possession has been transferred, the existing holder can change his mind, cancel the indorsement, and further negotiate the instrument to another person.

The key to determining whether possession has been transferred is whether the transferor has placed the instrument out of his control. Thus, when the transferor gives the instrument to his own agent for delivery to the transferee, delivery does not take place until the agent transfers possession of the instrument to the transferee. Because it is still in the possession of his agent, the transferor retains control of the instrument. In contrast, handing the instrument to the transferee's agent or mailing the instrument to the transferee is a delivery because upon these acts being taken, the instrument is no longer in the transferor's control.

There are some circumstances in which requiring an actual transfer of physical possession of the instrument may seem unnecessarily technical and unjust. Under these circumstances, a court may find that a good faith purchaser of an instrument, although lacking physical possession of the instrument, has constructive possession of it and therefore qualifies as the holder. For example, a transaction may be structured such that an instrument is

9. U.C.C. §3-201(a).
10. U.C.C. §1-201(14).
11. U.C.C. §3-201, Official Comment 1.

deposited with an escrow holder pending performance by the payee of certain duties. After the payee has performed these duties, the instrument should be deemed to be constructively delivered to the payee since, although he does not yet have physical possession of the instrument, he, and not the person depositing the instrument, is the only person who has the right to its possession. "Constructive possession" (sometimes called "constructive delivery") will not be found where the alleged transferor retains control of the instrument in that he may request its return from the third party. But where the instrument is, for all practical purposes, delivered to the transferee, the mere fact that it remains in the possession of a third person will not defeat delivery.

e. Negotiation Through Involuntary Transfer of Possession

In most situations, negotiation occurs through a voluntary transfer of possession by the holder or remitter.[12] However, although the actual transfer of possession is necessary for the transferee to become a holder, the transfer need not be voluntary. For example, a thief or finder of an instrument payable to bearer becomes the holder even though the transfer of possession was involuntary.

Assume that a check payable to bearer is stolen from Bill by Jim. Jim does not qualify as a holder in due course and therefore would be subject to Bill's claim of ownership.[13] However, if Jim negotiated the check to Ace Check Cashing Service, Ace may qualify as a holder in due course and take the instrument free of Bill's claim of ownership. The result would be the same if the check was stolen from the drawer before its delivery to Bill. Jim, not being a holder in due course, would take subject to the drawer's defense of nondelivery. However, once the check was negotiated to Ace Check Cashing Service, Ace would take free of the defense of nondelivery.

f. Obligation Must Run to Possessor

The possessor must, in addition to having possession of the instrument, be the person to whom the obligation contained in the instrument runs. All instruments are issued as either payable to order or to bearer.[14] Ase discussed in Chapter 1, when an instrument is payable to bearer, transfer of possession

---

12. U.C.C. §3-201, Official Comment 1.
13. U.C.C. §3-305(a)(2).
14. U.C.C. §3-109.

alone is sufficient for its negotiation.[15] To negotiate an instrument payable to order, the instrument must also be indorsed.

g. Indorsement

An *indorsement* sufficient to negotiate an instrument must be written by or on behalf of the holder[16] or his authorized agent.[17] A forged or unauthorized indorsement is not effective to negotiate the instrument. In Chapter 4 we will discuss situations in which the person whose indorsement is forged or unauthorized is estopped or otherwise precluded[18] from denying the authenticity of the indorsement.[19] Leaving aside these cases for the time being, if an indorsement in the chain of title is forged or unauthorized, no transferee subsequent to the unauthorized or forged indorsement can become a holder.

Assume, for example, that a check is made payable to Dan. Dan loses the check and the finder, Fred, forges Dan's indorsement on the check. Fred transfers the check for value to Gina. Gina thereafter deposits the check in her bank account at Wells Fargo Bank which demands payment from the payor bank, Bank of America. (See Figure 2.3.)

Because Dan's indorsement was forged, neither Fred, Gina, nor Wells Fargo Bank are holders of the check. As a result, Bank of America has no obligation to make payment on the check. If it does make payment, Dan will have the right to recover the amount of the check from Bank of America on a theory of conversion, which is discussed in Chapter 4. The result would be the same if Fred transferred the check without signing Dan's name. Unless Dan himself or through an authorized agent indorses the check, no subsequent person can become a holder of the check. This is the reason why it is safe to mail a check. Unless it reaches the intended payee, no one has the legal right to cash or negotiate the check.

15. U.C.C. §3-201(b).
16. U.C.C. §3-201(b). An indorsement written by one other than a holder is sufficient for the undertaking of the indorser's contract, U.C.C. §3-415(a); U.C.C. §3-204(a), but it is not sufficient to negotiate instrument.
17. The authority may be actual or apparent. However, an attempted indorsement by an agent who has exceeded his authority is an unauthorized indorsement.
18. U.C.C. §3-406.
19. U.C.C. §3-201, Official Comment 3.

FIGURE 2.3

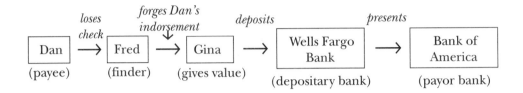

h.   Types of Indorsements

Two types of indorsements can be used to negotiate an instrument:[20] a special indorsement and a blank indorsement.[21] A special indorsement identifies the person to whom it is payable.[22] If the check is payable to Bill, Bill specially indorses the check by making it payable to John and by Bill signing his own name. No words of negotiability, for example, "order of," are required for a special indorsement. It is only necessary that the indorsement identify the person to whom it is payable. Both "Pay to the order of John Jones /s/ Bill," "To John, /s/ Bill," and "Pay to John Jones /s/ Bill" are special indorsements.

A "blank indorsement" is an indorsement that is not payable to an identified person.[23] It can consist of the unaccompanied signature of the holder or her signature accompanied by such phrases as "pay to bearer," "pay to holder," "pay to bank," or "pay to cash."[24] An instrument indorsed in blank becomes payable to bearer and any person who possesses the instrument becomes its holder. This is why it is dangerous to sign your name on the back of a check before reaching the bank to cash or deposit the check. If the check is lost or stolen, the check, being indorsed in blank, is payable to bearer and

20. The holder's indorsement is effective to negotiate the instrument even if accompanied by words of assignment, guaranty, condition, waiver, or the like. U.C.C. §3-204(a). An indorsement that transfers a security interest in the instrument is effective as an unqualified indorsement. U.C.C. §3-204(c).

21. There are two other types of indorsements. An "anomalous indorsement" is an indorsement made by a person who is not the holder of the instrument. U.C.C. §3-205(d). It does not negotiate the instrument or affect the manner in which the instrument may be negotiated. U.C.C. §3-205, Official Comment 3. The only effect of an anomalous indorsement, which usually is made by an accommodation party, is to undertake liability as an indorser. U.C.C. §3-205, Official Comment 3. A "restrictive indorsement" is effective to negotiate the instrument, U.C.C. §3-206(a), although it may prevent a subsequent holder from becoming a holder in due course. U.C.C. §3-206(e).

22. U.C.C. §3-205(a).

23. U.C.C. §3-205(b).

24. U.C.C. §3-205, Official Comment 2. Use of the words "pay to _____" with no one's name filled in is also a blank indorsement.

any finder becomes the holder. To guard against this risk, any holder of an instrument indorsed in blank may convert the blank indorsement into a special indorsement by writing over the signature of the indorser the name of an indorsee.[25] If Bill indorses a check in blank and delivers the check to John, in order to avoid the risk of losing the check while indorsed in blank, John may write over Bill's indorsement the words "Pay to John." The check is now payable to John and John must indorse the check before any one else can become its holder.

i. Indorsement Must Be Written on Instrument

As a general rule, an indorsement must be written on the instrument itself. This rule makes sense. If an indorsement could be written on a separate unattached piece of paper, a potential purchaser of the instrument may be deceived into believing that he is the holder of the check. For example, assume that Bill indorsed, on a separate piece of paper, the check to Dan. Bill steals the check back from Dan and sells the check to Gene. Because Bill's indorsement to Dan is not on the check, Gene has no way of knowing that Bill's indorsement to Gene does not make Gene the holder of the check. To prevent this possibility, the general rule is that the indorsement must be written on the instrument itself.

j. Exception: An Allonge

At times, space or other considerations require that an indorsement be written on a separate piece of paper. As long as the separate piece of paper, called an "allonge," is affixed to the instrument, the indorsement on that separate piece of paper is sufficient to negotiate the instrument.[26]

---

25. U.C.C. §3-205(c); U.C.C. §3-205, Official Comment 2.

26. U.C.C. §3-204(a). Under the old version of Article 3, an allonge could only be used if there was not sufficient space on the instrument to write the indorsement. The rationale was that the fact that the back of the instrument was completely filled with indorsements would give notice to the purchaser that there might be a separate paper containing additional indorsements. This limitation was omitted in present Article 3. Under present Article 3, it makes no difference whether or not there is sufficient room on the instrument for the indorsement. The new rule, thus, provides no real safeguards against the possibility that the purchaser will be

k. Manner of Negotiation Depends upon Last Indorsement

The initial categorization of an instrument can be changed by the way in which the instrument is indorsed.[27] An instrument becomes payable to order or payable to bearer depending upon whether the last indorsement is a special or a blank indorsement.[28] If the last indorsement is a special indorsement, the instrument is payable to the order of the special indorsee and can be negotiated only by his indorsement.[29] An instrument originally payable to an identified person may be negotiated by delivery alone if the last indorsement is in blank. For example, assume that Shelan receives a check payable to "cash." Shelan may indorse the check "Pay to Gina, Shelan" and deliver the check to Gina. The check is now payable to the order of Gina. In order for Gina to negotiate the check, she must indorse it. If Gina indorses the check by simply writing "Gina," the check is again payable to bearer and may be negotiated by delivery alone.

2. As to Whom an Instrument Is Payable in Specific Situations

There are only so many names in this world. As a result, few names designate only one person. When an instrument is payable to a name that designates more than one person, to which specific person is the instrument payable? Many related questions also arise. When a check is made payable to "John Smith," can any person named John Smith cash the check? Can the intended John Smith cash the check if his name is misspelled and his real name is "Jon Smith?" What if a check is made payable to "John Smith, Professor of Law, Loyola Law School," can John Smith cash this check even though he no longer teaches at Loyola Law School? These and numerous similar questions arise by the thousands each day. The answers that the Code gives to these questions are of vital importance to the ability of negotiable instruments to be an effective means of transferring funds. As we have briefly discussed, a negotiable instrument can only be negotiated or discharged if it is indorsed by the proper

---

unaware of possible subsequent indorsements if the allonge is detached from the instrument. Apparently, the drafters believed that the possibility of this occurrence was so negligible as to be outweighed by the practical advantages of allowing an indorsement to be written on a separate piece of paper.

27. U.C.C. §3-109(c).

28. U.C.C. §3-205.

29. U.C.C. §3-109(c).

payee. In order to know who is the proper payee, we must examine several rules found in Articles 3 and 4.

The basic rule is this: The person to whom an instrument is initially payable is determined by the intent of the person signing as the issuer, in the name of the issuer, or on behalf of the issuer of the instrument whether or not that person is authorized.[30] You may wonder "Why does the intent of the issuer control when it is impossible for a person paying or purchasing the instrument to know what the issuer intended?" The simple answer is that no other rule makes any better sense. There are too many people and organizations with the same or similar name. A negotiable instrument would be too hazardous for an issuer to use if he had to risk, notwithstanding due care, that the instrument may be cashed by some stranger who just so happened to have the same name. As we will discuss in Chapter 4, where the issuer has allowed such a stranger to acquire the instrument, he may be precluded by his own negligence from claiming that the proceeds of the instrument were paid to the wrong person.

The "issuer" is the drawer of a draft or the maker of a note.[31] If the drawer of the check intends John Smith, the lawyer who used to teach at Loyola Law School, to be the person to whom the instrument is payable, no other person, including other persons named John Smith, can indorse the check. An indorsement by another John Smith is completely ineffective to negotiate the check.[32]

An instrument is payable to the person intended by the signer even if the payee is identified by a name other than his real name.[33] Thus, if John Smith, former law professor, is intended by the drawer to be payee of a check, his indorsement is effective even though the drawer somehow believed that his name was "Jim Smith" and made the check so payable.[34] Similarly, his indorsement is sufficient even if the drawer misspelled his name "John Smythe." However, where a payee is designated in a name other than his true name, an indorsement in either the payee's true name or the name appearing on the instrument (or in both) is effective to negotiate the instrument.[35] Thus, he may indorse the instrument John Smith or John Smythe. The name appearing on the instrument does not have to bear any resemblance to the payee's true name as long as the payee is the person actually intended by the

---

30. U.C.C. §3-110(a).
31. U.C.C. §3-105(c); U.C.C. §3-110, Official Comment 1.
32. U.C.C. §3-110, Official Comment 1.
33. U.C.C. §3-110(a).
34. U.C.C. §3-110, Official Comment 1.
35. U.C.C. §3-204(d); U.C.C. §3-204, Official Comment 3.

designation.[36] As a result, if the check mistakenly identifies John Smith as "Jim Scott," he may indorse the check in his real name, John Smith, or by signing "Jim Scott." Subsequent transferees for value or collection can require the payee to indorse in both names.[37] The payor can require a receipt signed in both names.[38] If the presenter refuses to give a receipt in both names, the payor may, without dishonor, refuse to pay the instrument.

Sometimes an instrument may be signed by more than one person as maker or drawer. For example, a corporate check may require the signature of both the president and the treasurer. In an unusual situation each signer may intend that a different person be the person designated as the payee. If this happens, the instrument is payable to any person intended by any one of the signers.[39] If a check made payable to "John Smith" is signed by two trustees of a trust, one of whom intends that the payee be John Smith, former law professor, while the other intends that the payee be John Smith, the former track star, the check is payable to either the former law professor or the former track star.[40] The indorsement of either person will effectively negotiate the instrument.

Even if the drawer's signature on the check is forged, the payee is the person whom the signer, who in this case is the forger, intended. As a result, if Henry forges the drawer's name, making the check payable to "John Smith," while intending the check to be payable to Henry himself, Henry is the proper person to indorse the check and not John Smith. We will leave for Chapter 4C all of the consequences and variations of this rule when applied to a forged or unauthorized drawer's signature.

When no person actually signs the check, it is necessary to have some rule as to whose intent determines the identity of the payee.[41] Where the signature of the issuer is made by automated means, such as by a checkwriting machine, the identity of the payee is determined by the intent of the person who supplied the name (or other identification) of the payee, whether or not the person was authorized.[42] For example, if an employee of Steel Company uses Steel Company's checkwriting machine to issue a check to a payee identified by the name "Jeff Jay," the actual identity of the payee depends upon whom the employee intended to identify by the name "Jeff Jay." This rule applies both where the person supplying the name to the checkwriting machine is an

---

36. U.C.C. §3-110(a); U.C.C. §3-204, Official Comment 3.
37. U.C.C. §3-204(d); U.C.C. §3-204, Official Comment 3.
38. U.C.C. §3-204(d); U.C.C. §3-204, Official Comment 3.
39. U.C.C. §3-110(a).
40. U.C.C. §3-110, Official Comment 1.
41. U.C.C. §3-110, Official Comment 1.
42. U.C.C. §3-110(b).

authorized employee or, for example, where a person having nothing to do with the company feeds names of fictitious payees to the computer listing the accounts payable.[43] These issues will be further discussed in Chapter 4C.

a. Words of Description

Questions arise as to whose indorsement is sufficient to negotiate the instrument when a person is named with words describing her as taking the instrument in a particular capacity. For example, an instrument may be made payable to "John Jones, president of Smith Corp.," "Sally Jesse, trustee for the Young Children's Trust," or "Jane Mortimer, executor of the Samuel Mortimer estate."

Section 3-110(c) sets forth rules to permit the identity of the person entitled to discharge, enforce, or negotiate the instrument to be determined from the face of the instrument itself. These rules are only meant to determine who may act as the holder; they do not determine which party is the equitable owner of the instrument, as between the corporation, estate, trust, or other principal or beneficiary, and the individual named as payee.[44]

Instruments made payable to a named person with the addition of words of description can, with rare exception, be placed into one of the following five categories:[45] (1) an account number either with or without the name of the account holder; (2) an agent or similar representative of an identified person; (3) a trust, estate, or a person described as a trustee or representative of the trust or estate; (4) a fund or organization that is not a legal entity; or (5) an office or a person described as holding an office.

When a description does not fit into one of the categories of section 3-110(c), the additional words should be treated as surplusage. Thus, instruments payable to "John Smith, Professor of Law, Loyola Law School" or "John Smith, Father of Jane Smith" are payable to John Smith unconditionally whether or not John Smith is the father of Jane Smith or works at Loyola Law School. Similarly, if an instrument describes a person as being in a particular capacity, but does not name the represented person, for example, "John Smith, Trustee," or "John Smith, President," the instrument is payable to John Smith unconditionally.

Where Payable to Account Number. Sometimes a check may be made payable to a specific account number either with or without the name of the

---

43. U.C.C. §3-110, Official Comment 1.
44. U.C.C. §3-110, Official Comment 3.
45. U.C.C. §3-110(c)(1); U.C.C. §3-110(c)(2)(ii); U.C.C. §3-110(c)(2)(i); U.C.C. §3-110(c)(2)(iii); U.C.C. §3-110(c)(2)(iv) respectively.

account owner, for example, "Pay to the order of Acct # 1234" or "Pay to the order of John Jones, Acct # 5678." Where only the account number is identified, the check is payable to the person who owns the bank account so numbered.[46] Only the person who owns the account may indorse the check for purposes of negotiating it, and only that person can become its holder.[47] Even if the drawer intends that the check go to Mary Jones, if account # 1234 belongs to John Smith, the check may only be indorsed by John Smith.

When an instrument states both a name and an account number and the name and the account number refer to different persons,[48] the instrument is payable to the named person whether or not the person in fact owns the account.[49] Thus, even if John Jones does not have an account # 5678 (the account being owned by Fran George), the check is payable to John Jones.[50] The risk that the wrong account has been credited is placed upon the bank accepting the item for deposit. A depositary bank taking such a check for collection warrants to subsequent collecting banks, to the payor bank, or other payor, that the amount of the check was credited to the proper payee's account.[51] The bank must credit the proceeds of the check to an account belonging to John Jones. The bank is liable to subsequent banks if the check is deposited in account # 5678 because it is a simple task for the depositary bank to determine whether account # 5678 belongs to John Jones.

Payable to Agent for Identified Person.   When an instrument is made payable to a named person with words describing him as an agent or representative of a specified person, such as "Gary Williams, President of Blue Note Records," the instrument is payable to either the represented person, the representative, or a successor of the representative.[52] Thus, either Blue Note Records, Gary Williams, or the current president of Blue Note Records may act as the holder of the instrument. Blue Note Records may, through any agent, enforce, negotiate, or discharge the instrument. Gary Williams also has the right to act as the holder even though he is no longer, nor ever was, the President of Blue Note Records.

This rule applies to any type of agent or representative, including attorneys, if certain conditions are met. First, the instrument must specifically

---

46. U.C.C. §3-110(c)(1).

47. U.C.C. §3-110, Official Comment 2.

48. U.C.C. §3-110, Official Comment 2.

49. U.C.C. §3-110(c)(1).

50. U.C.C. §3-110, Official Comment 2.

51. U.C.C. §4-205(2); U.C.C. §4-205, Official Comment; U.C.C. §3-110, Official Comment 2.

52. U.C.C. §3-110(c)(2)(ii); U.C.C. §3-110, Official Comment 3.

name the agent or officer;[53] for example, "Gary Williams, president of Blue Note Records," or "Gary Williams, agent for Blue Note Records." This section would not apply if the instrument simply states "President of Blue Note Records" without naming Gary Williams. The check would then be payable to whoever is the president of Blue Note Records. Second, the name of the principal must appear in the designation.[54] This section would be inapplicable to a check payable to "Gary Williams, President." Third, the agency relationship must be spelled out. The section would not be applicable to a check payable to "Gary Williams for Blue Note Records."

Payable to Office or Officer. An instrument made payable to the office or officer, for example, "Gary Williams, Mayor,"[55] is payable to either the named person, Gary Williams, whether he is or ever was mayor, the present mayor, or a successor to the mayor.[56] Or, if the instrument is made payable to "President of Blue Note Records," the instrument is payable to whoever is the president of Blue Note Records when the check is negotiated or cashed.

Payable to Fund, Organization, Trust or Estate. Where an instrument is payable to a fund or organization that is not a legal entity, including any informal organization or club,[57] the instrument is payable to a representative of the members of the fund or organization.[58] Any representative of the members of the fund or organization can indorse the instrument.[59] When an instrument is payable to a trust, an estate, or a person described as trustee or representative of a trust or estate, the instrument is payable to the trustee, the representative, or the successor of either, whether or not the instrument also names the beneficiary or estate.[60] The person designated as the beneficiary has no right to negotiate, discharge, or enforce the instrument.

b. Two or More Payees

Sometimes an instrument may be made payable to more than one person. The question then arises as to whether one of the named payees alone may negotiate, enforce, or discharge the instrument or whether all of the payees

53. U.C.C. §3-110(c)(2)(ii).
54. U.C.C. §3-110(c)(2)(ii).
55. U.C.C. §3-110, Official Comment 3.
56. U.C.C. §3-110(c)(2)(iv).
57. U.C.C. §3-110, Official Comment 3.
58. U.C.C. §3-110(c)(2)(iii).
59. U.C.C. §3-110, Official Comment 3.
60. U.C.C. §3-110(c)(2)(i); U.C.C. §3-110, Official Comment 3.

must act together. The answer to this question depends upon whether the instrument is payable to the payees jointly or in the alternative.

This distinction is crucial. If an instrument is payable "jointly," all payees must participate in any negotiation, discharge, or enforcement of the instrument.[61] An instrument may not be enforced without the action of all joint payees. In contrast, an instrument payable in the alternative may be negotiated, discharged, or enforced by any payee who is in possession of the instrument.[62] For example, an instrument payable to "John and Mary" may be negotiated only if John and Mary both indorse the instrument. If the instrument is made payable to "John or Mary," the instrument may be negotiated by either John's or Mary's indorsement.

In most situations it is easy to determine whether a particular instrument is payable jointly or in the alternative. Instruments payable "to X and Y" are payable to X and Y jointly, while instruments payable "to P or R," or "to P and R in the alternative" are payable to P or R in the alternative. An instrument payable "to P/R" is payable to either P or R because "/," called a "virgule," means "either . . . or."[63]

When it is unclear whether an instrument is payable alternatively or jointly, the instrument is deemed to be payable in the alternative.[64] For instance, an instrument made payable "to P and/or R" is treated as if made payable "to P or R."[65] By treating an ambiguous instrument as payable in the alternative, the person dealing with any of the payees is able to treat that payee as the holder and rely upon his indorsement alone.

Sometimes it is difficult to determine whether an instrument is payable to two payees or whether it is payable to one payee with words of description. For example, how should a check payable to "John Smith, Loyola Law School" be treated? Is it payable to John Smith himself with the words Loyola Law School being ignored as mere surplusage? Should it be treated as being payable to John Smith and Loyola Law School jointly? Or should it be treated as being payable to John Smith and Loyola Law School in the alternative. To protect potential purchasers, it makes the most sense to treat the instrument as being ambiguous as to whether it is payable to the payees jointly or in the alternative, and therefore treat it as payable to John Smith and Loyola Law School in the alternative.[66]

61. U.C.C. §3-110(d); U.C.C. §3-110, Official Comment 4.
62. U.C.C. §3-110(d); U.C.C. §3-110, Official Comment 4.
63. U.C.C. §3-110, Official Comment 4.
64. U.C.C. §3-110(d); U.C.C. §3-110, Official Comment 4.
65. U.C.C. §3-110, Official Comment 4.
66. U.C.C. §3-110(d).

3. Holder Status of Collecting Banks

Because of the importance of efficiency in the bank collection process, special rules have been established to enable a depositary or other collecting bank to become a holder of an item without obtaining its transferor's indorsement.

Often a customer may forget to indorse a check that he has deposited in his bank for collection. Clearly, by depositing the check, the customer intends that the bank collect the check for him. Should the bank's status as holder of a check depend upon whether the customer has remembered to indorse the check? The answer is clearly in the negative. By depositing the check, the customer implicitly requests that the bank do whatever is necessary to collect the check for him. He would have no reason to deny the bank the right to indorse for him. In fact, the Code provides that whether or not his indorsement appears on the check, the customer is liable on the check in the event of its dishonor as though he had indorsed the check.[67]

Under agency law a depositary bank collecting the check or other item for its customer has the implied power to indorse for its customer. But should the depositary bank's holder status depend upon whether it performs the mechanical act of signing its customer's name? An affirmative answer would be placing form over substance. Requiring this act has no purpose. For these reasons the Code provides in section 4-205 that a depositary bank may become a holder of an item even though its customer fails to indorse the item.[68] If a customer delivers an item to a depositary bank for collection, the depositary bank becomes a holder of the item at the time it receives the item if the customer at the time of delivery was a holder of the item.[69] It is irrelevant whether the customer indorses the item. Allowing a depositary bank to become a holder without the necessity of obtaining its customer's indorsement makes it possible for businesses to use lock-box arrangements under which customer checks are mailed directly to the depositary bank without the need for the bank to engage in the functionless act of sending millions of checks through an indorsement machine.[70] In place of the indorsement, subsequent collecting banks, the payor, and the drawer are protected in that the depositary bank warrants to them that the amount of the item was paid to the customer or deposited to the customer's account.[71]

Section 4-205 applies only if the holder of the item delivers the item to the depositary bank for the purpose of engaging the bank to collect the item for

67. U.C.C. §4-207(b).
68. U.C.C. §4-205(1).
69. U.C.C. §4-205(1); U.C.C. §4-205, Official Comment.
70. U.C.C. §4-205, Official Comment.
71. U.C.C. §4-205(2); U.C.C. §4-205, Official Comment.

him. For example, if a check is made payable jointly to a contractor and a sub-contractor in payment for work performed jointly by them and the contractor deposits the check into his bank account, the bank does not become a holder of the check if the subcontractor did not participate in delivering the check to the bank or if the contractor was not authorized to act on behalf of the sub-contractor. Even had the contractor indorsed the check to the bank, the bank would not have become a holder because the subcontractor's indorsement was missing. Similarly, a bank does not become a holder of a note payable to its customer when the customer delivers the note as security for a loan and not for the purpose of having the bank collect the note for him. However, it is not necessary that the holder maintain an account at the bank in order for section 4-205 to apply as long as the holder delivered the item so that the bank could collect the item for her. For example, if a New York businesswoman, in Los Angeles for a business meeting, requests that Bank of America collect a check for her even though her checking account is at Chase Manhattan Bank in New York, section 4-205 applies. Upon collection of the check, Bank of America may remit the funds to the businesswoman by, for example, issuing a cashier's check to her.

A similar problem exists in regard to subsequent banks in the check collection process. Must each bank in the check collection process go through the act of indorsing the check? This would again be inefficient and somewhat functionless. As a result, section 4-206 allows transfers between banks to be made by virtue of any agreed method that identifies the transferor bank.[72] No indorsement by the transferor bank is required.[73] Any symbol that identifies the transferor is sufficient. The transferee bank may become a holder by complying with section 4-206 as long as its transferor bank was a holder even though the transferor bank failed to indorse the item.

The test for whether a bank has properly identified itself is simple: Can its identity be traced?[74] In most cases, stamping of an item with the bank's transit number is sufficient identification to transfer the item. Any "method" of identification may be used. There need only be some sort of formal or informal agreement.

72. U.C.C. §4-206.
73. U.C.C. §4-206, Official Comment.
74. U.C.C. §4-206, Official Comment.

B. VALUE

Looking at this next example makes it clear why a holder must take an instrument for value in order to acquire holder-in-due-course status. Assume that Jim purchases a car from John in payment for which Jim executes a promissory note payable to John. The car, it turns out, was stolen. John indorses the note as a present to his daughter, Jane, who is ignorant of the fact that the car is stolen. Jim refuses to pay the note when the police come to take back the car. By now, John has vanished. Should Jim be liable to Jane on the note? The answer is a clear "no." It would make no sense to allow Jane to have a windfall at Jim's expense. Jane loses nothing by being denied recovery from Jim.

The case of a gratuitous transfer is simple; however, trying to determine what else should or should not constitute value involves a far more complex inquiry than in the case of a simple gift. Value is related to, but not identical with, consideration. Value is judged in terms of what the holder gave for the instrument and not what the obligor received for his original issuance or transfer of the instrument. For example, assume that Allen issues a note to Rip-U-Off T.V. Sales in payment for a television to be delivered to him by Rip-U-Off T.V. Sales. Rip-U-Off T.V. Sales has the practice of immediately selling its notes to Finance Company. The television set is not delivered to Allen. Does Allen have a defense that he can assert against Finance Company? In order to make this determination, we must examine both the concepts of consideration and of value. Because the television set was never delivered to Allen, Allen has not received the agreed-upon *consideration*. Allen therefore has the defense of *failure of consideration*. Whether he can assert this defense against Finance Company depends upon whether Finance Company qualifies as a holder in due course. One of the requirements for holder-in-due-course status is that Finance Company take the instrument *for value*. As we will shortly see, if Finance Company has already paid Rip-U-Off T.V. Sales for the note, Finance Company would have taken the note for value and therefore possibly qualified as a holder in due course. However, if Finance Company, although promising to pay Rip-U-Off T.V. Sales for the note, had not yet made payment, Finance Company would not have taken the note for value. Although Finance Company's promise is *consideration* for the note, it is not *value*. To qualify as a holder in due course, Finance Company must take the note for value.

The definition of value was developed to take into account the unique needs of negotiable instruments law. Before we examine these particular needs, it will be useful to lay out the basic definition of value found in Article 3. We will examine later in this section a rule found in Article 4 as to what constitutes value in determining whether a collecting bank may qualify as a holder in due course.

An instrument is issued or transferred for value if:[75]

1. the instrument is issued or transferred for a promise of performance, to the extent the promise has been performed; or
2. the transferee acquires a security interest or other lien in the instrument other than a lien obtained by judicial proceeding; or
3. the instrument is issued or transferred as payment of, or as security for, an antecedent claim against any person, whether or not the claim is due; or
4. the instrument is issued or transferred in exchange for a negotiable instrument; or
5. the instrument is issued or transferred in exchange for the incurring of an irrevocable commitment to a third person by the person taking the instrument.

1.   Promise of Performance as Value

As you can tell, a holder may take an instrument for value under one of five alternative standards. An instrument is issued or transferred for value where it is issued or transferred for a promise of performance to the extent that the promise has been performed.[76] "Promise of performance" is a synonym for consideration. Any promise that would constitute consideration so as to uphold a return promise under the contract law of the applicable jurisdiction constitutes a promise of performance under Article 3. As you may remember from your course in Contracts, in order for a promise to constitute consideration for a return promise, the promisor must either promise to confer a legally recognized benefit upon the promisee or promise to suffer a legally recognized detriment. For example, a promise to render legal services would be consideration for the maker's promise contained in a note because the maker is acquiring the right to the promisor's legal services—a right he did not have prior to the promise. Furthermore, a nephew's promise to his uncle that he will refrain from drinking, smoking, and gambling until he is 21 years of age would be a legally recognized detriment as long as the nephew had the legal right to drink, smoke, or gamble. Thus, his promise to do so would be con-

---

75. U.C.C. §3-303(a)(1); U.C.C. §3-303(a)(2); U.C.C. §3-303(a)(3); U.C.C. §3-303(a)(4); U.C.C. §3-303(a)(5) respectively.
76. U.C.C. §3-303(a)(1).

sideration for his uncle's issuance of the note to him. Examples of consideration are limitless. Consideration may consist of a promise to sell a car, to perform services, to transfer title to land, and so on.

In order to constitute consideration, the legally recognized benefit or detriment must be bargained for. In other words, the promisee must be seeking the benefit or detriment that the promisor is promising. As long as a legally recognized benefit or detriment is bargained for, such promise constitutes consideration even if it is disproportionately small as compared to the face value of the instrument. For example, assume that Mary, maker of a note in the amount of $5,000 payable to Paul, is on the verge of bankruptcy. Paul needs cash. Finance Company agrees to pay Paul $100 for the note. Although $100 is far less than the face value of the note, Paul has bargained for that sum and therefore Finance Company's promise to pay the $100 constitutes consideration. Finance Company takes the note for value once it pays Paul the $100. In contrast, if Mary's father wants to help Mary out by giving her a note in the amount of $10,000 in exchange for her car worth $100, the car will not constitute consideration for the note. The father was not seeking to acquire Mary's car by issuing the note. Rather, he was making Mary a gift of the note. Thus, Mary did not take the note for value or, at least, not beyond the $100 value of the car.

An important limitation, however, is that the promise of performance is only value for the purposes of negotiable instruments law to the extent that it is executed or performed.

For example, assume that John issues a note for $1,000 to Car Dealer in payment for a car to be delivered. Car Dealer sells the note to Bank for $800. Bank does not take the note for value until it pays Car Dealer the $800. Why is this? Until Bank has paid Car Dealer for the note, Bank will lose nothing by not being allowed to recover from John on the note.

The issue of whether Bank has taken the note for value will only arise if Bank learns that John has a defense to his obligation to pay the note. Unless John has a defense, Bank can recover from John even if Bank does not take the note for value. However, if John has a defense, Bank can recover from him only to the extent that Bank gives value for the note prior to obtaining notice of his defense.[77] Assume that Bank has promised to pay Car Dealer in two installments of $400 each. If Bank learns of John's defense after paying the first installment, Bank should refuse to pay Car Dealer the second installment of $400. The reason—Bank should not be permitted to increase John's loss by attempting to deprive him of his right to raise his defense. If Bank refuses to pay Car Dealer, is Bank liable for breaching its promise to Car Dealer to pur-

---

77. U.C.C. §3-302(d).

chase the note for $800? The answer is "no." Once Bank discovers that the note is subject to a claim, defense, or claim in recoupment, it has the right, under ordinary contract law, to suspend the remainder of its counter-performance (paying the remaining $400).[78] By not making the payment, Bank can prevent the loss to John.

This is not really unfair to Bank. A negotiable instrument is only a promise to pay money. Bank is not deprived of some needed commodity as in the case of a contract to purchase goods. Bank loses only the benefit of its bargain (the profit that it would have made upon the purchase of the note). However, Bank has the right to recover any loss from Car Dealer.

Assuming that Bank has paid only $400, how much can Bank recover from John? When a holder has only partially performed the agreed-upon consideration, the holder has the rights of a holder in due course to the extent of the fraction of the amount payable under the instrument equal to the value of the partial performance ($400) divided by the value of the promised performance ($800).[79] Because, prior to learning of John's defense, Bank had paid Car Dealer $400 of the promised $800, Bank has paid one-half of the agreed consideration ($400/$800 = 1/2). Bank can therefore recover $500, which is one-half of the amount due ($1,000/2 = $500).[80] Bank in this way gets the profit attributable to the percentage of the purchase price that it promised to pay. Since Bank paid half of the purchase price, it gets half of its anticipated profit ($200/2 = $100).

2. Security Interest in Instrument as Value

A holder takes an instrument for value to the extent that it acquires a security interest in or a lien on the instrument otherwise than by legal process.[81] The lien or security interest may be acquired in different ways. A secured party who is granted a security interest in the instrument by means of a voluntary transfer by the debtor, usually an Article 9 security interest, takes the instrument for value. If, for example, Rip-U-Off T.V. Sales needs additional cash to purchase new inventory, it may borrow the money from Wedontcare Bank, by negotiating Allen's, and other buyers', notes as security for repayment of the loan. Thus, Wedontcare Bank becomes a holder for value to the extent that it has

---

78. U.C.C. §3-303, Official Comment 2.
79. U.C.C. §3-302(d); U.C.C. §3-302, Official Comment 6, Case #5.
80. U.C.C. §3-302, Official Comment 6.
81. U.C.C. §3-303(a)(2); U.C.C. §3-303, Official Comment 3.

acquired a security interest in the notes. We will discuss, later in this section, additional ways in which a collecting bank may acquire a security interest in instruments collected for its customer.[82]

A holder of an instrument may also acquire a lien in an instrument by operation of law.[83] A lien upon an instrument acquired by operation of law constitutes the taking of the instrument for value. Liens acquired by operation of law include common law or statutory banker's liens. The reason that the law grants liens to these categories of individuals is to protect what the law views as important interests. Bankers rely upon the existence of these liens in conducting their business.

In contrast, a lien acquired by judicial process, for example, attachment, garnishment, or execution, does not constitute value.[84] A lien by judicial process is acquired after the debt to the creditor arose. The creditor is usually using the judicial process in a desperate attempt to salvage whatever payment he can to satisfy the debt. He does not rely upon the lien in advancing the credit or in otherwise refraining from collecting the debt. There is no reason to treat him as a holder in due course thus allowing him to cut off the legitimate defenses of the maker or drawer.

A lienholder or secured party takes the instrument for value only to the extent of the amount owed on the underlying debt.[85] Assume that as security for a $1,000 loan from Bank, Car Dealer grants to Bank a security interest in John's note in the amount of $5,000. The car is not delivered and John refuses to pay the note. At the time of enforcement, Car Dealer owes Bank $1,000 plus $200 interest. Assuming Bank otherwise qualifies as a holder in due course, Bank may enforce the note only for the amount that is owed on the underlying obligation ($1,200).[86] Article 3 phrases this rule in a rather confusing manner. If the person obliged to pay the instrument (John) has a defense, claim in recoupment, or claim to the instrument that may be asserted against the person who granted the security interest (Car Dealer), those rights may be asserted only to an amount payable under the instrument ($5,000) that does not exceed the amount of the unpaid obligation secured at the time of enforcement ($1,200).[87] If the car was delivered and John had no defense, even though Bank only gave value to the extent of $1,200, Bank could enforce the note for the entire $5,000. However, under Article 9 Bank would have to pay the surplus $3,800 to Car Dealer.

---

82. U.C.C. §3-303, Official Comment 3; U.C.C. §4-210.
83. U.C.C. §3-303(a)(2); U.C.C. §3-303, Official Comment 3.
84. U.C.C. §3-303(a)(2); U.C.C. §3-303, Official Comment 3.
85. U.C.C. §3-302(e).
86. U.C.C. §3-302(e), Official Comment 6, Case #6.
87. U.C.C. §3-302(e).

3. *Payment or Security for Antecedent Debt as Value*

The third type of value is the taking of the instrument in payment of or as security for an antecedent debt. When an instrument is issued or transferred in payment of or as security for an antecedent claim against any person, the instrument has been issued or transferred for value whether or not the claim is due.[88] For example, assume that Rip-U-Off T.V. Sales owes money to Sally Lawyer for legal services rendered. If Rip-U-Off T.V. Sales negotiates Allen's note in payment for the services, Allen's note is transferred for value. The debt Rip-U-Off T.V. Sales owes Sally is an antecedent claim. Taking the note in payment of the claim is value. The same would be true even if Sally had originally given Rip-U-Off T.V. Sales a year to pay the fees; making the debt not even due yet. Sally need not give any new consideration for the note such as extending the time for Rip-U-Off T.V. Sales to pay the debt.[89]

The antecedent claim need not be against the transferor; a claim the holder has against any person is sufficient. For example, if Robert Ripoff, president of Rip-U-Off T.V. Sales, makes a note to Sally in payment for Rip-U-Off T.V. Sales' debt to Sally, Sally takes the note for value even though the debt was owed by Rip-U-Off T.V. Sales and not by Robert Ripoff.

Why is the giving of an instrument in payment of or as security for an antecedent debt considered value? What has the holder lost?[90] Sally was already owed the money. She was unsecured. Now she has the right to recover from Allen despite his defense. Is not Sally getting a windfall at Allen's expense? Maybe. However, the rationale for this rule is that if a person who takes a check or note for a debt could not be assured that she would take it free from any claims or defenses to the instrument, she would refuse to take the instrument in payment and would demand cash instead. Because most debts are paid by checks or other negotiable instruments, chaos may ensue.

---

88. U.C.C. §3-303(a)(3).

89. U.C.C. §3-303, Official Comment 4.

90. When a negotiable instrument is taken for an obligation, the obligation is discharged if the instrument is a cashier's, certified, or teller's check or suspended if the instrument is an uncertified check or note. U.C.C. §3-310(a). In this sense the holder has suffered a loss by either completely losing his right to recover on the underlying obligation, in the case of a bank check, or having his right to recover on the underlying obligation delayed until the uncertified check or note is dishonored. These consequences are discussed fully in Chapter 3F.

B. Value

4. *Negotiable Instrument or Irrevocable Obligation as Value*

When a negotiable instrument or an irrevocable obligation to a third person is given in exchange for an instrument, the holder takes the instrument for value.[91] For example, assume that Wedontcare Bank purchases the note that Allen gave to Rip-U-Off T.V. Sales in payment for the television set by issuing a check payable to Rip-U-Off T.V. Sales. Assume also that the television set was defective and Allen had the defense of failure of consideration. After receiving the check, Rip-U-Off T.V. Sales negotiates the check to a holder in due course. The holder in due course could fully recover from Wedontcare Bank.[92] Wedontcare Bank, therefore, to be made whole, needs to be able to recover on Allen's note free from Allen's defense. The possibility that a holder in due course might acquire the check and thereby deny Wedontcare Bank the right to refuse to pay the check distinguishes Wedontcare Bank from a holder who simply has promised to pay for the note. It makes no difference whether a subsequent holder in due course in fact acquires the check. Wedontcare Bank gives value because Wedontcare Bank itself is exposed to liability. Wedontcare Bank is exposed to personal liability because its promise runs to the holder in due course of the check. Wedontcare Bank would have no right to refuse to pay the holder in due course of its check if Wedontcare Bank receives notice of Allen's defense.

Likewise, an "irrevocable commitment to a third person" is a commitment that cannot be rescinded in the event that the holder learns of a claim, defense, or claim in recoupment to the instrument in return for which the holder had given his commitment. A typical example of an irrevocable commitment to a third person is a letter of credit.

For example, assume that Buyer wants to purchase goods from Seller. Seller does not trust Buyer and therefore asks Buyer's bank to issue a letter of credit under which the bank promises to pay Seller as long as Seller delivers to the bank certain designated documents. If the bank issues the letter of credit in exchange for a negotiable instrument transferred to it by Buyer, the bank takes the instrument for value even though it has yet to perform under the letter of credit. The reason is simple. Even if the bank learns that the instrument is subject to a defense, it cannot refuse to honor its letter of credit. The promise in the letter of credit is an unconditional promise made to Seller directly.

---

91. U.C.C. §3-303(a)(4); U.C.C. §3-303(a)(5).
92. U.C.C. §3-303, Official Comment 5.

5. Taking for Value by Collecting Bank

In addition to the five types of value listed in section 3-303, a collecting bank can, under section 4-210, take an item for value by acquiring a security interest in the item under Article 4. A collecting bank acquires a security interest in an item and any accompanying documents or the proceeds of either the item or the documents:[93]

1. in the case of an item deposited in an account to the extent to which credit given for the item has been withdrawn or applied;
2. in the case of an item for which it has been given credit available for withdrawal as of right, to the extent of the credit given whether or not the credit is drawn upon or there is a right of charge-back; or
3. if it makes an advance on or against the item.[94]

Section 4-210 grants a security interest to a collecting bank specifically in order to encourage the bank to give its customers immediate use of funds on deposited items. As we will examine, by allowing its customer to draw against the uncollected funds, the collecting bank acquires a security interest in the item. Because the security interest constitutes the taking of the item for value, the collecting bank, assuming that it meets the other requirements for holder-in-due-course status, qualifies as a holder in due course. This may prove useful to the bank in the event that the item is dishonored (on account of a stop payment order or otherwise) and its customer is unable to repay the funds withdrawn. In this event, the collecting bank will be able to recover from the drawer of the item despite any defense he may have against the customer.

Section 4-210, however, is not the exclusive means by which a collecting bank may acquire a security interest in an item. A collecting bank may, like any other lender, acquire a traditional security interest outside of section 4-210 by, for example, entering into an Article 9 security agreement with its customer. The advantage of complying with section 4-210 is that the security interest in the proceeds of the item and accompanying documents is effective under Article 9 even though the bank does not fulfill the requirements of Article 9.[95]

---

93. U.C.C. §4-210. The security interest granted under section 4-210 is in addition to, and not in lieu of, the bank's general common-law lien and right of setoff.

94. U.C.C. §4-210(a)(1), (2) and (3).

95. U.C.C. §4-210(c). As long as the requirements of section 4-210 are met, the bank is relieved of certain requirements of Article 9: (1) no need for a written security, U.C.C. §4-210(c)(1); (2) the security interest is automatically perfected without the need to file a financing statement, U.C.C. §4-210(c)(2), or take possession, U.C.C. §9-304; and (3) the bank's security interest has priority over conflicting perfected security interests in the item, its proceeds, and accompanying documents, U.C.C. §4-210(c)(3). However, once the bank has

B. Value

A collecting bank obtains a security interest in an item and any accompanying documents (for example, bills of lading) and the proceeds of either in the case of an item deposited in an account to the extent to which the credit given for that item has been withdrawn or applied.[96] Under this provision the collecting bank only acquires a security interest to the extent that the bank allows the customer to use the funds. Assume that a customer opens a checking account at his bank with a deposit of a check in the amount of $5,000. Before the deposited check is collected from the payor bank, the collecting bank pays a $4,000 check drawn by its customer. The depositary bank is a holder for value of the check to the extent of $4,000, the amount of the check that the customer drew upon. The bank is not a holder for value as to the remaining $1,000, the amount of the check still in the customer's account, because if the $5,000 check is returned unpaid, the bank can debit (charge-back) the customer's account for the remaining $1,000.

The collecting bank also acquires a security interest to the extent that the bank has applied part or all of the credit in payment of a debt owed to it by its customer. For example, assume that at the time a check in the amount of $5,000 is deposited in the customer's account, the account is overdrawn in the amount of $3,000. The bank acquires a security interest in the check to the extent that it applies the check to the overdraft. Thus, if the bank applies the check to the $3,000 overdraft, the collecting bank has a security interest in the check in the amount of $3,000.

Likewise, a collecting bank also has a security interest in an item to the extent that credit given for the item is available for withdrawal as a matter of right, whether or not the credit is drawn upon or there is a right of charge-back.[97] This may occur because the bank has an arrangement with its customer under which the customer has the right to draw upon funds that have not yet been collected by the bank. Even absent an express agreement with its customer, the bank may have a duty under section 4-215 or under Regulation CC to allow the customer to draw upon uncollected funds. Section 4-215(e) provides when a credit given by a bank for an item in a customer's account

---

received final settlement for the item, the security interest is extinguished. U.C.C. §4-210(c). Because the security interest includes the proceeds of the item and its accompanying documents, whatever consideration is received in exchange for either is subject to the bank's security interest. U.C.C. §9-306(1). The security interest ceases to be effective if the bank relinquishes possession of the item or accompanying documents for purposes other than collection. U.C.C. §4-210(c).

96. U.C.C. §4-210(a)(1).
97. U.C.C. §4-210(a)(2).

becomes available as a matter of right.[98] These sections are discussed in Chapter 5.

A collecting bank also has a security interest in an item to the extent that the bank makes an advance on or against the item. A security interest arises whether or not the item is deposited into the customer's account. For example, assume that a New York businesswoman needs to obtain funds from a check drawn upon Wells Fargo Bank. She needs the cash immediately. Having no account in Los Angeles, she requests that Bank of America not only collect the check for her, but also advance her the funds. If Bank of America does so, it has a security interest in the check to the extent of the advance.

When several items are simultaneously deposited by the customer into his account and the bank allows the customer to write checks against the account or applies the credit against a debt owed by the customer, the question arises as to which items the bank's security interest attaches. The rule is that when credits given for several items deposited at one time, or pursuant to a single agreement, are withdrawn or applied in part, the bank's security interest remains upon all the items, any accompanying documents, or the proceeds of either.[99] For instance, assume that when the customer's account contains no funds, the customer simultaneously deposits five items in the amounts of $1,000, $2,000, $3,000, and $4,000, $5,000. The customer withdraws $3,000. The bank has a security interest on each of the five items to the extent of $3,000. As soon as $3,000 is collected from any of the items, the bank is made whole and the security interest in all of the items is extinguished.

Credits first given are deemed to be first drawn upon.[100] Thus, where items are not deposited simultaneously, the security interest attaches to the items in the order in which they were deposited. Assume, in our example above, that the items were each deposited on different days in the order in which they are listed. Of the $3,000 withdrawn, the first $1,000 would be deemed to have been withdrawn against the $1,000 check. As a result, the bank would have a security interest in the check for its entire face amount of $1,000. The remaining $2,000 would be deemed to have been withdrawn

98. Under §4-215(e)(1), credit given to its customer may be withdrawn by the customer as a matter of right when the bank has had a reasonable time to receive return of the item and the item has not been received within that time. U.C.C. §4-215, Official Comment 11. If a bank is both the depositary bank and the payor bank, the credit is available as a matter of right on any item that is finally paid at the opening of the bank's second banking day following receipt of the item. U.C.C. §4-215(e)(2). Although section 4-215(e) determines when the customer has the right to use the funds, the section is subject to Regulation CC, EFTA, and to any state funds availability legislation. U.C.C. §4-215(e); U.C.C. §4-215, Official Comment 11.
99. U.C.C. §4-210 (b); U.C.C. §4-210, Official Comment 2.
100. U.C.C. §4-210(b).

against the second check deposited, the $2,000 check. The bank would then have a security interest in the $2,000 check for its entire face amount. The bank would have no security interest in the remaining three checks. As a consequence, the bank would not be a holder for value of any of the remaining three checks. This consequence assumes significance if the drawer of either of the first two checks becomes insolvent. In this event, the bank, not being a holder in due course of any of the three remaining checks, will not be able to recover on these checks if any of the drawers of these other checks have a defense to their obligation to pay.

C. GOOD FAITH AND NOTICE

As difficult as it was to determine what should constitute the giving of value for holder-in-due-course status, it was even more difficult to establish standards for determining what type of notice, knowledge, or pre-purchase behavior should disqualify a purchaser from holder-in-due-course status. On the one hand, it was important to ensure that no one be able to unfairly achieve holder-in-due-course status. On the other hand, if the rules allowed a court to use 20/20 hindsight to determine whether the purchaser should have realized that something was wrong, it would be dangerous for any person to purchase an instrument. Even if that person was truly innocent of any improper motive or knowledge, he would have to risk a costly trial to prove, or fail to prove, as the case may be, that he should be accorded holder-in-due-course status. In its attempt to balance these interests, Article 3 adopted two separate requirements for holder-in-due-course status: the requirement that the holder take in good faith and the requirement that the holder be without notice of any problems in the instrument itself or in the transaction involving the issuance or negotiation of the instrument.

1. Good Faith

A basic question arose as to whether good faith should be judged subjectively by looking at whether the specific individual in fact was pure at heart and lacked any improper knowledge or purpose or whether good faith should be judged objectively by a reasonable person standard—that is, whether a reasonable person in the holder's shoes would have known that something was wrong.

The standard adopted by the Code is partially subjective and partially objective. The subjective part of the standard is found in the requirement that the particular holder be "honest in fact" in the transaction.[101] For example, assume that a very naive person is approached on the street by a person who, in offering to sell him a $1,000 paycheck for $300, told the naive prospective purchaser that the seller's wife was sick and that the seller needed cash immediately to have her admitted into the hospital. If the naive person, in purchasing the check, truly believes the story, the purchase would be in good faith despite the fact that no other person in the world may have believed the story.

Although the failure to inquire into suspicious circumstances does not, by itself, amount to a lack of good faith, facts may be so suspicious that the trier of fact will not believe the holder's assertion that he was honest in fact. Where, for instance, a $3,000 note is purchased by the holder for $500, the trier of fact may find that the holder lacked good faith even under the purely subjective test of "honesty in fact." Such a finding may actually be required absent a plausible justification for such a large discount. Similarly, evidence that the holder was grossly negligent may lead the trier of fact to conclude that the holder desired to evade knowledge that an investigation would disclose. Under these circumstances, the court could find a lack of good faith.

In addition to the honesty in fact standard, good faith also requires "the observance of reasonable commercial standards of fair dealing."[102] This adds an objective standard as to the fairness of the holder's conduct.[103] However, the duty of the holder to comply with reasonable commercial standards extends only to his obligation of fair dealing. The holder has no duty to exercise due care with respect to the purchase. As a consequence, as long as the holder acts in a fair manner, and without actual awareness of any problem, his purchase is in good faith even though a reasonable person in his position would have realized that some problem existed with the instrument or transaction.

A simple example may illustrate the difference between the obligations of fair dealing and due care. Assume that a sinister-looking character named Simon asks the teller at Bank of Gotham to cash a check for him. The check is a paycheck payable to Dudley, one of the bank's own customers. The $2,000 paycheck is indorsed by Dudley in blank. Simon has no account at Bank of Gotham. The teller refers Simon to a bank officer. Although Simon presents no identification to the officer, the officer, believing Simon's story that he had lost his wallet, cashes the check. It turns out that Simon had acquired the

101. U.C.C. §3-103(a)(4).
102. U.C.C. §3-103(a)(4).
103. U.C.C. §3-103, Official Comment 4.

check by stealing Dudley's wallet. Has the bank acted in good faith? The answer is "yes." It is true that the officer was negligent. There is little doubt that a reasonable banker would not have cashed the check without seeing Simon's identification. However, the officer's failure was in neglecting to exercise due care. By cashing the check, the officer was not attempting to obtain an unfair advantage for the bank or to unduly prejudice Dudley. Therefore, he did not fail to observe reasonable commercial standards of fair dealing.

Let us change the facts a little. Assume that the bank officer refused to cash the check without seeing Simon's identification. After again telling the bank officer that he has no identification, Simon offers to take $800 for the paycheck. The bank officer accepts Simon's offer. Here, the bank has failed to observe reasonable commercial standards of fair dealing. By purchasing the check at a large discount, the bank officer was attempting to profit at his customer's expense.

In the vast majority of cases, a holder will lack good faith because he has notice of a claim or defense. For example, Finance Company may know that the car dealer from whom it is purchasing a note does not intend to deliver the car to the maker of the note. There will be times, however, when, although the holder does not know of any specific problem in the underlying transaction itself, it may still be found not to have taken the instrument in good faith. For example, Finance Company may know that a car dealer is very thinly capitalized and that, as a result, the car dealer will sooner or later default on its obligations to deliver cars to the makers of the notes. As to any individual note, Finance Company knows of no present or prospective inability on the car dealer's part. However, Finance Company does not act in good faith. It has failed to live up to the reasonable commercial standards of fair dealing in the trade because Finance Company is knowingly taking advantage of the situation. Finance Company purchases the notes at a great discount solely because the car dealer is saving money by not living up to the promises made to the makers of the notes.

2. Notice

There are many facts of which a potential holder may have notice that may indicate that something is wrong with the transaction or with the instrument. When a person has notice of these facts, there is no reason to encourage him to purchase the instrument; and if he does purchase the instrument, his equities should be less than those of the person holding the claim or raising the defense. Therefore, a purchaser who has notice of a proscribed fact is completely denied holder-in-due-course status. He takes subject to all claims, defenses, and claims in recoupment whether or not related to the one of which he has notice. If, for example, he knows that there is a small breach of warranty claim in recoupment that could be asserted by the maker against the payee, he also takes subject to a claim of an unrelated third party to ownership of the instrument. Although this may seem unfair to the purchaser, the occasional unfairness of this all-or-nothing rule is outweighed by the simplicity of its application.

A holder cannot become a holder in due course if he has notice of any number of different infirmities in the instrument or in any underlying transaction by which the instrument was issued or negotiated. Specific infirmities will be discussed in the next section. In general, a purchaser may not have notice of any claim to the instrument described in section 3-306, or of a defense or claim in recoupment of any party as described in section 3-305(a).[104] The claims, claims in recoupment, and defenses available under sections 3-305(a) and 3-306 are discussed in Chapter 2E.

In order for notice to be effective, it must be received at such time and manner as to give the purchaser a reasonable opportunity to act upon it.[105] A purchaser that receives in the mail at 9:00 A.M. a list of stolen certificates of deposit will not necessarily have time to open his mail and read the list before purchasing a certificate of deposit at 9:30 A.M. Once a purchaser becomes a holder in due course, notice subsequently obtained does not destroy his holder-in-due-course status. In our example, if the purchaser of the certificate of deposit reads the list at 10:00 A.M. and discovers that the certificate was stolen, this subsequently-discovered knowledge does not destroy his holder-in-due-course status. The rationale is that once he has already given value in good faith and without any proscribed notice, he deserves protection. Because value has already been given, it is too late for him to do anything about the notice when it is finally received.

A purchaser may have notice in three possible ways:[106]

1. he may have actual knowledge of the infirmity;
2. he may have received a notification of the infirmity; or
3. from all the facts and circumstances known to him at the time in question he may have reason to know that the infirmity exists.

A purchaser *has actual knowledge of* an infirmity when he is subjectively aware of the existence of the claim, defense, or claim in recoupment.

---

104. U.C.C. §3-302(a)(2)(vi); U.C.C. §3-302(a)(2)(vi) respectively.
105. U.C.C. §3-302(f).
106. U.C.C. §1-201(25)(a); U.C.C. §1-201(25)(b); U.C.C. §1-201(25)(c) respectively.

C. Good Faith and Notice

a. Notification

A person *receives a notice or notification* when

1. it comes to his attention; or
2. it is duly delivered at the place of business through which the contract was made or at any other place held out by him as the place for receipt of such communications.[107]

Notification is effective even though the holder did not actually read the notification and thereby acquire actual knowledge of the claim, defense, or claim in recoupment. Notification, instead, depends upon a formal act whereby the purchaser receives a notice or notification of the infirmity. The assumption is that if the purchaser receives a notice or notification, he is likely to read it and thereby learn of the claim, defense, or claim in recoupment. The risk that he will not have in fact read the notification is outweighed by the danger of perjury if the holder were permitted to deny having read the notification.

To constitute a notice or notification, the communication must, if read, inform the reader of the existence of the claim, defense, or claim in recoupment. Not only must the information constituting the infirmity be contained in the notice or notification, but the information must be presented in such a way that it will likely be read by the holder. For example, information contained in a newspaper or magazine should not constitute notification. A person has no obligation to read every portion of a newspaper or magazine. Of course, if the person in fact reads the newspaper or magazine, he may have acquired actual knowledge of the relevant information. On the other hand, a letter, an agreement, or prospectus accompanying the instrument, or a booklet containing a list of stolen instruments, should be read and therefore should suffice as notification.

The purchaser must have received the notification. This usually requires that the existence of the notification, although not necessarily its content, come to the purchaser's attention. When the existence of the notice or notification has been pointed out to the purchaser and placed in his control, the purchaser is deemed to have received it. For instance, the handing of the notification to the purchaser constitutes receipt. Placing of the notice or notification on his desk should constitute receipt only if he is informed of or discovers its presence.

Under certain limited circumstances, a purchaser is deemed to have

---

107. U.C.C. §1-201(26).

received a notice or notification even when the notice has not come to his attention. A purchaser receives a notice or notification when it is duly delivered to either of the following: (1) the place of business through which the contract was made;[108] or (2) at any other place held out by the purchaser as the place of receipt of such communications. One's home address or post office box should be a place held out by the purchaser as the place of receipt of such communications.

b.   Reason to Know

A purchaser may also have notice of an infirmity if from all of the facts and circumstances known to him at the time in question, he has reason to know that the infirmity exists.[109] Two tests have been adopted by courts for determining whether a purchaser has *reason to know* of a claim, defense, or claim in recoupment. One test, called the "duty to inquire" test, is whether a reasonable person from all the facts and circumstances known to the purchaser would have further investigated and thereby discovered the existence of the claim, defense, or claim in recoupment. This test is objective, allowing the court to determine whether the holder as a reasonable person should have, through the exercise of reasonable diligence, discovered the defense, claim, or claim in recoupment. A majority of courts have rejected the duty to inquire test in favor of the inferable knowledge test.

Under the "inferable knowledge" test, a person has reason to know of a claim, claim in recoupment, or defense where the only reasonable conclusion he could reach from the facts known to him is that the claim, claim in recoupment, or defense exists. Unlike the duty to inquire test, the purchaser does not have a duty to investigate further if circumstances are such that a reasonable person would have been suspicious. Under the inferable knowledge test, the issue is whether the purchaser could have reasonably inferred the probable existence of the claim, claim in recoupment, or defense from the facts known to him. Under the inferable knowledge test, the holder may assume an innocent explanation for a suspicious circumstance, while under the duty to inquire test, he must investigate to determine whether the suspicious circumstance indicates that some infirmity exists in the instrument or underlying transaction.

Certain facts do not give notice under either test. Public filing or recording of a document does not of itself constitute notice of a defense, claim in

---

108. U.C.C. §1-201(26)(b).
109. U.C.C. §1-201(25)(c).

recoupment, or claim to the instrument.[110] Likewise, knowledge that an instrument was issued or negotiated in return for an executory promise (a promise to perform in the future) or accompanied by a separate agreement does not give a purchaser notice of a claim, defense, or claim in recoupment. Knowledge of an executory promise does not impose upon the purchaser the duty to inquire as to whether the promise has been performed. The purchaser has notice of a defense or claim in recoupment only if he has notice that a breach has already occurred.

Thus, if Finance Company knows that Car Dealer has agreed to deliver a Mazda RX7 to Maker, Finance Company has no affirmative duty to determine whether the car has been delivered. Of course, knowledge of further facts may indicate that a breach has occurred. If Finance Company hears that Car Dealer has been terminated as a Mazda dealer, Finance Company would have the duty to find out, under the duty to inquire test, whether the car had already been delivered. Assuming Car Dealer did not already have the car in stock, Finance Company would have reason to suspect that Car Dealer, having been terminated as a Mazda dealer, will not be able to deliver the car.

Even under these circumstances, Finance Company would probably not have notice under the inferable knowledge test. Finance Company could assume that Car Dealer had already acquired the cars that it had resold. However, if Finance Company also knew that Car Dealer had no Mazda RX7s on order or on its lot at the time of termination, Finance Company could infer from these facts that Car Dealer will breach its promise.

In many situations, whether the holder is deemed to have notice of a claim, defense, or claim in recoupment depends upon which test the court adopts. For example, a finance company or bank that regularly purchases notes from the same retailer may know of defenses previously asserted by other customers of the retailer. Under the inferable knowledge test, notice of a defense to any specific note will not be imputed to the finance company or bank in this situation. Even if the finance company or bank knew of many complaints from other customers, such complaints would not indicate that there is a defense to the specific instrument at issue. On the other hand, under the duty to inquire test, a court may find that the numerous prior complaints give rise to a duty on the part of the finance company or bank to investigate this specific transaction. If the investigation would have revealed a defense, the finance company or bank will be deemed to have notice of the defense.

A second situation in which the result depends upon which test the court adopts is where an instrument is purchased at a substantial discount. Under the inferable knowledge test, the purchaser is not imputed with notice of a

---

110. U.C.C. §3-302(b); U.C.C. §9-309.

claim, defense, or claim in recoupment solely because of his knowledge of the discount alone.[111] The holder has the right to assume that another, more innocent, reason accounts for the discount. The holder may assume, for example, that the large discount is a result of a substantial risk that the maker is insolvent or of the seller's urgent need for immediate cash. The holder need not attempt to discover the actual reason. In contrast, under the duty to inquire test, a purchaser is required to investigate why the instrument is selling at such a large discount.[112] If the discount is because of a claim, defense, or claim in recoupment, the purchaser is deemed to have notice of it.

There is a subjective element to both tests. Under either test the question is whether "from all the facts and circumstances known" to him, the purchaser has reason to know of the defense, claim in recoupment, or claim. These facts and circumstances include, among others, those comprising the claim, defense, or claim in recoupment, the reliability of the source of the information, the purchaser's knowledge of the business or type of transaction involved, and any facts the purchaser discovers from his own investigation. An attorney may have reason to know of a defense under circumstances where an elderly widow who has never engaged in a business transaction might not.

c. When Notice Imputed to Organization

Banks and large corporations present unique concerns in analyzing whether and when they have notice of a defense, claim in recoupment, or claim to the instrument. These concerns center on when notice obtained by an agent will be imputed to his principal and when such notice is effective.[113] "Organization" is defined as including "a corporation, government or governmental subdivision or agency, business trust, estate, trust, partnership or association, two or more persons having a joint or common interest, or any other legal or commercial entity."[114] Despite the fact that an individual principal acting through an agent is not technically an "organization," the same rules for determining whether notice to the agent is imputed to the principal should apply whether the principal is an organization or an individual.

Notice to an organization is effective for a particular transaction from the

111. For a case under former Article 3, see Hatton v. Money Lenders & Assoc. Ltd., 39 U.C.C. Rep. Serv. 1336, 127 Ill. App. 3d 577, 82 Ill. Dec. 826, 469 N.E.2d 360 (1984) (large discount did not put buyer on notice; buyer did a quick inquiry).

112. For a case under former Article 3, see In re Nusor, 123 B.R. 55, 13 U.C.C. Rep. Serv. 2d 773 (Bankr. 9th Cir. 1991) (discount itself not sufficient to charge buyer with notice, but a factor).

113. U.C.C. §1-201(27).

114. U.C.C. §1-201(28).

C. Good Faith and Notice

earlier of the time the notice either: (1) is brought to the attention of the individual conducting the transaction; or (2) should have been brought to his attention had the organization exercised due diligence.[115]

"Due diligence" requires that the organization maintain reasonable routines for the communication of significant information from individuals who have the duty to forward information to the person conducting the transaction along with reasonable compliance with the procedures established. The reasonableness of the routine depends upon the importance of the information to be communicated. If it is a reasonable business practice to deliver mail twice a day, the individual conducting the transaction, and thus the organization, is deemed to obtain notice when that individual receives the mail and has had a reasonable time to review the mail and not when the mail was first delivered to the mail room. On the other hand, if an officer of a bank learns that a person has just attempted to sell a stolen certificate of deposit to a neighboring bank, the officer should inform the tellers of this fact immediately rather than through interoffice mail the next day. In this case, the teller should be deemed to have notice of the theft shortly after the officer learns of it.

As long as the organization is in reasonable compliance with its established procedures, notice will not be imputed to the organization until the information actually reaches the party conducting the transaction. If, for example, the organization has a reasonable routine for distributing mail, notice will be effective only when a misplaced letter is actually delivered and not when it should have been delivered had it not been misplaced. However, if there are no established procedures or if the procedures are not generally followed, notice will be effective from the moment that the information would have reached the party conducting the transaction had there been reasonable procedures in place at the time.

Only two groups of individuals are required to forward information that they have received.[116] The first group is composed of those individuals who have actual authority as part of their regular duties to receive and communicate such information. A teller in a bank, the bank president, and the receptionist would seem to have as part of their duties the obligation to forward any type of mail or other notification they receive. A security guard or a janitor may not have such a duty.

In the second group is any person who has reason to know of the transaction and that the transaction would be materially affected by the information. For example, if a teller who hears that a customer has been indicted on criminal fraud charges knows that the bank is contemplating buying an instru-

---

115. U.C.C. §1-201(27); U.C.C. §1-201, Official Comment 27.
116. U.C.C. §1-201(27).

ment from that person, the teller is required to forward this information to the person conducting the transaction.

3. Specific Types of Prohibited Notice

a. Notice That an Instrument Is Forged or Altered or Otherwise Irregular

A purchaser cannot be a holder in due course if the instrument, when issued or negotiated to the holder, bears such apparent evidence of forgery or alteration or is otherwise so irregular or incomplete as to call into question its authenticity.[117] Of course, the purchaser also cannot be a holder in due course if he has actual knowledge or has been notified of a forgery or alteration. But even without actual knowledge or notification, a purchaser is imputed with notice of any irregularity visible from the face of the instrument itself.

The standard is whether the instrument on its face is so suspect that a reasonable person would question its authenticity. The purchaser's particular knowledge is relevant in determining whether the particular irregularity should have alerted the purchaser to a claim, defense, or claim in recoupment. For example, a bank officer might know that the signature of a certain bank on a cashier's check is always printed. The bank officer will be deemed to have notice of a forgery if the signature is handwritten while most other purchasers will not be deemed to have such notice from the appearance of the check itself. Of course, a purchaser who makes a thorough investigation and finds an innocent explanation for an apparent irregularity may thereafter qualify as a holder in due course.

There will be times when even a clear alteration will not incite suspicion in a reasonable person. The alteration must not only be apparent upon reasonable inspection, but not reasonably susceptible of an innocent explanation. For example, the crossing out of "1995" and adding of "1996" on an instrument negotiated in January 1996 may indicate simply that the maker had forgotten that the year had changed. In this situation, the holder would have no duty to inquire as to the reason for the alteration.

---

117. U.C.C. §3-302(a)(1).

b.   Notice That Instrument Is Overdue or Has Been Dishonored

Despite the fact that there may be many innocent explanations for why an instrument is overdue or has been dishonored, there is little commercial reason to encourage the purchase of overdue or dishonored instruments. For this reason, a purchaser is denied holder-in-due-course status if he has notice that an instrument is overdue or has been dishonored or that there has been an uncured default with respect to payment of another instrument issued as part of the same series.[118]

The relevant issue is whether the purchaser has notice that the instrument is overdue or has been dishonored, not whether the instrument, in fact, is overdue or has been dishonored. A purchaser without notice that an instrument is overdue or has been dishonored may become a holder in due course even though the instrument has been in fact dishonored or is overdue.

We discuss in Chapter 3 under what circumstances an instrument has been dishonored. In this section, we will discuss when an instrument is overdue. A check is "overdue" the day after the day demand for payment is duly made or 90 days after its stated date, whichever is earlier.[119] For example, if a check dated March 1 is presented on April 1, the check is overdue if it is not paid by April 2. If presentment is not made by June 1 (90 days after the check's date), the check is overdue on that date. Because it is unlikely that a potential purchaser will know if demand or presentment has been made (unless there is a stamped notation on the check that it has been dishonored), in most situations the 90-day period will be the relevant one. The rationale for the 90-day limitation is that any purchaser of a check should generally be suspicious where the previous holder retains the check for more than 90 days.

Any other instrument payable on demand becomes overdue at the earlier of either: (1) the day after the day demand for payment is duly made;[120] or (2) when the instrument has been outstanding for a period of time after its date that is unreasonably long.[121] To determine if an unreasonably long period of time has passed, courts are instructed to look at the circumstances of the particular case in light of the nature of the instrument and usage of trade.

Almost all instruments payable in installments, and many instruments payable at a stated date, include a provision (called an "acceleration clause") allowing the holder to demand that the entire principal and interest be immediately due if any number of the enumerated events have occurred. The most

---

118. U.C.C. §3-302(a)(2)(iii).
119. U.C.C. §3-304(a)(1); U.C.C. §3-304(a)(2).
120. U.C.C. §3-304(a)(1).
121. U.C.C. §3-304(a)(3); U.C.C. §3-304, Official Comment 1.

typical accelerating event is a default in the payment of one or more installments. Once the instrument has been accelerated, causing the entire principal amount to be immediately due, the instrument becomes overdue on the
day after the accelerated due date.[122]

Absent acceleration, an instrument payable in installments becomes overdue upon default for nonpayment of an installment. The instrument remains
overdue until the default is cured.[123] Therefore, a purchaser should inquire as
to whether previous installments have been paid. If a note is payable monthly
in ten installments on the first of every month, and the first passes without payment, the note becomes overdue. Once payment of that installment is made,
the note is no longer overdue. Absent acceleration, an instrument not payable
in installments is overdue on the day after its due date.[124] A purchaser taking
after its due date has reason to know that the instrument is overdue.

As long as there is no default in the payment of the principal amount, the
instrument is not overdue simply because there is a default in the payment of
interest.[125] Cash flow problems often cause a maker to be late in the payment
of interest and do not indicate to the holder that there is any problem in the
underlying transaction. Similarly, knowledge that there has been a default in
the payment of interest is not notice that the instrument is overdue. The circumstances change where the instrument allows the holder to accelerate the
principal in the event of a default in the payment of interest. In this event, the
principal amount will also be due and therefore the instrument becomes overdue the day after the acceleration.

c. Notice of a Breach of Fiduciary Duty

There are many situations in which an agent, officer, trustee, or other
fiduciary embezzles funds of his principal by use of a negotiable instrument.
For example, a treasurer of a corporation may write a corporate check to
American Express Company to pay his own personal credit card bill. A president of a small corporation may deposit a check payable to the corporation
into his own personal bank account. When this occurs, a question arises as to
whether either American Express Company or the president's depositary bank
is a holder in due course. If either qualifies as a holder in due course, it will
take free of the claim by the corporation that the treasurer or president misused corporate funds. However, as we discuss in Chapter 2E(2)(d), if either

122. U.C.C. §3-304(b)(3).
123. U.C.C. §3-304(b)(1); U.C.C. §3-304, Official Comment 2.
124. U.C.C. §3-304(b)(2).
125. U.C.C. §3-304(c); U.C.C. §3-304, Official Comment 2.

purchaser does not qualify as a holder in due course, it will be liable to the corporation for the proceeds of the check.

Establishing rules to determine whether a purchaser has notice of a breach of fiduciary duty and therefore is denied holder-in-due-course status is difficult. On the one hand, the person often in the best position to prevent the misuse of funds is the first person to whom the instrument is negotiated. On the other hand, negotiable instruments would cease being truly negotiable if a potential purchaser or a depositary bank had to inquire of the principal as to whether the fiduciary is properly using the funds whenever an instrument written by or payable to the principal is negotiated by a fiduciary.

The rules found in Article 3 do a fairly good job of balancing these interests. The rules apply when a represented person (Article 3's name for the principal) makes a claim to an instrument or its proceeds on the grounds that the transaction is a breach of fiduciary duty.[126] A "represented person" is the principal, beneficiary, partnership, corporation, or other person to whom the fiduciary owes a duty.[127] A "fiduciary" is defined as "an agent, trustee, partner, corporate officer or director, or other representative owing a fiduciary duty with respect to an instrument."[128] Fiduciaries include, among others, an executor of an estate, a guardian of a minor or incompetent, any officer or other agent of a corporation, trust, or partnership, or an attorney.

A fiduciary is usually only authorized to negotiate an instrument for the benefit of the represented person. If the fiduciary breaches his duty by negotiating the instrument for his own or for someone else's benefit, the represented person has an equitable claim of ownership to the instrument or its proceeds.[129] The rules for determining whether the holder has *notice* of a breach of fiduciary duty only apply where (1) the instrument is taken from a fiduciary for payment or for collection or for value and (2) where the taker *knows* that the person with whom he is dealing is a fiduciary.[130] This means that in order for the holder to be found to have *notice* of a breach of fiduciary duty, the holder must have *actual knowledge*[131] that the person with whom he is dealing is a fiduciary. For example, assume that Jim Jones is the treasurer of Oasis Corporation. Jim Jones deposits a check payable to Oasis Corporation into his personal bank account at Bank of America. The check is properly indorsed by Oasis Corporation. Therefore, Bank of America does not have actual knowledge that Jim Jones is the treasurer for Oasis Corporation. Bank

---

126. U.C.C. §3-307(b)(iii).
127. U.C.C. §3-307(a)(2).
128. U.C.C. §3-307(a)(1).
129. U.C.C. §3-307, Official Comment 2.
130. U.C.C. §3-307(b)(i); U.C.C. §3-307(b)(ii); U.C.C. §3-307, Official Comment 2.
131. U.C.C. §1-201(25); U.C.C. §3-307, Official Comment 2.

of America does not have notice that Jim Jones breached his fiduciary duty to Oasis Corporation in depositing the check into his own bank account.

Assuming that the holder knows that the person from whom he took the instrument is a fiduciary, one of three rules may apply to determine whether the holder has notice of a breach of fiduciary duty and therefore is imputed with notice of the represented person's claim to the instrument (or its proceeds).[132]

The first rule covers instruments made payable to the represented party or to the fiduciary as such. For example, if the issue is whether Jim Jones, treasurer of Oasis Corporation, has breached his fiduciary duty, this rule would apply if the instrument was made payable either to "Oasis Corporation" (the represented person) or to "Jim Jones, Treasurer of Oasis Corporation" (the fiduciary in his fiduciary capacity).

A taker of such an instrument has notice of a breach of fiduciary duty if the instrument is (1) taken in payment of or as security for a debt known by the taker to be the personal debt of the fiduciary; (2) taken in a transaction known by the taker to be for the personal benefit of the fiduciary; or (3) deposited in an account other than that of the fiduciary as such or of the represented person.[133] If Jim Jones negotiates the check in payment of his personal debt or to purchase goods or other property for his personal benefit, the rule applies. If Jim Jones deposits the check in his personal bank account, the rule also applies. However, if Jim Jones has set up a bank account "Jim Jones for the benefit of Oasis Corporation," the rule would not apply because the check would be deposited in an account of Jim Jones as fiduciary and not in Jim Jones' personal account.

It must be remembered that the taker does not have notice of the breach of fiduciary duty unless he has *actual knowledge* that the transaction is (1) for the personal benefit of the fiduciary or (2) in payment of or as security for a personal debt of the fiduciary.[134] Mere knowledge that a person negotiating the instrument is or was a fiduciary neither gives notice to nor imposes a duty upon the taker to inquire of the claim of the represented person. For example, suppose Jim Jones negotiates a check payable to Oasis Corporation to MasterCard in payment of his personal credit card bill. Unless MasterCard has actual knowledge that the credit card purchases were personal rather than business-related, MasterCard does not have knowledge that the transaction was for Jim Jones' personal benefit. Of course, if Jim Jones negotiates a check payable to Oasis Corporation in payment of a loan that Bank of America

---

132. U.C.C. §3-307(b)(1).
133. U.C.C. §3-307(b)(2).
134. U.C.C. §3-307, Official Comment 2.

C. Good Faith and Notice

knows, from the loan application, to be for his personal benefit, Bank of America has notice of his breach of fiduciary duty. Notice is imputed in this situation because it is very likely that Jim had no authority to use the check to pay off his car loan. For similar reasons, a bank is imputed with notice of the breach of fiduciary duty where a fiduciary deposits such a check into his own personal account.[135]

The second rule covers instruments issued by the represented person or the fiduciary as such directly to the taker. This will occur when Oasis Corporation (the represented person) or Steve Smith, as guardian for Sally Smith, writes a check to the taker. For example, the president of Oasis Corporation may have written a check payable to MasterCard or Steve Smith as guardian for Sally Smith may have written a check to Harry's Men's Store. In these situations the taker is deemed to have notice in the exact same circumstances as when the instrument is payable to the represented person himself;[136] namely, when the instrument is (1) taken in payment of or as security for a debt known by the taker to be the personal debt of the fiduciary; (2) taken in a transaction known by the taker to be for the personal benefit of the fiduciary; or (3) deposited in an account other than that of the fiduciary as such or of the represented person.[137] Notice is imputed to the taker because it is unusual for a represented person to pay a debt of the fiduciary by issuing a check directly to the taker.[138] If Steve attempts to pay for a suit with a check drawn on Sally Smith's guardianship account, Harry's Men's Store should inquire as to whether this use of guardianship funds is proper. The balance weighs in favor of protecting the represented person (Sally Smith) because, in most of these situations, such use of the funds will be improper. In the unlikely event that Steve had the right to write the check for his own personal benefit, Steve has breached no duty and Sally will have no right to recover from Harry's Men's Store.

The third rule covers instruments payable to the fiduciary personally, whether drawn by the represented person or by the fiduciary himself. For example, the rule covers a check issued by Oasis Corporation and payable to Jim Jones. Because it is not unusual for the represented party to pay or reimburse the fiduciary by issuing a check directly to him,[139] the taker has notice of a breach of fiduciary duty only where it has *actual knowledge* of the breach.[140]

---

135. U.C.C. §3-307(b)(2)(i); U.C.C. §3-307, Official Comment 3.
136. U.C.C. §3-307(b)(4).
137. U.C.C. §3-307(b)(2).
138. U.C.C. §3-307, Official Comment 5.
139. U.C.C. §3-307, Official Comment 4.
140. U.C.C. §3-307(b)(3).

If, for example, Jim negotiates the check to Bank of America in payment for his personal bank loan, Bank of America does not have notice of a breach of fiduciary duty unless it not only knows that the check was used for the benefit of Jim personally but also knows that the check was not intended by Oasis Corporation to be so used. If the rule was otherwise, a bank could never safely allow an employee to deposit a paycheck into his own account.

d.   Notice of Discharge

As we will examine in a subsequent section, there are many situations in which a party is discharged from liability on an instrument under circumstances that do not cast doubt upon the obligation of any other party. For example, a co-maker may have been released by the holder and the release noted on the note. This has no effect upon whether his co-maker is likewise discharged. For this reason, notice of discharge of a party, other than discharge in an insolvency proceeding, is not notice of a defense. As a result, a holder who has notice of a party's discharge can still qualify as a holder in due course.[141] However, despite the fact that he may qualify as a holder in due course, he will take subject to any discharge of which he has notice.

Discharge in insolvency proceedings of a maker, drawer, or acceptor is treated differently. In the first place, as discussed in Chapter 2E(1)(b), it is specifically listed as a defense available against all persons including a holder in due course without notice of the insolvency.[142] Secondly, if a taker knows that the maker, drawer, or acceptor (the people ultimately liable on an instrument) has been discharged in insolvency proceeds, that taker should not be granted holder-in-due-course status, which would allow him to cut off the defenses of other parties to the instrument (in most cases, the indorsers).

D.   DENIAL OF HOLDER-IN-DUE-COURSE STATUS TO CERTAIN CLASSES OF PURCHASERS

Certain holders, even after meeting all of the requirements contained in section 3-302(a), do not thereby become holders in due course.[143] The desire

---

141. U.C.C. §3-302(b); U.C.C. §3-302, Official Comment 3.
142. U.C.C. §3-302, Official Comment 3.
143. Even though not qualifying as a holder in due course in his own right, such a pur-

to increase the negotiability of instruments is outweighed in the case of these holders by the need to protect the right of the obligors to raise their defenses. There are four categories of holders who cannot by their purchase become a holder in due course.

1. Acquisition by Taking Over Estate

First, a person who acquires an instrument by taking over an estate or other organization that previously held the instrument cannot by such acquisition become a holder in due course.[144] For example, assume that Jones made a note payable to Smith. Upon Smith's death, the executor, even if otherwise meeting all of the requirements for holder-in-due-course status, would take subject to all of the claims in recoupment and defenses to which Smith would be subject. There is no reason that Smith's death should deprive Jones of his right to raise his defenses or claims in recoupment. As we will see, if Smith himself was a holder in due course, the executor would acquire Smith's rights as a holder in due course.

2. Purchase in Execution, Bankruptcy, or Creditor's Sale

Second, a purchaser of the instrument in an execution, bankruptcy, or creditor's sale or similar proceeding or under legal process cannot become a holder in due course.[145] For example, when a state bank becomes insolvent, the state bank commissioner sells the bank's assets, including its negotiable instruments, at a judicial sale. Another bank or other financial institution may purchase all or some of these negotiable instruments. The purchasing institution realizes that because of the bank's insolvency, it is quite possible that the obligors on the instruments may have a claim or defense against the payee bank. Because the purchasing institution does not expect to take the instruments free of the obligor's claims or defenses, it will pay a lower price for the instruments. The same reasons apply to denying protection to attaching, garnishing, or executing creditors. Just the mere fact that there are creditors who are levy-

---

chaser is a transferee and therefore, under the shelter provision, is entitled to all of his transferor's rights. If his transferor was a holder in due course, the transferee is entitled to all of his transferor's rights as a holder in due course. U.C.C. §3-302, Official Comment 5.

144. U.C.C. §3-302(c)(iii); U.C.C. §3-302, Official Comment 5.
145. U.C.C. §3-302(c)(i); U.C.C. §3-302, Official Comment 5.

ing legal process like garnishment or execution indicates that the current holder of the instrument (their debtor) has financial problems. These creditors certainly recognize that their debtor's financial problems may also cause the debtor to be unable to satisfy its other obligations. These obligations may include duties owed to the obligors of the instruments being sold. The levying creditors, therefore, will pay lower prices for the instruments because of these potential defenses.

3.   Purchase in Bulk Transaction

Third, a person cannot become a holder in due course by purchase of an instrument as part of a bulk transaction not in the regular course of the transferor's business.[146] There are two different types of *bulk transactions* contemplated by this section. The first type is a bulk sale of instruments for the purpose of liquidating the holder's assets in preparation for the termination of his business. Assume, for example, that Stereo Shack, a retailer of stereo equipment, decides to go out of business. For this purpose it offers to sell to Finance Company all notes received from the purchasers of stereo equipment. When this offer is made to Finance Company, should not it wonder whether there are any obligations that Stereo Shack owes to these purchasers? Maybe Stereo Shack has not delivered all of the equipment or has commitments under long-term service contracts to these purchasers. If Stereo Shack is no longer in business, these purchasers may have defenses to their obligations to pay the notes. There is no reason to encourage Finance Company to purchase these notes by offering it holder-in-due-course status.

Finance Company is denied holder-in-due-course status regardless of whether it knows or has reason to know that its purchase is part of a bulk transaction not in the regular course of Stereo Shack's business. Finance Company has the duty prior to the purchase to determine whether Stereo Shack is making the sale in the regular course of its business or as part of the winding up of its business.

In contrast, there are some businesses, like new car dealerships, that as a regular and legitimate business practice sell all notes obtained from the sale of their cars so as to acquire sufficient cash to purchase new inventory. Financing of this type is desirable and should be encouraged. As a result, a purchaser of a substantial portion or all of the instruments sold by the car dealership in the regular course of the car dealership's business is not prevented from acquiring holder-in-due-course status by the purchase.

---

146. U.C.C. §3-302(c)(ii); U.C.C. §3-302, Official Comment 5.

D. Denial of Holder-in-Due-Course Status

The second type of bulk transfer is where there is a change in the organizational structure of the holder so that, even though the same actual entity retains the instruments, there has technically been a transfer from one entity to another.[147] For example, when a partner is added or withdraws from a partnership, the new partnership is deemed to be a different entity than the old partnership. In order for the new partnership to be the holder of an instrument, it is necessary that the instrument be indorsed from the old partnership to the new partnership. Clearly, this negotiation is in form only and should not result in the new partnership acquiring protection against defenses or claims to the instrument that the old partnership did not have. For this reason, even if the new partnership technically gives value to the old partnership by assuming its debts, the new partnership should not, by the transfer, acquire holder-in-due-course status. Similar situations in which the new entity acquires no greater rights than the old entity include the reorganization or merger of a corporation or the purchase by one bank of the assets of another bank facing insolvency.

An exception to these rules involves the purchase by the Federal Deposit Insurance Corporation ("FDIC"), the Federal Savings and Loan Insurance Corporation ("FSLIC"), or the Resolution Trust Corporation ("RTC") of the assets of an insolvent bank. Under federal common law, the FDIC, the FSLIC, or the RTC may become a holder in due course of a note even though it purchased the note in a bulk transaction not in the regular course of the seller's business[148] or acquired the note by taking over an insolvent bank.[149] This exception is discussed in Section I of this chapter.

4. Consumer Notes

Based upon a need to protect consumers against overreaching by retailers, the Federal Trade Commission, as well as most state legislatures, has enacted rules or statutes affecting the ability of a holder of an instrument, issued in a consumer transaction, to take free of the consumer's defenses. A consumer transaction is one in which a natural person uses a negotiable instrument (other than a check that is not postdated) to purchase goods or services to be used primarily for personal, family, or household purposes.

147. U.C.C. §3-302, Official Comment 5.
148. For a case under former Article 3, see Federal Sav. & Loan Ins. Corp. v. Murray, 853 F.2d 1251, 8 U.C.C. Rep. Serv. 2d 56 (5th Cir. 1988) (FSLIC is holder in due course under federal common law even though it purchased notes in bulk and not in regular course of business of seller's business.).
149. U.C.C. §3-302, Official Comment 5.

The problem that the Federal Trade Commission and many state legislatures were trying to rectify was simple. A thinly capitalized retailer or contractor would, usually through sharp sales practices, get a consumer to purchase goods or services to be delivered or rendered in the future by executing a promissory note, also due at a subsequent date. The retailer or contractor would immediately sell the note to a finance company. The services would never be rendered or the goods never delivered. But when the consumer attempted to raise this failure of consideration as a defense, the finance company would claim immunity from the defense by claiming to be a holder in due course. When the consumer attempted to recover from the retailer or contractor, the consumer would discover that the retailer either could not be found or was insolvent.

a. FTC Rule

Several years ago,[150] the Federal Trade Commission promulgated a rule aimed at preventing financers of negotiable instruments from taking an instrument free from a consumer's defenses. Under the "Trade Regulation Rule Concerning Preservation of Customers' Claims and Defenses,"[151] a seller in the business of selling goods to consumers must put the following legend in its consumer credit contracts:

NOTICE

ANY HOLDER OF THIS CONSUMER CREDIT
CONTRACT IS SUBJECT TO ALL CLAIMS AND
DEFENSES WHICH THE DEBTOR COULD ASSERT
AGAINST THE SELLER OF GOODS OR SERVICES
OBTAINED [PURSUANT HERETO OR] WITH THE
PROCEEDS HEREOF. RECOVERY HEREUNDER BY
THE DEBTOR SHALL NOT EXCEED AMOUNTS
PAID BY THE DEBTOR HEREUNDER.[152]

A seller who fails to include such a legend commits an unfair or deceptive act or practice within the meaning of section 5 of the Federal Trade Commission Act.

Where the required language is included, the holder takes subject to the

150. The rule was promulgated on May 14, 1976. 41 Fed. Res. 20022.
151. Bureau of Consumer Protection, Federal Trade Commission, Guidelines on Trade Regulation Rule Concerning Preservation of Consumers' Claims and Defenses, 16 C.F.R. §433.2.
152. Preservation of Consumers' Claims and Defenses (Federal Trade Commission Trade Regulation Rule), 16 C.F.R. §433.2(a) & (b).

D. Denial of Holder-in-Due-Course Status

consumer's claims and defenses.[153] The note remains negotiable but there can be no holder in due course, thus allowing the consumer to assert any of his defenses against the holder.[154] Assume that Jean purchases home improvements from ABC Construction Co. in payment for which she executes a note for $3,000. If the note contains the FTC legend, House Finance, the purchaser of the note, takes subject to Jean's defense that the improvements were never made. Under the terms of the FTC clause, the holder (House Finance) is liable to the consumer (Jean) up to, but no more than, the funds received by the holder (House Finance) from the consumer (Jean) pursuant to the instrument.[155] Assume that although Jean had paid $1,000 on the note to House Finance and $1,000 to ABC Construction Co., the improvements were never made. If House Finance sued Jean for the remaining $1,000, Jean could assert her defense of failure of consideration against House Finance. Furthermore, Jean could assert her counterclaim against House Finance to the extent of $1,000 (the amount paid by her to House Finance). In contrast, if she had paid all $2,000 to ABC Construction Co., she would have no affirmative right of recovery from House Finance because she would have paid nothing under the note to it.

The FTC rule has its limitations. First, only sellers who are regularly engaged in selling or leasing goods or services to consumers are subject to the rule.[156] Second, only "consumer credit contracts" must contain the legend. A "consumer credit contract" is "any instrument which evidences or embodies a debt arising from a 'Purchase Money Loan' transaction or a 'financed sale.'"[157] A "financed sale" is, generally, any extension of credit by a seller to a consumer to purchase goods.[158] A "purchase money loan" is a loan from a creditor "which is applied, in whole or substantial part, to purchase goods or services from a seller who (1) refers consumers to the creditor or (2) is affiliated with the creditor by common control, contract, or business arrangement."[159] In other words, the rule basically covers only those loans where the

---

153. U.C.C. §3-106(d).

154. U.C.C. §3-106(d).

155. See Bureau of Consumer Protection, Federal Trade Commission, Guidelines on Trade Regulation Rule Concerning Preservation of Consumers' Claims and Defenses at ¶11,394 (CCH Consumer Credit Guide 1976). See Ford Motor Credit Co. v. Morgan, 404 Mass. 537, 536 N.E.2d 587, 8 U.C.C. Rep. Serv. 2d 524 (1989) (where note contains required FTC legend, consumer may maintain affirmative action against holder for return of monies paid to holder only where seller's breach is so substantial that court is persuaded rescission and restitution are justified).

156. Supra, note 149, at §433.1(j).

157. Supra, note 149, at §433.1(i).

158. Supra, note 149, at §433.1(e).

159. Supra, note 149, at §433.1(d).

creditor and particular seller have established a formal or informal relationship with one another aimed at financing consumer purchases.[160] For example, if ABC Construction Co. and House Finance have an arrangement under which ABC Construction Co. refers its purchasers to House Finance who then makes the loan to Jean, the transaction is a purchase money loan.

When the seller fails to include the required language in its consumer contracts, it violates the FTC rule and is subject to either a cease and desist order (an order forbidding it from engaging in such practices)[161] or a civil action by the FTC.[162] Unless authorized by state law,[163] a consumer has no private right of action for violation of this rule.[164] Where the legend is omitted, a holder in due course takes free of the consumer's defenses. It can be argued, however, that a person in the business of financing consumer sales has notice that the legend should have been included and therefore is not a holder in due course.

b.   State Legislation

Many states have also enacted legislation that preserves, to varying degrees, the ability of a consumer to raise defenses against a holder of the note. This legislation has taken diverse forms. It is beyond the scope of this book to cover all of the applicable state laws.

The most influential legislation, which has been adopted by many states,[165] is the 1969 version of the Uniform Consumer Credit Code ("UCCC"), which provides that a seller or lessor in a consumer credit sale or consumer lease may not take in payment a negotiable instrument (other than a check). A holder is not in good faith and thus cannot qualify as a holder in due course if it takes a negotiable instrument with notice that the instrument is issued in violation of the UCCC. By being denied holder-in-due-course status, the holder takes the instrument subject to the consumer's defenses and claims in recoupment. Regular financers of commercial paper who know of this rule are prevented from becoming holders-in-due-course. At the same

---

160. Supra, note 151, at ¶¶11,396 - 11,401.

161. 15 U.S.C. §45.

162. 15 U.S.C. §57b.

163. For an example of a state statute providing a private right of action, see Mass. Gen. Laws Ann., ch. 93A, §2 (West 1984 & Supp. 1991).

164. See Holloway v. Bristol-Myers, 485 F.2d 986 (D. D.C. 1973); Carlson v. Coca-Cola Co., 483 F.2d 279 (9th Cir. 1973).

165. Idaho, Indiana, Oklahoma, S. Carolina, Utah, Wyoming, and Colorado (which have made major textual changes in the section).

time, a purchaser who does not regularly purchase consumer paper is usually unaware of the requirements of the UCCC and therefore may become a holder in due course who takes the instrument free of the consumer's defenses.[166]

Some state legislation, including those states adopting the 1974 version of the UCCC,[167] make an assignee of a consumer credit sale, whether or not a holder in due course, subject to all of the consumer's claims and defenses.[168] Other states adopt statutory schemes that preserve the right of a consumer to raise defenses and claims against a holder in due course to the extent that the consumer gives notice of his claim or defense to the holder within a set period of time, either after his purchase or after notice of the negotiation to the holder.[169]

E. DEFENSES, CLAIMS TO THE INSTRUMENT, CLAIMS IN RECOUPMENT, AND DISCHARGES

Any holder or person with the rights of a holder (collectively called a "person entitled to enforce an instrument") may recover on the instrument against the obligor in the absence of a claim to the instrument, defense, claim in recoupment, or discharge.[170] A "defense" is any ground a party may have that is sufficient to permit him to avoid all or some of his liability on the instrument. For example, the duty of a buyer of goods to pay for the goods is usually conditioned upon the seller delivering the goods.[171] If the seller fails to deliver the goods, the buyer may raise failure of consideration as a defense to the note that he gave evidencing his obligation to pay for the goods. However, if payment of the note is not conditioned, either expressly or constructively,

---

166. U.C.C. §3-305(b).

167. Iowa, Kansas and Maine.

168. Uniform Consumer Credit Code §3-404 (1974). Other states, although not enacting the UCCC, also permit a consumer to raise all claims and defenses even as against a holder in due course. See N.C. Gen. Stat. §25A-25 (1986); Ga. Code Ann. §96-908 (Harrison 1976 & Supp. 1989); Wash. Rev. Code Ann. §63.14.020 (1966 & Supp. 1991); Ohio Rev. Code Ann. tit. 13 §§1317.031, 1317.032 (Anderson 1979 & Supp. 1990).

169. See, e.g., Arizona, Ariz. Rev. Stat. Ann. §44-145 (1987) (a holder cannot be a holder in due course for a period of 90 days after receipt by the debtor of the goods or services).

170. U.C.C. §3-308(b).

171. U.C.C. §3-305, Official Comment 3.

upon performance of the breached promise, the buyer will not have a defense to his obligation to pay. Once the goods are delivered, the buyer is now obligated to pay for the goods.

If the goods turn out to be defective and in breach of the seller's warranty that the goods are merchantable, the buyer cannot use breach of warranty as a defense to his obligation to pay for the goods. However, the buyer does have a claim for damages that can be asserted against the seller as a set-off against the buyer's duty to pay for the goods. This set-off is called, under Article 3, a claim in recoupment. A "claim in recoupment" is a set-off that arises from the same transaction out of which the instrument arose. Not to be confused with a claim of recoupment, a "claim to the instrument" is any claim of a property or possessory interest in the instrument or its proceeds, including a claim to rescind a negotiation and to recover the instrument or its proceeds. Where an instrument payable to bearer is stolen from the owner, the owner has a claim to the instrument.

Where the obligor attempts to assert one of these grounds for his refusal to make payment, the person entitled to enforce the instrument's right to recover depends, to a large extent, upon whether he has the rights of a holder in due course. When the person entitled to enforce the instrument attempts to recover on an instrument, the obligor (the person who has promised to pay the instrument from whom the holder is attempting to recover) or a claimant (a prior owner of the instrument who claims that he still owns the instrument) may attempt to deny the holder the right to recover. There are many grounds that may be asserted by the obligor or claimant.

Let us begin by examining the defenses and claims of recoupment that may be asserted against any person, whether or not that person has the rights of a holder in due course.

1.   Defenses and Claims in Recoupment to Which All Persons Take Subject

a.   Defenses and Claims in Recoupment Assertible Against Holder Itself

The person entitled to enforce the instrument (sometimes, for simplicity's sake, to be called a "holder"), whether or not qualifying as a holder in due course, takes subject to any defense or claim in recoupment assertible against the holder himself.[172] This means that whenever a holder attempts to recover

---

172. U.C.C. §3-305, Official Comment 2.

from an obligor, the obligor may raise any defense or claim in recoupment that the obligor himself has against the holder arising out of the transaction by which the holder acquired the instrument.

For example, assume that Bob, as drawer, issues a check to Carl's Auto, as payee, in payment for a used car. The car has a defective transmission. Carl's Auto was unaware of this problem. Because it took the check for value, in good faith and without any proscribed notice, Carl's Auto qualifies as a holder in due course (there is no prohibition against a payee being a holder in due course). Bob may assert the breach of warranty as a claim in recoupment against Carl's Auto even though Carl's Auto is a holder in due course because it arose out of the transaction in which the check was issued. In contrast, assume that Bob had done business with Carl's Auto before. A few months earlier, Bob had purchased a truck for his business. The truck has defective brakes in violation of the warranty that Carl's Auto gave to Bob on the truck. Because the transaction in which Bob purchased the truck was a different one from the transaction out of which the check was issued, Bob may not raise the breach of warranty on the truck as a claim in recoupment in Carl's Auto's action on the check.[173] As we will later see, if Carl's Auto negotiates the check to Don, who takes the check as a holder in due course, Bob may not even raise his claim in recoupment on the car as a defense to Don's action on the check because the claim in recoupment is not one assertible against Don himself.

b. Real Defenses

There are also four defenses, nicknamed "real defenses,"[174] which are regarded as protecting such important interests that all holders, even ones acquiring the status of holder in due course, take subject.

Infancy. The first defense is infancy. To the extent that the obligor's infancy is a defense to a simple contract, it is also a defense available against any party (including a holder in due course).[175] Thus, if in the applicable jurisdiction a 16-year-old boy can defend against liability on an ordinary contract because he is under the age of majority, he may likewise defend against his liability on a negotiable instrument on the same basis.[176] Because allowing an infant to raise infancy as a defense is intended to protect the state's interest, the infant's right to raise this defense is subject to all of the state's limitations on his right to defend against liability on a simple contract.

---

173. U.C.C. §3-305(b).
174. U.C.C §3-305, Official Comment 1.
175. U.C.C. §3-305(a)(1)(i); U.C.C. §3-305, Official Comment 1.
176. U.C.C. §3-305, Official Comment 1.

Incapacity, Duress, or Illegality.   The second real defense is legal incapacity, duress, or illegality to the extent that such defenses render the obligation of the obligor a nullity.[177] Unlike in the case of infancy, these defenses are real defenses *only if statutory or case law makes the transaction void.*[178] A transaction is void when it has no effect whatsoever. In contrast, a transaction is voidable when a party has the option to either enforce or avoid the contract. Where the transaction is merely voidable, the defense is a personal defense that is not available against a person having the rights of a holder in due course. Incapacity may include, among others, mental incompetency arising from the party's insanity, or statutory incapacity to execute the instrument arising from a corporation's exceeding its corporate powers under its articles of incorporation or under state law.

Depending upon the applicable state law, duress sufficient as a real defense may require the threat of physical injury or merely a threat of economic injury, for example, withholding of a license to act as a commodities broker unless the instrument is signed. In most states the threat of physical injury makes an obligation void while a threat of economic injury, for example to prosecute the obligor's son for theft, only makes the obligation voidable.

The real defense of illegality is far narrower than may appear at first glance. Because the illegality must make the obligation of the obligor void, there are few situations in which illegality will qualify as a real defense. In most situations illegality will only make the obligation voidable. Typical examples of illegality that may constitute a real defense include use of the instrument to pay a gambling debt, as a bribe, or to purchase known stolen property.

Fraud in the Factum.   The third real defense is sometimes called "fraud in the factum." One of the primary reasons why an obligor on a negotiable instrument is denied the right to raise any defense against a holder in due course is that he voluntarily sent a promise contained in the instrument into the marketplace knowing that it may be acquired by a holder in due course who would cut off any right he has to raise his defenses. Where the obligor has not knowingly or carelessly sent the instrument into the marketplace, it would be unfair to deny him the right to raise his defenses.

For example, assume that one of the hundreds of fans on any given day who ask Michael Jordan for an autograph has Jordan sign a piece of paper that, unknown to Jordan, contained a promissory note. Should Jordan be liable on the note? Clearly not. To guard against this and other situations

---

177. U.C.C. §3-305(a)(1)(ii).
178. U.C.C. §3-305, Official Comment 1.

where an obligor unknowingly signs a negotiable instrument, any holder takes subject to the defense that the obligor has been induced by fraud to sign the instrument where he neither knows nor has a reasonable opportunity to learn of its character or its essential terms (called "fraud in the factum").[179]

Notwithstanding the unfairness to an obligor in holding him liable on such an instrument, allowing the obligor to escape liability undercuts the negotiability of instruments. The person purchasing the note, ignorant that Jordan did not intend to issue the note, not only qualified as a holder in due course, but may have also relied upon Jordan's reputation in making his purchase. Because the obligor's protection is at the expense of a holder in due course, the two requirements for the assertion of the real defense of fraud in the factum are strictly construed.

The first requirement is that the obligor must have signed the instrument without knowledge of its character or its essential terms. An obligor is ignorant of an instrument's character where he is under the impression that he is signing something other than a promise to pay money. An obligor would be ignorant of the instrument's essential terms where, for example, he believes that he is signing a note payable in two years when in fact it is payable on demand.[180] Other examples would include where the note contains a different principal amount or rate of interest than the obligor thought he had agreed to.

The second requirement is that the obligor must have neither knowledge nor a reasonable opportunity to learn of the character or essential terms of the instrument.[181] In evaluating this requirement, the obligor's education, business experience, literacy and intelligence are taken into consideration.[182] Needless to say, most of the cases in which the defense is raised involve consumers with little business experience.

The obligor cannot raise the defense if he, under the circumstances, should have discovered the character and essential terms of the instrument. Where the obligor had the opportunity to, but did not, read the instrument, the defense will seldom be available. Absent an excellent reason, the loss should be suffered by the obligor because his carelessness in not reading the instrument caused the loss. There will be times when his failure to read the instrument will be excused. For example, the payee may have switched papers after the obligor read what he believed was the instrument that he was signing or the payee may have occupied a position of such confidence with the obligor that the obligor was lulled into believing that he need not read the instrument.

179. U.C.C. §3-305(a)(1)(iii); U.C.C. §3-305, Official Comment 1.
180. U.C.C. §3-305, Official Comment 1.
181. U.C.C. §3-305(a)(1)(iii); U.C.C. §3-305, Official Comment 1.
182. U.C.C. §3-305, Official Comment 1.

If the obligor is illiterate and cannot read the instrument, he will not be able to raise the defense where a third person, like a spouse or friend, was available to read the instrument to him. In these situations, his failure to ask the third person to read it to him would be regarded as sufficient carelessness to impose the loss upon him.

Discharge in Insolvency Proceeding. The fourth defense is the obligor's discharge in insolvency proceedings.[183] "Insolvency proceedings" is defined as including bankruptcy regardless of whether the debtor is insolvent.[184] The discharge is effective against all takers of the instrument because a discharge in bankruptcy or other insolvency proceeding is for the purpose of allowing the obligor to make a new start. However, the obligor has a defense only as to those debts that are actually discharged in the insolvency proceeding.

2. *Defenses Available Only Against a Person Without the Rights of a Holder in Due Course*

a. Ordinary Defenses

Whether or not the holder takes free of other defenses or claims in recoupment and claims to the instrument depends upon whether the holder has the rights of a holder in due course. Except as already discussed, the defense of any party is cut off when the instrument is acquired by a holder in due course.[185]

In contrast, a person not having the rights of a holder in due course takes subject to

1. any defense which would be available on a simple contract;[186] and
2. any defense of the obligor stated in Article 3[187] which include:
   a. non-issuance of the instrument;
   b. conditional issuance;
   c. issuance for a special purpose;[188]
   d. failure to countersign a traveler's check;[189]
   e. modification of the obligation by a separate agreement;[190]

183. U.C.C. §3-305(a)(1)(iv); U.C.C. §3-305, Official Comment 1.
184. U.C.C. §1-201(22); U.C.C. §3-305, Official Comment 1.
185. U.C.C. §3-305(b).
186. U.C.C. §3-305(a)(2).
187. U.C.C. §3-305(a)(2); U.C.C. §3-305, Official Comment 2.
188. U.C.C. §3-105(b); U.C.C. §3-305, Official Comment 2.
189. U.C.C. §3-106(c); U.C.C. §3-305, Official Comment 2.
190. U.C.C. §3-117; U.C.C. §3-305, Official Comment 2.

      f. payment that violates a restrictive indorsement;[191]

      g. issuance without consideration or for which the promised performance has not been given;[192] and

      h. breach of warranty when a draft is accepted.[193]

Let us look at an example of one of the defenses spelled out in Article 3—conditional issuance of an instrument. Assume, for example, that John makes a note payable to Sam. The note is delivered by John to Sam on the condition that Sam pay certain of John's bills. Sam fails to pay any of John's bills. Sam, despite failing to meet the condition, negotiates the note to Carol. Even though the condition was not met, Sam's negotiation to Carol was effective to make Carol a holder of the note. If Carol qualifies as a holder in due course, she takes free of John's defense that the condition upon which the note was delivered was not satisfied. However, if Carol does not have the rights of a holder in due course, she takes subject to the defense.[194]

As against a person not having the rights of a holder in due course, the obligor may defeat his liability on an instrument by raising the same defenses that would be available to him if the obligation arose out of an ordinary contract.[195] Potential defenses include, among others, nonperformance of a condition precedent, want of consideration,[196] partial or complete failure of consideration, mistake, unconscionability, fraud, duress, illegality, infancy, incapacity, or usury.

No Consideration Necessary for Instrument Taken for Antecedent Debt. The above rule is, however, subject to one exception. Under ordinary contract law, a promise is not supported by consideration where the promisor has already received the benefit. For example, assume that Karen has purchased goods from Sally pursuant to an oral contract under which Karen agrees to pay for the goods in 90 days. A week later, Karen sends Sally a check. Is there consideration supporting Karen's promise to pay the check? (Look back at our discussion of consideration in Chapter 2B.) The answer under ordinary contract

---

191. U.C.C. §3-206(f); U.C.C. §3-305, Official Comment 2.

192. U.C.C. §3-303(b); U.C.C. §3-305, Official Comment 2.

193. U.C.C. §3-417(b); U.C.C. §3-305, Official Comment 2.

194. U.C.C. §3-305(a)(2); U.C.C. §3-306, Official Comment 2.

195. U.C.C. §3-305(a)(2).

196. Section 3-303(b) provides that the drawer or maker of an instrument has a defense if the instrument is issued without consideration ("want of consideration"). The antecedent obligation may be that of a party other than the obligor on the instrument. U.C.C. §3-303(a)(3); §3-303, Official Comment 4. The obligor may raise any defense he has arising out of the antecedent debt as a defense to his liability on the instrument.

law is "no." Since Karen already acquired the goods, Sally gave Karen no consideration for the issuance of the check. Sally did not even extend the time that payment is due. However, under Article 3, the promise contained in Karen's check is enforceable despite the absence of consideration because no consideration is necessary for an instrument given in payment of or as security for an antecedent obligation of any kind.[197]

What in Article 3 tells us this? Unfortunately, this conclusion is reached in a circuitous manner. Section 3-303(b) simply states that if an instrument is issued for value, the instrument is also issued for consideration.[198] Then, section 3-303(a)(3) provides that an instrument is issued or transferred for value if it is issued or transferred as payment for, or as security for, an antecedent claim against any person (this means the obligor or some third person), whether or not the claim is due (even though Karen's debt was not due for 90 days). We discussed this definition of value at length in Section 2B.

Let us now explore the application of this exception in more depth. Under this exception, as long as the obligee (Sally) is owed a debt (called an "antecedent obligation"), any instrument that Sally receives either in payment of or as security for that debt is enforceable despite the absence of true consideration. The debt may be one owed by the obligor (Karen) herself or it may be a debt owed by some third person (for example, Karen's husband, mother, brother, or a corporation of which Karen is a shareholder).

Because the instrument is in effect given in consideration for the debt, the obligor (Karen) may raise any defense she has arising out of the antecedent obligation as a defense to her liability on the instrument. For example, if Karen had been discharged on the debt, no antecedent debt would exist, and consequently, she could raise want of consideration as a defense to the instrument. However, as long as the statute of limitations has not run on the antecedent obligation at the time the instrument was executed, the fact that the statute of limitations has since run on the antecedent obligation does not make the instrument unenforceable. Assume that in 1990, Karen had entered into an oral contract with Sally to make certain payments to Sally. In 1993 Karen issues a note to Sally payable on demand. Assume that the statute of limitations expired on the oral contract in 1994. Despite this fact, Karen remains liable to Sally under the note and may not assert the running of the statute of limitations on the oral contract as a defense to her obligation to pay the note. Even if Karen's note is given in payment of or as security for an antecedent debt of her mother, Karen can raise any of her mother's defenses on the underlying obligation to defeat her obligation to pay the note.

197. U.C.C. §3-303(a)(3).
198. U.C.C. §3-303(b); U.C.C. §3-303, Official Comment 1.

E. Defenses and Discharges

The rule eliminating the need for consideration when an instrument is given in payment of or as security for an antecedent obligation can be abused. For example, this rule could theoretically be used to make what otherwise would be a gift into an enforceable obligation. Assume that Father owes $100 to Son. Father issues a note to Son for $50,000 payable in 20 years to be accelerated upon Father's death. Upon the death of Father, Son demands that the executor make payment of the note. The executor claims that the note is not supported by consideration. Son asserts that the note was given in payment of an antecedent obligation (the $100 debt owed by Father to Son) and therefore is enforceable absent consideration. It is unlikely that the drafters of Article 3 intended that the rule be used in this fashion. To the extent that the note does not represent payment for the antecedent debt, a court would probably not enforce the note. Thus, the court would probably only enforce this note to the extent of the $100 debt plus interest.

Another problem sometimes arises where the antecedent obligation is that of a third person. For example, assume that Husband borrows money from a bank and executes on May 1, 1995, a note payable on April 30, 1996. On November 1, 1995, the bank asks the Wife to indorse the note. Because this is an antecedent obligation of Husband, no consideration is needed for Wife's indorsement. Husband and Wife get divorced. Husband becomes insolvent and the bank sues Wife. Wife argues that she should not be liable because the bank gave no consideration in the form of an extension of the time given to Husband to make payment or in forbearing to sue Husband. However, because no consideration is necessary under Article 3, she will be liable.[199]

b. Claims in Recoupment

As we discussed at the beginning of this section, a contract contains certain obligations that are not conditions to the other party's performance. If payment of an instrument is not conditioned, either expressly or constructively, upon performance by the obligee of the breached promise, failure of such performance does not provide a defense to the obligor. Thus, the obligor still has the duty to pay the instrument. However, breach of the obligee's promise will give rise to a claim for damages that the obligor can use as a set-off against the amount owed on the instrument. If the set-off arises from the same transaction in which the instrument is issued, it is called a "claim in recoupment." A claim in recoupment is assertible against any person not hav-

---

199. In fact, Wife may have a remedy against the bank under the Equal Credit Opportunity Act, Pub. L. No. 93-495 §502 (eff. Oct. 28, 1975) and Resolution B promulgated thereunder, which limits the situations in which a creditor can require a spouse's signature.

ing the rights of a holder in due course. Assume that Buyer issues a note to Car Dealer for $10,000 in payment for a new car. Car Dealer transfers the note to Finance Company, which, having purchased the note after it is overdue, does not qualify as a holder in due course. The car has a defective transmission, which would cost $1,500 to repair. Being a person without the rights of a holder in due course, Finance Company takes subject to the claim in recoupment that Buyer has against the payee Car Dealer because the claim arose from the transaction that gave rise to the instrument.[200] If Finance Company qualified as a holder in due course, it would take free of the claim of recoupment.[201]

The claim of recoupment may be asserted against the transferee only to the extent that it reduces the amount owing on the instrument at the time the action is brought.[202] There is no right to an affirmative recovery on the recoupment for amounts already paid. For example, assume that Sally makes a note payable to Charley Contractor for work performed on Sally's house. The note is payable $100 per month for 36 months. Charley negotiates the note to his cousin Vinny, who, knowing that Charley's work was faulty, does not qualify as a holder in due course. Sally pays $500 to Vinny. Sally now discovers that the work is faulty and has a breach of contract claim in recoupment for the entire $3,600. However, because there is no affirmative recovery for amounts already paid (the $500 paid to Vinny), Sally can defeat Vinny's action for the remaining $3,100 but can recover nothing from him. She would have to recover the $500 from Charley Contractor.

As against the transferee (Vinny), the obligor (Sally) cannot raise a setoff from a transaction other than the one that gave rise to the instrument.[203] For example, if Charley had also sold Sally a car that proved to be defective, Sally could not raise the claim arising from the sale of the car as a claim in recoupment against Vinny. It is unfair to make the transferee bear the risk of wholly unrelated claims since the transferee was not a party to the unrelated transaction. Whether a claim arose from a transaction is not determined by Article 3.

c. Defenses and Claims in Recoupment of Other Persons

With the exception of an accommodation party (see discussion in Chapter 3), an obligor may only raise his own defenses. He may not attempt to raise

---

200. U.C.C. §3-305(a)(3).
201. U.C.C. §3-305(b).
202. U.C.C. §3-305(a)(3); U.C.C. §3-305, Official Comment 3.
203. U.C.C. §3-305, Official Comment 3.

a defense or claim in recoupment of another party to the instrument,[204] nor may the other party intervene in the action to raise the defense himself. For example, assume that David issues a check to Paul. Paul negotiates the check to Henry in payment for a car. Because the car has a defective transmission, Paul has a claim in recoupment against Henry for breach of the warranty of merchantability. David may not raise Paul's breach of warranty claim against Henry. David is liable to Henry. Paul's breach of warranty claim in recoupment should not allow David to avoid liability. Similarly, Paul may not intervene and raise his breach of warranty claim in Henry's action against David. Henry has the right to recover from David. Paul must bring a separate action against Henry. Of course, if Henry sues Paul on his indorser's contract, Paul may raise the breach of warranty as a claim in recoupment. In this event Paul is raising his own claim in recoupment to defend against his own liability. The results would be the same if Paul had a defense rather than a claim in recoupment.

d.   Claims to the Instrument

So far we have been concerned with the ability of a holder to take free of a party's claims in recoupment or defenses to his liability on the instrument. Now we shift gears to look at whether or not the property ownership rights of a holder in an instrument are superior to those of another person claiming property or possessory rights in the instrument.

Again, as in the case of defenses and claims in recoupment, the determining factor is whether the holder qualifies as a holder in due course. A person with the rights of a holder in due course takes free of all claims to the instrument.[205] Similarly, a prior negotiation may not be rescinded once an instrument is acquired by a person having the rights of a holder in due course.[206] In contrast, a person who lacks the rights of a holder in due course takes the instrument subject to all valid claims of a property or possessory interest in the instrument or its proceeds, including a claim to rescind a negotiation and to recover the instrument or its proceeds.[207]

Article 3 does not define what constitutes a valid claim to an instrument. This determination is left to the subject jurisdiction's personal property law. However, in most jurisdictions, claims to an instrument include both equitable and legal claims of ownership. Claims to an instrument also include a secured

---

204. U.C.C. §3-305 (c); U.C.C. §3-305, Official Comment 4.
205. U.C.C. §3-306.
206. U.C.C. §3-202(b).
207. U.C.C. §3-306.

party's right to possession of the instrument under his security agreement as well as the right of a lienholder to possession of the instrument.[208]

A "legal claim of ownership" arises where the owner of an instrument claims that he has been wrongfully and involuntarily deprived of its possession. Where the instrument is issued or indorsed to the order of the owner and does not bear his indorsement at the time it is stolen, the issue is simple. The owner will always have the right to recover the instrument because there can be no holder in due course of such an instrument. Until he indorses the instrument, no subsequent person can become its holder.

Assume that Sam made an instrument payable to Carl. The instrument is stolen by Ted who forges Carl's indorsement, adds his own indorsement, and then sells the instrument to Jane, who purchases the instrument in good faith and without notice of the forgery or of any other infirmity. (See Figure 2.4.)

FIGURE 2.4

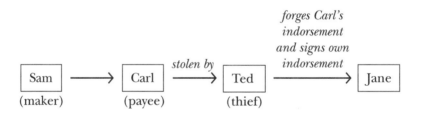

Jane, not being the holder of the instrument (because Sam did not indorse the instrument) is not a holder in due course. Carl can recover the instrument from Jane. However, if the instrument was payable to bearer or if Carl had indorsed the instrument prior to Ted's theft, Jane would be a holder.[209] As a result, although Carl would have a legal claim of ownership to the instrument, Jane would still be its holder. If Jane qualified as a holder in due course, Jane would take free of Carl's claim of ownership. If, however, Jane did not qualify as a holder in due course, Carl would be able to reclaim the instrument from Jane.

---

208. U.C.C. §3-306, Official Comment.

209. See Lawrence, Making Cashier's Checks and Other Bank Checks Cost Effective: A Plea for Revision of Articles 3 and 4 of the Uniform Commercial Code, 64 Minn. L. Rev. 275, 307 (1980). Although a legal claim of ownership may arise where an instrument payable to order has been stolen, a purchaser could never be a holder and therefore never a holder in due course of such an instrument.

E. Defenses and Discharges

An "equitable claim of ownership" arises where a prior owner claims that he voluntarily negotiated the instrument under circumstances giving him the right to rescind the negotiation and regain title to the instrument.[210] An equitable claim of ownership can arise from any ground that under state law gives the party a right to rescind the transaction in which he negotiated the instrument.[211] These grounds might include, among others, fraud, duress, mistake, illegality, breach of trust, infancy, incapacity, and nondelivery of the instrument.

Any person may assert his own claim of ownership against a person not having the rights of a holder in due course. In the example discussed previously, Carl may sue to obtain possession of the instrument from Jane. The same would be true if Carl had an equitable claim of ownership. Assume that Carl was defrauded into indorsing the instrument. Jane, having notice of this fact, does not qualify as a holder in due course. Carl may recover the instrument from Jane.

When the party being sued on the instrument does not have a claim or defense of his own, unless the claimant is made a party to the action and asserts his own claim to the instrument, the obligor may not use the claim to defeat the holder's action.[212] Thus, if Jane sues Sam, Sam may not raise Carl's equitable claim of ownership to the instrument.[213] However, if Sam gets Carl to intervene in the action, Carl may assert his own claim. If the claim is valid and if Jane is not a holder in due course, Sam will be required to pay Carl and not Jane.

There is one situation in which the obligor may raise a claim of a third person even if the claimant is not a party to the action. A third party claim may be asserted where the obligor knows that the holder is in wrongful possession of a stolen instrument.[214] If Carl, in the original example, told Sam that Ted stole the instrument from him, Sam may raise Carl's claim of ownership against Jane even if Carl is not a party to the action. If Sam pays Jane notwithstanding his knowledge of the claim of theft, Sam is not discharged and remains liable to Carl. Section E (e)(1) of this chapter discusses why Sam is not discharged by his payment. Because of this risk of liability, the obligor (Sam) needs to be able to defend against the holder's (Jane's) action even when the true owner (Carl) is not a party to the action.

---

210. See Lawrence, supra note 209, at 307.
211. U.C.C. §3-306, Official Comment; see also Lawrence, supra note 209, at 307.
212. U.C.C. §3-305(c); U.C.C. §3-305, Official Comment 4.
213. In the original example where Carl's indorsement was forged, Jane could not recover from Sam because she was neither a holder nor a person with the rights of a holder.
214. U.C.C. §3-602(b)(2).

e. Discharges

An obligor has another basis upon which to defeat the holder's action, in addition to asserting a defense or claim in recoupment. The obligor may contend that he has been partially or fully discharged from liability on the instrument. The most common ground for discharge is payment of the instrument. However, there are numerous grounds of discharge:

1. payment (section 3-602);
2. tender of payment (section 3-603);
3. cancellation or renunciation (section 3-604);
4. impairment of right of recourse or of collateral (section 3-605);
5. reacquisition of the instrument by a prior party (section 3-207);
6. fraudulent alteration (section 3-407);
7. acceptance of a draft by a bank (sections 3-414(c) and 3-415(d));
8. acceptance varying a draft (section 3-410);
9. unexcused delay in presentment or notice of dishonor (section 3-414(f) and (d) and section 3-415(c) and (e));
10. lost, destroyed, or stolen cashier's checks, teller's checks, or certified checks (section 3-312); or
11. any other act or agreement with such party that would discharge his simple contract for the payment of money (section 3-601(a)).

This list includes only those discharges arising under Article 3. A party may also be discharged by statutory or common law independent of Article 3. For example, a party's obligation on a negotiable instrument may be discharged through insolvency proceedings or under a statute regulating the use of negotiable instruments in gambling transactions.

Let us examine the effect of a discharge by looking at an example. Assume that Joe makes a note payable to Paul who indorses the note to Hank. Hank releases Paul from liability on the instrument by a writing renouncing Paul's obligation to pay the instrument. Thereafter, Hank negotiates the note to Ralph. (See Figure 2.5.)

Paul's discharge is not effective against Ralph if Ralph qualifies as a holder in due course and does not have notice of the discharge when he took the instrument.[215]

215. U.C.C. §3-601(b); U.C.C. §3-601, Official Comment.

FIGURE 2.5

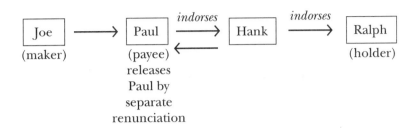

What effect would it have if Ralph had notice of Paul's discharge? A discharge is treated differently than a defense or claim in recoupment in that a holder's having notice of the discharge does not deprive the holder of due-course status.[216] Thus, Ralph would still be a holder in due course and could enforce the instrument against Hank. However, Paul's discharge is effective against Ralph even though Ralph is a holder in due course because he has notice of the discharge.[217] Of course, if Ralph does not qualify as a holder in due course, Paul's discharge would be effective against him.

The rule protecting a subsequent holder in due course against a discharge of which he had no notice poses a danger to an obligor. The liability of an obligor who has been discharged may be resurrected if the instrument is subsequently acquired by a holder in due course who is without notice of the discharge. Let us look at another example. Assume that, in purchasing a television set from Radio Shack, Bernice executes a note payable to Radio Shack in monthly installments of $50 for 24 months. After two months, Bernice obtains a small inheritance and decides to pay off the note. She sends a check in full payment. However, instead of returning the note to her, Radio Shack sells the note to Bank of Santa Monica. If Bank of Santa Monica qualifies as a holder in due course and does not have notice of the payment, Bank of Santa Monica takes free of Bernice's discharge. Bernice is left with the task of recovering her payment from Radio Shack. What lesson should Bernice learn from this experience? She should have protected herself against the possibility of a subsequent holder in due course acquiring the instrument without notice of her discharge by either requiring surrender of the note upon making payment or by requiring Radio Shack to mark the instrument "paid."

We discuss some of the grounds for discharge here. Other grounds for discharge are discussed in other sections of this book.

216. U.C.C. §3-601, Official Comment.
217. U.C.C. §3-601(b); U.C.C. §3-601, Official Comment.

Discharge by Payment.   The usual manner in which an instrument gets discharged is by payment. No problems arise in the case of 99 percent of all instruments. The party obliged to pay the instrument as a routine matter makes payment to the holder. The holder accepts the payment and then either returns or destroys the instrument. Let us examine, however, how payment constitutes a discharge and what potential problems may arise.

The basic rule is that an instrument is paid (1) to the extent that payment is made (2) by or on behalf of a party obliged to pay the instrument and (3) to a person entitled to enforce the instrument.[218] The person making payment is discharged to the extent of the payment. Payment of each installment of an installment note discharges the maker to the extent of the payment made.

Discharge Personal to Party Making Payment.   Discharges are personal to the person making payment. When a party pays the instrument, that party obtains a discharge. The instrument itself is not discharged. The party himself (or a person on his behalf) has to make the payment. Because a payor bank pays a check on behalf of the drawer, the drawer is discharged to the extent of the payment.

Let us look at an example of the effect of the rule that the party making payment and not the instrument is discharged. Assume that Paul (maker) makes a note payable to Sam (indorser) who indorses the note to Sela (person entitled to enforce the instrument). Sam pays Sela. Sam's payment to Sela provides him with a discharge of his indorser's liability. Should Paul be discharged? The obvious answer is "no." Paul is the one who should ultimately pay the note. Paul is not discharged by Sam's payment. Upon payment, Sam (as an indorser who paid the note) may recover from Paul.[219]

Payment Must Be Made to Person Entitled to Enforce Instrument.   Payment discharges the party obliged to pay only if payment is made to the person entitled to enforce the instrument. A person entitled to enforce an instrument is basically a holder or a person who has the rights of a holder (usually by a transfer from a holder).[220] Leaving aside for the moment the situation in which the obligor has notice that another person claims ownership of the instrument, the obligor is discharged by his payment to a person entitled to enforce the instrument.[221] This rule has two important consequences. First, as long as the

218. U.C.C. §3-602(a); U.C.C. §3-602, Official Comment.
219. U.C.C. §3-412.
220. A person not in possession of the instrument who is entitled to enforce it pursuant to section 3-309 or 3-418(d) is also a person entitled to enforce the instrument. These very limited situations are discussed elsewhere in the book.
221. U.C.C. §3-602(a).

person to whom payment is made is the person entitled to enforce the instrument, it is irrelevant whether the person entitled to enforce the instrument is the owner of the instrument. For example, payment to a thief of an instrument payable to bearer discharges the party making the payment.

Secondly, the party making payment is not discharged if he pays someone who is not a person entitled to enforce the instrument. Thus, the payor is not discharged by payment to a person who traces his title through a forged or missing indorsement. Similarly, payment to one of two joint payees does not discharge the obligor if the other joint payee does not indorse the instrument.

Because payment only to the person entitled to enforce the instrument discharges the payor, the party making payment should demand to see the instrument before making payment. Take, for example, Paul's note to Sam. Assume that because Paul does not know that Sam has negotiated the note to Sela, Paul pays Sam without first demanding to see the note. Paul is not discharged by his payment. Sam, not being in possession of the note, is not a person entitled to enforce the instrument, and therefore payment to Sam does not discharge Paul. Paul remains liable to Sela, the person entitled to enforce the instrument. Paul may, of course, recover the payment from Sam. However, it is likely that Sam will not be around to pay Paul.

Adverse Claim to Instrument.   Sometimes the person entitled to enforce the instrument is not the owner of the instrument. Under the traditional law of conversion of personal property, the party making payment would not be discharged if he paid a person other than the true owner. This rule, however, would cause havoc if applied to negotiable instruments. Without notice of the claim of another person to ownership of the instrument, payment to the apparent owner (the person entitled to enforce the instrument) must provide the payor with a discharge. Otherwise, it would not be safe to pay any instrument. Where Sela presents the instrument properly indorsed by Sam, Paul must be able to pay Sela without worrying whether or not she is the true owner of the instrument.

What would happen if Paul knew that Sam had a claim of ownership to the instrument? Sela may have defrauded Sam into indorsing the instrument to her. Sam may have called up Paul and requested that he not pay Sela. Should Paul be able to ignore Sam's plea and pay Sela? And, if he does so, should he be liable to Sam for conversion if it turns out that Sam was the rightful owner of the instrument? Must he refuse to pay Sela, thus forcing him to defend a lawsuit by her? Placing Paul in this predicament is not fair to him. His mere knowledge of Sam's claim to the instrument should not deny Paul a discharge if he pays Sela in spite of Sam's claim. The rule is that Paul is discharged to the extent of his payment to Sela (the person entitled to enforce the instrument) even though payment is made with knowledge of a claim to the instrument by Sam.[222]

Right of Adverse Claimant to Prevent Payment. Sam, the person claiming ownership of the instrument (also called the "adverse claimant"), however, has the ability to prevent payment. Payment to Sela (the person entitled to enforce the instrument) does not discharge Paul (the person making payment) if Sam's claim is valid and enforceable against Sela and either one of the following two exceptions apply: (1) Sam obtains an injunction against payment and Paul pays Sela even though he has knowledge of the injunction; or (2) Paul accepts from Sam indemnity against loss resulting from Paul's refusal to pay Sela.[223]

Injunction Against Payment. The first exception applies where the claimant has obtained an injunction prohibiting payment. For example, assume that Sam obtains an injunction enjoining Paul from paying Sela. The injunction denies Paul a discharge only if he has knowledge of the injunction. Until Paul has knowledge of the injunction, Paul is discharged by his payment to Sela. However, once Paul has knowledge of the injunction, Paul will be liable to Sam if Sam ultimately proves that he is entitled to rescind the negotiation to Sela and, therefore, is the true owner of the instrument.

As a safeguard against the possibility of inconsistent results, a court will not grant an injunction unless Sela (the person entitled to enforce the instrument), Sam (the claimant), and Paul (the party obliged to pay) are all subject to the court's jurisdiction. By requiring all parties to be present, the court's decision as to whether Sam or Sela is entitled to be paid by Paul will be binding on both Sam and Sela. This will relieve Paul from the fear that Sela will file a separate action and obtain a judgment that she, and not Sam, is entitled to payment.

Even if Paul pays in violation of the injunction, Paul is not liable to Sam unless Sam has a valid claim of ownership that would be effective against Sela (the person entitled to enforce the instrument). If, for example, Sam has no right to rescind the negotiation to Sela, Sam has no valid claim of ownership and Sela is therefore rightfully entitled to payment. Similarly, if Sela had negotiated the instrument to Gary, who qualified as a holder in due course, because a holder in due course takes free of all claims to an instrument, payment to Gary likewise discharges Paul from liability to Sam.[224]

---

222. U.C.C. §3-602(a).
223. U.C.C. §3-602(b)(1).
224. U.C.C. §3-306.

E. Defenses and Discharges

Indemnification of Obligor. The second exception is where Paul (the obligor) accepts indemnity from Sam (the claimant). Instead of seeking an injunction, Sam could ask that Paul refuse to pay Sela. In order to protect Paul, Sam would offer to indemnify Paul against any losses and expenses incurred in defending against Sela's action. Paul has no obligation to accept Sam's offer of indemnity. If Paul refuses the offer of indemnity, he is discharged by his payment to Sela. If, however, Paul accepts the indemnity but still pays Sela, Paul will be liable to Sam provided that Sam has a valid claim to the instrument enforceable against Sela.

Indemnification of the obligor is not effective to prevent the obligor's discharge where the instrument involved is a bank check. Assume that Norm acquires a cashier's check from Bank of America for the purpose of purchasing a car from Rick's Auto. Norm discovers, immediately upon handing over the cashier's check to Rick's Auto, that he has been defrauded. If Norm has sufficient time to obtain an injunction, he could prevent Bank of America from being discharged by its payment to Rick's Auto.[225] Not having time to obtain an injunction, however, Norm offers to indemnify Bank of America if it will refuse to pay Rick's Auto on the cashier's check. Bank of America agrees. Bank of America pays the cashier's check by mistake. Despite its agreement to accept the indemnity, Bank of America is discharged by its payment to Rick's Auto (the person entitled to enforce the instrument). Bank of America may, however, be liable to Norm for breach of the indemnity agreement. The exception for cashier's and other bank checks is intended to discourage an obligated bank from refusing to pay a bank check.

Exception for Stolen Instruments. There is one situation in which a person making payment is not discharged even though the claimant did not obtain an injunction or supply indemnity to the payor. Paul is not discharged if he knows that the instrument is stolen and pays Sela knowing that she is in wrongful possession of the instrument.[226] If Sam informs Paul that Sela stole the instrument from him, Paul is not discharged even if Sam neither offers to indemnify Paul nor obtains an injunction against payment. If Sela did not steal the instrument from him, Paul will be discharged by his payment to Sela. Similarly, even if Sela did steal the instrument, if she has subsequently negotiated the instrument to a holder in due course, Paul's payment to the holder in due course discharges him.

---

225. U.C.C. §3-602, Official Comment.

226. U.C.C. §3-602(b)(2). Because the obligor is not discharged by such payment, he is entitled to raise the third party's claim of theft as a defense under section 3-305(c) to an action brought by the person entitled to enforce the instrument even if the third party is not a party to the action.

The rationale behind denying a discharge to Paul in these circumstances is twofold. First, by denying Paul a discharge, Paul will be less likely to pay a thief or a person holding through a thief, which will make it more difficult for a thief to profit from his activity. Second, it is usually a fairly straightforward factual matter as to whether a theft has occurred. This limits the possibility of inconsistent results in the obligor's actions against the holder and against the owner. What constitutes a "stolen" instrument is not entirely clear. There would appear to be no reason not to treat lost instruments as stolen instruments. However, where the instrument has been embezzled, difficulties of proof as to whether the embezzler had the right to use the funds make the possibility of inconsistent results much higher than where the question is whether the instrument is stolen. For this reason, embezzled instruments should not be treated as stolen instruments.

Discharge by Tender of Payment.   Assume that a few years ago, when the interest rate was very high, you had to borrow $10,000 at 15 percent interest per annum. The note you signed was due in six years. You have come into a little money now and want to pay the note in full. There are still three years remaining on the note. You offer to pay the $10,000 with interest for the three years that you have had use of the money. The holder refuses to accept the payment. He demands that you make payment at the end of the term or at least pay the present value of the remaining interest. Can he do this? The answer is "yes." He bargained for the right to be paid the full interest for the duration of the term of the instrument and is entitled to be paid such interest.[227] As a result, the person entitled to enforce the instrument may refuse a tender of payment before the instrument is due unless he is paid the full interest due under the instrument.

However, the story changes once the person entitled to enforce the instrument has received his bargained-for exchange. The person entitled to enforce the instrument may not refuse an offer of payment for the purpose of continuing the accrual of interest payable after the instrument is due. The mechanism for achieving this result is the rules regarding discharge by tender. An effective "tender of payment" discharges the obligation of the obligor to pay interest after the due date on the amount tendered.[228]

A similar situation involves the rights of an indorser or accommodation party. Assume that your cousin had indorsed the note as a favor to you. You, as maker, tender full payment on the due date of the note. The holder, for some reason, refuses the tender. Immediately thereafter, you run into some eco-

227. U.C.C. §3-603(b).
228. U.C.C. §3-603(c).

nomic reversals and can no longer pay the holder. The holder then demands that your cousin pay the note. Is your cousin liable to the holder? The answer is "no." Upon the holder's refusal of your tender, an indorser or an accommodation party (your cousin) who has a right of recourse with respect to the obligation to which the tender relates (a right of recourse against you) is discharged to the extent of the amount tendered.[229] The holder should not be permitted to deny your cousin or any other indorser or accommodation party a discharge by refusing to accept the tender. No legitimate reason existed for the holder to refuse the tender.

The law governing tender of payments under a simple contract determines whether a co-maker, co-acceptor, or co-indorser is discharged to the extent of his right of contribution. The rule is generally that a co-obligor is discharged to the extent of his right of recourse. Thus, assume that you and your cousin were co-makers of a note signed for the benefit of both of you. You offered to pay the entire amount of the note. The holder refuses the tender. Because your cousin would have a right to contribution in the amount of one-half of the note in the event that he had paid the note in full, your cousin would be discharged in the amount of one-half of the amount due under the note.

Requirements for Tender.   The tender of payment must be made to the person entitled to enforce the instrument (or to a person to whom that person has directed that payment be made).[230] Other than this, the manner and effect of the tender is governed by the principles of law applicable to tender of payment under a simple contract.

The obligor need not tender the full payment of the instrument. Assume that John made a note to Bill in the amount of $1,000 payable with interest. John tenders partial payment in the amount of $500. At the time of tender, John owed $100 in interest on the note. Between the time of tender and the time of trial, additional interest in the amount of $300 accrued. To what extent is John discharged? John is only discharged for $150, which is the amount of interest accruing after his tender on the amount tendered. He is not discharged as to the principal amount ($1,000), interest accruing prior to the time payment was tendered ($100), interest on the principal amount that was not tendered ($150), or as to costs or attorney's fees. What if John had tendered the entire $1,000 before the note was due? John would still owe the principal amount of $1,000 and the pre-maturity interest of $100 (even though

---

229. U.C.C. §3-603(b); U.C.C. §3-603, Official Comment.
230. U.C.C. §3-603(a); U.C.C. §3-603, Official Comment.

accruing after the tender),[231] but would be discharged for any interest accruing after maturity.[232]

How does an obligor tender payment? To tender payment, an obligor must not only offer to make payment and produce the money, but he must be willing and able to immediately transfer the money to the person entitled to enforce the instrument. In most jurisdictions, a tender must be unconditional. In some states, a tender is not effective unless it is kept open until payment is finally accepted by the person entitled to enforce the instrument or until a judgment is rendered. Some courts require that the amount tendered be paid into court.

In most states the tender must be made in cash and not by a negotiable instrument. However, in some situations if the person to whom the tender is made does not object to payment by check or other instrument, his failure to object to the medium of payment may constitute a waiver of the objection. As a result, if the holder refuses to accept the tender but does not object to the tender of a check instead of cash, many jurisdictions treat the tender as proper.

There is one situation in which a party need not actually tender payment to comply with the requirements for a discharge. If presentment is required with respect to an instrument, and the obligor is able and ready to pay on the due date at every place of payment stated in the instrument, the obligor is deemed to have made tender of payment on the due date to the person entitled to enforce the instrument.[233] For example, as we will cover in Chapter 3, a note payable at a bank on a stated date is not dishonored unless presentment is made at the bank.[234] If the maker of the note has sufficient funds at the bank on the date due and has ordered the bank to make payment, the maker is deemed to have tendered payment on the due date. It was the obligation of the holder to make presentment. Had presentment been made, the note would have been paid and therefore, the holder's delay in making presentment should not entitle him to any interest accruing after the due date. Similarly, the holder should not be allowed to proceed against indorsers or accommodation parties who would have been discharged had he presented the note on time.

Discharge by Cancellation or Renunciation.   The person entitled to enforce the instrument may, if she desires, discharge any party to the instrument even

---

231. U.C.C. §3-603(c).
232. U.C.C. §3-603.
233. U.C.C. §3-603(c); U.C.C. §3-603, Official Comment.
234. U.C.C. §3-502(a)(2).

though she has received no payment or other consideration for the discharge. The manner of doing so will usually be by cancellation or renunciation.

Discharge by Cancellation.   A person entitled to enforce an instrument may, without consideration, discharge any party to the instrument in any manner apparent on the face of the instrument or indorsement.[235] For example, the holder may cancel the instrument by tearing it up, writing "void," "discharged," "paid," or other such language on the instrument or by crossing out the party's signature. The cancelled instrument need not be delivered to the party discharged. Thus, a person entitled to enforce the instrument may cancel one party's signature while retaining the right to further negotiate the instrument.

Discharge by Renunciation.   A person entitled to enforce the instrument may also, without consideration, discharge any party to the instrument by renouncing his rights in a signed writing.[236] For example, I could discharge you from liability on a note by writing, "I release Reader from liability on the note executed on January 1, 1996." The writing must evidence my present intention to renounce my rights rather than be a promise to cancel the instrument in the future. A writing stating "I will surrender the note" or "I promise to renounce my rights to the instrument" is not effective as a renunciation because it does not indicate a present intent to renounce my rights.

A renunciation is ineffective unless the party intends to renounce his rights. The requisite intent may be proven by delivery of the renunciation to the party sought to be discharged. However, as long as the party intends to renounce his rights, the renunciation need not be delivered to the person discharged thereby. For example, if the holder has informed the party to be discharged of the renunciation, the fact that the holder has yet to mail the renunciation does not make it ineffective.

If given a choice, a party to be discharged should prefer that the discharge be by a means other than renunciation. The problem with renunciation is that a subsequent purchaser of the instrument will have no way of

---

235. U.C.C. §3-604(a). The following are only some of the possible methods of cancelling an instrument:

1. Marking the instrument "Paid," "Void," "Cancelled," or "Discharged";
2. Tearing up or shredding the instrument;
3. Cutting out, crossing out, or erasing the signature of the party discharged;
4. Writing an "X" across the face of the instrument; or
5. Cutting out or erasing an essential portion of the instrument.

236. U.C.C. §3-604(a).

knowing of the discharge. In contrast, cancellation of the instrument, requiring notation on the face of the instrument itself, will always give notice of the discharge to any subsequent purchaser.

Discharge by Surrender. A party is also discharged upon surrender of the instrument to the party to be discharged.[237] To constitute a surrender, the instrument must be returned to the party with the intent to discharge him. When the party to be discharged has possession of the instrument, the intent to discharge him is presumed unless the person entitled to enforce the instrument provides a satisfactory explanation for the other party's possession of the instrument.

Unintentional, Mistaken or Fraudulently Procured Cancellation, Renunciation, or Surrender. A cancellation, renunciation, or surrender of an instrument is ineffective if it is unintentional, unauthorized, or procured by fraud or mistake. For example, accidentally tearing or mutilating an instrument does not discharge the affected parties. Returning an instrument to an obligor for safekeeping or accompanied with a request for payment likewise does not result in the obligor's discharge.

There is no discharge where an instrument is mistakenly marked "Paid" either as a result of a clerical error or because the person entitled to enforce the instrument mistakenly believed that payment had been made in full. In determining whether a mistake vitiates the discharge, all of the rules of equity come into play. For example, assume that Mary makes a note payable to Gail who negotiates the note to Hank. Hank's secretary, believing that Hank had told her that the note had been paid, marked the note "Paid" and notified Gail that payment had been made. Believing the note to be paid, Gail loans other money to Mary. Because of the mistake by Hank's agent, Gail was induced to make loans she would not have made had she known that she may be required to pay Hank on this note. Hank may not assert mistake as grounds for denying Gail a discharge after Gail has relied upon Hank's notification that the note had been paid by Mary.

A common mistake involves the exchange of old notes for new notes that, unknown to the person entitled to enforce the notes, contain a forged indorsement or are missing a required indorsement. Assume in our example above that Mary asks for an extension of time to pay the note. Hank tells Mary that he will return the original note to her if both Mary and Gail sign a new note. Mary forges Gail's indorsement on a new note. Hank's surrender of the original note does not operate as a discharge of Gail. Hank surrendered the

---

237. U.C.C. §3-604(a).

note upon the mistaken belief that Gail was liable on the new note. Since Gail is not liable, Hank's surrender was a mistake and does not result in Gail's discharge.

Where the mistake is in Hank's belief as to the legal consequences of an intended discharge, most courts are unwilling to allow him to rescind the cancellation or surrender. For instance, assume that although both Mary and Gail sign the new note, Hank took the new note without knowing that the cancellation not only discharged unpaid but accrued interest on the original note but also released his security interest in the collateral under the original note. This mistake will not allow him to avoid Gail and Mary's discharge on the original note.

Discharge of Simple Contract. Under section 3-601(a), a party is discharged from his liability on an instrument to another party by any act or agreement with such party that would discharge his simple contract for the payment of money.[238] The primary effect of this section is to recognize the possibility of a discharge by an agreement that neither constitutes payment under section 3-602 nor cancellation or renunciation under section 3-604. For instance, an oral agreement supported by consideration is usually sufficient to discharge a party on a contract to pay money.

Satisfaction by means other than the payment of money also provides a discharge under section 3-601(a). Similarly, a "novation," which is a new agreement intended to substitute for the old agreement, may provide a discharge. Even an agreement implied in the conduct of the parties may be sufficient to provide a discharge.

F. ADMISSIBILITY OF EVIDENCE EXTRINSIC TO THE INSTRUMENT

As we discussed in Chapter 1, a negotiable instrument is intended to be a simple unconditional promise or order unencumbered by a multitude of additional promises. Although we also saw that, in fact, some negotiable instruments are quite complex, the vast majority of negotiable instruments are not. In most cases the instrument will not contain the entire agreement of the parties. There will almost always be an underlying oral or written agreement out of which the instrument arose. When the obligor on the instrument wants to

238. U.C.C. §3-601(a).

raise a defense or claim in recoupment to his obligation to pay, the question arises as to the extent evidence of the underlying oral or written agreement can vary or supplement the terms of the instrument.

For example, assume that Mary issues a note to Bret in the sum of $1,000 in payment for the purchase of a car. Can Mary introduce evidence in Bret's action on the note that they had a separate oral agreement that she be entitled to a $200 deduction if the car does not pass a smog inspection? If Bret negotiates the note to his bank, can Mary introduce this evidence in the bank's action to enforce the note? Article 3 does not provide a complete answer to these questions. It leaves part of this answer to the parol evidence rule applicable under the governing common law.

1. Admissibility of Separate Agreement

The rule is that an obligor's (Mary's) duty to pay an instrument may be modified, supplemented, or nullified by a separate agreement (the oral agreement to reduce the principal by $200) between the obligor (Mary) and a person entitled to enforce the instrument (Bret).[239] However, the instrument must be issued or the obligation incurred either (1) in reliance on the agreement or (2) as part of the same transaction giving rise to the agreement.[240] Introduction of evidence of this separate agreement is, however, explicitly made subject to the parol evidence rule.[241] Because the agreement was part of the same transaction in which the instrument was issued, Mary may introduce evidence of this agreement unless it is barred by the parol evidence rule.

The agreement would be a defense available against any person other than a holder in due course without notice of the agreement.[242] Therefore, the agreement may be asserted as a defense against any person not having the rights of a holder in due course. If the bank does not qualify as a holder in due course, Mary may introduce evidence of the agreement as a defense to her liability on the note even though the bank did not have notice of the agreement. It is also admissible against a holder in due course who had notice of the agreement when he took the instrument. Thus, even if the bank qualified as a holder in due course, if it had notice of the agreement when it took the instrument, it takes subject to the agreement.

239. U.C.C. §3-117.
240. U.C.C. §3-117.
241. U.C.C. §3-117.
242. U.C.C. §3-117; U.C.C. §3-117, Official Comment 1.

F. Admissibility of Evidence

The separate agreement may be either an oral agreement or a written agreement and must be a bargain between the parties.[243] A letter or other communication by one of the parties alone, not being an agreement, may not vary the terms of the note.[244] For example, if Mary had written a letter telling Bret that it is unfair that she be required to pay the full price if the car cannot pass a smog inspection, this letter will not provide a defense unless Bret agreed to the reduction.

An agreement can be part of the same transaction even though the agreement was neither executed contemporaneously[245] with the instrument or obligation nor referred to in the instrument.[246] Because the agreement need only be a part of the same transaction in which the "obligation" was incurred, that transaction need not be the one in which the instrument was issued. It may be any transaction in which a party undertakes liability on the instrument. For example, if, at the same time that Bob indorses a draft to Carl, Bob and Carl agree that Bob will not be called upon to pay the draft unless Carl is unable to collect from Abe, Bob's liability is conditioned upon Carl's inability to collect from Abe.

Even if the separate agreement meets the conditions above, evidence of the agreement must also be admissible under the applicable parol evidence rule (called under Article 3 "applicable law regarding exclusion of evidence of contemporaneous or previous agreements").[247]

2. *The Parol Evidence Rule*

The parol evidence rule generally provides that no prior written agreement and no prior or contemporaneous oral agreement is admissible to vary or contradict the terms found in a writing intended by the parties to be the final

---

243. An agreement is "the bargain of the parties in fact found in their language or by implication from other circumstances including course of dealing or usage of trade or course of performance as provided in this Act." U.C.C. §1-201(3).

244. See Crosby v. Jordan, 123 Ga. App. 83, 179 S.E.2d 537, 8 U.C.C. Rep. Serv. 1050 (1970) (check given by payee to maker of note not written agreement modifying note).

245. See Gensplit Fin. Corp. v. Link Power & Mach. Corp., 36 U.C.C. Rep. Serv. 588 (S.D. N.Y. 1983) (question of fact whether part of same transaction when writing executed two years before).

246. For a case under former Article 3, see Merchants Natl. Bank & Trust Co. v. Professional Men's Assn., Inc., 409 F.2d 600, 6 U.C.C. Rep. Serv. 337 (5th Cir. 1969) (not all transaction documents referred to main agreement), cert. denied, 396 U.S. 1009, 24 L. Ed. 2d 501, 90 S. Ct. 567 (1970).

247. U.C.C. §3-117.

expression of the parties' agreement as to those terms.[248] Evidence of a written agreement entered into contemporaneously with the instrument is always admissible.

A negotiable instrument, by its nature, is seldom intended to include the complete terms of the parties' agreement. Therefore, the parol evidence will seldom bar introduction of additional terms that do not contradict the terms of the instrument. For example, an agreement permitting the holder to obtain attorney's fees will not be barred by the parol evidence rule as long as the instrument does not specifically provide otherwise. However, to be negotiable, an instrument must contain an unconditional promise or order to pay the holder. Consequently, at least on the surface, any condition to payment contradicts the terms of the instrument.

Does this mean that evidence of any condition to payment is inadmissible? The answer has generally been in the negative. The distinction between the types of evidence courts have and have not admitted appears to rest more upon the credibility of the evidence offered than upon its nature. The key factor appears to be the likelihood that the parties would have entered into the alleged agreement. It is, for instance, more likely that Mary and Bret would agree that delivery of the car be a condition to payment than that she would obtain a $200 reduction in price if the car did not pass a smog inspection. Courts, of course, have not rested their decisions upon this standard. In justifying their decisions as to whether a particular agreement is admissible, courts have made some questionable distinctions.

Courts hold generally that parol evidence is not admissible to prove a condition precedent to the obligation to pay.[249] Thus, it would appear that the obligor may not introduce parol evidence of an agreement that the instrument will be paid only out of the profits of a venture; that collateral will be realized upon prior to commencement of an action on the instrument;[250] or that the holder will look to the other obligor first.[251] In contrast, courts differ as to whether evidence tending to show that the promise to pay is a sham or

---

248. See Farnsworth, 2 Farnsworth on Contracts 198 (1990).

249. For cases under former Article 3, see Akin v. Dahl, 661 S.W.2d 914, 38 U.C.C. Rep. Serv. 230 (Tex. 1983) (prior written agreement under which the maker and payee had agreed that any note would be payable only upon death of maker was not admissible into evidence since it went to prove condition precedent to the promise to pay and not to effectiveness of instrument itself).

250. For a case under former Article 3, see Texas Export Development Corp. v. Schleder, 519 S.W.2d 134, 16 U.C.C. Rep. Serv. 1016 (Tex. App. 1974).

251. For a case under former Article 3, see Metro Natl. Bank v. Roe, 675 P.2d 331, 37 U.C.C. Rep. Serv. 1183 (Colo. App. 1983).

that the note would never be enforced against the obligor is admissible.[252] One can argue that the obligor is not attempting to change the terms of the instrument when the obligor attempts to prove that the instrument was never intended to create a legal obligation.[253]

However, some of this same evidence may be admissible if the obligor characterizes the evidence in other ways. Evidence that delivery of the instrument was for a special purpose or is conditional on some act or event may always be introduced.[254] For example, an indorser may show that his indorsement was not to be effective until four other indorser/guarantors also signed.[255] Evidence of any defense may also be introduced. The distinction between conditions precedent to the payment of an instrument and defenses is sometimes tenuous. For example, evidence that the maker's obligation to pay is conditioned upon the payee's delivery of contracted goods shows a failure of consideration if the goods are not delivered as well as a condition to his promise to pay. Phrasing it as a failure of consideration rather than as a non-fulfillment of a condition will make it more likely that the evidence will be admitted. Instead of trying to show that the agreement was a sham, evidence may be introduced to show that the instrument was never to take effect.[256] In addition, evidence to explain ambiguities contained in the instrument is always admissible.[257]

Evidence is also always admissible if it is not introduced in an attempt to vary, contradict, or add to the terms of the instrument.[258] An obligor may thus prove by parol evidence any of the following:

---

252. Compare Grossman v. Banco Industrial de Venezuela, C.A., 534 So. 2d 773, 7 U.C.C. Rep. Serv. 2d 1527 (Fla. App. 1988) (maker may not introduce evidence that payee told him that he would not have to pay note) and First Natl. City Bank v. Metal Trading Co., Ltd., 71 F.R.D. 363, 20 U.C.C. Rep. Serv. 701 (S.D. Fla. 1976) with Herzog Contracting Corp. v. McGowen Corp., 976 F.2d 1062, 18 U.C.C. Rep. Serv. 2d 1170 (7th Cir. 1992) (maker may introduce evidence that note was not intended to create legal obligation) and Cosmopolitan Fin. Corp. v. Runnels, 2 Haw. App. 33, 625 P.2d 390, 31 U.C.C. Rep. Serv. 146 (1981) (evidence admissible that note executed solely to deceive bank examiners).

253. See Herzog Contracting Corp. v. McGowen Corp., 976 F.2d 1062, 18 U.C.C. Rep. Serv. 2d 1170 (7th Cir. 1992).

254. U.C.C. §3-305(a)(2).

255. For a case under former Article 3, see Long Island Trust Co. v. International Inst. for Packaging Educ., Ltd., 38 N.Y.2d 493, 381 N.Y.S.2d 445, 344 N.E.2d 377 (1976).

256. See Jordan, "Just Sign Here—It's Only a Formality": Parol Evidence in the Law of Commercial Paper, 13 Ga. L. Rev. 53, 66-67 (1978).

257. See Farnsworth, Farnsworth on Contracts §7.8 (1990).

258. See Farnsworth, 2 Farnsworth on Contracts 198 (1990).

1. that a holder is not in due course[259] or had notice of the accommodation status of the obligor;
2. that the obligor had been discharged by payment, cancellation, accord and satisfaction, or otherwise;
3. the date an undated instrument was issued;
4. the order in which indorsers have signed;
5. that indorsers have agreed that they would be liable in a different order;
6. that two or more parties signed as part of the same transaction and therefore are jointly and severally liable;[260]
7. the identity of the party signing the instrument;[261]
8. the authority or lack thereof of a party signing for another party; or
9. whether an agent is personally liable when he signs the instrument in a manner which does not clearly designate the name of his principal.[262]

G.   TRANSFER OF INSTRUMENT AND SHELTER PROVISION

1.   What Is a Transfer?

When an instrument is transferred, the transfer vests the transferee with all of the rights of his transferor.[263] In other words, the transferee steps into the shoes of his transferor. An instrument is "transferred" when it is delivered by a person other than its issuer (that is, the maker or drawer) in order to give the right to enforce the instrument to the person receiving delivery.[264] Vest-

---

259. See Jordan, "Just Sign Here—It's Only a Formality": Parol Evidence in the Law of Commercial Paper, 13 Ga. L. Rev. 53, 63 (1978).

260. See Grimes v. Grimes, 47 N.C. App. 353, 267 S.E.2d 372, 29 U.C.C. Rep. Serv. 1332 (1980) (parol evidence admissible to show a different relationship intersese).

261. U.C.C. §3-401, Official Comment 2

262. U.C.C. §3-402, Official Comment 2.

263. U.C.C. §3-203(b). There is one distinction: the transferee obtains his transferor's right to negotiate the instrument only if the transfer is by negotiation. U.C.C. §3-203, Official Comment 1.

264. U.C.C. §3-203(a). Issuance of an instrument is not a transfer since, to constitute a transfer, the instrument must be delivered by a person other than the issuer. U.C.C. §3-203, Official Comment 1.

ing the rights of the transferor in the transferee makes sense. What difference does it make which particular person is attempting to enforce the instrument? If Joe wants Tom to collect the instrument for him, why should the obligor care? Tom only steps into Joe's shoes. Tom obtains no greater rights than Joe had unless Tom, on his own, qualifies as a holder in due course. So why would the obligor care if the plaintiff is Tom rather than Joe? With a couple of very narrow exceptions, the answer is that he would not care.

Before examining the consequences of a transfer, let us explore the two requirements that must be met for an instrument to be transferred. First, the transferor must deliver the instrument to the transferee. We have discussed delivery previously in this chapter. Until the instrument is delivered, the intended transferee obtains no rights in the instrument. Second, the transferor must intend, by the delivery, to vest in the transferee the right to enforce the instrument so that as between the two of them the transferee is the proper party to enforce the obligation. The transferor does not have to intend to vest ownership in his transferee, he just must intend to give the transferee the right to enforce the instrument.[265] For example, if Joe delivers the instrument to Tom for the purpose of having Tom collect the instrument for Joe, the requisite intent is present. In contrast, a thief who steals the instrument from Joe is not a transferee because Joe did not intend to vest in the thief the right to enforce the instrument. Similarly, where Joe asks his attorney to safeguard the instrument for him, Joe does not transfer the instrument to his attorney because he does not intend for his attorney to have the right to enforce the instrument. He only intends that his attorney look after the instrument for him.

2. Right to Indorsement of Transferor

A transfer may or may not result in the transferee becoming the holder of the instrument. Where the instrument is payable to bearer, the transfer will always make the transferee the holder. If the transferor, however, fails to indorse an instrument payable to his order, the transferee will not become a holder of the instrument by virtue of the transfer alone.

When an instrument payable to order has been transferred without the transferor's indorsement, the transferee may, depending upon the parties' agreement, have the right to compel the transferor's indorsement. The presumption is that, unless otherwise agreed, whenever a transfer is for value, the parties intended that the transferee become the holder of the instrument. As

---

265. U.C.C. §3-203, Official Comment 1.

a consequence, absent a contrary agreement, when the transfer is for value, the transferee has the specifically enforceable right to obtain the transferor's unqualified indorsement (we cover in Chapter 3 indorsements without recourse).[266] This gives the transferee both the right to become the holder and the safeguard of having the transferor's liability as an indorser.[267]

In contrast, absent a contrary agreement, the transferee has no right to require an indorsement of an instrument payable to bearer or of an instrument payable to order that is not transferred for value. In the case of an instrument payable to bearer, there is no need to have the transferor's indorsement in order to make the transferee the holder. The only purpose would be for the transferor to undertake liability as an indorser. Absent an agreement to the contrary, the presumption is that no such liability was intended. When the transfer is not for value, the transferee is lucky to get what he already received and should not impose any further upon the transferor.

3. The Shelter Provision

The most important aspect of the rule that the transferee obtains the rights of his transferor is a corollary rule nicknamed the "shelter provision." Under the shelter provision, a transferee may acquire the rights of a holder in due course through the transfer even though the transferee does not himself qualify as a holder in due course.[268] A transferee of a holder in due course takes free of all claims to the instrument, defenses, and claims in recoupment to the same extent as would his transferor/holder in due course.[269] In addition, the transferee obtains all of his tranferor's other rights under Article 3 including, among others:

1. the presumption that once the obligor's signature is established, production of the instrument entitles the person entitled to enforce the instrument to recover unless the obligor establishes a defense;
2. the right to demand payment of the instrument;
3. discharge of the instrument upon payment to the transferee;
4. the right of the transferee to enforce the obligation in his own name; and
5. the right to collect attorney's fees and interest if provided for in the instrument.

266. U.C.C. §3-203(c); U.C.C. §3-203, Official Comment 3.
267. U.C.C. §3-415(a); U.C.C. §3-203, Official Comment 3.
268. U.C.C. §3-203(b).
269. U.C.C. §3-305(b); U.C.C. §3-306.

G. Transfer of Instrument and Shelter Provision

The transferee also is entitled to any rights the transferor inherited from his own transferor. If Joe, a holder in due course, gave a note as a gift to Mary, who subsequently gave the note to Jane, Jane acquires all of Joe's rights as a holder in due course.

There are numerous situations in which the only way for a transferee to acquire the rights of a holder in due course is through the shelter provision. The most obvious situation is where the transferee has failed to obtain his transferor's indorsement and therefore, is not a holder of the instrument. Some other situations in which the transferee is not a holder in due course in his own right are (1) a donee or other person who did not take the instrument for value, or (2) a person who took the instrument in bad faith or with notice of a claim to the instrument, claim in recoupment or defense. The shelter provision can also bestow the rights of a holder in due course upon a holder who does not qualify as a holder in due course because he (a) purchased the instrument at a judicial sale or took it under legal process, (b) acquired it in taking over an estate, or (c) purchased it as part of a bulk transaction not in the regular course of the transferor's business.[270] Finally, as will be discussed in the next chapter, an accommodation party who, upon making payment, obtains possession of the instrument is a transferee and acquires the rights of his transferor.

a. Transferee's Rights No Greater Than Transferor's

Since the rights vested in the transferee are purely derivative, they can be no greater than those possessed by his transferor and are subject to the same limitations. The transferee obtains only the *rights* of his transferor as a holder in due course; he does not obtain the *status* of a holder in due course. He can only obtain the status of a holder in due course by meeting its requirements himself. If the transferor/holder in due course takes free of a claim of ownership, claim in recoupment, or defense, so will his transferee. Conversely, if the drawer has a claim in recoupment good against the transferor/holder in due course arising out of direct dealings between the drawer and the holder in due course, the transferee also takes subject to this claim in recoupment.

Take as an example Ellen issuing a note payable to Beth, who qualifies as a holder in due course. Beth gives the note as a gift to Charles, her brother. Not having taken the note for value, Charles does not become a holder in due course. He does, though, step into Beth's shoes and may recover from Ellen to the same extent as could Beth. If Ellen has a claim in recoupment that is

---

270. U.C.C. §3-302(c)(i); U.C.C. §3-302(c)(iii); U.C.C. §3-302(c)(ii), respectively.

assertible against Beth, Charles takes subject to this same claim in recoupment. If, however, Charles gave value for the note and thus independently met the requirements for holder-in-due-course status, he would take the note free of Ellen's claim in recoupment.[271]

b. Exceptions to Shelter Provision

There are situations in which the shelter provision could be abused. For example, Hank may have defrauded Linda into issuing a note payable to Mark, who is completely innocent of any knowledge of the fraud. Mark may have paid value for the instrument. If Hank purchases the note from Mark, should Hank take free of Linda's defenses? This would not be right. To protect against such manipulation, there is an exception to the shelter provision: No transferee who has himself engaged in any fraud or illegality affecting the instrument can acquire the rights of a holder in due course through transfer directly or indirectly from a holder in due course.[272] The transferee need not have been a prior party to the instrument itself. A party who had participated in a fraud upon the obligor is barred by this exception even though the obligor may have no claim against him arising out of the prior transaction. In contrast, a person who has not engaged in fraud can acquire the rights of a holder in due course even though he had notice of the fraud. Thus, if the note was purchased by George who knew of Hank's fraud, but was not a party to the fraud, George could acquire Mark's rights as a holder in due course.

4. Reacquisition by Prior Holder

There will be times when a person who had previously been a holder of an instrument reacquires the instrument. For example, James may have made a note payable to Ace Business Machines ("ABM") in payment for the purchase of a computer. ABM may have sold the note as part of its normal financing to Crest Financial. When James begins missing payments, Crest Financial may request that ABM repurchase the note. The note may be reacquired by ABM through either negotiation or transfer.[273]

If the reacquisition is by Crest Financial indorsing the note back to ABM, ABM thereby again becomes the holder of the instrument. If, however, Crest Financial forgets to indorse the note to ABM, ABM cannot become a holder

271. U.C.C. §3-305(b).
272. U.C.C. §3-203(b).
273. U.C.C. §3-207; U.C.C. §3-207, Official Comment.

until Crest Financial indorses the note. This would require ABM to return the note to Crest Financial for its indorsement. This act of obtaining Crest Financial's indorsement has little purpose. To relieve ABM of this largely unnecessary act, ABM is given the right to cancel any indorsement not necessary to its chain of title, thereby enabling it to become the holder of the instrument.[274] ABM may therefore cancel its own indorsement to Crest Financial. Cancellation of an indorsement can be accomplished by simply crossing out the indorsement. At this point, the instrument is now again payable to ABM; ABM can further negotiate the instrument.[275] Assume instead that Crest Financial sold and negotiated the note to Home Finance. Home Finance then transferred the note back to ABM. (See Figure 2.6.)

FIGURE 2.6

ABM may cancel Crest Financial's indorsement to Home Finance in addition to ABM's indorsement to Crest Financial. ABM is the holder again because the note is now again made payable to ABM.

Having the right to cancel intervening indorsements is useful where a transaction has fallen through. For example, Paul may obtain a cashier's check payable to himself, which he indorses to Kate as a good faith deposit for the purchase of real estate. When the deal is not consummated, Kate returns the check to Paul without indorsing it. Paul may cancel his own indorsement to Kate and thereby become the holder again.

Although a few courts have held otherwise, reacquisition of an instrument should not give the reacquirer his prior status as a holder in due course. Although he may regain his original rights through the shelter provision, he can become a holder in due course only if he fulfills the requirements for becoming a holder in due course at the time he reacquires the instrument. If he reacquires the instrument after it is overdue or after he has obtained notice of a defense, he will not himself qualify as a holder in due course.

---

274. U.C.C. §3-207.
275. U.C.C. §3-207; U.C.C. §3-207, Official Comment, Case #1.

The reacquirer's cancellation of intervening indorsements discharges any indorser whose indorsement has been cancelled.[276] By the cancellation, subsequent purchasers are deemed to have notice of the cancelled indorser's discharge.

In order for the reacquirer to have the right to cancel intervening indorsements, the instrument must have been transferred to him. This requires both (1) that his transferor intend to confer upon him the right to enforce the instrument; and (2) physical return of the instrument to the reacquirer. A reacquirer cannot cancel intervening indorsements unless, through the transfer, he has the right to enforce the instrument. Otherwise, a prior holder could steal the instrument from the present holder and then cancel all intervening indorsements, thereby entitling him to payment of the instrument. This would defeat the protection a specially indorsed instrument affords to its owner.

H. DEFENSES AND CLAIMS TO BANK CHECKS

1. Right of Bank to Raise Claims and Defenses to Its Obligation to Pay a Bank Check

In Chapter 1 we defined a cashier's check as a check that is drawn by a bank upon itself and a teller's check as a check drawn by one bank upon another bank. Despite the difference in form, teller's checks and cashier's checks are functionally equivalent. Sometimes a bank will issue a cashier's check or teller's check to pay one of its own obligations much in the same way that a customer may use a personal check.[277] For example, if Bank of America wants to pay its attorney, it will issue a cashier's check to its attorney. Because a certified check is a check drawn upon the customer's account, a certifying bank has no occasion for using a certified check to pay one of the bank's own obligations.

On other occasions, a customer for her own use may purchase a cashier's or teller's check from a bank or have the bank certify one of her own

276. U.C.C. §3-207; U.C.C. §3-207, Official Comment.
277. See Lawrence, Making Cashier's Checks and Other Bank Checks Cost-Effective: A Plea for Revision of Article 3 and 4 of the Uniform Commercial Code, 64 Minn. L. Rev. 275, 285 (1980).

checks.[278] For example, Jamie may buy a cashier's check from Wells Fargo Bank in order to purchase a car from Nissan World. In this event, two separate transactions are involved. Wells Fargo Bank sells the check to Jamie and then Jamie negotiates the check to Nissan World.

A person receiving payment from the customer by a certified, cashier's, or teller's check (collectively sometimes called "bank checks") feels the same sense of security as if he had received payment in cash.[279] This sense of security is eroded to the extent that the bank may refuse payment on a bank check. Article 3 seeks to discourage a bank from refusing, at its customer's request, payment of a bank check.[280] To this end, special rules were drafted to govern the bank's right to refuse payment on a bank check when used in a transaction by its customer.[281] These rules only apply when a bank check is used by its customer or other purchaser. When a bank uses a cashier's or teller's check for its own purposes, these special rules do not apply. The reason for this exception is simple. By definition any check that a bank issues will either be drawn upon itself, in which case it is a cashier's check, or drawn upon another bank, in which case it is a teller's check. A bank, like any other drawer, needs to issue checks to pay its rent, to pay for supplies, and to pay its employees. When the drawer bank uses a teller's or cashier's check for its own purposes, it needs to have the same right to refuse payment as does any other drawer. When, however, the check is purchased by a third person, all parties expect that the check will provide more security than does an ordinary check.

Cashier's, teller's, and certified checks are treated the same for purposes of determining the bank's right to refuse payment. A bank refusing to pay a cashier's or certified check is treated the same as a bank stopping payment of or dishonoring a teller's check.[282] The drawer bank of a teller's or cashier's check and the accepting bank on a certified check are called the "obligated bank".

In formulating rules governing bank checks, the Code attempted to balance the need to protect the expectation of the check's recipient that he is receiving a cash-like instrument with the need to protect the user of the check from being defrauded by the recipient. Despite the difficulty of this task, the Code has succeeded reasonably well in reaching a balance.

---

278. See Lawrence, supra note 277, at 285.
279. U.C.C. §3-411, Official Comment 1.
280. U.C.C. §3-411, Official Comment 1; U.C.C. §3-602, Official Comment.
281. "Obligated bank" means the acceptor of a certified check or the issuer of a cashier's check or teller's check bought from the issuer. U.C.C. §3-411(a); U.C.C. §3-411, Official Comment 2.
282. U.C.C. §3-411(b).

To begin with, the bank retains the same right as a drawer of a personal check to raise defenses or third-party claims. All of the rules we have covered regarding the ability of a drawer to defeat the holder's actions apply to bank checks. In our example above, assume that for some reason Wells Fargo Bank refuses to pay Nissan World on the cashier's check that Jamie purchased from it. Wells Fargo Bank's right to raise any defense is governed by the same rules that would apply if Wells Fargo Bank was an ordinary drawer being sued on its personal check.

However, in order to discourage Wells Fargo Bank from raising a defense or claim that is not valid against Nissan World, Wells Fargo Bank is assessed a penalty if it wrongfully refuses to pay the cashier's check (or any other bank check). The penalty is a way of protecting Nissan World from the expense that it thought it had avoided by demanding payment by cashier's check. An obligated bank that wrongfully refuses to pay a bank check is liable to the person asserting the right to enforce the check for any expenses and loss of interest resulting from the nonpayment.[283] The most important aspect of this penalty is that a court may award as expenses any attorney's fees resulting from the nonpayment, including the fees expended in bringing the action against the obligated bank.[284] The penalty is increased where the obligated bank knows that the failure to pay the check will cause the holder to suffer additional losses. Thus, the holder may recover consequential damages if the obligated bank refuses to pay the check after receiving notice of the particular circumstances giving rise to these damages.[285] For example, if Nissan World needed the funds to purchase another car for sale to a subsequent purchaser, Nissan World's loss of profits on this sale could be recovered as damages if notice of this fact was communicated to Wells Fargo Bank in time enough for Wells Fargo Bank to make payment to Nissan World, thereby avoiding the loss.

The Code only wants to discourage a bank from refusing to pay when its duty to pay is clear.[286] As a result, the obligated bank (Wells Fargo Bank) is not liable for expenses or consequential damages if its refusal to pay occurs because the bank:

1. suspends payments;
2. has reasonable grounds to believe that the bank's claim or defense is available against the   person entitled to enforce the instrument;

---

283. U.C.C. §3-411(b).
284. U.C.C. §3-411, Official Comment 2.
285. U.C.C. §3-411(b).
286. U.C.C. §3-411, Official Comment 3.

3. has reasonable doubt that the person is entitled to payment; or
4. if payment is prohibited by law.[287]

Thus, where Wells Fargo Bank suspends payment (is insolvent) and can-not make payment of the check, it will not be liable for expenses and conse-quential damages. Where Wells Fargo Bank is reasonable in questioning whether the person demanding payment is Nissan World, Wells Fargo Bank has the right to refuse payment until it receives adequate proof as to the pre-senter's identity.[288] Similarly, if Wells Fargo Bank has a defense of its own in that Jamie had paid for the cashier's check with a forged check, Wells Fargo Bank would be able to raise this defense against Nissan World if Nissan World did not qualify as a holder in due course. Wells Fargo Bank is not liable for either consequential damages or expenses, whether or not it is successful in raising the defense, as long as the bank reasonably believes both that it has such a defense and that Nissan World is subject to the defense. This requires that Wells Fargo Bank have reasonable grounds to believe that Nissan World is not a holder in due course. If Nissan World qualifies as a holder in due course, it will take free of Wells Fargo Bank's defense. In this event, even if Wells Fargo Bank was reasonable in its belief, because Wells Fargo Bank had use of the funds during the delay, it is liable to Nissan World for interest on the funds.

In contrast, Wells Fargo Bank receives no protection against expenses and consequential damages if it unsuccessfully attempts to raise a third party's (Jamie's) claim to the instrument. Under section 3-305(c), Wells Fargo Bank may be relieved of liability to Nissan World if Jamie defends the action for the bank by successfully asserting her claim. For example, Jamie may believe that Nissan World defrauded her into purchasing a defective car. If Jamie has the right to rescind the transaction because of Nissan's fraud, Wells Fargo Bank could raise Jamie's claim as a defense to Nissan's action on the cashier's check.[289] If, however, Jamie cannot prove the right to rescind, Jamie's mere breach of warranty defense cannot be used by Wells Fargo Bank as a defense. Even if Jamie does have a valid claim to the cashier's check, if the cashier's check has been negotiated by Nissan World to a holder in due course, the holder in due course will take free of Jamie's claim to the check.[290]

If Wells Fargo Bank could assert with impunity what turns out to be Jamie's invalid claim, the cash-like nature of bank checks would be defeated. Nissan World would have gained little by taking a cashier's check rather than Jamie's personal check. As a result, Wells Fargo Bank is given the choice. If

287. U.C.C. §3-411(c).
288. U.C.C. §3-411, Official Comment 3.
289. U.C.C. §3-202; U.C.C. §3-411, Official Comment 3.
290. U.C.C. §3-306.

Jamie's claim turns out to be valid, Wells Fargo Bank has no liability to Nissan World or any subsequent non-holder in due course. However, if the claim is invalid or if a subsequent holder in due course acquires the check, Wells Fargo Bank is liable to the person entitled to enforce the check for expenses and consequential damages, where appropriate.[291]

Of course, Wells Fargo Bank would not be liable if Jamie had payment enjoined by an appropriate court (enjoining payment is discussed earlier in this chapter). Jamie will not be able to obtain an injunction unless the court believes that Jamie has a reasonable chance to prevail on the merits of the case. Seldom will Jamie have the time or money to obtain an injunction against Wells Fargo Bank paying the check. Jamie can, if she desires, offer to indemnify Wells Fargo Bank to encourage it to refuse to pay Nissan World. In reality, Wells Fargo Bank will not even consider refusing to pay without such an agreement. This means that Jamie will be paying not only any liability that Wells Fargo Bank incurs to Nissan World but also, whether or not successful, all of Wells Fargo Bank's own expenses in defending the action.

However, the bank has no obligation to accept the offer of indemnity. It can pay Nissan World and obtain a discharge despite Jamie's offer. Even if it does accept her offer of indemnity, payment to Nissan World still discharges its obligation on the check.[292] The bank may, however, be liable to Jamie for breach of the indemnity agreement.

2. Rights of Remitters of Cashier's and Teller's Checks

When a cashier's or teller's check is made payable to someone other than the purchaser, the purchaser is called the remitter of the check. A "remitter" is a person who purchases an instrument from its issuer where the instrument is payable to an identified person other than the purchaser.[293] For example, Isaac may request that Crocker Bank issue a cashier's check payable to Hayes because Isaac is purchasing land from Hayes. Because the check is not payable to Isaac, Isaac is not the holder of the check. He is the remitter. Once Isaac delivers the check to Hayes, Hayes becomes the owner of the check.

Not being the payee, Isaac is not a party to the instrument. As a result, Isaac is not a person entitled to enforce the instrument, which can cause problems where Isaac wants Crocker Bank to refund him the money he paid for the

291. U.C.C. §3-411, Official Comment 3.
292. U.C.C. §3-602(b)(1); U.C.C. §3-602, Official Comment.
293. U.C.C. §3-103(a)(11).

check if the deal with Hayes falls through. If Isaac has not yet delivered the check to Hayes, Isaac is still the owner and is ultimately entitled to the money. On the other hand, if Isaac delivered the check to Hayes, but somehow reacquired possession of the check, Hayes and not Isaac is entitled to payment. Because of uncertainty as to whether Isaac or Hayes is the owner of the check, Crocker Bank cannot safely pay Isaac without risking liability to Hayes. The bank is discharged only by its payment to a person entitled to enforce the instrument.[294] If the check had been delivered to Hayes, Hayes would be the person entitled to enforce the check. The bank may therefore be liable to Hayes for conversion if it pays Isaac. However, if the bank refuses to pay Isaac, what can Isaac do where he is legitimately the owner because the transaction was not completed?

Because of this dilemma, most courts have held that unless the bank has reason to suspect that the payee (Hayes), rather than the remitter (Isaac), is the owner of the instrument, the bank may discharge its obligation by paying the remitter (Isaac).[295] This result makes sense. It is very unusual for a remitter to re-obtain possession of a cashier's or teller's check after its delivery to the payee. In most cases the remitter will in fact deserve payment because the transaction has fallen through.

I. FEDERAL HOLDER-IN-DUE-COURSE STATUS

With all of the bank and savings and loan association (collectively referred to as "banks") insolvencies during the past two decades, the Federal Deposit Insurance Corporation ("FDIC") and the Resolution Trust Company ("RTC") have been called upon to take over and run many failed banks and savings and loan associations. Prior to its abolition in 1989, the Federal Savings and Loan Insurance Corporation ("FSLIC") acted both as an insurer and as the conservator and receiver of failed savings and loan associations. Now the RTC has taken over these functions.

The FDIC may assume two different roles when a bank fails. The FDIC, as a *receiver* of the failed bank, may manage and protect the failed bank's assets. The FDIC, *in its corporate capacity*, insures the depositor's accounts. All of the

---

294. U.C.C. §3-602(a).

295. See Gillespie v. Riley Management Corp., 59 Ill. 2d 211, 319 N.E.2d 753, 16 U.C.C. Rep. Serv. 150 (1974); Bunge Corp. v. Manufacturers Hanover Trust Co., 37 A.D.2d 409, 325 N.Y.S.2d 983 (1971), order aff'd, 31 N.Y.2d 223, 335 N.Y.S.2d 412, 286 N.E.2d 903 (1972).

same powers that the FDIC has regarding banks, the RTC has regarding savings and loan associations.

Upon a bank's failure, the FDIC has several options. The FDIC may, in the unusual case, attempt to operate the failed bank back into good health. Often, instead, the FDIC will close the bank and liquidate its assets. As receiver of the closed bank, the FDIC succeeds to all of the failed bank's rights to any instruments held by the bank. The FDIC, as receiver, will attempt to recover on the negotiable instruments it holds and then pay to the failed bank's depositors the pro rata share of the bank's assets to which they are entitled. To the extent that the depositors are not fully paid, the FDIC will make up the difference (up to its insurance limits) in its capacity as insurer.

Instead of closing the bank and liquidating its assets, the FDIC, as receiver of the failed bank, can, in what is called a "purchase and assumption agreement," attempt to sell the failed bank's good assets to another bank. The failed bank's good assets will include those negotiable instruments held by the failed bank that are easily collectible. The negotiable instruments that are harder to collect ("bad assets") are retained by the FDIC. In consideration for the good assets, the acquiring bank agrees to pay in full the failed bank's depositors. The transaction is called a "purchase and assumption agreement" because the acquiring bank both purchases the assets of the failed bank and assumes the debts of the failed bank. The FDIC, in its corporate capacity as insurer, pays the acquiring bank the difference between the fair market value of the assets purchased and the amount that the acquiring bank is required to pay to the failed bank's depositors. The FDIC, in its corporate capacity, then purchases the failed bank's bad assets from itself in its receivership capacity and attempts to collect on these bad assets to replenish its insurance fund.

Because a purchase and assumption transaction is for the purpose of keeping the bank open, it must be completed in a swift manner. As a matter of ordinary course, it is often arranged with the acquiring bank overnight. In order to consummate the transaction, the FDIC must quickly estimate the value of the good assets that it sells to the acquiring bank. It does not have time to examine the files to determine if there are defenses that could be asserted against the instruments acquired in the transaction.

In both receivership and purchase and assumption transactions, the question arises as to whether the FDIC or the RTC may become a holder in due course of the purchased instruments. Prior to 1994, certain things were clear. Federal common law, and not the Code, determined whether the FDIC or the RTC in purchasing notes is a holder in due course.[296] Federal courts had

296. See Federal Deposit Ins. Corp. v. Wood, 758 F.2d 156, 40 U.C.C. Rep. Serv. 937 (6th Cir. 1985); Federal Deposit Ins. Corp. v. Leach, 772 F.2d 1262, 40 U.C.C. Rep. Serv. 937 (6th Cir. 1985).

I. Federal Holder-in-Due-Course Status

adopted a doctrine called the "federal holder in due course doctrine" to determine whether the FDIC or the RTC qualified as a holder in due course. The federal holder in due course doctrine applied only to negotiable instruments.[297] By executing an instrument that is not negotiable, the obligor naturally assumed that he could use any of his defenses against any transferee of the instrument. The mere fact that the bank failed was no reason to deny the obligor his bargained-for right. Such a denial would have given a windfall to the FDIC or the RTC, which knew that it was an instrument that was not negotiable.

Courts had generally agreed that the federal holder in due course doctrine applied to the FDIC and the RTC when they acquired instruments in a purchase and assumption transaction. In a purchase and assumption transaction, any loss suffered by virtue of a miscalculation as to the value of the assets would have been borne by the FDIC or the RTC (in other words, the public). Because the purpose of a purchase and assumption transaction is to protect the bank's depositors, the interests of the bank's depositors and the public were felt to outweigh the right of the makers of the acquired notes to raise their defenses. In contrast, most courts held that the federal holder in due course doctrine did not apply when the FDIC or RTC took over the operation of a failed bank in their receivership capacity.[298] When they acted as a receiver, they were simply liquidating the bank's assets. As such, they were merely continuing to operate the business of the failed bank and did not purchase the instrument for their own account.

However, courts were not consistent as to what the FDIC or the RTC must prove in order to acquire holder-in-due-course status. All courts agreed that it was easier for the FDIC or the RTC to qualify under the federal holder-in-due-course standard than under the standard adopted by Article 3. In the first place, under Article 3, a purchaser of an instrument in a bulk transaction not in the ordinary course of the transferor's business cannot thereby become a holder in due course. In contrast, under the federal holder-in-due-course standard, purchase in bulk by the FDIC or the RTC of the failed bank's instruments did not deny the FDIC or the RTC holder-in-due-course status.

---

297. See Resolution Trust Corp. v. 1601 Partners, Ltd., 796 F. Supp. 238, 19 U.C.C. Rep. Serv. 147 (N.D. Tex. 1992).

298. See Desmond v. Federal Deposit Ins. Corp., 798 F. Supp. 829, 20 U.C.C. Rep. Serv. 2d 196 (D. Mass. 1992) (does not apply); Federal Deposit Ins. Corp. v. Trans Pacific Indus., 14 F.3d 10, 22 U.C.C. Rep. Serv. 2d 1074 (5th Cir. 1994) (does not apply). But see Campbell Leasing, Inc. v. Federal Deposit Ins. Corp., 901 F.2d 1244, 12 U.C.C. Rep. Serv. 2d 138 (5th Cir. 1990) (applies; the 5th Cir. in the *Trans Pacific Indus.* case held otherwise even though it did not mention this decision).

Other than this point upon which all courts agreed, courts were not consistent in the criteria that they applied in determining whether the FDIC or the RTC qualified as a holder in due course. For instance, the 6th Circuit Court of Appeals in Federal Deposit Insurance Corporation v. Wood[299] held that the FDIC qualified as a holder in due course even though it took the instrument with notice that it was overdue while, under similar facts, the 3d Circuit Court of Appeals in Federal Deposit Insurance Corporation v. Blue Rock Shopping Center[300] held that the FDIC was not a holder in due course where it acquired an instrument that was overdue. Most courts seemed to require that the FDIC and the RTC take the instrument in good faith and without actual knowledge of any defense to the instrument.[301]

A transferee from the FDIC or RTC obtained all of the rights that the FDIC or RTC had as a holder in due course under the federal holder in due course doctrine.[302] By protecting the transferee, the market for the instruments acquired by the FDIC or the RTC was preserved.

Even where the FDIC or the RTC does not qualify as a holder in due course, proving a defense was more difficult against the FDIC and the RTC than against holders under Article 3. Proof of any defense was governed by the *D'Oench, Duhme* doctrine, under which defenses had to be based upon documents and not upon secret agreements.[303] Many courts required that defenses be proved through the failed bank's formal and board approved records.[304] However, even the fact that proof of the defense is contained in the failed bank's files did not make evidence of the agreement admissible unless the FDIC or the RTC had actual knowledge of the defense. A doctrine similar to the *D'Oench, Duhme* doctrine was codified in 12 U.S.C. §1823(e), as amended

---

299. 758 F.2d 156, 40 U.C.C. Rep. Serv. 937 (6th Cir. 1985).

300. 849 F.2d 600 (3d Cir. 1988).

301. See Federal Saving & Loan Ins. Corp. v. Mackie, 949 F.2d 818, 16 U.C.C. Rep. Serv. 2d 1097 (5th Cir. 1992); Federal Deposit Ins. Corp. v. Cremona Co., 832 F.2d 959, 4 U.C.C. Rep. Serv. 2d 1111 (6th Cir. 1987).

302. See Federal Deposit Ins. Corp. v. Newhart, 892 F.2d 47, 10 U.C.C. Rep. Serv. 2d 257 (8th Cir. 1989) (Where FDIC is granted holder-in-due-course status under federal common law, its transferee obtains the rights of a holder in due course.).

303. See Resolution Trust Corp. v. Montross, 944 F.2d 227, 15 U.C.C. Rep. Serv. 2d 1249 (5th Cir. 1991); Federal Deposit Ins. Corp. v. Byrne, 736 F. Supp. 727, 13 U.C.C. Rep. Serv. 2d 427 (N.D. Texas 1990).

304. See Resolution Trust Corp. v. Juergens, 965 F.2d 149, 18 U.C.C. Rep. Serv. 2d 484 (7th Cir. 1992); Federal Deposit Ins. Corp. v. Hershiser Signature Properties, 777 F. Supp. 539, 16 U.C.C. Rep. Serv. 2d 702 (E.D. Mich. 1991) (FDIC does not obtain knowledge from information that could have been obtained through reading of acquired bank's files); Federal Deposit Ins. Corp. v. Turner, 869 F.2d 270, 8 U.C.C. Rep. Serv. 2d 1094 (6th Cir. 1989) (presence in file of letters signed by one party only cancelling guaranty did not give FDIC notice of defense).

in 1989 by the Financial Institutions Reform, Recovery, and Enforcement Act (FIRREA), which provided that no agreement that had the result of diminishing the interests of the FDIC in any assets acquired by it (whether as a purchaser or a receiver of any insured bank or savings and loan) was valid against the FDIC unless such agreement was (1) in a writing that was (2) executed by the bank contemporaneously with the acquisition of the note and (3) was approved by the board of directors of the bank and reflected in the minutes of the board.

The fate of the federal holder in due course and *D'Oench, Duhme* doctrines became very cloudy in 1994 when the United States Supreme Court issued its opinion in O'Melveny & Myers v. FDIC.[305] In *O'Melveny & Myers*, the FDIC, as receiver for a failed California bank, sued O'Melveny & Myers, the attorneys for the bank, for professional negligence and breach of fiduciary duty for failing to inform the bank of the ultra vires acts of the bank's officers. O'Melveny & Myers defended by asserting that under California law, knowledge of the officers' misconduct would be imputed both to the bank and to the FDIC as the bank's receiver. The FDIC claimed that federal common law, and not California law, applied to determine whether such knowledge would be imputed to the FDIC. In holding that California law governed, the Supreme Court stated that it would not "adopt a court-made rule to supplement federal statutory regulation that is comprehensive and detailed; matters left unaddressed in such a scheme are presumably left subject to the disposition provided by state law."[306] The court found that FIRREA was an exclusive grant of rights to the FDIC as receiver, which could not be supplemented by federal common law.

Although the court in *O'Melveny & Myers* did not address the continued vitality of the federal holder-in-due-course or *D'Oench, Duhme* doctrines, subsequent federal circuits have decided that the *D'Oench, Duhme*, other than as codified in 12 U.S.C. §1823(e),[307] and the federal holder-in-due-course doctrine have been preempted by FIRREA.[308] As a result, the viability of the federal holder-in-due-course or *D'Oench, Duhme*, other than as codified in 12 U.S.C. §1823(e), doctrines appears questionable.

---

305. 114 S. Ct. 2048, 129 L. Ed. 2d 67 (1994).

306. Id. at 114 S. Ct. at 2054.

307. See Divall Insured Income Fund Limited Partnership v. Boatmen's First Natl. Bank, 69 F.3d 1398 (8th Cir. 1995); Murphy v. Federal Deposit Ins. Corp., 61 F.3d 34 (D.C. Cir. 1995).

308. See Divall Insured Income Fund Limited Partnership v. Boatmen's First Natl. Bank, 69 F.3d 1398 (8th Cir. 1995); RTC v. Maplewood Investments, 31 F.3d 1276, 24 U.C.C. Rep. Serv. 2d 119 (4th Cir. 1994); FDIC v. Massingill, 30 F.3d 601, 24 U.C.C. Rep. Serv. 2d 1073 (5th Cir. 1994).

CHAPTER 3

Nature of Liability on Instruments

A. LIABILITY OF ISSUER, DRAWER, ACCEPTOR, AND INDORSER

Though not known by most people, the mere act of signing one's name anywhere on a negotiable instrument will, in most cases, obligate the signer to pay the instrument. However, the conditions precedent to a signer's liability vary depending upon the capacity in which the party signs. There are four basic capacities in which a party may sign a negotiable instrument:

1. an issuer of a note or cashier's check;
2. the drawer of a draft;
3. the acceptor of a draft; and
4. an indorser.

There are two other capacities in which a party may undertake liability on an instrument. First, a person may sign as an accommodation party. An "accommodation party" is a person who signs for the purpose of guarantying the obligation of another signer to the instrument. An accommodation party may sign in any of the above four capacities. Second, a person may incur certain obligations merely by transferring the instrument even if he never signs it. In this section we will discuss the liability of an issuer, drawer, acceptor, and indorser. In addition, we will discuss the role of a drawee. The liability incurred by a transferor of an instrument and the role of an accommodation party are discussed later in this chapter.

149

1.   *Obligation of Issuer*

The Code calls the person who signs a note or cashier's check the "issuer." However, the issuer of a note is commonly called the "maker." The issuer promises to pay the instrument according to its terms at the time the instrument was issued.[1] The duty of the issuer to pay the instrument is owed to the person entitled to enforce the instrument (this usually is the holder).[2] If an indorser has paid the instrument, the issuer also has the duty to pay the indorser.[3] For example, assume John makes a note payable to Bill who indorses the note to David. David, as the holder of the note, may enforce John's promise to pay the note. In addition, if Bill pays David, John has the duty to pay Bill because Bill is an indorser who has paid the note.

The maker (issuer) of a note literally promises to pay the payee. A simple note may read: "I, John, promise to pay to the order of Bill the sum of $1,000 on demand. (s) John." A maker of a note is what may be called a "primary" party. When Bill or David wants to be paid, John is the person from whom they will demand payment.

There are no conditions to John's obligation to pay the note. He is simply liable to pay the note when it is due. If John fails to make payment on the date due, Bill may immediately commence suit without notice or demand. Because, in our example, the note is payable on demand, Bill can file a lawsuit against John without previously asking for payment as long as the statute of limitations has not run. The result would be the same if the note was payable on January 1, 1995. If the note was not paid on that date, Bill could, at any time thereafter, file his lawsuit. Is this unfair to John? Not really. Since Bill would rather get paid than go through a lawsuit to compel payment, it is unlikely that Bill would file a suit without first asking John for payment.

The obligation of an issuer of a cashier's check is identical to that of a maker of a note. Do not be misled by the form of a cashier's check. A cashier's check seems, like any other check, to be an order given by the drawer to the drawee to pay the payee. However, in the case of a cashier's check, the issuing bank is both the drawer and the drawee of the check. This means that just like the maker of a note, the holder will demand payment directly from the issuing bank. Assume that Bank of America issues a cashier's check payable to Bill. Being a cashier's check, the check is drawn by Bank of America, as drawer,

---

1. U.C.C. §3-412; U.C.C. §3-412, Official Comment 1. In the rare case in which the instrument was never voluntarily transferred by the maker and therefore never issued, the maker is obliged to pay the note according to its terms at the time it first came into the possession of a holder. U.C.C. §3-412; U.C.C. §3-412, Official Comment 1.

2. "Person entitled to enforce" is defined in U.C.C. §3-301.

3. U.C.C. §3-412.

upon itself as drawee. When Bill wants to be paid, just as with John's note, Bill will demand that Bank of America pay the check. Just like John, Bank of America cannot expect that anyone but itself will be called upon to make payment.

2. *Obligation of Drawer*

Despite the unilluminating nature of the word "drawer," the role of the drawer of a draft is fairly simple. As an example, let us look at a typical personal check.

Bob opens a bank account at Wells Bank by depositing $1,000 cash in an account. It is clear that Wells Bank now owes Bob $1,000. Bob can ask for the money back or draw checks on his account up to $1,000. So if Bob owes Jill $300, he can write a check to Jill in the amount of $300. As we know, a check is an order by a drawer to a drawee to pay the payee. So here, Bob is ordering Wells Bank to pay $300 to Jill. Jill gets paid the money Bob owes her by cashing the check.

On the face of the check itself, Bob does not expressly make any promise to Jill. By writing the check Bob is simply ordering Wells Bank to pay Jill. However, this is deemed by the Code to be an implied promise that if Wells Bank does not pay the check upon presentment that Bob will pay Jill. Thus, Bob, as the *drawer*, promises that if the check is dishonored, he will pay the unaccepted draft (the check) according to its terms at the time it was issued.[4] Bill, as drawer, makes this promise to the person entitled to enforce the draft (in this case Jill) and to any indorser who pays the draft.[5]

Bob expects Wells Bank to pay the draft. Bob has funds set aside with Wells Bank to pay the draft, and expects that the draft will result in his debt to Jill being paid. For this reason, unless Wells Bank refuses to pay the draft, Bill will not be liable. In other words, dishonor by Wells Bank, the drawee, must occur to cause Bill to be liable as drawer. We will discuss later how Bob's liability may be discharged by a delay or a failure to make presentment of the draft. Ultimately, however, Bill is the one who is expected to pay the debt represented by the draft. Bill is in reality the primary party on an unaccepted draft.[6] Bill's liability as drawer is not conditioned upon notice of dishonor, with one exception.[7] There is little reason to require Jill to communicate

---

4. U.C.C. §3-414(b). In the unlikely event that the draft was not issued, he promises to pay according to its terms at the time it first came into possession of a holder. U.C.C. §3-414(b).

5. U.C.C. §3-414(b).

6. U.C.C. §3-414(b); U.C.C. §3-414, Official Comment 2.

7. The exception is where a draft is accepted by a non-bank in which case the drawer is treated as an indorser under §3-415(a) and (c). U.C.C. §3-414(d).

notice of the dishonor to Bill as he knows or will find out soon from Wells Bank if the check is not paid.

a.   Effect of Acceptance on Drawer's Liability

Does the drawer's liability change if a draft is accepted? As we will cover in the next section, a drawee of a draft may accept the draft. By accepting the draft, the drawee promises to pay the draft as accepted. The effect on the drawer's liability of acceptance by the drawee varies depending upon whether the draft is accepted by a bank or by a non-bank.

The drawer is discharged when a draft is accepted by a bank because the bank now becomes liable as an acceptor.[8] The rationale for the drawer's discharge is that the holder has the bank's commitment to pay the draft. The holder will look to the bank's assets instead of to the drawer's assets. If, for some reason, the holder wants both the drawer's and the bank's promise to pay the draft, the holder may achieve this goal by having the drawer indorse the accepted draft. By indorsing the draft, the drawer undertakes liability as an indorser.

In contrast, a drawer is not discharged if a draft is accepted by a non-bank. When the acceptor is not a bank, there is no reason to assume that the holder would be satisfied in looking to the acceptor's assets only rather than also to the drawer's assets. For this reason, the drawer remains liable. However, because the holder has, by presenting the draft for acceptance, impliedly agreed to look initially to the acceptor for payment, the drawer's obligation becomes the same as that of an indorser.[9] In effect, the non-bank acceptor becomes primarily liable, and the drawer becomes a guarantor of the acceptor's payment.

b.   Draft Drawn Without Recourse

A drawer may disclaim liability on any draft which is not a check[10] by writing on the draft the words "*without recourse.*" "Without recourse" is a disclaimer of a party's promise to pay an instrument. A drawer is not permitted to draw a check without recourse because that would leave no one liable on the check.

There are situations in which it may make sense for a drawer to draw a draft without recourse. Assume that Seller wants Factor to finance his sale to Buyer. In so doing, Seller may use a documentary draft. Seller draws without

---

8. U.C.C. §3-414(c); U.C.C. §3-414, Official Comment 3.

9. U.C.C. §3-414(d); U.C.C. §3-414, Official Comment 4.

10. U.C.C. §3-414(e); U.C.C. §3-414, Official Comment 5.

recourse a draft upon Buyer payable three months after the goods are delivered. Accompanying the draft is a bill of lading that would enable Buyer to acquire the goods. You can refresh your memory as to how a documentary draft transaction works by referring back to Chapter 1. The draft is made payable to Factor. Before deciding to purchase the draft, Factor runs a credit check on Buyer and determines that Buyer is a good credit risk. Factor pays Seller the face amount of the draft less a discount for Factor assuming the credit risk. Because Seller drew the draft without recourse, Seller is not liable in the event that Buyer refuses to pay the draft. Factor, for all practical purposes, is financing the purchase for Buyer.

3.   Drawee and the Obligation of an Acceptor

The "drawee" is the person whom the drawer orders to pay the draft. In our example of a check above, Wells Bank is the drawee of the check. What effect does it have upon Wells Bank that it has been named as drawee on the check? Absent an agreement with Bill under which Wells Bank promises to pay checks drawn upon it, the answer is none. The mere fact that a person is named as drawee of a draft does not by itself impose any obligation upon that person to pay the holder of the draft. Any other rule would create chaos since, although a drawee will usually have an established relationship with the drawer, there is no requirement that such be the case. The mere fact that Bill draws a draft upon Wells Bank cannot impose any liability on Wells Bank.[11]

a.   Draft Not Assignment of Funds

When Bill draws a draft upon an account that he has at Wells Bank, does he vest in Jill, the payee, any right to the funds in this account? The simple answer is "no." A check or other draft does not of itself operate as an assignment of any of the drawer's funds held by the drawee.[12] The holder has no right to proceed directly against the drawee. Wells Bank, the drawee, is only liable to Bill, the drawer. Wells Bank is not liable to Jill, the holder, unless Wells Bank accepts the draft. When a drawee accepts a draft, it becomes an acceptor. Under other circumstances, a drawee may incur liability to the holder.

---

11. For example, Bill could have checks printed up indicating that he has an account with Wells Bank when no such account exists. Or Bill could write a check for $100,000 on an existing account at Wells Bank even though Bill's account contains only $1.

12. U.C.C. §3-408.

These circumstances arise completely independently of the drawee's liability as drawee and are discussed in Chapter 5.

b.   Acceptance

When a draft is presented to the drawee for acceptance and the drawee accepts the draft, the drawee becomes liable as an acceptor. "Acceptance" is the drawee's signed agreement to pay the draft as presented.[13] Acceptance of a draft must be distinguished from payment of a draft. When a draft is presented for payment, the drawee honors the draft by making payment to the person entitled to enforce the draft. Once payment is made, the drawee has no further obligation to that person. In contrast, when a draft is presented for acceptance, the person entitled to enforce the draft is not asking that the drawee pay the draft. Rather he is asking that the drawee sign or, in other words, "accept" the draft. The act of acceptance obligates the drawee to pay the amount of the draft to the person entitled to enforce the draft.[14] In the event that the drawer or an indorser is required to pay the draft, the acceptor has a duty to make payment to such party.

Upon acceptance, the "acceptor" becomes the primary party obligated to pay the draft. There are no conditions to the acceptor's obligation to make payment. As in the case of a maker of a note, once the draft is due, the acceptor is obligated to make payment. If the acceptor fails to make payment on the date due, the person entitled to enforce the draft may immediately commence an action against the acceptor without giving notice to or making a demand upon the acceptor to make payment.

An effective acceptance[15] must be (1) in writing, (2) appear on the instrument, (3) be signed by the drawee, and (4) either delivered to the holder or the holder must be notified.[16] Oral acceptance, an oral promise to accept, or a purported acceptance contained in a separate writing are not effective as an

---

13. U.C.C. §3-409(a).

14. U.C.C. §3-413(a).

15. A draft may be accepted even though it has not been signed by the drawer, is incomplete, overdue, or has been dishonored. U.C.C. §3-409(b).

16. U.C.C. §3-409(a). Unlike the obligation of other parties to a negotiable instrument, an acceptance can become effective when the holder is notified of the acceptance even though the accepted draft has not been delivered to him. U.C.C. §3-409(a); U.C.C. §3-409, Official Comment 2. This enables the acceptance to be effective sooner. The notification must indicate that there has been a written acceptance and must be sent to the holder or to another person at the holder's direction. The notification is not effective if it merely indicates tentative approval.

acceptance.[17] The acceptance may consist of the drawee's signature alone.[18] The signature need not be accompanied by words like "Certified," or "Accepted." Although the signature of an acceptor is usually written vertically across the face of the draft, the drawee's signature may be written anywhere on the draft, including on its back.

4. Obligation of Indorser

"Indorser" is a catch-all category that covers anyone that signs an instrument in any capacity other than as a drawer, acceptor, or maker. A signature is deemed to be an indorsement regardless of the signer's intent unless the accompanying words, terms of the instrument, place of signature, or other circumstances unambiguously indicate that the signature is made for a purpose other than as an indorsement.[19] This has both an upside and a downside for the signer. The upside is that treating the signature as an indorsement entitles the signer to the benefit of conditions and protections that drawers, makers, and acceptors do not get. This includes the requirement that notice of dishonor be given to the indorser. The indorser is also protected by being discharged if the holder has done anything to impair the indorser's recourse to any prior party or to any collateral posted by a prior party. The downside is that a person who has signed an instrument for a purpose other than to incur liability thereon may unknowingly become liable to pay the instrument. For example, a witness who signs for verification purposes only is liable as an indorser unless he indicates that he is only signing as a witness.

a. Indorsers in Chain of Title and Anomalous Indorsers

There are two distinct purposes for which a person may indorse an instrument. The first purpose, discussed in Chapter 2, is where the holder of the instrument wants to negotiate the instrument to a third person. Return to our example of Bob drawing a check payable to Jill. If Jill indorses the check to Sally, Jill's indorsement of the check to Sally not only operates to make Sally

---

17. U.C.C. §3-409(a). The drawee's oral promise to the holder to accept a draft may be enforceable under contract law. A drawee may be liable in tort where it intentionally or negligently misinforms the holder that the drawer's account has adequate funds to cover the draft. U.C.C. §3-408, Official Comments 1 and 2. A drawee may make a specific promise to the drawer that the draft will be accepted, giving the holder rights as a third-party beneficiary.

18. U.C.C. §3-409(a); U.C.C. §3-409, Official Comment 2.

19. U.C.C. §3-204(a); U.C.C. §3-204, Official Comment 1.

the holder of the check, but also obligates Jill to pay the check if dishonored. The presumption is that Sally not only wants title to the check, but also Jill's promise to pay the check. As discussed below, where Jill wants to avoid liability, she can indorse the instrument without recourse.

The second purpose of indorsing an instrument is where a person, for some reason or other, wants to undertake liability on an instrument which he did not draw, make, or hold. This person is called an "anomalous indorser." He is given this title because his indorsement is not in the chain of title. In other words, his indorsement is not needed to negotiate the instrument. If, for example, Sally refuses to purchase the check unless Jim, Jill's brother, also promises to pay the check, Jim's signature would be that of an anomalous indorser. It is anomalous because Jim's signature was not necessary to make Sally the holder of the check. Jill's indorsement alone was sufficient. In virtually all cases, an anomalous indorser is undertaking liability as a guarantor of payment by another party to the instrument. For purposes of the indorser's obligation, an anomalous indorser and an indorser in the chain of title are treated the same.

b.   Indorser's Promise

An indorser promises that if the instrument is dishonored, he will pay the amount of the instrument according to its terms at the time of his indorsement.[20] An indorser is liable according to all the instrument's terms, including any provisions for attorney's fees or interest. An indorser's obligation to pay is owed to the person who is entitled to enforce the instrument or to a subsequent indorser who pays the instrument.[21] Assume that the check drawn by Bob and payable to Jill is indorsed by Jill to Sally. Sally indorses the check to Grocer who indorses and deposits the check into his bank account at Crocker Bank. Upon presentment to Wells Bank, the check is dishonored. (See Figure 3.1)

Because Crocker Bank is the person entitled to enforce the check, Crocker Bank may recover from any indorser, which includes Grocer, Sally, and Jill. If Sally pays Crocker Bank, Sally may recover from Jill. Jill's obligation runs to Sally because Sally is a subsequent indorser. However, Sally may not recover from Grocer because Grocer's obligation does not run to Sally since Sally is not a subsequent indorser.

---

20. U.C.C. §3-415(a).
21. U.C.C. §3-415(a).

A. Liability of Parties

FIGURE 3.1

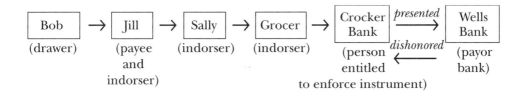

c. Indorsement Without Recourse

An indorser may disclaim liability on his indorser's contract by indorsing the instrument "without recourse";[22] the precise words "without recourse" are not required as long as words having an equivalent meaning are used. An indorser may want to indorse without recourse where he is only intending to transfer title to the instrument and does not wish to incur any personal liability on the instrument. For example, where a check is made payable jointly to an attorney and his client, the attorney may want to indorse the check so that his client can cash the check. However, because the attorney has no desire to become liable to subsequent purchasers of the check, he indorses the check "Attorney, without recourse." Despite the fact that the attorney, by such an indorsement, disclaims any liability as an indorser, he still faces the possibility of liability as a transferor of the check. A person who receives consideration for transferring an instrument makes certain warranties. These warranties, called "transfer warranties," are discussed in Chapter 3C.[23]

d. Conditions to Indorser's Obligation

Only when the instrument has been dishonored and any necessary notice of dishonor has been given, may the holder then seek to recover from the indorser.[24] Dishonor is always a condition to an indorser's obligation.[25] An indorser is not the primary party expected to make payment. His contract requires payment only if the maker, drawee, or acceptor refuses to make pay-

22. U.C.C. §3-415(b).
23. In addition, by transferring the check, the attorney also makes certain presentment warranties to the person who pays the check. These warranties are discussed in Chapter 4A(3).
24. The person entitled to enforce the instrument need not proceed first against the maker, drawer, acceptor, or prior indorser. Neither must he attempt to realize on the collateral.
25. U.C.C. §3-415(a).

ment. Thus, unless the instrument is dishonored by one of these parties, the indorser has no duty to pay. Unless excused, the indorser's obligation may not be enforced unless notice of dishonor is given.[26] An indorser has no reason to expect that the instrument will be dishonored and, in many cases, the indorser will have no way of knowing that payment has not been made. For this reason, notice of dishonor is made a condition to the indorser's liability. However, once these conditions are met, the holder may commence an action to recover from any of the indorsers, no matter in what order they signed. In our example above, Crocker Bank may recover from Jill, for example, without attempting to recover from Sally or Grocer.

An indorser is discharged if a check is not presented for payment or given to a depositary bank for collection within 30 days after his indorsement.[27] For example, assume that the check drawn by Bob is delivered to Jill on March 1st. Jill indorses the check on March 5th and delivers it to Sally who indorses the check on April 1st and delivers the check to Grocer. Grocer deposits the check in his account at Crocker Bank on April 27th. The check is presented to Wells Bank for payment on May 3d. (See Figure 3.2.)

FIGURE 3.2

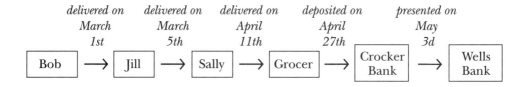

Because the check was not deposited for collection or presented for payment within 30 days after her indorsement, Jill is discharged. However, Sally is not discharged. Although the check was not presented for payment within 30 days of her indorsement, it was deposited for collection within the 30-day period.

This 30-day rule applies only to checks. A delay in presenting any instrument other than a check does not discharge an indorser. Although a delay in presentment does not discharge an indorser, an indorser is discharged with respect to any instrument if a necessary notice of dishonor is not given.[28] However, most notes contain boilerplate language that waives the obligation

26. U.C.C. §3-503; U.C.C. §3-415, Official Comment 2.
27. U.C.C. §3-415(e).
28. U.C.C. §3-415(c); U.C.C. §3-503(a).

of the holder to give notice of dishonor to the indorsers. Because in this event notice of dishonor is excused, the indorsers are not discharged by their failure to receive timely notice of dishonor. Notice of dishonor and when notice is excused are discussed later in section B of this chapter.

B. PRESENTMENT, DISHONOR, NOTICE OF DISHONOR—CONDITIONS TO DRAWER'S AND INDORSER'S LIABILITY

Once a drawer or an indorser signs an instrument, it is usually assumed that his involvement with the instrument is complete. When the drawer issues a check, with sufficient funds in his account, it is assumed that the payee will receive payment from the payor bank. An indorser, whether on a note or a draft, has even more reason to believe that payment will be made since the indorser seldom expects to be called upon to pay the note or draft. Under the terms of any instrument, the drawee, maker, or acceptor is the person by whom payment is to be made. The drawer or indorser should not be bothered with a demand for payment unless the drawee, maker, or acceptor refuses to pay. For these reasons, dishonor of the instrument by the maker, drawee, or acceptor is a condition precedent to the liability of a drawer or an indorser.[29]

The rules for determining whether an instrument has been dishonored are not always easy to understand. The first requirement for a dishonor is that the drawee, acceptor, or maker refuse or fail to pay or accept the instrument. If the instrument is paid, there can be no dishonor. If a draft is accepted but not yet paid, the holder must see if the acceptor will make payment before he seeks to recover from the drawer or indorser. However, a refusal or failure to pay or accept is not a dishonor unless the instrument has been properly presented for payment or acceptance. Since presentment can be excused, when it is, dishonor occurs if the instrument is not duly accepted or paid.[30] Thus, in order for an instrument to be dishonored, the instrument first must either be presented or presentment must be excused.[31]

29. U.C.C. §3-414(b); U.C.C. §3-415(a); U.C.C. §3-502, Official Comment 1.
30. U.C.C. §3-502(e); U.C.C. §3-502, Official Comment 7.
31. U.C.C. §3-502.

1.   *Presentment*

"Presentment" is a demand for payment or acceptance. There are no formal requirements. Although no particular language must be used, immediate payment or acceptance must be demanded. The mere demand itself is the presentment. The reason for this rule is that if the party being requested to pay or accept intends to dishonor the instrument, there is no reason to require the presenter do anything more than make the demand.

However, presentment must be made by or on behalf of a person entitled to enforce the instrument.[32] Thus, presentment may be made by the person himself or by his agent. In the case of a check, a collecting bank usually makes the demand on behalf of the person entitled to enforce the check. Presentment for payment must be made to the drawee or to a party obliged to pay the instrument (the maker of a note or the acceptor of an accepted draft). Presentment for acceptance must be made to the drawee.

a.   Manner of Presentment

Presentment may be made by any commercially reasonable means including by oral, written, or electronic communication.[33] Presentment may be made over the telephone. Absent an agreement regarding electronic truncation, the person to whom presentment is made may require that the instrument be exhibited.[34] Presentment may also be made by mail.[35] Section 4-212 explicitly authorizes a collecting bank to make presentment by sending a written notice in lieu of the instrument. If mailing written notice of presentment is commercially reasonable under the circumstances, the presentment should be effective even where not made by a collecting bank. Presentment by mail is effective when received.

b.   When Presentment Effective

Presentment is effective when the demand for payment or acceptance is received by the person to whom presentment is made.[36] If the party to whom

---

32. U.C.C. §3-501(a). Presentment is effective if made to any one of two or more makers, acceptors, drawees, or other payors. U.C.C. §3-501(b)(1). There is no need to present the instrument to the other makers, acceptors, or drawees in the event that payment or acceptance is refused.
33. U.C.C. §3-501(b)(1).
34. U.C.C. §3-501(b)(2)(i); U.C.C. §3-501, Official Comment.
35. U.C.C. §3-504(2)(a)(1989).
36. U.C.C. §3-501(b)(1).

presentment is made has a cut-off hour for the receipt and processing of instruments, and presentment is made after the cut-off hour, the party may treat the presentment as having occurred on the next business day.[37] The bank may not set a cut-off hour earlier than 2 P.M. Thus, if presentment is made at 3 P.M. on Friday and the bank has established a 2:00 P.M. cut-off hour, presentment is deemed to have been made on Monday since Saturday and Sunday are not business days.

c. Where Presentment Can Be Made

Where can presentment be made? In the absence of a Federal Reserve Regulation, clearinghouse rule, or contrary agreement, presentment can be made anywhere even if the instrument specifies a particular place of payment or acceptance. There is one exception. If the instrument is payable at a bank in the United States, the instrument must be presented at the bank specified.[38] In the absence of a Federal Reserve Regulation, clearinghouse rule, or contrary agreement, an instrument can always be presented at the place of payment.[39] Thus, where the party expected to pay or accept cannot be found, the instrument may be presented at its place of payment. However, this rule does not apply to checks. Regulation CC determines where a check may be presented.[40]

d. Rights of Party to Whom Presentment Made

A party cannot safely pay or accept an instrument unless it receives certain assurances from the presenter. Once the demand for payment or accep-

37. U.C.C. §3-501(b)(4).

38. U.C.C. §3-501(b)(1). The place of payment is the place, if any, specified in the instrument. Where no place of payment is specified in the instrument, the address of the drawer or maker stated in the instrument is the place of payment. If no address is stated, the place of payment is any place of business of the drawee or maker. Where the drawee or maker has no place of business, the place of payment is the residence of the drawee or maker. U.C.C. §3-111.

39. U.C.C. §3-501(b)(1).

40. U.C.C. §3-111. Presentment may be made: (1) at a location to which delivery is requested by the paying bank, 12 C.F.R. §229.36 (b)(1); (2) at an address of the bank associated with the routing number on the check, 12 C.F.R. §229.36 (b)(2); (3) at any branch or head office if the bank is identified on the check by name without address, 12 C.F.R. §229.36 (b)(3); or (4) at a branch, head office, or other location consistent with the name and address of the bank on the check if the bank is identified on the check by name and address, 12 C.F.R. §229.36 (b)(4). Presentment can be made directly to the computer processing center of the bank if so instructed by payor bank. 12 C.F.R. §229.36 (b)(1), App. E.

tance is made, the party to whom presentment is made has the right to demand, without thereby dishonoring the instrument, that the presenter do certain things. He may demand exhibition of the instrument to verify that the presenter has actual possession of the instrument.[41] To be assured that the proper person is being paid, he may demand reasonable identification from the presenter and, if presented on behalf of another, reasonable evidence of the agent's authority.[42] To protect himself against the claim that payment was not made, a person who makes payment may demand a signed receipt on the instrument or surrender of the instrument if payment in full is made.[43]

If the presenter fails within a reasonable time to comply with one of these authorized requests,[44] the presentment is invalidated. It is as if presentment had never been made. Once all authorized demands have been satisfied, the time within which acceptance or payment must be made commences to run.

e.   Effect of Delay in Presentment

The effect of a delay in presentment varies depending upon whether the party is the drawer or an indorser. An indorser of a check is discharged from his indorser's liability if a check is not presented for payment or given to a depositary bank for collection within 30 days after his indorsement.[45] An indorser is not discharged by a delay in presentment as to any instrument other than a check.

A drawer will only be discharged by a delay in presentment in very limited circumstances. He is not discharged by a delay in presentment of any draft other than a check. Even where the draft is a check, the drawer is discharged only when he is hurt by the delay. The presenter of a check is given 30 days from the check's stated date to present the check for payment or give the check to a depositary bank for collection. If the check is not presented or given for collection within this 30-day period, the drawer is discharged to the extent that he is deprived of funds maintained with the drawee because the drawee has suspended payment after the expiration of the 30-day period and

41. U.C.C. §3-501(b)(2)(i); U.C.C. §3-501, Official Comment. Exhibition of the instrument cannot be demanded if the parties have agreed otherwise as in an agreement allowing for electronic presentment. U.C.C. §3-501, Official Comment.
42. U.C.C. §3-501(b)(2)(ii).
43. U.C.C. §3-501(b)(2)(iii).
44. In addition, without dishonoring the instrument, the party to whom presentment is made may (1) return the instrument for lack of a necessary indorsement; or (2) refuse payment or acceptance for failure of the presentment to comply with the terms of the instrument, an agreement of the parties or other applicable law or rule.
45. U.C.C. §3-415(e).

failed to make payment on the check.[46] The drawer is only hurt where the drawee bank has gone insolvent (suspends payment) during the delay in presentment, thereby depriving the drawer of funds otherwise available to pay the check.

For example, assume that a check dated July 1st was not given to a depositary bank for collection until August 15th. If the payor bank went insolvent on August 8th, the drawer would be entitled to a discharge. However, if the bank went insolvent on July 29th, the drawer would not have been discharged because even if the check had been presented within the 30-day period (on July 30th), the drawer would have still lost his funds. The drawer is only deprived of funds if the bank either has no insurance coverage or if there is a significant delay in obtaining full payment of the insurance proceeds.[47] In those cases, the drawer may discharge his liability on the check by assigning his rights against the drawee to the person entitled to enforce the instrument.[48] The holder, although no longer having recourse against the drawer, obtains the drawer's rights against the drawee bank. Most banks and savings and loans are insured by the Federal Deposit Insurance Corporation ("FDIC"), which covers each depositor up to $100,000.[49] Thus, it is unlikely that any loss will be suffered by a holder.

f. When Presentment Excused

When a presentment or a delay in presentment is excused, presentment is treated as having been made within the prescribed time limits. Presentment is excused if it cannot be made by the exercise of reasonable diligence.[50] Reasonable diligence does not require a party to expend a tremendous amount of money, time, or effort; the effort need only be reasonable under the circumstances. The standard is an objective one as opposed to the subjective inability of the party himself. Thus, if an ordinary person with reasonable diligence could not present the instrument, it is irrelevant that the party himself made no effort to present the instrument. The typical situation in which this excuse applies is when the presenter cannot locate the party to whom presentment must be made. Where no place of payment is specified in an instrument, presentment is excused if the presenter cannot with reasonable diligence locate either the home or business address of the party to whom presentment is to be made.

---

46. U.C.C. §3-414(f); U.C.C. §3-414, Official Comment 6.
47. U.C.C. §3-414, Official Comment 6.
48. U.C.C. §3-414(f); U.C.C. §3-414, Official Comment 6.
49. 12 U.S.C. §1821(a).
50. U.C.C. §3-504(a)(i).

Presentment is also excused as to the drawer where the drawer has instructed the drawee not to pay or accept a draft, or where the drawee is not obligated to the drawer to pay the draft.[51] This situation typically occurs when a stop payment order is issued by the drawer of a check. The rationale for this rule is that by having instructed the drawee not to pay the draft, the drawer has no expectation that the draft will be paid. The holder's fault in not presenting the draft caused no harm to the drawer who already fully expected that the draft would not be paid. However, presentment is not excused as to an indorser (assuming that he did not order payment stopped). This exception is somewhat curious. It is true that the indorser, unlike the drawer, expects that the draft will be paid. But if the stop order is effective, the failure of the holder to present the draft will not be the cause of any loss to the indorser. Only if the drawee would have paid the draft over the stop payment order does the holder's failure to present the draft harm the indorser.

Similarly, presentment is excused where the drawer or an indorser has no reason to expect or right to require that the instrument be paid or accepted.[52] An indorser has no reason to expect that an instrument will be paid when, for example, he asserts an adverse claim upon the party obliged to pay. Presentment is also excused where a drawer knows that he has insufficient funds in his account to cover the draft or that the drawee is nonexistent.

Whenever presentment is unnecessary to enforce the obligation of the drawer or indorser pursuant to the terms of the instrument, presentment is excused.[53] Presentment is also excused whenever the party sought to be charged has waived the particular proceeding.[54]

Presentment would be an idle gesture where the maker or acceptor repudiates the obligation to pay the instrument or is in insolvency proceedings.[55] If the maker has died, it may be difficult tracking down the executor or administrator so as to make the presentment. Rather than requiring the party to undergo the potentially futile and time-consuming act of presentment, presentment is excused under all of these circumstances.[56] Notice of dishonor is still required because the indorser may be unaware of the death, insolvency proceedings, or repudiation.

51. U.C.C. §3-504(a)(v).
52. U.C.C. §3-504(a)(iv).
53. U.C.C. §3-504(a)(iii).
54. U.C.C. §3-504(a)(iv); U.C.C. §3-504(b)(ii).
55. U.C.C. §1-201(22) defines "insolvency proceedings."
56. U.C.C. §3-504(a)(ii).

B. Conditions to Liability

2. *Dishonor*

a. Dishonor of Demand Note

A note payable on demand is dishonored if: (1) presentment is duly made to the maker and (2) the note is not paid on the day of presentment.[57] It makes no difference when presentment is made. Presentment can be made one day or five years after issuance.

b. Dishonor of Note Not Payable on Demand

A note that is not payable on demand is dishonored if it is not paid on the day it becomes payable.[58] No presentment is required in order for the note to be dishonored. A note payable on January 1, 1997, is dishonored if it is not paid on that date. The holder can commence a lawsuit against the maker on January 2d even though payment was never demanded. Two types of notes are not dishonored unless presentment has been made. Neither a note payable at or through a bank nor a note whose terms require presentment is dishonored unless presentment is duly made and the note is not paid on the day it becomes payable or on the day of presentment, whichever is later.[59] For example, if the note is payable on June 1st at Bank of America, and presentment is not made until August 1st, the note is dishonored on August 1st.

c. Dishonor of Check

The rules for determining whether a check has been dishonored are quite complex. They will be briefly explained here, but you will not understand their significance until we cover the bank collection process in Chapter 6.

There are two ways in which a check presented to the payor bank (other than for immediate payment over the counter) may be dishonored. (When a check is presented to the payor bank for immediate payment in cash over the counter, the rules for determining dishonor are the same as for other drafts payable on demand.) First, a properly presented check is dishonored if the payor bank properly returns the check or sends notice of dishonor or nonpayment in compliance with §§4-301 and 4-302.[60] Sections 4-301 and 4-302 set

57. U.C.C. §3-502(a)(1); U.C.C. §3-502, Official Comment 3.
58. U.C.C. §3-502(a)(3).
59. U.C.C. §3-502(a)(2); U.C.C. §3-502, Official Comment 3
60. U.C.C. §3-502(b)(1); U.C.C. §3-502, Official Comment 4.

out the time and procedure that a payor bank must follow to make a proper dishonor of a check. Most dishonored checks fall into this category. Under this procedure, the payor bank must promptly return the check to the presenting bank with an indication that payment has been refused (or a notice in lieu of the check if the check is not available for return).[61] The second manner in which a check is dishonored is if the bank not only fails to promptly return the check (or send notice of nonpayment) but also fails to provisionally settle for the check and thus becomes accountable for the check under §4-302.[62] Further discussion of this type of dishonor will be deferred to Chapter 5.

d.   Dishonor of Other Demand Drafts

A draft payable on demand is dishonored if presentment for payment is duly made to the drawee and the draft is not paid on the day of presentment.[63] This applies to checks in only one situation. Checks presented over the counter for immediate payment in cash are dishonored if they are not paid on the day of presentment. Thus, if Bob draws on Wells Bank a check payable to Jill, Wells Bank dishonors the check if despite Jill's presentment for payment over the counter, Wells Bank does not pay the check on the day of presentment. Wells Bank also dishonors the check if it tells Jill that it will not pay the check.

e.   Dishonor of Drafts Not Payable on Demand

The rules for dishonor are more complex for a draft payable at a stated date. For example, assume that Bob draws a draft upon Wells Bank to Jill

---

61. In addition, a payor bank has certain duties under Regulation CC as to the time and manner in which the bank returns a check. These duties are discussed in Chapter 5E(7).

62. U.C.C. §3-502(b)(1); U.C.C. §3-502, Official Comment 4. A drawee bank that is not also the depositary bank becomes accountable for the amount of a check if it has not made a settlement for the check by midnight of the day of presentment. U.C.C. §4-302; U.C.C. §3-502, Official Comment 4. If the drawee bank is also the depositary bank, it becomes accountable for the check if it does not pay the check or return it or send notice of dishonor by its midnight deadline. U.C.C. §3-502, Official Comment 4. In these circumstances, because the payor bank has not settled for the check, the check has not yet been paid. U.C.C. §3-502, Official Comment 4. This situation is to be contrasted with the situation where the payor bank makes a provisional settlement for the check but fails to return the check or give notice of dishonor or non-payment by its midnight deadline. In this case, the settlement becomes final and the check is finally paid. U.C.C. §4-215; U.C.C. §3-502, Official Comment 4. The person entitled to enforce the check has already received the funds and therefore, the check is paid and not dishonored. U.C.C. §3-502, Official Comment 4.

63. U.C.C. §3-502(b)(2); U.C.C. §3-502, Official Comment 4.

payable on June 1st. Jill is now confronted with a choice. If she presents the draft for payment on or after June 1st and payment is not made, the draft will be dishonored.[64] Or Jill may present the draft for acceptance before June 1st.[65] Jill has the right to know whether Wells Bank will honor the draft when it becomes due. Jill, therefore, has the right to present the draft for Wells Bank's acceptance any time before the due date. If Wells Bank refuses to accept the draft on the day it is presented,[66] Jill has an immediate cause of action against Bob on the draft.

Where a draft is payable a fixed number of days after acceptance (called "after sight"), the exact date payment is due is not fixed until the draft has been accepted. A draft payable a fixed number of days after sight must therefore be presented for acceptance to determine when payment is due.[67] The draft is dishonored if presentment for acceptance is duly made, and the draft is not accepted on that day.[68]

f. Dishonor of Accepted Draft

Once a draft is accepted, the holder must present the draft to the acceptor for payment. An accepted draft payable on demand is dishonored if presentment for payment is duly made, and the draft is not paid on the day of presentment.[69] An accepted draft not payable on demand is dishonored if presentment for payment is duly made, and payment is not made on the day it becomes payable or on the day of presentment, whichever is later.[70] For exam-

---

64. U.C.C. §3-502(b)(3)(i). Dishonor of an unaccepted documentary draft occurs according to the rules applicable to other unaccepted drafts. However, payment or acceptance may be delayed without dishonor until no later than the close of the drawee's third business day following the day on which payment or acceptance is required under §3-502(b). U.C.C. §3-502(c). A drawee of a documentary draft is given a longer period to determine whether to pay a draft because of the time necessary to examine the accompanying documents. U.C.C. §3-502, Official Comment 5. The period given coincides with the one prescribed under §5-112 for documentary drafts drawn under a letter of credit. U.C.C. §3-502, Official Comment 5.

65. U.C.C. §3-502(b)(3)(ii); U.C.C. §3-502, Official Comment 4. If a draft is dishonored because timely acceptance of the draft was not made, and the person entitled to demand acceptance consents to a late acceptance, the draft is treated as never having been dishonored from the time of the acceptance. U.C.C. §3-502(f); U.C.C. §3-502, Official Comment 8. If the draft is subsequently presented for payment and is dishonored, the dishonor occurs at that time. U.C.C. §3-502, Official Comment 8.

66. U.C.C. §3-502(b)(3)(ii); U.C.C. §3-502, Official Comment 4.

67. U.C.C. §3-502, Official Comment 4.

68. U.C.C. §3-502(b)(4); U.C.C. §3-502, Official Comment 4.

69. U.C.C. §3-502(d)(1); U.C.C. §3-502, Official Comment 6.

70. U.C.C. §3-502(d)(2); U.C.C. §3-503, Official Comment 6.

ple, an accepted draft payable on August 1st but presented for payment on July 25th is not dishonored until August 1st.

3. Notice of Dishonor

The time within which notice of dishonor must be given depends upon whether or not the instrument is an item taken for collection by a collecting bank. Unless excused,[71] a delay in giving notice of dishonor discharges an indorser on any type of instrument.[72] In contrast, a delay in giving notice of dishonor does not discharge a drawer.[73]

a. Time Within Which Notice of Dishonor Must Be Given

Where an instrument is not taken by a collecting bank for collection, notice of dishonor must be given within the 30 days after the day on which the instrument is dishonored.[74] Because written notice is deemed to be given when sent,[75] the notice can be mailed on the thirtieth day. If the maker dishonors a note on May 1st, all indorsees are entitled to notice of dishonor by May 31st. For example, assume that Paul, as payee, indorses the note to Kate, who indorses the note to Dan. The note is dishonored on April 1st by the maker. Dan has the option to give notice only to Kate or also to Paul. Because Dan is looking only to Kate for payment, Dan on April 23d gives notice of dishonor to Kate only. Kate has until May 1st to give notice of dishonor to Paul. If Kate does not give notice to Paul by May 1st, Paul is discharged from liability as an indorser.[76]

Where an instrument is taken by a collecting bank for collection, the collecting bank must give notice of dishonor before midnight of the next banking day following the banking day on which the bank receives notice of dishonor.[77] For example, if a collecting bank receives notice of dishonor on Friday, it must give notice of dishonor by midnight on Monday, the next banking day. Persons other than a collecting bank must give notice of dishonor

71. U.C.C. §3-504(c).
72. U.C.C. §3-415(c).
73. U.C.C. §3-503, Official Comment 1.
74. U.C.C. §3-503(c); U.C.C. §3-503, Official Comment 2.
75. U.C.C. §1-201(26).
76. U.C.C. §3-415(c).
77. U.C.C. §3-503(c).

within 30 days following the day on which the person receives notice of dishonor.[78] Assume that a check is indorsed by Paul to Kate to Dan. Assume that Dan receives notice of dishonor on August 1. Dan can give notice of dishonor to either Paul only, Kate only, or to both Paul and Kate. Assume that he gives notice of dishonor to Kate on August 15th. Notice of dishonor is timely as to Kate. Kate now has until September 14th (30 days from the date Kate received notice of dishonor) to give notice of dishonor to Paul. If, instead, Dan waits until September 3d and gives notice of dishonor to both Paul and Kate, the notice is late and both are discharged. Ironically, in this latter example, Paul received notice earlier than he did in the previous example. If Dan gives only Kate notice of dishonor on September 3d, the notice is late and Kate is discharged. Kate should have no right to give notice of dishonor to Paul. Paul should also be discharged.

b. Manner of Giving Notice of Dishonor

Notice of dishonor may be given by any commercially reasonable means. It may be oral, electronic, by telephone or written.[79] Any terms that adequately identify the instrument and indicate that the instrument has been dishonored or not paid or accepted is sufficient. Return of an instrument given to a bank for collection is sufficient notice of dishonor.

The notice must sufficiently identify the instrument so that the recipient can determine which parties he must pursue. An error in the description that does not mislead the party notified will not invalidate the notice. Written notice is effective when sent even though it may never be received.[80] Providing that notice of dishonor is effective even though never received is not unfair to the intended recipient of the notice. Under §3-503(c), the time within which a party must give notice as to an item collected by a collecting bank does not commence until the giver has himself received notice; therefore, the recipient still has 30 days to give notice no matter when he actually receives notice.

c. When Notice of Dishonor Excused

If notice of dishonor itself or a delay in its performance is excused, notice of dishonor is treated as though it was given within the prescribed time limits. A delay in giving notice of dishonor is excused if the delay is caused by circumstances beyond the control of the person giving the notice, and the per-

---

78. U.C.C. §3-503(c); U.C.C. §3-503, Official Comment 2.
79. U.C.C. §3-503(b).
80. U.C.C. §1-201(26).

son giving notice exercises reasonable diligence after the cause of the delay ceases to operate.[81] The delay is excused as long as the circumstances would deter a person of ordinary prudence from giving notice.

The following are examples of some of the circumstances that might excuse a delay in the giving of notice of dishonor: (1) illness; (2) suspension of communication facilities; (3) war; (4) suspension of commercial intercourse between countries; [82](5) unforeseen absenteeism of employees or strike; or (6) inability to locate party to whom notice must be given.

Whenever notice of dishonor is unnecessary to enforce the obligation of the party to pay the instrument pursuant to the terms of the instrument, notice of dishonor is excused as to that party.[83] Notice of dishonor is also excused whenever the party sought to be charged has waived notice of dishonor.[84] A waiver of presentment also waives notice of dishonor.[85]

C.   TRANSFEROR'S LIABILITY

A negotiable instrument is a type of personal property. A purchaser of an instrument expects the instrument to be authentic and to provide for legally enforceable obligations. When a person receives consideration for transferring an instrument, he makes certain warranties as to the authenticity and the enforceability of the instrument. These warranties are called the "transfer warranties" and are undertaken by any person who transfers an instrument and receives consideration for the transfer. The transfer warranties are to be distinguished from the presentment warranties that are given to the person making, paying, or accepting the instrument. The presentment warranties are discussed in Chapter 4A(3).

The transfer warranties are in addition to and independent of any liability undertaken by that person as an indorser. However, because these warranties are given only by transferors who receive consideration, neither anomalous indorsers[86] nor transferors who have given the instrument as a gift make these transfer warranties.

81. U.C.C. §3-504(c).
82. U.C.C. §4-109(b).
83. U.C.C. §3-504(b)(i).
84. U.C.C. §3-504(a)(iv); U.C.C. §3-504(b)(ii).
85. U.C.C. §3-504(b).
86. Indorsements made by persons who were not holders at the time of their indorsement. U.C.C. §3-205(d).

C. Transferor's Liability

Any person who transfers an instrument for consideration makes the transfer warranties even if he does not indorse the instrument.[87] Thus, where a person transfers an instrument either without indorsing the instrument or by indorsing it "without recourse," the transferor undertakes the transfer warranties although not the indorser's contract.[88] Where there is an unexcused delay in making presentment or giving notice of dishonor,[89] although a person's liability as indorser may be discharged, he remains liable on his transfer warranties as the two operate independently. Similarly, a transferor may nevertheless have breached his transfer warranty even though he is not liable on his indorser's contract because the instrument is not yet due. For example, assume that Alice makes a note payable in two years to Bob who transfers the note by indorsement to Carl. As soon as Carl discovers that Bob has breached one of his transfer warranties, Carl may bring an action to recover for breach of the warranty even though because the note is not yet due, Bob is not yet liable on his indorser's contract.

1. To Whom Transfer Warranties Made

Outside of the bank collection process, a transferor makes the transfer warranties to his transferee and if the transfer is by indorsement, also to subsequent transferees.[90] Thus, when the transferor does not indorse the instrument, he makes the warranty only to his immediate transferee. If he indorses the instrument, he makes the warranty to all subsequent transferees. The reason an indorser's warranty runs to all subsequent transferees is that these subsequent parties may have relied upon his signature in purchasing the instrument. In reality, as we will see, whether he indorses the instrument or not will seldom have an effect on the ultimate allocation of the loss.

Let us return to the check that Bob issues to Jill. Assume the following chain of transfers. Jill indorses the check in blank and transfers it to Sally who transfers, without indorsement, the check to Grocer who indorses and transfers the check to Check Cashing Service. (See Figure 3.3.)

---

87. U.C.C. §3-416(a); U.C.C. §3-416, Official Comment 1.
88. U.C.C. §3-415(b).
89. U.C.C. §3-415(c) and (e).
90. U.C.C. §3-416(a).

FIGURE 3.3

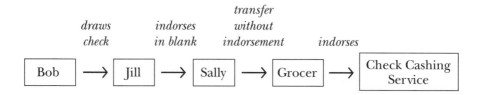

Since Sally did not indorse the check, she makes the transfer warranties only to Grocer. In the event of a breach of warranty, Check Cashing Service may sue Grocer or Jill, but not Sally. Its inability to sue Sally will probably not affect the ultimate allocation of the loss. In the first place, since Jill is liable to Sally, if Check Cashing Service recovers from Jill directly, the loss falls on the person (Jill) who is ultimately liable for breach of the warranty. If Check Cashing Service sues Grocer, Grocer may recover from Sally. Since Grocer is Sally's immediate transferee, Sally makes the warranties to Grocer. Sally will then recover from Jill.

If the instrument enters the bank collection process, any customer of a collecting bank that transfers the item and receives a settlement or other consideration makes the warranties to its transferee and to any subsequent collecting bank.[91] Whether or not the customer indorses the instrument, the customer makes the transfer warranties to all subsequent banks. Thus, assume that Check Cashing Service deposits the check in its account in Crocker Bank and Crocker Bank transfers the check to Interstate Bank for presentment to Wells Bank. (See Figure 3.4.)

FIGURE 3.4

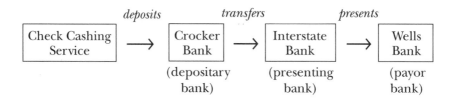

91. U.C.C. §4-207(a).

C. Transferor's Liability

Even if Check Cashing Service does not indorse the check, it makes the transfer warranties to both Crocker Bank and Interstate Bank.

2. *Content of Transferor's Warranties*

The five transfer warranties are specifically designed to allocate certain risks to the transferor. The transferor warrants that:

1. he is a person entitled to enforce the instrument;
2. all signatures are authentic and authorized;
3. the instrument has not been altered;
4. the instrument is not subject to a defense or claim in recoupment of any party that can be asserted against the warrantor; and
5. the warrantor has no knowledge of any insolvency proceedings commenced with respect to the maker or acceptor, or, in the case of an unaccepted draft, the drawer.[92]

The major difference between liability of an indorser and that of a transferor is that, with the exception noted below, a transferor does not guarantee the solvency of other parties to the instrument while an indorser, in effect, undertakes such a guarantee. We can see this difference in our example above. Assuming that Bob and Jill are insolvent, Grocer will suffer the loss. Check Cashing Service can recover from Grocer on its indorsement. However, Grocer cannot recover from Sally. Sally did not breach her transfer warranty. Because she did not indorse the check, she did not undertake liability as an indorser. Had she indorsed the check, Grocer could have recovered from his or her indorser's obligation.

a. Warranty That Transferor Is a Person Entitled to Enforce the Instrument

A transferor warrants that he is a person entitled to enforce the instrument.[93] This is basically a warranty that there are no unauthorized or missing indorsements that prevent the transferee from becoming a person entitled to enforce the instrument.[94] An example will help make operation of this warranty clear. Assume the following transaction. Bob draws a check payable to Jill

---

92. U.C.C. §3-416(a).
93. U.C.C. §4-207(a)(1); U.C.C. §3-416(a)(1).
94. U.C.C. §3-416, Official Comment 2.

who transfers by indorsement the check to Joan. Joan loses the check. Fred finds the check and forges an indorsement in Joan's name to Diane. Diane indorses the check to Dave. Upon presentment the check is dishonored. (See Figure 3.5.)

FIGURE 3.5

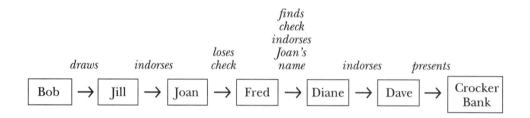

Dave sues Diane, Fred, Joan, and Jill. Which of these persons are liable for breach of the transfer warranty that they are a person entitled to enforce the check? Jill does not breach her warranty. When Jill transferred the instrument, she was a person entitled to enforce the instrument. Because Joan did not voluntarily deliver the check to Fred, Joan did not transfer the check and therefore does not make the transfer warranties. Because Joan's indorsement is forged, Fred is not a person entitled to enforce the instrument. He therefore breaches his transfer warranty.[95] Even though Diane was unaware that the indorsement was forged, she nonetheless breaches this warranty because she is not a person entitled to enforce the instrument.

b.   Warranty That All Signatures Are Authentic and Authorized

A transferor warrants that all signatures are authentic and authorized.[96] A forged or unauthorized signature of a drawer, maker, indorser, or acceptor breaches this warranty. When only an anomalous indorsement (an indorsement not in the chain of title) is forged or unauthorized, a subsequent transferor breaches the warranty that all signatures are authentic and authorized

---

95. Fred makes this warranty to Dave even though Fred did not indorse the check in his own name. Under U.C.C. §3-403(a), Fred's unauthorized signing of Joan's name is effective as Fred's own signature. Therefore, in essence, Fred has indorsed the check to Diane.

96. U.C.C. §4-207(a)(2); U.C.C. §3-416(a)(2).

although he does not breach the warranty that he is a person entitled to enforce the instruments. Because an anomalous indorsement is not in the chain of title, a subsequent transferor may still be a person entitled to enforce the instrument. In contrast, when an indorsement in the chain of title is forged or otherwise unauthorized, the transferor breaches both the warranty that he is a person entitled to enforce the instrument and the warranty that all signatures are authentic and authorized.

c. Warranty of No Alteration

A transferor warrants that the instrument has not been altered.[97] A transferee of an instrument expects that the instrument purchased will be enforceable according to its terms at the time of purchase. We discuss what constitutes an alteration in Chapter 4C. For our purposes now, just assume that an alteration is any unauthorized change in the terms of the instrument. Let us look at an example. Assume that Bob draws a check in the amount of $50 payable to Jill. Jill transfers by indorsement the check to Fred who raises the check to $500 and transfers by indorsement the check to Diane. Diane transfers the check by indorsement to Rick. The check is dishonored upon presentment. (See Figure 3.6.)

FIGURE 3.6

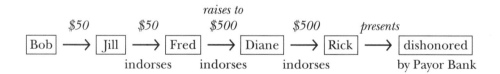

Rick sues Diane, Fred, and Jill. Because the check was not altered at the time that Jill transferred the check, Jill does not breach the warranty that the check has not been altered. However, both Fred and Diane breach this warranty.

Alteration also includes the unauthorized addition of words or numbers to an incomplete instrument. Assume that Bob, who is going out of town, asks his friend Jill to arrange to have his air conditioning system repaired. Bob leaves a check payable to Fred, the air conditioning repairman, with Jill. Because Bob does not know how much Fred will charge, he leaves the amount

---

97. U.C.C. §3-416(a)(3); U.C.C. §4-207(a)(3).

blank. However, Bob tells Jill not to pay more than $100. The bill comes to $700. Jill fills out the check for the entire $700. Fred cashes the check at Check Cashing Service. Upon presentment to the Bank of America (the payor bank), the check is dishonored because Bob does not have sufficient funds in his account to cover the check.

We will discuss in Chapter 4C that Check Cashing Service, being a holder in due course, could enforce the instrument against Bob for the entire $700.[98] This would, however, require that Check Cashing Service prove that it has taken the instrument for value, in good faith and without notice of the alteration. Check Cashing Service may choose, instead, to recover from Fred for breach of his warranty that the instrument has not been altered. To recover from Fred, Check Cashing Service would not have to prove its holder-in-due-course status. Fred would then be left with the task of recovering from Bob.

d. Warranty That Transferor Not Subject to Any Defense or Claims in Recoupment

A transferor warrants that the instrument is free from any defense or claim in recoupment of any party that can be asserted against the warrantor.[99] In essence, the transferor warrants that if he were to sue any party on the instrument, none of these parties would have a defense or claim in recoupment that could be asserted against him. A transferor who is a holder in due course himself breaches this warranty only to the extent that he would be subject to a defense or claim in recoupment. Such defenses or claims in recoupment include only "real defenses" or defenses assertible against the holder in due course himself.[100] Review Chapter 2 as to what defenses and claims in recoupment are assertible against a holder in due course. The transferor breaches this warranty even if the transferee is a holder in due course who would take the instrument free from the particular defense or claim in recoupment.[101]

Some examples may make this warranty more clear. Assume that Bob draws a check payable to Jill for the purchase of a car. Because the car has a defective transmission, Bob has a claim in recoupment against Jill. Jill has no notice of the defect in the transmission and therefore is a holder in due course. Jill negotiates the check to Sally, who takes as a holder in due course. Being a holder in due course who has not dealt with Bob, Sally can recover

---

98. U.C.C. §3-407(c).

99. U.C.C. §3-416(a)(4); U.C.C. §4-207(a)(4); U.C.C. §3-416, Official Comment 3.

100. U.C.C. §3-305(b).

101. U.C.C. §3-416, Official Comment 3.

from Bob notwithstanding Bob's claim in recoupment. However, in order to recover from Bob, Sally must prove that she is a holder in due course. Sally may not want to go to the trouble and expense of litigating her holder-in-due-course status. Sally can avoid this trouble and expense by proceeding against Jill for breach of Jill's warranty that no defenses or claims in recoupment are good against Jill. Even though Jill is a holder in due course, she takes subject to Bob's claim in recoupment because she dealt with him. If Sally negotiates the check to Wells Bank, she does not breach the warranty she made to Wells Bank since she is not subject to Bob's claim in recoupment.

e. Warranty of No Knowledge of Insolvency Proceedings

A transferor does not warrant that prior parties are solvent or that the transferee will not have difficulty in collecting from prior parties.[102] A transferor does warrant that it has no knowledge of insolvency proceedings with respect to the maker, acceptor, or drawer of an unaccepted item.[103] A transferor who knows that insolvency proceedings have been instituted against one of the above three parties in essence commits a fraud by not informing her transferee of this fact. No warranty is made as to the transferor's lack of knowledge of any insolvency proceedings instituted against an indorser. The distinction between the insolvency of the drawer, maker or acceptor and that of an indorser makes sense. It is expected that the instrument will be paid by one of the above three parties. In contrast, it is unlikely that the holder expects to recover from prior indorsers, which explains why the transfer warranty only covers the drawer, maker, or acceptor of an instrument.

D. ACCOMMODATION PARTIES

1. Who Is an Accommodation Party?

When a lender ("creditor") contemplates extending credit to a borrower ("debtor"), the creditor may have doubts about the ability of the debtor to repay the loan. In many situations, the debtor does not have adequate collateral to fully secure the loan. When this happens, the creditor may demand that

---

102. U.C.C. §3-416, Official Comment 4.
103. U.C.C. §3-416(a)(5); U.C.C. §4-207(a)(5); U.C.C. §3-416, Official Comment 4.

the debtor find a third person to agree, along with the debtor, to repay the loan. This third person is called a "surety."

Assume that Smith Family Corporation, a newly formed corporation desiring to operate a drugstore, wants to borrow start-up money from Jones State Bank. A great deal of this money is to be used for advertising and similar purposes that do not involve the purchase of assets in which Jones State Bank can take a security interest. Jones State Bank requires Jim Smith to personally guaranty the loan to Smith Family Corporation. Jones State Bank is the creditor. Smith Family Corporation is the debtor and Jim Smith is the surety. Jim Smith is a surety because, although both Smith Family Corporation and Jim Smith are bound to repay Jones State Bank, between Smith Family Corporation and Jim Smith, Smith Family Corporation ultimately should be the one that is paying the obligation.

Article 3 has its own rules regarding suretyship. Under Article 3, rather than being called "surety" and "debtor," the parties are called, respectively "accommodation party" and "accommodated party." Here is the rule for determining whether a person is an accommodation party:

> If an instrument is issued for value given for the benefit of a party to the instrument ("accommodated party"), and another party to the instrument ("accommodation party") signs the instrument for the purpose of incurring liability on the instrument without being a direct beneficiary of the value given for the instrument, the instrument is signed by the accommodation party "for accommodation."[104]

There are very specific requirements for determining who qualifies as an accommodation party. A person is an accommodation party only when both the surety and the debtor sign the same instrument. If both Jim Smith and Smith Family Corporation sign the same promissory note, Jim Smith is the accommodation party and Smith Family Corporation is the accommodated party. As an accommodation party, Jim Smith's rights and obligations are governed by Article 3. These obligations are set forth in §§3-116, 3-305, 3-415, 3-419, and 3-605.[105]

---

104. U.C.C. §3-419(a).

105. See PEB Commentary on the Uniform Commercial Code, Commentary Concerning Suretyship Issues Under Sections 3-116, 3-305, 3-415, 3-419, and 3-605, Final Draft (February 10, 1994), Issue 1, Discussion.

To the extent that these sections do not resolve a particular issue regarding the rights or duties of the surety, the general law of suretyship is applicable pursuant to §1-103. See PEB Commentary on the Uniform Commercial Code, Commentary Concerning Suretyship Issues Under Sections 3-116, 3-305, 3-415, 3-419, and 3-605, Final Draft (Feb. 10, 1994), Issue 1, Discussion.

D. Accommodation Parties

If Jim Smith signs a *separate* guaranty agreement instead of signing the note made by Smith Family Corporation, Jim Smith is not an accommodation party. He is still a surety and his rights as a surety are governed by the general law of suretyship. Similarly, where Jim Smith signs his own note to guarantee a debt owed by Smith Family Corporation, Jim Smith is a surety, but not an accommodation party. His rights as a surety are again governed by general suretyship law. Under the general law of suretyship, Jim Smith will be entitled to most of the same rights to which an accommodation party is entitled under Article 3.[106]

a. Collection Guaranteed

There is a special class of accommodation parties under Article 3 that assumes a more limited undertaking than other accommodation parties. Where "collection guaranteed" or equivalent words are added to a signature, the signer undertakes only a guaranty of collection.[107] If an accommodation party guarantees collection, he is obliged to pay the amount due only if the holder can not collect from the accommodated party. This inability to collect from the accommodated party must be evidenced by either (1) execution of judgment against the accommodated party being returned unsatisfied, (2) insolvency of or institution of insolvency proceeding against the accommodated party, (3) inability to serve the accommodated party with process, or (4) otherwise being apparent that payment cannot be obtained from the accommodated party. To have this limited liability as a guarantor of collection, the signature of the party must be accompanied by words that unambiguously indicate that he intends to guarantee only collection of the instrument.

b. Test for Determining Who Is Accommodation Party

The test to determine if a person is an accommodation party is whether he has received a direct benefit from the value given for the instrument. Only if he is not a direct beneficiary of the value given for the instrument can he be

---

106. These rights include, among others, the rights of subrogation, see Restatement (3d), Suretyship, Council Draft No. 2, §§23-27 (April 2, 1993); Simpson, Handbook of the Law of Suretyship, 205-223 (1950), and the right of reimbursement. See Restatement (3d), Suretyship, Council Draft No. 2, §§18-21 (April 2, 1993); Simpson, Handbook of the Law of Suretyship, 224-237 (1950).

107. U.C.C. §3-419(d); U.C.C. §3-419, Comment 4.

an accommodation party.[108] Assume that your sister asks you to co-make a note with her in order for her to purchase a car. You are an accommodation party since the benefit of the value given for the note, namely the car, went to your sister and not to you. In contrast, if the car was to be used by both you and your sister, you would be a direct beneficiary of the proceeds paid for the instrument and therefore not an accommodation party.

The fact that a person receives an indirect benefit from the value given for the instrument will not deny that person accommodation party status. So, in the above example, even if you benefit indirectly because you no longer have to drive your sister around, you will still be an accommodation party.

The definition of accommodation party contains a subtle, seemingly illogical, distinction. In order for a person to be an accommodation party, the value given for the "issuance" of the instrument must go to the accommodated party. Where you and your sister co-made the note to the car dealer for your sister to purchase a car, the value given for issuance of the note went to your sister, the accommodated party. Being that the value given for the issuance of the note was for the benefit of your sister, you qualified as an accommodation party.

In contrast, if the value given for the issuance of the instrument is not for the benefit of the accommodated party, even though value given for the negotiation of the instrument is for her benefit, you do not thereby qualify as an accommodation party. For example, assume that your sister receives a paycheck from her employer. Because she is visiting you from out of town, she needs to cash the check at your bank. Your bank requires that you also indorse the check. You are not an accommodation party. The check was originally issued for the work your sister performed for her employer. The value received by your sister, namely the cash from the bank, is from the negotiation and not the issuance of the check. Despite the fact that you are not an accommodation party, you are still an indorser and may be entitled to the same rights and defenses as an accommodation party. In addition, you are a surety and entitled to whatever rights a surety has under the general law of suretyship.

c. Accommodation Party Liable in Capacity in Which She Signs

An accommodation party has a type of dual personality. On the one hand, because he is usually doing the accommodated party a favor (or at the least is not intended to be ultimately liable as between the two of them), he is granted some special rights and defenses. On the other hand, since he has signed a

---

108. U.C.C. §3-419, Official Comment 1.

negotiable instrument, he is liable in whatever capacity he has signed, that is, indorser, maker, acceptor, or drawer. Although an accommodation party usually signs as either a co-maker or an anomalous indorser,[109] he may sign the instrument as a maker, drawer, acceptor, or indorser.

Except for those parties guarantying collection only, an accommodation party is obliged to pay the instrument in the capacity in which he signs.[110] Thus, if the accommodation party signs as an indorser, he undertakes the indorser's contract[111] under which the accommodation party's promise to pay is conditioned upon dishonor and its requisite notice of dishonor.[112] The liability of an accommodation party who signs as a maker or acceptor is not conditioned upon dishonor or notice of dishonor.

2. *Relationship between Accommodation and Accommodated Parties*

As should be apparent from the above discussion, the accommodated party is the person who is benefitting from the accommodation party undertaking liability on the instrument. Where you, as a favor to your sister, co-sign a note in order for her to obtain a loan to purchase a car, your sister should ultimately be the one to pay off the loan. If your sister makes the payment, she should have no right to recover any of the payment from you. For this reason, you as an accommodation party are not liable on the instrument to the party accommodated (your sister), nor are you liable for contribution to the accommodated party in the event of payment by the accommodated party.[113] Conversely, if the holder obtains payment from you (the accommodation party), you may recover the entire amount from your sister. You were merely doing your sister a favor. It would be preposterous for her to be able to refuse to reimburse you. An accommodation party (you) who pays an instrument is entitled to reimbursement from the accommodated party (your sister).[114]

---

109. U.C.C. §3-419 (b); U.C.C. §3-419, Official Comment 1.

110. U.C.C. §3-419(d); U.C.C. §3-419(b).

111. U.C.C. §3-419, Official Comment 4.

112. U.C.C. §3-415. As a result, a holder does not have to resort to the collateral before pursuing the indorser.

113. U.C.C. §3-419(e).

114. A question arises as to whether an accommodation party who has paid the instrument may obtain reimbursement from the accommodated party if the latter party had a defense to payment of the instrument. If the accommodation party was unaware of the defense, it is clear that he has a right of reimbursement. See PEB Commentary on the Uniform Commercial Code, Commentary Concerning Suretyship Issues Under Sections 3-116, 3-305, 3-415, 3-419,

This promise is implied in the relationship whether or not the accommodated (your sister) party makes any express promise.

The accommodation party's right of reimbursement[115] does not require that the accommodation party fully pay the instrument. However, the right of reimbursement only allows the accommodation party to recover from the accommodated party the amount that the accommodation party paid on the instrument. If you pay the car dealer $100 of the $2,000 loan balance, you can recover the $100 from your sister. Possession of the instrument is not necessary in order for you to exercise your right of reimbursement.

The accommodation party has other rights against the accommodated party.[116] The accommodation party, upon payment of the instrument, is entitled to enforce the instrument against the party accommodated.[117] Upon full payment, the accommodation party obtains all of the rights on the instrument and as to any collateral[118] of the party he paid. This permits the accommodation party to enforce the instrument according to all of its terms including any provision for attorney's fees or interest. In other words, upon payment of the instrument, the accommodation party takes the place of the holder as regards the accommodated party. You, as the accommodation party, obtain the car dealer's rights as holder of the note. If the car dealer retained a security interest in the car to secure the note, you now have the security interest and become the secured party.

Questions may arise as to who is the accommodation party and who is the accommodated party. One scenario is where, for example, Modern Door Corporation is planning to issue a note to Sommer, which Sommer plans to

---

and 3-605, Final Draft (Feb. 10, 1994), Issue 3, Discussion. If the accommodation party is aware of the defense, ordinarily he would not be entitled to reimbursement. See PEB Commentary on the Uniform Commercial Code, Commentary Concerning Suretyship Issues Under Sections 3-116, 3-305, 3-415, 3-419, and 3-605, Final Draft (Feb. 10, 1994), Issue 3, Discussion. However, the Code leaves it to the general law of suretyship to determine whether in a specific case reimbursement is justified. See PEB Commentary on the Uniform Commercial Code, Commentary Concerning Suretyship Issues Under Sections 3-116, 3-305, 3-415, 3-419, and 3-605, Final Draft (Feb. 10, 1994), Issue 3, Discussion.

115. U.C.C. §3-419(e).

116. The accommodation party has a third possible right. Under the general law of suretyship, if the accommodated party fails to pay the instrument when due, the accommodation party may bring a suit in equity to compel his performance. This right of exoneration does not affect the right of the person entitled to enforce the instrument to immediately recover from the accommodation party. There is no reason to believe that Article 3 in any way eliminates the right of exoneration. See PEB Commentary on the Uniform Commercial Code, Commentary Concerning Suretyship Issues Under Sections 3-116, 3-305, 3-415, 3-419, and 3-605, Final Draft (Feb. 10, 1994), Issue 2, Discussion.

117. U.C.C. §3-419(e); U.C.C. §3-419, Official Comment 5.

118. U.C.C. §3-419(e); U.C.C. §3-419, Official Comment 5.

sell to a bank. The bank has indicated that it will not purchase the note unless a financially stable third party indorses the note. Sommer requests that the president of Modern Door Corporation indorse the note. The question becomes: Is the president accommodating Modern Door Corporation or Sommer? The issue is only relevant as to whom Sommer may seek to recover from upon default by Modern Door Corporation. If the president is accommodating Modern Door Corporation, Sommer can recover from the president personally upon its payment to the bank. If the president is accommodating Sommer, Sommer may not recover from him. In this case, the issue is one of fact. Was the president doing this as a favor to Sommer or was Modern Door Corporation obtaining some type of advantage or benefit because of his indorsement?

The second scenario involves two persons both acting as accommodation parties. The issue here is the relationship between these two accommodation parties. In the absence of an agreement to the contrary, where two parties sign in the same capacity in accommodation for another party, the accommodation parties are co-sureties. Being co-sureties, they are jointly and severally liable. For example, assume that both you and your brother-in-law sign as accommodation-makers for your sister. Because neither you nor your brother-in-law received a direct benefit, you are both accommodation parties and are presumed to be co-sureties and as such are jointly and severally liable.[119] After one of you pays the instrument, you have a right of contribution from the other as a co-surety.[120] Thus, if you make payment, you can obtain half of the amount you paid from your brother-in-law.

In our example, however, the presumption that both you and your brother-in-law are co-sureties may be rebutted. You and your brother-in-law may have an express or implied understanding that because your sister is his wife, he, and not you, will be ultimately liable in the event that your sister does not pay. In this event, you are an accommodation party for both your brother-in-law and your sister. If you make payment, you may recover fully from your brother-in-law. If he makes payment, even though he may recover from your sister, he may not recover from you.[121] This is called a sub-suretyship relationship. Although both you and your brother-in-law are sureties for your sister, you are a sub-surety for your brother-in-law.

---

119. U.C.C. §3-116(a). See PEB Commentary on the Uniform Commercial Code, Commentary Concerning Suretyship Issues Under Sections 3-116, 3-305, 3-415, 3-419, and 3-605, Final Draft (Feb. 10, 1994), Issue 4, Discussion.

120. U.C.C. §3-116(b). See PEB Commentary on the Uniform Commercial Code, Commentary Concerning Suretyship Issues Under Sections 3-116, 3-305, 3-415, 3-419, and 3-605, Final Draft (Feb. 10, 1994), Issue 4, Discussion.

121. U.C.C. §3-419(e).

3. Defenses Available to Accommodation Party

Because an accommodation party receives no direct benefit and incurs liability so that the accommodated party can receive the benefit, the accommodation party is deemed for practically all purposes to have bargained for whatever consideration is received by the accommodated party. His obligation is supported by any consideration given to the accommodated party for the issuance of the instrument. As a result, his obligation may be enforced whether or not the accommodation party himself received any consideration.[122]

In most situations, the accommodation party in fact does receive true consideration. This is because consideration includes benefits flowing to a third party. For example, if a father buys a car for his son, the father's promise to pay for the car is supported by the car given to the son. The car is the benefit that the father is bargaining for. However, as long as the instrument was issued for value for the benefit of the accommodated party, the accommodation party may not raise the defense of lack of consideration even though he has in fact received no benefit in any form. For instance, assume that the son had borrowed money from a bank to purchase the car. The bank, although the loan is not yet in default, asks that the father indorse the note. The father obliges. Although the father obtained nothing that would qualify as consideration for either himself or his son, the defense of want of consideration is unavailable to the father.[123] The defense of want of consideration is not available to the father because consideration, as discussed in Chapter 2, may take the form of an antecedent debt. The father does not have the defense of want of consideration because any consideration the son (the accommodated party) received is deemed to have been received by the father (the accommodation party).

a. Right of Accommodation Party to Raise Accommodated Party's Defenses

We saw in Chapter 2E(2)(c) that an indorser (or other party) has no right to raise defenses of other parties to the instruments. There is, however, one exception to this rule. Unlike an indorser, an accommodation party stands in the shoes of the accommodated party. Thus, with a few exceptions, the accommodation party may raise any of the accommodated party's defenses or claims of recoupment.[124] For example, if the car is not delivered, the son has the

122. U.C.C. §3-419(b); U.C.C. §3-419, Official Comment 2.
123. U.C.C. §§3-303; 3-419.
124. U.C.C. §3-305(d).

defense of failure of consideration. The father may raise this defense. If the car has defective brakes, the son has a claim in recoupment for breach of warranty. The father may raise this claim in recoupment. Denying the father the right to raise his son's defenses would allow the creditor a windfall at the father's expense.

In contrast, the accommodation party should not be permitted to raise a set-off of the accommodated party, which arises out of a separate transaction.[125] Any separate transaction between the son and the creditor are of no concern to the father. The creditor obtained the father's accommodation on this particular instrument and should expect payment from the father. If the father could raise a set-off from a separate transaction in which the creditor owes the son money, the father would have the ability to, in effect, force the son to raise this set-off, possibly against the son's will.

The right of the accommodation party to raise the accommodated party's defenses is subject to an exception. The accommodation party may not raise as a defense to his own obligation to pay the accommodated party's discharge in insolvency proceedings, infancy, or lack of legal capacity.[126] He is not allowed to raise these three defenses because these are the precise risks that the creditor was attempting to avoid by obtaining the signature of the accommodation party. For example, one of the primary reasons why a lender will ask that a corporate officer act as an accommodation party for the corporation is to guard against the possibility that the corporation may file for bankruptcy. If the corporate officer could raise the corporation's discharge in bankruptcy as a defense to his obligation to pay the lender, the lender loses the sole benefit of obtaining the officer's guaranty. Similarly, a minor could never purchase any goods on credit if the minor's father could raise the child's minority as a grounds for defeating his obligation to pay on his guaranty.

b. Accommodation Party's Own Defenses

The accommodation party may also have defenses of his own. An accommodation party may raise any of his own real defenses against any person.

---

125. U.C.C. §3-305(a)(3). However, under the general law of suretyship, there are certain situations where the surety may have the right to raise an unrelated setoff against the obligee. These include where the principal obligor has assigned the claim to the surety or consented to its use or where the principal obligor is made a party to the action. See Restatement (3d), Suretyship, Council Draft No. 3, §31 (April 8, 1994). Under these circumstances, although the accommodation party would not have the right to raise the defense under U.C.C. §3-305(a)(3), the rules of civil procedure of the subject jurisdiction may allow the setoff to be asserted as a counterclaim.

126. U.C.C. §3-305(d).

These defenses include infancy, incapacity, duress, illegality, fraud in the factum, and discharge in insolvency proceedings.[127] For example, the accommodation party's own discharge in bankruptcy is a defense against any holder of the instrument. However, because the accommodation party steps into the shoes of the accommodated party, he may be denied the right to raise defenses that the accommodated party could not raise. For example, if the accommodated party is not subject to usury laws, the accommodation party cannot raise the defense of usury even though he would otherwise be entitled to such a defense.[128]

An accommodation party may want to assert as a defense that the consideration promised to him by the accommodated party has failed or that the instrument was used for a purpose different than as agreed or that a condition precedent to the effectiveness of his signature was not fulfilled. For example, a partner's signature in accommodation for his partner may be conditioned on the note being used for a partnership purpose. If the note is used for the accommodated party's personal purpose, the accommodation party may want to defend against his own liability on the grounds that the note was used for a purpose different than as agreed. Any such defense is clearly unavailable against a holder in due course.[129] However, even where the holder is not in due course, such defenses should be unavailable as against any taker who was unaware of the condition (or special purpose) at the time he took the instrument.[130] A holder, whether or not qualifying as a holder in due course, who is without notice of the condition (or special purpose) has been misled and should take free of this defense. Most courts rest their decision in these cases on the grounds that the parol evidence rule bars evidence that the accommodation party had an understanding with the accommodated party (or with the payee) that he would be liable only under certain conditions.[131]

127. U.C.C. §3-305(a)(1).

128. See Artistic Greetings, Inc. v. Sholom Greeting Card Co., 36 A.D. 2d 68, 318 N.Y.S. 2d 623, 8 U.C.C. Rep. Serv. 1294 (1971).

129. U.C.C. §3-305(b).

130. For a case under former Article 3, see Armstrong v. Armstrong, 714 F. Supp 451, 10 U.C.C. Rep. Serv. 2d 1277 (D. Colo. 1989) (payee not aware of agreement not subject to agreement between co-makers that one of co-makers would not be liable on note).

131. For cases under former Article 3, see Commerce Natl. Bank in Lake Worth v. Baron, 336 F. Supp. 1125, 9 U.C.C. Rep. Serv. 1376 (E.D. Pa. 1971); First Natl. City Bank v. Cooper, 50 A.D.2d 518, 375 N.Y.S.2d 118, 18 U.C.C. Rep. Serv. 159 (1975); Marine Midland Trust Co. of New York v. Couphos, 3 U.C.C. Rep. Serv. 66 (N.Y. Sup. Ct. 1965); Peters, Suretyship Under Article 3 of the Uniform Commercial Code, 77 Yale L.J. 854-858 (1968).

D. Accommodation Parties

4. Discharge of Indorsers and Accommodation Parties ("Suretyship Defenses")

When the accommodation party pays the instrument, she has a right to recover from the accommodated party.[132] Similarly, an indorser who pays may recover from the drawer, maker, acceptor, or prior indorser.[133] Both an accommodation party and an indorser who pays the instrument step into the shoes of the person who was paid and acquire that person's rights through the doctrine of subrogation. These include any rights that person had on the instrument and to any collateral acquired from the primary obligor. For example, if Betty acts as an accommodation party for Alice and is called upon to pay Cindy, Betty acquires Cindy's rights on the instrument and to any collateral Alice may have given to secure the loan. Betty can, therefore, obtain repayment of the money she paid Cindy by selling the collateral Alice gave to secure the loan. Betty will suffer the loss only if the collateral is insufficient to repay the debt and Alice is unable to pay the deficiency.

If Cindy causes harm to Betty's recourse against Alice or to the collateral, Betty is injured to the extent of the harm. To the extent an indorser or accommodation party is injured by any unjustifiable action of the person entitled to enforce the instrument (Cindy), the injured indorser or accommodation party may be discharged under §3-605.[134]

---

132. U.C.C. §3-419(e).

133. U.C.C. §3-412; U.C.C. §3-413(a); U.C.C. §3-414(b); U.C.C. §3-415(a). Of course, an accommodated indorser is liable to the accommodation party whether that party is another indorser, the maker, acceptor, or drawer.

134. Where neither §3-419 nor §3-605 codifies a defense traditionally available to a surety, it is unclear to what extent the defense is available to an accommodated party. Although §1-103 permits principles of law and equity to supplement the provisions of Article 3 to the extent that they have not been displaced by the particular provisions of Article 3, it is not clear to what extent §§3-605 and 3-419 were intended to displace other traditional suretyship defenses. For instance, some pre-Code cases and statutory law discharged a surety in the event that the creditor failed to proceed promptly against the debtor after being requested to do so. The Permanent Editorial Board has left this issue somewhat vague in commenting that to the extent that a right or duty has not been displaced by the particular provisions of Article 3, the general law of suretyship is applicable pursuant to §1-103 of the Code. Unfortunately no insight was given by the Board as to which defenses have been displaced. See PEB Commentary on the Uniform Commercial Code, Commentary Concerning Suretyship Issues Under Sections 3-116, 3-305, 3-415, 3-419, and 3-605, Final Draft (Feb. 10, 1994), Issue 2, Discussion.

Courts were divided under former Article 3 as to whether Article 3 pre-empted statutory surety law. For cases under former Article 3, Compare First Natl. City Bank v. Valentine, 61 Misc. 2d 554, 306 N.Y.S.2d 227, 7 U.C.C. Rep. Serv. 53 (N.Y. Sup. Ct. 1969) (not preempted) with Still v. Citizens Bank, 6 U.C.C. Rep. Serv. 813 (Okla. App. 1969) (preempted); Philadelphia Bond & Mortgage Co. v. Highland Crest Homes, Inc., 235 Pa. Super. 252, 340 A.2d 476, 17 U.C.C. Rep. Serv. 158 (1975) (preempted).

The various rules found in §3-605 by which an indorser or accommodation party may be discharged are commonly referred to as "suretyship defenses." In studying the following materials, you should keep in mind that many notes signed by indorsers or accommodation parties contain boilerplate clauses by which the accommodation party or indorser waives the right to assert these suretyship defenses. As we discuss later in this section, this waiver will prevent the accommodation party or indorser from raising the suretyship defenses.

The right to a discharge under §3-605 is limited to accommodation parties and indorsers.[135] An indorser is, for all practical purposes, treated as an accommodation party for prior parties to the instrument.[136] Other parties in the position of a surety or persons who sign separate guaranty agreements or other instruments that are not negotiable are not covered by §3-605.[137] For example, when a buyer of a house assumes the seller's obligation as maker of the mortgage note, although the seller is now in the position of a surety, he is not covered under §3-605(e) because the buyer is not a party to the note. This is subject to one minor exception. As we will cover, §3-605 (e) also deals with the effects of impairment of collateral upon the rights of a non-accommodation co-obligor.[138]

a.   Release of Principal Debtor

One interesting provision of §3-605 is that release of the principal debtor does not discharge an accommodation party or indorser.[139] For example,

---

Although Revised Article 3 does not decide how these issues are to be treated, the Code should be held to pre-empt such statutory and case law that requires the holder to first attempt to recover from the maker or acceptor. The accommodation party can always pay the holder and immediately proceed against the accommodated party himself. By adding the words "collection guaranteed," the accommodation party can require the holder to first attempt to recover from the maker or acceptor. It would be anomalous to find that such statutory or case law survives enactment of the Code since the accommodation party would be given greater protection than is given to one guaranteeing collection only.

135. U.C.C. §3-605(a). Indorsers include a drawer of a draft accepted by a non-bank drawee. U.C.C. §3-414(d).

136. U.C.C. §3-605, Official Comment 1.

137. See PEB Commentary on the Uniform Commercial Code, Commentary Concerning Suretyship Issues Under Sections 3-116, 3-305, 3-415, 3-419, and 3-605, Final Draft (Feb. 10, 1994), Issue 1, Discussion.

138. U.C.C. §3-605(f); U.C.C. §3-605, Official Comment 1.

139. Even though discharge of the accommodated party by cancellation or renunciation does not discharge the accommodation party under §3-605(b), a question arises as to whether the surety can raise the cancellation or renunciation as to defense under §3-305(d). Section 3-305(d) provides that, with certain exceptions not relevant here, an accommodation party may

assume that Alice makes a note payable to Creditor which Betty indorses as an accommodation party. Even if Creditor, for whatever reason, releases Alice, Creditor may recover in full from Betty.

This rule is phrased as follows in its technical manner: Discharge of the principal debtor by cancellation or renunciation[140] does not discharge the surety.[141] Cancellation and renunciation were discussed in Chapter 2. Why is this rule not unfair to the surety? Because the surety is not harmed. Notwithstanding release of the principal debtor, the surety retains both her right of recourse on the instrument and her right of reimbursement against the principal debtor.[142] Needless to say, in reality Alice is not really released. Once Betty pays Creditor, Betty will then proceed against Alice. The purpose of this rule is to allow the Creditor to make a settlement with Alice without obtaining Betty's consent.

b.   Extensions and Modifications

A different rule applies when the person entitled to enforce the instrument grants an extension to the debtor or otherwise modifies the debtor's obligation to pay the instrument. In many respects this rule seems counterintuitive. As a matter of business practice, however, the difference in treatment between releases and extensions or modifications is justified.

An accommodation party or indorser having a right of recourse against a principal debtor may be entitled to a discharge in the event that the person

---

assert the acccommodated party's defenses. However, allowing the accommodation party to raise the defense of cancellation or renunciation would undercut the rule adopted in §3-605(b). As a result, the Permanent Editorial Board has issued a commentary making it clear that the accommodation party may not raise the accommodated party's discharge by cancellation or renunciation as a defense under §3-305(d). See PEB Commentary on the Uniform Commercial Code, Commentary Concerning Suretyship Issues Under Sections 3-116, 3-305, 3-415, 3-419, and 3-605, Final Draft (Feb. 10, 1994), Issue 9, Discussion. However, if there was a disputed claim that was settled by an accord and satisfaction, the accord and satisfaction may be raised as a defense by the accommodation party under §3-305(d) because §3-605(b) was not intended to apply to disputed claims. See PEB Commentary on the Uniform Commercial Code, Commentary Concerning Suretyship Issues Under Sections 3-116, 3-305, 3-415, 3-419, and 3-605, Final Draft (Feb. 10, 1994), Issue 9, Discussion.

In contrast to §3-605, under the Restatement(3d), Suretyship, release of the principal debtor discharges the surety unless the creditor reserves its rights against the surety. See Restatement (3d), Suretyship, Council Draft No. 4, §35 (March 30, 1995).

140. In other words, a release of the principal debtor by the person entitled to enforce the instrument. U.C.C. §3-604(a).

141. U.C.C. §3-605(b); U.C.C. §3-605, Official Comment 3.

142. U.C.C. §3-419(e); U.C.C. §3-605, Official Comment 3.

entitled to enforce the instrument modifies the obligation of or grants an extension to the principal debtor.[143] The accommodation party is only discharged if the person entitled to enforce the instrument either (1) has actual knowledge of the accommodation or (2) has notice of the accommodation (a) from an indication on the instrument that the party has signed as "guarantor," "surety," or "accommodation party" or (b) from the fact that the signature is an anomalous indorsement which is presumed to be made in the capacity of an accommodation party.[144]

c.   Extensions

An extension granted to the principal debtor only discharges the surety to the extent that the extension causes the surety a loss with respect to his right of recourse against the principal debtor.[145] The extension must take the form of an agreement, whether or not binding, under which the person entitled to enforce the instrument gives more time to the principal debtor to pay the instrument. The mere failure to enforce the instrument when due or to foreclose upon the collateral does not constitute an extension. Thus, if the creditor, whether intentionally or by neglect, fails for two years to attempt to collect from the principal debtor, the creditor's failure is not an extension and does not discharge the surety even if the principal debtor does not go insolvent until long after the due date. In contrast, the rule will apply and discharge the surety if the creditor agrees that the principal debtor may delay payment for a week, and the delay causes a loss to the surety.

The surety is only discharged to the extent that he can prove that he suffered a loss resulting from the extension.[146] In a majority of situations, an extension will not cause the surety a loss. In fact, the extension will more than likely increase the chances of the debtor being able to pay the debt. For this reason, the burden is placed upon the surety to prove that he suffered a loss by virtue of the extension. The surety must prove that the principal debtor could have made at least partial payment at the time that the instrument was

143. U.C.C. §3-605(d); U.C.C. §3-605(c).

144. U.C.C. §3-419(c); U.C.C. §3-605(h).

145. U.C.C. §3-605(c); U.C.C. §3-605, Official Comment 4. Acceptance of a postdated check suspends the underlying obligation under §3-310(b)(1) and therefore constitutes the granting of an extension.

Similar to §3-605, the Restatement (3d), Suretyship, provides that when the creditor grants an extension to the debtor, the surety is discharged to the extent that the extension has caused the surety to suffer a loss. See Restatement (3d), Suretyship, Council Draft No. 2, §36 (April 2, 1993).

146. U.C.C. §3-605, Official Comment 4.

originally due, but is now insolvent or became insolvent at the extended due date. However, proof that the principal debtor had assets at the time that the instrument was originally due does not necessarily mean that those assets would have been used to pay the debt or been available for execution or attachment.

Often, the surety will be unaware that the creditor has given the principal debtor an extension. In these cases, the surety has no opportunity to protect himself. His only recourse is to try to prove that he suffered a loss by virtue of the extension. If, on the other hand, the surety learns ahead of time about the extension, the surety has certain options. The surety is not bound by the extension agreement and therefore may pay the instrument and obtain reimbursement from the principal debtor.[147] However, the surety does not have to make payment on the original due date. The person entitled to enforce the instrument may not enforce the obligation against the surety until the extended due date. As a result, the surety may wait for the creditor to sue him if payment is not made by the principal debtor on the extended due date. When sued by the creditor, the surety may attempt to prove that suffered a loss because of the extension. However, the surety's failure to pay the creditor on the original due date and proceed against the principal debtor at that time may be a factor in determining whether he has suffered a loss.

d.   Modifications

When the person entitled to enforce the instrument agrees to materially modify the obligation of the principal debtor, with or without consideration, the surety is discharged to the extent that the modification causes a loss with respect to the surety's right of recourse against the principal debtor.[148] The

---

147. See U.C.C. §3-419(e). See also PEB Commentary on the Uniform Commercial Code, Commentary Concerning Suretyship Issues Under Sections 3-116, 3-305, 3-415, 3-419, and 3-605, Final Draft (Feb. 10, 1994), Issue 7, Discussion. The rationale behind this rule depends upon whether the accommodation party is an indorser or co-maker. If he is an indorser, his liability does not arise until the instrument is dishonored. The instrument cannot be dishonored until the principal debtor fails to pay upon presentment that cannot be made until the extended due date. If the accommodation party is a co-maker, he may raise, under §3-305(d), the principal debtor's defense that the note is not yet due. On the other hand, if the accommodation party, knowing that the principal debtor's financial condition can only worsen, wants to pay the instrument now and immediately proceed against the principal debtor, he may do so.

148. U.C.C. §3-605(d); U.C.C. §3-605, Official Comment 5. Under the Restatement (3d), Suretyship, the surety is completely discharged if the modification results in a substituted contract or imposes risks on the surety that are fundamentally different from those imposed under the original contract. In the case of any other modification, the surety is discharged to the extent that he is caused to suffer a loss thereby. See Restatement (3d), Suretyship, Council Draft No. 4, §37 (March 30, 1995).

burden of proving the absence of a loss to the accommodation party in the case of a modification is placed upon the creditor.

This allocation of the burden of proof is accomplished by presuming that the loss suffered by the surety is equal to the amount of his right of recourse. Unless the creditor can prove that the loss is a lesser amount, the surety is completely discharged.[149] Modifications are treated differently than extensions because they are less common than extensions and are more likely to be detrimental to the surety.

Let us look at an example of a modification by which the principal sum is increased from $100,000 to $125,000. The surety, not having agreed to the modification, is only liable for $100,000. The surety has the benefit of the presumption that the increase in principal caused the surety a loss in the entire amount of $100,000. In other words, had the note not been modified, the debtor would have been able to either pay the entire $100,000 or at least have reimbursed the surety for the entire amount. However, the creditor may introduce evidence that the debtor's inability to pay was caused by a total collapse of his business and that the collapse would have occurred no matter what the amount of the principal was. In this case, the creditor has rebutted the presumption thus denying the surety a discharge.

e. Burden of Proof Where Both Modification and Extension

Questions often arise as to who has the burden of proof where an agreement both materially modifies the obligation of the principal debtor and also grants an extension.[150] Does the surety have the burden of proving that he suffered a loss on account of the extension or will he have the benefit of the presumption that the modification has caused him a loss to the extent of the amount of the obligation? The answer is that he may enjoy the benefit of the presumption of a loss. If neither the surety nor the creditor introduce any evidence as to the absence or presence of any loss, the surety is completely discharged because of the presumption in the case of modification. If evidence is introduced as to the presence or absence of loss, the court will have to determine the effect the modification and extension had upon the ability of the surety to recover from the principal debtor.

---

149. U.C.C. §3-605(d); U.C.C. §3-605, Official Comment 5.

150. See PEB Commentary on the Uniform Commercial Code, Commentary Concerning Suretyship Issues Under Sections 3-116, 3-305, 3-415, 3-419, and 3-605, Final Draft (Feb. 10, 1994), Issue 8, Discussion.

f. Consent and Waiver

Any party who consents to a modification or to an extension is not discharged.[151] There are no formal requirements for the consent. The surety's consent may be given, in advance as in the instrument itself, at the time of the modification or extension, or even after the modification or extension.[152] A waiver (intentional relinquishment of a known right) contained in an instrument or in a separate agreement is effective whether the waiver contains language specifically or generally indicating that the party waives defenses based upon §3-605.[153]

g. Impairment of Collateral

Let us return to our example of you co-making a note with your sister so that she can purchase a car. If the car dealer takes a security interest in the car to secure repayment of the debt, you may expect that you will not have to pay the debt until the car is repossessed and sold. If you have this belief, you will be disappointed. The car dealer does not have to go through the effort and expense to convert the car into cash before proceeding against you. However, you are protected to some degree by the car dealer having acquired a security interest in the car. Upon your payment, you are entitled to the car dealer's security interest in the car.[154] Therefore, you may repossess and sell the car to obtain repayment. Because you have the right to the collateral upon payment, the car dealer owes you a duty not to impair this right. For example, if the car dealer released the security interest in the car to your sister, the car dealer denies you the ability to be made whole. For this reason, you are discharged by the car dealer's action up to the value of the car.

This rule, of course, is not phrased that simply:

> If the obligation to pay an instrument is secured by an interest in collateral (the car), and the person entitled to enforce the instrument (the car dealer) impairs the value of the collateral (by releasing the security interest), the obligation of an indorser or accommodation party (you) having a right of recourse against the obligor (your sister) is discharged to the extent of the impairment.[155]

---

151. U.C.C. §3-605(i); U.C.C. §3-605, Official Comment 8.
152. U.C.C. §3-605, Official Comment 2.
153. U.C.C. §3-605(i).
154. U.C.C. §3-605, Official Comment 6.
155. U.C.C. §3-605(e); U.C.C. §3-605, Official Comment 6. Because §3-605 applies only to indorsers and accommodation parties, the principal debtor is not entitled to a discharge under Article 3 in the event that the person entitled to enforce the instrument has impaired the value

h.   Discharge of Co-obligors

A similar rule applies where the creditor impairs the value of collateral given by a party who is jointly and severally liable with the party claiming a discharge. When two parties are jointly and severally liable, each party can be required to pay the holder in full. However, upon payment, the party making payment has the right to contribution from the other party.

For example, assume that you and your sister co-make a note to borrow money to start a business. Being co-makers, you and your sister are jointly and severally liable. Upon your payment in full, you may recover one-half of your payment from your sister. Assume that your sister pledged certain stock certificates to secure this loan. If the creditor returns the stock certificates to your sister, you are thereby hurt in your attempt to recover from your sister her share of the obligation. The stock certificates could have been used by you to pay the debt. Your loss is not in the entire amount of the debt because had the entire amount been paid by the selling of the certificates, your sister could have recovered one-half of the amount from you. You are therefore only discharged to the extent that you are harmed by the impairment. The rule is phrased as follows:

> If a person entitled to enforce the instrument (the creditor) impairs the value of the interest in the collateral (by releasing the stock certificates), the obligation of any party who is jointly and severally liable with respect to the secured obligation (you) is (are) discharged to the extent that the impairment causes the party asserting the discharge (you) to pay more than he (you) would have been obliged to pay (the value of the stock certificates or however much more you paid over one-half of the debt, whichever is less).[156]

An accommodation party who is denied the right to a discharge because the holder does not know or have notice of his accommodation status may use this rule to achieve a partial discharge. For example, you may have co-made the note with your sister in order to enable her to start a business. You neither indicated on the note itself nor told the holder that you were acting as an accommodation party for your sister. However, as a co-maker, you would be entitled to a discharge to the extent discussed above.

---

of the collateral pledged by the principal debtor. However, if the collateral is personal property, U.C.C. §9-507(1), the principal debtor may have a right to obtain damages, and under certain circumstances, a complete discharge as a result of the secured party's failure to comply with the requirements of Article 9. If the property is real property, the law as to real property security must be consulted.

The Restatement (3d), Suretyship, contains a rule similar to U.C.C. §3-605(e). See Restatement (3d), Suretyship, Council Draft No. 2, §38 (April 2, 1993).

156. U.C.C. §3-605(f); U.C.C. §3-605, Official Comment 7.

D. Accommodation Parties

i. When Is Collateral Impaired?

Impairment of collateral occurs when some act or omission on the part of the person entitled to enforce the instrument causes the collateral to be no longer available to satisfy the instrument. The person entitled to enforce the instrument will only be found to have impaired the collateral if he has breached some duty respecting the collateral.[157] This duty may arise from an agreement, a common law duty of due care, or some statutorily imposed duty. For example, if the collateral is destroyed by fire or stolen, the creditor has impaired the collateral if he breached a duty to insure against or to use reasonable care to protect against such loss.[158] Similarly, the person entitled to enforce the instrument may fail to sell stock or other property in his possession before a decline in its price. Whether he has impaired the collateral depends upon whether he breached a duty he had to make such a sale.

Unless otherwise agreed, where the collateral is property in the possession of the person entitled to enforce the instrument, he has the duty to use reasonable care in its custody and possession. If the collateral is personal property, the standard of reasonable care is governed by §9-207.[159] Reasonable care in the case of an instrument, mortgage, or chattel paper includes taking any necessary steps to preserve rights against prior parties.[160] Where the creditor is granted a security interest in certain personal property, the creditor has the duty to obtain priority for the security interest by filing notice of the interest in the appropriate governmental offices or by otherwise properly perfecting the interest.

Any act or omission that results in a diminution of the value of the collateral is an impairment. Article 3 contains a non-exclusive list of certain acts that constitute impairment of collateral.[161] The first act is the failure to obtain or maintain perfection or recordation of the interest in collateral. An example would be the creditor's failure to file an Article 9 financing statement that results in the creditor not acquiring a perfected security interest in the collateral. The second act is the release of collateral without substitution of collateral of equal value. If the creditor obtains from the debtor a diamond ring as collateral for a loan, the creditor has impaired the value of the collateral if he

---

157. U.C.C. §3-605(g).

158. For cases under former Article 3, see Commerce Union Bank v. May, 503 S.W.2d 112, 14 U.C.C. Rep. Serv. 146 (Tenn. 1973) (bank had no contractual duty); Arlington Bank & Trust v. Nowell Motors, Inc., 511 S.W.2d 415, 15 U.C.C. Rep. Serv. 146 (Tex. App. 1974) (bank had contractual duty to insure).

159. U.C.C. §3-605(g).

160. U.C.C. §9-207(1).

161. U.C.C. §3-605, Official Comment 6.

releases the diamond ring to the debtor without obtaining any substitute collateral of equal value. The third act is the failure to perform a duty to preserve the value of the collateral owed to the debtor, surety, or person secondarily liable. If the creditor had the duty to insure the collateral and has failed to do so, he has breached this duty. The final enumerated act is the failure to comply with applicable law in disposing of collateral. If the creditor has violated the rules contained in Article 9 for selling collateral upon default, the creditor has impaired the collateral. It is beyond the scope of this book to attempt to provide a complete list of every act that might constitute the impairment of collateral.

j.   Discharge Only Where Notice of Accommodation

An accommodation party can only be discharged under §3-605(e) if the person entitled to enforce the instrument knows of the accommodation or has notice of the accommodation under §3-419(c).[162] Without notice of the party's accommodation status, the creditor may have no reason to suspect that his actions will harm the accommodation party. For example, assume that your sister asks you to sign in accommodation so that she can purchase a car. The car dealer asks you to sign as maker of the note and your sister to indorse the note. The car dealer takes a security interest in the car as collateral. The car dealer sells the note along with the security interest in the car to Finance Company. Finance Company releases title of the car to your sister. You are not discharged by the action of Finance Company unless Finance Company knew or had notice of your accommodation status. When Finance Company released the car to your sister, Finance Company did not know that it was hurting you. Since you signed as maker of the note, Finance Company believed that you were to be ultimately liable and that upon your payment, you would not have recourse to your sister who signed as an indorser.

k.   Extent of Discharge

The formula for determining the extent of the impairment seems more difficult than it really is. In reality, the surety is discharged to the extent of the amount that the creditor's actions hurt the surety. The Code provides two alternative formulas for determining the extent of the impairment. The first formula applies when the debt is fully secured. A debt is fully secured when the value of the collateral is equal to or greater than the amount owed on the

---

162. U.C.C. §3-605(h).

obligation. The first formula is stated as follows: "the value of an interest in collateral is impaired to the extent that the value of the interest is reduced to an amount less than the amount of the right of recourse of the party asserting the discharge."[163]

Assume that a creditor released his security interest in the collateral, a car worth $20,000. The principal debtor sells the car and loses the money. The remaining debt is $15,000. Because the car is no longer in the hands of the debtor and no longer subject to the security interest, the value of the collateral is now reduced to 0. Obviously, the surety is hurt to the extent of $15,000. Had the security interest not been released, the surety, upon payment, could have looked to the car for repayment. Because the car is no longer subject to the security interest, the surety has no way of recovering the $15,000 he would otherwise have to pay to the creditor. Using the terminology found in the Code, the value of the interest in the collateral has been reduced (to 0), which is $15,000 less than the amount of the right of recourse. Therefore, the surety is discharged as to the entire $15,000. If the car was still worth $2,000, the surety would be discharged in the amount of $13,000.

The second formula applies when the debt is undersecured, in other words, whenever the debt is greater than the value of the collateral. In this case the measure is phrased in terms of how much greater the debt is undersecured because of the impairment: "the value of an interest in collateral is impaired to the extent that the reduction in value of the interest causes an increase in the amount by which the amount of the right of recourse exceeds the value of the interest."[164]

Assume that the car, as in the above example, is worth $20,000. However, the debt is $50,000. Before the creditor released the security interest, the creditor was $30,000 undersecured. If the surety was forced to pay the debt of $50,000, he would be entitled to a security interest in the car, which interest would have a value of $20,000. Thus, the surety loses $20,000 as a result of the creditor releasing the security interest. Using the terminology found in the Code, the difference between the right of recourse ($50,000) and the present value of the collateral (0) is $50,000. Because of the impairment, the deficiency is now $50,000 rather than $30,000. Therefore the increase in the amount by which the amount of the right of recourse exceeds the value of the interest is $20,000.

163. U.C.C. §3-605(e)(i); U.C.C. §3-605, Official Comment 6. Under the Restatement (3d), Suretyship, the surety is discharged to the extent that such impairment would otherwise increase the difference between the maximum amount recoverable by the surety pursuant to its subrogation rights and the value of the collateral. See Restatement (3d), Suretyship, Council Draft No. 2, §38 (April 2, 1993).

164. U.C.C. §3-605(e)(ii); U.C.C. §3-605, Official Comment 6.

The party seeking the discharge bears the burden of proof as to both the fact of impairment and the amount of the loss.[165] For example, if the impairment is the failure of the creditor to perfect a security interest in the collateral, the loss is the extent to which a person who would not otherwise have priority to the collateral obtains such priority.[166] If he cannot prove a loss, he is not discharged.[167] Where released collateral is worthless, where a lien would have had priority even if the security interest had been perfected, or where substitute collateral is worth as much as the original collateral, there is no loss.

Where the party seeking the discharge is jointly and severally liable with the person who gave the collateral to the creditor, the party is discharged only to the extent that the impairment causes him to pay more than he would have been obliged to pay, taking into account his right of contribution.[168] Assume that Bob and Abe co-make a note. Abe gives to Carl, the payee, a security interest in property worth $1,000 as collateral. Because Carl fails to perfect the security interest, the interest is voided in Abe's bankruptcy. After payment to Carl, Bob would have a right of contribution against Abe in the amount of $500. As a result, Bob is discharged to the extent of $500. If Bob receives a portion of this amount in Abe's bankruptcy, Bob's loss is reduced by the amount he receives.

l.   Consent to Impairment

A party will be denied a discharge if he has consented to the act constituting the impairment.[169] The consent may be express or implied. For example, if a corporate officer, who has indorsed a note made by the corporation, negotiates for the release of collateral given by the corporate maker, the officer as an indorser will probably be found to have consented to the release and

---

165. U.C.C. §3-605(e); U.C.C. §3-605(f).

166. For a case under former Article 3, see Bank South v. Jones, 185 Ga. App. 125, 364 S.E.2d 281, 5 U.C.C. Rep. Serv. 2d 644 (1988) (accommodation party's discharge, where holder has failed to perfect security interest, can be no greater than the value of the collateral at the time of impairment).

167. For cases under former Article 3, see Farmers State Bank v. Cooper, 227 Kan. 547, 608 P.2d 929, 28 U.C.C. Rep. Serv. 733 (1980); Beneficial Fin. Co. v. Lawrence, 30 N.W.2d 114, 30 U.C.C. Rep. Serv. 1358 (N.D. 1980); First Natl. Bank v. Beaty, 2 U.C.C. Rep. Serv. 2d 1437 (Tenn. App. 1986) (there was no unjustifiable impairment of collateral where a bank advanced additional funds to principal debtor which had the effect of subordinating the guarantor's security interest since without the advance, security interest would have been worthless); Schause v. Garner, 590 P.2d 1316, 25 U.C.C. Rep. Serv. 1396 (Wyo. 1979).

168. U.C.C. §3-605(f); U.C.C. §3-605, Official Comment 7.

169. U.C.C. §3-605(i). This consent may be given in advance, in the instrument itself, or after the act of impairment. U.C.C. §3-605(i).

thus be denied a discharge in his role as indorser.[170] However, knowledge of the act impairing the collateral will not be deemed to be consent where the surety's silence does not unambiguously indicate his lack of objection to the release. The surety may assume that the creditor realizes that by impairing the collateral, that he is discharging the surety.

Consent should be somewhat narrowly construed. Consent to the granting of an extension to the maker to pay the instrument should not be held to be a consent to the release of the collateral. Similarly, consent to substitute or exchange collateral should not be construed as permission for the release of collateral.

E.   LIABILITY OF AGENTS, PRINCIPALS, AND CO-OBLIGORS

1.   Liability of Represented Person

When a corporate officer signs his name as drawer of a corporate check, is the corporation liable on the check? When a partner signs the partnership's name to a promissory note, is the partnership liable on the note? In other words, when is the principal liable on a negotiable instrument signed by its agent or other representative? Before we answer this question, it should be pointed out that Article 3 uses its own terminology. In Article 3, a principal is referred to as the "represented person." The agent is referred to as the "representative."

A represented person is liable on an instrument if the representative is authorized to sign for the represented person. The law of agency determines whether the representative is authorized to sign for the represented person.[171] An authorized signature by an agent or other representative[172] is effective as the signature of the represented person.[173] The issue comes down to one of authority. Was the representative authorized to sign for the represented per-

170. See McGhee v. First State Bank & Trust Co., 793 S.W.2d 133, 13 U.C.C. Rep. Serv. 2d 194 (Ky. App. 1990) (when accommodation party actively negotiated renewal, question of fact whether accommodation party consented to extension).

171. U.C.C. §3-402, Official Comment 1. See generally Restatement of the Law, Second, Agency 2d (1957).

172. "Representative" includes an agent, an officer of a corporation or association, a trustee, executor or administrator of an estate, or any other person empowered to act for another. U.C.C. §1-201(35).

173. U.C.C. §3-402(a); U.C.C. §3-402, Official Comment 1.

son? Under the law of agency, the authority of the representative may be actual authority, apparent authority, or inherent agency power. If the representative was, however, not authorized to sign for the represented person, the signature will not operate as the represented person's signature[174] unless the represented person ratifies it or is otherwise precluded from contesting it.

Actual authority is where the represented person has given the representative the right to act for him. Actual authority may be implied or express. The representative is expressly authorized to sign for the represented person where the represented person either verbally or in writing authorizes the agent to sign for him.[175] Express authority will often take the form of a power of attorney, an oral authorization, or a corporate resolution. If a corporate resolution requires the signature of two officers, the signature of only one officer is not sufficient to obligate the corporation.

Implied authority is authority evidenced by the represented person's conduct rather than his words.[176] For example, where the represented person does not object to the representative's signing of checks on his behalf, the represented person impliedly authorizes the representative to sign checks for him.

A representative may be found to have the power to bind the represented person even though he does not have either implied or express authority to do so. This arises where the representative is found to have apparent authority. Apparent authority is when the represented person has made such manifestations to the third party as to make the third party believe the representative is authorized even though the representative is not actually authorized to act for the represented person.[177] For example, where the representative in the presence of the represented person indorses a check for the represented person, the represented person may have apparently authorized the representative to indorse checks for him. Depending upon all the facts, the third party may be led to believe that the representative is authorized to sign for the represented person because the represented person did not object to the representative so doing. It is irrelevant that later the represented person told the representative that he had no right to sign for him.

Inherent agency power is the power, not derived from actual or apparent authority, that an agency has solely from the agency relation and that exists for

---

174. U.C.C. §3-403(a).

175. See Harold Reuschlein & William Gregory, Handbook on the Law of Agency and Partnership 37-38 (2d ed. 1990).

176. See Harold Reuschlein & William Gregory, supra note 175, at 41-44; Restatement of the Law, Second, Agency 2d §7, Comment c (1957).

177. See Harold Reuschlein & William Gregory, supra note 175, at 57-64; Restatement of the Law, Second, Agency 2d §8 (1957).

the protection of persons harmed by dealing with the agent.[178] Inherent agency power subjects the represented person to contractual liability when the representative has acted improperly in entering into a contract.[179] For example, assume that although the treasurer of a corporation has the general authority to sign promissory notes for the corporation, he does not have the authority to sign a note in excess of $100,000. If the treasurer signs a note for $150,000, he may be found to have inherent agency power to sign the note even though he neither had actual nor apparent authority to do so. Similarly, if the treasurer signed a note for $85,000 to purchase property for his own uses, he may be found to have inherent agency power even though he is not authorized to sign the corporation's name for his own purposes.

Where an authorized representative signs an instrument, the signature is effective even though the representative was not authorized to use the instrument for the particular purpose for which it was used.[180] For example, assume that Paul, president of Simon Industries, has the authority to indorse checks for Simon Industries. However, Paul has no authority to use Simon Industries' funds for his own personal use. If Paul indorses a check payable to Simon Industries to Bank of America in payment for his own mortgage, Paul's indorsement is effective to make Bank of America the holder of the check even though Paul was not authorized to negotiate the check for that purpose. Whether Simon Industries has an action against Bank of America depends upon whether Bank of America had notice of Paul's breach of fiduciary duty. This issue is discussed in Chapter 2.

Any mark or symbol used by the representative that is intended to signify the represented person is sufficient to bind the represented person. The representative may sign the name of the represented person either with or without the agent's own name or capacity, for example, "Simon Industries," "Simon Industries, by Paul, President," or "Simon Industries, by Paul." The symbol does not even have to be the name of the represented person, for example, "SI".

If a representative is authorized to sign on behalf of the represented person, the representative may sign his own name alone, for example, "Paul." If a

178. Restatement of the Law, Second, Agency 2d §8A (1957).

179. Id. at Comment b.

180. For cases under former Article 3, see Bank South, N.A. v. Midstates Group, Inc., 185 Ga. App. 342, 364 S.E.2d 58, 5 U.C.C. Rep. Serv. 2d 634 (1987) (principal's signature authorized where agent had apparent authority to indorse certificate of deposit even though not authorized to use certificate of deposit for the purpose for which it was used); Rohrbacher v. Bancohio Natl. Bank, 171 A.D.2d 533, 567 N.Y.S.2d 431, 14 U.C.C. Rep. Serv. 2d 1122 (1991) (Because attorney had authority to indorse for client on condition that the proceeds be deposited in escrow account, attorney's indorsement is authorized even though he cashed check and embezzled funds.).

person acts or purports to act as a representative and signs an instrument with either his name or the name of the represented person, the represented person is bound by the signature to the same extent the represented person would be bound if the signature appeared on a simple contract.[181] The represented person is liable on the instrument even though neither his signature nor his identity appears thereon to the extent the representative is authorized to act on his behalf. Thus, an undisclosed principal is liable on an instrument to the same extent that he is liable on an ordinary contract.

2.   Liability of Representative

Care must be taken by a representative when signing for the represented person. Otherwise, the representative may find that he has unintentionally become personally liable on an instrument that he intended to sign solely on behalf of the represented person.

A representative should know the extent of his authority. If the representative is not authorized to sign for the represented person or exceeds his authority in making the signature, the signature will operate as the signature of the representative personally.[182] As a consequence, the representative will be personally liable in whatever capacity the signature was made. For example, if a purchasing agent for a buyer is authorized to negotiate the purchase, but is not authorized to sign or issue negotiable instruments, the agent's unauthorized drawing of a check in the buyer's name will make the purchasing agent personally liable as drawer of the check.

Even when the representative is authorized to sign for the represented person, a failure to sign in the proper form may subject him to personal liability on the instrument. The possibility of personal liability poses little danger to the representative of a solvent represented person. Although she may be personally liable, being authorized, she will have a right of recourse against the represented person for any liability incurred to the holder.[183] However, if the represented person is insolvent or not amenable to process, the representative may have to absorb the loss. The holder will be able to recover from the representative while the representative may not be able to recover from the represented person.

---

181. U.C.C. §3-401(a); U.C.C. §3-401, Official Comment 1. U.C.C. §3-402, Official Comment 1.

182. U.C.C. §3-403(a); U.C.C. §3-403, Official Comment 1.

183. See Harold Reuschlein & William Gregory, supra note 175 at 148-152.

E. Liability of Agents, Principals, and Co-obligors

Let us examine the different ways in which a representative may have signed on behalf of the represented person. Assume that Paul is president of Simon Industries and is authorized to sign instruments on its behalf. If Paul signs the instrument "Simon Industries" without adding his own name, Paul is not personally liable on the instrument.[184] The reason is simple; Paul is not liable because his signature does not appear on the instrument. Paul should not be liable since he was authorized to act on behalf of Simon Industries. The payee only intended that Simon Industries be liable on the instrument. Subsequent holders could not be misled because no one could have assumed that Paul (his name not appearing on the instrument) intended to be liable on the instrument.

Where Paul's name does appear on the instrument, the manner in which he signs becomes especially important. Paul can ensure that he is not personally liable by making it clear that he is signing only on behalf of Simon Industries.

An authorized representative (Paul) who signs his own name to an instrument is not personally liable if the signature shows unambiguously that it is made on behalf of a represented person (Simon Industries) who is identified in the instrument.[185] The signature must both identify the represented person and make it clear that the representative is merely signing on his behalf. However, the instrument need not contain the legal name of the represented person.[186] Any name which reasonably identifies the represented person is sufficient.

When the representative signs his name together with his representative capacity and the represented person's name, it is clear that the representative is not personally liable.[187] For example, a signature such as "Simon Industries, by Paul, President" unambiguously indicates that the representative is signing on behalf of the represented party.[188] It is not necessary for the representative to indicate the office he occupies as long as he clearly indicates that he is signing on behalf of the represented party, for example, "Simon Industries by Paul" or "Simon Industries, Paul, Authorized Signer." The representative may still, however, be liable on any oral or written promise he makes to personally pay or guarantee the debt.

Of course, there will be times when it is unclear whether Paul has unambiguously signed on behalf of Simon Industries. For example, if the name "Simon Industries" does not directly precede or follow Paul's name and capac-

---

184. U.C.C. §3-401(a).
185. U.C.C. §3-402(b).
186. U.C.C. §3-402, Official Comment 2.
187. U.C.C. §3-402 (b)(1).
188. U.C.C. §3-402, Official Comment 2.

ity, it may not be clear whether Paul is signing for himself personally or for Simon Industries. There must be some logical connection between the location in the instrument of the name "Simon Industries" and Paul's name. Although not without question, a note whose body reads "Simon Industries promises to pay" and that is signed "Paul, President," should be found to unambiguously indicate that Paul is signing on behalf of Simon Industries. In contrast, where Paul signs a note "Simon Industries, Paul", it is unclear whether Paul is signing his name as an agent for Simon Industries or whether he is signing to undertake personal liability.

Where it is ambiguous whether the form of the signature is made in a represented capacity or where the represented person is not identified in the instrument, different rules apply. For example, Paul may sign "Paul," or "Paul, President" or "Simon Industries, Paul." Under these circumstances, subsequent purchasers of the instrument may be misled into believing that Paul is personally liable on the instrument. The expectations of these parties should be and are protected. Even though Paul did not intend to be personally liable, his carelessness may have misled subsequent purchasers and therefore, he, rather than they, should suffer any loss. For this reason, the representative (Paul) is personally liable to a holder in due course who takes the instrument without notice that the representative was not intended by the original parties to the instrument to be personally liable.[189] Of course, if the holder in due course has notice that Paul was not supposed to be personally liable, the holder has no expectation that needs to be protected. In that case, Paul is not liable to such a holder.

As to any other person, Paul is liable on the instrument unless Paul proves that the original parties to the instrument did not intend that he be personally liable. To avoid liability, Paul must prove an actual agreement, whether express or implied, with the payee that he was not to be personally liable.[190] Paul's undisclosed intention not to undertake personal liability is not sufficient.

There is one exception to these rules. The exception involves a representative signing as drawer of a check bearing the name of the represented person. An authorized representative who signs as drawer on a check that is payable from an account of the represented person without indicating his representative status is not liable as long as the represented person is identified on the check, and the signature is an authorized signature of the represented person.[191] In other words, even if Paul in signing a check on the account of

---

189. U.C.C. §3-402(b); U.C.C. §3-402, Official Comment 2.
190. U.C.C. §3-402(b)(2); U.C.C. §3-402, Official Comment 2.
191. U.C.C. §3-402(c); U.C.C. §3-402, Official Comment 3. A question arises as to whether the representative can be liable for overdrafts. A representative should not be liable for overdrafts in that he is not liable on the check itself and has no contractual obligation to reimburse

E. Liability of Agents, Principals, and Co-obligors

Simon Industries and bearing its name, signs only "Paul" without any indication that he is acting on behalf of Simon Industries, Paul does not incur personal liability. The reason is simple. No one is going to believe that Paul, when signing a Simon Industries' check, intends to incur personal liability.

3. Liability of Persons Signing in the Same Capacity in the Same Transaction

There are many situations in which two or more persons sign an instrument in the same capacity. Paul may co-make a note with his brother Art. Or Paul and Art may both indorse the note. Under these circumstances, a question arises as to Paul and Art's liability to each other and to the holder. Separate rules applies when persons sign (1) as makers, acceptors, and drawers or (2) as indorsers.

Except as otherwise specified in the instrument, two or more persons who sign an instrument as makers, acceptors, or drawers are liable jointly and severally in the capacity in which they sign.[192] By being jointly and severally liable, the holder may proceed against either party individually (Paul or Art) or against all of the parties together (Paul and Art). With one exception,[193] unless the parties otherwise agree, a party having joint and several liability is entitled to contribution from his joint and several obligors to the extent available under applicable law.[194] This means that if Paul is forced to pay the note,

---

the bank. Because the liability of a customer to a bank for an overdraft arises out of its contractual relationship with the bank and the representative was authorized to request the loan on behalf of the corporation and the bank did not rely upon the personal liability of the representative, the representative should be absolved of liability.

192. U.C.C. §3-116(a). If an instrument clearly specifies, liability of the parties can be exclusively joint or several. Where the parties are jointly liable, under the common law, the obligee could not generally sue one of the joint promisors without joining all other living promisors. See Farnsworth, Contracts 407, n. 28 (2d ed. 1990). However, in some states, statutes and, in other states, procedural reforms have eliminated compulsory joinder. See Farnsworth, Contracts 407, n.28 (2d ed. 1990). Where liability is several, any promisor may be sued without joinder of the other. Neither "I promise to pay" nor "we promise to pay" is sufficiently clear to defeat imposition of joint and several liability. However, language such as, "we jointly promise to pay" or "we severally promise to pay" is sufficient. If an instrument contains a promise by one of two signers, the other signer is an indorser and not a maker. For example, where an instrument reading "John promises to pay" is signed by both John and Steve, Steve is an indorser.

193. Remember when a party co-signs an instrument as an accommodation for his co-signer, the accommodated co-signer is liable for the full amount and may not seek contribution from the accommodation co-signer. U.C.C. §3-419(e).

194. U.C.C. §3-116(b).

he may recover half from Art. Of course, if the note was made by Paul, Art, and Carly, then each would be liable, as between each other, for one-third of the amount. There is a presumption of equal liability, which may be overcome by evidence either that Paul and Art had agreed between themselves to a different allocation,[195] or that Paul and Art had benefitted in unequal portions. Even if a party (Paul) having joint and several liability is discharged by some act of the holder, his discharge does not affect the right of his joint and several obligor (Art) to receive contribution from the discharged party (Paul).[196]

Generally, indorsers are not jointly and severally liable.[197] The reason is simple. Assume that a note is made by Mick to Rod who indorses the note to Elton who indorses it to John, the holder. Upon default by Mick, John sues Rod and Elton. Although both Elton and Rod have indorsed the note, it is clear that Elton, being a subsequent indorser in the chain of title, has a right to recover in full from Rod. Elton was relying upon Rod's indorsement when he purchased the note.

There are two situations in which indorsers are presumed to be jointly and severally liable.[198] First, copayees who indorse an instrument are jointly and severally liable unless one payee is accommodating the other payee, or they agree to be liable otherwise than as jointly and severally. If a note is made payable to Paul and Art and both indorse the note to Carly, it is presumed that upon payment by Paul, he can recover half from Art. Second, persons who sign as anomalous indorsers for the purpose of accommodating the maker are jointly and severally liable unless one anomalous indorser is acting as a sub-surety for the other anomalous indorser. Where Paul makes a note to Bank of Liverpool for the purpose of obtaining a loan, and Ringo and George indorse the note as an accommodation to Paul, it is presumed that Ringo and George are, between each other, agreeing to be equally liable. If however, Ringo asks that George indorse the note as a favor for both him and Paul, George may be the surety for Paul and the sub-surety for Ringo in which case George may recover in full from Ringo upon payment. For a more complete discussion of this issue see Chapter 3D.

---

195. See PEB Commentary on the Uniform Commercial Code, Commentary Concerning Suretyship Issues Under Sections 3-116, 3-305, 3-415, 3-419, and 3-605, Final Draft (Feb. 10, 1994), Issue 4, Discussion.   •

196. U.C.C. §3-116(c); U.C.C. §3-116, Official Comment 1.

197. U.C.C. §3-116(a); U.C.C. §3-116, Official Comment 2.

198. U.C.C. §3-116(a); U.C.C. §3-116, Official Comment 2. See PEB Commentary on the Uniform Commercial Code, Commentary Concerning Suretyship Issues Under Sections 3-116, 3-305, 3-415, 3-419, and 3-605, Final Draft (Feb. 10, 1994), Issue 4, Discussion.

F. EFFECT OF TAKING AN INSTRUMENT ON THE UNDERLYING OBLIGATION

Let us begin with an example. John purchases a car for $10,000. As payment for the car, John issues a note payable in equal installments over three years. Although John is current in his payments, the car dealer wants the remainder of the purchase price now. Can the car dealer sue John on the underlying sales contract even though John is not in default on the note yet? Or, assuming that John fails to make a payment on the note, can the car dealer sue John on the underlying sales contract or is the car dealer limited to an action on the note? These questions raise the issue as to the effect that taking an instrument has on the underlying obligation for which the instrument was taken. The effect of payment by instrument upon the underlying obligation depends upon whether the instrument is a bank instrument, such as a cashier's check or teller's check, or an instrument on which a bank is not the obligor.

1. Ordinary Instruments

First, we will examine the situation of an ordinary non-bank instrument (referred to as an "ordinary instrument"). Unless the parties otherwise agree, taking an ordinary instrument for an underlying obligation is treated as only conditional payment of the obligation. Thus, when John gave his note to the car dealer, the car dealer could not sue him on the sales contract. The obligation is suspended to the same extent that the obligation would be discharged if payment had been made in money.[199] This is simpler than it sounds. If John's note was intended to cover the full purchase price of the car, John's obligation under the sales contract would be suspended as to the total amount. If, on the other hand, John's note was in the amount of $4,000 and was intended only to be in part payment for the car, the car dealer could still sue John for the remaining $6,000.

While an underlying obligation is suspended, no action of any type, including law suits or setoffs, may be taken to enforce the obligation. The obligation is treated as not yet due. Where an uncertified check is taken, suspension of the obligation continues until the check is either dishonored, paid or certified.[200] If the check is paid or certified, the obligation is discharged to

---

199. U.C.C. §3-310(b); U.C.C. §3-310(c); U.C.C. §3-310, Official Comment 3.

the extent of the amount of the check.[201] Where a note is taken, suspension of the obligation continues until dishonor of the note or until it is paid.[202] The obligation is discharged to the extent that the note is paid.[203]

The effect of dishonor depends upon whether the person who is enforcing the instrument is also the person to whom the underlying obligation is owed. The person who is enforcing the instrument is the person who is bringing the action on the instrument. The person to whom the underlying obligation is owed is, in our example, the car dealer. Where the person entitled to enforce the instrument is also the person to whom the underlying obligation is owed (the car dealer brings the action on the note), the person (the car dealer) may enforce either the instrument or the obligation once the instrument is dishonored.[204] He retains all of his rights on both the instrument and the underlying obligation. If the underlying sales contract has a provision for attorney's fees and interest, he may then also recover his attorney's fees and interest.

However, the car dealer may have sold the note to Finance Company. In this case, where the person entitled to enforce the instrument (Finance Company) is not the person to whom the underlying obligation is owed (Car Dealer), it (Finance Company) may only enforce the instrument.[205] If the note does not contain a provision for attorney's fees or interest, Finance Company, having the right to enforce neither the attorney's fees provision nor the provision for interest found in the contract, has no right to interest or attorney's fees.

Where the underlying obligor is discharged on the instrument, he is also discharged on the underlying obligation.[206] When John pays the note, he is discharged on the note and on the underlying sales contract. Discharge is available even where the underlying obligor is not a party to the instrument. For example, assume that instead of borrowing money from Car Dealer, John had borrowed money directly from Finance Company. Finance Company makes a check payable to Car Dealer on John's behalf. Discharge of Finance Company on the check discharges John on the underlying sales contract. If the check is dishonored, Car Dealer may maintain an action against John on the underlying sales contract and against Finance Company on the check. Car Dealer, of course, can be paid only once. If the check had instead been made payable to

200. U.C.C. §3-310(b).
201. U.C.C. §3-310(b)(1).
202. U.C.C. §3-310(b)(2).
203. U.C.C. §3-310(b)(2).
204. U.C.C. §3-310(b)(3); U.C.C. §3-310, Official Comment 3.
205. U.C.C. §3-310, Comment 3.
206. U.C.C. §3-310(a) and (b)(1) and (2).

John who indorsed it to Car Dealer, discharge of John on the check also discharges John on the underlying sales contract.[207]

2.   Bank Checks

Unless otherwise agreed, if a certified check, cashier's check, teller's check, or any other instrument on which a bank is a maker or an acceptor[208] is taken for an obligation, the obligation is discharged to the same extent as had payment been made in cash.[209] The debt is discharged and the taker of the bank instrument is left to recover on the instrument against the bank. The rationale is that the parties intended by use of a bank instrument to allocate the risk of the bank's insolvency to the taker who could immediately present the bank instrument for payment. Any delay is his fault.

There will be times when the taker does not want to assume the risk of the bank's insolvency. He may want to know that the debtor will be responsible even if the bank goes insolvent. There are two ways that this can be accomplished. The parties may expressly agree that the debtor remains liable on the underlying obligation despite payment by bank instrument. Alternatively, the debtor may indorse the bank instrument. Although the underlying obligation will still be discharged, any liability that the obligor may have as an indorser on the instrument is not discharged.[210]

3.   Taking Instrument for Underlying Obligation

In order for an instrument to affect the underlying obligation, the instrument must be "taken" for the underlying obligation.[211] Mere delivery of the instrument to the obligee (Car Dealer) by the obligor (John) does not result in the obligee having taken the instrument for the underlying obligation. Car Dealer must perform some act of accepting the instrument in either conditional or absolute payment of the obligation. Whether the obligee has accepted the instrument in payment of the obligation is often a difficult question of fact.

Unless previously authorized by Car Dealer as an acceptable form of payment, Car Dealer's receipt by mail of an instrument does not constitute taking

---

207. U.C.C. §3-310(b)(3); U.C.C. §3-310, Official Comment 3
208. U.C.C. §3-310(c); U.C.C. §3-310, Official Comment 5.
209. U.C.C. §3-310(a); U.C.C. §3-310, Official Comment 2.
210. U.C.C. §3-310(a); U.C.C. §3-310, Official Comment 2.
211. U.C.C. §3-310(a) and (b).

of the instrument for the underlying obligation. Car Dealer can promptly return the instrument to John. John cannot unilaterally impose upon Car Dealer payment by a negotiable instrument. However, if Car Dealer deposits or negotiates the instrument, Car Dealer will have taken the instrument for the obligation. Borderline situations arise where the obligee retains the instrument but does not negotiate or deposit it. In one case under former Article 3,[212] a bank teller accepted a money order in payment of an overdue installment on a mortgage. Although the bank immediately returned the money upon review of its files by the appropriate employee, the bank was deemed to have taken the instrument in payment of the mortgage.

G. ACCORD AND SATISFACTION BY USE OF INSTRUMENT

Many of us have tried to resolve a dispute with a creditor by writing on the back of a check words like "Cashing of this check is the creditor's acceptance of this check as payment in full for any obligations owed by drawer to creditor."[213] But did we really know whether, when the check was cashed, we were relieved from any further obligation to the creditor? When we received a check bearing such words, could we cross out the words and cash the check? If we did, could we sue for the remainder of the obligation? The answers to these questions are important. However, the answers were not always clear or uniform.

Article 3 attempts to answer questions like these by establishing rules that are fair to both the debtor and the creditor. The answers are set out in §3-311 but apply only under certain well-defined conditions. The first condition is that the debtor tender an instrument in good faith and in full satisfaction of the claim.[214] Good faith requires not only honesty in fact but also the observance of reasonable commercial standards of fair dealing.[215] For example, an insurance company does not act in good faith where it sends a check in an unreasonably small amount knowing that the insured is destitute.[216] Similarly,

---

212. See Savings & Loan Assn. v. Tear, 435 A2d 1083, 32 U.C.C. Rep. Serv. 1152 (Me. 1981).
213. U.C.C. §3-311, Official Comment 1.
214. U.C.C. §3-311(a). The debtor has the burden of proof on this issue.
215. U.C.C. §3-103(a)(4).
216. U.C.C. §3-311, Official Comment 4.

a business does not act in good faith where it prints settlement language on all checks whether or not any dispute is involved.

The second condition is that the claim must be either unliquidated or subject to a bona fide dispute.[217] This tracts the common law requirement that in order for payment of less than the full amount to discharge the debt, the debtor must pay more than the undisputed portion of the debt. The debtor must give something to the creditor in consideration for release of the remainder of the debt. The something is payment of some of the disputed portion of debt. [218] The third condition is that the instrument must have been paid.[219] In other words, the instrument must have been cashed by the creditor or by a subsequent holder.

Subject to two exceptions, the claim is discharged only if the instrument, or accompanying written communication, contains a conspicuous[220] statement that the instrument is tendered in full satisfaction of the debt.[221] The statement may be written on the front or back of the check itself or in an accompanying letter. It must, however, be written in a conspicuous manner. This means that it must be so written that a reasonable person ought to have noticed it.[222] The debtor is discharged even if the creditor strikes out the language indicating payment in full or otherwise indicates his protest.

1. Exception for Lock Box Accounts

Large companies like Pacific Bell or Southern California Edison often require customers to make payments directly to a lock box located at the depositary bank or to one of its own post office boxes from which a clerk receives the checks, records the payment, and forwards the check to the depositary

---

217. U.C.C. §3-311(a)(2); U.C.C. §3-311, Official Comment 4.

218. The Code reserves for other rules of law the issue as to whether a debt may be discharged by payment of less than the amount owed. U.C.C. §3-311, Official Comment 4.

219. U.C.C. §3-311(a). Certification of a check is treated as equivalent to payment of the check. U.C.C. §3-311, Official Comment 4.

220. Under §1-201(20) a statement is conspicuous if it is "so written that a reasonable person against whom it is to operate ought to have noticed it." Almost any statement on a check would be conspicuous. U.C.C. §3-311, Official Comment 4. This is especially true in the case of an individual claimant where the notice is written above the place where he indorses the check. U.C.C. §3-311, Official Comment 4.

221. U.C.C. §3-311(b); U.C.C. §3-311, Official Comment 4. The debtor has the burden of proof on these issues.

222. U.C.C. §1-201 (10).

bank.[223] In either case, the employee's duties are merely the mechanical recording of the payment. Speed requires that the employee not read any accompanying correspondence or anything written on the back of the check. Lock box account arrangements greatly reduce the cost of doing business. The first exception attempts to facilitate efficiency in processing payments by providing that:

> A claim is not discharged if the organization proves that, within a reasonable time before the tender, (1) it sent a conspicuous statement to the debtor notifying him that checks or other communications regarding disputed debts must be sent to a designated person, office or place and (2) that the instrument or communication was not received by the designated person, office or place.[224]

The statement must be sent to the customer a reasonable time before the tender is made.[225] Thus, the statement must notify the customer that if he wants to dispute a claim, he must send the payment to a special address designated by the creditor. By having disputed claims sent to a special address, the creditor can ensure that the person processing the lock box account can continue to ignore any writing accompanying the payment, while still making available to the debtor an avenue for contesting claims.

2.   *Exception For Returning Payment*

There is a second exception that applies to all creditors who do not require that claims be sent to a special address. Under this exception, the claim is not discharged if the creditor proves that it had tendered repayment of the amount of the instrument within 90 days of its payment.[226] This protects the creditor from an inadvertent cashing of a check by allowing the creditor to recognize its error and correct it within 90 days.

However, these two procedures by which an organizational creditor can protect itself are mutually exclusive. The creditor may either require that "full payment" checks be sent to a specified person who determines whether the accord and satisfaction should be accepted and the check cashed, or it may cash all checks and thereafter reject any accord by returning the payment

---

223. U.C.C. §3-311, Official Comment 5.

224. U.C.C. §3-311(c)(1).

225. U.C.C. §3-311, Official Comment 5. The reasonable time requirement can be satisfied by notice on the billing statement itself.

226. U.C.C. §3-311(c)(2); U.C.C. §3-311, Official Comment 6.

within 90 days. If it sets up a separate address, it may not use the second exception by returning checks sent to that address in the 90-day period.

3. Limitation on Exceptions

Because both of these exceptions can be abused, both exceptions are subject to a limitation. The debtor may prove that within a reasonable time before collection of the instrument was initiated, the creditor or its agent who had direct responsibility with respect to the disputed obligation knew[227] that the instrument was tendered in full satisfaction.[228]

An agent has direct responsibility with respect to disputed obligations when he has the authority to settle the matter. A chief executive officer of a corporation probably would not be found to have such responsibility since, although he has general responsibility for the operations of the organization, he does not have direct responsibility for resolving small disputes.[229]

If the debtor succeeds in his proving that the creditor, or the agent who had responsibility for overseeing disputed obligations, knew that the check was tendered in full payment before the check was deposited for collection, the creditor cannot use either of the exceptions. It is extremely unlikely that any person having such authority would be processing checks sent to the lock box account. Because a clerk processing checks does not have authority to settle matters, the debt would not discharged even if the clerk saw the full satisfaction language before depositing the check. Therefore, a debtor will seldom be able to preclude the creditor from claiming that the debt was not discharged where the check was sent to a lock box account. However, the right of the creditor to return the payment within 90 days may very well be precluded by this limitation. If the debtor clearly indicated on the check or accompanying letter that the check was sent in full satisfaction of the disputed claim, and the check and any accompanying letter were sent to a person with authority to settle the claim, the debtor will probably be found to have proven that the limitation applies.

---

227. Knowledge, and not mere notice, is required. U.C.C. §3-311, Official Comment 6. An organization claimant is deemed to have knowledge when the person having responsibility for settlement has the requisite knowledge. U.C.C. §3-311, Official Comment 7; see also U.C.C. §1-201(27).

228. U.C.C. §3-311(d); U.C.C. §3-311, Official Comment 7.

229. U.C.C. §3-311, Official Comment 7; see also U.C.C. §1-201(27).

H. PROCEDURAL ISSUES INVOLVING NEGOTIABLE INSTRUMENTS

1. Who May Sue on a Negotiable Instrument

Besides holders, three other groups of people have the right to enforce an instrument. These people fall into the category of a "person entitled to enforce" an instrument. A "person entitled to enforce" an instrument includes:

1. the holder of the instrument;
2. a nonholder in possession of the instrument who has the rights of a holder;
3. the owner of a lost instrument under §3-309; and
4. a person from whom payment has been recovered under §3-418(d).[230]

The first category, a holder of the instrument, has already been previously discussed in Chapter 2. The second category, a nonholder in possession of the instrument who has the rights of a holder, includes several types of persons. A transferee of a holder who fails to obtain the indorsement of his transferor acquires, by the transfer, the rights of a holder.[231] For example, if Alice, as payee, gives or sells a note to Beth but fails to indorse the note, Beth, on account of the absence of indorsement, is not a holder of the note. However, because Alice transferred the note to her, Beth has Alice's rights as a holder and is, in her own right, a person entitled to enforce the instrument. An accommodation party who pays the holder obtains the rights of the holder through subrogation. The accommodation party may enforce the instrument in her own name. Similarly, an indorser who pays the holder also acquires the right to enforce the instrument against prior parties. The third category comprises certain owners of lost or stolen instruments. The requirements for having this right are discussed in Chapter 3I. Finally, as we will discuss in Chapter 4, §3-418 allows a payor who made payment by mistake to recover its payment from certain recipients. In the event that payment is recovered, the instrument is treated as if it had been dishonored and the person from whom the payment has been recovered becomes the person entitled to enforce the instrument.[232]

230. U.C.C. §3-301.
231. U.C.C. §3-301, Official Comment.
232. U.C.C. §3-418(d).

2.   Burden of Proof in Negotiable Instruments Cases

There are substantial procedural advantages that simplify and expedite actions involving negotiable instruments. These include simpler pleading requirements, favorable allocation of the burden of proof, and the creation of certain rebuttable presumptions.

A person entitled to enforce the instrument (we will call him the plaintiff here) establishes a prima facie case for recovery where he (1) establishes that the obligor's signature is effective, (2) produces the instrument, and (3) proves that he is a person entitled to enforce the instrument.[233] If the plaintiff's claim is that he is the holder, he must prove each element of holder status. If the instrument was originally made payable to the plaintiff himself or to bearer, the plaintiff need only prove that he is in possession of the instrument in order to prove that he is the holder.[234] If the instrument was originally made payable to another person and indorsed to the plaintiff or in blank, the plaintiff must also establish the effectiveness of each indorsement in his chain of title. If the plaintiff's status as a person entitled to enforce the instrument arises from being a transferee of a holder, he must prove both that the instrument has been transferred to him and that his transferor had the rights of a holder.[235] To establish that his transferor was a holder or had the rights of a holder, the plaintiff must prove the effectiveness of every indorsement necessary to his transferor's chain of title. In any case, the plaintiff cannot recover unless he produces the instrument itself.[236] A copy of the instrument is not sufficient.

3.   Proving Signatures

After proving that he is a person entitled to enforce the instrument, the plaintiff must establish the authenticity of the obligor's signature.[237] For example, if the plaintiff is suing John as maker of the note, the plaintiff must prove that

---

233. U.C.C. §3-308(b); U.C.C. §3-308, Official Comment 1; U.C.C. §3-308, Official Comment 2; U.C.C. §3-308(a).

234. U.C.C. §1-201(20).

235. U.C.C. §3-308, Official Comment 2.

236. U.C.C. §3-308(b); U.C.C. §3-308, Official Comment 2. There are two exceptions to this rule. The first exception is if the instrument has been lost, destroyed, or stolen, the owner of such an instrument, after complying with the requirements of §3-309, is entitled to the same rights and presumptions that would have been available under §3-308 if he had produced the instrument. U.C.C. §3-309(b). The second exception is for a person from whom a payment has been recovered pursuant to §3-418. U.C.C. §3-418(d).

237. U.C.C. §3-308(a); U.C.C. §3-308, Official Comment 1. If the signature was made by an

John's signature is authentic in order to recover from John. Although a party claiming under a signature (the plaintiff) has the burden of establishing its effectiveness, a signature is deemed effective unless specifically denied by the defendant (John).[238] Thus, in his answer to the complaint, John must specifically deny that his signature is authentic. If John fails to do so, the signature is deemed to be authentic. A general denial to the complaint is not sufficient.

Even if John contests the signature, the plaintiff is entitled to a presumption that the signature is genuine and authorized.[239] The presumption requires that the trier of fact find the signature to be genuine or authorized unless and until the obligor has introduced sufficient evidence to support a finding that the signature is either not genuine or unauthorized.[240] Once sufficient evidence is introduced, the presumption completely disappears. To rebut the presumption, John need only testify that his signature is not genuine and submit a sample of his true signature. However, most courts would hold that a mere denial of the signature's genuineness is insufficient to overcome the presumption. If the presumption is overcome, the plaintiff has the burden of proving that it is more probable than not that the signature is genuine or authorized.

4. Burden on Obligor to Prove Defense

Once the plaintiff has established his prima facie case by (1) establishing that he is a person entitled to enforce the instrument, (2) producing the instrument, and (3) proving the authenticity of the obligor's signature, he will recover against the obligor unless a defense or a claim in recoupment is established by the obligor.[241] The obligor cannot defend by proving that the plain-

---

agent, the plaintiff must prove the authority of the agent to sign for the obligor. In an action to enforce the instrument against a person as an undisclosed principal, the plaintiff has the burden of establishing that the defendant is liable on the instrument as a represented person under §3-402(a). U.C.C. §3-308(a).

238. U.C.C. §3-308(a); U.C.C. §3-308, Official Comment 1.

239. U.C.C. §3-308(a); U.C.C. §3-308, Official Comment 1. There is no presumption of genuineness or authorization if the purported signer has died or become incompetent before proof of the signature is required. U.C.C. §3-308(a); U.C.C. §3-308, Official Comment 1. However, where the signature at issue belongs to someone other than the deceased or incompetent, as where the contested signature is an indorsement in the holder's chain of title, the presumption still applies. U.C.C. §3-308(a).

240. U.C.C. §1-201(31); U.C.C. §3-308, Official Comment 1.

241. U.C.C. §3-308(b); U.C.C. §3-308, Official Comment 2.

tiff is not a holder in due course. Absent a defense or a claim in recoupment, any person entitled to enforce the instrument is entitled to recover against the obligor even if that person is not a holder in due course. These defenses and claims in recoupment include any authorized in Article 3 (discussed in Chapter 2) including, among others, any defense or claim in recoupment specified in §3-305, that the obligor signed only in a representative capacity, that the instrument has been materially altered, or that the obligor is discharged by payment, cancellation or otherwise.

5.   After Defense Proved, Duty of Plaintiff to Prove Holder-in-Due-Course Status

Even if the obligor has established a defense or claim in recoupment, the plaintiff will still recover if he proves that he is immune to the defense or claim in recoupment. He may do so by proving that he is a holder in due course or has the rights of a holder in due course.[242] To accomplish this, he must prove that he satisfies every requirement for holder-in-due-course status. He must prove that he took the instrument for value, without notice of any of the proscribed facts and in good faith. Due to the difficulty of finding objective facts showing the presence of good faith, he may only be able to assert that he was in good faith. In recognition of this problem, some courts require the obligor to introduce some evidence of the holder's lack of good faith before requiring the holder to prove his good faith.[243] Other courts find that the holder's testimony that he was honest in fact and that he acted in accordance with reasonable commercial standards of fair dealing is sufficient to uphold a finding in his favor absent contrary evidence.[244] If the obligor introduces evidence of

---

242. U.C.C. §3-308(b); U.C.C. §3-308, Official Comment 2.

243. For cases under former Article 3, see In re Williams Bros. Asphalt Paving Co., 59 B.R. 71, 1 U.C.C. Rep. Serv. 2d 794 (Bankr. W.D. Mich. 1986) (although burden of proof of holder-in-due-course status is upon bank/holder, where there is no evidence of absence of good faith, holder-in-due-course status is presumed); Corn Exchange Bank v. Tri-State Livestock Auction Co., 368 N.W.2d 596, 41 U.C.C. Rep. Serv. 845 (S.D. 1985) (in support of its holding that depositary bank/holder met its burden of proof, court stated that there was no evidence of absence of good faith).

244. For cases under former Article 3, see First International Bank of Israel, Ltd. v. L. Blankstein & Son, Inc., 59 N.Y.2d 436, 465 N.Y.S.2d 888, 452 N.E.2d 1216, 36 U.C.C. Rep. Serv. 565 (1983) (statement enough); DH Cattle Holdings v. Kuntz, 15 U.C.C. Rep. Serv. 2d 178, 568 N.Y.S.2d 229 (N.Y. App. Div. 1991) (Transferee of holder in due course obtained summary judgment upon affidavit of vice-president of holder in due course/transferor that transferor took the note in good faith and without any notice of defense.).

lack of good faith, the holder should introduce evidence of any investigation the holder undertook before purchasing the instrument.

Even if the plaintiff succeeds in proving that he is a holder in due course, the plaintiff will be denied recovery if the defendant proves a defense effective against a person having the rights of a holder in due course. These defenses include "real defenses," defenses or claims in recoupment that the defendant has against the plaintiff itself, or a discharge of which the plaintiff has notice.[245]

6.   Statute of Limitations

The Code sets out the statute of limitations period within which actions upon an instrument must be brought.[246] The forum state's law determines whether any circumstances will toll the running of the statute of limitations or will revive debts barred by the statute.

Generally, an action on a note payable at a definite time must be commenced within six years of the day after it is due, or if accelerated, within six years of the accelerated due date.[247] An action on a note payable on demand must be brought within six years after demand has been made.[248] If payment has not been demanded, any action is barred if none of the principal or interest has been paid for a continuous period of ten years.[249] An action on a personal check or other unaccepted draft must be brought within three years after dishonor or ten years after the date of the draft, whichever is earlier.[250]

I.   ENFORCEMENT OF LOST, DESTROYED, OR STOLEN INSTRUMENTS

1.   Lost, Destroyed, or Stolen Ordinary Instruments

Let us begin with an example. John, having sold his car to Alice, claims that he has lost the check Alice gave him in payment for the car. John requests that

245. U.C.C. §3-305(b).
246. U.C.C. §3-118, Official Comment 1.
247. U.C.C. §3-118(a).
248. U.C.C. §3-118(b).
249. U.C.C. §3-118(b).
250. U.C.C. §3-118(c); U.C.C. §3-118, Official Comment 3.

I. Enforcement of Lost Instruments

Alice give him a replacement check. John tells her that he needs the money. Alice does not really know John. Is it safe for Alice to give John a replacement check? The short answer is "no." John may have already negotiated the check. If he did and the new holder qualifies as a holder in due course, the new holder would take free of Alice's defense that she was discharged by her issuance of the new check to John. Even if John did not negotiate the check to a third party, if he indorsed the check in blank before it was lost, a purchaser of the check from the finder could himself become a holder in due course who would take the check free of Alice's defense of discharge by payment. But what if John is really telling the truth? One of the protections of receiving a negotiable instrument rather than cash is the safety from theft provided by an unindorsed instrument. How can John get his money? Article 3 provides the answer.

Article 3, in §3-309, provides a vehicle that while enabling John to enforce the instrument also protects Alice against the possibility of double liability. Under §3-309, John, being the person entitled to enforce an instrument which is lost by destruction, theft or otherwise, may maintain an action as if he had produced the instrument.[251] To protect Alice, a court cannot enter judgment in favor of John unless it finds that Alice is adequately protected against any loss that might occur by reason of a claim by another person to enforce the instrument.

a. Adequate Protection

Alice needs protection both against the possibility that John lied about losing the check, which may expose her to double liability, and also against expenses incurred by her in defending against an unsuccessful action brought by a person who acquired possession of the check bearing John's forged indorsement. Section 3-309 permits the court to require John to supply security to indemnify Alice against these losses or expenses.[252] A court has the discretion as to the amount and type of security required to be posted. The amount should be sufficient to protect the obligor not only against liability in the face amount of the instrument but also for all expenses incurred in defending the action, including attorney's fees and court costs. Security may not always be necessary. Where many years have elapsed without any attempt to present the instrument or where the owner is clearly financially stable, there may be little reason to require any security at all.

Unless John has property he could post as collateral, the usual way by

---

251. U.C.C. §3-309(b); U.C.C. §3-309, Official Comment.
252. U.C.C. §3-309(b); U.C.C. §3-309, Official Comment.

which John would supply security to indemnify Alice would be to purchase a "lost instruments bond." However, John may have trouble securing such a bond. Even if John were able to afford to pay the high premium charged by the bonding company, the company may refuse to issue the bond if it regards the circumstances of its loss to be suspicious. If he cannot obtain a lost instruments bond, John may be unable to provide protection deemed adequate by the court.

b.   What Must Be Proved

There are certain facts that John must prove to recover under §3-309. If he proves these facts, he may recover on the instrument as though he had produced the instrument itself.[253] However, although John may enforce the instrument, he may not enforce the obligation for which the instrument was given.[254] If John were allowed to sue Alice on the underlying obligation itself, this would permit him to shift to Alice the risk that the check was lost in bearer form and acquired by a holder in due course.

John must first prove that he was in possession of the instrument and entitled to enforce it when the instrument was lost.[255] This requires that he prove that he was either a holder or had the rights of a holder at the time he lost possession.[256] John must also prove that the loss of possession was not a result of his transfer of the instrument or of a lawful seizure of the instrument.[257] If he transferred the instrument or if it had been garnished or attached, John no longer has the right to enforce the instrument. John must also prove that he cannot reasonably obtain possession of the instrument because it was either destroyed, lost, or in the wrongful possession of an unknown person or a person that cannot be found or is not amenable to service of process.[258] John cannot maintain this type of action if he is able to reacquire possession of the instrument. When the person entitled to enforce the instrument knows who has possession of the instrument, he must bring an action against that party to recover the instrument.[259] Finally, John must prove the terms of the instru-

253. U.C.C. §3-309(b).
254. U.C.C. §3-310(b)(4); U.C.C. §3-310, Official Comment 4.
255. U.C.C. §3-309(a).
256. Proof that the plaintiff was named as the payee is insufficient absent proof that the instrument had been delivered to him or that the right of ownership had otherwise been transferred by the drawer to him.
257. U.C.C. §3-309(a)(ii).
258. U.C.C. §3-309(a).
259. Similarly, the owner of an instrument which has been paid by a payor bank over a forged indorsement has no action under §3-309. His action is against the payor bank or the depositary bank for conversion.

ment[260] including any terms necessary to make the instrument negotiable. This may be accomplished by the introduction of a photocopy, by his testimony or by introduction of the agreement pursuant to which the instrument was executed.[261]

2. Lost, Destroyed, or Stolen Bank Checks

A different set of rules apply when a bank check (a cashier's, teller's, or certified check) is lost, destroyed, or stolen. Let us look at an example that will illustrate the reasons why a special set of rules is needed. Jim is moving from New York to Los Angeles. He goes to his bank and withdraws his entire savings in the form of a cashier's check. Upon his arrival in Los Angeles, his wallet is stolen. He asks the bank to reimburse him for the amount of the check. The bank tells him that it cannot reimburse him unless he posts security in the amount of the check in order to protect the bank against the chance that he had indorsed the check before its loss. Jim does not have assets sufficient to post adequate security. Jim asks the bank how long will it be before the bank can be sure that it will not have to pay the check to someone else. The bank tells Jim that it could be forever. Although this may sound strange, the bank's statement is true. An action on a cashier's check must be brought within three years after demand for payment has been made by the person entitled to enforce the check.[262] However, the claim is never barred because there is no limitation upon the time within which demand must be made. Fortunately, Jim is not completely out of luck. The rules in §3-312 provide a mechanism for Jim to obtain a refund for the amount of the check within a reasonable period of time without the expense of posting security.[263] At the same time, these rules protect the bank against the possibility of double liability.

The class of persons who may use §3-312 is quite limited. Only the drawer or payee of a certified check and the remitter or payee of a teller's or cashier's

---

260. U.C.C. §3-309(b).

261. For cases under former Article 3, see Crawford v. 733 San Mateo Co., 854 F.2d 1220, 8 U.C.C. Rep. Serv. 2d 75 (10th Cir. 1988) (introducing copy of original note sufficient); Gutierrez v. Bermudez, 540 So. 2d 888, 9 U.C.C. Rep. Serv. 2d 1310 (Fla. App. 1989) (plaintiff established prima facie case for recovery when she testified that original note and mortgage had disappeared after she placed them in her desk, identified copies of documents, and testified that note remained unpaid).

262. U.C.C. §3-118(d); U.C.C. §3-118, Official Comment 3.

263. U.C.C. §3-312, Official Comment 1.

check ("claimant") may proceed under §3-312.[264] An indorsee of any of these bank checks is denied the advantages of §3-312 and must proceed as if he were suing on an ordinary instrument under §3-309.[265]

a.   Manner of Asserting Claim

To comply with §3-312, Jim (the claimant) must send a communication to the bank issuing the bank check (the issuing bank on a cashier's check, the drawer bank on a teller's check, and the certifying bank on the certified check) describing the check with reasonable certainty and requesting payment of the amount of the check.[266] This communication must be accompanied by a declaration of loss.[267] A declaration of loss is a written statement made under penalty of perjury which states that: (1) the declarer (Jim) lost possession of the check; (2) the declarer (Jim) is the drawer or payee of a certified check or payee or remitter of a teller's or cashier's check; (3) the loss of possession was not the result of a transfer by the declarer (Jim) or of a lawful seizure; and (4) the declarer (Jim) cannot reasonably obtain possession of the check because either the check was destroyed, its whereabouts cannot be determined, or it is in the wrongful possession of an unknown person or a person that cannot be found or is not amenable to service of process.[268]

b.   When Claim Is Effective

By complying with these simple requirements, Jim has asserted a valid claim under §3-312. However, Jim will not be reimbursed immediately. Because the issuing bank is not given any security to protect the bank against the possibility of double liability, the bank must be protected by other means.

---

264. U.C.C. §3-312(a)(3)(ii).

265. U.C.C. §3-312, Official Comment 2. U.C.C. §3-312, Comment 2 states that "Limitation to an original party or remitter gives the obligated bank the ability to determine, at the time it becomes obligated on the check, the identity of the person or persons who can assert a claim with respect to the check. The bank is not faced with having to determine the rights of some person who was not a party to the check at that time or with whom the bank had not dealt."

266. U.C.C. §3-312(b); U.C.C. §3-312, Official Comment 2. The communication must be received in a reasonable time for the bank to act upon it before the check is paid. U.C.C. §3-312(b)(iii). The claimant must also provide reasonable identification if so requested by the obligated bank. U.C.C. §3-312(b)(iv). The obligated bank has no right to insist upon any other conditions. U.C.C. §3-312, Official Comment 2. For example, the obligated bank may not require the posting of a bond or other security. U.C.C. §3-312, Official Comment 2.

267. U.C.C. §3-312(b).

268. U.C.C. §3-312(a)(3)(i)–(iv), respectively.

I. Enforcement of Lost Instruments

The issuing bank is protected by the imposition of a 90-day waiting period during which the bank may, with impunity, pay the person entitled to enforce the check. Of course, if Jim did not indorse it, the person paid would not be the person entitled to enforce the instrument and therefore the bank would not be discharged by its payment.[269]

Jim's claim only becomes effective at or after 90 days following the date of issuance of the cashier's or teller's check or of the acceptance of the certified check.[270] After the 90-day period, the issuing bank becomes liable to Jim (the claimant).[271] If the bank had not already paid a person entitled to enforce the check, the bank must now pay Jim (the claimant).[272] Payment to Jim (the claimant) discharges the bank's liability to a person entitled to enforce the check. The issuing bank is then freed from its obligation to pay the person entitled to enforce the check.[273]

What happens, however, if Jim did in fact indorse the bank check before he lost it, or worse yet, if he had negotiated the bank check and lied in his declaration? Under these circumstances, a holder in due course may have acquired the bank check. If a holder in due course presents the bank check after the bank pays Jim, the issuing bank may pay the holder in due course. Jim then is obliged to repay the bank.[274] If the bank refuses to pay the holder in due course, Jim must pay the holder. In addition, the declaration of loss made by Jim is a warranty of the truth of the statements contained therein.[275] The warranty runs to any party suffering a loss because of a breach of the warranty. This includes the obligated bank and any person entitled to enforce the check.[276] Of course, this is not a perfect system. The issuing bank has no duty to pay the person entitled to enforce the instrument. If Jim is insolvent, that person will suffer the loss. In some ways, this makes sense. The loss was caused by the person's failure to present the check for 90 days. The holder could have presented the check and received payment.

---

269. U.C.C. §3-312(b)(2); U.C.C. §3-312, Official Comment 3.

270. U.C.C. §3-312(b)(1); U.C.C. §3-312, Official Comment 3.

271. U.C.C. §3-312, Official Comment 4, Case #3. Of course, if the person to whom payment is made is not the person entitled to enforce the check because, for example, his chain of title includes a forged indorsement, the obligated bank is not discharged by its payment. U.C.C. §3-312, Official Comment 4, Case #3.

272. U.C.C. §3-312(b)(4); U.C.C. §3-312, Official Comment 4; U.C.C. §3-312, Official Comment 3.

273. U.C.C. §3-312(b)(3); U.C.C. §3-312, Official Comment 3.

274. U.C.C. §3-312(c); U.C.C. §3-312, Official Comment 3.

275. U.C.C. §3-312(b); U.C.C. §3-312, Comment 3.

276. U.C.C. §3-312, Official Comment 2.

CHAPTER 4

Forgery, Alteration, and Other Fraudulent Activity

There are many ways in which a person who wants to improperly acquire funds can do so by use of a negotiable instrument. We have already discussed how a fiduciary can misuse the proceeds of an instrument intended for the benefit of the represented person. In this chapter, we will discuss six other fraudulent activities involving instruments:

1. forgery of (a) the drawer's signature on a draft or other check, (b) the maker's signature on a note; or (c) the acceptor's signature on a draft;
2. forgery of the payee's or indorsee's signature on an instrument ("forged indorsement");
3. alteration of an instrument by, for example, raising the amount for which the instrument is payable ("alteration");
4. payment of an instrument in violation of a restrictive indorsement ("restrictive indorsement");
5. check kiting; and
6. fraudulent encoding of a check ("MICR fraud").

A. FORGED SIGNATURES

1. Introduction

Subject to certain exceptions, a forged or otherwise unauthorized signature is ineffective as the signature of the person whose name is signed.[1] An

---

1. U.C.C. §3-403(a); U.C.C. §3-403, Official Comment 2.

unauthorized signature may be an outright forgery or a signature by an agent in excess of his actual or apparent authority.[2] For example, assume that Allen, vice president of May Corporation, has no authority to draw checks on May Corporation's account. Allen's drawing of a check on May Corporation's account has the same effect as a stranger stealing May Corporation's checkbook and drawing a check on its account. Allen, not being authorized to sign checks for May Corporation, is for all practical purposes a forger.

The fact that a forged signature has no effect as the signature of the person whose name is forged has two distinct consequences:

1. The person whose signature is forged is not liable on the instrument; and
2. If there is a forged indorsement in the chain of title, no person following the forged indorsement can be a holder of the instrument.

a. Person Whose Signature Is Forged Not Liable

The person whose signature is forged is not liable on the instrument.[3] Thus, in the event that the check is dishonored by Payor Bank, May Corporation is not liable to the holder of the check. Similarly, in the event that Payor Bank pays the check, Payor Bank may not charge May Corporation's account. Why not? Because May Corporation did not authorize Payor Bank to pay the check.

Does Payor Bank after paying the check have recourse against anyone on the check? A forged signature is effective as the signature of the forger in favor of a person who in good faith pays the instrument or takes it for value.[4] Payor Bank may recover from Allen. It is as if Allen had signed the check in his own name. Allen is liable in the capacity in which he signed. In this case Allen is liable as the drawer of the check. In a vast majority of the cases, however, the forger either cannot be located or is insolvent.

Furthermore, May Corporation may still be liable on the check. If May Corporation's negligence allowed Allen to commit the forgery, May Corporation may be precluded from denying that the signature on the check was its

---

2. U.C.C. §1-201(43); U.C.C. §3-403, Official Comment 1. Where two or more signatures are required to constitute the signature of an organization, and one of the signatures is lacking, the signature of the organization is unauthorized. U.C.C. §3-403(b); U.C.C. §3-403, Official Comment 4.

3. U.C.C. §3-401(a).

4. U.C.C. §3-403(a); U.C.C. §3-403, Official Comment 2.

signature. In this event, if Payor Bank had refused to pay the check, the holder could recover from May Corporation on its drawer's obligation. If Payor Bank paid the check, Payor Bank could debit May Corporation's account just as if May Corporation's signature was authorized. We will discuss negligence and other grounds for preclusion later in this chapter.

b.   Forged Indorsement in Chain of Title

When an indorsement in the chain of title is forged, no person following the forged indorsement can become a holder of the instrument. This, of course, assumes that the instrument is not payable to bearer or indorsed in blank. When an instrument is payable to bearer or indorsed in blank, the instrument is negotiated by delivery alone. No indorsement is necessary. For this reason, a forged indorsement has no effect on the chain of title. Assume, for example, that a check is made payable to Paul. After indorsing the check in blank, Paul loses the check. The finder of the check, in cashing the check at his brother's bank, forges his brother's indorsement. Because his brother's indorsement was not necessary to negotiate the check to the depositary bank, the depositary bank qualifies as a holder despite the forged indorsement.

The issue that arises when there is a forged indorsement in the chain of title is who owns the instrument—the person whose indorsement is forged or the person who now possesses the instrument and claims through the forged indorsement? Absent a ground for preclusion, the person whose indorsement is forged owns the instrument. For example, assume that Fred forges Julia's indorsement on a check made payable to Julia. Fred then transfers the check to Raoul. Raoul is not the holder of the check. Because only a holder can indorse an instrument for purposes of its negotiation,[5] an unauthorized indorsement does not negotiate the check. Until Julia indorses the check no one other than she can become its holder. If Payor Bank pays Raoul, the drawer of the check is not discharged. Payor Bank may not debit Drawer's account.[6] Drawer is still liable to Julia.

However, in some cases the law may preclude a person from claiming that an indorsement is forged or may treat the forged indorsement as effective as the indorsement of the payee. For example, Drawer may have been negligent in mailing the check to a person having a name similar to Julia's who then improperly indorses the check. Or Julia's bookkeeper may have indorsed the check in Julia's name. We will later examine the situations in which a forged indorsement is effective to negotiate an instrument thereby making the indorsee the holder of the instrument.

5. U.C.C. §3-201(b).
6. U.C.C. §4-401(a).

Taken as a whole, the rules found in Articles 3 and 4 for determining which party suffers the loss resulting from a forged signature provide a comprehensive scheme of loss allocation. Unfortunately, these rules are not organized by the cause of the loss. Rather they are organized by the liability assumed by different parties to the instrument. As a result, understanding the loss allocation scheme requires reference to many diverse rules. Before we proceed to examine the allocation of loss in different situations, we must briefly examine the rules governing transfer warranties, presentment warranties, recovery of payments made by mistake, and conversion.

2.   *Transfer Warranties*

We have already discussed in Chapter 3 that any person who transfers an instrument and receives consideration makes certain warranties to his transferor and, in certain cases, to subsequent transferees. Remember, there are two warranties that are relevant in determining the allocation of loss where a signature is forged. First, a transferor warrants that he is a person entitled to enforce the instrument.[7] This is basically a warranty that there are no unauthorized or missing indorsements that prevent the transferee from becoming a person entitled to enforce the instrument.[8]

Second, a transferor warrants that all signatures are authentic and authorized.[9] Thus, a forged or unauthorized drawer's, maker's, indorser's, or acceptor's signature breaches this warranty. An anomalous indorsement (an indorsement not in the chain of title) also violates this warranty. We discussed anomalous indorsements in Chapter 3. Because an anomalous indorsement is not in the chain of title, a person taking the instrument following the anomalous indorsement may still be a person entitled to enforce the instrument. As a result, the taker does not breach the warranty that he is a person entitled to enforce the instrument. In contrast, when an indorsement in the chain of title is forged or is otherwise unauthorized, the transferor not only breaches the warranty that he is a person entitled to enforce the instrument, but he also breaches the warranty that all signatures are authentic and authorized.

---

7. U.C.C. §4-207(a)(1); U.C.C. §3-416(a)(1).
8. U.C.C. §3-416, Official Comment 2.
9. U.C.C. §4-207(a)(2); U.C.C. §3-416(a)(2).

A. Forged Signatures

3. Presentment Warranties

Certain risks should not be borne by the person making payment. In order to protect the person making payment, he is given certain warranties when an instrument is presented for payment. These warranties are called the "presentment warranties." We will speak primarily in terms of presentment warranties made to the payor. However, the same warranties that are given to the drawee when a draft is presented for payment are given also to the drawee when a draft is presented for acceptance.

a. Persons Who Make the Presentment Warranties

The presentment warranties are made by the person who obtains payment or acceptance as well as by any prior transferor.[10] Let us look at an example. Assume that Jim draws a check payable to Don. Don loses the check. Don's indorsement is forged by Gil who indorses the check in blank and gives the check as a present to his daughter Sally. Sally deposits the check in her bank account at Wells Bank, which sends the check for collection to Crocker Bank, which presents the check for payment to Bank of America. Bank of America pays the check. (Figure 4.1.)

FIGURE 4.1

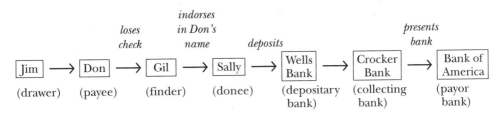

10. U.C.C. §4-208(a) and (d); U.C.C. §3-417(a) and (d). Section 3-417 provides warranties identical to those given under §4-208 except that §4-208 extends its coverage to items.

The presentment warranties cannot be disclaimed with respect to checks. U.C.C. §4-208(e); U.C.C. §3-417, Official Comment 7. Payor banks rely upon the presentment warranties in paying checks. Because checks are processed by automated means, a payor bank would not notice a disclaimer of the presentment warranties even if written conspicuously on the face of the check. If the warranties on presentment could be disclaimed, a payor bank would have to choose between forgoing the protection afforded by the presentment warranties or forgoing the efficiency that automated processing affords. U.C.C. §3-417, Official Comment 7. As to other items, a warranty may be disclaimed by an agreement among the parties to the transaction.

Crocker Bank, as the person that obtained payment, in addition to prior transferors Gil, Sally, and Wells Bank, all make the presentment warranties to Bank of America. Even though Gil did not receive consideration for the check, he still makes the presentment warranties. Even though Sally did not indorse the check, she still makes the presentment warranties. Furthermore, Wells Bank, although only an agent for collection, also makes the presentment warranties. Crocker Bank, the person presenting the item for payment, makes its warranties as of the time of presentment while the prior transferors, Gil, Sally, and Wells Bank, make their warranties as of the time of their transfer.[11] Thus, where an indorsement later in the chain of title is forged, only transferors following the forged indorsement breach their presentment warranty that they are a person entitled to enforce the instrument.

b. To Whom Presentment Warranties Are Made

The presentment warranties are made to any payor or acceptor who acts in good faith.[12] The fact that the payor or acceptor was negligent in making payment or acceptance does not deny it the right to receive these warranties.[13] For example, even if an alteration is so obvious that it should have been noticed by the payor bank, the payor bank may still recover from the presenter for breach of the warranty that the check has not been altered.

c. Warranties Made to Drawee of Unaccepted Draft

The drawee of an unaccepted draft is given three warranties:

1. that the warrantor is entitled to enforce the draft or authorized to obtain payment or acceptance on behalf of a person entitled to enforce the draft;
2. that the warrantor has no knowledge that the signature of the drawer is unauthorized; and
3. that the draft has not been altered.[14]

The basic measure of damages for breach of a warranty made to the drawee is damages equal to the amount paid less the amount that the drawee

11. U.C.C. §4-208(a)(ii); U.C.C. §4-208(d).
12. U.C.C. §4-208(a) and (d); U.C.C. §3-417(a) and (d)(1).
13. U.C.C. §4-208(b); U.C.C. §3-417(b).
14. U.C.C. §4-208(a); U.C.C. §3-417(a).

is entitled to receive from the drawer plus expenses and loss of interest arising from the breach.[15] For example, if the drawee makes payment of $1,000 on a check bearing a forged indorsement, the drawee would be entitled to $1,000 damages plus interest on the use of the funds between the time of the payment and the time of the judgment. Damages are in the full amount of the draft in the case of a forged indorsement because the drawee has no right to recover anything from the drawer. In contrast, assume that a check has been raised from $50 to $500. In this case, the basic measure of damages would be $450 plus interest and expenses since the payor bank could recover $50, the original amount of the check, from the drawer. Although there is no express provision authorizing them, attorney's fees are not necessarily excluded.[16] The drawee may have the right to recover attorney's fees under the phrase "expenses . . . resulting from the breach."[17]

d. Warranties Made to Other Payors

All payors, other than drawees of unaccepted drafts, receive only the warranty that the warrantor is entitled to enforce the instrument or is authorized to obtain payment on behalf of a person entitled to enforce the instrument.[18] These payors include drawers or indorsers to whom a dishonored draft has been presented for payment, makers of notes, and acceptors of drafts.[19] Damages for breach of this warranty are an amount equal to the amount paid plus expenses and loss of interest resulting from the breach.[20] As in the case of a drawee, attorney's fees may be granted to the payor as expenses.

Unlike the drawee of an unaccepted draft, neither the drawer nor the maker is given a warranty that the presenter lacks knowledge of the unauthorized nature of the maker's or drawer's signature.[21] A drawer or maker should

15. U.C.C. §4-208(b); U.C.C. §3-417(b). Breach of a presentment warranty is a defense to the drawee's liability as an acceptor to the same extent to which the acceptor would be entitled to damages had payment been made. U.C.C. §4-208(b); U.C.C. §3-417(b).

16. U.C.C. §3-417, Official Comment 5.

17. U.C.C. §3-415, Official Comment 5.

18. U.C.C. §4-208(d); U.C.C. §3-417, Official Comment 4.

19. U.C.C. §4-208(d); U.C.C. §3-417(d).

20. U.C.C. §4-208(d); U.C.C. §3-417(d)(2); U.C.C. §3-417, Official Comment 5.

21. U.C.C. §3-417, Official Comment 4. Similarly, no warranty is made to the acceptor of a draft that the warrantor lacked knowledge of the unauthorized nature of the drawer's signature. The acceptor as the drawee of an unaccepted draft was given a warranty that the warrantor lacked knowledge as to the unauthorized nature of the drawer's signature. U.C.C. §3-417, Official Comment 4. As a result the acceptor may recover both from the person presenting the

be able to determine whether his signature is authentic. Even absent a warranty, a drawer or maker could recover, under §3-418(a) or (b), any payment made to a presenter who had knowledge of the forgery at the time he took the instrument. Having such knowledge, the presenter would not have taken the instrument in good faith and therefore would not be protected under §3-418(c). We discuss §3-418 next.

e.   When Cause of Action Accrues

A cause of action for breach of a presentment warranty accrues when the claimant has reason to know of the breach.[22] The breach occurs when the item is paid or accepted. Notice of a claim for breach of a presentment warranty must be given to the warrantor within 30 days after the claimant had reason to know of the breach and could ascertain the warrantor's identity. Failure to give notice discharges the warrantor's liability to the extent of any loss caused by the delay in giving notice of the claim.[23] The extent of the warrantor's loss suffered as a result of the payor's delay in giving notice is a question of fact.

4. *Recovery by Payor of Payment Made by Mistake*

Payment of an instrument may be based upon a mistaken belief. For example, Freddy, an experienced forger, forges Jim's signature as drawer of a check payable to Sally. Sally negotiates the check to Don in payment for the purchase of a car. Don is unaware that Jim's signature is forged. Don deposits the check in his checking account at Wells Bank, which presents the check for payment to Bank of America. Bank of America, not noticing that Jim's signature is forged, pays the check. (See Figure 4.2.)

---

draft for acceptance, if he knew of the unauthorized nature of the drawer's signature, and from persons who transferred the draft prior to its acceptance who had such knowledge. U.C.C. §3-417, Official Comment 4. The acceptor could also recover under U.C.C. §3-418(a) from any person presenting the acceptance for payment who had knowledge of the unauthorized nature of the drawer's signature when he took the acceptance.

22. U.C.C. §4-208(f); U.C.C. §3-417(f).
23. U.C.C. §4-208(e); U.C.C. §3-417, Official Comment 7.

A. Forged Signatures

FIGURE 4.2

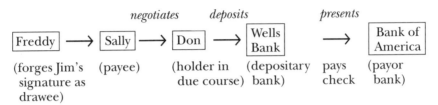

Upon receiving his bank statement, Jim notices the forgery and demands that Bank of America recredit his account. Because Jim did not authorize Bank of America to debit his account, Bank of America must recredit his account.[24] This means Bank of America will suffer the loss unless it is allowed to recover the mistaken payment from Wells Bank, Don, or Sally. Freddy, by now, has disappeared. Can Bank of America recover the payment from Wells Bank, Don, or Sally? We have just seen that neither Sally, Don, nor Wells Bank warrant to Bank of America, the payor bank, that Jim's (the drawer) signature is authentic. Sally, Don, and Wells Bank would only breach their presentment warranty if they had knowledge that Jim's signature was forged. We will now examine §3-418, which provides a potential ground upon which Bank of America may recover the payment.

We will limit our examination of §3-418 here to the question as to whether a drawee of a draft may recover a payment made upon the mistaken belief that the drawer's signature is authorized. The question as to whether a drawee, who has accepted a draft on a mistaken belief that the drawer's signature is authorized, may revoke its acceptance raises the identical issue as does whether the drawee can recover a payment based upon a mistaken belief. The drawee can revoke its acceptance in the identical circumstances that it could recover the payment had payment been made instead. The same question arises when the payor bank mistakenly pays an instrument drawn upon insufficient funds. We will examine this question in connection with check kiting in Chapter 4D. We will cover in Chapter 4A(6) whether a maker, acceptor, drawer, or indorser who, on a mistaken belief, pays an instrument bearing his or her forged signature can recover the payment.

The rule for determining whether a drawee who pays a draft bearing a forged drawer's signature can recover the payment is as follows:

> A drawee who pays a draft on a mistaken belief that the signature of the drawer was authorized, may recover the amount of the draft from the person

---

24. U.C.C. §4-401(a).

to whom payment was made or for whose benefit payment was made. However, the payment may not be recovered from a person who took the instrument in good faith and for value or who in good faith changed position in reliance on the payment ("protected persons").[25]

Thus, where Bank of America pays a check bearing Jim's unauthorized signature as drawer, Bank of America can recover the payment from Don or Wells Bank unless they are protected persons. Bank of America's right to recover the payment is not affected by its failure to exercise ordinary care.[26] Bank of America may not recover from Sally because payment was not made to her or for her benefit.

a.   Protected Persons under §3-418

There are two classes of protected persons.[27] The first class of protected persons includes any person who takes the instrument in good faith and for value. Thus, assume that Don himself presented the check to Bank of America and immediately upon payment the teller, realizing that Jim's signature was forged, demands the payment back. Because Don took the check in good faith and for value, the payment may not be recovered from him even though he did not rely upon the payment.

The second class of protected persons includes any person who has in good faith changed position in reliance on the payment. The issue is not whether the person acted in good faith in the transaction in which he acquired the instrument. Instead, the determinative issue is whether his act of reliance on the payment is in good faith. A person who obtains payment with knowledge of the mistake does not act in good faith when he changes position in reliance on the payment.

A person who did not qualify as a holder in due course because he had notice of a claim or defense can still be protected if he acted in good faith when he relied upon the payment. Assume that Don knew that the car he sold to Sally had defective brakes in breach of an express warranty. However, Don did not release the car to Sally until he cashed the check. Don is protected because he has changed position in good faith reliance on the payment even though, because he knew of Sally's defense, he did not take the check in good faith.

It is often difficult to determine what constitutes a change of position in reliance on payment. To make this determination, reference must be made to

---

25. U.C.C. §3-418(a); U.C.C. §3-418(c); U.C.C. §3-418, Official Comment 1.
26. U.C.C. §3-418(a).
27. U.C.C. §3-418(c).

the law of restitution of the subject jurisdiction. In many situations it is easy to determine whether the recipient has changed position in reliance on the payment. For example, a seller who releases the goods only after learning that the check has been paid has changed position in reliance on the payment. An agent who turns over the payment to his principal also changes position in reliance on the payment. For example, when Wells Bank allows Don to withdraw the funds represented by the check, Wells Bank changes position in reliance on the payment. Another example of good faith reliance is where Don gives the money received in payment to the American Red Cross as a charitable donation.[28] In contrast, if Don uses the money to pay his mortgage payment or gas bill, he would not be found to have changed position in reliance on the payment. This is because he would have been required to have made these payments even if Bank of America had not paid the check.

In between these extremes are cases in which the recipient makes an expenditure for his own benefit as, for instance, in purchasing a car or going on a vacation. If he would not have made these expenditures but for the payment, he qualifies as a protected person. In these cases, it can be argued that he should be deemed to have changed position only to the extent that he no longer retains the value of the goods purchased. For instance, if the recipient of the mistaken payment purchases a car that has depreciated in value to the extent of $1,000, it can be argued that he has changed position only to the extent of the $1,000. On the other hand, some courts may find that since he never would have made the purchase but for the payment, he should not be forced into the position of attempting to resell the property.

A transferee of a protected party should also be protected against the payor's right of restitution. Assume that Don gives the check to his sister, Aida, as a gift. Aida obtains payment. Unless a transferee of a protected person is also protected, the payor could recover the payment from Aida. If Don, however, obtains payment himself and gives the money to Aida, the payor could not recover the payment. Denying Aida protection in the first scenario but not in the second scenario makes little sense.

b. Consequences When Payment Is Recovered

In the event that payment is recovered, the instrument is treated as having been dishonored.[29] The person from whom payment is recovered is given

---

28. This is, of course, assuming that Don would not have otherwise made the donation. If he would have, he has not changed position on account of the payment.
29. U.C.C. §3-418(d); U.C.C. §3-418, Official Comment 2.

the rights of a person entitled to enforce the dishonored instrument. As a result, this person can enforce the instrument against the drawer, maker, or indorser just as if it had been dishonored on its initial presentment. Wells Bank, or its customer Don, may recover from Fred or Sally. In addition, because the instrument is deemed to have been dishonored, Don may also enforce the underlying sales contract.

5. Conversion

The right that the owner of an instrument has to recover from the obligors on the instrument is a property right worthy of protection just like the ownership right to any tangible property. Just as when someone deprives the owner of tangible personal property of its possession, whenever a person interferes with an owner's right to possession of an instrument, that person may be liable to the owner in tort for conversion.

a. When Taking by Transfer Constitutes Conversion

Article 3 expressly states that the law of conversion of personal property applies to instruments.[30] However, in addition, Article 3 specifically provides that certain acts constitute conversion. For example, it is specifically stated that an instrument is converted if it is taken by transfer, other than by negotiation, from a person not entitled to enforce the instrument.[31] Careful analysis of this rule will make its scope clear.

There are two requirements. First, the instrument must be taken by a transfer that is not a negotiation. Remember that negotiation of an instrument payable to bearer requires simply transfer of possession. For this reason, there can be no conversion of an instrument payable to bearer. In contrast, where the instrument is payable to the order of a specified person, that person must indorse the instrument in order for it to be negotiated. Therefore, if an instrument is transferred without the indorsement of the person to whom it is payable, it may be converted. For example, assume that a check is made payable to Jim. Don steals the check and purports to indorse the check in Jim's name to Gene. Because Don's indorsement was not effective to negotiate the instrument, Gene may be liable for conversion.

30. U.C.C. §3-420.
31. U.C.C. §3-420(a).

Second, the transferee must have acquired the instrument from a person not entitled to enforce the instrument. This requirement is met in the above example. Gene has not acquired the instrument from a person entitled to enforce the instrument. Don is not a person entitled to enforce the instrument. He is not a holder because the instrument was not indorsed to him by Jim. He is not a transferee of a holder since Jim did not voluntarily transfer possession of the instrument to him. Therefore, Gene has converted the instrument. If Jim had transferred the instrument to Don but had forgotten to indorse the instrument, Don would have Jim's rights as a holder, which would make Don a person entitled to enforce the instrument. Therefore Gene would not be liable for conversion. Although Don's indorsement would not make Gene a holder, Gene would be a person entitled to enforce the instrument. Gene's liability for conversion does not depend upon whether he has knowledge (or even reason to believe) that he lacks the right to possess the instrument.[32] Further, it is irrelevant whether Gene purchased the instrument, received the instrument as a gift, or whether he subsequently sold or donated the instrument.

b. When Payment Constitutes Conversion

Similarly, an instrument is converted if a payor bank makes payment with respect to the instrument to a person not entitled to enforce the instrument or to receive payment.[33] An instrument is likewise converted when a collecting bank takes the instrument for collection from a person not entitled to enforce the instrument or to receive payment.[34]

Thus, if Gene deposits the check in his account at Wells Bank, which presents the check for payment to Bank of America, both Wells Bank and Bank of America have converted the instrument. Wells Bank has taken the check from a person not entitled to enforce the instrument and Bank of America has made payment to such a person. Thus, collection or payment by a bank of an instrument bearing a forged indorsement, missing indorsement, or containing only one of two joint payee's indorsements is conversion.[35] As we will discuss later, a depositary bank is also liable for conversion when it applies value given for an instrument in a manner inconsistent with a restrictive indorsement.

---

32. See W. Page Keeton, Dan Dobbs, Robert Keeton & David Owen, Prosser and Keeton on Torts 92 and 93 (5th ed. 1984).

33. U.C.C. §3-420(a); U.C.C. §3-420, Official Comment 1.

34. U.C.C. §3-420(a); U.C.C. §3-420, Official Comment 1.

35. U.C.C. §3-420, Official Comment 1.

Although not specifically mentioned in Article 3, any person who makes payment of an instrument to a person not entitled to enforce the instrument is liable for conversion. This includes payment by the drawee, maker, acceptor, and drawer. In addition, a payor is liable for conversion whenever its payment does not effect a discharge under §3-602(a). In Chapter 2 we covered when a payor is not discharged by its payment. Generally, a payor is not discharged by its payment to the person entitled to enforce the instrument if there has been a properly asserted adverse claim by the true owner.

c. Liability of Representative for Conversion

A person who holds an instrument solely as a representative of another person exercises sufficient dominion and control over the instrument to be liable for conversion.[36] This means that, absent exemption from liability, a messenger who took the check to the bank to have it cashed would be liable to the true owner for conversion. Because there is no reason to hold persons like messengers liable when they are only acting as conduits, Article 3 provides protection from liability for agents or representatives under certain conditions.

A representative[37] who has, in good faith, dealt with an instrument or its proceeds on behalf of one who was not the person entitled to enforce the instrument is not liable to that person in conversion or otherwise beyond the amount of any proceeds that it has not paid out.[38]

The representative must act in good faith[39] to avoid liability for conversion.[40] Thus, if the messenger was not aware that the person for whom he was acting was not entitled to enforce the instrument, the messenger is not liable for conversion. The representative is relieved of liability only to the extent that it has paid out the proceeds of the instrument. Where the messenger retains a portion of the proceeds, he should be required to return the proceeds to the true owner rather than to his principal.

36. See W. Page Keeton, Dan Dobbs, Robert Keeton & David Owen, Prosser and Keeton on Torts 95 (5th ed. 1984).

37. A "representative" includes "an agent, an officer of a corporation or association, and a trustee, executor or administrator of an estate, or any other person empowered to act for another." U.C.C. §1-201(35).

38. U.C.C. §3-420(c).

39. "Good faith" means both honesty in fact and the observance of reasonable commercial standards of fair dealing. U.C.C. §3-103(a)(4).

d. Liability of Depositary Bank for Conversion

There is one exception to this rule. Although a depositary bank acts as its customer's agent in collecting the instrument, a depositary bank is liable for conversion whether or not it acts in good faith or retains any of the proceeds from the check.[41] There is a logical reason for this exception. All representatives, including depositary banks, are liable to the payor for breach of their presentment warranty that they are a person entitled to enforce the instrument.[42] Thus, even if the depositary bank was not liable to the owner of the instrument for conversion, the depositary bank would usually suffer the loss unless it could recover from its customer.

In our example, if Wells Bank, the depositary bank, were liable for conversion, Jim, the payee whose indorsement was forged, would be able to directly recover from Wells Bank. If, instead, Jim recovered from Bank of America, the payor bank, Bank of America would then be required to recover from Wells Bank for breach of its presentment warranty. Wells Bank would suffer the loss unless it could recover from Gene. Why should Jim be forced to recover from Bank of America who then would be required to recover from Wells Bank, if Jim could just directly recover from Wells Bank? There is no logic in denying him recovery against Wells Bank.

e. Intermediary Collecting Bank Not Liable for Conversion

In contrast, any intermediary collecting bank is relieved of liability for conversion when it acts in good faith and retains none of the proceeds from the check. Thus, any bank to which Wells Bank transferred the check for collection would not be liable to Jim for conversion. Denying Jim the right to recover from intermediary collecting banks makes sense. If Jim recovered from the bank, the intermediary collecting bank would just recover from Wells Bank for breach of its transfer warranty that Wells Bank is a person who is entitled to enforce the instrument. Wells Bank would ultimately be liable for the loss. Because in all likelihood Wells Bank will have adequate funds to pay Jim, there is no reason to involve the intermediary collecting bank in the matter.

---

40. U.C.C. §3-420(c).
41. U.C.C. §3-420(c).
42. U.C.C. §3-417(a). If it received consideration for the transfer, it is liable for breach of

f.   Payee's Right to Bring Action for Conversion

In addition to the question as to who may be liable for conversion, the issue arises as to who may bring an action for conversion. The proper party to bring an action for conversion of an instrument is the person who, before the theft or loss, was the person entitled to enforce the instrument.[43] Where an instrument is payable to the order of an identified person whose indorsement is forged, otherwise unauthorized, or missing, the right of that person to enforce the instrument depends upon whether the instrument had been delivered to him. Thus, in our example, whether Jim has the right to bring an action for conversion depends upon whether the check was delivered by the drawer to Jim.

If the drawer had not yet delivered the check to Jim, Jim may not bring an action for its conversion.[44] Whether an instrument has been delivered was discussed thoroughly in Chapter 2. The mere fact that the instrument is made payable to Jim does not confer any rights in him. Until the instrument has been delivered, Jim still retains the right to sue the drawer on the underlying obligation. Once the instrument is delivered to Jim, Jim has the right to enforce the instrument against the drawer or prior indorsers. The right to enforce the instrument gives Jim a sufficient property right to give him standing to bring an action for conversion.

g.   Issuer Has No Right to Bring Action for Conversion

An action for conversion may not be brought by the drawer, acceptor, or other issuer of the instrument.[45] The drawer is not harmed by the act of conversion. Assume, in our example above, that before the check was delivered to Jim, the check was stolen from the mail. The check is cashed by the thief. Bank

---

43. U.C.C. §3-420, Official Comment 1.

44. U.C.C. §3-420(a)(ii); U.C.C. §3-420, Official Comment 1.

45. U.C.C. §3-420(a). It appears that a remitter of a cashier's, teller's, or other bank check should have an action for conversion when the instrument is stolen or lost prior to its delivery to the payee. Since the remitter is not the holder of the check, it can be argued that she has no enforceable property right in the instrument. She may be viewed more like a drawer in that upon improper payment, she would have an action against the issuing bank for breach of contract. However, a remitter is different from a drawer in that the issuing bank itself, not the remitter, is the party obliged to pay the check. While it makes little sense to say that a drawer has a property right in his own promise, it makes a lot of sense to say that the remitter, prior to delivery, has a property right in the issuing bank's promise. A remitter should be found to have an action for conversion on a bank check.

of America debits the drawer's account and remits the funds to Wells Bank. Does Wells Bank possess funds belonging to the drawer? No. Because the indorsement was forged, Bank of America had no right to debit the drawer's account. The drawer has an adequate remedy against Bank of America for recrediting of his account. The drawer therefore suffers no loss from the improper payment and has no need to sue the depositary bank. He is, therefore, denied the right to maintain an action for conversion.[46]

h. Defenses to Conversion Action

When Jim, whose indorsement has been forged, sues the payor or depositary bank for conversion, the payor or depositary bank may defend the action by proving that Jim's negligence substantially contributed to the making of the forged indorsement.[47] Upon such proof, Jim would be precluded from asserting the forgery.[48] However, any failure of the payor or depositary bank to exercise ordinary care in paying or taking the instrument will result in allocating the loss between the bank and Jim to the extent to which each party's failure contributed to the loss.

There are other situations in which Jim may be denied the right to recover for conversion. Jim may be precluded from maintaining an action for conversion where he is precluded by estoppel or by ratification from denying that the indorsement is authorized or authentic. Estoppel and ratification are discussed in Chapter 4C. Jim has no right to sue for conversion where he has received the proceeds from the instrument. Similarly, where an indorsement is effective under §§3-404 (Impostors and Fictitious Payees) or 3-405 (Employer's Responsibility for Indorsements by Employees), also discussed in Chapter 4C, neither a subsequent purchaser nor the payor converts the instrument.

i. Measure of Damages for Conversion

The measure of damages for conversion is presumed to be the amount payable including interest, but recovery may not exceed the amount of plaintiff's interest in the instrument.[49] The defendant may prove liability in a lesser amount by introducing evidence of the insolvency of all of the obligors or proving a defense valid against the owner. The converter may also defend by proving that the owner actually received the proceeds.

46. U.C.C. §3-420(a)(i); U.C.C. §3-420, Official Comment 1.
47. U.C.C. §3-406(a).
48. U.C.C. §3-406.
49. U.C.C. §3-420(b); U.C.C. §3-420, Official Comment 2.

A difficult question arises as to whether punitive damages are available in an appropriate case. On the one hand, §3-420(b) provides that as to conversion actions under §3-420(a), damages may not exceed the amount of the plaintiff's interest in the instrument. Similarly, §1-106(1) provides that penal damages are not recoverable under the Code except as specifically provided therein or by "other rule of law." On the other hand, in spite of §1-106(1) and similar language in the predecessor to §3-420,[50] courts under former Article 3 allowed punitive damages in appropriate cases.[51] Because the award of punitive damages usually requires proof of particularly aggravated misconduct coupled with a malicious, reckless, or otherwise wrongful state of mind, it would seem that such damages should be available in an appropriate case.

j.   Statute of Limitations for Conversion

The statute of limitations on an action for conversion of an instrument expires three years after the cause of action accrues.[52] The cause of action accrues when the act of conversion occurred. In the case of a payor, the cause of action accrues on the date of payment. In the case of a purchaser, the cause of action accrues on the date of his purchase. The statute is not tolled simply because the owner is ignorant of the conversion.[53]

6.   *Allocation of Loss Where Signature of Maker or Acceptor Unauthorized*

The allocation of loss when an instrument bears the unauthorized signature of the maker or acceptor depends, to a large degree, upon whether the maker or acceptor pays the instrument. For example, assume that Allen forges John's name as maker of a note made payable to Peter. Peter indorses the note to Sally. Since Allen was not authorized to sign for John, Allen's signing of John's name does not operate as John's signature. (See Figure 4.3.)

---

50. U.C.C. §3-419(2)(1989).

51. For a case under former Article 3, see McAdam v. Dean Witter Reynolds, Inc., 896 F.2d 750, 10 U.C.C. Rep. Serv. 2d 1085 (3d Cir. 1990) (Account executive of Dean Witter would obtain checks payable to customers of Dean Witter and forge their indorsements. Depositary bank would cash these checks for account executive, even ones as large as $475,000. Bank was in bad faith where it deliberately broke its own rules. Jury award of punitive damages affirmed. Punitive damages may be awarded under §3-419 because conversion is a tort.).

52. U.C.C. §3-118(g).

53. For a case under former Article 3, see Husker News Co. v. Mahaska State Bank, 460 N.W.2d 476, 13 U.C.C. Rep. Serv. 2d 46 (Iowa 1990).

A. Forged Signatures

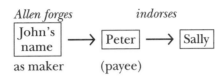

a. Where Payment Not Made

Let us first assume that John, upon recognizing that his signature is forged, refuses to pay Sally. In the absence of estoppel, ratification, or negligence, John is not liable because he did not sign the note.[54] We will discuss in Chapter 4C the consequences of John being precluded by estoppel, ratification, or negligence from asserting that his signature was forged. Will Sally suffer the loss? This depends upon whether Sally can locate Allen or Peter and whether Allen or Peter has reachable assets. Peter gives to Sally a transfer warranty that all signatures on the instrument are authentic and authorized.[55] (See Chapter 4A(2).) Peter transferred the note for consideration and by indorsement. Sally, therefore, may recover from Peter. In addition, Sally can recover from Peter on his indorser's contract.[56] (See Chapter 3.) If Sally recovers from Peter, Peter may recover from Allen. The loss from the forgery is sent back down the chain of title to the first solvent party following the forger. Sally can also recover from Allen on his maker's contract since his unauthorized signature makes him liable also as the maker of the note.[57] (See Chapter 4A(1).)

b. Where Payment Made

Assume that John, however, fails to recognize that his signature on the note is forged and pays Sally. Whether John may recover the payment from Sally depends upon whether Sally is a protected person under §3-418. (See Chapter 4A(4).) If Sally is a good faith purchaser for value or has relied in good faith on the payment, she is protected from John's action in restitution and therefore John may not recover the money from Sally. If Sally neither relied upon the payment nor is a good faith purchaser for value, John would be entitled to recover the payment from her.[58] Neither the maker nor the

54. U.C.C. §3-401(a).
55. U.C.C. §3-416(a)(2).
56. U.C.C. §3-415(a).
57. U.C.C. §3-403(a).
58. U.C.C. §3-418(c).

acceptor is given any warranty as to the authenticity of his own signature and therefore John may not recover from Sally or Peter on a theory of breach of presentment warranties. The maker or acceptor should know his own signature and must suffer the loss if the signature is unauthorized.[59] Of course, if Allen is solvent and available for process, John can recover from him.

7.   Allocation of Loss Where Signature of Drawer Unauthorized

When the signature of the drawer is forged or otherwise unauthorized, which party suffers the loss depends in large part upon whether the drawee (payor bank in the case of a check) pays the draft (or check). Assume that Jane, the office manager of The Smoke Shop, having no authority to sign checks for her employer, forges the treasurer's (an authorized signer for The Smoke Shop) signature on a check payable to David, Jane's husband. David, knowing of the forgery, deposits the check in his bank account at Security Bank, which allows him to withdraw the uncollected funds. Security Bank presents the check to Wells Bank, the payor bank. (See Figure 4.4.)

FIGURE 4.4

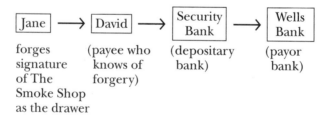

a.   Where Drawee Makes Payment

First, assume that Wells Bank pays the check. Wells Bank may not debit The Smoke Shop's account. Because The Smoke Shop did not sign the check, absent a ground precluding it from claiming that the signature was not authentic, the check is not properly payable and therefore Wells Bank may not

---

59. U.C.C. §3-417, Official Comment 4.

charge The Smoke Shop's account.[60] Wells Bank may properly debit The Smoke Shop's account if The Smoke Shop was negligent in allowing the unauthorized signature to be made or in reviewing its bank statement, or was otherwise precluded from asserting the unauthorized nature of its signature. (See Chapter 4B.) Can Wells Bank recover the proceeds from Security Bank or from David? The applicable rule is that in the absence of a breach of a presentment warranty, payment by the drawee (Wells Bank) cannot be recovered from a person who took the instrument in good faith and for value or who in good faith changed position in reliance on the payment ("protected party").[61] (See Chapter 4A(4).) Neither the presenter nor prior transferors warrant that the drawer's signature is genuine. The only warranty they make is that they have no knowledge that the drawer's signature is unauthorized.[62] (See Chapter 4A(3).) If Security Bank is not a protected person because it neither gave value to David nor relies upon the payment, Wells Bank may recover the payment from Security Bank under a common law right of restitution for payments made by mistake.[63] (See Chapter 4A(4).)

However, if Security Bank is a protected party because it took the instrument in good faith and for value or relied in good faith on the payment, Wells Bank may not recover the payment from it. Wells Bank can, however, recover from David. Not only is he not a protected person under §3-418 because he had knowledge of the forgery, but he has also breached the presentment warranty of lack of knowledge that the drawer's signature is not genuine. If David is insolvent, Wells Bank ultimately suffers the loss since Wells Bank cannot debit The Smoke Shop's account.

Why, you may ask, does the payor bank suffer the loss? I wish that I could give you some logical explanation. All of the proferred explanations appear to be more like rationalizations. One explanation is that the drawee is in a better position than the holder to determine whether the drawer's signature is valid. But even though a payor bank may have a sample of its customer's signature, the rule cannot be based upon its ability to spot the forgery because liability is imposed upon the payor bank even where the forgery is perfect. Rather, the true explanation seems to lie in history. After Lord Mansfield held in Price v. Neal[64] that the drawee suffers the loss when it pays a draft over a forged drawer's signature, courts without question began to follow the rule. Banks, being the parties primarily affected by the rule, began obtaining insurance

---

60. U.C.C. §4-401(a).
61. U.C.C. §3-418 (c).
62. U.C.C. §4-208(a)(3); U.C.C. §3-417(a)(3).
63. U.C.C. §3-418(a) and (c).
64. 3 Burr. 1354, 97 Eng. Rep. 871 (K.B. 1752).

covering this risk.[65] Once banks factored the cost of insurance into the price charged for checking accounts, there became no reason to change the rule. The cost of the insurance was simply spread to all checking account customers.

b. Where Drawee Does Not Make Payment

If Wells Bank does not pay the check, Security Bank can recover from David and any prior transferors for breach of their transfer warranty that all signatures are authentic and authorized.[66] Each prior transferor may then recover from his transferor as well as from any prior transferor who indorsed the check. If David had transferred by indorsement the check to Jim who deposited the check in his checking account at Security Bank, Security Bank could recover from both David and Jim on their transfer warranty. Because the check was not paid, Security Bank may also charge back Jim's account.[67] (See Chapter 5.) Because the instrument was dishonored, the holder can recover from prior indorsers on their indorser's contract.[68] The holder may also recover from Jane as drawer of the check because her unauthorized signature makes her liable in the capacity in which she signs.[69] The loss from the forgery is sent back down the chain of title to the first solvent party following the forger.

The Smoke Shop only suffers the loss if it was negligent[70] or otherwise precluded from asserting that its signature was unauthorized. If it is so precluded, Security Bank as a person who took the check in good faith and for value may recover from The Smoke Shop on its drawer's contract. (See Chapter 4C.)

c. Where Drawer Makes Payment

There may be occasions where Security Bank demands that The Smoke Shop make payment of the check after Wells Bank refuses to make payment. Assuming that The Smoke Shop pays Security Bank, the question may arise as to whether The Smoke Shop may recover the payment. The Smoke Shop may not recover the payment if Security Bank is a protected person under §3-418.

65. See generally Farnsworth, Insurance Against Check Forgery, 60 Colum. L. Rev. 284 (1960); Whitney, Rubin & Stabbe, Twenty Years of the Uniform Commercial Code and Fidelity and Surety Bonding—Some Random Observations, 18 Forum 670 (1983).
66. U.C.C. §3-416(a)(2); U.C.C. §4-207(a)(2).
67. U.C.C. §4-214(a).
68. U.C.C. §3-415(a).
69. U.C.C. §3-403(a).
70. U.C.C. §3-406(a).

A. Forged Signatures

(See Chapter 4A (4).) Not only is the drawer given no warranty that its signature is authorized, but it is not even given a warranty that the presenter lacks knowledge of the unauthorized nature of the drawer's signature.[71] The drawer should be able to determine whether its signature is authentic.

This rule is, however, somewhat suspect. Although the drawer should know his own signature, it is questionable whether his fault in not recognizing the forgery is greater than the holder's culpability in knowing that the signature is a forgery. This may be especially true where the drawer is a bank or corporation since the person making payment is not usually the same person who signed the instrument. In fact, where the presenter had knowledge of the forgery before he paid value or relied upon the payment, the presenter will suffer the loss. By having such knowledge, he will not qualify as a protected person and therefore the drawer may recover the payment under §3-418. (See Chapter 4A (4).) If, on the other hand, the presenter acquired the check for value and in good faith and only thereafter learned of the forgery, the drawer will not be able to recover from the presenter. By having taken the check for value and in good faith, the presenter would be a protected person under §3-418(c) and therefore the drawer would not be able to recover the payment from him.

8. Application of Rules Where Indorsement Is Unauthorized

The rights of the parties where there is an unauthorized indorsement in the chain of title depend upon whether the instrument has been delivered to the payee. Let us first look at an example of an unauthorized indorsement occurring prior to delivery of the instrument to the payee.

a. Allocation of Loss Where Check Not Delivered to Payee

Let us take, as a hypothetical, a check drawn by Dan Drawer upon Security Bank payable to Paul Payee in payment for legal services rendered. Fred Forger steals the check prior to its delivery to Paul. Fred forges Paul's indorsement and cashes the check with Local Grocer who deposits the check in his checking account at Wells Bank, which sends the check for collection to Crocker Bank, which presents it for payment to Security Bank. Security Bank

---

71. U.C.C. §3-417, Official Comment 4.

pays the check. We will assume that Fred Forger is insolvent. In the event that he is not, he will ultimately suffer the loss. (See Figure 4.5.)

FIGURE 4.5

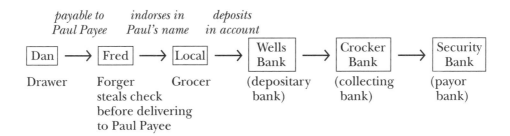

Since the check was not delivered to Paul, Paul has no rights to or upon the check.[72] However, because the check was not "taken" for the underlying obligation,[73] Paul retains whatever rights he had against Dan on the underlying obligation to pay for the legal services. What right does Security Bank have to recover its payment? Security Bank cannot debit Dan's account because the check was not properly payable.[74] Dan's order to Security Bank was to pay Paul Payee. Paul neither indorsed the check nor received the proceeds. As a result, Security Bank did not honor Dan's order to pay Paul and therefore has no right to debit Dan's account. Security Bank can only debit Dan's account if he is negligent or is otherwise precluded from asserting that the indorsement was unauthorized.[75]

Security Bank's recourse is against Crocker Bank, Wells Bank, or Local Grocer for breach of their presentment warranty that they are a person entitled to enforce the instrument.[76] Because Paul's indorsement was forged, no party after the forged indorsement qualifies as a holder. Since Paul did not voluntarily transfer the check to Fred Forger, neither Fred Forger nor any subsequent transferee has the rights of a holder. Crocker Bank (the presenter) and Wells Bank and Local Grocer (prior transferors) each warrant that the warrantor is, or was, at the time the warrantor transferred the item, entitled to enforce the item. Because none of these parties were holders or had the rights of a holder, each of these three parties breaches his presentment warranty that

72. U.C.C. §3-420(a).
73. U.C.C. §3-310(b).
74. U.C.C. §4-401(a); U.C.C. §4-401, Official Comment 1.
75. U.C.C. §§3-404; 3-405; 3-406; 4-406.
76. U.C.C. §4-208 (a)(1): U.C.C. §3-417(a)(1).

he is a person entitled to enforce the instrument. This warranty is made to the drawee of an unaccepted draft and to the payor of any other item.[77] This presentment warranty may be breached in three situations: (1) where an indorsement in the chain of title is unauthorized; (2) where an indorsement necessary to the chain of title is missing; or (3) where the person receiving the payment or acceptance is not authorized to act on behalf of a person with the rights of a holder.[78]

Crocker Bank may recover from Wells Bank or Local Grocer on their transfer warranty that they are a person entitled to enforce the instrument.[79] If Crocker Bank recovers from Wells Bank, Wells Bank in turn may recover from Local Grocer on his transfer warranty that he is a person entitled to enforce the instrument. Local Grocer could have likewise recovered from Fred Forger had Fred been solvent.

If, because of the drawer's negligence or other grounds for preclusion (See Chapter 4C), Security Bank could, but fails to, debit the drawer's account, Security Bank may not shift the loss to the presenter or prior transferor by way of the presentment warranties.[80] This is because §4-208(c) provides that the person making the presentment warranty may defend by proving that the indorsement was effective under §§3-404 (impostors and fictitious payees) or 3-405 (employer's responsibility for fraudulent indorsement by employee) or that the drawer is precluded under §3-406 (negligence) from asserting against the drawee the unauthorized indorsement. The warrantor may also prove that the unauthorized indorsement was ratified[81] (see Chapter 4C) or that the proceeds reached the intended payee. By allowing the warrantor to use defenses that the drawee could have used as grounds to debit the drawer's account, the drawee is prevented from attempting to shift the loss from its customer (the drawer) to the warrantor.

Crocker Bank and Wells Bank have an additional remedy if Security Bank does not pay the check. In that event, Crocker Bank may charge back Wells Bank's account and Wells Bank in turn may charge back Local Grocer's account for the amount of the check.[82] (See Chapter 5 for a collecting bank's right to charge back its customer's account.) If the draft or check is dishonored, each transferee in turn will have the same right to recover from prior

---

77. U.C.C. §4-208(a)(1) and (d); U.C.C. §3-417(a)(1) and (d)(1); U.C.C. §3-417, Official Comment 2.

78. U.C.C. §3-417; Official Comment 2, U.C.C. §4-208(a)(1) and (d)

79. U.C.C. §4-207(a)(1).

80. U.C.C. §4-208(c); U.C.C.§3-417(c).

81. U.C.C. §3-403(a).

82. U.C.C. §4-214(a).

transferors on their transfer warranty that they are a person entitled to enforce the instrument as in the case of the draft or check having been paid.[83]

Absent grounds for preclusion, neither Crocker Bank, Wells Bank, nor Local Grocer may recover from Dan. Since Paul's indorsement is unauthorized, none of these parties can acquire holder status. Not being holders, they may not recover from Dan on his drawer's contract. The result would be different if Dan were negligent or otherwise precluded from asserting the unauthorized nature of the indorsement.[84] At that point, if the check was dishonored, Crocker Bank, Wells Bank, or Local Grocer could recover from Dan on his drawer's contract. Dan's negligence would preclude him from denying that the party in possession of the check is its holder. However, if Crocker Bank, Wells Bank, or Local Grocer themselves are negligent, the loss will be split to the extent that each party's negligence contributed to the loss.

Does Dan have any rights against Crocker Bank or Wells Bank? Although Dan clearly has the right to compel Security Bank to recredit his account, Dan may prefer to sue Crocker Bank or Wells Bank. There is no compelling legitimate reason why Dan would prefer to sue Crocker Bank or Wells Bank rather than Security Bank. Because Dan is the customer of Security Bank, Security Bank is more familiar with Dan than is Crocker Bank or Wells Bank. Security Bank has a better basis for determining the legitimacy of Dan's claim that he was not at fault in causing the forged indorsement to be made. For this reason, Dan is denied the right to sue Crocker Bank or Wells Bank either for conversion[85] or for breach of the presentment warranty that they are a person entitled to enforce the instrument.[86]

b. Allocation of Loss after Delivery to Payee

Let us now look at the allocation of loss after the check has been delivered to Paul Payee. We will use the same hypothetical except that we will assume that Fred Forger, who is now insolvent, steals the check from Paul Payee, forges Paul Payee's indorsement, and cashes the check with Local Grocer, which deposits the check in its own account at Wells Bank. Local Grocer was permitted by Wells Bank to draw against the uncollected funds, took full advantage of this permission, and then used the money for his own benefit.

83. U.C.C. §3-416(a)(1); U.C.C. §4-207(a)(1).
84. U.C.C. §3-406; U.C.C. §3-404; U.C.C. §3-405.
85. U.C.C. §3-420(a).
86. U.C.C. §3-417, Official Comment 2.

A. Forged Signatures

Payee's Rights If Instrument Not Paid.   After delivery to the payee, the payee's rights depend upon whether the instrument has been paid. If the check is still missing, Paul may recover on the check from Dan by complying with the requirements for the enforcement of lost, destroyed, or stolen instruments.[87] The requirements for enforcement of a stolen or lost instrument were discussed in Chapter 3. Paul may not recover from Dan on the underlying obligation for legal services.[88] If the check is found prior to payment, Paul may recover possession of the check from the possessor, whether it is Wells Bank, Crocker Bank, or Local Grocer. Since none of these parties have the rights of a holder in due course (because Paul's indorsement is forged, no subsequent person can be a holder or, ipso facto, a holder in due course), they take subject to Paul's claim of ownership. Once Paul recovers possession of the check, he may present the check for payment, and if it is not paid, he can recover from Dan on his drawer's contract or on the underlying obligation. The party required to return the check can then recover from his transferor[89] and any prior transferors, who have indorsed the draft following the forged indorsement, for breach of their transfer warranty that they are a person entitled to enforce the draft.[90] Paul will be precluded from asserting the unauthorized nature of his signature if he is negligent.[91] However, if the other party is negligent, the loss will be allocated according to the extent of their respective negligence.[92]

Assume that Paul recovers possession of the check from Crocker Bank. Crocker Bank, however, will not ultimately suffer the loss.[93] It can charge back[94] the account of Wells Bank or recover from either Wells Bank or Local Grocer for breach of their transfer warranty that they are a person entitled to enforce the instrument.[95] Wells Bank has the same rights as against Local Grocer. If Paul is negligent or otherwise precluded from asserting the unauthorized nature of his indorsement, he may be denied the right to recover the instrument. If he is precluded, Wells Bank, Crocker Bank, or Local Grocer, depending upon who now possesses the check, can recover from Dan on his drawer's contract or from Paul on his indorser's contract.

---

87. U.C.C. §3-310(b)(4). See U.C.C. §3-309.

88. U.C.C. §3-310(b)(4);U.C.C. §3-310, Official Comment 4.

89. Assuming that the transferor had received consideration for the transfer.

90. U.C.C. §3-416(a)(1); U.C.C. §4-207(a)(1).

91. U.C.C. §3-406.

92. U.C.C. §3-406(b).

93. U.C.C. §3-415(a).

94. U.C.C. §4-214(a).

95. U.C.C. §4-207(a)(1).

Payee's Rights If Instrument Paid. Assume now that Security Bank pays the check. What are Paul's rights? Paul may recover from Security Bank for conversion.[96] (See Chapter 4A(5).) Instead, he may recover from Wells Bank or Local Grocer for conversion. However, because an intermediary bank is not liable for conversion, Paul may not recover from Crocker Bank. If Paul is negligent or otherwise precluded from asserting the unauthorized nature of his indorsement, he may be precluded from recovering from Security Bank, Wells Bank, or Local Grocer. (See Chapter 4C.) If one of these parties is negligent, Paul may recover a part of his loss from it.[97]

Who will ultimately suffer the loss? The first solvent party after the person who made the unauthorized indorsement bears the loss. Security Bank may recover the payment from Crocker Bank, Wells Bank, or Local Grocer for breach of their presentment warranty that they are a person entitled to enforce the instrument.[98] Crocker Bank can recover from Wells Bank and Local Grocer for breach of their transfer warranty that they are a person entitled to enforce the instrument[99] and Wells Bank can likewise recover from Local Grocer. However, if Paul is negligent, the warrantor will have a defense to Security Bank's action for breach of warranty.[100]

B. ALTERATIONS AND INCOMPLETE INSTRUMENTS

1. Alterations

Let us start with an example. Peter draws a check in the amount of $50 payable to John. John alters the check by raising the amount to $500 and negotiates the check to Dentist, in payment of his bill. Dentist deposits the check in his account at Wells Bank, which presents the check to Bank of America. Bank of America pays the check and debits Peter's account. (See Figure 4.6.)

96. U.C.C. §3-420(a); U.C.C. §3-420, Official Comment 3.
97. U.C.C. §3-406(b).
98. U.C.C. §4-208(a)(1).
99. U.C.C. §3-416(a)(1); U.C.C. §4-207(a)(1).
100. U.C.C. §4-208(c).

B. Alterations and Incomplete Instruments

FIGURE 4.6

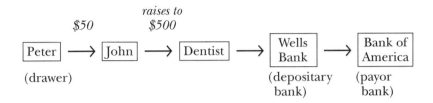

In examining his returned checks, Peter discovers the alteration and demands that Bank of America recredit his account for the extra $450. Is Bank of America obligated to do so? If so, can Bank of America recover from any of the prior parties? Who ultimately suffers the loss? These are the questions that we will examine in this section.

a. What Is an Alteration?

An "alteration" is any unauthorized change in an instrument that attempts to modify in any respect the obligation of any party.[101] As discussed later, any unauthorized addition of words or numbers or other change to an incomplete instrument relating to the obligation of any party is also an alteration.

Any change in the terms of an instrument that changes the contract of any party is an alteration. An alteration could be a change in, among other terms, the sum payable, the date of execution, the date of payment, the number or amount of an installment, the place of payment, the currency in which payment is due, or the name of the payee or of any other party. By John raising the amount of the check from $50 to $500, John altered the check. Most alterations are, in fact, increases in the amount that the instrument is payable.

Alterations can take any form. Words or numbers may be added to an instrument[102] or words or numbers may be omitted by erasure, crossing out, cutting off of a portion of the instrument, or removing part of an instrument along a perforation. Any change, no matter how small or benign, is an alteration. An increase in the amount payable by one penny is an alteration. Similarly, a reduction in the sum payable is also an alteration.

An instrument is not altered if the change does not affect the obligation of a party in any respect.[103] For example, the writing of administrative information in the margin or on the back of the instrument, the changing of the

101. U.C.C. §3-407(a); U.C.C. §3-407, Official Comment 1.
102. U.C.C. §3-407(a)(ii); U.C.C. §3-407, Official Comment 2.
103. U.C.C. §3-407(a).

principal amount to show a payment made or to show the total of the interest and principal payable are not alterations. The addition of a co-maker or surety does not affect the contract of the maker and is therefore not an alteration.

An instrument is not altered if the terms of the contract are not changed as a result of the purported alteration. For example, because words control figures,[104] a change in the figures only is not an alteration. Thus, where the instrument provides in one place that it is payable in the amount of "five hundred dollars," and in another place that it is payable in the amount of "$5," a change in the figures so that it now reads "$500" is not an alteration. Because the words indicated that the instrument is payable in the sum of $500 and the words control the figures, the instrument is payable in the sum of $500. Where an instrument is payable "with interest," interest is payable at the judgment rate from the time interest first accrues.[105] Thus, if the judgment rate of interest is added to the instrument, the instrument has not been altered because no contract has been changed. Addition of the place of payment is not an alteration if the instrument would have been payable at that place in any event.

b.   Allocation of Loss

The rules for allocating loss in the event of an alteration are simple. In the absence of his own negligence, assent, or preclusion, a party who signs an instrument only promises to pay the instrument according to its terms at the time he signed the instrument.[106] The party is not liable beyond the amount for which the instrument was payable at the time he signed the instrument. Thus, because the check was payable for $50 when Peter signed it, Bank of America may only debit Peter's account in the amount of $50. In the event that Bank of America had refused to pay the check, Wells Bank could recover only $50 from Peter. However, because John and Dentist indorsed the check when it was payable in the amount of $500, Wells Bank could have recovered $500 from either of these parties.

A party whose failure to exercise ordinary care substantially contributes to an alteration is precluded from asserting the alteration as against a person who in good faith pays the instrument or takes it for value or collection.[107] The negligent party, a party who assents to the alteration, or a party who is other-

---

104. U.C.C. §3-114.
105. U.C.C. §3-112(b).
106. U.C.C. §3-412; U.C.C. §3-413(a); U.C.C. §3-414(b); U.C.C. §3-415(a).
107. U.C.C. §3-406(a).

wise precluded from asserting the alteration may thus be liable on the instrument as altered.[108]

c.   Payment by Drawee

In the case of a check or other unaccepted draft, the allocation of loss does not depend upon whether the drawee has paid or accepted the draft. If the drawee pays the draft, the drawee may debit the drawer's account only in the amount as originally drawn by the drawer[109] unless the drawer is negligent or otherwise precluded from asserting the alteration. Bank of America may only debit Peter's account in the amount of $50. In the absence of grounds for precluding the drawer, the drawee may recover from any person obtaining payment or acceptance or any previous transferor for breach of the presentment warranty that the draft has not been altered.[110] Bank of America may recover the remaining $450 from Wells Bank, Dentist, or John.

The party from whom the drawee recovers can recover from his transferor[111] and any prior transferors[112] for breach of their transfer warranty that the draft had not been altered.[113] If Wells Bank reimburses Bank of America, Wells Bank may recover $450 from John or Dentist for breach of their transfer warranty that the instrument has not been altered.

d.   If Check Not Paid

If the check has not been paid, the person entitled to enforce the instrument has these same rights as against prior transferors for breach of their transfer warranty of no alteration and the right to recover up to the amount for which the instrument was payable at the time of their indorsement against prior indorsers on their indorser's obligation.[114] Thus, Wells Bank can recover $50 from Peter. It can recover $450 from John or Dentist on their transfer warranty that the instrument has not been altered. Or, instead, it can recover $500 from either John or Dentist on their indorser's contract. In addition, Wells Bank has the right to charge back Dentist's account for the amount of the check upon its dishonor. We will discuss the right of chargeback in Chapter 5.

---

108. U.C.C. §3-407(b); U.C.C. §3-407, Official Comment 1.
109. U.C.C. §4-401(d)(1).
110. U.C.C. §3-417(a)(2); U.C.C. §4-208(a)(2).
111. Assuming the transferor received consideration for the transfer.
112. Assuming the prior transferor indorsed the instrument.
113. U.C.C. §3-416(a)(3); U.C.C. §4-207(a)(3).
114. U.C.C. §3-415(a).

e.   Where Drawer, Maker, or Acceptor Pays

Where the drawer, maker, or acceptor makes the payment, the result is different. For example, assume that a note is made in the amount of $50 by Sam and payable to Gabriel. Gabriel raises the note to $500 and negotiates the note to Hank for value. Hank presents the note to Sam for payment. If Sam recognizes that the note has been altered and refuses to pay Hank, Hank can recover only $50 from Sam. Hank must recover the remaining money from Gabriel for breach of his transfer warranty that the note has not been altered. However, if Sam pays the note for the entire $500, he may have to suffer the loss unless he can recover from Gabriel. Hank does not warrant to Sam that the note has not been altered. No warranty is given to the drawer, maker, or acceptor that the instrument has not been altered.[115] These individuals should know the terms of the instrument at the time of their engagement and should not pay the instrument if it has been altered. Although Sam can certainly recover from Gabriel, Gabriel will probably not be solvent. If Sam does pay the note in the altered amount, Sam may have the right to recover the $450 from Hank under §3-418 if the law of restitution allows such recovery but only if Hank does not qualify as a person who took the instrument in good faith and for value or who in good faith changed position in reliance on the payment.[116] (See Chapter 4A(4.)) Where the instrument is not paid or the payment is recovered, the loss will flow down the chain of title through the transfer warranties to the first solvent party after the alterer.

f.   Discharge of Party Whose Obligation Is Affected

A deterrent effect is provided in the Code against persons altering instruments. A fraudulently made alteration discharges a party whose obligation is affected by the alteration unless that party assents to the alteration or is precluded from asserting the alteration.[117] The party affected is discharged as a means of discouraging the holder from attempting to alter the instrument. The holder is punished for his attempt to gain an advantage by the fraudulent alteration by being completely denied the right to enforce the instrument against the party whose contract was changed.

Thus, Gabriel could not enforce the instrument whatsoever against Sam. Any transferee, other than one who takes the instrument for value, in good

---

115. U.C.C. §3-417, Comment 4.
116. U.C.C. §3-418(b) and (c).
117. U.C.C. §3-407(b).

faith, and without notice of the alteration, also takes subject to Sam's discharge.[118] A payor bank or other drawee paying a fraudulently altered instrument or a person taking it for value, in good faith, and without notice of the alteration, may enforce the instrument according to its original terms.[119] If Hank took the instrument for value, in good faith, and without notice of the alteration, he could recover $50 from Sam. Otherwise, he would simply stand in Gabriel's shoes and recover nothing from Sam.

g. Alteration Must be Fraudulent

An alteration does not discharge the party whose obligation is affected unless the alterer had a fraudulent intent in making the alteration.[120] An alteration is fraudulent when the alterer intends to achieve an advantage for himself to which he has reason to know he is not entitled. Thus, where the holder erroneously believes that the party has authorized or consented to the alteration or completion or that he has the right to alter the instrument to reflect the true agreement of the parties, the fact that no such consent or authorization actually exists or that he has no such right does not make the alteration fraudulent.

Where a party is discharged because the instrument has been fraudulently altered, the discharge is personal to the party discharged. Only the party whose obligation is affected by the alteration is discharged by the alteration.[121] However, if a party is discharged because of an alteration, any party having a right of recourse against the discharged party is also discharged.[122]

When an alteration is not fraudulent, the instrument may be enforced according to its original terms.[123] For instance, where the holder has not acted fraudulently in adding a provision for interest, the instrument may be enforced to its full extent except for the provision for interest.

2. Incomplete Instruments

Sometimes a person may sign an instrument containing blank spaces to which he intends to add additional terms. As a matter of business, and for that mat-

---

118. U.C.C. §3-407(c); U.C.C. §3-203(b).
119. U.C.C. §3-407(c); U.C.C. §3-407, Official Comment 2.
120. U.C.C. §3-407(b); U.C.C. §3-407, Official Comment 1.
121. U.C.C. §3-407(b); U.C.C. §3-407, Official Comment 1.
122. U.C.C. §3-407, Official Comment 1.
123. U.C.C. §3-407(b).

ter, common sense, such a practice is not wise. However, there may be some legitimate reasons to do so. As an example, a drawer, who is going out of town, may give a check to his neighbor to be used to pay for repairs on the drawer's house. Because the drawer does not know how much the repairs will cost, the drawer may fill in the repair company's name as payee and leave the check blank for his neighbor to fill in the amount. In a vast majority of these cases, the neighbor will fill in the proper amount and no problem will arise. Similarly, where a person trusts his lawyer to complete loan documents, the person may sign a note in blank and leave it to his lawyer to fill in the remaining terms of the note.

a. What Is an Incomplete Instrument?

When the signer intends that the instrument as signed be completed by the addition of words or numbers, the instrument is called an "incomplete instrument."[124] In order for an instrument to be an incomplete instrument, it must contain a blank space for the missing term to be supplied. However, an instrument is not incomplete where it lacks the issuer's signature. Thus, an instrument whether or not otherwise complete is not an incomplete instrument where the drawer or maker has yet to sign the instrument. The determination as to whether an instrument is complete is to be made by looking at the face of the instrument itself. The subjective intent of the drawer or maker is not relevant.[125] The question that must be asked is "Does the appearance of the instrument indicate that the drawer intended to add words or numbers?" If the answer is "yes," then the instrument is an incomplete instrument. If the answer is "no," then it is not. Clearly, a mere signature on a blank piece of paper does not qualify as an incomplete instrument.

Some incomplete instruments do not contain all of the terms required for negotiability.[126] In this case, the instrument is not yet negotiable and cannot be enforced until completed.[127] Where, for example, the instrument does not contain the amount payable, it is not a negotiable instrument until the amount is inserted. There are not many terms that are required to make an instrument negotiable. In addition to the sum payable, these terms include: a promise or order;[128] the date if the time of payment is a fixed period after

---

124. U.C.C. §3-115(a); U.C.C. §3-115, Official Comment 1.
125. U.C.C. §3-115(a); U.C.C. §3-115, Official Comment 1.
126. U.C.C. §3-115(b); U.C.C. §3-115, Official Comment 1.
127. U.C.C. §3-115(b); U.C.C. §3-115, Official Comment 3.
128. U.C.C. §3-104(a).

date;[129] or the words "order" or "bearer."[130] A check may be negotiable even though it does not contain "order" or "bearer" words.[131] For this reason, a check complete except for the omission of "order" or "bearer" words is not an incomplete instrument.

Where the instrument already contains all of the terms necessary for negotiability, it is negotiable even though it may leave a blank space for other terms.[132] Such an instrument may be enforced according to its terms even if it is not completed.[133] Because an instrument to be negotiable does not need to state a rate of interest, an instrument that leaves a blank space for insertion of the rate of interest is negotiable even though incomplete. Because an instrument that omits the name of the payee, for example, "Pay to _____," is payable to bearer, the instrument is negotiable even before insertion of the payee's name. However, leaving a blank space for the payee's name means that the instrument is also incomplete. An instrument is a negotiable incomplete instrument where there is a blank space for any of the following terms, among others: the date of issue unless the instrument is payable a fixed period after date; the date of payment; the place of payment; or a provision for attorney's fees.

b.   Effect of Completing Instrument

Where the completion of an incomplete instrument is authorized, an incomplete instrument may be enforced as completed.[134] Where the neighbor, in our example above, fills in the proper amount for the repairs, the check may be enforced in the amount completed. This rule, of course, makes sense. The homeowner, by authorizing his neighbor to complete the check, has agreed to be bound by the check as completed. The payor bank that pays the instrument may debit the homeowner's account in the amount as completed.[135] Authority for completion of an incomplete instrument may be either express or implied.

Where the completion is unauthorized, the completion is treated as though it were an alteration.[136] However, there are certain differences in the consequences of an unauthorized completion as compared to an ordinary

---

129. U.C.C. §3-108(b).
130. U.C.C. §3-104(a)(1).
131. U.C.C. §3-104(c).
132. U.C.C. §3-115(b); U.C.C. §3-115, Official Comment 1.
133. U.C.C. §3-115(b), U.C.C. §3-115, Official Comment 2.
134. U.C.C. §3-115(b).
135. U.C.C. §4-401(d)(2); U.C.C. §4-401, Official Comment 4.
136. U.C.C. §3-115(c); U.C.C. §3-115, Official Comment 3.

alteration. By leaving open a blank or space, the issuer has made it easy for the alterer to pass off the completion as authentic. For this reason, the issuer takes the risk that the instrument will be completed contrary to her authority. A payor bank acting in good faith may enforce the instrument as completed even though the completion was unauthorized.[137] Thus, even if the homeowner told the neighbor that the amount could not exceed $100, the payor bank may debit the homeowner's account for the entire amount of the check where the neighbor writes in $500 as the amount payable. Similarly, if the repair company is unaware of this limitation, the repair company can enforce the check for the entire $500. A person taking the instrument for value, in good faith, and without notice of the improper completion may enforce the instrument according to its terms as completed.[138]

C.   GROUNDS OF PRECLUSION

There are many grounds that cause an unauthorized signature or alteration to be treated as though it was authorized. In this section we will examine the following grounds of preclusion:

1. ratification (§3-403(a));
2. estoppel (§1-103);
3. negligence (§3-406);
4. failure of customer to examine his bank statement (§4-406);
5. making instrument payable to impostor or fictitious payee (§3-404); and
6. employer's responsibility for fraudulent indorsement by an employee (§3-405)

1.   Ratification

An unauthorized signature may become effective as the signature of the person whose name is signed if ratified by that person.[139] Ratification is a fairly

137. U.C.C. §3-407(c); U.C.C. §3-407, Official Comment 2.
138. U.C.C. §3-407(c); U.C.C. §3-407, Official Comment 2.
139. U.C.C. §3-403(a); U.C.C. §3-403, Official Comment 3. Both a forgery and a signature by an agent in excess of his authority may be ratified. U.C.C. §3-403, Official Comment 3.

C. Grounds of Preclusion

straightforward doctrine. Ratification is the election by the person whose name is signed to treat the unauthorized signature as though it were originally authorized by him.[140] For example, assume that Mary, John's wife, signs John's name as co-maker of a note for the purchase price of a car. The simple fact that Mary is John's wife does not give her authority to sign his name to an instrument. When Mary comes home with the car, she tells John that she has purchased the car by signing his name as co-maker of the note. John uses the car on a regular basis. Although Mary's signing of John's name was not originally authorized, John, by using the car, evidences an intention to treat the unauthorized signature as though originally authorized by him. Therefore, John has ratified the signature. It is now effective as his signature as though he had originally signed the note himself. John cannot later revoke the ratification.

The law of agency of the subject jurisdiction determines whether a person has ratified an unauthorized signature. Before John can be found to have ratified his signature, he must either (1) have full knowledge of all of the relevant facts involved or (2) know that he is making a decision without possessing all of the relevant facts.[141] For example, if Mary told John that the note was in the amount of $10,000 when it fact the note was for $20,000, John would not be found to have ratified his signature because he did not have full knowledge of all of the relevant facts involved. In contrast, if Mary told John only that she had signed a note in payment for the car and John did not inquire as to the amount of the note, John would have ratified the signature. In this latter situation, John knows that he is making a decision without possessing all of the relevant facts.

Ratification may be either express or implied.[142] An implied ratification occurs where the conduct of the person whose name is signed can be explained or justified only on the assumption that he has adopted the signature as his own. Ratification will be implied when the ratifier, like John, retains the proceeds of the instrument with full knowledge of all relevant facts. A ratification is also implied where the party whose signature is forged fails to object after full knowledge that the proceeds of the instrument have been placed in his bank account. To avoid ratification, the party must return the proceeds upon obtaining knowledge of the forgery and of deposit of the proceeds in the account. Ratification may also be implied if the party is silent

---

140. U.C.C. §3-403, Official Comment 3. Ratification is effective even where there is no detrimental reliance on the part of the person asserting the ratification. See Restatement (2d), Agency §82, Official Comment c.

141. See Harold Reuschlein & William Gregory, Handbook on the Law of Agency and Partnership, 75 (2d ed. 1990).

142. U.C.C. §3-403, Official Comment 3.

under circumstances where a person who did not intend to ratify the signature would have informed the holder of the unauthorized signature. In order to constitute ratification, the silence must be explainable only on the theory that the party intended to adopt the signature as his own.

Because the party whose name is signed has adopted the signature as his own, the unauthorized signer is no longer liable on the instrument. If Jim, an agent for Morehouse Steak Co., having no authority to sign drafts for the company, signs a draft in purchase of cattle, Morehouse Steak Co.'s ratification releases Jim from liability on the draft. However, the ratification neither affects Morehouse Steak Co.'s rights against Jim for his unauthorized signing of the draft nor affects any criminal liability Jim may have incurred by the unauthorized signature.[143] Morehouse Steak Co. may recover from Jim any loss caused by the unauthorized signature.

2. *Estoppel*

A party may be estopped to deny the authenticity of a signature.[144] A party is estopped where he represents that the signature is authentic, and the holder or payor relies to his detriment on such representation. However, there is no estoppel where the holder or payor has not relied upon the representation. The representation may take the form of a failure to speak when a duty to speak exists. Before silence will estop the person whose name is signed, the person must know of the unauthorized signature. For example, if an authorized agent of Morehouse Steak Co. sees Jim sign the draft and says nothing, Morehouse Steak Co. would be estopped from denying that Jim was authorized.

3. *Preclusion Through Negligence*

Let us begin with an example. John receives, as a gift, a check drawn by his father upon Bank of America in the amount of $1,000. John carelessly leaves his wallet containing the check and all of his identification on a desk in the Los Angeles Public Library. The wallet is stolen. John does not tell his father to stop payment on the check. A week later, a person, looking quite similar to John, goes to Bank of America and asks to have the check cashed. The bank teller carefully looks at the identification and watches while the person

143. U.C.C. §3-403, Official Comment 3.
144. U.C.C. §1-103.

indorses the check. The indorser's signature is very much like the signature on John's driver's license. The teller gives the person $1,000. John sues Bank of America for conversion. Should Bank of America absorb the loss? The answer should be apparent. John's negligence in not only leaving his wallet with his identification on the desk but also in failing to inform his father so that the father could issue a stop payment order caused Bank of America to pay the check. Bank of America in no way was at fault in cashing the check. Clearly, John should suffer the loss. Under the Code, in fact, John will suffer the loss: "A person whose failure to exercise ordinary care substantially contributes to an alteration or to the making of a forged signature is precluded from asserting the alteration or forgery against a person who, in good faith, pays the instrument or takes it for value or for collection."[145]

Any person who is negligent, whether the person is an acceptor, drawer, maker, or indorser, may be precluded from asserting the alteration or forged signature. The signature does not have to be that of the negligent person himself. A drawer who negligently sends a check payable to John Jones to the wrong John Jones will be precluded from asserting that the indorsement was not effective where the check is signed by the wrong John Jones.

a. Who May Assert the Preclusion

Only certain persons, however, may assert the preclusion.[146] The class of protected persons includes the following:

1. Any person who in good faith[147] pays the instrument. In our example above, Bank of America may assert John's negligence because Bank of America, the payor bank, paid the check in good faith;
2. Any person who in good faith takes the instrument for value. If the thief had negotiated the check to Check Cashing Service, which in good faith had paid the thief for the check, Check Cashing Service could preclude John from claiming that the indorsement was forged; and

---

145. U.C.C. §3-406(a). A fine distinction must be kept in mind. Section 3-406 applies only to a forged signature, whether made by an agent not authorized to sign the represented person's name or by a stranger. Where an agent without authority signs his own name as authorized agent for the represented party, the represented party's signature is unauthorized, rather than forged, and therefore not covered by §3-406. Whether the represented person is liable for an unauthorized agent's actions is determined by the subject jurisdiction's law of agency. U.C.C. §3-406, Official Comment 2.

146. U.C.C. §3-406(a); U.C.C. §3-406, Official Comment 1.

147. Good faith means both honesty in fact and the observance of reasonable commercial standards of fair dealing. U.C.C. §3-103(a)(4).

3. Any person who, in good faith, takes the instrument for collection. For example, if Check Cashing Service, had deposited the check in its account at Wells Bank, Wells Bank, having taken the check for collection, could preclude John from claiming that the indorsement is forged even though Wells Bank had not given value for the check.

b. Comparative Negligence

John thus suffers the loss unless he can either recover from the person who took the check from him or prove that the person asserting the preclusion, whether it be Bank of America, Wells Bank, or Check Cashing Service, itself failed to exercise ordinary care and that the failure substantially contributed to the loss. In this event, the loss is allocated according to principles of comparative negligence.[148] Thus, if the person cashing the check did not look at all like John, Bank of America would have been negligent in cashing the check and therefore the loss would be split between John and Bank of America. The Code gives, however, absolutely no guidance as to how this split should take place. The burden of proving the failure of the taker or payor to exercise ordinary care is on the person precluded (John).[149]

c. Drawer's Negligence May be Asserted Against Payor Bank

A payor bank has an incentive to recredit its customer's account even though the customer is negligent. For example, assume that Dan drew a check payable to Alice Faye. Carelessly looking up her address in a telephone book, he mails the check to the wrong Alice Faye. The wrong Alice Faye deposits the check in her account at Crocker Bank, which presents the check for payment to Union Bank. Union Bank pays the check. Upon Dan's complaint, Union Bank recredits Dan's account and sues Crocker Bank for breach of its presentment warranty that it is a person entitled to enforce the instrument. Crocker Bank is not a person entitled to enforce the instrument because the wrong Alice Faye indorsed the check. Since Union Bank itself is not negligent, Crocker Bank would not appear to be able to preclude Union Bank from claiming that the indorsement was forged. Crocker Bank would, it seems, have to pay Union Bank and then proceed to attempt to recover from Dan.

However, there is no reason to allow Union Bank to impose this burden

148. U.C.C. §3-406(b).
149. U.C.C. §3-406(c).

C. Grounds of Preclusion

on Crocker Bank. Because of Dan's negligence, Union Bank should have refused to recredit his account. To ensure that Union Bank does so, a member of the protected class of takers (Crocker Bank) may assert the drawer's (Dan's) failure to exercise ordinary care in defending an action brought by the payor bank (Union Bank) for breach of the presentment warranty that the instrument has not been altered or the person was entitled to enforce the instrument.[150]

d. What Person Asserting Preclusion Must Prove

The party claiming that the negligent party is precluded from asserting that the unauthorized signature or alteration is not effective must prove two separate elements: (1) that the party to be precluded failed to exercise ordinary care; and (2) that the failure substantially contributed to the making of the forged signature or alteration.

e. Failure to Exercise Ordinary Care

The Code defines "ordinary care" in general terms:[151] "Ordinary care" in the case of a person engaged in business means observance of reasonable commercial standards, prevailing in the area in which the person is located, with respect to the business in which the person is engaged.[152]

The test as to whether a party has exercised ordinary care is the traditional tort test for negligence: whether the party's actions were reasonable considering the foreseeability of the loss, the magnitude of the potential loss and the cost of the means required to eliminate the risk of loss.[153] The question is left for the court or the jury to decide in light of the circumstances in the particular case including reasonable commercial standards that may apply.[154] The burden of proving the failure to exercise ordinary care is on the person asserting the preclusion.[155]

Let us examine some typical instances in which a person may be found to have been negligent. In some situations, giving a check to a third party for delivery to the payee so greatly increases the possibility of a forgery that the

150. U.C.C. §4-208(c); U.C.C. §3-417(c).
151. U.C.C. §3-406, Official Comment 1.
152. U.C.C. §3-103(a)(7).
153. See W. Page Keeton, Dan Dobbs, Robert Keeton & David Owen, Prosser and Keeton on the Law of Torts, at pp.169-173 (5th ed. 1984).
154. U.C.C. §3-406, Official Comment 1.
155. U.C.C. §3-406(c).

drawer will be precluded from asserting the subsequent forgery. Whether the drawer has failed to exercise ordinary care depends upon the likelihood that, under the circumstances, the third person would forge the payee's indorsement. For example, assume that David's car is damaged in an accident. David has the car towed to Ripoff Repair Shop. Loss Insurance Company, without telling David, issues a check for the repairs payable jointly to Ripoff Repair Shop and David. Ripoff Repair Shop forges David's indorsement on the check but never finishes the repairs. Loss Insurance Company may be found to be negligent in giving the check directly to Ripoff Repair Shop without telling David. In contrast, had Loss Insurance Company dealt with Ripoff Repair Shop on many occasions in the past without any incidents, Loss Insurance Company may be found not to have been negligent. Similarly, sending a check to David's attorney would probably be found not to have been negligent.

Careless business practices can result in an increased possibility of forgery. For example, Automobile Dealer, in a plan to defraud Finance Company, may submit to Finance Company loan applications and supporting loan agreements supposedly from prospective car buyers. Finance Company, without verifying any of the information on the loan applications, makes the loan and sends the checks to Automobile Dealer. Automobile Dealer forges the payees' indorsements on these checks. Finance Company is negligent in failing to verify the applications' authenticity.

A drawer also fails to exercise ordinary care where he allows a signature stamp to be accessible to nonauthorized personnel even though the stamp is not used by the drawer to sign checks. Use of the signature stamp by the nonauthorized personnel would give the appearance to third parties that the drawer had in fact signed the check.

An employer may also be precluded from denying the effectiveness of a signature forged by an employee where the employer has failed to exercise ordinary care in either hiring or supervising the employee. For instance, a company should not without good reason hire a bookkeeper who has a background of forgery or embezzlement or who has a gambling or drug problem. If such a bookkeeper is hired, he should be watched carefully. Even in less obvious cases, the employer has a duty to exercise ordinary care in supervising its employees. For instance, when a bookkeeper is authorized both to write checks and to reconcile the books, a periodic audit by another person should be performed.

It is unlikely that a court would hold a drawer to have failed to exercise ordinary care simply because he was not careful in guarding his blank check forms. Anyone can have checks printed up with another person's name and account number imprinted on them. Losing a checkbook without any accompanying identification does not greatly increase the chance of a forgery.

C. Grounds of Preclusion

Although a party does not have a duty to draw or make an instrument such that it cannot be altered, she must use reasonable care to prevent its alteration.[156] When the numbers or words signifying the amount due on the instrument are written so as to leave space open for additional words or numbers to be inserted, the party drawing or making the instrument will usually be found to have failed to exercise ordinary care.[157] If the instrument reads "in the amount of _____ two dollars," a subsequent party can add the words "two thousand and," thereby easily raising the amount to $2,002. It also may be negligent to leave a space open at the beginning or end of the line containing the payee's name so as to make it easy for the payee's name to be altered. The leaving of a space at the end of a sentence or between lines is probably not a failure to exercise ordinary care even though additional provisions, for example, for attorney's fees or interest, could be added to the instrument.

Certain other precautions should be exercised in preparing an instrument. Although there is no duty to use indelible ink, a protectograph machine, or sensitized paper, the use of a pencil or easily erasable ink may constitute the failure to exercise ordinary care. However, if the paper upon which the instrument is written tends to show any minor erasure, the use of a pencil or erasable ink might not be a failure to exercise ordinary care. It would also seem that if the payor bank informs the drawer that forgery and alteration has become a problem and that, as a result, the bank is offering, at no additional charge, sensitized paper that shows any changes or checks that provide other safeguards, a court could find the drawer's failure to use such checks to be negligent. If the bank is only willing to furnish such checks at a much higher price, it may be reasonable, in light of the low risk of alteration, for the drawer to refuse to purchase and use such checks.

f. Failure of Payor Bank to Exercise Ordinary Care

In reading the following materials, it is important to remember that irrespective of whether or not the payor bank exercises ordinary care, the payor bank has no right to charge the drawer's account when it pays an instrument bearing a forged indorsement or forged drawer's signature unless the drawer is negligent or would otherwise be precluded from claiming that the indorse-

---

156. U.C.C. §3-406, Official Comment 1
157. U.C.C. §3-406, Official Comment 3, Case No. 3.

ment or signature was unauthorized.[158] When the drawer is negligent or otherwise precluded, the drawer will attempt to prove that the payor bank failed to exercise ordinary care so as to cause the loss to be split between them.

When a check is presented to the payor bank by a presenting bank, the payor bank will almost certainly be found to have exercised ordinary care in paying the check even though the check contains a forged indorsement.[159] A payor bank cannot know if an indorsement is forged and thus may rely upon the presenting bank's guaranty of prior indorsements in paying the check. A payor bank is held to a higher standard where the payor bank is also the depositary bank or where the item is presented over the counter for payment. In these cases, the bank fails to exercise ordinary care if it does not discover obvious irregularities in the identification of the person presenting the item for payment.[160]

When a payor bank makes payment over a forged drawer's signature, the question arises as to whether the payor bank has failed to exercise ordinary care in not detecting the forgery. For example, assume that Steve, secretary for Allen, forges Allen's signature as drawer on a check. The forged signature bears no resemblance to Allen's true signature. Bank of America pays the check. Bank of America refuses Allen's demand to recredit his account on the grounds that Allen was negligent in supervising Steve. Allen raises comparative negligence as a defense. He contends that because the forgery was so obvious, Bank of America was negligent in not recognizing that his signature was a forgery. Bank of America claims that it did not notice the forgery because it never visually examines any checks under $5,000. Allen contends that the fact

158. As we will discuss in Chapter 4C(4), a drawer may be precluded from asserting that an indorsement is unauthorized where the payee is an impostor or a fictitious payee or where as an employer it is responsible for an unauthorized indorsement by an employee.

159. In the case of payor banks, action or nonaction approved by Article 4 or pursuant to Federal Reserve regulations or operating circulars constitutes the exercise of ordinary care. U.C.C. §4-103(c). Additionally, in the absence of special instructions, action or nonaction consistent with clearing-house rules and the like or with a general banking usage not disapproved by Article 4 constitutes a prima facie case of the exercise of ordinary care. U.C.C. §4-103(c); U.C.C. §4-103, Official Comment 4. Although the Code gives some specific guidance as to what constitutes ordinary care in the case of banks, these rules are for the purpose of determining whether a bank is liable for its own negligence in the bank collection process. Seldom do they have any impact upon whether the bank has been contributorily negligent in the case of a forgery or alteration. We discuss these rules in Chapter 5.

160. For a case under former Article 3, See Consolidated Pub. Water Supply Dist. No. C-1 v. Farmers Bank, 686 S.W.2d 844, 40 U.C.C. Rep. Serv. 955 (Mo. App. 1985) (Payor bank which cashes checks payable to corporation containing handwritten indorsements may be found to have not acted in accordance with reasonable commercial standards even though it need not require an indorsement under §3-505.).

alone that Bank of America did not visually examine the check conclusively proves that Bank of America was negligent. Does Allen's contention have merit?

Banks objected to having the duty to visually inspect checks imposed upon them. Because banks are presented with thousands of checks each day, banks argued, they could not be expected to verify every drawer's signature. Forcing them to examine each check was, the banks argued, extremely inefficient. Not only were the number of forgeries so small compared to the number of legitimate checks that would have to be examined, but most forgeries could not be detected by even close inspection. The drafters of Article 4 agreed with the banks and adopted a very lenient standard of care for banks processing checks:

> Where a bank takes an instrument for processing for collection or payment by automated means, the bank need not visually examine the instrument in order for the bank to meet reasonable commercial standards if the failure to examine such instrument does not violate the bank's prescribed procedures and the bank's procedures do not vary unreasonably from general banking usage not disapproved by Article 3 or Article 4.[161]

Therefore, Bank of America's lack of visual examination of signatures does not conclusively demonstrate a lack of ordinary care or good faith as long as Bank of America's procedure is reasonable and commonly followed by other comparable banks in the area.[162] Because few banks visually inspect checks for forgeries or alterations, it is doubtful that Allen could successfully prove that Bank of America's failure to visually inspect the check was unreasonable and therefore negligent.

By the way, this standard applies not only to whether a payor bank is required to visually examine a check to discover alterations or a forged drawer's signature, but also to whether a depositary or other collecting bank which uses automated means to process checks for collection must verify its customer's indorsement.

g. **Substantially Contributes**

In order for the failure to exercise ordinary care to preclude the negligent party, the failure must substantially contribute to the making of the

161. U.C.C. §3-103(a)(7).
162. U.C.C. §4-406, Revised Official Comment 4.

forgery or alteration.[163] The simplest case where the failure to exercise ordinary care substantially contributes to the forgery is where the drawer is negligent in allowing unauthorized personnel access to a facsimile signature machine. By allowing such access, the forgery, looking identical to an authentic signature, would be impossible to detect.

Although the negligence does not have to make detection of the forgery or alteration more difficult as in the example of the facsimile signature machine, the negligence must have been a contributing cause and a significant factor in enabling the forgery or alteration to have been made. For example, where Brother and Sister are in a bitter estate contest and Brother is in dire need of money, Drawer's negligence in handing a check to Brother for delivery to Sister would be a significant factor and a contributing cause in Brother's forging Sister's indorsement. Although Brother still has to convince a subsequent purchaser or payor that Sister's indorsement is authentic, Drawer's negligence in delivering the check to a person of questionable integrity made the forgery more likely.

In many situations, although a person may have been negligent, the person is not precluded because the negligence did not substantially contribute to the forgery or alteration. Where the negligence had no effect on the likelihood of the forgery or alteration occurring or of its success, the negligence will not have substantially contributed to the making of the forgery or alteration. Generally, the mailing of a check to a person other than the payee does not substantially contribute to the resultant forgery even though it may constitute the failure to exercise ordinary care. The forger must still convince the purchaser or payor that he is the payee.

But where the check is mailed to a different person having the same name as the intended payee, the ability of the forger to pass himself off as the payee is greatly increased. Thus, if the sender fails to exercise ordinary care in sending the check to a person bearing the same name as the payee, the sender's failure will be deemed to contribute substantially to the forged indorsement.[164] However, this may not necessarily be the case. For example, assume that Drawer is negligent in addressing a check intended for Fay Wray, King Kong's wife, to Fay Wray, the singer. Despite this negligence, if the check is stolen from Fay Wray, the singer, before she has a chance to mail it back to Drawer, Drawer's negligence would not have been a contributing cause in the indorsement being forged.

---

163. U.C.C. §3-406(a); U.C.C. §3-406, Official Comment 2.
164. U.C.C. §3-406, Official Comment 3, Case No. 2.

C. Grounds of Preclusion

4. *Impostors, Fictitious Payees, and Employer's Responsibility for Unauthorized Indorsements by Employees*

There are three grounds where, even absent proof of any specific negligence regarding the instrument, a forged indorsement is deemed to be effective to negotiate the instrument. The first two grounds, issuance of an instrument to an impostor or to a fictitious payee, involve behavior of the drawer or maker in issuing an instrument that is so likely to result in a forged indorsement that the loss is initially placed upon the drawer or maker. The third ground involves an employer's responsibility for the actions of its employees. This latter ground, discussed in the next subsection, provides that the employer will initially suffer the loss whenever an employee to whom the employer has entrusted responsibility as to instruments forges the indorsement of the payee. In any of these three situations where the person taking the instrument or paying the instrument is negligent, comparative negligence principles apply to split the loss.

a. Introduction to Impostor Rule

"Impostor" is defined as a person who "by use of the mails or otherwise induces the issuer to issue the instrument to the impostor, or to a person acting in concert with the impostor, by impersonating the payee of the instrument or a person authorized to act for the payee."[165]

In other words, an impostor is a person who pretends to be the payee or an agent for the payee. For example, Ivan Impostor is an impostor if he pretends to be Newt Gingrich and asks you to give him a check for his upcoming Congressional campaign. Ivan Impostor would also be an impostor if he claimed that he was a member of Gingrich's campaign committee and asked for a check payable to Gingrich.

b. Introduction to Fictitious Payee Rule

While the drawer or maker in the case of an impostor believes that the instrument will be cashed by the named payee, this is not true in the case of a fictitious payee. A "fictitious payee" is either a person who is not intended to have any interest in the instrument or is a nonexistent person.[166]

---

165. U.C.C. §3-404(a).
166. U.C.C. §3-404(b).

For example, Tax Defrauder, for tax purposes, wants cancelled checks indicating that he has made charitable contributions. To obtain these cancelled checks, Tax Defrauder may make checks payable to American Cancer Society intending to cash the checks himself. American Cancer Society is a fictitious payee because Tax Defrauder intended that the American Cancer Society have no interest in the instrument. Similarly, if Tommy Treasurer wants to embezzle money from his employer, he may write a check payable to Ace Hardware intending to cash the check himself. Ace Hardware is a fictitious payee. Review the discussion in Chapter 2 as to how the intent of the maker or drawer determines the identity of the payee.

c.   Need for Indorsement

What is the effect of the payee being an impostor or a fictitious payee? In the case of both impostors and fictitious payees, an indorsement by any person in the name of the payee is effective in favor of a person who, in good faith, pays the instrument or takes it for value or for collection.[167] Thus, Tommy Treasurer's indorsement in the name of Ace Hardware is effective to negotiate the check. As long as there is an indorsement in the name of Ace Hardware, it need not be written by Tommy Treasurer or by a person acting in concert with him. The indorsement may be written by anyone. Furthermore, the indorsement need not be in the exact name of Ace Hardware. As long as it is in a name substantially similar to that of the named payee, it is sufficient to negotiate the instrument.[168] Leeway is given because even in the most innocent of situations, the drawer's or maker's designation of the payee may not be entirely accurate. Especially where a corporate name is different from its trade name, an indorsement in a similar trade name will not arouse suspicion. If the discrepancy is reasonable, the indorsement is effective. Furthermore, as long as the instrument is deposited in a depositary bank to an account in a name substantially similar to that of the payee, the depositary bank is the holder of the instrument regardless of whether the instrument is indorsed.[169]

Impostors are treated differently than fictitious payees for purposes of determining whether an indorsement is necessary in order for the person in possession of the instrument to be its holder. In the case of a fictitious payee, because no person was the intended payee, any person in possession of the instrument is its holder.[170] Thus, even before any indorsement is made in the

---

167. U.C.C. §3-404(a) and (b)(2).
168. U.C.C. §3-404(c); U.C.C. §3-405(c).
169. U.C.C. §3-404(c)(ii); U.C.C. §3-404, Official Comment 2, Case #5.
170. U.C.C. §3-404(b)(1).

C. Grounds of Preclusion

name "Ace Hardware," any person in possession of the instrument is its holder. In contrast, when Ivan Impostor pretends to be Newt Gingrich and asks you to give him a check for his upcoming Congressional campaign, until an indorsement in the name "Newt Gingrich" is made, no person, other than Newt Gingrich, can be its holder.[171]

d. Who May Assert That the Indorsement Is Effective

Where a fictitious payee or impostor is involved, an indorsement by any person in the name of the payee is effective to negotiate the instrument, thus making the indorsee its holder. This means that any person that acts in good faith may assert that the indorsement is effective against any other person. (Remember, in the case of negligence, that only the negligent party was precluded from asserting the forgery.) Assume, in our example above, that Ivan Impostor indorses the check to Local Grocer, who deposits the check into his bank account at Wells Bank, which presents the check for payment to Bank of America. Bank of America pays the check. (See Figure 4.7.)

FIGURE 4.7

Because Ivan's indorsement in the name of Newt Gingrich is effective, Local Grocer and Wells Bank are persons entitled to enforce the instrument. Neither Local Grocer nor Wells Bank breach their presentment warranty to Bank of America that they are persons entitled to enforce the check. Likewise, being persons entitled to enforce the check, their taking of the check is not conversion. Upon its payment to Wells Bank, Bank of America may charge your account.

The result would change if Local Grocer, Wells Bank, or Bank of America did not act in good faith or had failed to exercise ordinary care. A payor or taker who does not act in good faith may not assert that the indorsement is

---

171. U.C.C. §3-404(a).

effective.[172] When the taker or payor is negligent, the loss is allocated under comparative negligence principles between the drawer and the negligent party.[173] For example, assume that Ivan Impostor had deposited the check in an account under the name of "Newt Gingrich" that Ivan opened at Wells Bank. If Wells Bank had allowed Ivan to establish a bank account in the name of Newt Gingrich without asking for any identification, Wells Bank's negligence would have contributed to Ivan Impostor's ability to accomplish his mischief. You therefore have a cause of action against Wells Bank to recover a portion of the loss.[174]

e.   What Is an Impostor?

An impostor is one who represents himself as the named payee or a person authorized to act for the named payee and, by such representation, induces the issuer to issue the instrument to him or to a person acting in concert with him.[175] In essence, the drawer or maker is deemed to have made the instrument payable to the impostor under the assumed name of the named payee. When you made your check payable to Newt Gingrich believing that Ivan Impostor was Newt Gingrich, you in essence were making your check payable to Ivan under the name of Newt Gingrich. You may wonder what is so wrong with what you did. The answer is simply that you have made it extremely likely that the check will be cashed upon Gingrich's forged indorsement. You may feel that you should be protected because Ivan will have to prove that he is Newt Gingrich to get the check cashed. This may be true. But do you believe that Ivan chose the name Newt Gingrich at random? Quite the contrary. Ivan has either already established a bank account under this name or believes that he has other means of successfully cashing the check. Your fault in not making sure that he was Newt Gingrich allowed Ivan to accomplish his fraud. Now, if the depositary bank or payor bank was negligent in allowing Ivan to deposit or cash the check without proper identification, you will not have to suffer the entire loss. Under comparative negligence principles, you will be able to recover the portion of the loss from the negligent payor or depositary bank.

A person is also an impostor where he falsely represents himself to be the agent of the named payee.[176] Assume that Fred, representing himself to be an employee of the Water Company, induces the drawer to issue a check payable

172. U.C.C. §3-404(b)(2); U.C.C. §3-404, Official Comment 3.
173. U.C.C. §3-404(d); U.C.C. §3-404, Official Comment 3.
174. U.C.C. §3-404, Official Comment 3.
175. U.C.C. §3-404, Official Comment 1.
176. U.C.C. §3-404(a)

C. Grounds of Preclusion

to the Water Company. Fred indorses the check in the name of the Water Company. Fred's indorsement is effective to make the depositary bank a holder of the check. The loss would, however, probably be split between the depositary bank and the drawer because the depositary bank probably failed to exercise ordinary care when it permitted Fred to deposit the check into his own personal bank account.

The impostor rule applies whether the impostor acts in person, by mail, by telephone, or otherwise.[177] The manner of the imposture is irrelevant. For example, if upon receipt of a letter from Ivan Impostor, signed by him under the name of Newt Gingrich soliciting campaign contributions, you mail a check to the designated address, any person's indorsement in the name of Newt Gingrich will be sufficient to negotiate the check.

It is also irrelevant whether or not you in fact owe the named payee a debt. Where Fred, claiming to be an agent of the Water Company, asks that you write a check for this month's overdue bill, the impostor rule applies even though you really do owe Water Company the money. You should have asked for identification or called the Water Company to inquire as to Fred's authority.

The wrongdoer is not an impostor if he does not obtain the instrument by pretending to be the named payee. Where Fred steals the check from your mailbox and thereafter pretends to be an agent for the Water Company in cashing the check, the impostor rule does not apply. You were not culpable in any manner. Likewise, where the drawer by mistake mails the check to a person having the same name as the payee, the issuance was not induced by the impostor, and therefore, the section does not apply.

Fuzzy areas exist where it is unclear whether the impostor rule applies. For example, what if Brother forges Husband's name to a savings account withdrawal slip and asks that the bank issue a check payable to Husband. Or, what if Wife in filling out a loan application forges Husband's signature and then forges Husband's indorsement on the check payable to Husband.[178] In neither of these situations, does Brother or Wife pretend to be Husband. Courts were split as to whether the impostor rule found in the earlier version

---

177. U.C.C. §3-404(a).

178. Compare Broward Bank v. Commercial Bank, 547 So. 2d 687, 9 U.C.C. Rep. Serv. 2d 638 (Fla. App. 1989) (Impostor rule does not apply where husband took papers for loan home and brought them back with appearance of his wife's signature. He then forged his wife's indorsement on check.) with Franklin Natl. Bank v. Shapiro, 7 U.C.C. Rep. Serv. 317 (N.Y. Sup. Ct. 1970) (Impostor rule applies where wife forged husband's signature on loan documents and on check).

of the Code applied to these situations.[179] It is unclear how these situations differ from Brother or Wife writing a letter to the bank and signing Husband's signature to the letter and then to the forged withdrawal slip or loan application. Yet, in the latter situations, the impostor rule would apply. The impostor rule should also apply in the former situation.

f.   Payee Intended to Have No Interest in the Instrument and Fictitious Payee

There are three distinct situations where a payee is regarded as a fictitious payee. In all of these situations, the person signing as or on behalf of the drawer or maker intended that the payee have no interest in the instrument.

The first situation is where the person identified as the payee does not in fact exist.[180] For example, a check payable to Donald Duck or to the Lion King does not designate any person who could possibly indorse the instrument. It makes no difference whether the drawer knew that the payee is fictitious. Where he knows that the payee is fictitious, the drawer knows that the indorsement will not be made by the payee and therefore has no right to expect an indorsement by the named payee. Even where the drawer has no knowledge that the payee does not exist, he should absorb the loss because he is in the best position to determine whether the named payee exists.

The second situation is where the maker or drawer issues an instrument intending that the named payee have no interest in the instrument. Because the drawer or maker knows that there will be no proper indorsement, subject to the principle of comparative negligence, it is unfair to shift the loss to a subsequent purchaser or payor whose fault may be minimal. There is seldom, if ever, a legitimate reason for the maker or drawer to issue an instrument to a person whom he does not intend to have any interest in the instrument. In most of these situations, the drawer or maker is attempting to create the appearance of a payment so as to cover up some type of fraudulent or improper activity. Remember, for example, Tax Defrauder who was attempting to defraud the IRS by creating cancelled checks payable to the American Red Cross.

179. Compare Snow v. Byron, 580 So. 2d 238, 14 U.C.C. Rep. Serv. 2d 1132 (Fla. App. 1991) (No impersonation and therefore no imposture where estranged husband, who had forged wife's signature on letter authorizing broker to close account, forges wife's indorsement on check.) with Fidelity & Deposit Co. v. Manufacturers Hanover Trust Co., 63 Misc. 2d 950, 313 N.Y.S.2d 823, 7 U.C.C. Rep. Serv. 1142 (N.Y. Civ. Ct. 1970) (because the bank checked the wife's signature on the withdrawal slip against her signature card, the bank intended to deal with the person who forged the withdrawal slip, and therefore impostor rule applied).

180. U.C.C. §3-404(b)(ii); U.C.C. §3-404, Official Comment 2.

C. Grounds of Preclusion

The third situation is where an agent, employee, or officer signs on behalf of the drawer or maker intending the payee to have no interest in the instrument. In this situation, the actual signer is usually trying to defraud his employer. The agent, employee, or officer may attempt to hide his activity by padding the payroll or altering the records to show a debt owed to the named payee, or he may make no attempt at all to conceal his activity. For example, Tommy Treasurer may draw a check on behalf of Tune Corporation payable to Music Publishers intending to cash the check himself. Tommy Treasurer may cover up this fraud by mailing to Tune Corporation a phony bill from Music Publishers. Or, Music Publishers may have in fact submitted the bill. Even though the debt is actually owed to Music Publishers, the fact that Tommy Treasurer, the person signing the check on behalf of Tune Corporation, intends that Music Publishers not receive the proceeds, makes Music Publishers a fictitious payee.[181]

However, the rules for fictitious payees do not apply where the person signing for the issuer develops the intent to steal the instrument only after the instrument has been signed.[182] Thus, if Tommy Treasurer originally signed the check intending to pay Music Publishers, and only later decided to cash the check himself, Music Publishers would not be a fictitious payee. However, as we will discuss in the next section, Tommy Treasurer's indorsement would be effective since Tune Corporation had entrusted him with responsibility as to instruments.

g. Who Determines Whether Payee Is Intended to Have Interest in Instrument

In determining whether a payee is a fictitious payee, it is necessary to look at the intent of the "person whose intent determines to whom an instrument is payable." Sections 3-110(a) and (b) set out the rules for determining whose intent is relevant in determining to whom an instrument is payable. In most situations, it will be simple. It is usually the person who signs the instrument as the drawer or maker. But there are situations in which it is not all that clear. For example, where there are multiple signers, each signer may intend that the instrument be payable to a different person. In this case, the instrument is payable to any person intended by any of the signers. Thus, if any one of the issuers did not intend that the named payee have an interest in the check, the payee is a fictitious payee.[183]

---

181. U.C.C. §3-404(b)(i) and (ii); U.C.C. §3-404, Official Comment 2.
182. U.C.C. §3-404, Official Comment 2, Case No. 2.
183. U.C.C. §3-404, Official Comment 2, Case No. 3.

For example, assume that both Sally, the President, and Sandra, the Treasurer, must sign any corporate check. Sally draws up a check made payable to Sapphire Gem Company intending to cash the check herself. Although Sandra intends that Sapphire Gem Company receive the proceeds, Sally does not. As a consequence, the check is payable to either Sapphire Gem Company, to whom Sandra intended that the check be payable, or to Sally personally, to whom Sally intended the check to be payable. As a result, Sapphire Gem Company is a fictitious payee. When a check is signed automatically by a check-writing machine, the intent of the person who supplied the payee's name determines whether the payee is intended to have any interest in the check.[184]

h.   Double Forgeries

Where a person who forges the drawer's name also intends that the payee have no interest in the check,[185] the payee is a fictitious payee. This application of the rule has an impact upon whether the depositary bank or the payor bank suffers the loss where there is both a forged drawer's signature and a forged indorsement. As we discussed in an earlier section, when an indorsement is forged, the depositary bank breaches its presentment warranty that it is a person entitled to enforce the instrument. As a result, the depositary bank rather than the payor bank will suffer the loss where only an indorsement is forged. However, the depositary bank gives no warranty to the payor bank that the drawer's signature is authentic. As a result, the payor bank will usually suffer the loss when only the drawer's signature is forged.

So what is the result when there is both a forged drawer's signature and a payee whom the forger intends to have no interest in the check? The answer is that the payor bank suffers the loss because the check is treated as bearing only a forged drawer's signature. Because any indorsement in the name of the payee is effective to negotiate the instrument, the depositary bank is a person entitled to enforce the instrument. Therefore, the depositary bank does not breach its presentment warranty to that effect and the loss falls on the payor bank.

Let us look at an example. Thief steals Drawer's checkbook and forges Drawer's signature on a check that Thief makes payable to his sister Agnes. Thief intends that Agnes have no interest in the check. Thus, any indorsement in Agnes's name is effective to negotiate the check. Thief, after signing Agnes's name, asks his girlfriend to deposit the check in her bank account at Wells

---

184. U.C.C. §3-404, Official Comment 2, Case No. 4.
185. U.C.C. §3-404, Official Comment 2, Case No. 4.

Bank. Bank of America pays the check. Because Drawer's signature is forged, Bank of America may not debit the drawer's account[186] nor may it recover from Wells Bank for breach of a presentment warranty. Bank of America therefore suffers the loss. Treating this as a case of a forged drawer's signature rather than as a forged indorsement makes sense. Because Thief could have chosen the name of any accomplice as the named payee, forgery of the indorsement does not cause the loss.

i. Employer's Responsibility for Fraudulent Indorsement by Employee

When an employer hires an employee and gives the employee responsibility regarding instruments, the employer is liable when the employee forges an indorsement on an instrument. The loss is imposed upon the employer for two reasons. First, he has a duty to prevent the loss by carefully hiring and supervising his employees. Second, even where the employer is not at fault in any manner, he is still in the best position to prevent a loss by purchasing a fidelity bond governing misappropriations by employees. Therefore, subject to the principle of comparative negligence, the employer suffers the loss whether or not the employer is negligent.[187]

Two types of situations are covered by this rule. The first situation is an indorsement made in the name of the employer on an instrument payable to the employer.[188] For example, Sandra, bookkeeper of Diamonds-R-Forever, forges Diamonds-R-Forever's indorsement on a check payable to Diamonds-R-Forever. The second situation is an indorsement in the name of the payee on an instrument issued by the employer.[189] For example, Sandra takes a check issued by Diamonds-R-Forever and intended for Sapphire Gem Company and indorses the check in the name of Sapphire Gem Company.

The rule is that an indorsement in the name of the payee is effective in favor of any person who in good faith pays an instrument or takes it for value or for collection whenever an employer entrusts an employee with responsibility with respect to the instrument, and the employee or a person acting in concert with him makes a fraudulent indorsement.[190]

As in the case of impostors, the instrument must in fact be indorsed in the

---

186. U.C.C. §3-404, Official Comment 2, Case No. 5.
187. U.C.C. §3-405, Official Comment 1.
188. U.C.C. §3-405(a)(2)(i).U.C.C. §3-405, Official Comment 1.
189. U.C.C. §3-405(a)(2)(ii).U.C.C. §3-405, Official Comment 1.
190. U.C.C. §3-405(b).

name of the payee.[191] However, even without an indorsement, deposit in a bank to an account in a name substantially similar to the payee's name is sufficient to make the bank a holder of the check.[192]

If the person paying or taking the instrument fails to exercise ordinary care, and the failure substantially contributes to the loss, the person bearing the loss may recover from the person failing to exercise ordinary care to the extent that his failure contributed to the loss.[193]

In order for the indorsement to be effective under this rule, the employer must entrust an employee with responsibility with respect to the instrument.[194] "Employee" is broadly defined to include actual employees, independent contractors, and employees of an independent contractor retained by the employer.

More importantly, the employee must be entrusted with responsibility with respect to the instrument.

"Responsibility" means authority:

1. to sign or indorse instruments on behalf of the employer;
2. to process instruments received by the employer for bookkeeping purposes, for deposit to an account, or for other disposition;
3. to prepare or process instruments for issue in the name of the employer;
4. to supply information for determining the names or addresses of payees;
5. to control the disposition of instruments issued in the name of the employer; or
6. to act otherwise with respect to instruments in a responsible capacity.[195]

The prototypical employee who has been entrusted with responsibility regarding checks is a bookkeeper whose duties include the authority to process checks received by the employer for bookkeeping purposes.[196] Where the bookkeeper deposits one of the checks into his personal bank account, the

---

191. U.C.C. §3-405(b) and (c). As in the case of fictitious payees or impostors, the indorsement does not have to be in the exact name of the payee in order to negotiate the instrument. Any indorsement in a name substantially similar to the payee's name is sufficient. U.C.C. §3-405 (c) .

192. U.C.C. §3-405 (c).

193. U.C.C. §3-405, Official Comments 2 and 4.

194. U.C.C. §3-405(a)(1); U.C.C. §3-405(b).

195. U.C.C. §3-405(a)(3).

196. U.C.C. §3-405(a)(3)(ii).

C. Grounds of Preclusion

check is deemed to have been properly indorsed by the employer.[197] Similarly, an employee whose duties include entering addresses of suppliers into a computer has responsibility with regard to checks[198] since he has responsibility to supply information determining the names or addresses of payees.[199] Where the employee adds a fraudulent address for a real supplier, his indorsement of the check in the name of the supplier is effective. Likewise, because Sandra, as treasurer, has authority to sign instruments for Diamonds-R-Forever, Sandra's indorsement in the name of Sapphire Gem Company is effective even though she only developed the intention to steal a check after the check was issued to pay a bona fide debt owed to Sapphire Gem Company.[200] The rule also applies where a clerk who has authority to prepare checks fraudulently induces the treasurer to issue a check to a supplier and thereafter forges the payee's indorsement.[201]

However, an employee does not have responsibility with respect to an instrument just because he has access to instruments, or to blank or incomplete forms, as part of incoming or outgoing mail or otherwise.[202] Therefore, an indorsement by a mail room attendant in the name of the payee is not effective where he stole the check from the mailroom.[203]

5. Customer's Duty to Review Bank Statement

Even after a forgery or alteration has taken place, it is not always too late to prevent the loss. Let us look at an example. Sandra, treasurer of Diamonds-R-Forever, has a gambling problem. She owes bookies almost one hundred thousand dollars. To keep the bookies from taking more drastic measures, she has told them that she would pay them $2,000 per week. Not having the money, she forges Sally's name, the president of the company, as drawer of checks payable to phony suppliers. She then deposits the money in different accounts that she has opened for just this purpose. She forges $20,000 of these checks in February. Although the statement from the bank containing the checks forged in February arrives on March 10th, Diamonds-R-Forever does not examine the statement. Between March 10th and March 31st, Sandra forges

---

197. U.C.C. §3-405, Official Comment 3, Case No. 3.
198. U.C.C. §3-405, Official Comment 3, Case No. 5.
199. U.C.C. §3-405(a)(3)(iv).
200. U.C.C. §3-405(a)(3)(i); U.C.C. §3-405, Official Comment 2, Case No. 6.
201. U.C.C. §3-405, Official Comment 3, Case No. 7.
202. U.C.C. §3-405(3).
203. U.C.C. §3-405, Official Comment 3, Case No. 1.

$40,000 more checks. Although she has paid the bookies $16,000, she has put $24,000 into her various bank accounts. The bank statement containing the checks forged in March arrives on April 10th. The statement is finally examined on April 21st by Sally who immediately notifies Bank of America of the forgeries. Between April 11th and April 20th, Sandra has forged another $20,000 of checks. On April 20th, Sandra withdraws all of the funds from her accounts and flees the country. Who should be responsible for the loss—Bank of America upon whom the checks were drawn or Diamonds-R-Forever whose delay in examining the bank statement contributed to the loss?

It is pretty obvious that at least those losses that could have been prevented by the use of ordinary care on the part of Diamonds-R-Forever in reviewing its bank statement should be borne by it. The Code does this by imposing upon the bank customer a duty to examine her bank statement and accompanying items and to report to the bank any forgery of her own signature or any alteration. [204] The Code also has an absolute bar against contesting her forged signature or alteration if the customer does not report the alteration or unauthorized signature within one year after receipt of the statement or one year after the item has been made available to her.[205] Section 4-406 covers only forgeries of the customer's own signature. A customer has no duty under §4-406 to discover whether an indorsement is unauthorized. This is because the customer cannot, by examining the bank statement and returned items, determine whether the indorsement of another person has been forged. However, if the customer has reason to know that an indorsement has been forged, the customer may have a duty under the common law of negligence to report her suspicions to the bank.

a.   Applies to Items

Because the preclusion is found in Article 4, the term "instrument" is not used. Rather, the customer is precluded from asserting her unauthorized signature or an alteration on any "item." An "item" is any instrument or promise or order to pay money handled by a bank for collection.[206] It does not include electronic funds transfers, payment orders governed by Article 4A, or credit and debit card slips.[207] We have discussed the definition of "item" in Chapter 1.

---

204. U.C.C. §4-406(c).
205. U.C.C. §§4-406(c) and (f).
206. U.C.C. §4-406(c); U.C.C. §4-104(a)(9).
207. U.C.C. §4-104(a)(9).

b. Duty of Bank to Send Statement of Account to Customer

Virtually all banks send to their customers a statement of account indicating which items have been paid in the relevant period of time and the balance left in the account. Whether or not the bank has a duty to supply its customer with this statement of account depends purely upon its agreement with its customer.[208] However, the bank has an interest in sending such a statement. Unless the bank sends the customer such a statement, the customer has no duty to examine the statement and items and report to the bank her unauthorized signature or an alteration.

A bank that sends or makes available to a customer a statement of account showing payment of items for her account shall either return or make available to the customer the items paid or provide information in the statement of account sufficient to allow the customer to reasonably identify the items paid.[209]

Instead of returning the items to the customer or making them available to her, the bank may instead provide sufficient information in the statement of account to permit the customer to reasonably identify the items.[210] Recently, in an attempt to decrease costs, banks have begun to institute the cost-saving practices of check retention and check truncation. Under a check retention plan, the payor bank retains the check or other item instead of returning it to the customer along with the statement of account.[211] Under a check truncation agreement, the item is electronically presented to the payor bank with the collecting bank retaining the item.

When the item or its image is not furnished, what information is sufficient to permit the customer to identify the item? Section 4-406(a) sets out the

---

208. U.C.C. §4-406, Revised Official Comment 1. However, if items are not returned to the customer, the bank or other person retaining the items has the duty, for seven years after receipt of the items, to either retain the items or, if the items are destroyed, maintain the capacity to furnish legible copies of the items. U.C.C. §4-406(b). In addition, upon the customer's request, the payor bank must either supply the customer with the item or, if the item has been destroyed, supply a legible copy of the item within a reasonable time. U.C.C. §4-406(b); U.C.C. §4-406, Official Comment 3. However, the Code neither defines what constitutes a reasonable time, U.C.C. §4-406, Revised Official Comment 3, nor provides any sanctions for a bank's failure to return or furnish the item or a legible copy; nor does it regulate the fees that a bank may charge for furnishing the item or a copy. U.C.C. §4-406, Revised Official Comment 3. The only limitation upon the fee a bank may charge for this service is the power of courts to review the reasonableness of the fees under the doctrines of unconscionability or good faith and fair dealing. U.C.C. §4-406, Revised Official Comment 3.

209. U.C.C. §4-406(a).

210. U.C.C. §4-406(a); U.C.C. §4-406, Revised Official Comment 1.

211. U.C.C. §4-406, Revised Official Comment 3.

information that is deemed sufficient to reasonably identify the item.[212] In order to reduce costs to banks, the information required is only that information which is easily retrievable by computer, that is, the information contained on the MICR-encoded line. This information includes the number of the item, its amount and the date of payment.[213] A bank that supplies these three pieces of information retrievable from the MICR-encoded line fulfills its duty to sufficiently identify the item. Although a customer may find the payee's name and the date of the item useful in identifying the item, this information is not currently available through MICR encoding. As a result, despite the fact that omission of the payee's name may make it more difficult for customers who do not keep good records to determine whether an item is properly payable, the burden imposed on these customers is justified by the cost savings to all bank customers afforded by computer-generated statements.

c.   Customer's Duty to Examine Statement

To trigger the customer's duty to examine the statement, the payor bank may either send or make available the statement of account showing payment of the items.[214] The statement of account may be sent by mail or by any other usual means of communication, as long as it is properly addressed and all costs of postage or transmission are paid. As long as the statement is received by an authorized agent, the customer will be deemed to have received the statement even if that agent happens to be the person making the unauthorized signature or alteration.[215] Because the customer chose the agent to act on his behalf in examining the statement, the customer will be charged with whatever knowledge a reasonable examination by a loyal agent would have discovered.

The payor bank makes the statement of account available by holding it pursuant to a request by or instructions from its customer. The manner in which the bank makes the statement available to its customer must be reasonable.

Once the bank sends or makes available a statement of account or the items, the customer has the duty to exercise reasonable promptness in exam-

---

212. U.C.C. §4-406, Revised Official Comment 1.

213. U.C.C. §4-406(a); U.C.C. §4-406, Revised Official Comment 1.

214. U.C.C. §4-406, Revised Official Comment 1.

215. See, e.g., Westport Bank & Trust Co. v. Lodge, 164 Conn. 604, 325 A.2d 222, 12 U.C.C. Rep. Serv. 450 (1973) (wrongdoer was secretary responsible for paying bills and maintaining customer's checking account).

ining the statement or the items to determine whether any payment was unauthorized due to an alteration or because a purported signature by or on behalf of the customer was unauthorized.[216] If the customer should reasonably have discovered the unauthorized payment from the statement or items provided, the customer must promptly notify the bank of the relevant facts.

Reasonable care on the customer's part should at least include the reconciling of the statement of account with his records. However, determining whether the customer should have reasonably discovered an unauthorized payment depends upon the information the customer receives. If the bank chooses not to return the items, the customer will not be able to discover certain types of fraud.[217] For example, if the fraud is accomplished by altering the payee's name, the customer will be unable to discover the unauthorized payment unless either the item is returned or the statement of accounts furnished by the bank includes the payee's name. If, on the basis of the information furnished, the customer could not have reasonably discovered that the payment was unauthorized, he is not precluded from asserting the unauthorized nature of the payment.[218]

Whether the customer has exercised reasonable promptness in examining the statement is a question of fact in light of all of the circumstances of his situation. To provide certainty, a bank may, by agreement, limit the time within which a customer has to examine his bank statement and report any forgery or alteration.[219]

---

216. U.C.C. §4-406(c), U.C.C. §4-406, Revised Official Comment 1.

217. U.C.C. §4-406, Revised Official Comment 1.

218. U.C.C. §4-406, Revised Official Comment 1. When the customer notices an inconsistency between his records and the statement of account and requests a copy of the item, his duty of examination should commence upon receipt of the item or copy. Prior to receipt of the item or copy, the customer could not have examined the item or copy to determine whether it contained his unauthorized signature or alteration.

219. Courts have upheld bank/customer agreements giving the customer a period as short as 14 days to examine his bank statement and report his own unauthorized signature or alteration. Absent extenuating circumstances, however, it is unlikely that a delay of more than two or three weeks in examining a statement would be found to be reasonable. Extenuating circumstances may include the customer's illness, his being on vacation or, in the case of a corporate customer, a change in corporate control. However, the drafters of Revised Article 4, in light of the great increase in the volume of checks, U.C.C. §4-406, Revised Official Comment 3, increased from 14 days to 30 days the time limit within which a customer could be found to be reasonable in not discovering an alteration or forgery for purposes of being liable for repeat alterations or forgeries under §4-406(d)(2). Courts may view this to be an indication that it is unreasonable for a bank to require notification within any period less than 30 days. See Coine v. Manufacturers Hanover Trust Co., 16 U.C.C. Rep. Serv. 184 (N.Y. App. Term 1975) (court upheld 14-day limit on customer to report errors and forgeries).

d.   Customer's Duty to Report Forgery or Alteration

Once a customer examines the statement of account, the customer must report any forgery of the customer's own signature or alteration to his bank within a reasonable time. A short delay may be justified where the customer, prior to reporting the item as forged or altered, wants to determine whether the forger or alterer will pay the item. However, even in this event, a delay of more than a week may not be justified since the delay may make it more difficult for the payor bank to recover from the forger or alterer.

e.   Duty of Bank to Prove Loss

Even when a customer fails to comply with these duties, the customer is only precluded from asserting an unauthorized signature or alteration if the bank proves that it suffered a loss by reason of the failure.[220] The bank may have a difficult task in proving that the customer's failure caused the loss. Where a wrongdoer forges or alters only one check, he typically immediately withdraws the funds and either vanishes, becomes insolvent, or goes to jail by the time the check is paid and the statement is returned to the customer. The bank suffers the same loss whether or not the customer promptly discovers and reports the forgery or alteration. However, there will be times when the bank can prove a loss. In our example involving Sandra and Diamonds-R-Forever, Sandra had funds in her bank accounts after the time that Diamonds-R-Forever should have informed the bank of the forgeries. If the bank could have proven that it or Diamonds-R-Forever could have promptly identified Sandra as the forger, the bank would have suffered a loss to the extent that funds remained in her accounts.

Where the bank proves it suffered a loss, the customer is only precluded from asserting the loss due to the forgery to the extent of the loss suffered by the bank. If the bank can prove that Sandra had $20,000 in her account at the end of a reasonable time for the customer to report the forgery of checks for $30,000, Diamonds-R-Forever is precluded only to the extent of $20,000 and not up to the entire $30,000 face amount of the checks.

f.   Forgery or Alteration By Same Wrongdoer

The customer is also precluded from asserting an unauthorized signature or alteration by the same wrongdoer on any other item paid in good faith by

---

220. U.C.C. §4-406(d)(1); U.C.C. §4-406, Revised Official Comment 2.

the bank before it received notice from the customer of the unauthorized signature or alteration and after the customer had been afforded a reasonable period of time, not exceeding 30 days, in which to examine the item or statement of account and notify the bank.[221]

Let us return to our example of Sandra and Diamonds-R-Forever. When Diamonds-R-Forever received its bank statement on March 10th, it had a reasonable time not exceeding 30 days to examine the statement. The 30-day period expired on April 10th. Diamonds-R-Forever reported the forgeries to Bank of America on April 21st. The first question is, what constitutes a reasonable time for Diamonds-R-Forever to examine the statement and report the forgeries? If a court finds that 14 days was a reasonable time, it will prohibit Diamonds-R-Forever from asserting the forgery on checks paid after March 24th. A court could have found that ten days was the limit of a reasonable time. If so, it would preclude Diamonds-R-Forever from asserting the forgery on any check paid after March 20. Under any circumstances, Diamonds-R-Forever would be unable to assert the forgery on any check paid more than 30 days after it received the statement. The court must reach this result because any delay in excess of 30 days is deemed to be an unreasonable time for the customer to examine the statement of account and report any forgery or alteration.[222] The customer is not entitled to prove that a delay of more than 30 days was reasonable under the circumstances. The 30-day period begins to run from the day when the customer receives the statement, not from the day the statement was sent by the bank.

g. Notification by Customer

Once the customer notifies the bank of prior forgeries or alterations, the customer is not barred from recovering as to any items paid after the notification. There is no specific form required for the notification. The notification may be oral or in writing.

h. Comparative Negligence

If the customer proves that the bank failed to act in good faith in paying an item, the loss falls completely on the bank.[223] Even if the bank acts in good faith, the customer may prove that the bank failed to exercise ordinary care in paying the item and that the failure substantially contributed to the loss.

221. U.C.C. §4-406(d)(2); U.C.C. §4-406, Revised Official Comment 2.
222. U.C.C. §4-406, Revised Official Comment 2.
223. U.C.C. §4-406(e); U.C.C. §4-406, Revised Official Comment 2.

Where the customer meets this burden the loss is allocated between the customer and the bank according to the extent to which the customer failed to comply with his duties and the extent of the bank's failure to exercise ordinary care.[224] The customer bears the burden of proving that the bank did not exercise ordinary care. This is a question for the trier of fact. Neither Article 3 nor Article 4 gives any guidance as to the manner in which the trier of fact should allocate the loss.

i.   One-Year Preclusion

A customer must discover and report the customer's unauthorized signature or any alteration on an item within one year after the statement or item is made available to the customer. Failure to report the defect precludes the customer from asserting the alteration or unauthorized signature against the bank.[225] The customer's preclusion does not depend upon the bank's use of ordinary care. For example, assume that, in our example above, all of the checks forged by Sandra were returned by Bank of America to Diamonds-R-Forever on March 10th. If Diamonds-R-Forever reports the forgery by March 10th of the next year, Diamonds-R-Forever will not be precluded unless Bank of America proves that it suffered a loss on account of the delay. Even if Bank of America establishes a loss, Bank of America will suffer the loss to the extent that it failed to exercise ordinary care in paying the checks. However, if Diamonds-R-Forever does not report the forgeries by March 10th of the next year, Diamonds-R-Forever will be precluded from asserting the forgeries even if Bank of America had failed to exercise ordinary care in paying the checks.

The period of preclusion begins when the items are "made available" to the customer. The period is calculated separately as to each new statement. If the bank sends the statement to the customer, the period should commence from the moment the statement is received by the customer. Where the statement is otherwise made available to the customer, the one-year period should commence from the time when the customer receives notice from the bank that he may pick up the statement and items.

The one-year preclusion period is not a statute of limitations. As long as notice is given by the customer within the one-year period, the customer may commence his action any time within the applicable statute of limitations period.

Although the one-year period does not cover forged indorsements,[226] the

---

224. U.C.C. §4-406(e); U.C.C. §4-406, Revised Official Comment 2.
225. U.C.C. §4-406(f).
226. U.C.C. §4-406, Revised Official Comment 5.

general statute of limitations contained in Article 4 precludes a customer who delays more than three years after payment in filing an action from having his account recredited for a debit resulting from the payment of an item bearing a forged indorsement.[227]

Where a payor bank has the right to debit its customer's account because the customer is precluded under §§4-406(c),(d) and (f) (failure to report customer's forged signature or alteration after receipt of bank statement) or §3-406 (customer's negligence substantially contributing to a forgery or alteration) from asserting an unauthorized signature or alteration, the payor bank is not allowed to shift the loss from its customer to the presenting or depositary bank,[228] by recrediting the customer's account and recovering from the presenting bank for breach of its presentment warranty.[229]

D. OTHER FRAUDULENT ACTIVITY

1. *Restrictive Indorsements*

A "restrictive indorsement" is an indorsement that negotiates an instrument for a limited use written by or on behalf of the holder. There are two types of restrictive indorsements. First, an indorsement that signifies a purpose of deposit or collection.[230] For example, when James receives his paycheck, he may indorse it "for deposit only (s) James." James indorses the check in this manner to ensure that the check's proceeds are deposited in his bank account.

Second, an indorsement that states that payment is to be made to the indorsee as agent, trustee, or other fiduciary for the benefit of the indorser or another person ("trust indorsement").[231] For example, if Jim wants to negotiate a check for use by the estate of John Jones, Jim may indorse the check to Don, the executor of the estate, by stating "Don in trust for the estate of John Jones." By so doing, Jim intends that Don use the funds only for the benefit of the estate of John Jones.

Although a restrictive indorsement may affect the holder's ability to become a holder in due course,[232] it deprives an indorsee neither of holder

227. U.C.C. §4-111; U.C.C. §4-406, Official Comment 5.
228. U.C.C. §4-406(f); U.C.C. §4-406, Official Comment 5.
229. U.C.C. §4-208(c); U.C.C. §4-406, Revised Official Comment 5.
230. U.C.C. §3-206(c); U.C.C. §3-206, Official Comment 3.
231. U.C.C. §3-206(d).
232. U.C.C. §3-206(e) .

status[233] nor of the right to further negotiate or transfer the instrument.[234] For example, even if James, in the above example, loses his paycheck, Finder becomes the holder of the check since the check is payable in blank (James had not listed any one as the special indorsee). Finder may further negotiate the check to Auto Loan Co. in payment of his own debt in violation of the restrictive indorsement. Auto Loan Co. by virtue of the indorsement becomes the holder of the check. However, Auto Loan Co. cannot become a holder in due course because it applied the value inconsistently with the indorsement. Similarly, the payor bank has the right to refuse to pay Auto Loan Co. because such payment is inconsistent with the indorsement's effect.[235]

a.   For Deposit Indorsement

Although any term may be used that signifies a purpose of deposit or collection, the most common ones used are "for deposit," "for collection," or "pay any bank." By indorsing his paycheck, "for deposit, (s) James," James is indicating that the proceeds of the instrument can only be used to credit his bank account. James could instead have indorsed the check "for collection, (s) James." Such an indorsement would similarly indicate his intention that the proceeds be deposited into his bank account. James would likewise be indicating that the proceeds should be deposited into his bank account if he indorses the check "To Bank of America, for collection, (s) James." However, there will be times when James may want to appoint someone other than a bank as his agent to collect the funds for him. If he indorses the check "To Allen, for collection (s) James," it makes little sense to interpret this as requiring Allen to deposit the funds into James' account. As far as Allen knows, James may not even have a bank account. When James' indorsement names someone other than a bank as the special indorsee, the indorsement should be interpreted as a trust indorsement appointing Allen as James's agent for collection and James should assume the risk that Allen will not properly apply the funds.

Pay Any Bank.   A check may pass through the hands of several collecting banks on the way from the depositary bank to the payor bank. We discuss this collection process in Chapter 5. The depositary bank may want to ensure that the check will stay in banking channels. On the other hand, the deposi-

---

233. The one exception is in the case of an indorsement reading "pay any bank." Until specially indorsed by a bank, only a bank may become a holder of an instrument so indorsed. U.C.C. §4-201(b).

234. U.C.C. §3-206(a).

235. U.C.C. §3-206(f); U.C.C. §3-206, Official Comment 5.

D. Other Fraudulent Activity

tary bank does not want to have to use a separate indorsement stamp for each potential collecting bank. Therefore, it will stamp the check "pay any bank." The indorsement speeds up the collection process by eliminating the need for each collecting bank to specially indorse the check to the next collecting bank.

"Pay any bank" is a blank indorsement which limits holder status to banks.[236] Once an item has been indorsed "pay any bank," only a bank may acquire the rights of a holder until one of the following two events happens: (1) the item is returned to the customer initiating collection (James in our example); or (2) the bank specially indorses the check to a non-bank.[237] This second event is extremely rare.

When an item is indorsed "pay any bank," the proceeds must be deposited in either the indorser's or the collecting bank's account. Because of changes initiated by Regulation CC, use of the words "pay any bank" is no longer necessary. Under Regulation CC, any indorsement by a bank in the check collection process has precisely the same effect whether or not it includes the words "pay any bank."[238]

Effect of "For Deposit Only" Indorsement. Let us examine the effect of a "for deposit only" or similar indorsement. Assume that after James has indorsed the check "for deposit only, (s) James," Thief steals the check. Thief deposits the check in his account at Wells Bank, which sends it to Crocker Bank for collection, which presents the check to Bank of America for payment. Bank of America pays the check. Thief takes the money and runs. Who is liable to James? (See Figure 4.8.)

FIGURE 4.8

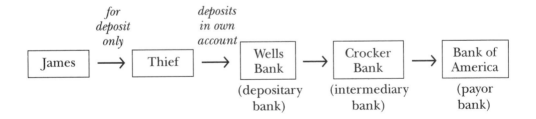

236. U.C.C. §4-201(b).
237. U.C.C. §4-201(b).
238. 12 C.F.R. §229.35(c). In fact, in order to eliminate confusion as to whom to return a check, Regulation CC prohibits any bank, other than a depositary bank, from indorsing a check "pay any bank." 12 C.F.R. §229.35(c), app. D and app. E at 518-519 (1993).

Any bank in the bank collection process, except a depositary bank, may disregard a "for deposit" or similar indorsement.[239] Thus, Crocker Bank (the intermediary bank) and Bank of America (the payor bank) may treat the check as having been indorsed by James in blank. Why is this? The answer is— because it is efficient to allow these banks to ignore the restriction. Wells Bank, the depositary bank, is still bound by the restriction. As a result, at least one bank in the collection process is always bound by the restriction. The odds are great that Wells Bank is solvent and therefore James can recover from it. Crocker Bank, the intermediary bank, and Bank of America, the payor bank, are permitted to ignore the restrictive indorsements so as to enable them to efficiently process in bulk the vast number of checks they receive.

Crocker Bank (the intermediary bank) is therefore not liable for conversion even though the value it gave to Wells Bank went into Thief's account and not to James' account. Moreover, Crocker Bank is deemed to have taken the check for value, even though it applied the value to the wrong account.[240] Likewise, Bank of America (the payor bank) is discharged by its payment to Thief's account[241] and therefore, is not liable to James for conversion.[242]

In contrast, Wells Bank (the depositary bank), whether it purchases the instrument or takes it for collection, converts the instrument unless Wells Bank pays James (the indorser) or applies the proceeds consistently with the indorsement (to James' account).[243] Wells Bank can only become a holder in due course to the extent that it applies the funds for James' benefit.[244] The result would be the same if Wells Bank was both the depositary bank and the payor bank. In this case, Wells Bank would likewise be liable to James. Being the only bank in the chain of collection, it is necessary that Wells Bank be liable whether in its capacity as depositary bank or payor bank. Similarly, if the check was presented to Bank of America (the payor bank) by Thief for immediate payment over the counter, Bank of America would be liable unless the funds were received by James.

In order to be consistent with the terms of a "for deposit" indorsement, the depositary bank must credit the bank account designated by the indorser. If James indorses the check "For deposit in account number 1234, (s) James," Wells Bank must credit account number 1234. If the indorsement does not specify a particular account, for example, "for deposit, (s) James," Wells Bank must merely deposit the proceeds in any of James' bank accounts. Bank of

239. U.C.C. §3-206(c)(4); U.C.C. §3-206, Official Comment 3.
240. U.C.C. §3-206(e).
241. U.C.C. §3-602(b).
242. U.C.C. §3-206(c)(4); U.C.C. §3-206, Official Comment 3.
243. U.C.C. §3-206(c)(2); U.C.C. §3-206, Official Comment 3.
244. U.C.C. §3-206(e).

D. Other Fraudulent Activity

America (the payor bank) can pay cash over the counter for the check as long as James receives the funds.

Any person, other than a bank, who purchases an instrument restrictively indorsed for collection or deposit is treated just like the depositary bank and is deemed to have converted the instrument unless the amount paid for the instrument is received by the indorser or applied consistently with the indorsement.[245] Such a purchaser can become a holder in due course to the extent that it applies the funds properly.[246]

b. Trust Indorsement

A so-called "trust indorsement"[247] is a restrictive indorsement that provides that payment is to be made to the indorsee as agent, trustee, or other fiduciary for the benefit of the indorser or of another person.[248] In other words, the person named as the indorsee must be designated as receiving the proceeds for the benefit of the indorser or of a third person. In order for an indorsement to qualify as a trust indorsement, it must expressly name the person for whose benefit the indorsee holds the proceeds. Examples of trust indorsements are "pay Allen as agent for Bob," "pay Allen in trust for the estate of Bob," "pay Allen as my agent," or "pay bearer in trust for Bob." Where the beneficiary is not named, the indorsement is not a trust indorsement, for example, "Pay to Allen, President." Similarly, where the instrument is indorsed to the beneficiary itself, the indorsement is not a trust indorsement, for example, "Pay to the Estate of Bob."

A trust indorsement is far less effective in fulfilling the intent of the indorser than is a "for deposit" indorsement. The effect of a trust indorsement differs depending upon whether the person deals directly with the indorsee when he makes payment, takes the instrument for collection, or purchases the instrument. Let us return to our original example of Jim indorsing a check "payable to Don, in trust for the estate of John Jones." Don goes to Check Cashing Service and asks that it cash the check. Don uses the check to buy himself a car. What effect does the trust indorsement have on Check Cashing Service?

Unless Check Cashing Service has notice of Don's breach of fiduciary

---

245. U.C.C. §3-206(c)(1); U.C.C. §3-206, Official Comment 3.

246. U.C.C. §3-206(c)(1); U.C.C. §3-206(e).

247. The term "trust indorsement" is not used in Revised Article 3. The term was used in the comments to old Article 3. U.C.C. §3-206, Official Comment 6 (1989). I continue to use the term here for the sake of convenience.

248. U.C.C. §3-206(d).

duty, Check Cashing Service who purchases the instrument from Don (the indorsee) can apply its value without regard to whether Don (the indorsee) violated a fiduciary duty to Jim (the indorser). This is also the rule as to whether a collecting bank properly applies credit or whether a payor makes proper payment.

We have already discussed in Chapter 2 under what conditions a person has notice of a breach of fiduciary duty. Check Cashing Service is only denied holder-in-due-course status if it has notice of the breach of fiduciary duty.[249] Check Cashing Service would only have notice of Don's breach of fiduciary duty if it took the check in payment of or as security for a debt known by it to be Don's personal debt or in a transaction it knows to be for the personal benefit of Don.[250] Unless Check Cashing Service knew that the proceeds would be used by Don personally, Check Cashing Service will qualify as a holder in due course and take free of the claim of ownership of the beneficiary (Estate of John Jones). In contrast, if Don had deposited the check in his own personal bank account at Sunshine Bank, the bank would not be a holder in due course. Sunshine Bank, not being a holder in due course, would then take subject to the claim of ownership of the beneficiary (the Estate of John Jones).[251] Similarly, a payor who has notice of the breach of fiduciary duty is not discharged by its payment.

Assume, instead, that after Check Cashing Service took the check from Don, it deposited the check in its personal account at Moonlight Bank. In this case Moonlight Bank did not take the instrument directly from Don (the indorsee). Therefore, Moonlight Bank is neither given notice nor otherwise affected by the restriction contained in the indorsement unless it knows that the fiduciary (Don) dealt with the instrument or its proceeds in breach of his fiduciary duty.[252] Thus, Moonlight Bank is a holder in due course and unaffected by the trust indorsement unless it knew that Don had used the funds for his own personal use. In the unlikely case that it had such knowledge, it would be denied holder-in-due-course status and would be subject to the claim of ownership of the beneficiary (Estate of John Jones).[253] Similarly, a payor that makes payment of the check would be liable for conversion only if it had actual knowledge that Don misused the funds.

The difference between these two rules is that the first taker, Check Cashing Service, is denied holder-in-due-course status if it has *notice* under §3-307

---

249. U.C.C. §3-206, Official Comment 4; U.C.C. §3-206(e).
250. U.C.C. §3-307(b)(2).
251. U.C.C. §3-306.
252. U.C.C. §3-206(d)(2).
253. U.C.C. §3-206, Official Comment 4.

of Don's breach of fiduciary duty. Moonlight Bank, which did not take the check directly from Don, is only denied holder-in-due-course status if it had actual *knowledge* of Don's breach of fiduciary duty.

2. *MICR Fraud*

As we will discuss further in Chapter 5, the payor bank is identified in three different ways on a check. First, the name of the payor bank is written in words on the face of the check. Second, the payor bank is identified by a set of numbers located in the upper right-hand corner of the check. Third, in order to enable banks to process checks by computer, the identity of the payor bank is indicated in magnetic numerical characters ("MICR") encoded on the bottom left-hand corner of a check. Because most checks are processed by computers reading the MICR line, a new type of fraud has arisen.

"MICR fraud" is accomplished by a perpetrator printing up phony checks with the name of one bank written on the face of the check and another bank designated on the MICR line. The perpetrator deposits the check in his bank account in the hope that the confusion caused by the differing designations will allow him to withdraw the funds before the check is returned unpaid.

Let us look at an example. Assume that the Riddler has a check printed up that indicates on its face that the check is drawn upon Beverly Hills Bank. However, the MICR encoded number identifies the payor bank as Puget Sound National Bank in the state of Washington. The Riddler deposits the check in an account he established at Austin State Bank in Texas. Austin State Bank, using a computer to sort checks, sends the check to Salt Lake City State Bank for the purpose of ultimate presentment to Puget Sound National Bank. As we will cover in Chapter 5, banks are required by Regulation CC to permit customers to withdraw funds within a set number of days depending upon whether the check is a local or a nonlocal check. Being a nonlocal check, Austin State Bank must allow the Riddler to withdraw the funds within five business days after the day of its deposit. The check reaches Puget Sound National Bank on the third day following deposit. Puget Sound National Bank, not being the actual drawee bank, believes that the check was wrongly encoded and thus on the fourth day returns the check by mail to Salt Lake City State Bank, which receives it on the fifth day. Salt Lake City State Bank, after visual examination of the check, notices that the drawee is Beverly Hills Bank. The check reaches Beverly Hills Bank on the seventh day. Because the alleged drawer has no account with Beverly Hills Bank, the check is dishonored. By the time that notice of nonpayment gets back to Austin State Bank, the hold on the uncollected funds has been removed and the Riddler has withdrawn the money.

Should Austin State Bank be upset at anyone? Does Austin State Bank have any recourse? The reason that Austin State Bank suffered the loss is that Puget Sound National Bank did not give notice to Austin State Bank that the drawer had no account with it. In the overwhelming majority of cases in which checks are not paid, the drawer, although having an account with the bank designated on the MICR line, either has stopped payment on the check or does not have sufficient funds in his account to cover the check. In these situations, the drawee bank (called a paying bank under Regulation CC) is required by Regulation CC to expeditiously return the check to the depositary bank[254] as well as to give notice of nonpayment by 4:00 P.M. on the second business day following the day of presentment on any item for $2,500 or more.[255] We will discuss these duties in Chapter 5. In our example above, had Puget Sound National Bank given such notice of nonpayment, Austin State Bank would not have suffered any loss. The notice would have arrived before the Riddler was allowed to withdraw the funds. Upon receipt of the notice, Austin State Bank would have revoked the credit given for the check and denied the Riddler the right to withdraw the funds.

Because the drawer has no account with Puget Sound National Bank, Puget Sound National Bank is not the drawee of the check. However, Puget Sound National Bank is a paying bank under Regulation CC. Any bank whose routing number appears on a check is deemed to be a paying bank even if it is not the drawee of the check.[256] As a result, Puget Sound National Bank has the duty to expeditiously return checks and to give prompt notice of nonpayment of large items. Since its failure to do so caused Austin State Bank the loss, Puget Sound National Bank will suffer the loss subject to the principle of comparative fault.[257]

3. Check Kiting

Check kiting is another type of check fraud that involves neither a forgery nor an alteration. The principal benefit to the wrongdoer of check kiting is that it makes interest-free loans available to him. The prototypical check-kiting scheme goes as follows. John opens up bank accounts at Security Bank and at

254. 12 C.F.R. §229.30.
255. 12 C.F.R. §229.33(a).
256. 12 C.F.R. §229.2(z).
257. 12 C.F.R. §229.38(c).

D. Other Fraudulent Activity

Crocker Bank with a deposit of $1,000 in each account. John knows that both Security Bank and Crocker Bank will allow him to immediately draw upon the uncollected funds and that it will take three days for the checks to reach the respective payor banks. On January 5th, John writes a check to Dan for $3,000 on his account at Security Bank in payment for goods purchased. On January 7th, John writes a $4,000 check upon his account at Crocker Bank, which he deposits in his account at Security Bank. On the same day, Security Bank gives John credit for the check. As a result when Dan presents the check to Security Bank, the check is paid. John's account at Security Bank is debited. He now has $2,000 in his account there.

But John must now worry about the check he wrote from his Crocker Bank account because he does not have adequate funds in this account to cover the check he wrote to Security Bank. He therefore on January 9th writes a check on Security Bank in the amount of $5,000 payable to Crocker Bank which he deposits in his account at Crocker Bank. Crocker Bank gives him immediately usable credit for the amount of the check. Thus, when the check payable to Security Bank is presented to Crocker Bank, his account, now showing $6,000, is sufficient to cover the check. On January 11th, John deposits a check for $6,000 in his Security Bank account drawn on his Crocker Bank account. He must, of course, continue writing checks from one account to the other to keep the kite going. The kite ends when he either deposits cash to cover the uncollected checks or when one of the banks refuses to pay checks drawn upon uncollected funds.[258]

Now assume that Crocker Bank begins to suspect the kite. What would make Crocker Bank suspect the kite? Because check kiting can pose a significant risk of loss for a bank, banks monitor accounts for indications of check-kiting behavior. For example, the fact that numerous checks are deposited into and written from an account may indicate that the drawer is engaged in a check kite. This possibility increases where there are large fluctuations in the balance of the account. Some banks have a computer program that automatically reports any sign of kiting.

If Crocker Bank suspects a kite, it may try to ensure that Security Bank rather than itself suffers the loss. Assume that Crocker Bank becomes suspicious around January 9th. At this point, Crocker Bank decides that it will not allow John to draw upon any deposits until Crocker Bank knows that the checks deposited have been paid by Security Bank. But this precaution alone will not prevent Crocker Bank from suffering the loss. On January 9th, John

---

258. See Town & Country State Bank of Newport v. First State Bank of St. Paul, 358 N.W.2d 387, 39 U.C.C. Rep. Serv. 1740, 1743 (Minn. 1984).

still owes Crocker Bank $3,000. The only way in which Crocker Bank will be made whole is if Security Bank pays the check John deposited on January 9th.

The question now arises as to whether Crocker Bank, now that it suspects a check-kiting scheme, has a duty to inform Security Bank of its suspicions. If it does, Security Bank will dishonor the January 9th check causing Crocker Bank to suffer the loss. If it does not, since Security Bank will pay the check and Crocker Bank will not pay the January 11th check, Security Bank will suffer the loss.

Most courts have held that a bank may, even with knowledge of a check-kiting scheme, dishonor checks drawn upon itself while at the same time presenting checks drawn upon the other bank.[259] There are some courts, though, which have implied that under the proper circumstances, there may be such a duty.[260] However, none of these courts have found such a duty under the particular facts of their case. On the other hand, Federal banking law imposes a duty upon national banks to report suspected kites to the Comptroller of Currency.[261]

Leaving aside the question as to whether Crocker Bank has a duty to inform Security Bank of its suspicions, a separate issue arises as to whether Security Bank may recover the payment made to Crocker Bank under §3-418 (See Chapter 4A(4)).

Two questions are involved. First, is there a mistake upon which restitution can be based? A strong argument can be made that because Security Bank knew that it was extending credit on uncollected funds, it was not under a mistake when it knowingly undertook the risk that the check will not be paid. Second, did Crocker Bank take the instrument in good faith? If Crocker Bank had notice of the kite when it took the check, it can be argued that it did not act in accordance with reasonable commercial standards of fair dealing and there-

---

259. See Citizens Natl. Bank v. First Natl. Bank, 347 So. 2d 964 (Miss. 1977) (no duty to inform); Mid-Cal Natl. Bank v. Federal Reserve Bank, 590 F.2d 761 (9th Cir. 1979); Cumis Ins. Socy. v. Windsor Bank & Trust Co., 736 F. Supp. 1226, 12 U.C.C. Rep. Serv. 2d 769 (D. Conn. 1990) (Although depository bank had reason to know of existence of check-kiting scheme, does not owe duty of disclosure to payor bank affected by scheme nor does it act in bad faith, and therefore not liable for losses of payor bank. Although depository bank started dishonoring checks deposited by payor bank while at the same time presenting checks to same bank, payment by payor bank final and cannot be recovered since it should be aware of the state of its customer's account); Alta Vista Bank v. Kobliska, 897 F.2d 930, 11 U.C.C. Rep. Serv. 2d 160 (8th Cir. 1990) (Bank owes no duty to notify another bank of its suspicion as to check-kiting scheme.).

260. See Community Bank v. U.S. Natl. Bank, 276 Or. 471, 555 P.2d 435, 20 U.C.C. Rep. Serv. 589 (1976); Community Bank v. Ell, 278 Or. 417, 564 P.2d 685, 21 U.C.C. Rep. Serv. 1349 (1977).

261. 12 C.F.R. §21.11(b)(2), (3).

D. Other Fraudulent Activity

fore did not take the instrument in good faith. If so, it would not be a protected person under §3-418(c). If a court finds both that the payment was a result of a mistake and that the Crocker Bank is not a protected person, Security Bank would be entitled to recover the payment. However, once Crocker Bank has relied upon the funds represented by the check, its subsequent knowledge of the kite will not defeat its protected status.

When a bank, although suspicious of a kite, is not consciously attempting to shift the loss to another bank, it is extremely unlikely that a court will attempt to impose liability upon that bank. In Town & Country State Bank v. First State Bank of St. Paul,[262] the court held that when the bank, although suspecting a kite, keeps the kite going for the purpose of trying to help the customer out of his cash flow problems, its presentment and payment of checks was not in bad faith since its intent was not to hurt the other banks especially since its own loss was increased by continuation of the kite.

262. 358 N.W.2d 387, 39 U.C.C. Rep. Serv. 1740, 1743 (Minn. 1984).

CHAPTER 5

The Bank Collection Process

A. INTRODUCTION TO CHECK COLLECTION PROCESS

Before we proceed further, it is necessary to have a basic understanding of the check collection process—that is, the process by which a holder converts a check into cash or credit from the payor bank. The check collection process is governed by Article 4, Federal Reserve Regulations J and CC, Federal Reserve Bank Operating Circulars, Clearing-House Rules, and agreements among banks. These regulations, operating circulars, clearing-house rules, and agreements are discussed in the next two subsections. Here we will lay out the basic elements of the check collection process and some effects that the rules of Article 4 and Regulation CC have on this process.

We will first examine the check collection process under Article 4. Assume that Depositor deposits a check drawn upon Bank of Albany into his account at Bank of Los Angeles. Bank of Los Angeles has no obligation to allow Depositor to draw upon the funds represented by the check until Bank of Los Angeles would have had a reasonable time to receive return of the check, had the check been dishonored by Bank of Albany.[1] In other words, Depositor will not have access to these funds until Bank of Los Angeles has a reasonable time to learn that payment of the check has been refused. It may take a long time for the bank to receive return of the check. How long it takes depends, to a large extent, upon the manner Bank of Los Angeles chooses to collect the check.

---

1. U.C.C. §4-215(e)(1).

Bank of Los Angeles has many ways of collecting the check. If it desires, Bank of Los Angeles could mail the check directly to Bank of Albany. In this event, payment would be made by Bank of Albany's crediting of the account of Bank of Los Angeles, if it has an account with Bank of Albany, or by sending a remittance draft (its own check) to Bank of Los Angeles. (See Figure 5.1.)

FIGURE 5.1

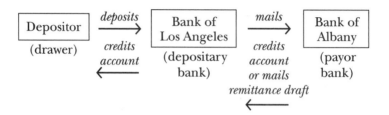

Bank of Los Angeles could, instead, send the check for collection through the Federal Reserve System. The *Federal Reserve System* is the central bank of the United States. Federal Reserve services are provided by a series of individual Federal Reserve Banks. One of the primary purposes of the Federal Reserve System is the expedited collection and return of items. There is a network of 12 Federal Reserve District Banks spread throughout the country as well as 25 additional branches of these banks. In this event, Bank of Los Angeles could send the check to the Federal Reserve Bank in its region, the Los Angeles Office of the 12th District of the Federal Reserve Bank.[2] The Los Angeles Federal Reserve Office will credit the account of Bank of Los Angeles and will then send the check to the New York City Office of the 2nd District of the Federal Reserve Bank, which will present the check for payment to Bank of Albany. In the event that the check is dishonored, the Los Angeles Federal Reserve Office will reverse the credit given to Bank of Los Angeles. (See Figure 5.2.)

2. See Federal Reserve System, Supplementary Information for Proposed Rule, 56 Fed. Reg. 4744-45 (1991).

A. Introduction to Check Collection Process

FIGURE 5.2

If Bank of Los Angeles so desires, it can send the check directly to the New York City Federal Reserve Office.

If Bank of Los Angeles and Bank of Albany are in the same city or county, they may be part of the same clearing house. A "clearing house" is an association of banks or non-bank payors like express companies or governmental agencies[3] regularly clearing items.[4] For example, the major banks in a particular city may establish a clearing house through which items are exchanged between the banks. A bank will present all of the checks drawn upon another member of the clearing house at a designated hour and that other member will present all of the checks drawn upon the first bank at the same time. If both banks are a part of the same clearing house, Bank of Los Angeles would deliver the check to the Bank of Albany through the clearing house. A credit would be given to Bank of Los Angeles for the check on the books of the clearing house. If the check was dishonored, Bank of Albany would simply return the check at a subsequent clearing and the credit would be reversed by the clearing house. (See Figure 5.3.)

---

3. U.C.C. §4-104, Official Comment 3.

4. U.C.C. §4-104(a)(4). Under Regulation CC, a "check clearinghouse association" is defined as "any arrangement by which three or more participants exchange checks on a local basis, including an entire metropolitan area. The term "check clearinghouse association" may include arrangements using the premises of a Federal Reserve Bank, but it does not include the handling of checks for forward collection or return by a Federal Reserve Bank." 12 C.F.R. §229.2(l). A check clearinghouse may include informal arrangements. However, it does not include direct exchanges between two banks. 12 C.F.R. §229(l), app. E, Commentary.

FIGURE 5.3

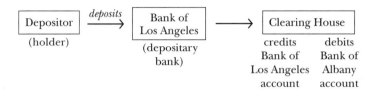

Each of the above methods of collection is fairly swift. Bank of Los Angeles will know quickly whether the check is dishonored. However, Bank of Los Angeles is not required to use one of these methods. As long as the route chosen is reasonably prompt considering its cost, Bank of Los Angeles can use any method it desires.[5] For the purpose of saving costs, Bank of Los Angeles could choose to send the check through a series of correspondent banks (banks having a relationship with each other for purposes of collecting checks). If this method of collection is used, Bank of Los Angeles would send the check to a bank with which it has established an account, Bank of Chicago, for example. Bank of Chicago, if it does not itself have an account at Bank of Albany, would send the check to a bank with which it has an account, Pittsburgh State Bank, for example. Pittsburgh State Bank, which has an account at Bank of Albany, would send the check directly to that bank. Because each bank has until midnight of the day after it receives the check to forward the check for collection,[6] a substantial delay may occur before the check reaches Bank of Albany. (See Figure 5.4.)

FIGURE 5.4

Forward Collection

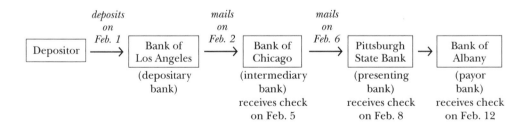

5. U.C.C. §4-204(a).
6. U.C.C. §4-202(b).

A. Introduction to Check Collection Process

Because settlements between banks are provisional under Article 4, when a check is returned unpaid it has to retrace the same path on its return route as it took in its forward collection trip so as to allow each provisional settlement to be revoked. If Bank of Los Angeles used a series of correspondent banks, the item would be returned from each bank to the bank from which the check was originally received.

The check collection process operates on the assumption that a check will be paid. Around 99 percent[7] of all checks are paid upon presentment. Notice is given by a payor bank only as to the nonpayment of a check, not as to its payment. This has both good and bad aspects. On the one hand, because notice need be given only as to 1 percent of all checks collected, the cost of check collection is greatly reduced. On the other hand, the depositary bank does not learn that a check has not been paid until it receives return of the check or notice of its non-payment. This may be a substantial period after the check had been deposited. (See Figure 5.5.)

FIGURE 5.5

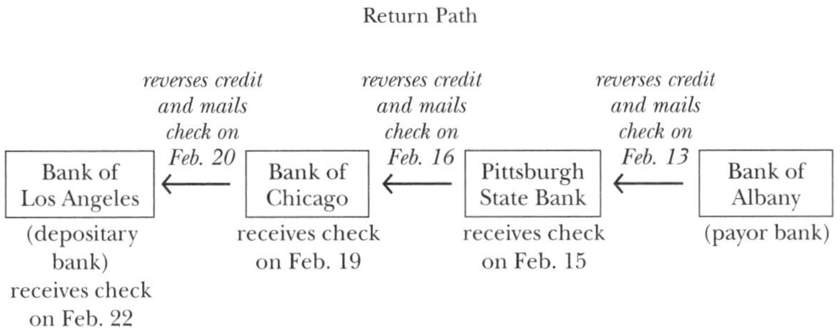

Return Path

You can see that it is possible that Bank of Los Angeles may not receive return of the check until three weeks after it provisionally credited Depositor's account. Allowing Depositor to withdraw the funds before that time exposes Bank of Los Angeles to the risk that the check would be dishonored and Depositor would have already spent the funds. Because of this risk, Bank of Los Angeles would be justified, under the mandate granted to it under §4-215(e)(1), in placing a three-week hold on the funds represented by the check. Even though, at times, it may in fact take three weeks for Bank of Los Angeles to learn of the check's return, in most cases Bank of Los Angeles, hav-

7. See Barkley Clark and Barbara Clark, The Law of Bank Deposits, Collections and Credit Cards 7-9 (rev. ed. 1995).

ing utilized a swifter means of collection, would have learned of the return far sooner. Because Bank of Los Angeles' account at the Federal Reserve Bank or its correspondent bank would then have been credited much earlier, Bank of Los Angeles would have had the interest-free use of Depositor's money for this period.

Recognizing that banks were abusing the rights granted to them under Article 4 to place holds on their customer's accounts, thereby obtaining interest-free use of their customer's funds, the Federal Reserve Board promulgated Regulation CC. Regulation CC has two substantive subparts. Subpart B provides mandatory availability schedules under which depositary banks must permit their depositors use of deposited funds within certain expedited deadlines. The potential loss to depositary banks that may be required to allow their customers use of funds prior to the time that the bank would otherwise learn of a check's dishonor has the effect of encouraging depositary banks to speed up the forward collection process. However, because payor banks are not affected by rules as to expedited funds availability, they would have no reason to expedite return of a check or notice of its dishonor. For this reason, subpart C provides rules that impose upon payor banks the duty to expedite the check return process so that depositary banks quickly learn of a check's dishonor.

Prior to the promulgation of Regulation CC, the forward collection process by which a check is sent from the depositary bank to the payor bank averaged 1.6 days to complete.[8] Not only is the forward collection process swift because of the large incentive for depositary banks to expedite the process so as to obtain earlier use of the funds, but also because of the use of MICR-encoding, which permitted automated handling of the checks. MICR-encoding is the magnetic ink character recognition numbers enscribed in the lower left-hand corner of a check. Look at the numbers designated "1" on the check in Figure 1.4 on page 17. The "12" designates the Federal Reserve District in which the payor bank is located. The "2" designates the Federal Reserve Bank within the district that serves the payor bank. The "0218" is the American Bankers Association number identifying the payor bank. By a computer reading these numbers, the check can be automatically sorted for delivery to the payor bank through the Federal Reserve System or otherwise.

In contrast, when a check was dishonored because the identity of the depositary bank was not generally micro-encoded on the check, the check on its return path had to be handled on an individual, rather than bulk, basis.[9] As

8. See Barkley Clark, The Law of Bank Deposits, Collections and Credit Cards 6-7 (3d ed. 1990).

9. See Barkley Clark, The Law of Bank Deposits, Collections and Credit Cards 6-7 (3d ed. 1990).

a result, the process by which a check was returned by the payor bank to the depository bank took an average of 5.2 days. During this trip, the check was handled by an average of 3.4 banks. Furthermore, having dishonored the check, the payor bank had no reason to ensure the check's prompt return to the depository bank.

Under the check collection process established by Regulation CC, upon dishonor of a check, the payor bank, in its return of the check to the depositary bank, will, in effect, treat the check as a check drawn upon the depositary bank by the customer of the depositary bank. The payor bank can return the check directly to the depositary bank. Alternatively, the payor bank can send the check through a returning bank. The returning bank then returns the check to the depositary bank.

The most important changes that resulted in the speeding up of the return process were two new duties placed by Regulation CC upon paying banks in the check return process. First, a duty to expeditiously return an unpaid item was imposed upon both the paying bank and returning banks. Second, a duty was imposed upon the paying bank to give prompt notice of nonpayment to the depositary bank as to any item in the amount of $2,500 or greater. Although the majority of the changes that Regulation CC made were in the return process, certain changes had to be made in the forward collection process so as to pave the way for the changes in the return process. These changes are discussed in a Chapter 6B.

B.   FEDERAL LAW: STATUTORY, REGULATORY, AND COMMON LAW

Articles 3 and 4 have been enacted by all 50 states and by the District of Columbia. However, there is substantial federal statutory and regulatory law that preempts any conflicting provisions of Article 3 or 4.[10] Furthermore, the rights and duties of the United States to a negotiable instrument are, to the extent not covered by statutory or regulatory law, governed by federal common law and not by Articles 3 and 4.

---

10. U.C.C. §3-102(c) provides that "Regulations of the Board of Governors of the Federal Reserve System and operating circulars of the Federal Reserve Banks supersede any inconsistent provision of this Article [3] to the extent of the inconsistency." U.C.C. §3-102, Official Comment 3; U.C.C. §4-102, Official Comment 1.

1.   *Regulations CC and J and Federal Reserve Bank Operating Circulars*

The bank collection aspects of Article 4 have been preempted to a fairly substantial extent by Congress' enactment of the Expedited Funds Availability Act,[11] and by the Federal Reserve Board's promulgation of Regulation CC[12] and Regulation J.[13] In contrast, their effect on Article 3 has been minimal.

Regulation CC was promulgated under the Expedited Funds Availability Act ("EFAA").[14] Section 609 of the EFAA delegated to the Federal Reserve Board broad authority to speed up and improve the check collection process. The Board issued Regulation CC for the purposes of providing earlier funds availability to bank customers and speeding up the return of dishonored checks. Subpart C of Regulation CC changes, to a substantial degree, the duties of banks in the check collection process. Regulation CC governs the collection of checks through any banking channel.

Regulation J was promulgated under authority granted to the Board of Governors of the Federal Reserve System by the Federal Reserve Act[15] to direct bank collection functions.[16] Regulation J,[17] which governs the collection of items through the Federal Reserve System, binds any bank that sends an item for collection through a Federal Reserve Bank.[18] Although Regulation J's rules largely resemble Article 4's rules, there are some differences, which will be pointed out where appropriate.

Where a check is sent for collection through a Federal Reserve Bank, both Regulations J and CC apply. Where a check is not collected through a Federal Reserve Bank, only Regulation CC applies. Where an item other than a check is collected through a Federal Reserve Bank, only Regulation J applies. Where an item other than a check is not collected through a Federal Reserve Bank, neither Regulation J nor CC applies.

In addition to Regulation J, when an item is sent for collection through a Federal Reserve Bank, collection of the item is also governed by Federal Reserve Bank operating circulars. Each of the 12 Federal Reserve Bank Dis-

---

11. 12 U.S.C. §4001 et seq.; U.C.C. §4-102, Official Comment 1.

12. 12 C.F.R. Pt. 229. Specifically, the check return collection aspects of Article 4 have been substantially preempted by Regulation CC. The forward collection aspects of Article 4 are, to a far lesser degree, preempted by Regulation CC.

13. 12 C.F.R. §210(b).

14. 12 U.S.C. §4001 et seq.

15. 12 U.S.C. §221 et seq.

16. U.C.C. §4-103, Official Comment 3.

17. 12 C.F.R. §210(b).

18. 12 C.F.R. §210.3.

tricts publishes operating circulars governing the rules for collection through the Federal Reserve Bank of that district and its branches.[19] Operating circulars of Federal Reserve Banks take precedence over inconsistent state law.[20] Thus, operating circulars that govern the details of check clearing may vary the effects of Article 4.[21] Operating circulars contain instructions to paying and collecting banks for the handling and paying of returned checks received by Federal Reserve Banks. For example, an operating circular may authorize a collecting bank that has an account with the Federal Reserve Bank of its own district to send for collection an item directly to a Federal Reserve Office in another district. Or, for another example, an operating circular may give the Federal Reserve Bank the right to encode an unencoded or a misencoded item with the amount of the item and the routing number of the payor bank.

Because Regulation J and Federal Reserve Bank operating circulars apply only to items collected through a Federal Reserve Bank, a question arises as to who is bound by the Regulation J or an operating circular. For example, is a payor bank that is not a member of the Federal Reserve System bound by Regulation J? Clearly, both Regulation J and Federal Reserve Bank operating circulars are binding on any party who has expressly assented to such regulations, or circulars, and on members of the Federal Reserve System who have, by their membership alone, expressed such assent. However, limiting the binding effect of the regulation and operating circulars only to those who have expressly assented to their applicability would seriously hinder the goal of uniformity. For example, the customer of the depositary bank that sent the item through the Federal Reserve Bank would not be governed by the regulation or operating circular. It made little sense to have the depositary bank bound by the regulation and circulars while having the real party in interest, its customer, not bound. Similarly, it made little sense to have a regulation or operating circular governing the payment of items if payor banks were not bound by the regulation or circular.

To broaden the binding effect of the regulation and operating circulars,

19. The circulars are substantially uniform throughout the country although each circular refers to actions by a particular reserve bank or branch. See Federal Reserve Bank, Twelfth District San Francisco, Circular 1, Check Collection and Return, Introduction (1.1) (July 1991). The operating circulars issued by the Federal Reserve Bank of each district apply to the handling of cash items that are accepted for forward collection, returned checks accepted for return and any form of payment that is received for such items. See Federal Reserve Bank, Twelfth District San Francisco, Circular 1, Check Collection and Return, Introduction (1) (July 1991).

20. U.C.C. §3-102, Official Comment 3.

21. U.C.C. §4-103, Official Comment 3; 12 C.F.R. §210.3(a).

Article 4 provides that Federal Reserve Regulations and operating circulars have the effect of agreements, whether or not specifically assented to by all parties interested in the items handled.[22] This provision could be read broadly to provide that all persons involved in the collection process are bound by the regulations and circulars. However, this would be unfair to any person who did not in some way agree to be bound. Courts have found such consent from nonmember banks and their customers as long as a claim of agency between the bank and a Federal Reserve Bank can be made.[23] As long as the agreement is with respect to the item being handled, the bank's customer (usually the owner of the item) is bound by any agreement that is made by the bank in the process of collecting the item for him even though he is not a party to the agreement.[24] By asking that the bank collect the item, the customer impliedly authorizes the bank to do anything that is reasonably necessary to collect the item. This would include making collection arrangements and agreements with other banks. Thus, it is only necessary that the nonmember bank be bound by an agency relationship to a Federal Reserve Bank. A nonmember payor bank for which MICR encodes a check so as to allow the check to be col-

22. U.C.C. §4-103(b); U.C.C. §4-103, Official Comment 3. Even without explicit authorization under Article 4, Federal Reserve Regulations and operating circulars preempt conflicting provisions of Article 4 via the supremacy clause. U.C.C. §4-103, Official Comment 3.

In contrast Regulation CC partially rejects §4-103(b), 12 C.F.R. §229.37, app. E at 515 (1995) in providing that neither Federal Reserve Rules, operating circulars nor clearing-house rules operate as agreements to vary the provisions of Regulation CC as to any party who has not specifically assented to or adopted, ratified, or is estopped to deny the applicability of the rule, regulation or circular. 12 C.F.R. §229.37, app. E at 515 (1995). It thus treats these regulations, rules and circulars the same as Article 4 treats ordinary agreements under §4-103(a) and refuses to give them the additional effect that §4-103(b) gives to them. 12 C.F.R. §229.37, app. E at 515 (1995).

23. See Community Bank v. Federal Reserve Bank of San Francisco, 500 F.2d 282, 14 U.C.C. Rep. Serv. 1407 (9th Cir. 1974), cert. denied, 419 U.S. 1089, 42 L. Ed. 2d 681, 95 S. Ct. 680 (1974), citing Report of the New York Law Revision Commission for 1955: Study of the Uniform Commercial Code 1262-1263.

Contrast Union National Bank v. Metropolitan National Bank, 265 Ark. 340, 578 S.W.2d 220, 26 U.C.C. Rep. Serv. 449 (1979) (Even though nonmember banks had a bin in the same room used by the clearing house and the member depositary bank placed checks payable by nonmember payor banks in the nonmember payor bank's bin, these physical circumstances were not sufficient to bind the nonmember payor bank to the earlier deadline established by the CACHA rule.) with Wells Fargo Bank, N.A. v. Hartford Natl. Bank and Trust Co., 484 F. Supp. 817, 28 U.C.C. Rep. Serv. 446 (D. Conn. 1980) (Payor bank obligated to give notice by wire under Operating Circular where item sent through private correspondent collecting banks and not a Federal Reserve Bank. Practice of following circular became agreement among banks).

24. U.C.C. §4-103, Official Comment 3.

lected through the Federal Reserve System has, by the act of encoding the check, established an agency relationship between the nonmember payor bank and Federal Reserve Banks that collect the check.[25] A similar agency relationship is established when a depositary bank sends an item for collection through the Federal Reserve System.[26]

2.   Federal Common Law

In the absence of a federal statute or regulation, if the United States is a party to an instrument, its rights and duties are governed by federal common law and not by the Code.[27] There is nothing in the Code that prevents a federal government instrument (other than money or an investment security) from qualifying as an instrument covered by Article 3 or as an item covered by Article 4. For example, an income tax refund check meets the requirements as both an Article 3 negotiable instrument and an Article 4 item. However, courts have held that, under the Supremacy Clause of the United States Constitution, Articles 3 and 4 are preempted by federal law whenever the rights of the United States government on an instrument are involved.

Because Congress neither adopted the Code as part of federal law nor any other comprehensive set of rules covering negotiable instruments, courts have fashioned a federal common law to determine the rights of the federal government on instruments issued by it and its agencies or divisions.[28] Generally, this federal common law is virtually identical to Articles 3 and 4. However, because of the need to protect taxpayers and the government largess, there are times in which courts have been unwilling to apply the provisions of the Code. For example, in determining whether the Federal Deposit Insurance Corporation, the Federal Savings and Loan Insurance Corporation or the Resolution Trust Company is a holder in due course of an instrument acquired in that agency's takeover of a failed bank or savings and loan, courts have adopted a federal common law holder-in-due-course standard far more

25. See Community Bank v. Federal Reserve Bank of San Francisco 500 F.2d 282, 14 U.C.C. Rep. Serv. 1407 (9th Cir. 1974), cert. denied, 419 U.S. 1089, 42 L. Ed. 2d 681, 95 S. Ct. 680 (1974), citing Report of the New York Law Revision Commission for 1955: Study of the Uniform Commercial Code 1262-1263.

26. See Sterling Natl. Bank & Trust Co. v. Savings Bank Trust Co., 19 U.C.C. Rep. Serv. 904 (N.Y. Sup. Ct. 1976) (bank that sends item for collection through Federal Reserve Bank subject to terms of operating letters), aff'd, 44 N.Y.2d 869, 407 N.Y.S. 2d 476, 378 N.E.2d 1046 (1978).

27. U.C.C. §4-102, Official Comment 1.

28. U.C.C. §3-102, Official Comment 4.

lenient than the standard contained in §3-302.[29] If the dispute does not involve the rights or duties of the United States government but rather those of other parties to a United States government instrument, Articles 3 and 4 apply. For example, if a co-maker of a note payable to the Federal Deposit Insurance Company is suing his co-maker for contribution, Article 3 would apply.

C.   VARIATION BY AGREEMENT

The rules set out in Article 4 regulating the bank collection process can be varied by agreement between the affected parties.[30] However, there are two limitations: Such an agreement may not disclaim a bank's liability for its own lack of good faith or failure to exercise ordinary care, nor may it limit the measure of damages resulting from its lack of good faith or failure to exercise ordinary care.[31] The parties may, however, determine by agreement the standards by which the bank's responsibility is to be measured if those standards are not manifestly unreasonable.[32]

29. See Federal Sav. & Loan Ins. Corp. v. Cribbs, 918 F.2d 447, 13 U.C.C. Rep. Serv. 2d 797 (5th Cir. 1990) (successor to FSLIC holder in due course even though bank had notice that note was overdue); Campbell Leasing, Inc. v. Federal Deposit Ins. Corp., 901 F.2d 1244, 12 U.C.C. Rep. Serv. 2d 138 (5th Cir. 1990) (FDIC holder in due course whether it acquired note in its corporate or its receivership capacity. FDIC does not have to meet state requirements for holder-in-due-course status and therefore takes free of personal defenses even though it had notice that note was overdue. Transferee of FDIC obtains rights of holder in due course.); Federal Deposit Ins. Corp. v. Wood, 758 F.2d 156, 40 U.C.C. Rep. Serv. 937 (6th Cir. 1985) (FDIC entitled to holder-in-due-course protection, even though it has notice that the instrument is overdue). But see Federal Deposit Ins. Corp. v. Blue Rock Shopping Center, 766 F.2d 744, 41 U.C.C. Rep. Serv. 1 (3d Cir. 1985) (FDIC is not holder in due course where instrument is overdue when acquired by it).

In addition, court decisions have conflicted as to whether old §3-405, and presumably will likewise conflict as to whether new §§3-404 or 3-405, are applicable to preclude the federal government from contesting the unauthorized nature of an indorsement. Compare United States v. Bank of Am. Natl. Trust & Sav. Assn, 438 F.2d 1213, 8 U.C.C. Rep. Serv. 962 (9th Cir. 1971) (§3-405 not applicable) with Bank of America Natl. Trust & Sav. Assn. v. United States, 552 F. 2d 302, 21 U.C.C. Rep. Serv. 812 (9th Cir. 1977) (§3-405 applicable).

30. U.C.C. §4-103(a); U.C.C. §4-103, Official Comment 2. Subpart C of Regulation CC which governs the check collection process may be varied by agreement except that no agreement can disclaim a bank's duties of due care or good faith. 12 C.F.R. §229.37.

31. U.C.C. §4-103(a); U.C.C. §4-103, Official Comment 2; U.C.C. §1-102(3).

32. U.C.C. §4-103(a).

C. Variation by Agreement

An "agreement" is the bargain of the parties as found in their language or by implication from other circumstances including course of dealing,[33] usage of trade or course of performance.[34] An agreement does not have to be a formal written document executed by the affected parties, as in a bank/customer contract.[35] It may be as simple and concise as a legend on a deposit ticket[36] or a letter sent by a depositary bank to the payor bank for the purpose of collecting a draft.

Agreements can be broken down into two types: interbank agreements and bank/customer agreements. Interbank agreements usually relate to various aspects of the check collection process. For example, an agreement between a depositary bank and a payor bank may give the payor bank more time in order to determine whether it will pay or dishonor a check. Interbank agreements are, with rare exception, binding on the customers of the respective banks.[37] As long as the agreement is with respect to the item being handled, the bank's customer (usually the owner of the item) is bound by any agreement that is made by the bank in the process of collecting the item for him even though he is not a party to the agreement.[38] By asking that the bank collect the item, the customer impliedly authorizes the bank to do anything that is reasonably necessary to collect the item. This would include making collection arrangements and agreements with other banks. Virtually all agreements made by a bank in a good faith attempt to collect an item for its customer are within the bank's implied authority to act on behalf of the customer. On a rare occasion, an agreement may be found to be in excess of its

---

33. See Southern Cotton Oil Co. v. Merchants Natl. Bank, 670 F.2d 548, 33 U.C.C. Rep. Serv. 632 (5th Cir. 1982) (collecting bank's 52-day delay in giving notice of dishonor reasonable due to course of dealings between it and depositary bank where notice of dishonor had previously been delayed up to 45 days).

34. U.C.C. §1-201(3); U.C.C. §4-103, Official Comment 2. Although the definition and effect of "course of performance" is contained in U.C.C. §2-208 rather than in Article 1, the definition of "agreement" in U.C.C. §1-201(3) incorporates the provisions of U.C.C. §2-208.

35. U.C.C. §4-103, Official Comment 2.

36. See Rapp v. Dime Sav. Bank, 64 A.D.2d 964, 408 N.Y.S. 2d 540 (1978), 24 U.C.C. Rep. Serv. 1220, aff'd, 48 N.Y.2d 658, 421 N.Y.S. 2d 347, 396 N.E. 2d 740, 27 U.C.C. Rep. Serv. 501 (1979) (collection agreement under which a 6 to 15 day hold would be placed on checks enforceable when it was printed on reverse side of bank's checking account deposit slips, posted in bank's branch offices and explained to checking account customers when account opened).

37. Official Comment 2 to U.C.C. §4-103 states: "[O]wners of items and other interested parties are not affected by agreements under this subsection unless they are parties to the agreement or are bound by adoption, ratification, estoppel or the like." Official Comment 3 to §4-103 adds ". . . they may become bound to agreements on the principle that collecting banks acting as agents have authority to make binding agreements with respect to items being handled."

implied authority when the agreement's purpose is to protect or favor the bank's own interests over its customer's or where, of course, the agreement violates an express understanding between the bank and its customer as to the scope of its authority.

One special type of interbank agreement is a "clearing-house rule." Clearing-house rules have the effect of agreements varying the rules of Article 4 for items collected through the clearing house.[39] Local clearing houses have long issued rules governing the details of clearing which may vary the effect of Article 4 on hours of clearing, media of remittance, time for return of misspent items, and similar issues. Clearing houses may be citywide or extend to banks throughout an entire county or region. Generally clearing-house rules may vary the provisions of Article 4 only as to functions traditionally exercised by clearing houses.

Clearing-house rules, and the like, have the effect of agreements under §4-103(a), whether or not specifically assented to by all parties interested in the items handled.[40] Clearing-house rules are clearly binding on any party who has expressly assented to such rules and on members of the clearing house who have, by their membership alone, expressed such assent.[41]

Since Article 4 is not a regulatory statute, it neither regulates the terms of the bank/customer agreement nor prescribes consumer protection constraints on bank/customer agreements.[42] Article 4 leaves the protection of bank customers to the individual state legislatures to enact legislation and to the courts to regulate abuse through normal contract doctrines such as unconscionability, public policy, and contracts of adhesion.

In fact, bank/customer agreements, being usually standardized agreements that the customer neither reads, understands, nor has any power to bargain for change, are virtually always contracts of adhesion. Like other contracts of adhesion, agreements by which a bank attempts to limit its customer's rights or disclaim the bank's own duties are closely scrutinized. Courts often have refused to enforce provisions found in a bank/customer agreement or on a deposit slip that cause hardship to the customer or result in unfair surprise. In one case, for example, the court refused to enforce a requirement found on a stop-payment order form that the bank is only obligated to stop

38. U.C.C. §4-103, Official Comment 3.
39. U.C.C. §4-103(b); U.C.C. §4-103, Official Comment 3.
40. U.C.C. §4-103(b); U.C.C. §4-103, Official Comment 3.
41. See Lockhart Sav. & Loan Assn. v. Republic Bank Austin, 720 S.W.2d 193, 3 U.C.C. Rep. Serv. 2d 699, (Tex App. 1986) (clearing-house rule binding upon members of clearing-house).
42. U.C.C. §4-101, Official Comment 3.

C. Variation by Agreement

payment of a check if all of the information is accurate, including the amount to the penny.[43]

The extent to which the customer actually has knowledge, or had a clear opportunity to acquire knowledge, will be instrumental in the court's decision as to whether it will enforce the provision. For example, in Rapp v. Dime Savings Bank of New York,[44] the court enforced an agreement giving the bank the right to place a reasonable hold on uncollected funds where the agreement was printed on the reverse side of the deposit slip, posted in all branch offices, and explained to individual checking account customers upon opening of their accounts.

A fertile area of dispute between courts concerns the charges that a bank may levy for services such as the return of checks drawn upon insufficient funds. The California Supreme Court in Perdue v. Crocker National Bank[45] remanded to the trial court to determine whether a charge of $6 per check for checks drawn on insufficient funds was unconscionable when the true cost to the bank of processing such checks was $.30 per check.[46] On the other hand, the New York Court of Appeals, in Howard L. Jacobs v. Citibank, N.A.,[47] held that the bank may levy any charge that is not in bad faith or grossly disproportionate to the bank's actual processing costs.[48]

A court may refuse to enforce a provision of a bank/customer agreement that it finds to be in violation of public policy. One ground of public policy

43. See Staff Serv. Assocs. v. Midatlantic Natl. Bank, 207 N.J. Super. 327, 504 A.2d 148, 42 U.C.C. Rep. Serv. 968 (1985).

44. 164 A.D. 2d 964, 408 N.Y.S. 2d 540, 24 U.C.C. Rep. Serv. 1220 (1978), aff'd, 48 N.Y. 2d 658, 421 N.Y.S. 2d 347, 396 N.E.2d 740, 27 U.C.C. Rep. Serv. 501 (1979). See also Tolbert v. First Natl. Bank, 312 Or. 485, 823 P.2d 965, 17 U.C.C. Rep. Serv. 2d 1204 (1991) (Where bank and customer agreed to specific charges for not sufficient funds checks and where customer was informed that charges may change and then informed that charges were changed, bank has not violated duty of good faith in amount charged.).

45. 38 Cal. 3d 913, 216 Cal. Rptr. 345, 702 P.2d 503 (1985).

46. Compare the decision of the Oregon Supreme Court in Best v. United States National Bank of Oregon, 78 Or. App. 1, 714 P.2d 1049, 1 U.C.C. Rep. Serv. 2d 6 (1986), aff'd, 303 Or. 557, 739 P.2d 554, 4 U.C.C. Rep. Serv. 2d 8 (1987), which held that it was a question of fact as to whether a $5 per check charge was a violation of the bank's implied covenant of good faith with the same court's decision in Tolbert v. First Natl. Bank of Oregon, 312 Or. 485, 823 P.2d 965, 17 U.C.C. Rep. Serv. 2d 1204 (1991), which held that where the bank and customer agreed to specific charges for insufficient funds checks and where the customer was informed that charges may change, the bank has not violated its duty of good faith in the amount charged for such checks.

47. 61 N.Y.2d 869, 474 N.Y.S.2d 464, 462 N.E.2d 1182, 37 U.C.C. Rep. Serv. 1648 (1989).

48. An interpretative ruling promulgated by the Office of the Comptroller of the Currency, 12 C.F.R. §7.8000, provided that the fee charged for insufficient funds checks was a business decision by a bank that could consider deterrence among other factors.

may be Article 4 itself. Article 4 establishes certain basic rights that bank cus-tomers assume are guaranteed them when they open up their checking account. For example, a court probably would not permit a bank to com-pletely eliminate any of the basic rights that Article 4 has granted to bank cus-tomers: the right to stop payment, the right to sue for wrongful dishonor, or the right to object to the payment of items not properly payable. A court may even refuse to permit a bank to eliminate the customer's right to issue an oral stop-payment order. In contrast, a reasonable agreement as to the manner of issuing a stop-payment order would certainly be enforced.

In contrast, for example, courts often enforce bank/customer agree-ments that greatly limit the time within which a customer may claim that a sig-nature or alteration is unauthorized.[49] For another example, it has been held that the right to a jury trial may be waived by an agreement in small print— so long as the agreement is neither unconscionable nor against public policy.[50]

D.   TYPES OF BANKS

We will now examine the duties of the different types of banks in the bank collection process. We discussed the process by which a check is collected from the payor bank earlier in this chapter. In this section, we will look at the dif-ferent types of banks in the check collection process. In section E, we will examine the duties of a payor bank. We will examine the duties of collecting banks in section K, and in section G, we will examine the deadlines by which a bank must let its customer withdraw deposited funds.

Let us begin with a hypothetical. Assume that your employer draws your paycheck on its account at Wells Bank. You deposit the paycheck in your bank account at Bank of America. What does Bank of America do when it receives your check? It first provisionally credits your account. Although it has no obli-gation to allow you to write checks or withdraw the provisional credits, often banks will do so if their customer is creditworthy. Bank of America will then attempt to present the check to Wells Bank in order to obtain payment for you.

49. See Simcoe & Erie Gen. Ins. Co. v. Chemical Bank, 770 F. Supp. 149, 15 U.C.C. Rep. Serv. 2d 1269 (S.D. N.Y. 1991) (14 days); Qassemzadeh v. IBM Poughkeepsie Employees Fed. Credit Union, 167 A.D.2d 378, 561 N.Y.S.2d 795, 13 U.C.C. Rep. Serv. 2d 833 (1990) (30 days to notify credit union of any discrepancy in account).
50. See David v. Manufacturers Hanover Trust Co., 59 Misc. 2d 248, 298 N.Y.S.2d 847, 6 U.C.C. Rep. Serv. 504 (N.Y. App. Div. 1969).

D. Types of Banks

In this effort, Bank of America sends the check to Crocker Bank for the purpose of presenting the check to Wells Bank for payment. Crocker Bank then presents the check for payment to Wells Bank.

When the Code or Regulation CC speaks of banks, it does not mean only those institutions that are officially called "banks." A "bank" is "any person engaged in the business of banking."[51] This includes, among others, commercial banks, savings banks, savings and loan associations, credit unions, and trust companies. Because the collection process and the bank/customer relations of savings and loan associations and credit unions are the same as commercial banks, the same rules apply to all of these financial institutions. Thus, the same rules apply whether you deposit your check at your local credit union, at a savings and loan association, or at Bank of America.

As you are all aware, most banks, like Bank of America, have many different branches or separate offices. The question arises as to whether these branches are treated as one bank or as different banks. A branch or separate office of a bank is treated as a separate bank for most purposes including computing the time within which an action must be taken, in determining where action may be taken or directed, or where notices or orders must be given.[52] This rule has many consequences, some of which we will examine in this chapter. For example, Crocker Bank's actions would not be a proper presentment if it attempted to present a check drawn upon the Beverly Hills branch of Wells Bank to the Santa Monica branch of Wells Bank.[53] Instead, Crocker Bank would be treated as having engaged the Santa Monica branch as the presenting bank to present the check to the Beverly Hills branch. Similarly, as we will see in Chapter 6C, if your employer issued a stop payment order to the Santa Monica branch of Wells Bank, the stop payment order would not be effective until it reached the Beverly Hills branch of Wells Bank.

Article 4 classifies banks into five categories:

1. depositary banks
2. payor banks
3. intermediary banks

---

51. U.C.C. §4-105(1).

52. U.C.C. §4-107. However, branches or separate offices of a bank are not treated as separate banks for all purposes. U.C.C. §4-107, Official Comment 4. For instance, the assets of the entire banking institution are still available for the discharge of liability incurred by a particular branch or separate office. U.C.C. §4-107, Official Comment 4. As to other issues, the drafters of Article 4 intentionally left to courts to resolve on a case-by-case basis for what purposes a branch ought to be considered a separate bank. U.C.C. §4-107, Official Comment 1.

53. U.C.C. §4-107, Official Comment 2.

4. collecting banks
5. presenting banks

Regulation CC has added two additional categories of banks: paying banks and returning banks. Figure 5.6 will be helpful in seeing the role of each bank in the check collection process.

FIGURE 5.6

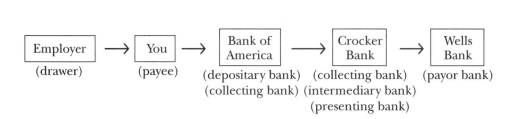

1. *Payor Bank*

A "payor bank" is "a bank that is a drawee of a draft."[54] The drawee is the person ordered in a draft to make payment.[55] Because your employer drew the check upon Wells Bank, Wells Bank is the drawee of the draft. Since it is also a bank, it is the payor bank.

When the item is not an ordinary check, it may be difficult to determine whether the bank is a payor bank or a collecting bank.[56] In Chapter 1 we covered items payable through a bank and items payable at a bank. When an item states that it is payable through a bank, the named bank is designated as a collecting bank through whom presentment must be made. The bank is not the drawee of the item and has no authority to pay the item. As a result, the bank is not a payor bank.[57]

When an item is payable at a bank, whether the bank is a payor bank depends upon which alternative of §4-106(b) the state has adopted. Alternative A to §4-106(b) treats an item payable at a bank as being drawn on the bank. Because the item is treated as being drawn on the bank, the bank at which the item is payable is a payor bank. Alternative B to §4-106(b), in contrast, treats the words "payable at" as identical to the words "payable through." An item payable "at" a bank is therefore simply payable "through" the bank.

54. U.C.C. §4-105(3).
55. U.C.C. §4-104(a)(8); U.C.C. §4-105, Official Comment 4.
56. Where a draft names a nonbank drawee and it is unclear whether a bank named in the draft is a co-drawee or collecting bank, the bank is a collecting bank. U.C.C. §4-106(c).
57. U.C.C. §4-106(a).

D. Types of Banks

As we discussed in the preceding paragraph, a bank through which an item is payable is a collecting bank and not a payor bank. Therefore, in a state adopting Alternative B to §4-106(b), the bank at which an item is payable is not a payor bank.

2. Paying Bank

Regulation CC created the classification of a "paying bank." Under Regulation CC, paying banks have duties above and beyond those imposed upon payor banks under Article 4.[58] "Paying bank" is a broader concept than "payor bank." In order to prevent MICR fraud (which we discussed in Chapter 4), the definition of a paying bank includes the bank whose routing number appears on a check even if it is not the true drawee bank. As a result, when a check is sent to a bank whose routing number was fraudulently encoded on the check, the bank has the duty, as does any paying bank, to expeditiously return the check and to give notice of nonpayment as to any large check. Furthermore, for some purposes (the bank collection functions), a bank through which a check is payable is a paying bank, even though the check is drawn upon another bank.[59] Thus, a bank through which a check is payable, although only having the duties of a collecting bank under Article 4, has the duties of a paying bank under Regulation CC.

3. Depositary Bank

A "depositary bank" is "the first bank to take an item even though it is also the payor bank unless the item is presented for immediate payment over the counter."[60] Bank of America is a depositary bank. When you deposited the check into your bank account at Bank of America, Bank of America became the depositary bank. Bank of America would still be the depositary bank had the check also been drawn upon Bank of America, making it is also the payor bank.[61] If a check is both drawn on and deposited in the same bank, the bank

58. Regulation CC duties include the duty of expeditious return, 12 C.F.R. §229.30(a), and the duty to give notice of nonpayment to the depositary bank on items in the amount of $2,500 or more. 12 C.F.R. §229.33(a).

59. 12 C.F.R. §229.2(z).

60. U.C.C. §4-105(2).

61. U.C.C. §4-105(2). U.C.C. §4-105, Official Comment 3. The bank also is both the depositary bank and the payor bank if the holder asks his bank to apply the check to a loan that the bank has made to him. U.C.C. §4-105, Official Comment 3.

first takes the check in its capacity as a depositary bank. Later, it will undertake its duties as a payor bank. The result would be different were you to demand payment for the check from Bank of America by presenting the check for immediate payment over the counter (whether or not you had an account at Bank of America). In other words, you walk up to a teller at the branch of Bank of America where the check was drawn and demand that the teller pay you cash for the check. In this situation, because Bank of America is not being asked to collect the check for you, it is only the payor bank and not a depositary bank.

4.   Collecting Bank

A "collecting bank" is "any bank handling an item for collection except the payor bank."[62] A depositary bank, as long as it is not also the payor bank, is a collecting bank. Thus, where Bank of America, the depositary bank, sends your paycheck to Crocker Bank for presentment to Wells Bank, both Bank of America and Crocker Bank are collecting banks. Suppose your paycheck had been drawn by your employer on Bank of America and you deposited the check in your account also at Bank of America. Since it was the payor bank, Bank of America would not be a collecting bank.

5.   Intermediary Bank

An "intermediary bank" is "any bank to which an item is transferred in the course of collection except the depositary or payor bank."[63] In our original example, only Crocker Bank is an intermediary bank. Wells Bank, being the payor bank, is not an intermediary bank. As the depositary bank, Bank of America is not, in addition, an intermediary bank. We have already seen in Chapter 4 that intermediary banks, unlike payor or depositary banks, are not liable for conversion when an instrument is paid over a forged indorsement.

---

62. U.C.C. §4-105(5).

63. U.C.C. §4-105(4). Where the payor is not a bank, the last bank in the process will usually also be an intermediary bank. U.C.C. §4-105, Official Comment 5.

6. *Presenting Bank*

A "presenting bank" is "any bank presenting an item except a payor bank."[64] A presenting bank can be a depositary bank, a collecting bank or an intermediary bank. Because Crocker Bank is the bank that presented the check to Wells Bank, Crocker Bank is the presenting bank. Bank of America is not a presenting bank because it did not present the check to Wells Bank.

7. *Returning Bank*

Regulation CC created the classification of "returning banks." A "returning bank" is any bank other than the paying or depositary bank that handles the item on its return or a notice in lieu of return of the item.[65] For example, if Wells Bank decides not to pay your paycheck, it must return the paycheck (or if the check is not available a notice of nonpayment) to Bank of America, the depositary bank. Wells Bank may decide to send the returned check back to Bank of America, not through Crocker Bank, but rather through Interstate Bank. It may do so because it has an agreement with Interstate Bank under which it receives a discounted rate for the service. Interstate Bank is a returning bank. Had Wells Bank returned the check through Crocker Bank, Crocker Bank would also be a returning bank. Regulation CC imposes special duties upon returning banks.[66]

E.   DUTIES OF PAYOR BANK

Let us return to the paycheck that you deposited in your account at Bank of America. Remember that Bank of America, the depositary bank, sent the check to Crocker Bank, the presenting bank, for presentment to Wells Bank, the payor bank. Assume that Crocker Bank presents the check to Wells Bank on Friday morning.

---

64. U.C.C. §4-105(6). Where the payor is not a bank, the last bank in the process will usually be also a presenting bank. U.C.C. §4-105, Official Comment 5.

65. 12 C.F.R. §229.2(cc).

66. 12 C.F.R. §229.31.

What does Wells Bank have to do when the check is presented to it? You would think that the answer would be easy. Wells Bank would look at the check, see if adequate funds are present and, if present, pay the check. If sufficient funds are not present, Wells Bank would return the check to Crocker Bank. Unfortunately, the payment process is anything but simple. The overwhelming number of checks presented for payment each day has made it necessary to structure a fairly complex payment and return process so as to result in a quick but reasonably cost-effective system for collecting, paying and returning checks and other items.

1.   Payor Bank's Duties in Paying Item

a.   How Long Does the Payor Bank Have to Pay or Return an Item?

How long after it receives the check does Wells Bank have to decide whether to pay or return the check? In making the determination of how long a payor bank should have to process an item for payment, a balance had to be struck between conflicting interests. Because checks are intended to be a substitute for cash, the holder of a check had to be able to immediately convert the check into cash. Ideally, this would necessitate that the payor bank be required to either pay or return the check on the day that the check is presented for payment. However, requiring the payor bank to make payment on the day of presentment would require the bank to employ a significant number of employees whose only purpose would be to enable the bank to immediately process checks. Banks would have to find space for these employees, and substantial costs would be added to the check collection system. Alternatively, banks could process checks overnight, no additional space would be required. Check processing could be performed in what would be office space not otherwise in use during the night hours. Furthermore, by having some leeway in time, banks could weather busy times without having to hire too many temporary employees.

Unfortunately, even allowing one additional day for the payor bank to process checks for payment results in a windfall to the payor bank at the expense of the owner of the check. During this additional day, Wells Bank, rather than you (the owner), has use of the drawer's money. This may not seem to be a big deal on any given check. But when you realize that billions of checks are paid every year, the total interest on the total number of the checks becomes very significant.

The payment, settlement, and return system devised by Article 4 and modified by Regulations CC and J attempts to balance these conflicting inter-ests. Because of the burden that it would impose, Article 4 does not generally require that a payor bank determine on the day of presentment whether to pay an item. Rather, the payor bank may defer this decision until the next banking day. However, in order to allow the presenting bank, and not the payor bank, to have use of the funds represented by the item during this addi-tional day, a condition to the right of the payor bank to have the additional day to process the item is placed on the bank. The payor bank must provisionally settle for the item on the day of its presentment.[67] The payor bank must, therefore, on the day the check is presented, settle with the presenting bank for the check. The settlement will, more often than not, involve crediting the presenting bank's account at a Federal Reserve Bank and debiting the payor bank's account. The manner in which a payor bank may settle for an item is discussed more fully later in this section.

The settlement is provisional only. The provisional nature of an interbank settlement is different than the provisional nature of the depositary bank's crediting of a customer's account upon deposit of an item. Remember when a depositary bank provisionally credits its customer's account, the bank has no duty to allow the customer to draw upon the credit. In contrast, the whole pur-pose of an interbank provisional settlement is to transfer the interest-free use of the funds from the payor bank to the presenting bank. This purpose would be defeated if the funds were not usable by the presenting bank. An interbank settlement is provisional only in the sense that upon nonpayment of the check, the settlement will be revoked.

This practice of settling on the day of the item's receipt and waiting one day before determining whether to pay an item is called "deferred posting."[68] In our example, if Wells Bank wants to defer posting of your paycheck, it must settle with Crocker Bank for the amount of the check, even before it has any idea whether your employer has sufficient funds in its account. If Wells Bank decides to return the check unpaid the next day, it has the right to revoke the settlement. If the provisional settlement included crediting of Crocker Bank's account with Wells Bank, Wells Bank would revoke the settlement by debiting Crocker Bank's account for the amount of the check.

67. U.C.C. §4-301, Official Comment 1.
68. U.C.C. §4-301, Official Comment 1.

b. What Must a Payor Bank Do to Have the Right to Defer Posting of an Item?

A payor bank has the right to defer deciding whether to pay a demand item (item payable on demand) only if it settles for the item before midnight of the banking day of receipt.[69] In our example, Wells Bank may defer its decision as to whether or not to pay your paycheck only if it gives Crocker Bank a settlement for the check before midnight on Friday night (the banking day that it received the check).

There is one situation in which a payor bank has no right to defer posting of an item. When a demand item is presented for immediate payment over the counter, a payor bank has no right to defer its decision as to whether to pay the item.[70] If, therefore, you want to receive payment of your paycheck immediately, you would go to the branch of Wells Bank on which the check was drawn and demand that it make payment of the check. In this event, Wells Bank would have to either pay the check or dishonor it on the day of presentment.[71] If Wells Bank does not make payment on that day, the check is dishonored, and you have an action against your employer.[72]

c. What If the Payor Bank Fails to Settle for a Demand Item on the Day of Its Receipt?

Settling for a demand item on the day of its receipt is the price that the payor bank must pay in order to have the right to defer its decision to pay the check until the next banking day. If it does not pay this price, it still has the option of dishonoring the item by returning it on the day of receipt.[73] However, if the payor bank neither settles for the item nor returns the item by midnight of the banking day of receipt, the payor bank is penalized by being accountable for the amount of the item.[74] This basically means that the payor bank becomes obligated to the holder to pay the item. We discuss accountability later in this section. When an item is presented by a Federal Reserve

---

69. U.C.C. §4-301(a).

70. U.C.C. §4-301 (a); U.C.C. §4-301, Official Comment 2.

71. U.C.C. §3-502(b)(2).

72. Because §4-302 does not cover items presented over the counter for payment, a bank does not become accountable if it delays paying or returning an item presented over the counter. U.C.C. §4-302 (a)(1).

73. U.C.C. §4-302, Official Comment 1.

74. U.C.C. §4-302(a)(1).

Bank, the payor bank does not even have until midnight on the day of receipt to settle for the item. The bank must settle by the close of Fedwire.[75]

There is one exception to the rule that a payor bank becomes accountable for an item if it does not return or settle for the item on the day of its receipt. This exception is for "on-us" items. An "on-us" is an item where the payor bank and depositary bank are the same bank. Thus, if both you and your employer bank with Wells Bank, the deposit of your paycheck in Wells Bank makes your paycheck an "on-us" item. Wells Bank does not need to provisionally settle with you on the day of receipt[76] in order to have the right to defer the decision of whether to pay or return the on-us item until the next banking day. This exception for "on-us items" makes sense. When an item is presented through another bank, Wells Bank can reasonably be assured that it will be able to recover the settlement in the event that the item is returned unpaid. However, if Wells Bank were required to settle with you on the day it received the item, it does not have the protection of a solvent presenting bank. Fraud would be made simple. For example, you could deposit a very large check drawn by a cohort in crime and, after receiving the settlement, withdraw the funds before Wells Bank decided to dishonor the check. By not allowing you access to the funds before Wells Bank determines whether the check is payable, this risk is eliminated. The exemption from settling with its customer on the day of receipt of the item is the only difference in treatment that is

75. 12 C.F.R., §210.9(a)(1); 57 Fed. Reg. 46953 (Oct. 14, 1992). Fedwire is defined in 12 C.F.R. §210.26(e) as "the funds-transfer system owned and operated by the Federal Reserve Banks that is used primarily for the transmission of payment orders. . . . Fedwire does not include the system for making automated clearing house transfers."

Section 210.9(a)(2) imposes an even more stringent requirement upon paying banks. A paying bank must settle with the Federal Reserve Bank or return the check by the end of the clock hour after the hour during which presentment had been made or by one hour after the scheduled opening of Fedwire, whichever is later. 12 C.F.R. §210.9 (a)(2)(i).

However, the only consequence of the bank not complying with the requirements of this section is that the paying bank would be subject to any applicable overdraft charges. If, for example, the paying bank receives a check at 12:30 P.M., the bank is liable for overdraft charges if it does not settle by 2:00 P.M. on the same day. 57 Fed. Reg. 46951 (Oct. 14, 1992).

Regulation CC also requires the paying bank to provide "same-day settlement" for certain checks. A paying bank must settle for a check by the close of Fedwire on the day of presentment, if the check is presented by 8:00 A.M. at a location designated by the paying bank. 12 C.F.R. §229.36(f)(1); 57 Fed. Reg. 46972-73 (Oct. 14, 1992).

The paying bank is accountable for a check presented in accordance with these requirements if it does not by the close of Fedwire on the business day it receives the check, return the check, or settle with the presenting bank by a credit to an account at a Federal Reserve Bank designated by the presenting bank.

76. U.C.C. §4-301(b); U.C.C. §4-301, Official Comment 4.

accorded to "on-us items" under Article 4. In all other respects, "on-us items" are treated the same as any other demand items.[77]

d. What Does It Mean to "Settle" for an Item?

If you read the definition of "settle," you might be misled as to what Wells Bank must do to comply with its duty to settle on the day it receives the paycheck. "Settle" is defined broadly to include "payment in cash, by clearing house settlement, in a charge or credit or by remittance, or otherwise as agreed."[78] However, Wells Bank does not have much leeway in the manner in which it may settle for the item because the purpose of requiring the payor bank to settle on the day of receipt is to give the presenting bank, and not the payor bank, use of the funds on that day. If, for example, Wells Bank were allowed to settle for the paycheck by sending back its own cashier's check, Crocker Bank would not have use of the funds on the day of settlement. Because the cashier's check would have to be presented for payment, Crocker Bank would not have use of the funds until it obtains payment of the cashier's check. For this reason, absent agreement, the presenting bank does not have to accept a remittance draft, that is, a cashier's or teller's check, in settlement.[79]

As to checks presented through a Federal Reserve Bank, Regulation J determines the manner in which a payor bank must settle with the presenting Federal Reserve Bank. Under Regulation J, the payor bank is required to settle by authorizing the Federal Reserve Bank to debit the payor bank's account at the Federal Reserve Bank.[80] Where the check or other item is not presented through a Federal Reserve Bank, the means through which it is presented determines to some extent the manner by which the payor bank must settle. Since most other settlements are between banks in the same clearing house, the rules of the clearing house will determine the manner of settlement.[81] Settlements between banks in the same clearing house often take the form of either (1) crediting and debiting the respective banks' accounts with the clearing house or (2) crediting of the presenting bank's account with the payor bank. Where two banks frequently exchange checks or other items with each

77. U.C.C. §4-214(c); U.C.C. §4-301(b); U.C.C. §4-301, Official Comment 4.
78. U.C.C. §4-104(a)(11).
79. U.C.C. §4-213, Official Comment 3. The same is true of an authority to charge an account of the bank making the settlement in the bank receiving the settlement. U.C.C. §4-213, Official Comment 3. The same result if the check is presented by a Federal Reserve Bank. Regulation J provides that a remittance draft, such a cashier's or teller's check, may be used only if the Federal Reserve Bank consents. 12 C.F.R. §210.9(a)(5); 57 Fed. Reg. 46957 (Oct. 14, 1992).

other, an agreement between these banks will determine the manner of the settlement. In the absence of an applicable clearing-house rule or agreement, the payor bank can require that the presenting bank accept a medium of settlement prescribed by Federal Reserve regulations or operating circulars.

Of course, the recipient may specify some other form of acceptable media.[82] Where the payor bank does not settle through an approved medium, no settlement occurs unless the presenting bank accepts the medium of settlement.[83] As we will see, this has severe consequences since the payor bank becomes accountable for the item if it has not properly settled for the item.

e. What Happens If, after Settling for the Item, the Payor Bank Decides to Dishonor the Item?

Assume that Wells Bank properly settles for the item on the day of its receipt. What does Wells Bank have to do if it decides that it will not pay the item after all? Wells Bank may revoke and recover the settlement if it returns the item (1) before it has finally paid the item and (2) before its midnight deadline.[84] If the item is unavailable for return,[85] Wells Bank may instead send[86] written notice of dishonor or nonpayment.[87]

Thus, if Wells Bank decides that the check should not be paid, Wells Bank

---

80. 12 C.F.R. §210.9(a)(5); 57 Fed. Reg. 46957 (Oct. 14, 1992). Of course, the payor bank may settle in cash instead if it desires. Id.

81. U.C.C. §4-213, Official Comment 1. In the rare case in which the means of settlement is not prescribed by agreement, Federal Reserve Regulation, operating circular, or clearinghouse rule, the only medium of settlement that must be accepted by the bank receiving the settlement is cash or a credit to an account in a Federal Reserve bank. U.C.C. §4-213(a)(1).

82. U.C.C. §4-213(a).

83. U.C.C. §4-213(b); U.C.C. §4-213, Official Comment 1.

84. U.C.C. §4-301(a)(1) and (2).

85. An item is not "unavailable" for return simply because the bank has difficulty finding the item. The item must in fact be unavailable for return. For example, where the item is held by a collecting bank under a check-retention plan, the item is unavailable. U.C.C. §4-301, Official Comment 2.

86. "Send" under §-201(38) means to "deposit in the mail or deliver for transmission." U.C.C. §4-301, Official Comment 6.

87. U.C.C. §4-301(a)(1) and (2). The notice of nonpayment or dishonor must be in writing and should contain sufficient information to allow the recipient to determine which item has been dishonored. Banks usually return an item with a return item letter indicating the reason for the return. Regulation CC requires that the paying bank wire advice of the nonpayment of items in the amount of $2,500 or greater. However, even though the advice of nonpayment may be by telephone, notice by telephone is not in writing and therefore is not sufficient notice for purposes of §4-302(a)(2).

must return it or, if the check is not available, provide written notice of dishonor or nonpayment before either of two events has occurred.

The first event is that the check must be returned or notice of nonpayment sent before Wells Bank makes final payment of the check. We discuss later in this section when a bank makes final payment of an item. The second event is that Wells Bank must return the item or send notice of nonpayment before its midnight deadline. A bank's "midnight deadline" is midnight of the banking day following the banking day on which the item was received.[88] Remember that your paycheck was received by Wells Bank on Friday. Because Saturday and Sunday are not banking days, the next banking day is Monday. Thus, Wells Bank has to return the check by midnight on Monday.

Wells Bank may not necessarily be regarded as having received the check on Friday for purposes of determining when it must settle for the check or revoke its settlement solely because the check was physically received on Friday. Two provisions have an effect on this determination. The first is §4-108, which allows Wells Bank to establish a *cut-off hour* after which the item is deemed to have been received by Wells Bank on the next banking day.[89] This cut-off hour can be no earlier than 2:00 P.M. If, for example, Wells Bank has established a cut-off hour of 2:00 P.M. and the check arrives after that hour on Friday, it will be deemed to have been received on Monday, the next banking day.[90] In this case, the midnight deadline would be midnight on Tuesday.

The second is §4-107, which provides that a separate branch's receipt of an item is not receipt by the payor branch. Thus, if the Tarzana branch of Wells Bank received a check on Friday drawn upon the Northridge branch, the check is not deemed to have been received by Wells Bank as payor bank on Friday. Rather, it is received when the Northridge branch either receives the check or should have received the check, had the Tarzana branch exercised due diligence. The result would be different if the Tarzana branch was the center at which the data processing of checks occurred. Delivery to an off-premises data processing center as requested by the payor bank constitutes receipt by the payor branch.[91] Thus, if the Northridge branch requests that all checks be presented to the Tarzana branch for processing, the check is

---

88. U.C.C. §4-104(a)(10).

89. For the purpose of allowing time to process items, prove balances, and make the necessary entries on its books to determine its position for the day, a bank may fix an afternoon hour of 2:00 P.M. or later, as a cut-off hour for the handling of money and items and the making of entries on its books. U.C.C. §4-108(a). If the close of its banking day is earlier than the cutoff hour, the bank may treat any item received after the close of its banking day as received on the next banking day. U.C.C. §4-108(b); U.C.C. §4-108, Official Comment 2.

90. U.C.C. §4-108(b); U.C.C. §4-108, Official Comment 2.

91. U.C.C. §4-204(c).

deemed to have been received by the Northridge branch the day it is received by the Tarzana branch.

There is one exception to a payor bank's duty to pay or return an item by its midnight deadline. The exception involves documentary drafts. We discussed the collection of documentary drafts in Chapter 1. Because the payor bank needs time to examine the documents in order to determine whether to pay a documentary draft, a payor bank has until the close of the third business day following presentment to determine whether to pay a documentary draft.[92]

f.   What Does the Payor Bank Have to Do If It Decides to Pay an Item?

Because Wells Bank has already settled for the item on the day of its receipt, the bank has nothing more to do if it decides to pay the item. Once the midnight deadline (or any earlier deadline set by agreement, clearinghouse rule, Federal Reserve regulation, or circular) has passed, the check is deemed to be paid.[93] At this point, Wells Bank is precluded from revoking its settlement.[94] We will discuss the ways in which a payor bank makes final payment later in this section.

g.   What Are the Consequences of a Payor Bank's Failure to Settle for an Item or to Timely Return the Item after Settlement?

We have seen that a payor bank has two major responsibilities. First, it must settle for a demand item[95] by midnight of the day of receipt. Second, it must pay or return the item by its midnight deadline. When the payor bank fails to perform either of these duties, the bank becomes accountable for the item.[96] This means that the payor bank is liable for the face amount of the

---

92. U.C.C. §3-502(c).

93. U.C.C. §4-215(a)(3).

94. U.C.C. §4-301(a).

95. Demand items include checks, demand certificates of deposit, demand notes, or demand acceptances payable at a bank in states adopting Alternative A to §4-106(b), and cashier's, certified, and teller's checks.

There is an exception for demand documentary drafts which are covered by §4-302(a)(2) rather than by §4-302(a)(1).

96. U.C.C. §4-302(a)(1); U.C.C. §4-302, Official Comment 1.

item.[97] The bank is penalized for its untimely actions by being liable in the face amount of the item whether or not the holder suffers any loss. Although the bank may be liable for pre-judgment interest, it is not liable for consequential damages or attorney's fees.[98] Once the bank finally pays the item by transferring usable funds to the presenting bank, the payor bank has discharged its obligation to account for the item.[99]

Because accountability is a punishment for the payor bank's tardiness, the payor bank is accountable for the item whether or not the item is properly payable.[100] Thus, even where the account does not contain sufficient funds or the item bears a forged drawer's signature, the bank nonetheless may be accountable for the amount of the item.

Payor Bank's Defenses Against Accountability.   The payor bank may raise certain defenses against its accountability on an item or, under certain circumstances, may recover a payment made on an item. We have already discussed in Chapter 4 the bank's right to recover payments made by mistake[101] as well as the warranties given to the payor bank upon presentment of an item.[102] These rights can be asserted either as a defense by the payor bank to its obligation to account for the item or affirmatively to recover a payment made.

For example, assume that Wells Bank is accountable for your paycheck because it did not give a settlement on the day it received the paycheck. When you seek to recover against Wells Bank on its duty to account (accountability) for the item, Wells Bank may defend by showing that the item contains a forged indorsement or has been altered, and that therefore you breached one of your presentment warranties. Wells Bank may also defend by proving that

97. U.C.C. §4-302, Official Comment 3.
98. However, the payor bank may be liable for expenses, including attorney's fees, incurred by the person entitled to enforce the item for breach of its warranty under Regulation CC that the item has been returned by the midnight deadline. 12 C.F.R. §229.34(a) and (c).
99. U.C.C. §4-302, Official Comment 3.
100. U.C.C. §4-302(a)(1).
101. Section 3-418(d) specifically authorizes a payor bank to recover a mistaken payment notwithstanding final payment under §4-215. U.C.C. §3-418, Official Comment 4. There is no reason to distinguish accountability under §4-302 and final payment under §4-215 for these purposes. The bank is accountable for an item for which it has not made final payment only where the bank has failed to settle for the item on the day of receipt.
Its failure to settle for the item should not deprive it of the right to defend against its accountability where it could recover the payment had it so settled. Furthermore, there is no reason to believe that the specific reference in §4-302(b) to the two defenses listed was intended to preclude payor banks from asserting a defense under §3-418.
102. U.C.C. §4-302(b).

you presented or transferred the paycheck intending to defraud Wells Bank.[103] For example, you and your employer may have devised a scheme by which you would present checks to Wells Bank knowing that there were insufficient funds in the account. You would present these checks in the hope that Wells Bank would make a mistake and become accountable for one or more of these checks. Wells Bank has the right to raise your plan to defraud it as a defense to its duty to account for the check. In addition, Wells Bank is given encoding, retention, and settlement warranties by Bank of America and Crocker Bank, the collecting banks. We discuss these warranties in section F of this chapter.

Warranties Given by Paying Bank upon Return of Item.   We discussed earlier in this chapter that under Regulation CC a paying bank that returns a check to the depositary bank is treated as if it was presenting a check drawn upon the depositary bank. Thus, if Wells Bank decides not to pay your paycheck, it will return the paycheck to Bank of America, the depositary bank. In so doing, the returned paycheck is treated as a check drawn by you on Bank of America and made payable to Wells Bank. Wells Bank sends the check to Interstate Bank (the returning bank), which settles with Wells Bank for the paycheck. Interstate Bank then returns the check to Bank of America, which settles with Interstate Bank. Bank of America now debits your account for the amount of the paycheck.

Let us assume that Wells Bank is accountable for the check because it did not return it by the midnight deadline. Wells Bank, as a result, had no right to return the paycheck and obtain reimbursement of its provisional settlement. Did Interstate Bank or Bank of America know this when they settled for the returned paycheck? The answer is "no." They would not have settled for the returned paycheck if they knew that the check was not returned on time. We have just seen that Bank of America may recover from Wells Bank on its duty to account for the item. Regulation CC gives Bank of America certain rights on the improperly returned check in addition to those rights Bank of America has under Article 4. Wells Bank warrants to Interstate Bank, Bank of America, and you (the owner of the check) that it returned the check by its midnight deadline (or any earlier time required by the Code, Regulation J, or Regulation CC).[104] Interstate Bank (the returning bank) gives Bank of America the same warranties. We discuss a returning bank's responsibilities in Chapter 5F.

---

103. U.C.C. §4-302(b); U.C.C. §4-302, Official Comment 3.

104. 12 C.F.R. §229.34(a)(1). It also warrants that it is authorized to return the check; the check has not been materially altered; and in the case of a notice in lieu of return, the original check has not been and will not be returned. 12 C.F.R. §229.34(a).

Wells Bank is already accountable for the amount of the check under Article 4 because the bank was late in returning the check.[105] However, Bank of America may choose to recover for breach of the warranty on returned checks given by Wells Bank because the damages available to it are more favorable than in its action against Wells Bank under §4-302(a). Although damages for breach of this warranty cannot exceed the consideration received by Wells Bank (the face amount of the check), the damages may include finance charges and expenses related to the returned check.[106] Expenses may include the depositary bank's attorneys' fees.[107]

h.   What Are the Payor Bank's Responsibilities on Documentary Drafts and Items not Payable on Demand?

The strict liability imposed on payor banks in the case of checks or other demand items is, as you will recall, for the purpose of speeding up the bank collection process. Imposing liability on the payor bank, even where the demand item was not properly payable, was intended as an incentive for the bank to promptly perform these duties. Similar interests are not involved where the item is a documentary draft (even if payable on demand) or an item not payable at a stated date. Typical items that are not payable on demand are (1) drafts drawn upon a bank payable at a stated date and (2) time notes and acceptances payable at a bank in states adopting Alternative A to §4-106(b) (in these states notes and acceptances payable at a bank are treated as drafts drawn upon the bank). These items are not cash-substitutes; rather, they serve both a payment and a credit function. Unlike checks, these items are hand-processed and, because they are not payable immediately upon their issuance, a substantially greater chance exists that these items will not be paid when the stated date for payment arrives.

Because speed in processing documentary drafts and time instruments is not an overriding concern, there is no need to force banks to process these items promptly by imposing strict liability upon the bank. There is a reason, however, to impose some restraints on the manner in which a payor bank handles these items upon presentment for payment. The payor bank has to be discouraged from delaying payment of these items for its own selfish purposes. For example, assume that a documentary draft presented to the bank is payable on February 1st and also that the drawer of the draft owes a debt to

---

105. U.C.C. §4-302(a).
106. 12 C.F.R. §229.34(d).
107. 12 C.F.R. §229.34(d), app. E at 508 (1995).

the bank, which will mature on February 5th. The payor bank has an incentive to delay payment of the draft until after February 5th so that sufficient funds remain in the account so as to allow the bank to set off the debt owed by its customer when the debt matures on February 5th.

A payor bank is accountable for the amount of a documentary draft (whether payable on demand or at a stated time) or other item not payable on demand only if (1) the item is properly payable and (2) the payor bank does not pay or accept the item or return it and any accompanying documents within the time limits allowed.[108]

We will discuss when an item is properly payable in Chapter 6. The holder of the item should not be entitled to a windfall simply because the payor bank was late in processing the item. As a result, unless the item was properly payable, meaning that sufficient funds were present in the customer's account and the item was authorized by the customer, the payor bank does not incur liability solely by its delay. However, because the Code wants to discourage banks from delaying payment for the purpose of favoring its own self-interest, the payor bank should be liable if, at any time during the period in which the bank retains the item, funds deposited to the customer's account exceed the amount of the draft.[109] Thus, if the drawer had adequate funds on February 5th to cover his draft, the bank should be accountable if it sets off the debt owed to the bank on February 5th rather than paying the documentary draft.

Article 4 does not expressly state the time within which a payor bank must pay, accept, or return an item to avoid accountability under §4-302(a)(2) for documentary drafts and time items. Section 3-502 states the appropriate deadlines where an item qualifies as an instrument under Article 3. In a case involving a documentary draft, the payor bank must pay or dishonor an item by the close of the third banking day following receipt of the documents or, upon the presenter's consent, a longer period.[110] Where a draft is payable on a stated date, a payor bank must make payment on the day of presentment or on the stated date, whichever is later.[111] These time limits may be extended by custom, course of dealing or agreement.

---

108. U.C.C. §4-302(a)(2).

109. See New Ulm State Bank v. Brown, 558 S.W.2d 20, 23 U.C.C. Rep. Serv. 389 (Tex. App. 1977); Suttle Motor Corp. v. Citizens Bank, 216 Va. 568, 221 S.E.2d 784, 18 U.C.C. Rep. Serv. 1031 (1976).

110. U.C.C. §3-502(c). U.C.C. §5-112(1) provides the same period in the case of a documentary draft drawn under a letter of credit.

111. U.C.C. §3-502(b)(3).

i.   Is the Midnight Deadline Ever Extended?

Emergencies. Sometimes emergencies happen that prevent a payor bank from settling for an item on the day of its receipt or from returning the item by its midnight deadline. For example, there may be a blackout of electricity in the city that prevents the bank from using its computer for processing checks. It would be unfair under these circumstances to hold the bank liable for an item when there is nothing that the bank could have done to have met its deadlines.

Both Article 4 and Regulation CC provide excuses for a bank's delay in meeting its deadlines when its failure to act within the specified time limits is caused by circumstances beyond the control of the payor bank and when the bank exercises such diligence as the circumstances require.[112] The bank is excused not only in meeting the time limits imposed by Article 4, but also those imposed by special instructions, by agreement, or by Federal Reserve regulations or operating circulars, clearing-house rules, or the like.

Two requirements must be met before a delay is excused.[113] First, the delay must be caused by circumstances beyond the bank's control such as interference with the mails by blizzards, floods, or hurricanes, other "Acts of God," wrecks, or disasters; suspension of payments by another bank; abnormal operating conditions such as substantial increased volume or substantial shortage of personnel during war or emergency situations; or interruption of communication or computer facilities.[114]

Second, the bank must exercise such diligence as the circumstances require. A bank seeking an excuse must prove that the circumstances not only caused the delay but that the circumstances were beyond the bank's control. The circumstances must be such that they could not be prevented by the bank through the exercise of reasonable care. For example, if a computer broke down because the bank failed to regularly service the computer, the delay is not excused because the breakdown was within the bank's control.

The bank must also prove that it exercised such reasonable diligence as the circumstances required. This requirement has two consequences. First, the bank must prove that it exercised reasonable diligence in anticipating the effects of any foreseeable events. For example, if a bank had reason to know that computers occasionally break down, the bank should have access to a back-up computer or other processing equipment in the event of a computer

---

112. U.C.C. §4-109(b); U.C.C. §4-109, Official Comment 3.

113. The requirements for excuse of a delay under §4-109(b) are identical to those for excusing a delay under 12 C.F.R. §229.38(e) (Regulation CC). U.C.C. §4-109, Official Comment 3.

114. U.C.C. §4-109(b); U.C.C. §4-109, Official Comment 3.

breakdown. If it does not have such access, the delay is not excused. Second, the bank must prove that once the circumstance arose, the bank acted with reasonable diligence.[115] If it would have been reasonable to process the items by hand, the bank should have done so rather than to wait for the computer to be fixed.

Special Extensions under Regulation CC. Regulation CC specifically provides for extensions of the midnight deadline in returning a check in two situations.[116] First, the midnight deadline is extended by one day if the paying bank uses a means of delivery that would ordinarily result in a check being received by the bank to which it is sent on or before the next banking day following the midnight deadline. For example, if instead of mailing a check before the midnight deadline, the payor bank sends the check by a courier who picks up the check at 3:00 A.M. (three hours after the midnight deadline), the midnight deadline is extended one day if the check would normally be delivered by the courier on the next banking day. As long as the means of delivery "ordinarily" results in next day receipt, the one-day extension is available to the bank even if there is an occasional delay. Second, the midnight deadline is extended further if a paying bank uses a highly expeditious means of transportation even if this means of transportation would ordinarily result in delivery after the receiving bank's next banking day. For example, if a paying bank in Los Angeles ships a returned check by air courier directly to the New York depositary bank, the midnight deadline is extended even if the check would normally be received by the New York depositary bank after its next banking day following the Los Angeles bank's midnight deadline.[117] Shipment cross country by air courier, even if initiated after the midnight deadline, is a highly expeditious means of transportation and would result in the depositary bank receiving the returned check sooner than had the check been mailed before the midnight deadline.

---

115. U.C.C. §4-109, Official Comment 3. Compare Port City State Bank v. American State Natl. Bank, 486 F.2d 196, 13 U.C.C. Rep. Serv. 423 (10th Cir. 1973) (bank's delay excused because of computer failure) with Blake v. Woodford Bank & Trust Co., 555 S.W.2d 589, 21 U.C.C. Rep. Serv. 383 (Ky. App. 1977)(the court refused to excuse the bank's failure to return the checks by its midnight deadline since the responsible employees had left the bank prior to midnight without leaving any instructions for the bookkeepers, and because the checks could have been returned on time had the employee placed the checks in the mail); Sun River Cattle Co. v. Miners Bank, 164 Mont. 237, 521 P.2d 679, 14 U.C.C. Rep. Serv. 1004 (1974)(court refused to excuse the bank's delay because the bank failed to introduce evidence of the actions it took once the checks reached the data-processing center).

116. 12 C.F.R. §229.30(c)(1).

117. 12 C.F.R. §229.30(c)(1), app. E. Commentary.

j. What Does It Mean When a Payor Bank Finally Pays a Check?

We have discussed the time limits within which a payor bank must act. We have seen that the payor bank may revoke its settlement as long as it acts before its midnight deadline and before it has finally paid the item. We now must examine when a payor bank finally pays an item ("final payment").

What is final payment? Final payment signifies the moment when an item is deemed to be paid. At this point in time, the drawer and indorsers are discharged from liability.[118] Upon final payment of your paycheck, your employer is no longer liable on the check. Similarly, you are no longer liable as an indorser of the check. Once it makes final payment, Wells Bank, as the payor bank, may no longer revoke its settlement. In addition, Bank of America, as the depositary bank, becomes accountable to you for the amount of the item.[119]

Payment in Cash.   The payor bank finally pays an item when it has done any one of three acts.[120] The first act constituting final payment is payment made in cash by the payor bank.[121] An item is paid in cash when, upon presentment over the counter to a teller, the teller pays cash for the check. When you take your paycheck to Wells Bank and demand that the teller give you cash for the check, the teller's act of handing you the cash is final payment of the check. The result may be different when both you and the drawer have an account at the same bank. Clearly, when you fill out a deposit slip listing first the check and then listing the same amount in the column reading "less cash," the bank has not finally paid the check. Rather, you have deposited the check into your bank account and your bank, in its role as depositary bank rather than as payor bank, has simply advanced you the funds against the check. Even where no deposit slip is filled out, your receipt of cash from your bank might not be final payment. To determine whether the bank has made final payment, it is necessary to read your depositor's contract. Your depositor's contract probably provides that any cash given for an on-us item is simply an advance that may be recovered in the event that the item is subsequently dishonored.

Settles for Item Without Reserving Right to Revoke.   The second act constituting final payment is when the bank settles for the item without reserv-

---

118. U.C.C. §4-215, Comment 8; U.C.C. §3-310(b).
119. U.C.C. §4-215(d).
120. U.C.C. §4-215(a).
121. U.C.C. §4-215(a)(1); U.C.C. §4-215, Official Comment 3.

ing a right to revoke the settlement under statute, clearing-house rule, or agreement.[122] Remember that on the day of receipt of an item, the payor bank must settle for the item in order to take advantage of deferred posting. If the payor bank settles for the item without reserving a right to revoke this settlement, the payor bank has finally paid the item. The reservation must be specifically authorized by statute, clearing-house rule, or other agreement. We have already seen, however, that the Code gives payor banks an automatic right to revoke a settlement it has made, if it meets the requirements specified in §4-301. This does not apply to checks presented for payment over the counter.

Thus, except for checks presented over the counter for payment in cash, banks seldom settle for an item without having a right to revoke the settlement. In addition to its right to revoke under §4-301, where the settlement is through a clearing house, a clearing-house rule will more than likely give the bank a right to revoke the settlement.[123] Where the payor bank is also the depositary bank, the depositor's contract or the receipt given upon deposit may likewise make the settlement provisional.

We will see in Chapter 5F(4) that Regulation CC deems all settlements in the forward collection process to be final.[124] Do not let this provision fool you. Regulation CC determines only whether a payor bank can revoke the settlement given to the presenting bank, not whether the payor bank intended in regards to the depositary bank or the owner to settle without retaining the right to revoke the settlement.[125]

Fails to Revoke Provisional Settlement by Midnight Deadline. The third act constituting final payment occurs when the bank has made a provisional settlement for the item and fails to revoke the settlement by the midnight deadline (or an earlier time established by clearing-house rule or agreement).[126] We have already examined the time and other requirements for revoking a provisional settlement. It should be noted that this third act only comes into play where the payor bank provisionally settles for an item. If the payor bank fails to make a provisional settlement, final payment does not take place under this subsection, even though the bank may be accountable for the item.

122. U.C.C. §4-215 (a)(2); U.C.C. §4-215, Official Comment 4.
123. U.C.C. §4-215, Official Comment 4. Clearing-house rules often provide that items exchanged and settled for by a specified time may be revoked any time up to a specified number of hours later. U.C.C. §4-215, Official Comment 4.
124. 12 C.F.R. §229.36(d).
125. 12 C.F.R. §229.36(d), app E. at 512 (1995).
126. U.C.C. §4-215(a)(3); U.C.C. §4-215, Official Comment 7.

There is a technical distinction (which may confuse you) between final settlement and final payment. This distinction really only applies when the payor bank settles by remittance draft, for example, cashier's or teller's check. An item is not finally paid if the provisional settlement does not become final.[127] This provision does not come into play where the settlement is by credit and debits (for example, Crocker Bank's account is credited at a Federal Reserve Bank and Wells Bank's account is debited at the Federal Reserve Bank). In this case, the settlement automatically becomes final upon payment being final.[128] Thus, if Wells Bank fails to revoke the settlement by its midnight deadline,[129] both the payment and the settlement are final.[130] That is the only occurrence necessary in order for Crocker Bank to have use of the funds.

Let us assume instead, that Bank of America (the depositary bank) sent your paycheck directly to Wells Bank (the payor bank). Wells Bank settled for your paycheck by sending to Bank of America a cashier's check. Later, Wells Bank refused to pay the cashier's check. At this point, unlike the case in which its account in the Federal Reserve Bank had already been credited, Bank of America does not have the funds represented by the check. Should your paycheck be deemed to have been paid? This would result in you having an action against Wells Bank on the cashier's check, but no action against your employer on the paycheck. The drafters of the Code felt that this would be unfair to you. Therefore, if the cashier's check sent in settlement is not finally paid, your paycheck is not finally paid.[131] This means that Wells Bank is accountable for your paycheck unless the bank returned it by the midnight deadline. Even if Wells Bank returned your paycheck by the midnight deadline, Wells Bank is liable on its cashier's check. Furthermore, your employer remains liable on your paycheck. You bargained for payment and not merely for the liability of Wells Bank.

2. Duties of Paying Banks under Regulation CC in Returning Unpaid Items

As we will discuss in section G of this chapter, depositary banks are required to make funds represented by deposited items available according to an expe-

---

127. U.C.C. §4-215(b).

128. U.C.C. §4-215, Official Comment 4.

129. Absent a contrary agreement or clearing-house rule, the time within which the settlement must be revoked is the bank's midnight deadline. U.C.C. §4-301(a).

130. U.C.C. §4-215(a)(3); U.C.C. §4-215, Comment 7.

131. U.C.C. §4-215, Official Comment 8.

dited schedule. When you deposit your paycheck in your account at Bank of America, it must allow you to withdraw the funds represented by your paycheck within a certain number of days.

Imposing the obligation upon a depositary bank to quickly make deposited funds available to its depositor exposes the bank to the risk that the depositor will withdraw the funds before the bank has learned that the check is not going to be paid by the payor bank. For example, assume that Bank of America is required to allow you to withdraw funds represented by the deposit of your paycheck within two days of your deposit of the check. You take advantage of this right and withdraw the funds on the second day. The check is not returned by Wells Bank, the payor bank, until the third day. You lose your job on the third day and have no money to repay Bank of America.

Obviously, Congress and the Federal Reserve Board did not intend to impose undue risks on the banks in requiring these depositary banks to expedite the availability of funds for their depositors. In order to protect depositary banks from these and similar risks, Regulation CC imposes two duties upon paying banks that result in a depositary bank learning more promptly that a check has not been paid: (1) the duty to expeditiously return unpaid items[132] and (2) the duty to give prompt notice of nonpayment of any item in the amount of $2,500 or greater.

In reviewing these two new duties imposed by Regulation CC upon paying banks, you should keep in mind that neither of these duties has an impact upon the time within which the bank has to determine whether to pay or return a check. As we discussed in Chapter 5E(1), with certain minor exceptions, a paying bank has until its midnight deadline to decide whether to pay or return a check.

a. Duty of Expeditious Return

A paying bank's duty to expeditiously return unpaid items requires the bank to return unpaid items in a manner that is likely to result in the item's prompt return to the depositary bank. Complying with this duty generally means that any unpaid item is returned prior to the time that the depositary bank must allow its customer to withdraw the uncollected funds. Thus, for the most part, Bank of America will learn that the check has not been paid prior to the time that it is required to allow you to withdraw the funds. There are two tests that a paying bank may meet in order to satisfy its duty of expeditious

---

132. 12 C.F.R. §229.30(a).

return: the two-day/four-day test or the forward collection test.[133] The paying bank satisfies its duty of expeditious return if it meets either of these tests.

b.   Two-Day/Four-Day Test

The "two-day/four-day test"[134] requires that the paying bank return an item in a manner such that it will normally be received by the depositary bank within certain time limits. The time limit for the depositary bank to receive the return of a local check is not later than 4:00 P.M. on the second business day after the check was presented to the paying bank.[135] A "local check" is a check drawn on or payable through or at a local paying bank.[136] A local paying bank is basically a paying bank that is located in the same Federal Reserve Bank check processing region as the depositary bank.[137] A "non-local check" is simply a check payable through a bank not located in the same check processing region as the depositary bank.[138] The time limit for the depositary bank to receive the return of a non-local check is not later than 4:00 P.M. on the fourth business day after presentment.[139] A "business day" is a calendar day other than Saturday or Sunday or certain enumerated holidays.[140]

For example, assume that your paycheck is a local check and that it was presented to Wells Bank on Friday. Wells Bank must return the check to Bank of America so that it would normally be received by Bank of America by 4:00 P.M. on Tuesday. Saturday and Sunday are not business days and therefore are not included in the calculation. If Tuesday was one of the enumerated holidays, the check must be sent so as to normally be received by Bank of America by Wednesday. Assuming that Tuesday is not a holiday, Wells Bank may mail the check to Bank of America if under normal circumstances the check would be received by Bank of America no later than Tuesday at 4:00 P.M. As long as the depositary bank would "normally" receive the check within the specified

---

133. 12 C.F.R. §229.30(a).

134. 12 C.F.R. §229.30(a)(1). These deadlines are extended to the next banking day when the last business day is not a banking day for the depositary bank.

135. 12 C.F.R. §229.30(a)(1)(i).

136. 12 C.F.R. §229.2(r).

137. Technically, "local paying bank" is defined as a bank that is located in the same check processing region as the physical location of the branch or proprietary ATM at which the check was deposited or where both the branch of the depositary bank and the nonproprietary ATM at which the check was deposited are located. 12 C.F.R. §229.2(s).

138. A "nonlocal check" means a "check payable by, through, or at a nonlocal paying bank." 12 C.F.R. §229.2(v). A "nonlocal paying bank" is a "paying bank that is not a local paying bank with respect to the depositary bank." 12 C.F.R. §229.2(w).

139. 12 C.F.R. §229.30(a)(1)(ii).

140. 12 C.F.R. §229.2(g).

time limit, it is irrelevant whether the particular depositary bank in fact received the check within the specified time.[141] In the case of a non-local check that is received by Wells Bank on Friday, it must be sent in a manner so as to be received by Bank of America by 4:00 P.M. on Thursday of the following week.

c. The Forward Collection Test

The second test is the forward collection test.[142] This test rests upon the assumption that by sending a check for collection, a depositary bank has an incentive to use a means of collection that is reasonably prompt. Why? Because whether or not the check is ultimately paid or returned, the depositary bank has a vested interest in the check promptly reaching the payor bank. The sooner the check is paid, the sooner the depositary bank will have use of the funds represented by the check. In addition, the sooner the check is returned, the less the possibility exists that the bank will have allowed withdrawal of the funds.

The "forward collection test" states that a paying bank returns a check in an expeditious manner if it does so in a manner that a similarly situated bank would normally handle a check drawn upon the depositary bank and deposited for forward collection in that bank by noon on the banking day[143] following the banking day on which the check was presented to the paying bank.[144] In other words, the payor bank has to act as though this was not a check that was presented for payment, but rather a check that has been deposited for collection. The payor bank must act as though its customer deposited the check by noon on the next banking day following the banking day that the check was in fact presented to the payor bank. If your paycheck was presented for payment on Friday, Wells Bank must treat the paycheck as if it were a check drawn by you upon Bank of America and deposited by your employer in its account at Wells Bank by noon on Monday. The standard is based on how similarly situated banks would collect such a check. Thus, where similarly situated banks would use an intermediary collecting bank or a Federal Reserve Bank to present the check to the payor bank, the paying bank may use an intermediary collecting bank or a Federal Reserve Bank to return the check.[145] But when similarly situated banks deliver their checks to the

141. 12 C.F.R. §229.30(a)(1), app. E at 497 (1995).
142. 12 C.F.R. §229.30(a)(2).
143. A "banking day" means "that part of any business day on which an office of a bank is open to the public for carrying on substantially all of its banking functions." 12 C.F.R. §229.2(f).
144. 12 C.F.R. §229.30(a)(2)(iii).
145. 12 C.F.R. §229.30(a)(2), app. E at 498, Example 4 (1995).

intermediary collecting bank by courier, the paying bank cannot mail the check to the returning bank, but must use a courier.[146]

If the paying bank satisfies the forward collection test, it is irrelevant whether in fact the check reaches the depositary bank quickly. There are three methods of returning a check, by which a paying bank is assured by Regulation CC of satisfying the forward collection test: (1) mailing the check directly to the depositary bank;[147] (2) sending the check to any Federal Reserve Bank for return to the depositary bank;[148] and (3) sending the check to any returning bank that agrees to return the check expeditiously.[149]

d.   Duty to Send Notice of Nonpayment

Large checks impose an especially serious risk to depositary banks. The magnitude of the potential loss justifies requiring the paying bank to exert a greater effort to ensure that the depositary bank will learn of the nonpayment before it allows its customer to withdraw the funds. For this reason, the paying bank has a duty to send notice of the nonpayment[150] of any check in the amount of $2,500 or greater directly to the depositary bank.[151]

The notice may be communicated in any way as long as it is received by the depositary bank by 4:00 P.M. on the second business day following the banking day on which the check was presented to the paying bank. Thus, if the check was presented on Wednesday to Wells Bank, the notice must be received by Bank of America by 4:00 P.M. on Friday. One effective method of informing the depositary bank is by telephone.

There will be occasions in which a paying bank, although having already paid the check, erroneously sends a notice of nonpayment. For example, the paying bank may have missed the midnight deadline in returning the check. By such failure, the payor bank has final payment of the check. Upon receiving the notice of nonpayment, the depositary bank charges back its deposi-

---

146. 12 C.F.R. §229.30(2), app. E at 498, Example 3 (1995).

147. 12 C.F.R. §229.30(a), app. E at 498 (1995).

148. 12 C.F.R. §229.30(a)(2), app. E at 497-498, Example 2 (1995).

149. 12 C.F.R. §229.30(a)(2), app. E at 498 (1995).
The returning bank need not have handled the check in the forward collection process.

150. The notice must contain the name and routing number of the paying bank, the name of the payee, the amount, the date of the indorsement of the depositary bank, the account number of depositor, the branch name or number of the depositary bank found in its indorsement, the trace number associated with the depositary's bank indorsement, and the reason for nonpayment. If the notice is in writing, it must include the name and routing number of the depositary bank found in its indorsement.

151. 12 C.F.R. §229.33(a).

tor's account for the amount of the check. However, because final payment has been made, the chargeback is improper. The depositary bank is liable for interest lost by its customer and possibly even for the wrongful dishonor of subsequent checks. All of this occurred because the paying bank sent an erroneous notice of nonpayment. To protect depositary banks from such erroneous notices, a paying bank that sends a notice of nonpayment warrants to its transferee bank, any subsequent transferee bank, the depositary bank, and the owner of the item[152] that it was authorized to send notice of nonpayment.[153]

However, the paying bank does not warrant that the notice of nonpayment is accurate and timely.[154] Damages for breach of these warranties may not exceed the consideration received by the paying bank plus finance charges and expenses related to the returned check.[155] In fact, depositary banks receive little protection from the warranty of notice of nonpayment. Because damages are limited to the consideration received, the paying bank is not liable for any liability incurred by the depositary bank to its customer for wrongful dishonor of the item.

e.   Liability for Violation of Paying Bank's Duties of Expeditious Return and Notice of Nonpayment

A bank is liable only for damages for breach of its duties of expeditious return or of transmitting notice of nonpayment if the bank fails to exercise ordinary care or act in good faith.[156] Plaintiff must prove that the bank has failed to comply. The measure of damages applicable depends on whether the bank failed to exercise ordinary care or failed to act in good faith. A paying bank that violates its duty of ordinary care is liable to the injured party for the amount of the check less the amount of loss that would have been incurred had ordinary care been used. The bank's failure to act in good faith gives rise to liability for all proximately caused damages. The bank is not liable for costs or attorney's fees incurred by the injured party.

Because Regulation CC adopts the principle of comparative negli-

152. 12 C.F.R. §229.34(b).
153. 12 C.F.R. §229.34(b)(2). The paying bank also warrants that the check has not been materially altered. 12 C.F.R. §229.34(b)(3).
154. 12 C.F.R. §229.34(b), app. E at 517-518 (1993).
155. 12 C.F.R. §229.34(d). The measure of damages is the same as for breach of warranty damages under U.C.C. §4-207(3). 12 C.F.R. §229.34(d), app. E at 508 (1995). In an appropriate case expenses may include attorney's fees.
156. 12 C.F.R. §229.38(a).

gence,[157] the damages for which a paying bank is liable are diminished in proportion to the amount of negligence or bad faith attributable to the plaintiff. For instance, when the depositary bank's negligence in failing to use a form of indorsement required by Regulation CC causes the paying bank to fail to meet its duty of expeditious return, the paying bank's liability to the depositary bank is reduced according to the degree of the depositary bank's negligence.

Although a paying bank may be liable on the same check both under Regulation CC for failing to expeditiously return a check and under the Code for failing to return the check by the midnight deadline, the owner may recover on either one of these causes of action but not on both.[158]

F.   DUTIES OF COLLECTING BANKS

We have examined the duties of Wells Bank as the payor bank on your paycheck. It is now time to examine the duties of Bank of America and Crocker Bank as collecting banks. We will see that both Bank of America, as depositary bank, and Crocker Bank, as an intermediary and presenting bank, are collecting banks.

When you, as the holder of your paycheck, deposit the paycheck in your bank account, you are asking your bank to undertake the job of collecting the check from the payor bank. You may believe that you are simply depositing the funds represented by your paycheck into your bank account. In fact, you are also impliedly asking that Bank of America act as your agent for the purpose of collecting the check.

Unless you clearly indicate to the contrary, Bank of America, as a collecting bank (which includes a depositary bank), is presumed to be your agent.[159] As the depositary and collecting bank, Bank of America's status as your agent automatically arises when you deposit a check or other item into your account. Even if you have no account with Bank of America, Bank of America becomes your agent for collection once you request that the bank collect the check for you. Whether you indorse the check "for collection,"[160] indorse it with your name only, or do not indorse it at all, the result is the same. Bank of America

---

157. 12 C.F.R. §229.38(c); 12 C.F.R. §229.38(c), app. E at 515-516 (1995).
158. 12 C.F.R. §229.38(b).
159. U.C.C. §4-201(a).
160. U.C.C. §4-201(a); U.C.C. §4-201, Official Comments 2 and 6.

is your agent for collection. There may be a case in which Bank of America wants to purchase the check from you rather than to simply act as your agent for collection. However, this happens very rarely.

When Bank of America sends the check for collection to Crocker Bank, a subsequent collecting bank (the same would be true if it sent the check to a Federal Reserve Bank for collection),[161] Crocker Bank as a collecting bank becomes your subagent.[162] Crocker Bank is responsible directly to you. Despite the fact that Crocker Bank was chosen by Bank of America, it is not the agent of Bank of America.

As collecting bank, Bank of America's agency status terminates when it finally settles with you for the item.[163] As we examined in the previous section on payor banks, this occurs in most situations when the payor bank has made final payment. At this point, Bank of America becomes indebted to you in the amount of the item, and your relationship with Bank of America is transformed from principal and agent to creditor and debtor.[164]

1.   *Collecting Bank's Simultaneous Status as Agent and Holder for Value*

Bank of America will provisionally settle with you by crediting your account for the amount of the paycheck when you deposit your paycheck there. This settlement is a settlement in name only. Except as provided in Regulation CC and discussed in section G, Bank of America has no obligation to allow you to withdraw the credit or draw checks against this credit until Bank of America receives a final settlement for the item, which is usually not until payment is final. This means that until Bank of America obtains final payment from Wells Bank, Bank of America may refuse to treat your account as containing the

---

161. 12 C.F.R. §210.6(a).

162. U.C.C. §4-201(a).

163. U.C.C. §4-201(a); U.C.C. §4-214(a); U.C.C. §4-214, Official Comment 3. Although with respect to checks, under Regulation CC §§229.31(c) and 36(d), all settlements between banks are final in both the forward and the return collection path, U.C.C. §4-201, Official Comment 4, this does not affect the time within which settlement is final between a depositary bank and its customer. 12 C.F.R. §229.36(d), app. E at 512 (1995).

164. U.C.C. §4-201, Official Comment 4. Upon deposit of an item, the depositary bank will usually provisionally settle with its customer for the item. However, subject to funds availability rules, the customer generally has no right to use the funds until the item is paid by the payor. Even if the customer has the right to use the funds under state or federal funds availability rules, the depositary bank has the right to seek a refund from the customer or charge back his account if the item is not finally paid.

funds represented by your paycheck. If you were relying upon these funds to cover checks you have written, you will be upset to know that Bank of America may rightfully dishonor any of these checks.

As a gesture of good will, Bank of America may allow you to draw on uncollected funds. The provisional nature of the settlement does not change just because Bank of America allowed you to draw on the uncollected funds.[165] Whether or not you were allowed to draw upon the provisional settlement, Bank of America may charge back your account or obtain a refund for the amount of any provisional settlement given to you if for any reason Bank of America does not receive a final settlement for the item.[166]

Unless you and Bank of America otherwise agree, you remain the owner of the paycheck. However, despite your continued ownership of the paycheck, Bank of America may nevertheless become a holder in due course of the check. For example, as we discussed in Chapter 2, if Bank of America allows you to draw against the provisional settlement, it obtains a security interest in the paycheck to the extent of the withdrawal.[167] Upon acquiring this security interest, Bank of America becomes a holder in due course of the check if it meets the other requirements for holder-in-due-course status.[168] In this way, Bank of America becomes a holder in due course, while retaining its agency status.

Because you own the item and Bank of America is its holder in due course, Bank of America enjoys the best of both worlds in the event that the item is dishonored. Should you become insolvent after drawing against the uncollected funds, Bank of America may, as a holder in due course, recover from your employer as the drawer and any indorsers even though they may have a claim, claim in recoupment, or defense to the instrument.[169] On the other hand, because you remain the owner of the item, the risk of loss from the insolvency of your employer (the drawer), Crocker Bank (the collecting bank), or Wells Bank (the payor bank) rests upon you.[170] This is because Bank of America has the right to charge back your account if, for any reason, it fails to receive a final settlement for the item.[171] We cover the bank's right of charge-back in the next subsection. Therefore, you, as the owner of the item,

---

165. U.C.C. §4-201, Official Comment 2.
166. U.C.C. §4-214(a).
167. U.C.C. §4-210(a).
168. U.C.C. §4-211.
169. U.C.C. §3-306(a),(b).
170. U.C.C. §4-201, Official Comment 4.
171. U.C.C. §4-214(a). The right of charge-back with respect to checks is limited to some extent by Regulation CC, 12 C.F.R. §229.36(d). U.C.C. §4-201, Official Comment 3.

and not Bank of America, are left to pursue the drawer, prior indorsers, or the insolvent bank.[172]

2. Right of Charge-Back or Refund

Unless otherwise agreed, any settlement that Bank of America as a collecting (depositary) bank makes with you (its customer) is provisional.[173] If, for any reason, Bank of America fails to receive a final settlement for the item, it may revoke the settlement given by it to you, charge back the amount of any credit given for the item to your account, or obtain a refund from you.[174] Bank of America retains its right of charge-back or refund, even if it allowed you to draw upon the uncollected funds,[175] or was required to allow you to use the funds under Regulation CC.[176]

Bank of America retains the right of charge-back or refund if, for whatever the reason, it fails to receive a final settlement for the item.[177] Your paycheck may have been dishonored because your employer had insufficient funds in his account or he may have stopped payment on the check. The payor bank may have gone insolvent. Bank of America's right of charge-back or refund is not even affected by any of these events nor by the failure of the bank itself or any other bank to exercise ordinary care.[178] Even though Bank of America's failure to exercise ordinary care in sending the item for collection caused the dishonor, it still may charge back your account. Of course, Bank of America remains liable to you for damages caused by its failure to exercise ordinary care in collecting the deposited item.[179]

Bank of America's failure to charge back your account or to collect a refund does not affect other rights the bank may have against other parties.[180] For example, Bank of America may, instead of charging back your account,

---

172. In the event that the payor bank is accountable for the item but has not finally settled for the item, the owner/customer has an action against the payor bank. U.C.C. §4-302; U.C.C. §4-201, Official Comment 4. The customer has some special rights in the event that a payor bank becomes insolvent under §4-216, and in the case of checks under Regulation CC §229.39.

173. U.C.C. §4-201(a); U.C.C. §4-201, Official Comment 3.

174. U.C.C. §4-214(a).

175. U.C.C. §4-214(d)(1); U.C.C. §4-201(a).

176. 12 C.F.R. 229.32(b), app. E at 506 (1995).

177. U.C.C. §4-214(a); U.C.C. §4-214, Official Comment 2; U.C.C. §4-214, Official Comment 5.

178. U.C.C. §4-214(d)(2); U.C.C. §4-214, Official Comment 5.

179. U.C.C. §4-214(d)(2); U.C.C. §4-214, Official Comment 6. Where the bank seeks a refund from its customer, the customer can raise the bank's failure to exercise ordinary care as a claim of recoupment.

sue your employer on its drawer's contract Conversely, even if you are discharged on your indorser's contract, Bank of America may charge back your account.

In order to exercise its right of charge-back or refund, Bank of America must:

(1) either
    (a) return the item or
    (b) send notification of the facts if the item is not available for return; and
(2) it must do so
    (a) by its midnight deadline or within a longer reasonable time after it learns the facts[181] or
    (b) if Bank of America is both the depositary bank and the payor bank, by its midnight deadline.[182]

A collecting bank returns an item when the item is sent[183] or delivered to the bank's customer or transferor or pursuant to its instructions.[184] Thus, the item is returned when it is personally delivered to the bank's customer or transferor or when it is sent. Because sending includes mailing the item, an item mailed before the bank's midnight deadline is returned in a timely manner.

The requirements for charge-back or refund are deceptive. Even if Bank of America does not act within the required time, Bank of America nevertheless may revoke its settlement, charge back your account or obtain a refund from you.[185] The only consequence of an untimely act by Bank of America is that it remains liable to you for any loss resulting from the delay.[186] However, you have the burden of proving this loss and it will often be a formidable task. Unless the drawer and all indorsers miraculously become insolvent or leave the jurisdiction in the period between when the item should have been

---

180. U.C.C. §4-214(e).

181. U.C.C. §4-214(a). A bank can learn of the fact of an item's nonpayment when it receives oral notification of the nonpayment. The bank can also learn of the facts by notice of dishonor received from the payor bank or by the notice of nonpayment received pursuant to Regulation CC.

182. U.C.C. §4-214(c). U.C.C. §4-301(a) and (b).

183. It is unclear whether a bank "sends" notice of the facts by orally notifying its customer or transferor of the nonpayment.

184. U.C.C. §4-214(b); U.C.C. §4-214, Official Comment 4.

185. U.C.C. §4-214(a); U.C.C. §4-214, Official Comment 3.

186. U.C.C. §4-214(a); U.C.C. §4-214, Official Comment 3.

returned (or the notice given) and when the item was in fact returned (or the notice given), you will probably be unable to prove a loss.

3.   Duty of Collecting Bank to Use Ordinary Care in Collecting and Returning Items

Both Bank of America and Crocker Bank, as collecting banks, owe a duty of ordinary care to you (their customer) in performing their collection and return duties.[187] A collecting bank must exercise ordinary care when it presents or sends an item for presentment,[188] chooses a route to forward an item for collection, sends notice of dishonor or nonpayment or returns the item, or settles for an item.

Part of Bank of America's duty to exercise ordinary care is its duty to act seasonably. As a collecting bank, Bank of America must take proper action before its midnight deadline following receipt of the item, notice, or settlement.[189] For example, if you deposit your check on Monday, Bank of America must send the check for collection by midnight on Tuesday. Taking action within a longer time considered reasonable may constitute the exercise of ordinary care, but the burden of establishing the timeliness of the action is upon Bank of America.[190] If, for example, your check was mutilated and Bank of America's computer could not read the MICR-encoded line, the fact that it was required to hand-process your check may justify it in missing the midnight deadline to send the check for collection. However, in most cases, where Bank of America fails to perform a routine duty by its midnight deadline, it is unlikely that it will be able to prove that it has exercised ordinary care. Even when the bank delays beyond its midnight deadline, its delay may be excused under §§4-109(a)[191] or (b) or permitted by an agreement[192] extending the time for performance.[193] For example, if a blackout of electricity in the city

187. U.C.C. §4-202(a); U.C.C. §4-201(a); U.C.C. §4-202, Official Comment 1.

188. U.C.C. §4-202, Official Comment 2.

189. U.C.C. §4-202(b); U.C.C. §4-202, Official Comment 3.

190. U.C.C. §4-202(b); U.C.C. §4-202, Official Comment 3.

191. Section 4-109(a) extends the time limits imposed upon a collecting bank that attempts to collect a specific item from a nonbank payor. The limited extension allows the payor to hold the item for additional time before being required to pay or dishonor the item. The right to grant an extension applies only to items that are drawn on or are payable by a non-bank payor. U.C.C. §4-109, Official Comment 1. A collecting bank may not grant an extension to a payor bank for payment of a check or other item. U.C.C. §4-109, Official Comment 1.

192. U.C.C. §4-103(a).

193. U.C.C. §4-202, Official Comment 3.

prevented Bank of America from processing the check by computer, Bank of America's delay in forwarding the check for collection may be excused. We have discussed §4-109(b) in section E of this chapter.

Bank of America is liable only for its own failure to exercise ordinary care. It is not liable for the insolvency, neglect, misconduct, mistake, or default of Crocker Bank or other bank or for loss or destruction of an item in transit or in the possession of others unless it failed to exercise ordinary care in choosing Crocker Bank or the other bank.[194]

a. Authorized Methods of Sending and Presenting Items

Bank of America has the duty to send the check by a reasonably prompt method when collecting your paycheck.[195] In determining whether a method is "reasonably prompt," Bank of America should consider any instructions it received from you, the nature of the item, the number of those items on hand, cost of collection, and the method generally used by it or others to present those items. Bank of America has a self-interest in choosing a reasonably prompt method to collect checks. The check must arrive early enough at Wells Bank so that it can inform Bank of America of the check's dishonor before Bank of America is required to allow you to withdraw the funds. In the case of instruments as to which Regulation CC does not apply, Bank of America may decide that the cost of the method of collection is a more important factor than is its speed. In this case, the question may arise as to whether the method chosen by Bank of America qualifies as a reasonably prompt method. Article 4 authorizes certain methods of collection.[196] These authorized methods include directly mailing, expressing, or messengering the item to the payor bank.[197]

b. Electronic Presentment

Technological advances combined with the great time and expense involved in physically transporting checks and other items from the depositary

---

194. U.C.C. §4-202, Official Comment 4.

195. U.C.C. §4-204(a); U.C.C. §4-204, Official Comment 1.

196. U.C.C. §4-204(b) and (c).

197. U.C.C. §4-204(b)(1); U.C.C. §4-204, Official Comment 2. Regulation CC contains one exception to the right of a bank to present a check directly to the payor bank. If a presenting bank wants to take advantage of the same-day settlement procedure authorized under §229.36(f), the bank may not present the check directly to the paying bank, if the paying bank has designated a different location for presentment pursuant to §229.36(f)(1).12 C.F.R. §229.36, app. E; 57 Fed. Reg. 46975 (Oct. 14, 1992).

F. Duties of Collecting Banks

bank through one or more collecting banks to the payor bank has ushered in a new way of collecting checks. This new way, called "electronic presentment" (or "check truncation"), involves the transferring of the content of the item rather than the item itself. For example, rather than Bank of America transmitting your paycheck to Crocker Bank, which then has to send it to Wells Bank for payment, Bank of America can retain the check[198] and send the demand for payment to Wells Bank electronically.

The only presently available efficient means of electronic presentment is through the information contained on the MICR-encoded line. The MICR-encoded line identifies the payor bank, the account number to be charged, the check's number, and the face amount of the check (usually encoded by the depositary bank). High-speed reader-sorters transmit the MICR line electronically to another computer or switch that, after combining the messages received from several sources, sends the information to the computer serving the payor bank. In development now is a second means of electronic presentment called "imaging technology"[199] which will allow the check's image to be electronically transmitted to the payor bank. When an item is presented electronically, a presentment notice is sent in the place of the item itself.[200] The item is deemed presented when the presentment notice is received.[201]

Bank of America would not unilaterally attempt to present your paycheck to Wells Bank electronically. Too many issues need to be resolved between the banks for either bank to proceed with an electronic presentment without an agreement resolving these potential issues. Therefore, they will have some sort of agreement for electronic presentment of items.[202] An "agreement for elec-

---

The Code fully approves direct sending only in the case of payor banks because of the countrywide acceptability of this practice, the need for speed, the general financial responsibility of banks, and Federal Deposit Insurance protection. U.C.C. §4-204, Official Comment 2. A collecting bank may send an item to a nonbank payor if authorized by its transferor. U.C.C. §4-204(b)(3).

In addition, it may send an item, other than documentary drafts, to a nonbank payor, if authorized by Federal Reserve regulation or operating circular, clearing-house rules, or the like. U.C.C. §4-204(b)(2). Direct sending of items to nonbank payors is limited because of questions as to the drawee's responsibility and the risk in permitting them to handle instruments calling for payment from themselves. U.C.C. §4-204, Official Comment 3.

198. The bank retaining the item then holds the item for a short period of time for return to the drawer upon his request. After a short period of retention, the bank microfilms and then destroys the item.

199. U.C.C. §4-110, Official Comment 1.

200. U.C.C. §4-110(a).

201. U.C.C. §4-110(b); U.C.C. §4-110, Official Comment 1.

202. U.C.C. §4-110, Official Comment 2.

tronic presentment" is an agreement,[203] clearing-house rule, or Federal Reserve regulation[204] or operating circular that provides that presentment of the item may be made by transmission of an image of an item or information describing the item ("presentment notice") rather than by delivery of the item itself.[205] The agreement may provide for procedures governing retention, presentment, payment, dishonor, and other matters concerning items subject to the agreement. The item may be retained by the depositary bank, kept by a customer of the depositary bank, or subsequently sent by the depositary bank to the payor bank.

The electronic presentment notice Bank of America sends to Wells Bank may contain inaccurate information. For example, Bank of America may have indicated that the amount payable was $30, rather than $300. In order to protect Wells Bank from losses caused by an inaccurate electronic presentment, the agreement governing the electronic presentment will probably allocate to Bank of America the loss resulting from the inclusion of the inaccurate information in the presentment notice.[206]

Section 4-209(b) reinforces the obligations of Bank of America by providing that a person who undertakes to retain an item pursuant to an electronic presentment agreement (Bank of America) warrants to subsequent collecting banks and to the payor bank (Wells Bank) or other payor that the retention complies with the check retention agreement.[207] The remedy for breach of this warranty is damages in the amount of the loss suffered, plus expenses and loss of interest.[208]

c. Measure of Damages for Failure to Exercise Ordinary Care

The measure of damages for a collecting bank's failure to exercise ordinary care in handling an item is the amount of the item reduced by an amount

---

203. This may take the form of individual agreements between banks that frequently do business together, U.C.C. §4-103(a); U.C.C. §4-110, Official Comment 2, or other multi-bank agreements. U.C.C. §4-103(b); U.C.C. §4-110, Official Comment 2.

204. Although Regulation CC §229.36(c) authorizes truncation agreements, it forbids truncation agreements from extending the time for return of items or otherwise varying the requirements of Regulation CC without the agreement of all parties interested in the check. U.C.C. §4-110, Official Comment 2.

205. U.C.C. §4-110(a); U.C.C. §4-110, Official Comment 1.

206. U.C.C. §4-110, Official Comment 3.

207. U.C.C. §4-209(b). If a customer of a depositary bank retains the item, the depositary bank also makes the warranty. U.C.C. §4-209(b).

208. U.C.C. §4-209(c).

that could not have been realized by the use of ordinary care.[209] In the absence of bad faith,[210] damages do not include consequential damages.[211] Upon a showing of bad faith, damages may include any other damages the party has suffered as a proximate[212] consequence.[213]

The fact that the customer has the burden of proving the actual loss[214] causes substantial problems for the customer. The customer may have a difficult time proving how much would have been realized for the item had the collecting bank exercised reasonable care. The simplest case for the customer would be if the drawer withdrew the funds after a reasonable time for presentment had expired but prior to the time that the check was ultimately presented. In this case, had the collecting bank presented the check within a reasonable time, the check would have been paid. However, because of its delay, no funds remained. But, if the funds were withdrawn during the reasonable time allowed for the bank to present the check, the customer cannot prove that he suffered any loss by virtue of the delay.

The customer may also successfully establish a loss if he proves that he has parted with money or property after the time that notice of dishonor should have been received. For example, assume that Customer agreed to sell to Buyer a diamond ring. Although Buyer pays by check, Customer and Buyer agree that Customer does not have to deliver the diamond ring until the check clears. After two weeks, Customer noticing that his bank had taken the hold off his account for the amount of the check (and thus assuming that the check had been paid), sends the diamond ring to Buyer. In reality, his bank had misplaced the check and did not forward the check for collection for three weeks. Upon presentment, the check was dishonored. Buyer has vanished. Customer has suffered a loss in the amount of the diamond ring's value on account of his bank's negligence in collecting the check.

---

209. U.C.C. §4-103(e); U.C.C. §4-103, Official Comment 6.

210. Although the Code provides no definition of bad faith, the Official Comments indicate that bad faith is the absence of good faith as defined in §3-103(a)(4). U.C.C. §4-103, Official Comment 6.

211. U.C.C. §4-103 (e).

212. "Proximateness" is to be tested by the ordinary rules in comparable cases; that is, the usual proximate cause test employed by the court in a common law negligence case. U.C.C. §4-103, Official Comment 6.

213. U.C.C. §4-103(e).

214. U.C.C. §4-103, Official Comment 6.

4.   *Duties of Depositary Bank under Regulation CC*

In addition to those duties imposed by Article 4, Regulation CC also imposes duties upon depositary banks in the collection of checks. Under the new check collection procedure adopted by Regulation CC, if your paycheck was returned unpaid by Wells Bank, it would treat the dishonored check as a check payable to Wells Bank drawn upon Bank of America (your depositary bank) by you (the person for whom Bank of America is collecting the check).

What is the reason for this fiction? Each bank along the collection path has already received a settlement for the check. When Bank of America sent the check to Crocker Bank, Crocker Bank settled for the check by paying Bank of America. On the day of presentment, Wells Bank paid Crocker Bank. In order to free Wells Bank to directly return the check to Bank of America rather than requiring it to send the check back to Crocker Bank, each of these settlements in the forward collection process is regarded as final.[215] To allow Wells Bank to recover its payment, the returned check is now treated as a check drawn by you upon Bank of America because ultimately it is you (or if you are not solvent, Bank of America) who must repay the money. To obtain this money, Wells Bank is treated as the payee of the imaginary check. Everyone is made whole after you have paid the check upon Bank of America charging back your account. You now have the returned check so that you can sue your employer, and Wells Bank has its money back.

Just as Wells Bank was required to settle with Crocker Bank on the day of presentment with funds that are usable on that day, Bank of America must settle with Wells Bank (or if the check is returned through a returning bank, the returning bank) in funds usable on the day that the check is received.[216] Bank of America fulfills this duty by settling for the check prior to the close of business on the banking day of receipt by one of the following means: a debit to its account at the returning or payor bank, cash, wire transfer, or another form of payment acceptable to Wells Bank (or the returning bank). As in the case of settlements in the forward collection process, the settlement by Bank of America is deemed to be final when made.[217]

There is another duty that Regulation CC imposes upon Bank of America as a depositary bank. Because the back of a check gets quite messy by the time that the check reaches the paying bank, it is sometimes very difficult for the paying bank to determine to which bank the dishonored check must be

---

215. 12 C.F.R. §229.36(d).
216. 12 C.F.R. §229.32(b).
217. 12 C.F.R. §229.32.

returned. Appendix D to Regulation CC[218] sets out requirements that depositary banks must meet in the form of permissible endorsements, the information that can be contained in an endorsement, and in the permissible location and ink color of indorsements.[219] These requirements ensure that the paying bank will be able to determine the identity of the depositary bank.

5. Duties of Returning Bank under Regulation CC

The role of returning bank was made necessary by the new procedure adopted by Regulation CC by which unpaid checks are returned from the payor bank to the depositary bank. As we discussed in the previous section, Crocker Bank's settlement for the check (as subsequent collecting bank) with Bank of America (as depositary bank) is final.[220] Similarly Wells Bank's settlement (as payor bank) with Crocker Bank was also final. Since Crocker Bank is now made whole, there is no need for the check to be returned through it. Wells Bank is free to choose a return path that does not involve Crocker Bank.

Regulation CC gives Wells Bank two options in determining how it will return the check to Bank of America for refund of the settlement Wells Bank gave to Crocker Bank.[221] Wells Bank can either return the check directly to Bank of America (the depositary bank) or it can send the check to another bank, called a "returning bank," for the purpose of returning the check to Bank of America. Although no bank is obligated to become a returning bank, it may engage in the service of returning checks because of the fees that are generated from such service.[222] Federal Reserve Banks have been authorized by the Federal Reserve Board to perform services as returning banks.

Let us assume that Wells Bank chooses Interstate Bank to act as the returning bank. In essence, Interstate Bank as the returning bank is acting as a collecting bank for the purpose of collecting a check drawn upon Bank of America, the depositary bank, by you. As a result, Interstate Bank must settle with Wells Bank by the same means that it would settle for a check received for forward collection drawn upon Bank of America.[223] As in the forward collec-

---

218. Information that must be contained includes the nine-digit routing number of the depositary bank, its name and location, and the indorsement date. There are limits on the indorsements of collecting and returning banks to ensure that the depositary bank's indorsement remains clear. 12 C.F.R. §229.35(a), app. D.

219. 12 C.F.R. §229.35(a).

220. 12 C.F.R. §229.36(d).

221. 12 C.F.R. §229.31(c), app. E at 504 (1995).

222. 12 C.F.R. §229.31(d).

223. 12 C.F.R. §229.31(c).

tion process, there can be more than one returning bank. In this event, each returning bank settles with the bank from which it received the check.

Just like the paying bank, Interstate Bank, as the returning bank, must return the item in an "expeditious manner."[224] In complying with this duty, the returning bank has the same options and duties as the paying bank. We discussed these duties in section E of this chapter. And like Wells Bank, Interstate Bank may return the check either directly to Bank of America or through another returning bank.[225] And like Wells Bank, Interstate Bank may either meet the forward collection test[226] or the two-day/four-day test.[227] There are only a couple of points that should be made regarding Interstate Bank's compliance with these tests. Under the forward collection test, Interstate Bank generally must process the check overnight.[228] However, unlike the paying bank, Interstate Bank (as a returning bank) is given an additional business day to return the check if it qualifies the check.[229] Qualifying a check means that Interstate Bank MICR encodes certain information on the check enabling the check to be processed by Bank of America or other returning banks by computer.[230]

In meeting the two-day/four-day test, the time within which Interstate Bank must act is measured beginning from the time when the check was presented to Wells Bank. This means that if Wells Bank must return the check so that it would normally be received by Bank of America by 4:00 P.M. on Tuesday, Interstate Bank also would have to return the check so that it would normally be received by Bank of America by 4:00 P.M. on Tuesday. Measuring the time within which Interstate Bank must act from the time from which the check was presented to Wells Bank may cause problems for Interstate Bank. The major problem is that Interstate Bank does not know whether Wells Bank has forwarded the check to it in a timely manner. If Wells Bank has delayed in forwarding the check to Interstate Bank, Interstate Bank may be unable to comply with the applicable deadline. To protect Interstate Bank against this

224. 12 C.F.R. §229.31(a).
225. 12 C.F.R. §229.31(a), app. E at 504 (1995).
226. 12 C.F.R. §229.31(a)(2).
227. 12 C.F.R. §229.31(a)(1).
228. 12 C.F.R. §229.31(a)(2). It may, though, establish cutoff hours for returns different than for forward collections, but the cutoff hour can be no earlier than 2:00 P.M. 12 C.F.R. §229.31(a)(2)(iii). If the check is received after the cutoff hour, it is treated as having been received the next day. As a result, the bank will have an additional night to process the check.
229. 12 C.F.R. §229.31(a)(2)(iii). Since qualifying a check allows for its swifter return, the returning bank is encouraged to do so by being allowed this additional day.
230. However, the returning bank takes a risk in qualifying a check in that it is liable for any damage caused by a negligent mistake in its encoding of the check. 12 C.F.R. §229.31(a), app. E at 503 (1995).

potential source of undeserved liability, Wells Bank will probably agree to indemnify Interstate Bank for any loss caused by a delay for which Wells Bank was responsible.

Interstate Bank (as returning bank) gives the same warranties to subsequent returning banks, to Bank of America, and to you (the owner of the check) as did Wells Bank. The most important of these warranties is that Wells Bank (as paying bank) has returned the check by its midnight deadline (or any earlier time under the Code, Regulation J, or Regulation CC).[231]

Just like a paying bank, a returning bank is only liable for failing to return a check in an expeditious manner if its failure to do so was the result of its failure to exercise ordinary care or to act in good faith.[232] A returning bank is liable for the same measures of damages as is a paying bank. The measure of damages for breach of the bank's duty of ordinary care is the amount of the check less the amount of loss that would have been incurred even if ordinary care had been used. The bank is liable for any additional damages proximately caused when it fails to act in good faith. Under the doctrine of comparative negligence,[233] the liability of a returning bank is diminished in proportion to the amount of negligence or bad faith attributable to the plaintiff.

6.   *Encoding Warranties*

When your paycheck is deposited in your account at Bank of America, Bank of America will encode the face amount of the check on the MICR line.[234] Bank of America may by mistake wrongly encode this information. Your paycheck drawn in the amount of $1,000 may be overencoded in the amount of

---

231. A returning bank also warrants that it is authorized to return the check, the check has not been materially altered, and in the case of a notice in lieu of return, the original check has not been and will not be returned. 12 C.F.R. §229.34(a). Damages for breach of warranty, in addition to the consideration received by the returning bank, may include finance charges and expenses related to the returned check. 12 C.F.R. §229.34(d).

Courts are given the discretion to award attorney's fees to a prevailing plaintiff. This authorization is found in the Commentary to §229.34(d), which adopts the warranty measure of damages found in U.C.C. §4-207(3). See 12 C.F.R. §229.34(d), app. E at 508 (1995).

232. 12 C.F.R. §229.38(a). A delay by a returning bank may be excused under §229.38(e) if the delay is caused by emergency conditions or other unforeseen circumstances. 12 C.F.R. §229.38(e). This excuse is identical to the excuse provision of §4-109.

233. 12 C.F.R. §229.38(c).

234. Actually some larger banks will encode items for correspondents who do not have encoding machinery. Also sometimes intermediary banks will do the encoding. A customer of a bank that is a payee on a large volume of checks may be equipped to encode the checks itself. U.C.C. §4-209, Official Comment 1. For a discussion of microencoding, see Chapter 5A.

$10,000. Conversely, your paycheck may be underencoded in the amount of $100. When the check reaches Wells Bank (the payor bank) Wells Bank's computer will treat the check as being payable in the encoded amount rather than in the amount in which the check was actually drawn.

If your paycheck was overencoded in the amount of $10,000, Wells Bank's computer will automatically treat the check as being drawn in the overencoded amount of $10,000. Wells Bank, however, can debit your employer's account only for $1,000, the amount for which the check was drawn.[235] If your paycheck is underencoded in the amount of $100, the check will be paid in that amount. Bank of America can recover the remaining $900 from Wells Bank because Wells Bank failed to return the check by its midnight deadline and is therefore accountable for the check under §4-302(a).[236] Since your employer wrote the check for $1,000, Wells Bank may debit its account for the remaining $900.[237] However, if your employer's account does not contain sufficient funds, Wells Bank will suffer a loss on account of the erroneous underencoding of the check.

In order to protect Wells Bank and subsequent collecting banks, any person who encodes information on an item warrants to any subsequent collecting bank and to the payor bank or other payor that the information is correctly encoded.[238] Although under Article 4, no warranty is made by any collecting banks that take the item after the bank that encoded the item,[239] under Regulation CC any bank that handles a check or a returned check warrants that the information encoded after issue in magnetic ink on the check or returned check is correct.[240]

Under Article 4, the person misencoding an item is liable to any person taking the item in good faith for the loss suffered, plus expenses and loss of interest incurred.[241] Thus, when Bank of America overencodes your check, Wells Bank has the right to recover from Bank of America the overencoded amount ($10,000) less the amount for which the check was properly payable

235. U.C.C. §4-209, Official Comment 2.
236. U.C.C. §4-302(a).
237. U.C.C. §4-209, Official Comment 2.
238. U.C.C. §4-209(a). If a customer of the depositary bank encodes the item, the depositary bank also makes this warranty. U.C.C. §4-209(a).
239. U.C.C. §4-209, Official Comment 1.
240. 12 C.F.R. §229.34(c)(3); 57 Fed. Reg. 46966 (Oct. 14, 1992).
241. U.C.C. §4-209(c). Damages for breach of the encoding warranty under Regulation CC cannot exceed the consideration received by the bank plus interest compensation and expenses relating to the check or returned check, if any. 12 C.F.R. §229.34(d); 57 Fed. Reg. 46972 (Oct. 14, 1992).

($1,000), in other words $9,000.[242] If the item was dishonored because it was overencoded, Bank of America is liable to Wells Bank for any damages for which Wells Bank is liable to its customer for wrongful dishonor.

If an item is underencoded, Bank of America is liable to Wells Bank in the amount that Wells Bank has not recovered from its customer. If the drawer's account does not contain sufficient funds, Wells Bank may recover the deficit from Bank of America without first pursuing your employer (the drawer).[243] Bank of America is then subrogated to Wells Bank's rights against your employer.

7. Regulation CC: Warranty of Settlement Amount

Crocker Bank will usually present to Wells Bank more than one check at a time. The checks will be presented in bulk and a single settlement amount will be demanded for all of the checks combined. Because Wells Bank (as payor bank) must settle for checks without having adequate time to verify the information transmitted to it by Crocker Bank, Crocker Bank makes a warranty under Regulation CC as to the accuracy of the settlement amount demanded by Crocker Bank.[244]

Damages for breach of this warranty cannot exceed the consideration received by Crocker Bank plus interest and expenses, if any.[245] A similar warranty is given by the paying and returning banks on returned checks.[246]

G. FUNDS AVAILABILITY UNDER REGULATION CC

We discussed earlier in this chapter how, prior to the promulgation of Regulation CC, a depositary bank may not discover for weeks whether a check

242. U.C.C. §4-209, Official Comment 2.
243. U.C.C. §4-209(a); U.C.C. §4-209, Official Comment 2.
244. 12 C.F.R. §229.34 (c).
245. 12 C.F.R. §229.34(d); 57 Fed. Reg. 46972 (Oct. 14, 1992).
246. This warranty is made by any bank returning a check. Each bank that transfers one or more checks or returned checks to a collecting, returning, or depositary bank and in return receives a settlement or other consideration, warrants to the transferee bank that the accompanying information, if any, accurately indicates the total amount of the checks or the returned checks transferred. 12 C.F.R. §229.34(c)(2); 57 Fed. Reg. 46972 (Oct. 14, 1992).

has been paid or dishonored. Thus, had your paycheck been drawn upon a bank located in another state, Bank of America may not even learn that the check was dishonored until several weeks later. To protect itself from you withdrawing the funds and your paycheck being subsequently dishonored, Bank of America might impose a hold of ten to fifteen business days upon your account for the amount of the check. This means that you would have no right to use the funds represented by your paycheck for two to three weeks. At the same time, if your paycheck is actually paid earlier, Bank of America's account at the Federal Reserve Bank or at the payor bank would be credited and accruing interest.

These extensive holds and the float (interest made by Bank of America with the corresponding loss of interest to you) generated such a serious problem that Congress enacted the Expedited Funds Availability Act ("EFAA"). Regulation CC was promulgated by the Federal Reserve Board pursuant to the authority delegated to it by Congress in the EFAA. We have already examined how Regulation CC has sped up the return of unpaid checks by requiring payor banks to expeditiously return unpaid checks and to give prompt notice of the dishonor of large checks. By these means, depositary banks are assured of quicker notice of a check's dishonor. We will now examine the mandatory availability schedules adopted by Regulation CC, which require depositary banks to allow customers use of deposited funds within specified times.

Congress did not leave the mandatory availability schedules for the Federal Reserve Board to adopt by regulation but, instead, carved the schedules in granite by writing them into the EFAA itself. Regulation CC (in subpart B) merely fleshes out the schedules provided in the EFAA. Under Regulation CC, depositary banks must allow their customers the right to withdraw funds within reasonable time periods corresponding with the likely time within which the bank would obtain notice of the item's nonpayment.[247] Regulation CC also contains provisions requiring a depositary bank to disclose its availability policies to its depositors.

1. Institutions Bound to Comply with the Mandatory Availability Schedule

Not all institutions are required to comply with subpart B of Regulation CC. Only when the institution is a "bank" for subpart B purposes and when the

247. The EFAA provisions can be preempted by state law only to the extent that the state law allows quicker availability. 12 U.S.C. §4007; 12 C.F.R. §229.20(a). In order to achieve uniformity, the state law can only preempt Regulation CC if the state law was adopted by September 1, 1989. 12 C.F.R. §229.20(a).

funds are deposited to an "account" must the institution comply with the requirements of subpart B. For subpart B purposes, "bank" is defined broadly to include almost every type of depositary institution regulated by federal law, including commercial banks, savings banks, savings and loan associations, credit unions, and United States branches of foreign banks.[248] Covered accounts[249] include virtually any account at a bank from which the account holder is permitted to make transfers or withdrawals. The transfer or withdrawal may be made by means of negotiable or transferable instruments, payment orders of withdrawal, telephone or electronic transfers of funds to third persons by ATM, remote service unit, other electronic device, or debit card.[250]

2. *Mandatory Funds Availability Schedule: Introduction*

Regulation CC effectively eliminates a depositary bank's interest-free use of the depositor's funds by two means. First, Regulation CC adopted the mandatory availability schedule, which provides a deadline by which a bank must make funds available to its depositor. Secondly, depositary banks are required to pay interest on interestbearing accounts no later than the business day on which the bank receives credit for the funds from its transferee bank.[251] As a consequence, from the moment Bank of America receives a settlement for the check from Crocker Bank, Bank of America must begin paying interest to you on your interestbearing account. Of course, there is no duty to pay interest on a noninterestbearing account.

Certain points are helpful to keep in mind. The first is that the mandatory availability schedule provides only the maximum time within which funds must be made available. Bank of America may allow you immediate use of the funds deposited even though it has the right to delay availability of the funds under the mandatory availability schedule. [252] The second point is that Bank

---

248. 12 C.F.R. §229.2(e)

249. "Account" further encompasses NOW accounts, share accounts in credit unions, and savings accounts in which funds are automatically transferred to cover overdrafts. Subpart B covers both consumer and business accounts.

Note, however, that "account" excludes interbank accounts, pure savings accounts, money market accounts, United States Treasury accounts, and accounts located in an office of a bank outside of the United States. 12 C.F.R. §229.2(a); 12 C.F.R. §229.2(a), app. E at 466 (1995).

250. 12 C.F.R. §229.2(a).

251. 12 C.F.R. §229.14(a). The bank is allowed to rely upon standard schedules from Federal Reserve banks, Federal Home banks, or correspondent banks as to typical availability.

252. 12 C.F.R. §229.19(c), app. E at 493 (1995).

of America's obligation to make funds available to you is subject to its right to charge back your account in the event that the check is returned unpaid. Thus, even though you have use of the funds, the money is not necessarily yours. If your paycheck is dishonored, Bank of America can charge back your account and, if your account does not contain sufficient funds, it can require you to refund the money. The third point is that your right to withdraw funds pursuant to the mandatory availability schedule is a matter of right. Bank of America may not charge you a fee for allowing you to withdraw the funds even if Bank of America has not yet received the funds itself.

Because the time within which funds must be made available depends on the day on which the funds were deposited, it is important to understand one of the more important rules for determining on which day funds have been deposited.[253] This rule is that if a deposit is made on a day that is not a banking day for the bank or is received after the bank's cut-off hour,[254] the deposit is considered to have been made on the next banking day.[255] For example, if Bank of America has established a 3:00 P.M. cut-off hour, a deposit made at 4:00 P.M. on Friday will be considered to have been deposited on Monday. Because it is made after the bank's cutoff hour, the deposit is considered to have been made the next banking day. Because neither Saturday nor Sunday are banking days for Bank of America, the next banking day is Monday. Under Regulation CC, neither Saturday nor Sunday are banking days because neither day is a business day. Only a business day can be a banking day for Regulation CC purposes. A "business day" is any day other than a Saturday, Sunday, or holiday.[256] A "banking day" is any *business day* on which an office of a bank is open to the public for substantially all of its banking functions.[257]

a.   Mandatory Availability Schedule: Next-Day Availability

The time by which funds must be made available to a depositor by the depositary bank under the mandatory availability schedule depends upon two

---

253. 12 C.F.R. §229.19(a). Another important rule is that when funds must be made available for withdrawal on a business day, the funds must be available for withdrawal at the start of business on that day. 12 C.F.R. §229.19(b). The start of the business day is the later of 9:00 A.M. or the time teller facilities, including ATMs, are available for customer withdrawals. The bank can set 9:00 A.M. for ATM withdrawals if it likes.

254. The cutoff hour must be 2 P.M. or later for teller facilities and noon or later for ATMs or other off-premise facilities. 12 C.F.R. §229.19(a)(5)(ii).

255. 12 C.F.R. §229.19(a)(5).

256. 12 C.F.R. §229.2(g).

257. 12 C.F.R. §229.2(f).

factors: (1) the speed with which the check or other deposit will more than likely be paid; and (2) the likelihood that the check or other deposit will be paid rather than dishonored.

Some types of deposits are so likely to be paid that the depositary bank is required to allow the depositor "next-day availability" of the funds.[258] This means that the funds must be made available at the start of business on the business day after the banking day on which the deposit was made. Funds deposited on Tuesday must be made available on Wednesday (the next business day). Wednesday need not be a banking day for the depositary bank as long as it is a business day.

The following types of deposits must be given next-day availability:

1. cash deposits made directly to a teller;[259]
2. deposits by electronic payment, including both wire transfers and ACH credit transfers;[260]
3. deposit of a United States Treasury check in the account of the payee;[261]
4. deposit of a United States Postal Service money order, Federal Reserve Bank check, or a Federal Home Loan Bank check in person to a teller in the account of the payee;[262]

258. 12 C.F.R. §229.10.

259. 12 C.F.R. §229.10(a)(1). In contrast, a cash deposit made to a proprietary ATM, night depository, or by mail need not be made available until the second business day after the banking day of deposit. 12 C.F.R. §229.10(a)(2). Deposits made to a nonproprietary ATM whether in cash or by check that otherwise would be entitled to next-day or second-day availability are available by the fifth business day after the banking day of receipt. 12 C.F.R. §229.12(f). The provisions of §229.10(c)(1)(vii) requiring the depositary bank to make up to $100 available on the next business day do not apply. 57 Fed. Reg. 36601 (August 14, 1992).

However, §4-215 (f), which requires next-day availability for non-teller cash deposits, pre-empts second-day availability provided under subpart B. 12 C.F.R. §229.20(a). The Federal Reserve Board has made a formal preemption rule that §4-213(5) makes deposits not in person available on the next day. 53 Fed. Reg. 32,356. Although §4-215(f) makes itself subject to applicable law stating a time of availability, the Federal Reserve Board has held that former §4-213(5), and presumably its successor §4-215(f), pre-empts Regulation CC, so the fact that §4-215(f) is subject to Regulation CC should have no effect.

260. 12 C.F.R. §229.10(b); "Automated Clearinghouse" is defined in 12 C.F.R. §229.2(b) as "a facility that processes debit and credit transfers under rules established by a Federal Reserve Bank operating circular on automated clearinghouse items or under rules of an automated clearinghouse association."

261. 12 C.F.R. §229.10(c)(1)(i). The payee deposit requirement reduces the risk of a forged indorsement. 12 C.F.R. §229.10(c), app. E at 475 (1995).

262. 12 C.F.R. §229.10(c)(ii)–(iii). Funds representing deposits from these types of checks are entitled to second-day availability if the check is not deposited in person to a teller. 12 C.F.R. §229.10(c)(2).

5. deposit of a state or local government check in person to a teller, in the account of the payee in a depositary bank located in same state as the unit issuing the check, and with a special deposit slip[263] or special envelope indicating the type of deposit;[264]
6. deposit of cashier's checks, certified checks, and tellers' checks[265] in person, to the account of the payee, and with a special deposit slip or envelope;[266] and
7. deposits of on-us checks[267] in a branch of a bank in the same state or processing region as the paying branch.[268]

Furthermore, one hundred dollars of the aggregate amount of all checks deposited (not counting those that are otherwise entitled to next-day availability) in any one banking day must be given next-day availability.[269] The $100 is in addition to the amount available under other next-day availability rules.[270] For example, when there is a $1,000 deposit of a cashier's check and $500 deposit of ordinary checks, the bank must make $1,100 available on the next business day.

263. Special deposit slips are required in order for a customer to obtain next-day availability of funds because state and local government checks do not have special MICR numbers that inform the depositary bank's computer that next-day availability is required. Under 12 C.F.R. §229.10(c)(3)(ii), banks must either provide these special deposit slips to customers or inform customers of how to obtain them.

264. 12 C.F.R. §229.10(c)(1)(iv). There is second-day availability where all of the other conditions are met but where the check is not deposited in person to a teller. 12 C.F.R. §229.10(c)(2).

265. Under 12 C.F.R. §229.2(i), cashier's checks are only those used for remittance purposes—they do not include expense checks used by banks to pay their own debts. Certified checks are defined in 12 C.F.R. §229.2(j) the same as under the Code. Teller's checks are defined in 12 C.F.R. §229.2(gg) as a check drawn by a bank on another bank or payable through or at a bank.

266. 12 C.F.R. §229.10(c)(1)(v). Where the other conditions are met, but the check is not deposited in person to a teller, the check is entitled to second-day availability. 12 C.F.R. §229.10(c)(2).

267. 12 C.F.R. §229.10(c)(1)(vi). Deposits made at off-premises ATMs or remote depositaries are not deemed deposits made at a branch of a bank and, therefore, are not entitled to next-day availability.

268. Check processing region is defined in 12 C.F.R. §229.2(m) as "the geographical area served by an office of a Federal Reserve bank for purposes of its check processing activities."

269. 12 C.F.R. §229.10(c)(1)(vii). The $100 availability rule does not apply to checks deposited at nonproprietary ATMs. 12 C.F.R. §229.10(c)(1)(vii) app. E at 476 (1995).

270. 12 C.F.R. §229.10, app. E at 476 (1995).

b. Mandatory Availability Schedule: Second-Day and Fifth-Day Availability

When a check is not entitled to next-day availability, it is entitled to availability either on the second or fifth business day after its deposit depending upon whether the check is a local or nonlocal check. We discussed in section E the difference between local and nonlocal checks.

Funds from a deposit of a local check must be made available on the second business day following the banking day of deposit.[271] For example, assume that Wells Bank and Bank of America are both located in the same check processing region because both banks are in the Southern California area. If you deposit your paycheck in your account at Bank of America on Thursday, Bank of America must make the funds available to you at the beginning of business on the following Monday.[272]

Funds from a deposit of a nonlocal check must be made available on the fifth business day after the banking day of deposit.[273] For example, if Wells Bank was located in Portland while Bank of America was located in Los Angeles, your paycheck would be a nonlocal check. If you deposited your paycheck on Tuesday, Bank of America would have to make the funds available for withdrawal on the following Tuesday.[274] Appendix B-2 to Regulation CC contains specific exceptions requiring earlier availability for certain nonlocal checks whose collection would occur, in general, earlier than as provided for under the mandatory availability schedule.[275]

---

271. 12 C.F.R. §229.12(b)(1).

272. 12 C.F.R. §229.12(b), app. E at 478 (1995). Second-day availability applies to some checks that do not comply with requirements for next-day availability: (1) any treasury check not deposited in an account of the payee. 12 C.F.R. §229.12(b)(2); (2) any United States Postal Service money order not deposited in an account of the payee. 12 C.F.R. §229.12(b)(3); and (3) local Federal Reserve Bank checks, Federal Home Bank checks, state or local government checks, and cashier's, certified, or teller's checks. 12 C.F.R. §229.12(b)(4).

273. 12 C.F.R. §229.12(c)(1)(i). Funds also must be made available on the fifth business day following the banking day of receipt for nonlocal Federal Reserve Bank checks, Federal Home Bank checks, state or local government checks, and cashier's, certified, or teller's checks that do not otherwise qualify for next-day availability. 12 C.F.R. §229.12(c)(1)(ii). Deposits made to a nonproprietary ATM whether in cash or by check that otherwise would be entitled to next-day or second-day availability must be made available by the fifth business day after the banking day of receipt. 12 C.F.R. §229.12(f). The provisions of §229.10(c)(1)(vii) requiring the depositary bank to make up to $100 available on the next business day do not apply. 57 Fed. Reg. 36601 (Aug. 14, 1992).

274. 12 C.F.R. §229.12(c), app. E at 479 (1995).

275. 12 C.F.R. §229.12(c)(2).

3.   *Extensions of Mandatory Availability Schedule*

a.   Extension for Cash Withdrawal

The availability schedules are a little deceptive in that there are provisions allowing the depositary bank to extend the time within which funds must be made available.[276] The most important provision is that the time within which funds must be made available may be extended for one business day for funds represented by deposited checks if the depositor attempts to withdraw the funds in cash or by similar means.[277]

For example, let us assume that your paycheck, a local check, was deposited on Thursday. Under the mandatory availability schedule, Bank of America must allow you to withdraw the funds by Monday. However, Bank of America may refuse to allow you to withdraw the funds until Tuesday if you attempt to withdraw the funds in cash, by an ATM or by a bank check. If this extension is invoked with regard to a local check, Bank of America must still make $400 of the check available by 5:00 P.M. on the second business day (on Monday), in addition to the required $100 of the check that must be given next-day availability (on Friday).[278] In contrast, if a check you drew on your account (which depends for its payment upon credit being given for your paycheck) was presented on Monday, Bank of America must honor the check.

The distinction between cash or cash-like withdrawals and drawing against the account by check makes sense. Assume that you deposit your local paycheck in Bank of America on Tuesday. According to the mandatory availability schedule, the funds must be available on your local paycheck at the opening of business on Thursday. But, it is unlikely that Chase Bank will hear of the nonpayment of your local paycheck until at least Thursday afternoon. If you could withdraw the funds in cash or similar means on Thursday morning, Bank of America would lose the opportunity to hear of the nonpayment before it is required to make the funds available. But if the question is whether Bank of America can dishonor a check that was drawn on it by you that arrives on Thursday morning, a different situation is presented. Since Bank of America does not need to decide whether or not to honor the check until

---

276. One provision for an extension is that the period may be extended one business day for deposits in depositary banks located in Alaska, Hawaii, Puerto Rico, and the Virgin Islands where the paying bank is not located in same state as the depositary bank. This does not apply to checks drawn on banks in these states or territories and deposited in the continental United States. 12 C.F.R. §229.12(e).

277. Similar means include electronic payment, cashier's, teller's, or certified check or other irrevocable commitment to pay. 12 C.F.R. §229.12(d).

278. 12 C.F.R. §229.12(d).

Friday, it has the opportunity to learn of the dishonor before it pays your check.[279]

b. Other Extensions

There are situations in which a depository bank would be exposed to an unreasonably high risk of loss if it were required to make funds available according to the mandatory availability schedule. To protect depository banks against undue risks of loss, Regulation CC provides several exceptions under which a depository bank may extend the time for the availability of funds.[280]

New Account Exception. The first exception is for new accounts.[281] Why is there a greater risk to the bank in the case of a new account? Simply because the bank does not know its customer. Picture Freddy Fraud setting up new bank accounts at many local banks under assumed names. Freddy deposits phony checks in these accounts in the hope that some of these banks will be forced under the mandatory availability schedule to allow Freddy to draw upon the funds before the bank learns that the check has not been paid. By allowing these banks to put an extended hold on these funds, they are assured of learning of the dishonor before Freddy withdraws the funds.

An account is new during its first 30 days if the customer did not have another account at the bank for at least 30 days prior to the opening of the account.[282] For example, when you first opened your account at Bank of America, the new account exception would apply for the first 30 days. However, if you already had a savings account at Bank of America for 30 days, the new account exception would not apply if you thereafter opened a checking account at the same bank. Under this exception, Bank of America may extend the hold on both local and nonlocal checks.[283] Although no maximum time is specified within which funds must be made available,[284] the bank is prohibited from extending the hold beyond a reasonable period of time.

279. 12 C.F.R. §229.12(d), app. E at 479 (1995).
280. 12 C.F.R. §229.13, app. E at 479-480 (1995).
281. 12 C.F.R. §229.13(a). The new account exception does not apply to cash and electronic payment deposits entitled to next-day availability. Furthermore, the first $5,000 of funds deposited on any one banking day must be made available according to the next-day availability rules where the customer deposits Treasury checks, United States Postal Service money orders, Federal Reserve Bank and Federal Home Loan Bank checks, state and government checks, and cashier's, certified, teller's, or traveler's checks. 12 C.F.R. §229.13(a)(ii). The remaining funds must be given availability no later than the ninth business day following the banking day of the deposit. 12 C.F.R. §229.13(a)(ii).
282. 12 C.F.R. §229.13(a)(2).
283. 12 C.F.R. §229.13(a), app. E. at 480-481 (1995).
284. 12 C.F.R. §229.13(a), app. E. at 480-481 (1995).

Large Deposit Exception.   The second exception is for large deposits.[285] The bank may extend the hold for local and nonlocal checks to the extent that the aggregate deposit on any banking day is more than $5,000. The mandatory availability schedule still applies to the first $5,000 of deposits on that day.[286] The $100 availability rule is also applicable. If you deposited a $10,000 Treasury check, and $10,000 in local checks on Monday, Bank of America must make the entire $10,000 Treasury check and $100 of the local checks available on Tuesday. Four thousand, nine hundred dollars of the funds from the local checks must be made available on Wednesday, and the remaining $5,000 can be deferred under this exception.

Returned and Redeposited Check Exception.   The third exception is for previously returned and redeposited checks.[287] This exception is based upon the premise that when a check has been dishonored once, there is a good chance that it will be dishonored again.

Repeatedly Overdrawn Exception.   The fourth exception applies whenever any account or combination of accounts of a single customer has been repeatedly overdrawn.[288] A customer who repeatedly overdraws his account is not a good credit risk. If a check is returned unpaid after he is allowed to withdraw the funds, the bank may not be able to recover the funds from him. Allowing the bank to extend the hold guarantees that the check will be paid before the customer can withdraw the funds.

Reasonable Cause to Doubt Collectibility Exception.   The fifth excep-

---

285. 12 C.F.R. §229.13(b). The exception does not apply to cash and electronic payment deposits. 57 Fed. Reg. 36593-4 (Aug. 14, 1992).

286. The exception applies even though the deposit is made to more than one account. 12 C.F.R. §229.13(b), app. E at 481 (1995).

287. 12 C.F.R. §229.13(c). The exception does not apply to cash or electronic payments. 57 Fed. Reg. 36593-4 (Aug. 14, 1992). The $100 availability rule applies. 12 C.F.R. §229.13(c), app. E. at 481 (1995). It also does not apply to checks returned due to a missing indorsement or postdating.

288. 12 C.F.R. §229.13(d). An account is repeatedly overdrawn if either (1) on six or more banking days within a six-month period, the balance was or would have been negative had checks been paid, 12 C.F.R. §229.13(d)(1) or (2) on two or more banking days within the six-month period, the balance was or would have been $5,000 or more overdrawn. 12 C.F.R. §229.13(d)(2). The days may be separate or consecutive. 12 C.F.R. §229.13(d), app. E at 481-482 (1995).

The exception does not apply where the depositor has an overdraft credit line. 12 C.F.R. §229.13(d), app. E at 481-482 (1995). The exception also does not apply to cash or electronic payments. 57 Fed. Reg. 36593-4 (Aug. 14, 1992) The $100 availability rule does not apply. 57 Fed. Reg. 36598 (Aug. 14, 1992).

tion applies where the bank has reasonable cause to doubt collectibility of a check.[289] For example, where the depositary bank receives notice from the paying bank that the check is being returned, the depositary bank should not be forced to allow the depositor to withdraw funds as to which the bank already knows that it has the right to recover.[290]

Emergency Condition Exception. The sixth exception is applicable in emergency conditions where there is an interruption of communications or computer or other equipment facilities, suspension of payments by another bank, war or other emergency conditions beyond the control of the depositary bank.[291] The exception applies only so long as the bank exercises such diligence as the circumstances require. Funds must be made available a reasonable time after the emergency ceases to exist or according to the mandatory availabiility schedule, whichever is later.[292]

Requirement of Notice. Because the depositor may be relying upon the mandatory availability schedule, the depositary bank must give notice to its depositor when it invokes one of these exceptions.[293] When a bank uses one

---

289. 12 C.F.R. §229.13(e). The exception applies to local and nonlocal checks under the second- and fifth-day availability schedules. 12 C.F.R. §229.13(e)(1). The exception does not apply to the deposit of cash or electronic payments. 57 Fed. Reg. 36593-4 (Aug. 14, 1992). The $100 availability rule does not apply. 57 Fed. Reg. 36598 (Aug. 14, 1992).

290. Other situations include where (1) the check is more than six months old, (2) the bank receives information from the paying bank which indicates that the check will not be paid, (for example, that the account is insufficient or that a stop-payment order has been issued), or (3) the check is presented prior to its postdate. 12 C.F.R. §229.13(e), app. E. at 482 (1995).

291. 12 C.F.R. §229.13(f). The $100 availability rule does not apply. 57 Fed. Reg. 36598 (Aug. 14, 1992).

292. 12 C.F.R. §229.13(h)(3).

293. 12 C.F.R. §229.13(g). The notice must state the customer's account number, the date of and amount of the deposit, the amount of the deposit that is being delayed, the reason the exception was invoked and, except as for the emergency conditions exception, the day the funds will be available for withdrawal. A model form of notice is contained in appendix C. The notice must be given at the time of the deposit if the deposit is made in person to a teller or other employee. If not made in person, the notice must be mailed or delivered to the customer no later than the close of the first business day after the banking day in which the deposit was made. If the facts justifying the hold do not become known until later, notice must be given by the first business day after the facts become known to the bank.

As to checks falling under the large deposit, redeposited checks, and repeated overdraft exceptions, when the account is a non-consumer account as defined in 12 C.F.R. §229.2(n), a one-time notice may be given prior to the notice required in 12 C.F.R. §229.13(g)(1) informing the customer that the bank may apply the exception under certain circumstances. 12 C.F.R. §229.13(g)(2) and (3).

of these exceptions to extend the time for withdrawal, the time may only be extended for a reasonable period of time,[294] which is presumed to be five business days for local checks and six business days for nonlocal checks.[295]

4. *Disclosure of Availability Policy*

Banks must disclose their availability policy to their customers in a clear and conspicuous manner.[296] The disclosure must contain the following information:[297]

1. a summary of the bank's general availability policy;
2. a description of any categories of deposits or checks used by the bank when it delays availability beyond the next day;
3. a description of any exceptions, time funds will be available and a statement that the bank will notify the customer of any hold;
4. a description of any case-by-case policies; and
5. a description of the difference between proprietary and non-proprietary ATMs.[298]

Generally, the bank must disclose their availability policy on newly opened accounts before the opening of the account.[299] The disclosures may be contained in the general information given to the new customer.[300] Certain disclosures are required on deposit slips, bricks and mortar locations (actual places where bank employees receive deposits), automated teller machines (ATMs), and upon the customer's request.[301]

---

294. 12 C.F.R. §229.13(h).

295. 12 C.F.R. §229.13(h)(4). For on-us checks, a reasonable period is presumed to be one day. 57 Fed. Reg. 3280 (Jan. 29, 1992). There is no presumption in the case of the new account exception. 12 C.F.R. §229.13 (g)(1); 57 Fed. Reg. 3281 (Jan. 29, 1992).

296. 12 C.F.R. §229.16(a); 12 C.F.R. §229.15(a).

297. 12 C.F.R. §229.16(b).

298. There are other miscellaneous disclosure requirements. For example, the bank must disclose the bank's business day cutoff hour.

299. 12 C.F.R. §229.17(a). There are exceptions for accounts opened by mail or by phone. 12 C.F.R. §229.17(a), app. E at 490 (1995).

300. 12 C.F.R. §229.17(b), app. E at 490 (1995).

301. 12 C.F.R. §229.18(a)–(d). "Automated teller machine" is defined in 12 C.F.R. §229.2(c) as "an electronic device at which a natural person may make deposits to an account by cash or check and perform other account transactions."

5. *Liability for Violation of Subpart B of Regulation CC*

Both public and private enforcement remedies are available for violation of subpart B. The primary regulator for the type of bank (for example, national banks, state banks, savings and loan institutions) committing the violation may obtain cease and desist orders, consent decrees, affirmative action orders, and suspension of officers and directors.[302]

Three types of damages are available to a party injured by a violation of subpart B or of any state law that supersedes any provision of subpart B.[303] First, the bank in violation is liable for any actual damages suffered by the person as a result of the breach.[304] Actual damages from an improper hold include loss of interest or use of the funds. Damages for wrongful dishonor of subsequent checks are not available.[305] Second, the bank is subject to a penalty of between $100 and $1,000, as determined by the court.[306] Third, if successful, the injured person may recover reasonable attorney's fees and costs.[307] In class actions, damages are limited to a total of $500,000 or 1 percent of net worth of the bank, whichever is less, with no minimum damages being required.[308] A bank may defend by proving that its violation was not intentional and resulted from a bona fide error notwithstanding the maintenance of reasonable procedures to avoid such errors.[309]

---

302. 12 C.F.R. §229.3. For national banks, this is the Comptoller of Currency; for state banks members of the Federal Reserve System, it is the Federal Reserve Board. For state banks that are not members of the Federal Reserve System and for federal savings banks, it is the Federal Deposit Insurance Corporation; for savings and loan institutions, it is the Federal Home Loan Bank Board and the Director of the Office of Thrift Supervision.

For insured credit unions, it is the National Credit Union Administration Board. For commercial and savings banks, Regulation CC compliance is enforced under §1818 of the Federal Deposit Insurance Act, 12 U.S.C. §1811. For savings and loan institutions, compliance is enforced under §1464(d) of the Home Owners Loan Act of 1933, 12 U.S.C. §1461. For federal credit unions and insured credit unions, compliance is enforced under the Federal Credit Union Act, 12 U.S.C. 1751.

303. 12 C.F.R. §229.21(a).

304. 12 C.F.R. §229.21(a)(1).

305. 12 C.F.R. §229.21(f). Except that if a wrongful dishonor occurs out of the same set of facts as does the violation of Regulation CC, the customer may recover attorney's fees expended proving facts common to both actions.

306. 12 C.F.R. §229.21(a)(2)(i).

307. 12 C.F.R. §229.21(a)(3).

308. 12 C.F.R. §229.21(a)(2)(ii)(B).

309. 12 C.F.R. §229.21(c)(1).

CHAPTER 6

Payor Bank/Customer Relationship

You receive your bank statement and notice that the balance in your account is much less than you thought it was. As you carefully review the bank statement and the returned checks, you get more and more angry. First, you notice that the check the Gas Company claims it never received was paid. It turns out that the check was stolen from your mailbox and paid on a forged indorsement. Second, you notice that a check you gave to Autos-R-Us as a deposit for the purchase of a new car was paid even though it was postdated and not supposed to be cashed for another two weeks. Autos-R-Us has never delivered the car and refuses to refund your deposit. Third, you notice that a check to Ripuoff T.V., on which you had placed a stop payment order because the television set you bought there was defective, had been paid despite your stop payment order. Fourth, you notice that, although your account contained no funds because the first three checks were paid a check you mailed to the American Red Cross as a charitable donation was paid. The payment resulted in an overdraft on your account for which the bank imposed a service charge. Fifth, the bank refused to pay the check you wrote to your landlord for your rent. The check would have been paid, had payment been stopped on your Ripuoff T.V. check. Your landlord is now attempting to evict you.

What are your rights against the bank as to these checks? Several issues arise as you determine your rights. First, can the bank debit your account when it pays a check bearing a forged indorsement? Second, can the bank debit your account when it makes early payment of a postdated check? Third, can the bank pay a check that then causes your account to be overdrawn? We will discuss these three issues in section A of this chapter. We will also examine in section A whether a bank can (1) pay a check that is stale, (2) pay a check after the customer has died or become incompetent, and/or (3) set-off against your account a debt you owe to the bank. In section B, we will discuss whether the bank was within its rights to refuse to pay your rent check. This question raises the issue of under what conditions a bank has wrongfully dishonored a check. Finally, in section C, we will examine whether a bank can debit your account when it pays a check over a valid stop payment order.

The relationship between the payor bank and you, its customer, is based upon the agreement that you and your bank entered into when you opened your account. In Chapter 5 we examined certain limitations on the freedom banks have to require their customers to contract away the customer's rights. In this chapter we examine rights given to the customer by Article 4. We begin by examining the instances in which a bank may pay an item and debit its customer's account.

A.   WHEN IS AN ITEM PROPERLY PAYABLE?

A payor bank may charge against its customer's account only items that are properly payable.[1] When is an item properly payable? The answer is really quite simple. An item is properly payable if it is both authorized by the customer and complies with the bank/customer agreement.[2] When a bank pays an item that is properly payable, the bank may debit its customer's account for the amount of the item. Conversely, when a bank pays an item that is not properly payable, it may not debit its customer's account.

In determining whether a check or other item is properly payable, reference must first be made to the agreement establishing the account between the customer and the bank. For example, many corporate accounts require that any check drawn by the corporation be signed by two officers. When this is the case, a check signed by one officer only is not properly payable. Secondly, the customer must authorize the payment. For example, where the drawer's signature has been forged, the check is not properly payable. Why not? It is not properly payable because the customer did not authorize the bank to pay the payee. The forger had no authority to tell the bank to pay the payee out of the customer's account. Similarly, the check on which the Gas Company's indorsement is forged is not properly payable. By drawing a check payable to the Gas Company, the customer had ordered the bank to make pay-

1. U.C.C. §4-401(a).
2. U.C.C. §4-401(a); U.C.C. §4-401, Official Comment 1.

ment only to the Gas Company or to its transferee. The bank had no authority to pay anyone else.

In certain situations, a bank may charge against its customer's account an
item that is not properly payable. For example, the bank may debit its customer's account if the funds actually reach the intended payee[3] or if the customer is precluded by negligence, estoppel, or ratification from asserting the
unauthorized nature of his own signature or that of an indorser. We examined
these grounds in Chapter 4B.

1. Items Creating Overdrafts

Was the bank proper in paying the check you wrote to the American Red Cross
despite the fact that you did not have adequate funds in your account to cover
the check? The answer is clearly "yes." The bank is in fact doing you a favor. If
you did not want the check paid, you should not have written it. By drawing an
item in an amount greater than the balance in your bank account, you
impliedly request that the bank advance you funds by paying the item.[4] The
bank may charge your account for an item even though it creates an overdraft
as long as the item is otherwise properly payable.[5] Although the bank has a
right to pay the item, it has no duty to pay an item that creates an overdraft,
absent an agreement to the contrary.[6] However, you may in fact have an agreement with your bank under which the bank must pay certain overdrafts. Your
agreement may take the form of a ready reserve agreement, an overdraft protection agreement or a similar agreement.

2. Postdated Checks

Was your bank within its rights in debiting your account upon its early payment of the postdated check to Autos-R-Us? You may be certain that the

---

3. See Ohio Bell Tel. Co. v. Banc Ohio Natl. Bank, 27 Ohio App. 3d 8, 499 N.E.2d 327, 2
U.C.C. Rep. Serv. 2d 1347 (1985) (whether properly payable depends not upon whether there
is an indorsement, but whether proper party receives proceeds).

4. When payment of a check drawn upon a joint account creates an overdraft, the non-sign-
ing co-account holder is not obligated to reimburse the bank unless the co-account holder who
signed the check was authorized to act for the other co-account holder or unless the non-sign-
ing co-account holder benefitted from the proceeds of the item. U.C.C. §4-401(b); U.C.C. §4-
401, Official Comment 2.

5. U.C.C. §4-401(a); U.C.C. §4-401, Official Comment 1.

6. U.C.C. §4-402(a).

answer is "no." You had not authorized your bank to pay the check prior to its date. You postdated the check just for that reason. By paying the check prior to its date, the bank defeated your purpose in giving such a check. If the bank could debit your account, there would be no purpose in postdating a check.

All of this is true. However, you have no idea how much of a problem it would have been for the bank to have noticed that your check was postdated, thereby allowing it to refuse payment until the stated date. Most banks process checks by sending the check through a computer, which reads the MICR-encoded line of the check. The computer determines whether or not to pay the check. Because the MICR-encoded line does not include the date of a check, the computer has no way of determining whether the check is post-dated.[7] If banks were not permitted to debit their customer's account on a check paid before its date, banks would have to visually examine each check before paying it. The cost of this visual examination would be staggering.

It is apparent that both you and your bank have conflicting, though important, interests at stake. Article 4 provides a procedure that attempts to protect both you and your bank's interests. As a basic rule, a bank may charge against its customer's account a check that is otherwise properly payable, even though payment was made before the date of the check.[8] However, you do have a way to protect yourself. Your bank may not properly pay a postdated check prior to its date if you have given notice to the bank of the postdating.[9]

The notice requirement means that the bank does not have to visually examine all those other checks that have not been postdated. Furthermore, since you are the one who wants to take advantage of postdating, you should pay the costs incurred by the bank. For this reason, the bank may charge a fee for acting on your postdating notice.[10]

The procedure for giving notice of postdating is the same as for placing a stop payment order on an item. Like a stop payment order, the postdating notice must describe the check with reasonable certainty and must be given in enough time to allow the bank a reasonable opportunity to act upon the notice before the check has been processed for payment or certified.[11] We discuss these procedures in section C. If, after proper notice of postdating has

---

7. U.C.C. §4-401, Official Comment 3.

8. U.C.C. §4-401(c).

9. U.C.C. §4-401(c); U.C.C. §4-401, Official Comment 3.

10. The Code does not regulate what fee a bank may charge. U.C.C. §4-401, Official Comment 3. However, a court may, under the doctrines of good faith and fair dealing or unconscionability, refuse to enforce the customer's promise to pay an excessive fee. U.C.C. §4-401, Official Comment 3.

11. U.C.C. §4-401(c); U.C.C. §4-401, Official Comment 3. As in the case of a stop payment order, the notice is effective for the period stated in §4-403(b). U.C.C. §4-401(c).

been given, the bank charges the check against the customer's account prior to the date of the check, the bank is liable for all damages resulting from the payment, including those damages resulting from the wrongful dishonor of subsequent items.[12] However, in the event of the bank's payment of a post-dated check in violation of a properly given notice, the bank has the same subrogation rights as it does when it pays an item in violation of an effective stop payment order.[13] We discuss these rights in section C.

3. Bank Not Obligated to Pay Check Six Months Old

How often will you wait six months before cashing a check? Hopefully, not often. There is almost no reason to do so. Yes, you may have forgotten about a small check you received. Or, you may have misplaced the check and been too embarrassed to ask for another. But in the vast majority of cases, when a check is six months old and has not yet been cashed, something is wrong. Most likely, the payee lost the check and had asked that the drawer send him a replacement check.[14] Because the staleness of a check (a check is stale if it is presented more than six months after its date) may indicate that a problem exists, a bank is given discretion as to whether to pay a stale check. Thus, a bank is under no obligation to its customer to pay a check presented more than six months after its date.[15] For example, a payor bank does not wrongfully dishonor a check when it refuses to pay one that bears the date January 1st and is presented on July 2d.

The bank may, on the other hand, pay a stale check in good faith and charge its customer's account for the amount of the check. This gives the bank an option as to whether to pay a stale check.[16] The bank needs this discretion because at times it may know that the drawer wants the check to be paid.

The fact that a check is stale does not affect the obligation of the drawer to pay the check. Notwithstanding the bank's dishonor of a stale check, the

12. U.C.C. §4-401(c); U.C.C. §4-401, Official Comment 3.

13. See Siegel v. New England Merchants Natl. Bank, 386 Mass. 672, 437 N.E.2d 218, 33 U.C.C. Rep. Serv. 1601 (1982).

14. U.C.C. §4-404, Official Comment. Certified checks are excluded because they are the primary obligation of the certifying bank which runs directly to the holder. U.C.C. §4-404, Official Comment. Therefore, the bank knows whether there is any problem with a certified check. By allowing a bank to refuse to pay a stale check, the bank can protect its customer's interests.

15. U.C.C. §4-404.

16. U.C.C. §4-404, Official Comment.

drawer remains liable to the person entitled to enforce the check. The drawer's liability is terminated only when the statute of limitations has run.[17]

4. Bank's Right of Setoff

You have borrowed money from your bank to purchase a car. You have agreed to make monthly payments of $400 payable on the first of every month. You are a little tight for money this month, and you decide that it is more important to pay your rent on time than to make your car payment. You send your landlord a check on the third of the month. The landlord presents the check to the bank on the fifth of the month. The check bounces. You go to your bank and demand to know why. The bank tells you that when you failed to make your car payment on time, it set off the car payment against your account on the second of the month. This left insufficient funds to pay your rent check. You look at both your bank/customer agreement and your loan agreement and do not see anything that authorizes the bank to charge the car payment against your account without your consent. You are irate. You are sure that the bank cannot do this.

Despite your outrage, the bank acted within its rights. The bank has the right to set off against its customer's account any matured debts the customer owes to the bank. However, there are certain limitations.[18] Setoff is available

17. U.C.C. §3-118.

18. Subject to a few exceptions, the bank may set off a debt owed to it by its customer only against an account belonging to the customer himself. A bank may not exercise its right of setoff if the bank has actual knowledge, see South Cent. Livestock Dealers v. Security State Bank of Hedley, Tex., 614 F.2d 1056 (5th Cir. 1980), reason to know, see Universal C.I.T. Credit Corp. v. Farmers Bank of Portageville, 358 F. Supp. 317, 13 U.C.C. Rep. Serv. 109 (E.D. Mo. 1973) (bank had enough facts to put it on inquiry as to interest of third party), that the funds in an account belong to a person other than the customer or that the funds are held in trust by the customer for another.

A bank has no right of setoff against an account where the designation of the account indicates that a third party has an interest in the account. See Energetics, Inc. v. Allied Bank, 784 F.2d 1300, 42 U.C.C. Rep. Serv. 1568 (5th Cir. 1986) (bank not permitted to set off a debt of its customer Republic Drilling against an account entitled "Well Account-Energetics" which contained prepayments by Energetics of drilling expenses.).

Some courts adopt the "equitable rule" that when a third party has an interest in an account, for example, a secured party claiming proceeds in an account, a bank, even without notice of the third party's interest, cannot exercise its right of setoff unless it has changed its position in reliance upon the reasonable belief that the account belongs solely to its depositor. See National Indem. Co. v. Spring Branch State Bank, 162 Tex. 521, 348 S.W.2d 528 (1961) (even though the bank had no notice that funds in an insurance agent's account were premiums he received in trust for his employer, the setoff was improper because the bank had not changed its position).

only if both the debt you owe the bank and the debt the bank owes you have matured.[19] Because your car payment was due on the first, the debt had matured, and the bank could set it off against your account. Similarly, the bank may set off against its customer's account a debt evidenced by a demand note even without making demand for payment or giving notice to the customer. A demand note is due at the holder's discretion. In contrast, the bank may not set off a debt that is not yet due. If the car payment was not due until the sixth of the month, the bank would have been improper in debiting your account prior to that date.

A bank is required to indicate in its records that it has exercised a setoff.[20] The book entry or other evidence of the setoff, however, may take place after the setoff is accomplished. Absent a statute to the contrary, there is no requirement that the bank give prior notice to the depositor before making the setoff.[21] Although there is also no requirement under the common law that a customer consent to a setoff, both state and federal law limit to some extent a bank's right of setoff as to a debt arising out of a consumer credit transaction. For example, under §169 of the Fair Credit Billing Act of 1974,[22] a bank credit card issuer (absent consent in writing) may not set off a debt arising from the use of the credit card against a deposit account of the credit card holder. Under California law, a bank may not set off a debt arising out of a consumer credit transaction against an account if the resulting balance is reduced to less than $1,000.[23]

There is a split in authority as to whether a bank can set off a debt of one account holder against an account jointly held. Some courts permit the bank to set off the debt against the entire account regardless of the respective interests of the account holders. See Burgess v. First Natl. Bank, 31 Colo. App. 67, 497 P.2d 1035 (1972). Other courts hold that the setoff may be exercised only to the extent of the respective interests of the account holders. See Peoples Bank v. Turner, 169 Md. 430, 182 A. 314 (1936).

19. See Bottrell v. American Bank, 773 P.2d 694, 9 U.C.C. Rep. Serv. 2d 583 (Mont. 1989) (setoff not available where debt not matured).

20. See Baker v. National City Bank of Cleveland, 511 F.2d 1016, 16 U.C.C. Rep. Serv. 298 (6th Cir. 1975).

21. There is apparently no requirement that the bank give notice within any specified time after the setoff absent a statutory requirement. One example of such a notice requirement is found in California. California requires that a consumer depositor be given notice no later than the day following the setoff so that the consumer can claim an exemption or that the debt is not due. Cal Fin. Code §864(c). See Bichel Optical Lab, Inc. v. Marquette Natl. Bank, 487 F.2d 906, 13 U.C.C. Rep. Serv. 738 (8th Cir. 1973).

22. 15 U.S.C. §1666h.

23. Cal. Fin. Code. §864(b).

5. Death or Incompetence of Customer

A check is simply an order by the customer to its bank to pay a sum of money to a payee. The order is revocable by the customer. As we will see, that is why the customer has the right to stop payment on a check. Just like any revocable power of attorney, the death or incompetency of the customer would terminate the order. However, any such consequence would be disastrous to the banking system. How can a bank know whether one of its customers is incompetent or has died? For this reason, banks are given the right to pay checks even after a customer has been adjudicated as incompetent or has died.

a. Effect of Incompetence

A customer's incompetence does not revoke the bank's authority to pay or collect an item or account for proceeds of its collection until the bank knows of the adjudication of incompetence and has a reasonable opportunity to act upon it.[24]

b. Effect of Death

Until the bank knows of the customer's death, the bank has the right to pay or collect an item.[25] Death of a customer does not revoke a bank's authority to pay or collect an item until the bank knows of the death, and has had a reasonable opportunity to act upon the knowledge. Even when the bank learns of its customer's death, the bank may, for ten days after the date of death, pay a check unless the bank is ordered to stop payment by a person

---

24. U.C.C. §4-405(a). The bank may also accept the item. U.C.C. §4-405(a). The adjudication of incompetency is not constructive notice to the bank of the customer's incompetence. U.C.C. §4-405, Comment 1. The bank must have actual knowledge of the adjudication, and a reasonable time must pass to permit that knowledge to reach the employee handling the item. Even after the bank knows that its customer is incompetent, the bank remains authorized to act on behalf of the customer in the collection or payment of an item until the judicial appointment or qualification of a personal representative for the customer.

25. U.C.C. §4-405(a). The bank may also account, accept, or certify for an item. The bank may also pay or account for an item. U.C.C. §4-405(a). The bank's right to pay or collect items upon death or incompetency applies to all phases of the bank collection process. It applies to any kind of item, to customers who own items as well as those who draw or make them, to the role of the bank as a collecting or payor bank, to carrying out transfers to third parties, and to other activities as well. U.C.C. §4-405, Official Comment 1.

claiming an interest in the account.[26] The bank is allowed to pay checks (but not other items) presented in the ten-day period after the date of death because most of these checks represent bona fide debts. Many of the checks are in payment of ordinary bills. Rather than making these creditors file a claim against the estate, it is simpler for the bank to pay the checks and have the executor or administrator of the estate recover any improper payment.[27]

Although a bank can pay a check after the customer's death, the bank has no duty to pay the check. The bank is not liable for wrongful dishonor if it refuses to pay a check after its customer has died.[28]

To ensure that the drawer has not been pressured shortly before his death to write checks, a bank may not pay a check with knowledge of its customer's death if ordered to stop payment by any person claiming an interest in the account.[29] Any surviving relative, creditor, or other person who claims an interest in the account may order the bank not to pay the check.[30] The bank is not required to determine whether the person's claim to the account has merit.

B. WRONGFUL DISHONOR

Remember our example at the beginning of this chapter in which you had written a check to your landlord for the rent? The bank dishonored the check, and now your landlord is attempting to evict you. Was the bank wrong

26. U.C.C. §4-405(b). The bank may also certify the check. The check, for obvious reasons, must have been drawn on or before the date of death. U.C.C. §4-405(b). This right is limited to checks. U.C.C. §4-405, Official Comment 2. Some state inheritance tax statutes, notwithstanding §4-405(b), forbid banks from paying checks after having obtained knowledge of the customer's death.

27. U.C.C. §4-405, Official Comment 2. Section 4-405(b) is not intended to affect the validity of any gift causa mortis or other transfer in contemplation of death. U.C.C. §4-405, Official Comment 2.

28. See Bank Leumi Trust Co. v. Bally's Park Place, Inc., 528 F. Supp. 349, 32 U.C.C. Rep. Serv. 1542 (S.D.N.Y. 1981).

29. U.C.C. §4-405(b). Such a notice has the same effect as a stop payment order. U.C.C. §4-405, Official Comment 3. As in the case of a stop payment order, the order may be oral or written. A bank which makes an improper payment under §4-405 has subrogation rights under §4-407.

30. U.C.C. §4-405, Official Comment 3. Any person claiming an interest in the estate may give the bank notice of a claim (including the person named in the will as the executor), even if the will has not yet been admitted to probate. U.C.C. §4-405, Official Comment 3.

in dishonoring the check? If so, do you have a cause of action against the bank? What damages can you recover? We will examine these questions in this section.

1.   Item Must Be Dishonored

In the previous section we covered the question as to when an item is properly payable. Subject to one exception,[31] a payor bank is liable to its customer for wrongful dishonor where it dishonors an item that is properly payable.[32] Notice that there are two conditions to the bank's liability for wrongful dishonor. The first condition is that the bank must dishonor the item. In Chapter 3 we discussed under what conditions an item has been dishonored. Generally, an item is "dishonored" when the payor bank refuses to pay an item that has been properly presented or as to which presentment has been excused.[33] For example, if the bank refuses to pay the item because the payee refuses to show identification, the bank has not dishonored the item. As you will recall, when an instrument is presented for payment, the payor may demand that the presenter exhibit reasonable identification. If the presenter fails to do so, the presentment is invalidated.

2.   Item Must Be Properly Payable

The second condition is that the item must be properly payable. As you will recall, an item is properly payable if it is authorized by the customer and is in accord with any agreement between the customer and the bank.[34] For example, an item that contains a forged indorsement or a forged drawer's signature is not properly payable. There is one major exception to this rule. Remember that an item is deemed to be properly payable, even though the payment would create an overdraft. This gives the bank discretion to decide whether or not it will advance you credit in the form of paying an item drawn upon insufficient funds.

However, the definition of "properly payable" was not intended to require that the bank pay items drawn on insufficient funds. If you draw a check for

---

31. Unless otherwise agreed, a payor bank may dishonor an item that is otherwise properly payable if payment of the item would create an overdraft. U.C.C. §4-402(a).

32. U.C.C. §4-402(a); U.C.C. §4-402, Official Comment 1.

33. U.C.C. §3-502(a)(2),(b) and (d).

34. U.C.C. §4-401(a).

B. Wrongful Dishonor

$1,000,000 upon an account containing only $5, the bank certainly cannot be liable for wrongful dishonor if it refuses to pay the check. To protect the bank against any such unwarranted liability, unless otherwise agreed a payor bank may dishonor an item that is otherwise properly payable if payment of the item would create an overdraft.[35] As a result, the bank is not liable for wrongful dishonor when it dishonors an item drawn upon insufficient funds. However, the bank may be liable for wrongful dishonor if it breaches an express agreement with its customer to honor overdrafts, for example, a ready reserve agreement or check overdraft protection. There may even be situations in which a court may find that a bank has through a course of performance impliedly agreed to cover overdrafts.[36]

3. Sufficient Funds in Account

In determining whether an item has been wrongfully dishonored, the pivotal question is whether the account contained sufficient funds to cover the item. This question is pivotal because liability for wrongful dishonor is absolute. A bank is liable for wrongful dishonor notwithstanding the fact that it exercised ordinary care in determining whether or not to pay the item.

The basic question is a simple one. Were there adequate funds in the customer's account to cover payment of the dishonored item? Whether adequate funds were in fact present almost always depends upon whether the bank's debit or credit of the customer's account was proper. For example, in writing the check to your landlord, you may have believed that because you deposited your paycheck in the account the day before, you had sufficient funds in your

---

35. U.C.C. §4-402(a).

36. U.C.C. §1-201(3). For example, a refusal to pay that creates an overdraft may be a wrongful dishonor if a bank has engaged in a pattern of honoring overdrafts and dishonors a particular overdraft without adequately notifying its customer of the change in policy. See, e.g., Murdaugh Volkswagen, Inc. v. First Natl. Bank, 801 F.2d 719, 2 U.C.C. Rep. Serv. 2d 25 (4th Cir. 1986). (Bank wrongfully dishonored checks when for first time in 20 years it placed a hold on an account for checks deposited and the account holder's checks bounced. The court affirmed the jury finding that the dishonors were in bad faith and that sufficient evidence existed for the jury to conclude that the withdrawal of immediate credit to the account caused the corporation to fail. Damages awarded were the total asset value of the corporation at the time of bankruptcy.)

However, in the absence of an express agreement, many courts refuse to find that payment of prior overdrafts imposes any obligation on the part of the bank to pay subsequent overdrafts. See Thiele v. Security State Bank, 396 N.W.2d 295, 3 U.C.C. Rep. Serv. 2d 686 (N.D. 1986) (no such course of dealing bound bank in light of provision in depositor's contract giving bank complete discretion).

account to cover the rent check. Whether the bank wrongfully dishonored your rent check depends upon whether you are correct in your assumption. Your bank does not have to allow you to immediately draw on your paycheck funds. As we discussed in Chapter 5, Regulation CC establishes deadlines by which a payor bank is required to allow you to draw on deposited checks. If your rent check was presented for payment prior to the established deadline that requires the bank to allow you to draw on your paycheck, the bank has no obligation to pay your rent check. If, however, the rent check was presented after the established deadline, the bank is required to have credited your account for the amount of the paycheck. Since your account should have contained the funds represented by your paycheck, it contained sufficient funds to pay your rent check. As a result, your bank has wrongfully dishonored your rent check. Or maybe your account contained insufficient funds because your paycheck bounced and, before you received notice of this fact, your bank charged back your account for the amount of the paycheck.

Conversely, whether your account contains adequate funds also depends upon whether the debits entered against your account are proper. A bank wrongfully dishonors any item where, but for an improper debit, the account would have contained sufficient funds to pay the item. For example, when the bank exercises its right of setoff or honors a writ of garnishment, a determination of whether your account contains adequate funds depends on whether exercise of the setoff or honoring of the writ of garnishment was proper. When the bank has properly exercised its right of setoff or properly honored a writ of garnishment,[37] your account may contain insufficient funds to pay your rent check.

On the other hand, if the bank improperly exercised a setoff against the account[38] or improperly honored a writ of garnishment, sufficient funds may have been present to cover your rent check. In our original example, your bank paid the Gas Company check upon a forged indorsement. Your bank has no right to debit your account when it pays a check bearing a forged indorsement or a forged drawer's signature. Had the bank not improperly charged the Gas Company check against your account, it would have contained sufficient funds to cover your rent check; therefore, your bank would be liable for wrongful dishonor.

37. See Farmers Coop. Elevator, Inc. v. State Bank, 236 N.W.2d 674, 18 U.C.C. Rep. Serv. 607 (Iowa 1975) (proper setoff); Texas Commerce Bank New Braunfels, N.A. v. Townsend, 786 S.W.2d 53, 11 U.C.C. Rep. Serv. 2d 919 (Tex. App. 1990) (bank not liable for wrongful dishonor when prior garnishment left insufficient funds in account to pay check).

38. See Morse v. Mutual Fed. Sav. & Loan Assn., 536 F. Supp. 1271, 34 U.C.C. Rep. Serv. 230 (D. Mass. 1982) (wrongful dishonor when bank froze customer's account without notice to customer).

4. Bank May Pay Checks in Any Order

There are a few provisions in Article 4 that affect whether a bank acts properly in debiting or in failing to credit your account. The payor bank has the right to pay checks drawn upon your account in any order that it desires.[39] The reason for this discretion is to allow the bank to process checks by computer without concern that a subsequently dated check had been paid while an earlier dated check was dishonored. Thus, assume that your check to the American Red Cross was issued after your rent check. You did this deliberately to ensure that there would be adequate funds in your account to pay the rent check. You were not concerned with whether the American Red Cross check was paid as it was a charitable donation. However, the bank processed and paid the American Red Cross check first. This left insufficient funds to pay your rent check. Had the American Red Cross check not been paid, there would have been sufficient funds to pay your rent check. Despite this, the bank was justified in dishonoring your rent check and was not liable for wrongful dishonor.

5. Bank May Debit Account Despite Its Negligence in Collecting Item

Similarly, you may have deposited a check a few weeks ago. Your bank may have credited your account for the amount of the check. However, in handling this check for collection, your bank may have negligently misplaced the check. By the time the check was sent to the payor bank, the drawer of the check was insolvent. Had your bank not misplaced the check, it would have been paid. As we examined in Chapter 5, you have a cause of action against your bank for the loss caused by its negligent mishandling of the check. Despite this cause of action, your bank may properly charge back your account for the amount of the check.[40] If, as a result of this chargeback, your account contains insufficient funds to pay your rent check, the bank is not liable for wrongful dishonor.

---

39. U.C.C. §4-303(b).
40. U.C.C. §4-214(d)(2).

6. *Time for Determining Whether Sufficient Funds Present*

A bank need only examine a customer's account once in deciding whether to dishonor an item for insufficient funds.[41] This examination may be made at any time during the period between the time when the bank received the item and when it returned the item (or gave notice in lieu of the item's return). Thus, assume that your rent check was received by your bank at 9:00 A.M. Your bank examines your account at 10:00 A.M. and determines that there are insufficient funds to cover the check. At 11:00 A.M. the bank credits your account with the amount of your paycheck. If you needed your paycheck credited to your account in order to cover your rent check, the bank may properly dishonor your rent check. Any credits added to the customer's account after the bank has examined the account are not considered in determining whether the account contains sufficient funds.[42] However, if your bank examined your account again at noon, the balance at the time of that later examination is used to determine whether there were adequate funds to pay your rent check. In the above example, because you had sufficient funds at noon to cover your rent check, your bank would have been liable for wrongful dishonor.

7. *Duty Owed Only to Customer*

A bank is liable only to its customer for wrongful dishonor of an item.[43] A payee or other holder of the item has no cause of action against the bank for wrongful dishonor of an item. Thus, your landlord has no cause of action against your bank for wrongful dishonor. The bank's duty was owed only to you.

Limiting the bank's duty to its customer has broad implications. Assume that you are the president of a small family-owned corporation. You are the only person authorized to sign checks for the corporation. Furthermore, everyone that does business with your corporation does so because of their faith in you personally. A check that you write to your major supplier is dishonored because of the bank's mistake. However, before the bank recognizes the mistake, the supplier has filed a criminal complaint against you for writing a check on insufficient funds. You are arrested. The members of your country

---

41. U.C.C. §4-402(c).
42. U.C.C. §4-402, Official Comment 4.
43. U.C.C. §4-402(b); U.C.C. §4-402, Official Comment 5.

club no longer talk to you and you are banished from the Rotary Club. Do you have an action for wrongful dishonor?

The answer is a disappointing "no."[44] Your corporation is the bank's customer, not you. The result would be the same if you were a partner in a partnership or a trustee of a trust. "Customer" is defined as any person either having an account with the bank or for whom the bank has agreed to collect the item.[45] "Person" includes an individual or an organization.[46] "Organization" includes corporations, trusts, partnerships, or other legal or commercial entities.[47] Even if you personally have an account with the bank, you are not the customer because it was not from your account that the check was to be paid.

However, nothing in Article 4 displaces any common law cause of action you may have against the bank.[48] Under tort law, when it is clearly foreseeable to a bank that a partner, trustee, or corporate officer will suffer a loss, the bank may be held to have a duty to the individual to use reasonable care in paying or dishonoring an item. The officer, trustee, or partner may possibly also have a cause of action for defamation.

8. Damages

A payor bank that wrongfully dishonors an item is liable to its customer for all damages proximately caused by the wrongful dishonor.[49] Thus, the Code adopts the tort test of proximate causation for determining the liability of a payor bank for damages caused by a wrongful dishonor. Whether damages are proximately caused by the wrongful dishonor is a question of fact to be determined on a case-by-case basis.

The customer has the burden of proving any actual damages that he has suffered.[50] Damages may include any damages suffered as a consequence of

---

44. U.C.C. §4-402, Official Comment 5.

45. U.C.C. §4-104(a)(5).

46. U.C.C. §1-201(30).

47. U.C.C. §1-201(28).

48. U.C.C. §4-402, Official Comment 5. See Agostino v. Monticello Greenhouses, Inc., 166 A.D.2d 471, 560 N.Y.S. 2d 690, 13 U.C.C. Rep. Serv. 2d 472 (1990) (Although corporate officer may not maintain cause of action for wrongful dishonor where checks drawn on corporate account, he may bring a negligence action against the bank under §1-103 where the dishonor had caused his arrest.).

49. U.C.C. §4-402(b).

50. U.C.C. §4-402(b).

the dishonor.[51] For example, if your landlord has you arrested and prosecuted for writing a check on insufficient funds, you can recover from your bank any damages suffered on account of the arrest and prosecution. These damages may include your costs of defense and any harm done to your reputation. If you are evicted because of the dishonor, you could recover any damages on account of the eviction. All of these damages are proximately caused by the dishonor. Similarly, if a check you wrote as a deposit on a house was wrongfully dishonored, you could recover any losses resulting from your inability to buy the house,[52] including loss of profits from an appreciation in the value of the house. If a profitable contract was terminated because one of your checks was wrongfully dishonored, you could recover any profits lost as a result of the termination.[53] If your reputation was harmed because checks sent in payment of your bills were wrongfully dishonored, you could recover damages for the loss to your reputation.[54] If a wrongful dishonor resulted in a customer's bankruptcy, a court could even award as damages the difference between the value of the customer's assets before and after dishonor.[55]

Although clearly foreseeable consequences of a wrongful dishonor are the embarrassment, emotional distress, and mental anguish that a customer suffers as a result of the dishonor, courts are reluctant to award a customer damages for these injuries because of the ease of fabricating such injuries. Many courts require that the bank's behavior be reckless or outrageous before such damages are awarded.[56]

Whether a bank is liable for punitive or other noncompensatory damages is left to the court's determination under §1-103 or §1-106.[57] However, when

51. U.C.C. §4-402(b); U.C.C. §4-402, Official Comment 3.
52. See Twin City Bank v. Isaacs, 283 Ark. 127, 672 S.W.2d 651, 39 U.C.C. Rep. Serv. 35 (1984).
53. See Murdaugh Volkswagen, Inc. v. First Natl. Bank, 801 F.2d 719, 2 U.C.C. Rep. Serv. 2d 25 (4th Cir. 1986) (damages may include injury to credit of corporation including value of assets on bankruptcy caused by loss of credit); Skov v. Chase Manhattan Bank, 407 F.2d 1318, 6 U.C.C. Rep. Serv. 170 (3d Cir. 1969) (awarded three years of lost profits where supplier stopped doing business with customer).
54. See Morse v. Mutual Fed. Sav. & Loan Assn., 536 F. Supp. 1271, 34 U.C.C. Rep. Serv. 230 (D. Mass. 1982) (mental suffering and loss of reputation damages available).
55. See In re Geri Zahn, Inc., 135 B.R. 912, 16 U.C.C. Rep. Serv. 2d 731 (Bankr. S.D. Fla. 1991) (where dishonor caused bankruptcy of customer, the customer's damages were the value of the assets before dishonor minus their value after dishonor).
56. See Morse v. Mutual Fed. Sav. & Loan Assn., 536 F. Supp. 1271, 34 U.C.C. Rep. Serv. 230 (D. Mass. 1987) (mental suffering and loss of reputation damages available); Twin City v. Isaacs, 283 Ark. 127, 672 S.W.2d 651, 39 U.C.C. Rep. Serv. 35 (1984) (damages for mental anguish available upon intentional dishonor).
57. U.C.C. §4-402, Official Comment 1.

the dishonor is willful and wanton, courts have allowed punitive damages for wrongful dishonor.[58] In one case,[59] punitive damages were awarded when a bank knowingly misrepresented the terms of a loan to lure a customer to switch its business to the bank and then failed to timely fund the line of credit and dishonored checks covered by the supposed line of credit.

C. CUSTOMER'S RIGHT TO STOP PAYMENT

1. *Introduction*

You will recall that in our example at the beginning of the chapter you had stopped payment on a check payable to Ripuoff T.V. because the television set was defective. Your bank, however, had paid the check in spite of the stop payment order. Can your bank debit your account for the amount of the check? Does it make a difference whether you had a legitimate reason for stopping payment? Must the bank honor any stop payment order? These are some of the questions that we will examine in this section.

a. Who May Stop Payment

As a customer, you have the right to stop payment of any item drawn on your account.[60] If the account is a joint account with your wife, either you or your wife could stop payment on the check. When there are two or more per-

---

58. See In re Brandywine Assocs., 30 U.C.C. Rep. Serv. 1369 (Bankr. E.D. Pa. 1980) (only available where malicious, oppressive, or reckless); Alaska State Bank v. Fairco, 674 P.2d 288, 37 U.C.C. Rep. Serv. 1782 (Alaska 1983) (punitive damages available where willful and wanton); Twin City Bank v. Isaacs, 283 Ark. 127, 672 S.W.2d 651, 39 U.C.C. Rep. Serv. 35 (1984) (punitive damages awarded).

59. See In re Geri Zahn, Inc., 135 B.R. 912, 16 U.C.C. Rep. Serv. 2d 731 (Bankr. S.D. Fla. 1991).

60. U.C.C. §4-403(a). Subject to a contrary agreement, checks presented after a customer closes a bank account are not properly payable. Once the account is closed, the authority given to the bank by the customer is revoked. To prevent liability for paying a check after the closing of an account, a bank should provide in its contract with its customer that the bank has authority to pay an otherwise properly payable check presented after the closing of the account.

The same basic rules apply when a check is paid after the customer has closed his account. U.C.C. §4-403(a). However, because of the infrequency of issues arising involving closing of an account we will speak in the text only of stop payment orders.

sons, each of whom is individually entitled to write items on an account, any of these persons may order payment stopped even if he or she is not the person who signed the item.[61] Thus, even if it was you who signed the check, your wife could stop payment on the check.

Although most stop payment orders are issued by a drawer of a check, a customer has the right to stop payment of any item payable by his bank from his account.[62] However, a person may stop payment only on an item payable from his account. For example, assume that you purchased a cashier's check from your bank to pay Ripuoff T.V. A cashier's check is drawn by and out of the account of the issuing bank. Because it is not payable from your account, you may not stop payment on the cashier's check.[63] The reason for this rule is simple. It is your bank's credit that is at stake and not yours. You should not have the right to impugn the bank's credit by stopping payment on one of its obligations. For the same reason, a payee or indorsee has no right to stop payment on a check or other item.[64] The only exception to this rule is that after the death of a customer, any person claiming an interest in the account may stop payment on any item payable from the deceased customer's account.[65] We covered this situation in section A of this chapter.

b.   Effect of Stop Payment Order

Some people are confused about the actual effect of a stop payment order. The only effect of the stop payment order is to prevent the holder from immediately obtaining possession of the funds represented by the item. Stop payment orders do not change who ultimately gets the funds because issuance of a stop payment order has no effect upon your liability as drawer of the item.[66] When payment is stopped, you (the drawer) will be sued by the holder.[67] As drawer, you will be obligated to pay the instrument unless you

---

61. U.C.C. §4-403, Official Comment 5. Or to close an account. U.C.C. §4-403, Official Comment 5. Similarly, when an organization requires two or more persons to sign an item on behalf of the organization, any person authorized to sign on behalf of the organization may by himself order payment stopped. U.C.C. §4-403, Official Comment 5. Or to close the account. U.C.C. §4-403, Official Comment 5.

62. U.C.C. §4-403(a); U.C.C. §4-403, Official Comment 3. These other customers include a maker of a note payable at a bank in a state adopting Alternative A to §4-106(b), U.C.C. §4-403 Official Comment 3, the drawer of a purchase money order (sometimes erroneously designated as the "remittter") and the drawer bank on a teller's check. U.C.C. §4-104(a)(5).

63. U.C.C. §4-403, Official Comment 4. This also applies to teller's checks.

64. U.C.C. §4-403, Official Comment 2.

65. U.C.C. §4-405(b); U.C.C. §4-403, Official Comment 2.

66. U.C.C. §4-403, Official Comment 7.

67. U.C.C. §3-414(b).

have a defense or claim in recoupment that is assertible against the holder.[68] In our example, you could raise a claim in recoupment that the defective television set was in breach of the warranty of merchantability. You would be able to defeat Ripuoff T.V.'s action to the extent that you would be entitled to damages for breach of the warranty. However, if Ripuoff T.V. negotiated the check to a holder in due course, you will not be able to raise your claim in recoupment or any other defense; therefore, you would be liable for the full amount of the item notwithstanding the stop payment order.[69] The true effect of the stop payment order is that it shifts the bargaining power. By stopping payment, you shift the burden and risk of litigation, as well as the risk of insolvency, to the holder. If payment is made to Ripuoff T.V., you must now sue it for your damages for breach of warranty. You not only bear the expense of paying a lawyer and court costs, but you bear the risk that a judgment against Ripuoff T.V. may not be collectible. If payment is stopped, Ripuoff T.V. or any subsequent holder must commence an action to recover from you. Because the holder must now expend the legal fees, you may be able to negotiate a favorable settlement.

2. Requirements for a Stop Payment Order

When you attempt to stop payment on a check or other item, your bank will probably require you to both pay a fee (sometimes as much as $25) and sign an exculpatory agreement relieving the bank of liability to you in the event that it fails to honor the stop payment order. You may wonder whether the bank can require you to pay this fee. Although nothing in Article 4 specifically answers this question, it would appear that the bank has the right to charge you a reasonable fee for the service of stopping payment on your check.[70] You will be more pleased with the answer as to whether the exculpatory agreement is effective. U.C.C. §4-103(a) specifically provides that no agreement can "disclaim a bank's responsibility for its lack of good faith or failure to exercise ordinary care." In most situations in which a bank pays an item over a valid stop payment, the bank will be found to have failed to exercise ordinary care. In these cases, any attempt by the bank to disclaim liability will be ineffective.[71]

Banks pay thousands of checks per day. You may have several checks out-

---

68. U.C.C. §3-305(a) and (b).

69. U.C.C. §3-305(b); U.C.C. §4-403, Official Comment 7.

70. If the fee is unreasonable, a court could refuse to enforce your promise to pay the fee on the grounds that the agreement is unconscionable or violates public policy. See Chapter 5C.

71. U.C.C. §4-403, Official Comment 7.

standing at any given moment. In order for your bank to stop payment on the Ripuoff T.V. check, it must have sufficient information to identify the check and adequate time to process the stop payment order before payment of the check. As we will examine later in this section, the stop payment order must be received at a time and in a manner that affords the bank a reasonable opportunity to act on the order before the bank has paid or accepted the check or substantially completed the process of payment.[72]

a. What Information Is Sufficient

Because of the bank's need for sufficient information to identify the check, a stop payment order is effective only if the order describes the check or other item with reasonable certainty.[73] A check or other item is identified with reasonable certainty when the bank is given sufficient information to enable it to identify the item on which payment is to be stopped.[74] In determining what information a bank can require its customer to specify in the stop payment order, the drafters of Article 4 were acutely aware of cost considerations. If the bank were to visually examine each check drawn on your account, the bank would not need much information to identify the check. The payee's name by itself would be sufficient. The date of the check or an approximation of the amount payable would also be sufficient if that were the only check written on that date or in that general amount. However, visually examining all of your checks would impose far too great a burden on the bank. Cost considerations require banks to be able to process stop payment orders by computer.

Thus, the standard for determining what information is sufficient is phrased in terms of what technological capabilities it is fair to require banks to employ. The test adopted by the Code is that the customer must meet the standard of what information allows the bank under the technology then existing to identify the item with reasonable certainty, unless there is a contrary agreement between the bank and the customer.[75] The state of current technology is such that the computers that banks find economically feasible can only be programmed to read the information contained in the MICR-encoded line.[76] Therefore, unless the customer supplies the bank with information that

---

72. U.C.C. §4-403(a). More specifically, your stop payment order must be received before the bank takes any action with respect to the item as described in §4-303. We cover this requirement later in this section.

73. U.C.C. §4-403(a). The same basic requirements are present for closing an account.

74. U.C.C. §4-403, Official Comment 5 (or as to which account is to be closed).

75. U.C.C. §4-403, Official Comment 5.

76. See Graziano, Computerized Stop Payment Orders Under the U.C.C.: Reasonable Care or Customer Beware?, 90 Com. L.J. 550, 556, 557 (1985).

is contained on the MICR-encoded line, the computer will not be able to identify the item upon which payment is to be stopped. The only information encoded on the MICR-line that would enable the computer to identify an individual check is either the check number or the amount payable.

Because most current computers used for processing checks can be programmed only to identify checks by either the precise amount payable or the precise check number, a mistake in one digit results in the computer failing to stop payment of the item. For example, if you indicated on the stop payment order that your check to Ripuoff T.V. was in the amount of $1,001, instead of its actual amount of $1,000, the computer would not be able to locate the check. This means that banks can require their customers to furnish either the exact check number or the exact amount payable. For those of us who do not keep accurate records, this will present a problem; however, the cost the bank would incur to use far more expensive computer programs outweighs the cost to us of keeping accurate records. Once technology allows banks to program their computers with more tolerance for error, less accurate information will be necessary for banks to process stop payment orders.

b. How Long Stop Payment Order Is Effective

A stop payment order may be either written or oral.[77] There is an advantage, however, in stopping payment by a written order. A written stop payment order is effective for six months from the date that it is given. By contrast, an oral stop payment order lapses within 14 calendar days. If there is a written confirmation of the oral order given within the 14-day period, the oral order is effective for six months beginning at the time the oral order was given. A stop payment order may be renewed for additional six-month periods with a written instruction given to the bank within the period during which a stop payment order is effective. An oral renewal is effective for 14 calendar days. There is no limit as to the number of times that a stop payment order may be renewed. Although a new stop payment order may be given after the original order has expired, the new order takes effect only from the date given.

When a stop payment order expires, it is as if the order had never been given, and the payor bank may in good faith pay the item (even though the

---

77. See U.C.C. §4-403(b); U.C.C. §4-403, Official Comment 6. Or to close the account. An order to close an account is effective the first time that it is given and remains effective once given. Because of the significance of closing an account, a court would probably uphold an agreement between the bank and its customer that an order to close an account must be in writing.

item had at one time been subject to a stop payment order). For example, assume that you originally issued a stop payment order on January 2d and that you attempted to renew the order on August 1st. Because the renewal was not within the six-month period, it is effective only from August 1st, the date received. Your stop payment order would have been ineffective between July 2d and July 31st. If the bank had paid the item any time between July 1st and July 31st, the bank's payment would have been proper.

3. Timeliness of Stop Payment Orders, Writs of Garnishment, Notices, and Setoffs

a. Stop Payment Orders

A stop payment order must be received at a time and in a manner that affords the bank a reasonable opportunity to act on the order before the bank has paid, accepted, or significantly processed the item.[78] It is clearly too late to stop payment on an item that has already been paid. Even before the item has been paid, there must come a time when the bank can safely pay the item without worrying about liability for failing to observe a subsequently received stop payment order.

Clearly, when the stop payment order is received by the bank before the bank has received the item for payment, the stop payment order is effective. However, even after the bank has received the item, a substantial period of time (possibly as long as 36 hours) may pass before the payor bank pays the item. When the stop payment order is received within this period of time, the question arises as to whether the stop payment order has arrived in time to be enforceable.

Section 4-303(a) sets out rules for determining at what point a stop payment order comes too late to prevent the payor bank from paying an item.[79] Section 4-303(a) provides that the payor bank may ignore a stop payment order once it has already paid the item, accepted a draft, or significantly processed a check for payment. Specifically, as will be discussed shortly, the stop payment order must be received before the occurrence of any of five specified events to be effective in preventing the bank from paying the item. Section 4-303(a), however, does not answer the question of whether a bank

78. U.C.C. §4-403(a). More specifically, your stop payment order must be received before the bank takes any action with respect to the item as described in §4-303. We cover this requirement later in this section.
79. U.C.C. §4-303, Official Comment 3.

that honors a late stop payment order is liable to the payee. The answer to this question is found in §§4-215 and 4-302(a) and discussed in Chapter 5.

Time by Which Stop Payment Order Must Be Received. Let us now examine the rule itself. A stop payment order arrives too late to terminate the bank's right or duty to pay an item if it comes after the earliest of one of five events.[80] Certainly, a stop payment order comes too late once the bank has already paid the item or become liable to the payee for the item. Once the money is paid or the bank has incurred liability, the customer's funds are gone, and the stop payment order is not effective.

This is the case in each of the first four specified events. The first event occurs when the bank accepts or certifies the item.[81] Upon acceptance or certification, the bank becomes liable on the item to the holder. Acceptance and certification were discussed in Chapter 3. The second event is when the bank pays the item in cash.[82] The third event is when the bank settles for the item without having a right to revoke the settlement under statute, clearing-house rule, or agreement.[83] The fourth event is when the bank becomes accountable for the amount of the item under §4-302.[84] We discussed the second, third, and fourth events in Chapter 5.

The fifth event occurs when, with respect to checks only, the stop payment order arrives after a cutoff hour established by the bank, or if no cutoff hour has been established, the stop payment order arrives after the close of the next banking day after the banking day on which the bank receives the check.[85] Assume that the bank does not establish a cutoff hour after which items are deemed to arrive on the next banking day. The bank closes each day at 5:00 P.M. A check is presented for payment on Tuesday. The stop payment order is too late if it arrives after 5:00 P.M. on Wednesday. If the bank had established a cutoff hour of 10:00 A.M., the stop payment order would have been too late had it arrived after 10:00 A.M. on Wednesday. Although the bank is not yet liable for the item by the time the stop payment order is deemed to be too late, the bank needs to know at what point in time it can safely pay an item without

80. U.C.C. §4-303(a).

81. U.C.C. §4-303(a)(1); U.C.C. §4-303, Official Comment 3. The time at which certification and acceptance is deemed to have occurred is discussed in Chapter 5.

82. U.C.C. §4-303(a)(2). The issue as to whether and when a bank has paid an item in cash is discussed in Chapter 5.

83. U.C.C. §4-303(a)(3). The issue as to when a bank has settled for an item without reserving a right to revoke the settlement is discussed in Chapter 5.

84. U.C.C. §4-303(a)(4); U.C.C. §4-303 Official Comment 5. The issue as to when and under what circumstances a bank becomes accountable for an item is discussed in Chapter 5.

85. U.C.C. §4-303(a)(5); U.C.C. §4-303, Official Comment 4.

worrying about a subsequent stop payment order. Therefore, once the earlier of either the cutoff hour or end of the next banking day has passed, the bank knows that it may safely pay the check (whether or not it receives a stop payment order after the designated hour but before actual payment).

Cutoff Hour.   A bank may not establish a cutoff hour earlier than one hour after the opening of the next banking day following the banking day on which the bank received the item.[86] If the bank opens for business at 9:00 A.M., it may not establish a cutoff hour prior to 10:00 A.M. on the next banking day following receipt of the item. For example, assume that 10:00 A.M. is established as the bank's cutoff hour. If the check is received by the bank on Tuesday, and a stop payment order is received on Wednesday at 9:59 A.M., the stop payment order is timely. A stop payment order that arrives at 11:30 A.M. on Wednesday is after the cutoff hour and is therefore too late.

Time to Process Stop Payment Order.   A bank needs time to process a stop payment order. For this reason, the stop payment order must arrive early enough to give the bank a reasonable time to act upon it prior to the time that the bank has done any of the above five specified events.[87] The bank must have a sufficient time for the stop payment order to be transmitted from the person receiving the order to the person who makes the decision to pay the item. Considering the pervasive presence of computers, "reasonable time" is probably a relatively short period.[88]

Branch Banking.   Most banks have many branches. If the branch at which you have your checking account is the Downtown Los Angeles Branch, must your stop payment order be sent to the Downtown Los Angeles Branch, or will a stop payment order issued to the Beverly Hills Branch be sufficient? As discussed in Chapter 5, each branch is considered to be a separate bank for most purposes. As a result, a stop payment order given to the Beverly Hills Branch will not be effective.[89] However, because the Beverly Hills branch is part of the same organization, it has a duty to forward the stop payment order to the

---

86. U.C.C. §4-303(a)(5); U.C.C. §4-303, Official Comment 4.

87. U.C.C. §4-303(a); U.C.C. §4-303, Official Comment 6. In the case of a setoff, because the bank itself is exercising the setoff, it needs no time to act upon the setoff. Therefore, the issue is simply whether the bank's actual exercise of the setoff occurred before one of the specified acts occurred. U.C.C. §4-303, Official Comment 6.

88. U.C.C. §4-303, Official Comment 6; see Chute v. Bank One, N.A., 10 Ohio App. 3d 122, 460 N.E.2d 720, 38 U.C.C. Rep. Serv. 949 (1983) (bank can place stop payment order in computer within very short time).

89. U.C.C. §4-107, Official Comment 2.

C. Customer's Right to Stop Payment

Downtown Los Angeles Branch.[90] The stop payment order will be effective when it is (or should have been) received by the Downtown Los Angeles Branch.

__Effect of Stop Payment Order Arriving on Time.__ Let us now first examine what happens when the stop payment order arrives prior to any of the five specified events. In this event, the payor bank has neither the right to pay the check nor a duty to its customer to pay the check. Thus, when a stop payment order comes in time to terminate the bank's right and duty to pay the check, the bank is liable to the drawer if in spite of the timely stop payment order, it pays the check.

__Effect of Stop Payment Order Arriving Too Late.__ What happens if a stop payment order comes too late? In this case, because the payor bank has the right to pay the check or other item,[91] it incurs no liability to the drawer by paying the item. Must the bank pay the item? Not necessarily. Although it has the right to pay the item, it may waive that right. Remember that it also has a duty to the customer to pay the item. However, by issuing the stop payment order, the drawer has, in effect, waived the bank's duty to pay the item. As a result, the bank is not liable to the drawer if it honors the stop payment order. Stopping payment was precisely what the drawer intended.

Under what circumstances will a bank honor a stop payment order that comes too late? The answer is—only when doing so will not cause it to be liable to the holder. When the bank is liable to the holder because it has made final payment under §4-215 or is accountable for the item under §4-302(a), the bank certainly cannot honor its customer's stop payment order. It already has, in essence, paid the item. We discussed in Chapter 5 the situations in which a payor bank is liable to the holder of an item. However, if the bank is not yet liable to the holder, the bank may honor the stop payment order as a favor to its customer. For example, assume that your bank has established a cutoff hour of 10:00 A.M. Your check to Ripuoff T.V. arrived at the bank on Tuesday. You call your bank at noon on Wednesday and ask that it stop payment on the check. If the bank has not already incurred liability to Ripuoff T.V. under one of the first four events, the bank may agree to stop payment of the check. Why might it do so? Because it wants to keep your goodwill.

---

90. U.C.C. §1-201(27); U.C.C. §4-107, Official Comment 4.
91. U.C.C. §4-303(a).

b. Priority Between Payment of Check and the "Legals"

Section 4-303(a) does not only apply to stop payment orders. It also applies to three other claims to the account out of which the item is drawn. These three other claims, nicknamed the "legals," include: (1) the payor bank learning that the drawer has filed a petition in bankruptcy, died, or become incompetent; (2) a creditor attaching or garnishing the bank account from which the item is to be paid; and (3) the bank setting off against the customer's account a debt owed to it by the customer.[92]

When there are sufficient funds in the account to pay the attaching creditor or to satisfy the bank's setoff and to pay the item that has been presented, there is no need to determine priority between the rights of the respective parties. However, when insufficient funds exist to pay both, to the extent that one of the legals is given priority over payment of the item, there may be insufficient funds left in the account to pay the item. For example, assume that your bank account contained $1,000 and that your rent check was $700. If one of your creditors garnished your account for a debt in the amount of $500 and the bank honored the garnishment, only $500 would remain in your account. As a result, there would be insufficient funds to pay your rent check.

Subsection 4-303(a) states a rule for determining the priority between the three legals and payment of the item. It answers the question of whether your bank is liable to you when it satisfies the garnishment instead of paying your rent check. Under §4-303(a), your bank is liable to you if it refuses to pay the item when the attachment or garnishment, setoff, or knowledge of your bankruptcy takes place after one of the same five events applicable in the case of a stop payment order.

Effect of Legal Arriving on Time. When a writ of attachment, garnishment, execution, or the like comes in time, the bank no longer has a duty to the customer to pay the check. As a result, if it refuses to pay the check, the bank is not liable to its customer for wrongful dishonor. Similarly, where a setoff is exercised by the bank in time, the bank has no duty to the customer to pay the check and thus may properly debit the customer's account. If the customer's account does not contain adequate funds to cover payment of the check, the bank may properly refuse to pay it.[93]

What happens if the bank, despite the fact that the legal is timely, pays the check? Is it liable to the creditor for whose benefit the writ was issued? Whether the payor bank is liable to the creditor is answered, not by Article 4,

---

92. U.C.C. §4-303, Official Comment 1.
93. U.C.C. §4-303, Official Comment 1.

but by the debtor-creditor law of the particular state.[94] The debtor-creditor law of most states would hold the payor bank to be liable to the creditor under these circumstances.[95] Similarly, if the bank acquires knowledge of the drawer's bankruptcy in time, the bank is liable to the trustee if it pays the check. Section 4-303 does not determine whether the trustee may recover the payment from the payee.[96]

Effect of Legal Arriving Too Late.   Recall that when a stop payment order came after one of the five specified events, the payor bank still had the option as to whether to honor the stop payment order. The bank does not have the same option in deciding whether to exercise its right of setoff or in honoring a writ of garnishment. When a writ of garnishment arrives after one of the five specified events has occurred, although the bank can waive its right to pay the check, it still owes a duty to its customer to pay the check. Unless its customer waives the duty, the payor bank will be liable to the customer for wrongful dishonor if it dishonors the check. Similarly, if the bank does not exercise its setoff in time, the bank breaches its duty to its customer if it refuses to pay the check.

The issue becomes a little more complex when the "legal" is the bank's knowledge of the drawer's bankruptcy. Assume your rent check was presented for payment on Tuesday. Although you filed a petition for bankruptcy on Monday, your bank did not learn of your bankruptcy until after the cutoff hour on Wednesday. As a result, the bank paid the check. Is the bank liable to your trustee in bankruptcy for the amount of the check? The answer is "no." It is true that at the moment that the petition is filed, all assets belong to your bankruptcy estate. However, the Bankruptcy Reform Act of 1978 is consistent with Article 4 in providing that the bank is not liable to the trustee for paying an item after the bankruptcy petition is filed as long as the bank does not have actual knowledge of the bankruptcy.[97]

94. See Pittsburgh Natl. Bank v. United States, 657 F.2d 36, 31 U.C.C. Rep. Serv. 1217 (1981) (§4-303 does not govern dispute between bank's right of setoff and federal tax lien); Aspen Indus., Inc. v. Marine Midland Bank, 52 N.Y. 2d 575, 439 N.Y.S 2d 316, 421 N.E. 2d 808 (1981) (§4-303 does not govern dispute between bank's right of setoff and garnishment).

95. See, e.g., Wilton Enter., Inc. v. Cook's Pantry, Inc., 230 N.J. Super. 126, 552 A.2d 1031, 8 U.C.C. Rep. Serv. 2d 128 (1988) (bank liable to creditor since levy came in time).

96. 11 U.S.C. §§549(a)(2)(A), 550(a).

97. 11 U.S.C. §542(c).

4. Damages for Payment in Violation of Stop Payment Order: Right to Recredit of Account

Let us examine the damages to which you would be entitled if your bank pays the Ripuoff T.V. check over your valid stop payment order. The mere fact that the bank has paid the check over your valid stop payment order entitles you to recover from the bank any damages you have suffered. Your bank is liable whether it failed to honor the stop payment order by accident or intentionally did so.[98] However, you have the burden of proving the amount of loss resulting from the payment contrary to the stop payment order.[99]

Although nothing in the Code states the appropriate measure of damages for payment over a valid stop payment order, the applicable measure is readily apparent. The measure is the difference between the amount paid by the bank and the amount that you would have been obligated to pay on the check had the stop payment order been honored by the bank. For example, assume that your check to Ripuoff T.V. was drawn in the amount of $1,000. Assume further that you had a $400 breach of warranty claim in recoupment that could have been asserted against Ripuoff T.V. had payment been stopped. First, assume that the bank pays Ripuoff T.V. Had payment been stopped, Ripuoff T.V. would have sued you for the $1,000. You would have asserted your $400 breach of warranty claim in recoupment against Ripuoff T.V. Thus, you would have been liable to Ripuoff T.V. for $600. Therefore, your damages arising from the bank's failure to stop payment of the check are the $400 that you could have avoided paying Ripuoff T.V. had payment been stopped.

However, assume instead that Ripuoff T.V. negotiated the check to Finance Company. If Finance Company qualifies as a holder in due course, it takes the check free of your claim in recoupment. Thus, even if payment had been stopped, you would have had to pay the entire $1,000 to Finance Company. As a result, you suffered no loss by virtue of the bank's failure to honor the stop payment order. Most checks are not negotiated by the payee to a third person, but are deposited into the payee's account at his bank. However, the possibility of a holder in due course acquiring the check is still great.

As we discussed in Chapter 2, when a depositary bank takes an item for collection, it may become a holder in due course if it allows its customer to draw upon the item or advances funds against the item. Thus, if Ripuoff T.V. had deposited the check in its bank account at Wells Bank, which allowed Ripuoff T.V. to withdraw the entire $1,000, Wells Bank would have been a

98. U.C.C. §4-403, Official Comment 7. Or to close the account.
99. U.C.C. §4-403(c). To close an account.

holder in due course of the check. As a holder in due course, it could have fully recovered from you. As a result, the bank's failure to honor the stop payment order did not cause you any loss.

There is one exception to this method of determining damages. Losses from the payment of an item contrary to a stop payment order may also include damages for the wrongful dishonor of subsequent items.[100] Unfortunately, it is not clear under what circumstances you are entitled to such damages. Assume that had the bank honored your stop payment order, there would have been sufficient funds in your account to pay your rent check. Has your bank wrongfully dishonored your rent check? The answer to this question is not as easy as it appears. This is because the Code does not indicate whether the initial debit by the bank is wrongful even if the customer cannot prove a loss resulting from the payment. The Code also does not indicate whether the customer's knowledge of the improper payment affects the bank's liability for wrongful dishonor of a subsequent item.

If you were unaware that the bank had failed to honor the stop payment order at the time you wrote the check to your landlord, your bank would be liable for wrongfully dishonoring your rent check. The result should not turn upon whether Ripuoff T.V. or Finance Company presented the check to your bank. Even though you would have been ultimately liable to Finance Company, your rent check would have been paid. However, courts under the previous version of Article 4 have indicated that where the bank would not have been ultimately required to recredit your account, it would not be liable for wrongful dishonor.[101] These cases appear to be misguided.

You should have no right to sue the bank for wrongful dishonor, however, if you already knew of the bank's payment of the Ripuoff T.V. check when you wrote your rent check. Under these circumstances, until you have proven to your bank that you suffered a loss due to the payment, your bank should have no obligation to recredit your account. Allowing you to create a wrongful dishonor by writing a check which you know will be dishonored is unjustifiable.

---

100. U.C.C. §4-403(c).

101. For cases under pre-amended Article 4 see Kunkel v. First Natl. Bank, 393 N.W.2d 265, 2 U.C.C. Rep. Serv. 2d 574 (N.D. 1986) (question of fact whether debit was proper where payment over valid stop payment order for bona fide debt caused several checks payable to suppliers to be dishonored); Chute v. Bank One, N.A., 10 Ohio App. 3d 122, 38 460 N.E.2d 720, 38 U.C.C. Rep. Serv. 949 (1983) (seems to intimate that an action for wrongful dishonor would be available only if debit is ultimately proved to be improper).

5. Payor Bank's Right of Subrogation on Improper Payment over a Valid Stop Payment Order and Otherwise

We have described the measure of damages to which you are entitled in the event that the bank has failed to honor your stop payment order. However, we have not discussed how the Code reaches this measure of damages. As mentioned, nothing in Article 4 specifies this measure.[102] The measure is arrived at by piecing together different provisions of the Code.

When your bank paid the Ripuoff T.V. check over your valid stop payment order, the bank lost its right to charge the payment to your account. However, denying the bank the right to charge your account will result in you being unjustly enriched by its mistake. If the bank has to recredit your account for the entire $1,000, you will have received a free television set worth $600. This is not fair. As a result, if a payor bank (your bank) has paid an item over the order of the drawer (you) to stop payment, to prevent unjust enrichment and only to the extent necessary to prevent loss to the bank by reason of its payment of the item, the payor bank is subrogated to the rights[103]

1. of any holder in due course on the item against the drawer or maker; and
2. of the payee or any other holder of the item against the drawer or maker either on the item or under the transaction out of which the item arose.

Thus, assuming that Ripuoff T.V. was the party paid, your bank would be subrogated to Ripuoff T.V.'s rights against you on the check and on the underlying obligation. Since Ripuoff T.V. could recover $600 ($1,000 purchase price minus the $400 breach of warranty damages) from you, your bank can also recover $600 from you. As a result, it has to recredit your account only for the $400 difference between the amount of the item and the amount to which it is subrogated to Ripuoff T.V.'s rights against you. Assuming that Finance

---

102. Nothing in the Code clearly specifies how the customer's burden of proof works in conjunction with the bank's right of subrogation. The most reasonable allocation is to require that the customer first prove that he issued an effective order. The bank should then be required to introduce evidence of the absence of loss on the customer's part by proving its subrogation rights under §4-407(1) or (2). If it fails to do so, a verdict should be directed in favor of the customer. However, once the bank proves its subrogation rights, the burden should shift to the customer to prove the existence of a defense effective against the payee or holder in due course and the amount of such a defense.

103. U.C.C. §4-407(1) and U.C.C. §4-407(2) respectively.

C. Customer's Right to Stop Payment

Company was the party paid, and since Finance Company could recover the entire $1,000 from you on the check, your bank can also recover $1,000 from you. As a result, it does not have to recredit your account at all.

Let us return to the example where the bank paid Ripuoff T.V. Even if your bank has to recredit your account for $400 only, it still is out of pocket that amount. Ripuoff T.V. still has the entire $1,000 even though you had a breach of warranty action against it for $400. In order to prevent Ripuoff T.V. from being unjustly enriched, your bank (the payor bank) is subrogated to your rights (as drawer) against Ripuoff T.V. (the payee) or any other holder of the item with respect to the transaction out of which the item arose.[104] Because you had a $400 breach of warranty action against Ripuoff T.V., your bank will also have the right to recover $400 from Ripuoff T.V. The payor bank usually has the right to recover only from the payee. Because subsequent holders, such as Finance Company, are not liable to the drawer for the payee's breach of contract, there will probably be no rights under which the payor bank may be subrogated against these subsequent parties.

As a result, the loss resulting from the improper payment is imposed on the party ultimately responsible for the loss. Assuming Ripuoff T.V. is solvent, the same party suffers the loss whether or not the bank honored the stop payment order. However, if Ripuoff T.V. is insolvent, whether you or your bank suffers the loss depends upon whether the check has been acquired by a holder in due course. You suffer the loss only if you would have suffered the loss had payment been properly stopped. If payment had been stopped, and Ripuoff T.V. sued you, you could have asserted your claim in recoupment. Because the payor bank's failure to honor the stop payment order denied you the ability to recover from the insolvent Ripuoff T.V., the payor bank must suffer the resultant loss. However, if the check had been acquired by Finance Company (a holder in due course), even if the payor bank honored the stop payment order, Finance Company would have recovered the entire amount from you. You would have been left with a worthless claim in recoupment action against the insolvent Ripuoff T.V. Because the payor bank's failure to stop payment of the check did not cause your loss, you must suffer the loss occasioned by Ripuoff T.V.'s insolvency.

Your bank has the burden of proving the claim to which it is subrogated. If your bank asserts your breach of warranty claim against Ripuoff T.V., your bank must prove that Ripuoff T.V. breached its warranty.

The bank's subrogation rights arise not only when a payor bank has paid a check over a valid stop payment order, but also in any situation in which the payor bank cannot charge its customer's account for the payment. These situ-

104. U.C.C. §4-407(3).

ations include, among others: a bank that has paid a note or accepted a draft payable at the bank in violation of a valid stop payment order in any state adopting Alternative A to §4-106(b);[105] a bank that makes an early payment of a postdated check in violation of a proper notice of the postdating issued by the drawer under §4-401(c);[106] and a bank that, with knowledge of its customer's death, pays a check more than ten days after the death.[107]

105. A question does arise in the case of drafts or notes payable at a bank where the state has adopted Alternative B to U.C.C. §3-121 where the bank wrongly pays the instrument even though it was not ordered to do so. The issue is whether allowing the bank a right of subrogation defeats the purpose of adoption of Alternative B which is to allow the drawer to choose which creditor to pay. Furthermore, not being the payor bank, the bank technically is not covered by §4-407.

106. See Peck v. Franklin Natl. Bank, 4 U.C.C. Rep. Serv. 861 (N.Y. Sup. 1967); Siegel v. New England Merchants Natl. Bank, 386 Mass. 672, 437 N.E.2d 218, 33 U.C.C. Rep. Serv. 1601 (1982).

107. U.C.C. §4-405(b).

CHAPTER 7

Wholesale Funds Transfers

A. WHAT IS A FUNDS TRANSFER?

General Motors ("GM") agrees to purchase computers from International Business Machines ("IBM") for a price of $5 million. IBM will not deliver the computers until the purchase price is paid. GM wants the computers immediately. How does it make payment? Does GM mail IBM a check? Sending a check will delay the purchase by several days while IBM awaits payment of the check. Does GM send a messenger to IBM with $5 million in cash? The messenger may be robbed while carrying the cash.

What GM will probably do is instruct its bank, Bank of America, by telephone to pay $5 million to IBM's account at Chase Manhattan Bank. Bank of America will then debit GM's account and wire instructions to IBM's bank, Chase Manhattan Bank, to credit IBM's account in that amount. Chase Manhattan Bank will credit IBM's account and, as a means of obtaining payment, debit the account that Bank of America maintains with it.[1] (See Figure 7.1.) The transaction will be completed on the same day with virtually no risk of anything going wrong.

---

1. See U.C.C. §4A-104, Official Comment 1, Case #2.

FIGURE 7.1

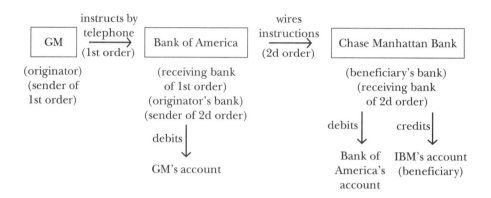

The form of payment used by GM in our example above is a funds transfer (also sometimes known as a "wire transfer" or a "wholesale wire transfer").[2] With certain exceptions discussed below, funds transfers are governed by Article 4A.[3] Prior to examining which funds transfers are governed by Article 4A, it is important to understand the terminology employed in Article 4A.

1.   Terminology of Funds Transfers

GM, in our example above, is the sender. A "sender" is the person giving the instruction to the receiving bank.[4] GM is also the customer of Bank of America. A "customer" is a person having an account with a bank or from whom a bank has agreed to receive payment orders.[5] Bank of America is the receiving bank. A "receiving bank" is the bank to which the sender's instruction is addressed.[6] Bank of America is the receiving bank because GM has instructed Bank of America to pay IBM.

IBM is the beneficiary. A "beneficiary" is the person to be paid by the ben-

2. Specifically, this type of funds transfer transmitted electronically between two banks is called a "wholesale wire transfer." While checks and credit cards are the most common form of payment as measured by the number of transactions per day, wholesale wire transfers far exceed all other payment systems as measured by dollar volume on a daily basis. Each wholesale wire transfer usually exceeds six figures. A majority of funds transfers covered by Article 4A are, in fact, wholesale wire transfers. See Prefatory Note, U.C.C., Article 4A (Official Text 1989).

3. U.C.C. §4A-102.

4. U.C.C. §4A-103(a)(5).

5. U.C.C. §4A-105(a)(3). One bank can be the customer of another bank. If Bank of America issues a payment order to Bank of Missouri, Bank of America is the customer of Bank of Missouri. Id.

6. U.C.C. §4A-103(a)(4).

eficiary's bank.[7] IBM is the beneficiary because GM has instructed Bank of America to cause Chase Manhattan Bank to pay IBM. Chase Manhattan Bank is the beneficiary's bank. A "beneficiary's bank" is "the bank identified in a payment order in which an account of the beneficiary is to be credited pursuant to the order or which otherwise is to make payment to the beneficiary if the order does not provide for payment to an account."[8] Chase Manhattan Bank is the beneficiary's bank because GM's payment order instructed Chase Manhattan Bank to credit IBM's account.

The instruction from GM to Bank of America is a payment order. A "payment order," is defined in part as "an instruction of a sender to a receiving bank, transmitted orally, electronically, or in writing, to pay, or to cause another bank to pay, a fixed or determinable amount of money to a beneficiary."[9] GM, the sender, gave an instruction orally, by telephone, to Bank of America, the receiving bank, to cause Chase Manhattan Bank to pay a fixed amount, $5 million, to a beneficiary, IBM.

Bank of America's wire to Chase Manhattan Bank is also a payment order. As to this payment order, Bank of America is the sender, Chase Manhattan Bank is the receiving bank and IBM is the beneficiary. There are, therefore, two payment orders in this funds transfer. The first payment order is the order from GM to Bank of America. The second payment order is the order from Bank of America to Chase Manhattan Bank. GM, as the sender of the first payment order, is the "originator" of the funds transfer.[10] Bank of America is the originator's bank.[11] An "originator's bank" is the receiving bank to which the payment order of the originator is issued if the originator is not a bank.[12] Where a bank is the originator, that bank is both the originator and the originator's bank. Assume, for example, that Bank of America owed IBM money for the purchase of computers. If Bank of America issued an instruction to Chase Manhattan Bank to pay IBM, Bank of America would be both the originator and the originator's bank.

2. What Is a Funds Transfer?

Now we can examine what makes the above transaction a funds transfer? A "funds transfer" is "the series of transactions, beginning with the originator's

---

7. U.C.C. §4A-103(a)(2).
8. U.C.C. §4A-103(a)(3).
9. U.C.C. §4A-103(a)(1).
10. U.C.C. §4A-104(c).
11. U.C.C. §4A-104(d).
12. U.C.C. §4A-104(d).

payment order, made for the purpose of making payment to the beneficiary of the order."[13] In our example, a series of transactions—the two payment orders—began with GM's (the originator) payment order, which was made for the purpose of making payment to IBM (the beneficiary of the order).

The term "funds transfer" includes "any payment order issued by the originator's bank or an intermediary bank intended to carry out the originator's payment order." Thus, Bank of America's wire and Chase Manhattan Bank's subsequent payment to IBM are part of the funds transfer originated by GM.

3. Manner of Making a Funds Transfer

There are many ways in which a funds transfer may be accomplished. The above example involved two payment orders: one from GM to Bank of America, and a second from Bank of America to Chase Manhattan Bank. However, a funds transfer may involve only one payment order. For instance, if both IBM and GM have an account with Bank of America, GM could instruct Bank of America to credit IBM's account. In this instance, Bank of America would be both the receiving bank and the beneficiary's bank.[14] This type of transaction is called a "book transfer" because the payment is accomplished by the receiving bank both crediting the account of the beneficiary and debiting the account of the sender.

A funds transfer may involve more than two payment orders.[15] Altering the facts of the original example, assume that Bank of America does not have an account at Chase Manhattan Bank. Bank of America may instruct any bank with which it has an account and which has an account with Chase Manhattan Bank[16] to pay $5 million to IBM's account at Chase Manhattan Bank. This bank, call it Bank of Missouri (or the "intermediary bank"), will debit Bank of America's account and then send a payment order to Chase Manhattan Bank which then will credit IBM's account and debit the account of Bank of Missouri.[17] (See Figure 7.2.)

13. U.C.C. §4A-104(a).
14. U.C.C. §4A-104, Official Comment 1, Case #1.
15. U.C.C. §4A-104, Official Comment 1, Case #3.
16. U.C.C. §4A-104(b) defines "intermediary bank" as a receiving bank other than the originator's bank or the beneficiary's bank.
17. U.C.C. §4A-104, Official Comment 1, Case #3.

A. What Is a Funds Transfer?

FIGURE 7.2

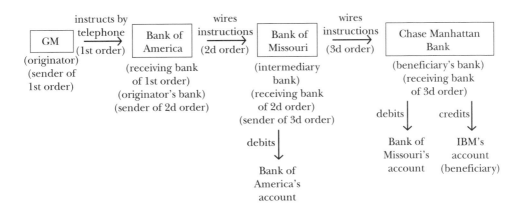

In this variation, there are three payment orders: one from GM to Bank of America, a second from Bank of America to Bank of Missouri, and a third from Bank of Missouri to Chase Manhattan Bank.

At times, the originator and the beneficiary may be the same entity.[18] For example, GM may have two separate accounts at Bank of America and may want Bank of America to transfer the funds from one account to the other. In other cases, Bank of America may be both the originator and the originator's bank. For example, Bank of America may owe money to IBM and issue a payment order for its own account.

4. Funds Transfer Must Be Between Banks

Because an instruction must be sent to a receiving bank requesting it to pay or to cause another bank to pay money to the beneficiary,[19] a funds transfer is limited to payments made through the banking system. A transfer of funds by an entity other than a bank is excluded.[20] Banks do not include companies, for example, Western Union, not engaged in the business of banking. Transfers of funds through Western Union, or similar companies, therefore, are not covered by Article 4A.

18. U.C.C. §4A-104, Official Comment 1.

19. U.C.C. §4A-103(a)(1).

20. "Bank" is defined as "a person engaged in the business of banking and includes a savings bank, savings and loan association, credit union, and trust company." U.C.C. §4A-105(a)(2). See also U.C.C. §4A-104, Official Comment 2.

5. *Other Requirements for Funds Transfer*

In addition to being an instruction from a sender to a receiving bank to pay, or to cause another bank to pay, a fixed amount of money to a beneficiary, an instruction to be a payment order must meet the following three requirements. First, the instruction cannot state a condition to the obligation to pay the beneficiary other than as to the time of payment.[21] For example, an instruction that states that Chase Manhattan Bank is to pay IBM only upon delivery of bills of lading covering 400 IBM PC computers is not a payment order.[22] Conditional orders are excluded because Article 4A is structured specifically to cover low price, high speed transactions in which the banks' actions are purely mechanical.

Second, the receiving bank must be paid or reimbursed by the sender.[23] In other words, the instruction must be sent by the person who is going to make the payment. When GM orders Bank of America to pay IBM, GM is both the sender and the person who will make payment to Bank of America. Therefore, the order is a payment order. In contrast, assume that GM has a preexisting arrangement with its California distributor that the distributor has the right to order Bank of America to transfer funds from GM's account to the distributor's account in payment for expenses incurred by the distributor. Under this arrangement, the distributor's order to Bank of America would not be a payment order. This is because the distributor would be the sender, but it is GM's account that is to be debited.

Third, the instruction must be transmitted by the sender directly to the receiving bank or to the sender's agent, funds-transfer system, or communication system for transmittal to the receiving bank.[24] GM must send the order directly to Bank of America or through someone whose sole purpose is to communicate the order to Bank of America. This requirement eliminates credit cards and checks from coverage under Article 4A.[25] In these types of transfers, the instruction is not sent directly to the receiving bank, nor through an agent of the sender, nor to a funds-transfer system or communication system for transmittal to the receiving bank. If GM sends a check to IBM, IBM presents the check for payment to Bank of America. GM does not send the check directly to the Bank of America. Similarly, if GM were to pay IBM by credit card, GM would not be directly ordering Bank of America to pay IBM. GM would, instead, give the credit card slip to IBM. As we discuss in Chapter 9,

21. U.C.C. §4A-103(a)(1)(i).
22. U.C.C. §4A-104, Official Comment 3.
23. U.C.C. §4A-103(a)(1)(ii).
24. U.C.C. §4-103(a)(1)(iii).
25. U.C.C. §4A-104, Official Comment 5.

IBM would then send the slip to Chase Manhattan Bank which would electronically send the information on the slip to Bank of America (assuming that the credit card was issued by Bank of America).

6. Funds-Transfer Systems

Although most payment orders are wire transfers involving electronic transmissions, the manner in which a payment order is sent does not determine the applicability of Article 4A.[26] If the other requirements of Article 4A are met, Article 4A applies to payment orders sent orally, electronically, or in writing.[27] A telephone instruction can qualify as a payment order.[28] The order may be transmitted directly by Bank of America to Chase Manhattan Bank, through an agent, or through a funds-transfer system or communication system.[29]

Most payment orders are sent through a funds-transfer system. A "funds-transfer system" is a wire transfer network, automated clearing house, or other communication system of a clearinghouse or other association of banks through which a payment order by a bank may be transmitted to the bank to which the order is addressed.[30]

The two principal funds-transfer systems are Fedwire and CHIPS. Fedwire and CHIPS carry out large currency transfers between banks for the settlement of transactions.[31] Fedwire, operated by the Federal Reserve System,[32] is an automated network connecting Federal Reserve banks.[33] Fedwire handles three kinds of messages: (1) transfers of account balances between banks having accounts with the Federal Reserve; (2) transfers of United States government and federal agency securities; and (3) certain other information related to payments.[34]

---

26. U.C.C. §4A-104, Official Comment 6.

27. U.C.C. §4A-103(a)(1).

28. U.C.C. §4A-104, Official Comment 6.

29. U.C.C. §4A-103(a)(1)(iii); U.C.C. §4A-104, Official Comment 6.

30. U.C.C. §4A-105(a)(5).

31. There is also Society of Worldwide Interbank Financial Telecommunication ("SWIFT"). SWIFT is purely a communications and message switching network with no payment capacity. Having no payment capacity, receipt over SWIFT of the sending bank's payment message gives no assurance to the receiving bank that funds, in fact, will be transferred.

32. See Carl Felsenfeld, Legal Aspects of Electronic Funds Transfers 75 (1988).

33. See Donald Baker & Roland Brandel, The Law of Electronic Fund Transfer Systems 11-3 (Rev. ed. 1996). In addition, there is a Network Management Control Center in Chicago. Id.

34. See Donald Baker & Roland Brandel, The Law of Electronic Fund Transfer Systems 11-7 (Rev. ed. 1996).

A typical Fedwire transfer operates in the following manner. Assume that Bank of America has an account at the San Francisco Federal Reserve Bank and Chase Manhattan Bank has an account at the New York Federal Reserve Bank. Bank of America sends a payment order to the San Francisco Federal Reserve Bank, which will then debit Bank of America's account with it and credit the account of the New York Federal Reserve Bank. The San Francisco Federal Reserve Bank will then issue an instruction to the New York Federal Reserve Bank to credit the account of Chase Manhattan Bank and debit the account of the San Francisco Federal Reserve Bank.[35] The New York Federal Reserve Bank will then advise Chase Manhattan Bank of the credit. (See Figure 7.3.)

FIGURE 7.3

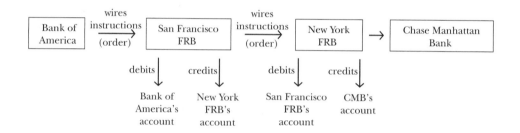

CHIPS is privately owned by the 12 New York banks that make up the New York Clearing House.[36] Although CHIPS processes some domestic funds transfers, its main purpose is to process international transfers between its members that act as intermediaries for foreign banking organizations with which they have a correspondent relationship.[37] Unlike Fedwire, a transfer through CHIPS is not a present transfer of funds.[38] In a CHIPS transaction, the sending bank will send its payment message to the receiving bank sometime during the banking day. Although the message instructs the receiving bank to pay the beneficiary, the message does not operate to transfer any funds from the sending bank to the receiving bank. Rather, the sending bank pays the receiving bank at the end of the banking day by ordering a Federal Reserve Bank to credit the receiving bank's account with the Federal Reserve Bank and to debit

35. U.C.C. §4A-107, Official Comment 1.
36. See Carl Felsenfeld, Legal Aspects of Electronic Funds Transfers 86 (1988).
37. See Donald Baker & Roland Brandel, The Law of Electronic Fund Transfer Systems 11-13 (Rev. ed. 1996).
38. See Carl Felsenfeld, Legal Aspects of Electronic Funds Transfers 87 (1988).

the sending bank's own account at the same Federal Reserve Bank.[39] As a result, the receipt of the payment message does not guarantee that the receiving bank will actually receive the funds. Because of this risk of nonpayment, CHIPS has adopted a loss sharing plan under which CHIPS participants contribute to a fund which is used to complete the settlement obligation of any participant unable to meet its obligations.[40]

Let us look at a typical CHIPS transaction. For example, assume that BMW, located in Germany, wanted to pay for computers purchased from IBM, located in New York. BMW would request its bank, Bank of Munich, to transfer funds to Chase Manhattan Bank (IBM's bank). Bank of Munich would send instructions by cable to European American Bank (its correspondent bank in the United States) to pay Chase Manhattan Bank. Assuming that the instructions arrive in the morning, European American Bank would, after verifying the instructions, send a payment message to Chase Manhattan Bank that same morning. Chase Manhattan Bank would then credit IBM's account. At the close of business that day, around 5:30 P.M., the CHIPS computer would prepare a report showing the net position between European American Bank and Chase Manhattan Bank.[41] This net position shows the net amount owed after offsetting the amount that European American Bank owes Chase Manhattan Bank from all of the payment orders it transmitted during the day against the amount that Chase Manhattan Bank owes European American Bank from all of the payment orders that it transmitted during that day. Whichever of the banks has transmitted a greater amount of funds will then be required to pay the other bank the difference. Payment will usually be made by debiting the paying bank's account and crediting the other bank's account at a Federal Reserve Bank.

A transfer can also be made through an automated clearing house ("ACH").[42] An ACH is especially useful when the originator makes numerous payments to different beneficiaries having accounts at different banks. For example, GM may have many suppliers to pay. GM will send instructions to Bank of America to pay all of these suppliers at their various banks. Assume that the list includes paying IBM at Chase Manhattan Bank and Westinghouse at Bank of Newport. This list of instructions will be sent to Bank of America either on a magnetic tape or in an electronic device. Bank of America will send

---

39. See Prefatory Note, U.C.C. Article 4A. See also Carl Felsenfeld, Legal Aspects of Electronic Funds Transfers 87 (1988).

40. See Nelson, Settlement Obligations and Bank Insolvency, 45 Bus. Law. 1473, 1478-1479 (1990).

41. See Donald Baker & Roland Brandel, The Law of Electronic Fund Transfer Systems 11-14 (Rev. ed. 1996).

42. U.C.C. §4A-107, Official Comment 2.

the tape or device to an ACH, which will process and repackage GM's instructions by separating out the instructions going to each particular bank and packaging these instructions with instructions from other originators to the same bank so that they can be transmitted together to that bank. The instruction to pay IBM at Chase Manhattan Bank will be combined with all other instructions received from other originators to pay beneficiaries at Chase Manhattan Bank. Similarly, the instruction to pay Westinghouse at Bank of Newport will be combined with other instructions to pay beneficiaries at Bank of Newport. The ACH will send these new packages of instructions to Chase Manhattan Bank and Bank of Newport respectively. (See Figure 7.4.) ACHs are operated by Federal Reserve banks and by other associations of banks.

FIGURE 7.4

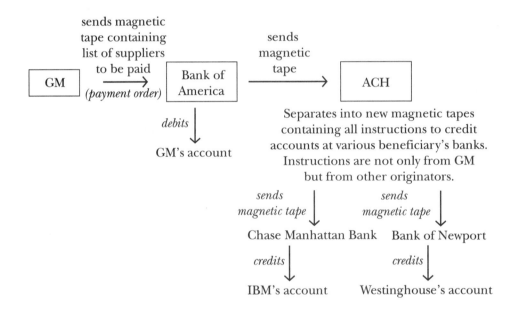

7. *Consumer Transactions Excluded*

Consumer transactions often present special concerns. Some funds transfers involving consumers are, as a result, not governed by Article 4A. Instead, they are governed by the Electronic Fund Transfer Act of 1978 ("EFTA").[43] The

---

43. U.C.C. §4A-108.

A. What Is a Funds Transfer?

EFTA is a federal statute covering many types of consumer electronic fund transfers. The EFTA and Article 4A are mutually exclusive.[44] Article 4A does not apply to a transaction if any part of the transaction is covered by the EFTA. For example, a funds transfer is not covered by Article 4A if the funds transfer is to a consumer account in the beneficiary's bank and made in part by Fedwire and in part by an automated clearinghouse. Because part of the transaction is governed by the EFTA, the entire transaction is excluded from Article 4A. If the transfer was made in whole through Fedwire and CHIPS (which are excluded from the EFTA), the transfer would be covered by Article 4A even though the transfer is effected for a consumer.[45]

8. Variation by Agreement

The provisions of Article 4A may be varied or even superseded by the agreement of the affected parties, a funds-transfer system rule, Federal Reserve Board regulations, or Federal Reserve bank operating circulars.

Except as otherwise provided in Article 4A, the rights and obligations of a party to a funds transfer subject to Article 4A may be varied by agreement of the affected party.[46] Even more importantly, except as otherwise provided in Article 4A, a funds-transfer system rule is effective even if it conflicts with an Article 4A rule.[47] Certain provisions of Article 4A specifically provide that, to the extent noted in these provisions, a funds-transfer system rule also may govern rights and obligations of parties other than participating banks using the system. These provisions are §4A-404(c) (governing the obligation of the beneficiary's bank to pay the beneficiary and give notice to the beneficiary), §4A-405(d) (provisional nature of settlement given by the beneficiary's bank to the beneficiary) and §4A-507(c) (choice of governing law). Aside from these explicit exceptions, however, a funds-transfer system rule can have a direct effect only on participating banks.[48]

The rule may, though, have an indirect effect on another party to the funds transfer even if the party does not consent to the rule.[49] For example, a rule might prevent execution of a payment order or might allow cancellation of a payment order with the result that a funds transfer is not completed. The rule operates directly only upon the participating bank sending the order and

44. U.C.C. §4A-108, Official Comment.
45. 15 U.S.C. §1693(a)(6)(B).
46. U.C.C. §4A-501(a).
47. U.C.C. §4A-501(b).
48. U.C.C. §4A-501, Official Comment 1.
49. U.C.C. §4A-501(b); U.C.C. §4A-501, Official Comment 1.

the participating bank receiving the order. Yet, by allowing cancellation of the order, both the originator and the beneficiary are indirectly affected. Had the rule tried to define rights and obligations of the non-participating originator and the beneficiary themselves, the rule would have no effect.

Section 4A-107 specifically provides that regulations of the Board of Governors of the Federal Reserve System supersede any inconsistent provision of Article 4A to the extent of the inconsistency.[50] The Board of Governors of the Federal Reserve System, pursuant to Federal Reserve Act §§13, 11(i), and 16 and the Expedited Funds Availability Act, has promulgated subpart B of Regulation J to govern transfers through Fedwire.[51] Regulation J incorporates the provisions of Article 4A to the extent that they are not inconsistent.[52]

Federal Reserve Banks issue operating circulars governing certain aspects of funds transfers.[53] Section 4A-107 makes it clear that an operating circular of a Federal Reserve Bank supersedes Article 4A to the extent that it is consistent. As a consequence, reference should be made to Regulation J and Federal Reserve Bank operating circulars, in addition to Article 4A, in determining the rights of parties to Fedwire transfers.

B.   OVERVIEW OF FUNDS TRANSFER

Let us return to our example of GM's $5 million computer purchase from IBM. GM issues a payment order to Bank of America, which then issues a payment order to an intermediary bank, Bank of Missouri, which in turn issues a payment order to Chase Manhattan Bank, the beneficiary's [IBM] bank. (See Figure 7.2.)

Subject to two minor exceptions,[54] acceptance of a payment order by a receiving bank, other than the beneficiary's bank, obligates the sender to pay the bank the amount of the sender's order.[55] Thus, upon acceptance by Bank of America, GM becomes obligated to pay Bank of America the amount of the order. Similarly, upon acceptance of the payment order sent by Bank of

50. U.C.C. §4A-107; U.C.C. §4A-501, Official Comment 1.

51. 12 U.S.C. §§342, 248(i) and (j), 248(o); 12 U.S.C. 4001; 12 C.F.R. §210.25-32; 12 C.F.R. §210.25.

52. 12 C.F.R. §210.25(b)(1).

53. U.C.C. §4A-107, Official Comment 3.

54. Section 4A-402(e) (suspension of payments by chosen intermediary bank) and §4A-303 (erroneous execution of payment order).

55. U.C.C. §4A-402(c);U.C.C. §4A-402, Official Comment 2.

America to Bank of Missouri, Bank of America becomes obligated to pay Bank of Missouri the amount of the order. This is the only obligation of the sender of a payment order; the sender has no liability to any subsequent party.[56] GM has no obligation to pay Bank of Missouri. GM's duty, as sender, to pay Bank of America does not arise until the execution date of the order.[57]

1.   Money-Back Guarantee

GM's obligation to pay Bank of America is dependent upon the funds transfer being completed. If the funds do not reach IBM, GM's obligation to pay Bank of America is discharged. In other words, the obligation of the sender is excused if the funds transfer is not completed because the beneficiary's bank does not accept the payment order.[58]

GM has a "money-back guarantee" that if the funds transfer is not completed, GM will receive its money back.[59] This means that if GM has not yet paid Bank of America, it is relieved of its obligation to pay Bank of America. If GM has made payment, Bank of America must refund the money to GM.[60] The same applies to Bank of America's obligation to pay Bank of Missouri. The money-back guarantee applies if, for any reason, Chase Manhattan Bank (the beneficiary's bank) does not accept the payment order.

The money-back guarantee has an effect on the allocation of a loss caused by an error or the insolvency of an intermediary bank. If the funds transfer was not completed either because of an error on the part of the Bank of Missouri or Bank of Missouri's insolvency, the loss falls upon Bank of America and not upon GM.[61] Bank of America must refund the money to GM and seek its recourse from Bank of Missouri. There is one exception to this rule. If GM instructed Bank of America to route the order through Bank of Missouri, GM is obligated to reimburse Bank of America if Bank of Missouri cannot refund the payment because of applicable law or because it has suspended payments.[62] Having chosen to use Bank of Missouri, GM, and not Bank of

---

56. U.C.C. §4A-402, Official Comment 3.

57. U.C.C. §4A-402(c). This is true even if Bank of America executes the order early.

58. U.C.C. §4A-402(c).

59. U.C.C. §4A-402, Official Comment 2. This right of the sender to be excused from payment may not be varied by agreement. U.C.C. §4A-402(f).

60. U.C.C. §4A-402(d). Subject to §4A-204 (duty to report unauthorized orders) and §4A-304 (duty of sender to report erroneously executed payment orders), interest is payable on the refundable amount from the date of sender's payment to the receiving bank.U.C.C. §4A-402(d).

61. U.C.C. §4A-402, Official Comment 2.

62. U.C.C. §4A-402(e).

America, suffers the loss.[63] To protect GM, it is subrogated to Bank of America's right to a refund from Bank of Missouri.[64]

2. *Issuance of Payment Order to Beneficiary's Bank*

When a payment order is issued to the beneficiary's bank, acceptance of the order by the beneficiary's bank obligates the sender to pay the beneficiary's bank the amount of the order.[65] For example, Bank of Missouri, which sent the order, is obligated to pay Chase Manhattan Bank upon Chase Manhattan Bank's acceptance of the order. Payment is not due until the payment date of the order.[66] The obligation of Bank of Missouri, the sender, to pay Chase Manhattan Bank arises on the payment date.[67] We discuss in section C how to determine the payment date. Upon acceptance by Chase Manhattan Bank, the obligation of GM to pay IBM for the computers is discharged and the obligation of Chase Manhattan Bank to pay IBM is substituted for it.

3. *Payment by Sender to Receiving Bank*

Let us return to the example of Bank of America sending its payment order directly to Chase Manhattan Bank. How does Bank of America actually transfer the funds to Chase Manhattan Bank in satisfaction of the payment order that it sent? The payment order does not alone result in Bank of America transferring funds to Chase Manhattan Bank. It only instructs Chase Manhattan Bank to pay IBM. There are three principal ways in which a sender can make payment: book transfer, Fedwire, or through a funds-transfer system like CHIPS.

a. Book Transfers

The simplest way for the sender to make payment is through a "book transfer." If Bank of America has an account with Chase Manhattan Bank,

---

63. U.C.C. §4A-402, Official Comment 2.

64. U.C.C. §4A-402(e); U.C.C. §4A-402, Official Comment 2. The right of a sender to a refund from the intermediary bank may not be varied by agreement. U.C.C. §4A-402(f).

65. U.C.C. §4A-402(b); U.C.C. §4A-402, Official Comment 1. Bank of Missouri's obligation to pay Chase Manhattan Bank is subject to §4A-205 (erroneous payment orders) and §4A-207 (misdescription of beneficiary).U.C.C. §4A-402(a).

66. U.C.C. §4A-402(b).

67. U.C.C. §4A-402, Official Comment 1.

B. Overview of Funds Transfer

Chase Manhattan Bank can obtain payment from Bank of America by debiting its account. Chase Manhattan Bank then credits IBM's account. It is called a "book transfer" because the entire transfer of funds is accomplished by entries in Chase Manhattan's books of account. If Bank of America has no account with Chase Manhattan Bank, it may send the payment order through Bank of Missouri, which will debit Bank of America's account with it. Upon receipt of the payment order, Chase Manhattan Bank will debit Bank of Missouri's account. Bank of Missouri's payment (or Bank of America if it has an account with Chase Manhattan Bank) to Chase Manhattan Bank is made when the debit is made assuming there are sufficient funds in Bank of Missouri's account at Chase Manhattan Bank to cover the debit.[68]

If it desires, Bank of America can instead make payment to Chase Manhattan Bank by crediting Chase Manhattan Bank's account with Bank of America (or causing Chase Manhattan Bank's account at another bank, like Bank of Missouri to be credited). In this event, payment occurs when Chase Manhattan Bank withdraws the credit.[69] If Chase Manhattan Bank does not withdraw the credit, payment occurs at midnight of the day on which Chase Manhattan Bank learns that the credit can be withdrawn.[70] Assume that Bank of America advises Chase Manhattan Bank that it has credited Chase Manhattan Bank's account in the amount of the order.[71] If Chase Manhattan Bank immediately withdraws the credit, payment occurs upon withdrawal. Chase Manhattan Bank may withdraw the credit by ordering, for example, that Bank of America pay a third party. If the credit is not withdrawn, payment does not occur until midnight of the day the funds are made available to Chase Manhattan Bank. This allows Chase Manhattan Bank time to reject the order if it so desires.[72]

When Bank of America and Chase Manhattan Bank transmit payment orders to each other under an agreement that settlement will be made at the end of the day (or at the end of some other specified period), the total amount owed with respect to all orders transmitted by Bank of America is set off against the total amount owed with respect to all orders transmitted by Chase Manhattan Bank. To the extent of the setoff, each bank has made payment to the other.[73] This becomes important in the event that either bank

68. U.C.C. §4A-403(a)(3); U.C.C. §4A-403, Official Comment 3. The same would hold true if the sender was not a bank. U.C.C. §4A-403(a)(3); U.C.C. §4A-403, Official Comment 3.

69. U.C.C. §4A-403(a)(2).

70. U.C.C. §4A-403(a)(2).

71. U.C.C. §4A-403, Official Comment 2.

72. Chase Manhattan Bank may want to reject the order if it does not have time to withdraw the credit and does not want to advance the beneficiary the amount of the credit. U.C.C. §4A-403, Official Comment 2.

73. U.C.C. §4A-403(c); U.C.C. §4A-403, Official Comment 4.

becomes insolvent. For example, Bank of America may go into insolvency proceedings when it has not yet paid some of the orders it has sent to Chase Manhattan Bank and also has not received payment on some of the orders it has received from Chase Manhattan Bank. Because of the setoff, each individual payment order sent by Bank of America is not treated as a separate liability nor is each individual payment order received by Bank of America treated as a separate asset. Rather, the amount owed by or owed to Bank of America is its net position after the setoff.

b.   Settlement Through Fedwire, Clearing House, and Funds-Transfer Systems

When either Fedwire is used or settlement is effected through a Federal Reserve Bank, settlements are made by a debit to the sender's account at the Federal Reserve Bank and a credit to the receiving bank's account at the Federal Reserve Bank.[74] Thus, if Bank of America uses Fedwire to send the payment order, the Federal Reserve Bank will debit Bank of America's account and will credit Chase Manhattan Bank's account.[75] Since Bank of America, the sender, is a bank, payment to Chase Manhattan Bank occurs when Chase Manhattan Bank receives the settlement through the Federal Reserve Bank.[76] The same principle applies when payment is made through a funds-transfer system or through a clearing house.[77]

c.   Multilateral Netting

A different rule applies when there is a funds-transfer system that nets obligations multilaterally among participants.[78] Assume that Chase Manhattan Bank and Bank of America are part of such a funds-transfer system. Chase Manhattan Bank receives final settlement when the settlement is completed in accordance with the rules of the system. If permitted by the rules of the system, Bank of America's payment obligation may be satisfied by Chase Manhattan Bank setting off, and applying against Bank of America's obligation, the right of Bank of America to receive payment from Chase Manhattan Bank of the amount of any other order transmitted to Bank of America through the system. If, for example, Chase Manhattan Bank sent a $5 million payment order to Bank of America on a separate transfer transmitted through

74. U.C.C. §4A-403, Official Comment 1.
75. 12 C.F.R. §210.31(a).
76. U.C.C. §4A-403(a)(1).
77. U.C.C. §4A-403(a)(1); U.C.C. §4A-403, Official Comment 1.

the same funds-transfer system, the duty of Bank of America to pay its order on the GM transfer is set off against the duty of Chase Manhattan Bank to pay its order on the other transfer.

To the extent permitted by the system, the aggregate balance of obligations owed by each sender to each receiving bank in the system may be satisfied by setting off, and applying against that balance, the aggregate balance of obligations owed to the sender by other members of the system.[79] The aggregate balance is determined after the right of setoff discussed above has been exercised. Assume the following payment obligations:

1. Chase Manhattan Bank owes Bank of America $3 million on payment orders it sent to Bank of America;
2. Bank of America owes Bank of Missouri $4 million on payment orders sent to it; and
3. Bank of Missouri owes Chase Manhattan Bank $2 million on payment orders it sent to Chase Manhattan Bank.

Chase Manhattan Bank will have an aggregate balance of minus $1 million ($2 million due from Bank of Missouri minus $3 million owed to Bank of America). Bank of America will have an aggregate balance of minus $1 million ($3 million due from Chase Manhattan Bank minus $4 million owed to Bank of Missouri). Bank of Missouri will have an aggregate balance of plus $2 million ($4 million due from Bank of America minus $2 million owed to Chase Manhattan Bank). Both Bank of America and Chase Manhattan Bank will have to pay the funds transfer system $1 million each. The funds transfer system will have to pay Bank of Missouri $2 million.

In drafting this provision, the drafters had in mind the CHIPS system of settlement in which settlement is not based on individual payment orders.[80] Rather, it is based upon the net credit or debit position of that bank with all the other banks using the system. As to any sender, all of his obligations are paid when he has a net credit position in accordance with the rules of the system.

d. Other Means of Settlement

When payment is by any other means, the time when payment of the sender's obligation to the receiving bank occurs is governed by the applicable

78. U.C.C. §4A-403(b).
79. U.C.C. §4A-403(b). Multilateral netting is valid even absent a mutuality of obligation. U.C.C. §4A-403, Official Comment 4.
80. U.C.C. §4A-403, Official Comment 4.

principles of law that determine when an obligation is satisfied.[81] This rule governs when the sender neither has an account with the receiving bank nor settles through a Federal Reserve Bank nor a funds-transfer system.[82] For example, a customer may pay the receiving bank for a payment order by making payment by check, cashier's check or cash. When a check is given in payment, U.C.C. §3-310 determines when payment has been made.

C. DUTIES AND LIABILITIES OF RECEIVING BANK

1. Duties of Receiving Bank in Executing Payment Orders

a. Duty of Receiving Bank to Accept Payment Order

What duty does Bank of America have to accept a payment order sent by GM? Absent an agreement to accept such order, the answer is "none."

A receiving bank, like Bank of America, is not obligated to accept a payment order and thus has no duties before it accepts the order.[83] Bank of America has a duty to accept a payment order only if it has made an agreement to accept the order or is bound by a funds-transfer system rule requiring acceptance of such orders.[84]

b. Rejection of Payment Order

Thus, Bank of America has the option of rejecting or accepting the order.[85] Why would Bank of America reject GM's order? There are many possible reasons. The order may be ambiguous as to the identity of the beneficiary or of the beneficiary's bank so that Bank of America cannot determine to whom to send the order.[86] Bank of America may have reached its credit limit

---

81. U.C.C. §4A-403(d).
82. U.C.C. §4A-403, Official Comment 5.
83. U.C.C. §4A-212; U.C.C. §4A-212, Official Comment.
84. U.C.C. §4A-209, Official Comment 3.
85. U.C.C. §4A-209, Official Comment 1.
86. U.C.C. §4A-210, Official Comment 1.

C. Duties and Liabilities of Receiving Bank

with Chase Manhattan Bank. Or, GM's account may contain insufficient funds and Bank of America may not want to extend credit to GM.

Bank of America, as receiving bank, can reject the payment order by giving notice of rejection to GM (the sender) orally, electronically, or in writing.[87] No particular words of rejection are required. The notice need only indicate that the bank rejects or will not pay the order.

c. Acceptance upon Execution

With one exception,[88] a receiving bank (if it is not also the beneficiary's bank) accepts a payment order only when it executes the order.[89] GM's order to Bank of America is a request for the bank to execute the order.[90] Bank of America accepts the payment order when it executes the order.[91] By executing the order, Bank of America incurs certain obligations to GM.[92] One of these obligations is to issue a payment order complying with GM's order.[93] It should be noted that execution occurs when Bank of America issues a pay-

---

87. U.C.C. §4A-210(a). Rejection is effective when the notice is given if transmission is by a means that is reasonable under the circumstances. U.C.C. §4A-210(a). If the means is unreasonable, rejection is effective when received. U.C.C. §4A-210(a). When the bank and the sender agree on a means of rejection, any means complying with the agreement is reasonable and any means not complying is unreasonable unless no significant delay in receipt results. U.C.C. §4A-210(a). If, however, the receiving bank suspends payment, unaccepted payment orders are deemed rejected at the time suspension of payments occurs. U.C.C. §4A-210(c); U.C.C. §4A-210, Official Comment 4. If such suspension occurs, acceptance does not occur under §4A-209(b)(3). U.C.C. §4A-210, Official Comment 4.

88. The exception is contained in U.C.C. §4A-209(d) and deals with the attempt to execute an order before its execution or payment date.

89. U.C.C. §4A-209(a); U.C.C. §4A-209, Official Comment 2. Because a receiving bank accepts the order only by executing it, notice of rejection is not necessary to avoid acceptance. U.C.C. §4A-210, Official Comment 1. However, generally, if the receiving bank cannot or will not execute the order it will give notice of rejection. U.C.C. §4A-210, Official Comment 1. Notice of rejection allows the sender to correct the order or seek other means of payment. U.C.C. §4A-210, Official Comment 1. The receiving bank may be liable for interest if it fails to give notice of rejection when it rejects a payment order despite the existence on the execution date of a withdrawable credit balance in an authorized account of the sender sufficient to cover the order. U.C.C. §4A-210(b). Under the preceding circumstances, if an account is non-interest bearing and the sender does not receive notice of rejection on the execution date, the bank is obligated to pay interest on the amount of the order. U.C.C. §4A-210(b).

90. U.C.C. §4A-209, Official Comment 1.

91. U.C.C. §4A-209(a); U.C.C. §4A-209, Official Comment 2.

92. U.C.C. §4A-302; U.C.C. §4A-209, Official Comment 1.

93. U.C.C. §4A-302(a)(1).

ment order intending to carry out GM's order.[94] Thus, Bank of America executes GM's order if, by mistake, Bank of America names Xerox instead of IBM as the beneficiary or issues the payment order in the amount of $500,000 instead of $5 million.[95] Bank of America may be liable for the damages GM has suffered due to the erroneous execution of the order.

d. Execution Date and Payment Date

Bank of America is obligated to issue the payment order on the execution date. "Execution date" is the day on which the receiving bank may properly issue a payment order executing the sender's order.[96] The execution date refers to the day that the payment order should be executed rather than the day that it is actually executed.[97] The "payment date," in contrast, is the day on which the amount of the order is payable to the beneficiary by the beneficiary's bank.[98] In other words, the payment date indicates the day the beneficiary is to receive payment.[99]

GM, as sender, may in its instructions set an execution date.[100] However, in most situations, GM is more concerned as to when IBM will receive the payment rather than when Bank of America will send the payment order. As a result, GM will probably only specify the payment date.

If GM's instructions state a payment date, the execution date is the payment date if the order can be transmitted by a means allowing payment to be made on the same date.[101] If the order can not be transmitted the same day, the execution date is an earlier date on which execution is reasonably necessary to allow payment to be made to the beneficiary on the payment date.[102] If GM has instructed Bank of America to send the payment order by mail, Bank of America would have to send the payment order a few days before the payment date in order to ensure that the letter reaches Chase Manhattan Bank by that date.

---

94. U.C.C. §4A-301(a); U.C.C. §4A-209, Official Comment 2. A payment order is issued when it is sent to, not when it is received by, the receiving bank. U.C.C. §4A-103(c). A payment order therefore can be issued although never received by the receiving bank.

95. U.C.C. §4A-209, Official Comment 2; U.C.C. §4A-301, Official Comment 1.

96. U.C.C. §4A-301(b).

97. U.C.C. §4A-301, Official Comment 2.

98. U.C.C. §4A-401; U.C.C. §4A-301, Official Comment 2.

99. U.C.C. §4A-401, Official Comment.

100. U.C.C. §4A-301(b); U.C.C. §4A-301, Official Comment 2. The date, however, cannot be earlier than the day the order is received. U.C.C. §4A-301(b). It would be absurd to require the receiving bank to execute an order before it receives it.

101. U.C.C. §4A-301(b); U.C.C. §4A-301, Official Comment 2.

102. U.C.C. §4A-301(b); U.C.C. §4A-301, Official Comment 2.

C. Duties and Liabilities of Receiving Bank

When an order is transmitted electronically, payment can be made on the same day as the order is sent. With the exception of ACH transfers, therefore, the execution date for funds transfers within the United States carried out electronically is the payment date.[103] If the transfer takes place through an ACH, execution will usually occur before the payment date. In ACH transactions, the beneficiary is usually paid one or two days after execution of the originator's payment order.

Where the payment date is not specified, the payment date is the day the order is received by Chase Manhattan Bank (the beneficiary's bank).[104] Where both Bank of America and Chase Manhattan Bank are part of a funds-transfer system, a rule of the system may determine the execution date.[105] If not, the execution date is the day the order is received by Bank of America.[106] Thus, when no payment date or execution date is set, the order usually is intended to be executed immediately.

Bank of America, as receiving bank, may set a cut-off time for receipt and processing of payment orders.[107] In determining whether an order is timely, an order received after the cut-off time may be treated by Bank of America as having been received at the opening of the next funds-transfer business day.[108] When an execution date, payment date, or other date on which a receiving bank is required to take action does not fall on a funds-transfer business day, the next day that is a funds-transfer business day is treated as that date unless stated in Article 4A to the contrary.[109]

e. Duties of Receiving Bank upon Acceptance of Payment Order

Bank of America, as receiving bank, has certain obligations upon the acceptance of a payment order.[110] Bank of America must issue a payment

---

103. U.C.C. §4A-301, Official Comment 2. Unless, of course, the order is received by the receiving bank after the payment date.

104. U.C.C. §4A-401.

105. U.C.C. §4A-301, Official Comment 2.

106. U.C.C. §4A-301(b);U.C.C. §4A-301, Official Comment 2.

107. U.C.C. §4A-106(a).

108. U.C.C. §4A-106; U.C.C. §4A-301, Official Comment 2.

109. U.C.C. §4A-106(b).

110. U.C.C. §4A-302(a).

A question exists as to whether the duties of a receiving bank (including a beneficiary's bank) are exclusively determined by Article 4A. Specifically, the question has arisen as to whether a receiving bank can be liable under tort law for failing to exercise ordinary care or for acting in bad faith. Article 4A itself, to some extent, provides an answer to this question. The comments to §4A-102 make it clear that when a particular provision specifies the duties of a

order on the execution date complying with GM's (sender) order.[111] The order should be executed on the execution date.[112] However, there will be times when an order will be executed before or after the date.

If GM's instruction states a payment date, Bank of America is obligated to transmit the order at a time and by a means reasonably necessary to allow payment to IBM (the beneficiary) on the payment date or as soon thereafter as is feasible.[113] If GM's instructions specify the means by which the payment order is to be transmitted, Bank of America must use those means.[114] If GM's instructions state that the funds transfer is to be sent by telephone, wire, or otherwise by the most expeditious manner, Bank of America is obliged to use the most expeditious manner available and to so instruct the intermediary bank.[115] Because GM, by use of these words, usually intends a same day transfer, Bank of America must use electronic or telephonic means.[116] When Bank of America is not otherwise instructed or if the instruction does not indicate that the most expeditious means should be used, Bank of America may transmit its payment order by first class mail or by any means reasonable under the circumstances.[117] When the instruction indicates the means by which the

---

receiving bank, resort to principles of law or equity outside of Article 4A is not appropriate to create rights, duties or liabilities inconsistent with those stated in Article 4A. For example, in determining whether a receiving bank has failed to properly cancel a payment order, because Article 4A clearly sets out the receiving bank's duties in that regard, the originator may not maintain a tort action against the bank for negligence. See Aleo Intl., Ltd. v. Citibank N.A., 160 Misc. 2d 950, 612 N.Y.S. 2d 540 (Sup. Ct. 1994).

However, where no provision in Article 4A addresses an issue, resort to common law tort principles should be available. For example, in Sheerbonnet, Ltd. v. American Express Bank, Ltd., 905 F. Supp. 127 (S.D.N.Y. 1995), Sheerbonnet, the seller of troop carriers, requested that the buyer of the carriers make payment by wire transfer to Sheerbonnet's bank, BCCI. The buyer wired the funds to American Express Bank (AEB) for payment to BCCI as beneficiary. AEB not only knew that Sheerbonnet was the ultimate beneficiary of the funds, but also that the Superintendent of Banking of the State of New York had ordered the seizure of all of BCCI's New York assets. Notwithstanding this knowledge, AEB accepted the payment. When the Superintendent requested the funds, AEB claimed the funds as a setoff against money that BCCI owed AEB. The court allowed Sheerbonnet to bring a tort action against AEB alleging that it accepted the payment order for the sole purpose of exercising its right of setoff even though it knew that Sheerbonnet was the true beneficiary of the order. Sheerbonnet's action was allowed because no particular provision of Article 4A determined the right of a receiving bank to accept a payment order under these circumstances.

111. U.C.C. §4A-302(a)(1).
112. U.C.C. §4A-302(a)(1); U.C.C. §4A-301, Official Comment 3.
113. U.C.C. §4A-302(a)(2).
114. U.C.C. §4A-302(a)(1).
115. U.C.C. §4A-302(a)(2).
116. U.C.C. §4A-302, Official Comment 1.
117. U.C.C. §4A-302(c);U.C.C. §4A-302, Official Comment 1.

order should be transmitted, Bank of America has the right to transmit the order through any other means that is as expeditious as the means stated.[118] For instance, even though GM instructs that the order be sent by telex, Bank of America may send the order by telephone.

Bank of America must follow GM's instructions concerning which funds-transfer system is to be used.[119] Bank of America may refuse to follow GM's instruction as to the choice of funds-transfer system to be used only if it in good faith determines that following the instruction is not feasible or would unduly delay completion of the funds transfer.[120] For instance, Bank of America may refuse to follow the instruction if it knows that there has been a computer breakdown that would slow execution of the order.[121]

Absent instructions to the contrary, Bank of America may execute a payment order by using any funds-transfer system reasonable under the circumstances.[122] It may, for example, use an ACH, Fedwire, or CHIPS.[123] However, Bank of America must exercise ordinary care. For example, it may not be commercially reasonable to use an ACH for a large transfer because the security and credit controls of ACHs generally are not as strict as are those of Fedwire or CHIPS.[124] Bank of America may issue a payment order directly to Chase Manhattan Bank (the beneficiary's bank).[125] Bank of America may, in the exercise of ordinary care, choose an intermediary bank to issue the order. For instance, it may issue the order through Bank of Missouri (an intermediary bank), which can expeditiously issue a conforming order to Chase Manhattan Bank.

Bank of America must follow GM's instructions concerning which intermediary bank is to be used.[126] Bank of America must send the order through the intermediary bank designated by GM because GM may have intended Chase Manhattan Bank to rely on obtaining a credit from the designated intermediary bank.[127] Bank of America, however, has the right to first route the order through another intermediary bank if Bank of America does not have a correspondent relationship with the designated intermediary bank or is subject to bilateral credit limitations with that bank.

---

118. U.C.C. §4A-302(c).

119. U.C.C. §4A-302(a)(1).

120. U.C.C. §4A-302(b).

121. U.C.C. §4A-302, Official Comment 2.

122. U.C.C. §4A-302(b)(ii).

123. U.C.C. §4A-302, Official Comment 2.

124. See Baxter & Bhala, Proper and Improper Execution of Payment Orders, 45 Bus. Law. 1447, 1456 (1990).

125. U.C.C. §4A-302(b)(ii).

126. U.C.C. §4A-302(a)(1).

127. U.C.C. §4A-302, Official Comment 2.

When Bank of America issues an order to Bank of Missouri (the intermediary bank), Bank of America is obligated to instruct Bank of Missouri according to GM's instructions.[128] For example, if GM instructs Bank of America to send the order by telex, Bank of America must instruct Bank of Missouri (the intermediary bank) to send the order to Chase Manhattan Bank by telex. Bank of Missouri is bound to follow the instructions given to it by Bank of America.

f.   Time When Payment Order Can Be Accepted

Bank of America, as the originator's bank, cannot accept GM's payment order until the execution date.[129] If Bank of America were also the beneficiary's bank, it could not accept the order until the payment date. These rules are designed to protect GM (the originator) against early execution of its payment order.

Assume that on April 1st, GM instructs Bank of America to make a payment on April 15th to IBM's account at Chase Manhattan Bank.[130] Bank of America's payment order to Chase Manhattan Bank mistakenly provides for immediate payment. Chase Manhattan Bank immediately releases the funds to IBM. Because Chase Manhattan Bank complied with Bank of America's order, Bank of America is required to pay Chase Manhattan Bank upon Chase Manhattan Bank's acceptance of the order. However, GM is not obligated to pay Bank of America until Bank of America has itself accepted the order. Bank of America cannot accept the order until the execution date. Because no execution date is stated, the execution date is deemed to be the date prior to the payment date on which execution must take place in order for the order to be received by Chase Manhattan Bank in time for it to make payment on the payment date. Therefore, no acceptance can occur by Bank of America until shortly before April 15th. Early payment has not injured GM because it is not required to pay Bank of America until the execution date.

If GM discovers on April 3d that it actually does not owe IBM the money, it may cancel its order[131] because it retains the absolute right to cancel its order before acceptance by Bank of America. As we will cover in Chapter 7E, upon cancellation, GM has no duty to pay Bank of America. Bank of America, as the originator of an erroneous funds transfer to IBM, has the burden of recovering from IBM.

128. U.C.C. §4A-302(a)(1).
129. U.C.C. §4A-209(d).
130. This is the example used in U.C.C. §4A-209, Official Comment 9.
131. U.C.C. §4A-211(b).

g. Right to Deduct Charges

Wire transfers are not free of charge. Bank of America will charge GM for the transfer. Can Bank of America simply deduct its charges and expenses from the amount of the payment order it sends to Chase Manhattan Bank? This may cause a serious problem for GM. Unless it knows that Bank of America will deduct its charges and expenses, GM will not know that it must increase the amount of the order to include the charges and expenses.[132] The deduction by Bank of America may result in its order to Chase Manhattan Bank being in an amount less than GM agreed to pay IBM causing GM to be in breach of its contract with IBM or to fail to comply with the terms of an option resulting in the loss of a favorable contract right.

For this reason, unless instructed by GM, Bank of America may not deduct its service charges or expenses from the money it receives from GM and then issue a payment order in an amount equal to the amount of GM's order less the amount of the charges or expenses.[133] Nor may it instruct Bank of Missouri (or any subsequent intermediary bank) to obtain payment of its charges in this manner. Furthermore, to protect GM from an unwarranted forfeiture, if Bank of America (or Bank of Missouri) improperly subtracts its charges from the order, GM still retains its contract or option rights.[134] We discuss this later point in section D. In contrast, Chase Manhattan Bank (the beneficiary's bank) may deduct its charges to IBM (the beneficiary) because this has no effect on the amount that GM (the originator) will be deemed to have paid IBM.

h. Damages for Breach of Duty by Receiving Bank

For what damages is Bank of America liable when it breaches its duty to properly execute GM's payment order? If Bank of America delays in executing GM's payment order, Bank of America is obligated to pay interest for the period of the delay.[135] Article 4A does not identify to whom the interest should be paid in a particular case. Normally, compensation will be owed to Chase Manhattan Bank (the beneficiary's bank), so that it can compensate IBM (the beneficiary) for the interest lost due to the delay.[136]

---

132. U.C.C. §4A-302, Official Comment 3.

133. U.C.C. §4A-302(d).

134. U.C.C. §4A-406(c); U.C.C. §4A-302, Official Comment 3.

135. U.C.C. §4A-305(a). The rate of interest is provided in §4A-506. U.C.C. §4A-305, Official Comment 1.

136. U.C.C. §4A-305, Official Comment 1.

If Bank of America (1) breaches an express agreement to execute an order,[137] (2) fails to complete an order it has accepted, (3) fails to use an intermediary bank designated by GM, or (4) issues an order that does not comply with the terms of GM's payment order,[138] Bank of America is liable for GM's expenses in the funds transfer and for incidental expenses and interest lost as a result of its failure to properly execute the order. Bank of America is liable to GM for reasonable attorney's fees only if a demand for the recoverable damages has been made by GM and refused by Bank of America before legal action is brought.[139] If there is an express agreement providing for damages, no attorney's fees are recoverable unless provided for in the agreement.[140]

Absent an express written agreement to the contrary,[141] consequential damages are not available to GM.[142] Exposing a receiving bank to the possibility of consequential damages is inconsistent with the low cost and high speed of wire transfers.[143] Because of the requirement of an express written agreement in which the bank assumes responsibility for consequential damages, the bank has the protection necessary to maintain reasonable rates. This allocation of loss makes sense. GM is in the best position to know of the importance of proper execution of the transfer. GM should send the order early enough so that it can verify receipt of the order by IBM, and resend the order if not received by IBM.

2. Erroneous Execution of Payment Order

What are the respective rights of the parties when Bank of America, as receiving bank, erroneously issues a payment order in the amount of $7 million when GM's order was actually $5 million? Conversely, what if Bank of America's order was less than GM's order? Who suffers the loss when Bank of America issues a duplicative order to Chase Manhattan Bank for the benefit of IBM? We discuss in this section the consequences of Bank of America's erroneous execution of a payment order.

---

137. U.C.C. §4A-305(d). If a receiving bank breaches an express agreement to accept a payment order, it is liable for damages as provided in the agreement or as provided in §4A-305. U.C.C. §4A-212; U.C.C. §4A-209, Official Comment 3. Liability may not be reduced by agreement. U.C.C. §4A-305, Official Comment 5.

138. U.C.C. §4A-305(b).

139. U.C.C. §4A-305(e).

140. U.C.C. §4A-305(e), Official Comment 4.

141. U.C.C. §4A-305(c).

142. U.C.C. §4A-305(a),(b) and (d).

143. U.C.C. §4A-305, Official Comment 2.

C. Duties and Liabilities of Receiving Bank

When Bank of America makes a mistake and improperly executes a payment order, two questions arise: (1) to what extent, if any, can Bank of America obtain reimbursement from GM? and (2) to what extent can Bank of America recover any excess payment from Chase Manhattan Bank (the beneficiary's bank)?

a. Duplicate Execution or Execution in Greater Amount

GM suffers no loss where Bank of America either executes a payment order in an amount greater than the amount of GM's order or issues a duplicate order to Chase Manhattan Bank. Not having authorized either payment in the greater amount or the duplicate payment, GM has no obligation to reimburse Bank of America, which is entitled only to payment according to GM's original order.[144]

Bank of America's recourse is to attempt to recover the excess amount from IBM (the beneficiary). Whether Bank of America has this right depends upon the common law governing mistake and restitution.[145] For example, if GM issues an order to pay IBM $5 million but Bank of America issues an order in the amount of $7 million, GM is liable to Bank of America for $5 million only.[146] Bank of America must seek the remainder from IBM. There are basically two rules that a court may apply in determining whether Bank of America may recover from IBM. One rule is the "mistake in fact rule." Because Bank of America made a mistake in fact in issuing the erroneous order to IBM, Bank of America may recover from IBM unless IBM detrimentally relied upon the payment. For example, IBM may have agreed to sell GM additional computers in reliance upon the larger payment. Unless IBM relied upon the payment, Bank of America can recover the mistaken payment. The second rule is the "discharge for value rule."[147] Under the discharge for value rule, IBM is entitled to retain the funds as long as it had given value to GM, had made no misrepresentations to Bank of America, and had no notice of the bank's mistake. Thus, if GM had owed IBM other debts equally at least $2 million, IBM could retain the payment even though IBM did not change position in reliance on the payment.

In either event, if, under the law of restitution, IBM can retain the excess payment, Bank of America would be subrogated to any rights that IBM had

---

144. U.C.C. §4A-303(a);U.C.C. §4A-402(c).

145. U.C.C. §4A-303(a).

146. U.C.C. §4A-303, Official Comment 2.

147. See Banque Worms v. BankAmerica International, 13 U.C.C. Rep. Serv. 2d 657 (N.Y. 1991).

against GM.[148] Thus, Bank of America could recover from GM on the debts owed to IBM which were discharged by the mistaken payment.

b.   Payment in a Lesser Amount

A different situation is presented when, for example, Bank of America issues its payment order in the amount of $3 million, while GM's payment order to it was in the amount of $5 million. In this event, Bank of America is entitled to payment from GM only for $3 million unless Bank of America issues an additional payment order for the remaining $2 million difference.[149] As we discussed in the previous section, Bank of America would also be liable to GM for failing to properly execute the payment order.

c.   Issuance of Order to Wrong Beneficiary

If Bank of America issues a payment order to Xerox as the beneficiary instead of properly issuing an order to IBM, GM is not obliged to pay Bank of America on the payment order.[150] Bank of America must seek reimbursement from Xerox, the beneficiary of the erroneous order, to the extent allowed by the law governing mistake and restitution. We have previously discussed the right to recover payments made by mistake.

d.   Duty of Sender upon Receipt of Notification of Error

If GM (the sender of a payment order that is erroneously executed) receives a notification from Bank of America that the order was executed or that GM's account was debited for the amount of the order, GM has the duty to exercise ordinary care to determine, on the basis of the information available to it, whether the order was erroneously executed and, if so, to notify Bank of America of the relevant facts within a reasonable time not exceeding

---

148. U.C.C. §4A-303, Official Comment 2.
149. U.C.C. §4A-303(b). Of course, when Bank of America executes GM's payment order by issuing a payment order in an amount less than the amount of GM's order for the purpose of obtaining payment of its charges for services and expenses pursuant to instruction of the sender, it may obtain reimbursement according to the sender's original order. U.C.C. §4A-303(b).
150. U.C.C. §4A-303(c).

90 days after the notification is received by GM.[151] The only penalty for GM's failure to perform this duty is that Bank of America is not obligated to pay interest on any amount refundable to GM for the time before the bank learns of the execution error.[152] Bank of America is not entitled to any other damages from GM for breach of this duty.

However, GM may be precluded from objecting to Bank of America's retention of its payment for the order if GM does not notify Bank of America of its objection within one year after GM received a notification reasonably identifying the order.[153] If GM does not give Bank of America notice of objection within the one-year period, GM is precluded from objecting to Bank of America's debit of GM's account or its retention of GM's payment on the grounds that the order was unauthorized, erroneously executed or not accepted by the beneficiary's bank.

D. DUTIES OF BENEFICIARY'S BANK

1. Acceptance of Payment Order

When Chase Manhattan Bank (the beneficiary's bank) accepts the payment order sent by Bank of America on behalf of GM (the originator) to IBM (the beneficiary), the funds transfer is complete.[154] Until acceptance by Chase Manhattan Bank, IBM has no assurance that it will receive the funds. Upon its acceptance of the payment order, however, Chase Manhattan Bank becomes indebted to IBM in the amount of the order.[155] Chase Manhattan Bank's indebtedness is substituted for the obligation of GM. Subject to certain exceptions discussed in Chapter 7D(2) and (3), once Chase Manhattan Bank accepts the payment order, GM's debt to IBM on the underlying contract of purchase is discharged.[156] IBM may look only to Chase Manhattan Bank for payment. Chase Manhattan Bank's duty is to make payment to IBM on the pay-

151. U.C.C. §4A-304. Under Regulation J, the sender has only 30 calendar days to notify a Federal Reserve Bank of an unauthorized or erroneously executed payment order. 12 C.F.R. §210.28(c).
152. U.C.C. §4A-304.
153. U.C.C. §4A-505; U.C.C. §4A-505, Official Comment.
154. U.C.C. §4A-104(a);U.C.C. §4A-406(a); U.C.C. §4A-406, Official Comment 1.
155. U.C.C. §4A-404(a).
156. See discussion in Chapter 7D(2).

ment date.[157] If acceptance occurs on the payment date, but after the close of its funds-transfer business day, payment is due on its next funds-transfer business day.[158]

Because Chase Manhattan Bank becomes liable to IBM upon acceptance of the payment order, it assumes the risk of Bank of America's insolvency if it accepts the payment order prior to its receipt of payment from Bank of America.[159] Chase Manhattan Bank is not relieved of its obligation to pay IBM just because Bank of America becomes insolvent and cannot make payment of its order. Chase Manhattan Bank's only recourse is against the insolvent Bank of America.

a. Manner of Acceptance

Acceptance by Payment.   Chase Manhattan Bank, as the beneficiary's bank, can accept the payment order in one of four ways.[160] First, Chase Manhattan Bank accepts the payment order when it pays IBM.[161] Thus, unless it has already accepted the payment order, when Chase Manhattan Bank makes payment to IBM, it accepts the payment order. Payment thus may have two consequences: (1) it can be the act that constitutes Chase Manhattan Bank's acceptance of the payment order,[162] and (2) it is the means by which Chase Manhattan Bank pays the obligation it incurs to IBM upon acceptance of the order.[163]

Chase Manhattan Bank will normally pay IBM by crediting IBM's account. If Chase Manhattan Bank credits IBM's account, payment occurs when one of three acts has taken place. The first act is that Chase Manhattan Bank notifies IBM of its right to withdraw the credit.[164] The second act is where Chase Manhattan Bank properly applies the credit to a debt of IBM.[165] For example, Chase Manhattan Bank may set off a debt owed to it by IBM or honor a writ of garnishment levied against IBM.[166] The third act is where Chase Manhattan Bank makes the funds otherwise available to IBM.[167] Under this third manner

---

157. U.C.C. §4A-404(a).
158. U.C.C. §4A-404(a).
159. U.C.C. §4A-405, Official Comment 2.
160. U.C.C. §4A-209(b)-(d).
161. U.C.C. §4A-209(b)(1)(i).
162. U.C.C. §4A-209(b)(1).
163. U.C.C. §4A-404(a).
164. U.C.C. §4A-405(a)(i).
165. U.C.C. §4A-405(a)(ii).
166. U.C.C. §4A-405, Official Comment 1.
167. U.C.C. §4A-405(a)(iii).

of payment, payment occurs when Chase Manhattan Bank allows IBM to use the funds even though Chase Manhattan Bank attempts to make IBM's retention of the funds provisional on receipt of payment from Bank of America. Thus, when Chase Manhattan Bank releases funds to IBM, payment occurs even though Chase Manhattan Bank classifies the funds "as a loan" or states that the funds must be repaid if the bank does not receive payment.[168] As a result, subject to two exceptions, a condition to payment or an agreement of the beneficiary to repay the bank is not enforceable.[169]

Chase Manhattan Bank can also make payment in other ways. It may give a check or cash to IBM. Whether and/or when payment is made by these other means is determined by the principles of law that govern when an obligation is satisfied by such means.[170] For example, when payment is by check, U.C.C. §3-310 determines whether and when payment has been made.

Acceptance by Notification.   Second, Chase Manhattan Bank accepts the payment order when it notifies IBM of the receipt of the order or that IBM's account has been credited for the order.[171] Mere notification that the order has been received is sufficient to constitute acceptance of the order, thereby obligating Chase Manhattan Bank to pay IBM. Of course, the notification does not operate as acceptance if the notice informs IBM that Chase Manhattan Bank is rejecting the order or that funds with respect to the order may not be withdrawn or used until receipt of payment from the sender of the order.

Acceptance by Beneficiary's Bank Receiving Payment.   Third, Chase Manhattan Bank accepts the payment order when it receives payment of the entire amount of the order.[172] Thus, even if Chase Manhattan Bank does not notify

---

168. U.C.C. §4A-405, Official Comment 2; U.C.C. §4A-209, Official Comment 5.

169. U.C.C. §4A-405(c). The two exceptions to this rule are found in U.C.C. §4A-405(d) and (e) and discussed in section 4(3) of this chapter.

170. U.C.C. §4A-405(b).

171. U.C.C. §4A-209(b)(1)(ii).

172. U.C.C. §4A-209(b)(2). Whether the bank has received payment is determined by U.C.C. §4A-403(a)(1),(2). The time at which the bank is deemed to have received payment of the sender's order depends upon the means by which the payment was made. If the sender is a bank and payment is made through a Federal Reserve Bank or through a funds-transfer system, payment is deemed to have been received when the settlement becomes final. U.C.C. §4A-403(a)(1). When a payment order is sent by means of Fedwire, final settlement occurs at the same moment that the payment order is received by the beneficiary's bank. U.C.C. §4A-209, Official Comment 6. At that moment, the Federal Reserve account of the beneficiary's bank is credited resulting in the bank receiving payment of the entire amount of the sender's order. U.C.C. §4A-209, Official Comment 6. Because the beneficiary's bank receives payment of the sender's order simultaneously with receipt of the order itself, the beneficiary's bank, without any choice in the matter, has accepted the payment order. U.C.C. §4A-209, Official Comment

IBM that the order has been received or make payment to IBM, Chase Manhattan Bank accepts the payment order when it receives payment of the order from Bank of America. This third manner of acceptance can only occur if the sender is a bank. By obtaining payment, Chase Manhattan Bank quite logically is deemed to have accepted the order, thus becoming liable to IBM. This means of acceptance has an intended collateral consequence when Chase Manhattan Bank receives payment and pays the wrong beneficiary. Assume that after Chase Manhattan Bank receives payment, it mistakenly pays IDS instead of IBM. Chase Manhattan Bank, despite its improper payment, accepted the order once it received payment of the order. By accepting the order, Chase Manhattan Bank becomes liable to IBM for the amount of the order.[173] Chase Manhattan Bank must then attempt to recover its payment from IDS under the law of restitution for payments made by mistake. If the beneficiary of the payment order does not have an account with the receiving bank, acceptance does not occur when the receiving bank obtains payment from the sender.[174]

Acceptance by Passage of Time. Fourth, Chase Manhattan Bank may accept a payment order by its inaction.[175] Unless Chase Manhattan Bank rejects the order, acceptance occurs automatically upon the opening of Chase Manhattan Bank's next funds-transfer business day following the payment date of the order if either of one of two conditions has occurred.

The first condition is that the amount of the order is fully covered by a withdrawable credit balance in an authorized account that Bank of America (the sender) maintains with Chase Manhattan Bank.[176] An authorized account is a deposit account of Bank of America (a customer) in the bank (1) designated by Bank of America (the customer) as a source of payment of payment orders issued by Bank of America (the customer) to the Chase Manhattan Bank[177] or, (2) if no account is designated, any account of Bank of

---

6. When the sender is a bank and makes payment by crediting an account of the beneficiary's bank with the sender bank or causing an account of the beneficiary bank at another bank to be credited, payment occurs at the earlier of (1) the moment when the credit is withdrawn or (2) at midnight of the day on which the beneficiary's bank learns that the credit may be withdrawn. U.C.C. §4A-403(a)(2).

173. U.C.C. §4A-209, Official Comment 6.

174. U.C.C. §4A-209(c). Acceptance also cannot occur in this fashion where the account has been closed, or the receiving bank is not permitted by law to receive credits for the beneficiary's account.

175. U.C.C. §4A-209(b)(3); U.C.C. §4A-209, Offical Comment 7.

176. U.C.C. §4A-209(b)(3)

177. U.C.C. §4A-105(a)(1).

D. Duties of Beneficiary's Bank

America (the customer) is an authorized account if payment from that account is not inconsistent with a restriction on the use of that account. Payment is effected by Chase Manhattan Bank debiting Bank of America's account.[178] Of course, acceptance does not occur unless there are sufficient funds available to cover the order. Because Chase Manhattan Bank may not know until the end of the day whether Bank of America (which may have engaged in numerous transactions that day) has a sufficient balance in its account to cover the transfer, Chase Manhattan Bank may defer its determination as to whether to accept the payment order until the opening of the next funds-transfer business day.

The second condition is that Chase Manhattan Bank has otherwise received full payment from the sender.[179] The main application of this second condition is where the sender is not a bank.[180] As discussed above, if the sender is a bank, acceptance occurs immediately upon Chase Manhattan Bank's receipt of payment of the order. Where the sender is not a bank, acceptance occurs after the requisite passage of time following Chase Manhattan Bank's receipt of payment.

If either of these two conditions is met, acceptance occurs automatically upon the opening of Chase Manhattan Bank's next funds-transfer business day following the payment date of the order. A "funds-transfer business day" is that part of a day during which the bank is open for the receipt, processing, and transmittal of payment orders and cancellations and amendments of payment orders.[181] The requirement that the bank have the capacity to perform all of these functions is important.[182] A bank's computer will often have the capability to receive payment orders even when the bank is not otherwise open. Thus, the fact that Chase Manhattan Bank's computer can receive a payment order on Saturday does not mean that Saturday is a funds-transfer business day. If Chase Manhattan Bank does not otherwise process payment orders on Saturday or Sunday, neither day is a funds-transfer business day. Therefore, if the payment date is Friday, acceptance occurs upon the opening of business on Monday.

Where the beneficiary of the payment order does not have an account with the receiving bank, acceptance cannot occur in this fourth way.[183]

---

178. U.C.C. §4A-209, Official Comment 7.
179. U.C.C. §4A-209(b)(3)
180. U.C.C. §4A-209, Official Comment 7.
181. U.C.C. §4A-105(a)(4).
182. U.C.C. §4A-105, Official Comment 2.
183. U.C.C. §4A-209(c). Acceptance also cannot occur in this fashion where the account has been closed, or the receiving bank is not permitted by law to receive credits for the beneficiary's account.

b. Rejection of Payment Order

Acceptance merely by the passage of time can be prevented if Chase Manhattan Bank gives timely notice of its rejection of the order.[184] Rejection must occur within one hour after the opening of Chase Manhattan Bank's next funds-transfer business day after the payment date.[185] If, in our example above, the payment date is Friday, assuming that its funds-transfer business day begins at 9:00 A.M., Chase Manhattan Bank must give notice of rejection before 10:00 A.M. on Monday. There is one exception to this rule. If Bank of America (the sender bank) does not open for business until later, Chase Manhattan Bank may give notice of rejection within one hour of the time that Bank of America's next funds-transfer business day begins.[186] The main relevance of this exception is where Bank of America is located in an earlier time zone than Chase Manhattan Bank. For example, if Bank of America is in Los Angeles and Chase Manhattan Bank is in New York, when Chase Manhattan Bank opens at 9:00 A.M. Eastern Standard Time, Bank of America will still be closed because it will be 6:00 A.M. Pacific Standard Time.[187] Chase Manhattan Bank has until 10:00 A.M. Pacific Standard Time (1:00 P.M. Eastern Standard Time) to give notice of its rejection to Bank of America.

Once Chase Manhattan Bank accepts the payment order, it may not reject the order later.[188] Likewise, once Chase Manhattan Bank rejects the payment order, it may not thereafter accept the order. Why, you may ask, should Chase Manhattan Bank be precluded from accepting the order after rejecting it? The answer is—to prevent the possibility of double payment to IBM. Upon notice of rejection being received by GM, it may have made payment to IBM through other means.[189] Of course, GM may consent to Chase Manhattan Bank's later acceptance of the order.

Chase Manhattan Bank can reject a payment order by giving notice of

184. U.C.C. §4A-209, Official Comment 8.
185. U.C.C. §4A-209(b)(3). If the notice of rejection is received by the sender after the payment date and the sender has a noninterestbearing authorized account, the beneficiary's bank must pay interest to the sender on the amount of the order. U.C.C. §4A-209(b)(3). Interest is calculated based on the number of days between the payment date to, and including, the date that the sender receives notice or learns that the order was not accepted. U.C.C. §4A-209(b)(3). If the withdrawable credit during this period falls below the amount of the order, the amount of interest is to be reduced accordingly. U.C.C. §4A-209(b)(3). The rate of interest is provided in §4A-506.U.C.C. §4A-209, Official Comment 8.
186. U.C.C. §4A-209(b)(3).
187. U.C.C. §4A-209, Official Comment 8.
188. U.C.C. §4A-210(d).
189. U.C.C. §4A-210, Official Comment 4.

rejection to the sender transmitted orally, electronically, or in writing.[190] No particular words of rejection are required. The notice need only indicate that Chase Manhattan Bank rejects or will not pay the order. Because the sender and the beneficiary's bank will usually be in direct electronic contact with each other, notice of rejection will usually be instantaneous.[191]

c. Liability for Failure to Make Prompt Payment

Breach of Chase Manhattan Bank's duty to make prompt payment to IBM subjects Chase Manhattan Bank to liability for consequential damages. If Chase Manhattan Bank refuses to pay IBM after proper demand by IBM and receipt of notice of the particular circumstances giving rise to such damages, IBM may recover consequential damages unless Chase Manhattan Bank proves that it did not pay because of a reasonable doubt concerning the right of IBM to the payment.[192]

Assume that IBM needs $5 million to exercise an option to purchase land to build a new factory. If Chase Manhattan Bank fails to make timely payment to IBM, Chase Manhattan Bank is liable for the damages IBM will suffer in not being able to exercise the option if IBM not only demands payment from Chase Manhattan Bank but also gives notice at the time of demand of the general type or nature of the damages that it will suffer.[193] If the damages are extraordinary, IBM also must give Chase Manhattan Bank notice of this fact.[194] For instance, if IBM's inability to exercise the option will cause it to lose $100 million due to the rapid rate of appreciation of real estate, IBM must inform Chase Manhattan Bank of this fact. Because Chase Manhattan Bank normally would not be aware that a $100 million loss would result from a $5 million transfer, IBM is not permitted to recover these extraordinary damages

---

190. U.C.C. §4A-210(a). Rejection is effective when the notice is given if transmission is by a means that is reasonable under the circumstances. If the means is unreasonable, rejection is effective when received. U.C.C. §4A-210(a). When the bank and the sender agree on a means of rejection, any means complying with the agreement is reasonable and any means not complying is unreasonable unless no significant delay in receipt results. U.C.C. §4A-210(a). If, however, the receiving bank suspends payment, unaccepted payment orders are deemed rejected at the time suspension of payments occurs. U.C.C. §4A-210(c); U.C.C. §4A-210, Official Comment 4. If such suspension occurs, acceptance does not occur under §4A-209(b)(3). U.C.C. §4A-210, Official Comment 4.

191. U.C.C. §4A-210, Official Comment 2.

192. U.C.C. §4A-404(a).

193. U.C.C. §4A-404, Official Comment 2.

194. Official Comment 2 to §4A-404 makes this clear when it approves the result reached in the pre-Code case of Evra Corporation v. Swiss Bank Corporation, 673 F.2d 951 (7th Cir. 1982) (The failure of the beneficiary's bank to complete a wire transfer for $27,000 caused the beneficiary to lose a valuable ship charter with resultant damages in the amount of $2 million. The court held that such damages were not foreseeable and therefore could not be recovered.).

unless it informs Chase Manhattan Bank that the damages may be of such a magnitude.[195]

Although Chase Manhattan Bank may defend against its liability for consequential damages by proving that its failure to pay resulted from a reasonable doubt concerning IBM's right to receive the payment, this exception rarely will be applicable.[196] To meet its burden of proof, Chase Manhattan Bank must prove, for example, that it did not know whether it in fact had received the payment and therefore whether acceptance had really occurred, or that it questioned whether the person demanding payment was authorized to act for IBM.

d. Duty to Notify Beneficiary

Chase Manhattan Bank, as the beneficiary's bank, also has the duty, under certain circumstances, to notify IBM (the beneficiary) of receipt of the order. If Chase Manhattan Bank accepts a payment order that requires payment to an account of IBM, it must give notice to IBM of receipt of the order before midnight of the next funds-transfer business day following the payment date.[197] Without this notice, IBM may be unaware that the funds have been received. If, however, the order does not instruct payment to an account of IBM (the beneficiary), Chase Manhattan Bank is only required to notify IBM if the order requires notification.[198] Where the order is to pay IBM rather than to credit one of its accounts, Chase Manhattan Bank's act of payment alone will give IBM notice that the funds have been received.

The notice requirement may be dispensed with by (1) an agreement between Chase Manhattan Bank and IBM or (2) a funds-transfer system rule of which IBM is informed before the funds transfer is initiated.[199] Notice may be given by any reasonable means under the circumstances, including by first class mail.[200]

The only penalty for the failure to give notice is that Chase Manhattan Bank must pay interest on the funds from the day notice should have been given to the day IBM learns of the bank's receipt of the payment order.[201]

---

195. U.C.C. §4A-404(a); U.C.C. §4A-404, Official Comment 2.

196. U.C.C. §4A-404, Official Comment 3. Chase Manhattan Bank may not argue that IBM had no "right to receive" the payment on the grounds that GM had a defense to the underlying contract. U.C.C. §4A-404, Official Comment 3.

197. U.C.C. §4A-404(b).

198. U.C.C. §4A-404(b).

199. U.C.C. §4A-404(c); U.C.C. §4A-404, Official Comment 4.

200. U.C.C. §4A-404(b).

Reasonable attorney's fees are recoverable by IBM only if its demand for interest is refused by Chase Manhattan Bank before an action is brought on the claim.

2. *Effect of Acceptance upon Underlying Obligation*

When GM makes payment by a funds transfer to IBM, its obligation to IBM on the underlying contract is discharged not when Bank of America sends the payment order to Chase Manhattan Bank, but only when Chase Manhattan Bank accepts the payment order.

Subject to three limited exceptions,[202] the originator of a funds transfer is deemed to have paid the beneficiary at the time the order is accepted by the beneficiary's bank.[203] Payment is accomplished by substituting the obligation of the beneficiary's bank for that of the originator.[204] Once Chase Manhattan Bank accepts Bank of America's payment order, the obligation of GM to IBM is discharged.

Payment by a funds transfer discharges the underlying obligation to the same extent as would payment in cash[205] unless all of the following conditions are met: (1) the means of payment was prohibited under the contract governing the underlying obligation; (2) within a reasonable time after receiving notice of the order, the beneficiary notified the originator of his refusal to accept the means of payment; (3) the funds were neither withdrawn by the beneficiary nor applied to his debt; and (4) the beneficiary would suffer a loss that could have reasonably been avoided if payment had been made in a way that complied with the contract. Applied to the GM example, assume that GM promised to pay IBM by a cashier's check drawn upon Bank of America. Instead, GM issued a payment order to Bank of America, which in turn issued a payment order that was accepted by Chase Manhattan Bank. Before IBM withdraws the credit, Chase Manhattan Bank becomes insolvent. IBM has the right to refuse the payment, thereby denying GM a discharge.[206] IBM then can

---

201. U.C.C. §4A-404(b).

202. The first exception is where the sender is allowed to cancel the payment order. U.C.C. §4A-211(e). This exception is discussed in section E of this chapter. The other two exceptions are contained in U.C.C. §4A-405(d) and (e) discussed in section D(3).

Rights of the originator or the beneficiary under §4A-406 may be varied only by an agreement of the originator and the beneficiary. U.C.C. §4A-406(d).

203. U.C.C. §4A-406(a).

204. U.C.C. §4A-406, Official Comment 1, 2.

205. U.C.C. §4A-406(b).

206. U.C.C. §4A-406, Official Comment 3.

assert its rights under the underlying contract for payment of the $5 million. GM cannot shift the risk of Chase Manhattan Bank's insolvency to IBM when the required means of payment did not provide for such an allocation of risk. Not being discharged, GM still has the duty to pay IBM the $5 million. Upon GM's payment to IBM, it is subrogated to IBM's right to receive payment from Chase Manhattan Bank on account of Chase Manhattan Bank's acceptance of the payment order.[207] If the contract between GM and IBM does not prohibit the use of a funds transfer as a means of payment, GM would be discharged when the transfer is completed.[208]

GM is only denied a discharge if the loss could reasonably have been avoided if payment had been made in a way that complied with the contract. Assume that although the contract required that payment be made by Fedwire, GM sent the order by CHIPS. Even if Chase Manhattan Bank thereafter becomes insolvent, GM is discharged because the failure to use the proper means of payment did not cause the loss to IBM.[209] If Fedwire had been used, the funds would have arrived at Chase Manhattan Bank, which only became insolvent afterwards.

GM may have authorized the subtraction of charges by Bank of America from the amount of the order without remembering this authorization when it sent the order. Or, Bank of America, without authorization, may have improperly deducted its charges from the payment order. When either of these two situations occurs, although the amount of the payment order as originally issued is for the proper amount, by the time it reaches IBM, it is in a lesser amount. This failure to pay the amount raises the issue whether GM has breached its underlying contract with IBM. If the payment order sent by Bank of America was in the amount of $4,999,950 instead of the original $5 million, has GM breached the underlying contract by failing to pay the entire $5 million? The answer to this question could be crucial if IBM required payment by a certain date as a condition to its obligation to deliver the computers. The answer is that GM has met its duty to make payment in a timely manner and its obligation is thus discharged [210] unless upon demand by IBM, GM does not pay it the amount of the deducted charges.[211] Because these charges are normally so small, it would be unfair to GM (the originator) to allow a forfeiture without giving it a chance to make up the deficiency.[212]

---

207. U.C.C. §4A-404(a); U.C.C. §4A-406(b); U.C.C. §4A-406, Official Comment 3.
208. U.C.C. §4A-406, Official Comment 2.
209. U.C.C. §4A-406, Official Comment 4.
210. U.C.C. §4A-406(b).
211. U.C.C. §4A-406(c).
212. U.C.C. §4A-406, Official Comment 5.

3. *Right to Recover Payment*

Generally once Chase Manhatttan Bank (the beneficiary's bank) makes payment to IBM (the beneficiary), Chase Manhattan Bank cannot recover the payment.[213] There are two exceptions to this rule.

Under the first exception, a funds-transfer system rule may provide that any payment made through the funds-transfer system is provisional until receipt of payment by Chase Manhattan Bank from Bank of America, its sending bank.[214] If Chase Manhattan Bank recovers the payment under this rule, both the acceptance by Chase Manhattan Bank and the payment by GM (the originator) to IBM (the beneficiary) are nullified.[215]

This exception is for the purpose of accommodating the unique characteristics of ACH transfers.[216] ACH transfers are done in batches. Chase Manhattan Bank will accept orders in a batch from different originators' banks. The custom in ACH transactions is for Chase Manhattan Bank to release the funds to IBM early on the payment date even though payment to Chase Manhattan Bank does not occur until later that day on the understanding that the settlement is provisional until Chase Manhattan Bank receives the payment itself.

There are three conditions to the bank's right to claim a refund under the first exception. First, the funds-transfer system rule must require that both IBM and GM be given notice of the provisional nature of the payment before the funds transfer is initiated.[217] Because GM is not a customer of Chase Manhattan Bank, Chase Manhattan Bank does not have the ability to ensure that GM receives notice. This is Bank of America's duty so the settlement is provisional even though notice in fact is not given to GM. GM's recourse is against Bank of America for any loss suffered by Bank of America's failure to give it proper notice.[218]

Second, IBM, Chase Manhattan Bank, and Bank of America must all agree to be bound by the rule.[219] Implicit in this requirement is that IBM must receive notice of the rule. [220] Notice can be given by, for example, providing IBM a copy of the system's operating rules.

213. U.C.C. §4A-405, Official Comment 2.

214. U.C.C. §4A-405(d).

215. U.C.C. §4A-405(d).

216. U.C.C. §4A-405, Official Comment 3.

217. U.C.C. §4A-405(d)(i). Notice does not have to be given separately as to each particular funds transfer but may be given once as to all future funds transfers. U.C.C. §4A-405, Official Comment 3.

218. U.C.C. §4A-405, Official Comment 3.

219. U.C.C. §4A-405(d)(ii); U.C.C. §4A-405, Official Comment 3.

220. U.C.C. §4A-405, Official Comment 3.

Third, Chase Manhattan Bank cannot have received payment of the order.[221]

The second exception is very narrow. The second exception was drafted with the CHIPS' rule for the multilateral netting of obligations in mind.[222] It is only applicable in the unlikely event that CHIPS fails to settle under its loss-sharing rule. Under the second exception, payment by Chase Manhattan Bank to IBM is provisional if: (1) the funds transfer included a payment order transmitted over a funds-transfer system (CHIPS) that (i) nets obligations multilaterally among participants, and (ii) has in effect a loss-sharing agreement among participants for the purpose of providing funds necessary to complete settlement of the obligations of one or more participants that do not meet their settlement obligations;[223] and (2) the funds-transfer system fails to complete the settlement pursuant to its rules.

Under these conditions, acceptance of the payment order by Chase Manhattan Bank is nullified.[224] No person obtains any rights or incurs any obligation based on Chase Manhattan Bank's acceptance. Chase Manhattan Bank is entitled to recover the payment from IBM. Furthermore, GM is deemed not to have paid IBM. Each sender in the funds transfer is excused from its obligation to pay its payment order because the funds transfer has not been completed.[225] The consequence of application of this exception is, in effect, that the transfer never occurred. Thus, each sender is entitled to a refund.

E.   CANCELLATION (STOPPING PAYMENT) OF PAYMENT ORDER

There are many situations in which the sender may want to stop payment of a payment order. In our example, GM (the sender) may have a defense arising out of the underlying transaction with IBM, or the order may be unauthorized, in a greater amount than intended, a duplicate of an earlier order, or sent to Xerox instead of IBM.[226] Under Article 4A, stop payment is called

---

221. U.C.C. §4A-405(d)(iii).
222. U.C.C. §4A-405, Official Comment 4.
223. U.C.C. §4A-405(e).
224. U.C.C. §4A-405(e).
225. U.C.C. §4A-405, Official Comment 4.
226. U.C.C. §4A-211, Official Comment 1.

E. Cancellation of Payment Order

"cancellation." To what extent can GM cancel the payment order? What happens if Bank of America fails to honor the cancellation order? We will explore these questions in this section.

1. *Effect of Cancellation*

There is no concept of wrongful cancellation of a payment order.[227] Either the cancellation is effective and rightful or it is ineffective and the attempt at cancellation is ignored. If GM issues a cancellation to Bank of America that is timely and proper, it is as if GM never issued the original payment order. A cancelled payment order cannot be accepted.[228] When an accepted order has been cancelled, the acceptance is nullified, and no person has any right or obligation based on the acceptance.[229] If GM's attempt at cancellation is not effective, it is liable on its payment order as if there had been no attempt at cancellation. An amendment of an order is simply the cancellation of one order and the reissuance of a corrected order.[230] Hence, the rules applicable to cancellations are also applicable to amendments.

2. *Right to Cancel Unaccepted Orders*

There is a substantial difference between the right of the sender to cancel an accepted payment order and one that has not yet been accepted. Before the receiving bank has accepted the order, the sender has the absolute right to cancel the order if the sender gives timely notice of cancellation.[231] GM has the absolute right to cancel any order that Bank of America has yet to accept. Granting GM this right does not harm Bank of America because it incurs no liability by being required to cancel the order since it had not accepted the order.[232]

GM must give Bank of America notice of cancellation at a time and in a manner that affords Bank of America a reasonable opportunity to act on the communication before Bank of America accepts the payment order.[233] Since

227. U.C.C. §4A-211, Official Comment 1.
228. U.C.C. §4A-211(e).
229. U.C.C. §4A-211(e).
230. U.C.C. §4A-211(e); U.C.C. §4A-211, Official Comment 1.
231. U.C.C. §4A-211(b).
232. U.C.C. §4A-211, Official Comment 3.
233. U.C.C. §4A-211(b).

execution of an order by Bank of America is its acceptance of the order, the cancellation must be received by Bank of America in sufficient time to ensure that the appropriate bank employee can prevent execution of the order.[234] Although execution by Bank of America, in and of itself, does not impose liability upon the bank, the payment order executed by Bank of America may be accepted by Bank of Missouri (the intermediary bank) or by Chase Manhattan Bank (the beneficiary's bank). In either event, Bank of America would become liable on the order.

Bank of America may fix a cut-off time on a funds-transfer business day for the receipt and processing of payment orders, cancellations, and amendments.[235] Different cut-off times may apply to payment orders, cancellations, or amendments, or to different categories of payment orders, cancellations, or amendments. If a payment order, cancellation, or amendment is received after the close of a funds-transfer day or after the appropriate cut-off time, Bank of America may treat the order, cancellation, or amendment as having been received at the opening of the next funds-transfer business day.

Payment orders are normally executed by the receiving bank on the execution date or on the next day.[236] Similarly, a payment order received by the beneficiary's bank is usually accepted on the payment date or on the next day. When the payment order is not executed within a few days of its execution date or accepted within a few days of its payment date, it is likely that there is some problem with the order. For example, the terms of the order may be ambiguous or the sender may not have sufficient funds to cover the payment order. After a few days, although the sender probably regards the unaccepted payment order as dead, he may have neglected to cancel the order. To protect the sender from an unexpected delayed acceptance, an unaccepted payment order is cancelled by operation of law at the close of the fifth funds-transfer business day of the receiving bank after the execution date or payment date of the order.[237] For example, if GM, in its payment order, instructed that payment be made to IBM on Monday, February 4th, the order, if not yet accepted by Chase Manhattan Bank, is cancelled by operation of law at the close of business on Monday, February 11th. An unaccepted payment order is also revoked by operation of law when the receiving bank knows of the sender's death or of his adjudication of incapacity by a court of competent jurisdiction and has a reasonable opportunity to act upon such knowledge before acceptance of the order.[238]

234. U.C.C. §4A-211, Official Comment 3.
235. U.C.C. §4A-106(a). A cut-off time may apply to senders generally. U.C.C. §4A-106(a).
236. U.C.C. §4A-211, Official Comment 7.
237. U.C.C. §4A-211(d): §4A-211, Official Comment 7.
238. U.C.C. §4A-211(g). Although Article 4A contains no rule as to the effect of the

3.   Cancellation of Accepted Order

Cancellation becomes much harder once the receiving bank accepts the order. Once the order has been accepted by Bank of America, cancellation is not effective unless either Bank of America agrees to the cancellation or a funds-transfer system rule allows cancellation without Bank of America's agreement.[239]

Even if Bank of America agrees to the cancellation, the cancellation is not effective unless Bank of America cancels the payment order it sent in execution of GM's order.[240] Bank of America becomes liable to Bank of Missouri (the intermediary bank) once Bank of Missouri accepts the order. If Bank of America is unable to cancel its order to Bank of Missouri, it will be obligated to reimburse Bank of Missouri. GM has no right to cancel its order if Bank of America cannot cancel its order to Bank of Missouri.

It is even harder to cancel an order that has been accepted by the beneficiary's bank. Upon acceptance by Chase Manhattan Bank, not only is Chase Manhattan Bank liable to IBM for the amount of the accepted order, but GM's liability to IBM on the underlying contract is discharged.[241] Subject to the exceptions discussed below, Chase Manhattan Bank, therefore, has no right to agree to cancellation of Bank of Missouri's order. Because Bank of Missouri's order to Chase Manhattan Bank is not cancelled, Bank of Missouri has no right to agree to the cancellation of the order sent by Bank of America.

There are only four situations in which the Chase Manhattan Bank (the beneficiary's bank) may agree to a cancellation.[242] First, Chase Manhattan Bank may agree to a cancellation if the payment order is unauthorized. A payment order is unauthorized when the originator's bank issues an order in the name of a customer as sender who has not authorized the order.[243] Suppose,

---

sender's bankruptcy, Bankruptcy Code §542(c), although not drafted with this purpose in mind, can be read to allow the receiving bank to charge the sender's account for the amount of the payment order if the receiving bank has executed the order in ignorance of the bankruptcy. U.C.C. §4A-211, Official Comment 6.

239. U.C.C. §4A-211(c); U.C.C. §4A-211, Official Comment 3. Consent by the receiving bank can be obtained at the time of the cancellation or contained in a preexisting agreement. U.C.C. §4A-211, Official Comment 3.

240. U.C.C. §4A-211(c)(1); U.C.C. §4A-211, Official Comment 3.

241. U.C.C. §4A-211, Official Comment 4.

242. U.C.C. §4A-211(c)(2); U.C.C. §4A-211, Official Comment 4. To ensure that these are the only situations in which cancellation is possible, a funds-transfer system rule is not effective to the extent that it conflicts with §4A-211(c)(2). U.C.C. §4A-211(h); U.C.C. §4A-211, Official Comment 8.

243. U.C.C. §4A-211, Official Comment 4, Case #1.

for example, an unauthorized employee of GM sends the payment order to Bank of America and Chase Manhattan Bank consents to the cancellation. Bank of America can then cancel its order to Bank of Missouri, which in turn can cancel its order to Chase Manhattan Bank. The right of cancellation exists whether or not the unauthorized order was effective against the customer as a verified order.[244] We will discuss in section F the difference between an unauthorized payment order and a verified payment order. Upon cancellation, the acceptance is nullified and Chase Manhattan Bank is entitled to recover the payment from IBM to the extent permitted by the law of mistake and restitution. In many cases of unauthorized transfers, the beneficiary will be a party to the fraud and therefore will have no right to retain the payment.

Second, a payment order duplicative of a payment order previously sent may be cancelled.[245] In most of these situations, the first payment order will have satisfied the originator's debt to the beneficiary and, therefore, the beneficiary will have no right to retain the proceeds from the duplicate order.[246] If, however, GM owes additional money to IBM, the proceeds from both orders may be retained by IBM under the law of restitution. We discussed the right of a beneficiary to retain funds sent by mistake in a previous section. If IBM can retain the funds, Chase Manhattan Bank is entitled to reimbursement from Bank of America.[247]

Third, a mistaken payment order may be cancelled if the beneficiary is not entitled to payment from the originator.[248] For example, assume GM mistakenly ordered Bank of America to pay $1 million to Xerox instead of to IBM.[249] Chase Manhattan Bank may recover the $1 million from Xerox unless prohibited by the law of restitution and mistake. If it is able to recover the money from Xerox, Chase Manhattan Bank may consent to cancellation of the order.

Fourth, a payment order issued by mistake may be cancelled if the order is in an amount greater than the beneficiary is entitled to receive from the originator.[250] For example, if, although GM owes IBM only $10,000, GM mistakenly ordered Bank of America to pay $1 million to IBM,[251] Bank of America may, with Chase Manhattan Bank's consent, cancel its payment order to Chase Manhattan Bank. In this event, GM may cancel its order to Bank of America.

244. U.C.C. §4A-202(b); U.C.C. §4A-211, Official Comment 4, Case #1.
245. U.C.C. §4A-211(c)(2)(i).
246. U.C.C. §4A-211, Official Comment 4, Case #2.
247. U.C.C. §4A-211(f); U.C.C. §4A-211, Official Comment 4, Case #2.
248. U.C.C. §4A-211(c)(2)(ii).
249. U.C.C. §4A-211, Official Comment 4, Case #3.
250. U.C.C. §4A-211(c)(2)(iii).
251. U.C.C. §4A-211, Official Comment 4, Case #4

However, because the $10,000 was properly owed to IBM, it may retain the $10,000. This will permit Chase Manhattan Bank to recover $10,000 from Bank of America, which in turn can recover $10,000 from GM.

The foregoing four situations are the only ones in which Chase Manhattan Bank may agree to a cancellation of a payment order. Chase Manhattan Bank has no right to agree to a cancellation because of any defense GM may have on the underlying transaction against IBM. A payment order is the equivalent of payment in cash. GM's recourse is against IBM on the underlying transaction.

After acceptance, Chase Manhattan Bank has no duty to agree to a cancellation even if one of the foregoing four situations exists.[252] Why would Chase Manhattan Bank refuse to agree to a cancellation? Chase Manhattan Bank may refuse to agree to the cancellation if, for example, it is not sure that one of the four situations exists. Chase Manhattan Bank may even refuse to agree to the cancellation solely because it does not want to risk its relationship with IBM by demanding repayment.

When the receiving bank agrees to a cancellation or is bound by a funds-transfer rule allowing cancellation without its consent, regardless of whether the cancellation is effective, the sender is liable to the bank for any loss and expenses (including reasonable attorney's fees) incurred by the bank as a result of the cancellation or amendment or the attempted cancellation or amendment.[253]

4. *Manner of Cancellation*

GM, the sender, may cancel its order orally, electronically or in writing.[254] Unless Bank of America agrees otherwise, when there is a security procedure in effect between GM and Bank of America, the cancellation is not effective unless it is verified pursuant to the security procedure.[255] We discuss in the next section the reasons why a receiving bank has the right to require that a payment order or cancellation be verified pursuant to a security procedure.

252. U.C.C. §4A-211, Official Comment 5.
253. U.C.C. §4A-211(f); U.C.C. §4A-211, Official Comment 5. This is unless otherwise provided in an agreement of the parties or in a funds-transfer system rule.
254. U.C.C. §4A-211(a).
255. U.C.C. §4A-211(a).

F. LIABILITY FOR UNAUTHORIZED
PAYMENT ORDERS

1. Liability for Authorized Orders

GM has the obligation, as sender, to reimburse Bank of America (the receiving bank) for the amount of any authorized payment order.[256] A payment order is authorized if GM either authorized the order or is otherwise bound by the order under the law of agency.[257] GM is bound not only when its agent has actual authority to send the order, but also when the agent has apparent authority or authority by estoppel.[258] Agency may be established by estoppel when a purported agent misrepresents his authority and the principal either intentionally or negligently fails to notify the bank that no such authority exists. Even when the order is not authorized, Bank of America may have the right to obtain reimbursement from GM if GM benefitted from payment of the order.

2. Liability for Unauthorized Orders

Most payment orders (as well as cancellations) are transmitted through electronic means.[259] In most situations, Bank of America will be acting upon an electronically transmitted message appearing on a computer screen.[260] There is no way for Bank of America to determine the identity or authority of the person sending the message. How does Bank of America know that the transmission containing the payment order is authentic and accurate? How does Bank of America know that an order sent electronically to Bank of America purportedly from GM instructing Bank of America to pay $5 million to IBM was sent by an employee of IBM? How does Bank of America know whether the employee of GM sending the order is authorized to do so? How does the bank know whether GM actually intended to send an order for $50,000? Since Bank of America could not know whether the order is authentic and accurate, it could not safely pay the order if it faced the possibility of not being able to recover from GM in the event that the order was not authorized or accu-

256. U.C.C. §4A-203, Official Comment 1.
257. U.C.C. §4A-202(a).
258. U.C.C. §4A-203, Official Comment 1.
259. U.C.C. §4A-201, Official Comment.
260. U.C.C. §4A-203, Official Comment 1.

rate. On the other hand, how can GM be liable for an order that it did not authorize?

There must be some way by which Bank of America can verify the authenticity and the accuracy of the transmission. Once Bank of America verifies the transmission, it must be able to safely send the payment order knowing that it can recover from GM. To protect GM, the method of verification has to be adequate to assure GM that if careful, it will not be liable for any unauthorized order.

3. Verified Orders

The mechanism that was adopted by Article 4A to assure authenticity and accuracy of a transmission is the security procedure.[261] If the security procedure can be designed to assure that the message can be sent only by authorized persons who alone have access to the information required by the security procedure, GM would have some assurance that any order that is authenticated pursuant to the security procedure is authorized. If Bank of America can treat as "authorized" any payment order that is authenticated pursuant to the security procedure, it can safely transmit the payment order. An order that passes upon being properly tested according to a security procedure is called a "verified payment order."[262] We will see that GM is liable for certain verified payment orders even if the order is unauthorized.

4. What Is a Security Procedure?

The key issue in determining whether a payment order is verified is whether the order passes after being properly tested according to a security procedure. A security procedure is a procedure by which the bank may test the authenticity and/or accuracy of the order.[263] By use of a security procedure, GM can protect itself from transmission error by adopting a procedure for confirming the name of the beneficiary or the amount of the order.[264] GM can help prevent embezzlement by authorized agents by use of a security procedure that prohibits Bank of America from accepting a payment order (1) that is not payable from an authorized account, (2) that is payable in an amount that

261. U.C.C. §4A-203, Official Comment 1.
262. U.C.C. §4A-202(b).
263. U.C.C. §4A-201, Official Comment.
264. U.C.C. §4A-203, Official Comment 3.

exceeds a defined credit balance or a set amount per transfer, or (3) that is payable to a person outside of a specified list of authorized beneficiaries. By properly utilizing a security procedure, Bank of America will know, prior to executing the order, whether GM will be obligated to reimburse it for the $5 million.

A "security procedure" is a procedure established by agreement of a customer and a receiving bank for the purpose of (1) verifying that a payment order or communication amending or cancelling a payment order is that of the customer or (2) detecting error in the transmission or content of the order, amendment, or cancellation.[265]

A security procedure may take any number of forms. A code or algorithm may be employed. There may be identifying words or numbers, encryption or callback procedures. However, because of the ease of forging a signature, the comparison of a signature on a payment order (or other communication) with an authorized specimen is not by itself a security procedure.[266]

To allow GM to modify established limitations, a security procedure often will contain a means by which a particular limitation can be lifted.[267] Unless the prescribed means of modifying the limitation is followed, Bank of America is not required to follow an instruction that violates a written agreement forbidding such payment.[268]

A procedure can constitute a "security procedure" only if it is established by an agreement between the customer and the receiving bank.[269] The term does not apply to procedures that the receiving bank unilaterally adopts to process payment orders.

5. Sender's Liability for Verified Payment Orders

Whether Bank of America or GM suffers the loss caused by an unauthorized or erroneous payment order depends on the existence of a security procedure and whether it has been followed.[270] The same rules apply to alterations of

265. U.C.C. §4A-201. The customer may impose these limitations either in a security procedure that is designed to detect any payment in violation of the specified limitations, in an instruction given unilaterally by the customer to the bank, or in a separate agreement between the bank and the customer forbidding the bank from executing any payment order in violation of the instruction or agreement. U.C.C. §4A-203, Official Comment 3.

266. U.C.C. §4A-201.

267. U.C.C. §4A-203, Official Comment 3.

268. U.C.C. §4A-202(b); U.C.C. §4A-203, Official Comment 3.

269. U.C.C. §4A-201, Official Comment.

270. U.C.C. §4A-201, Official Comment. The customer cannot agree to take more of the loss than provided for in Article 4A. U.C.C. §4A-202(f).

payment orders as apply to the unauthorized sending of original instructions.[271] The same rules also apply to amendments and cancellations to the same extent as they apply to the original payment order.

6.   Bank's Duty to Comply with Commercially Reasonable Security Procedure

Determining whether the customer is liable to the receiving bank for an unauthorized but verified payment order is a two-step process. The first step places the burden on the bank to prove that:[272]

1. the bank had an agreement with its customer providing that orders would be verified pursuant to a security procedure;
2. the security procedure is a commercially reasonable method of providing security against unauthorized payment orders; and
3. the bank accepted the payment order in good faith and in compliance with the security procedure and any written agreement or instruction of the customer restricting acceptance of payment orders issued in his name.[273]

7.   What Is a Commercially Reasonable Security Procedure?

The burden of making a commercially reasonable security procedure available is on the bank because it knows what procedures are possible and how well they will work.[274] The test is whether the procedure was reasonable for the particular bank and customer involved.[275] The bank is not an insurer. A procedure is not unreasonable simply because another one may have been better.

The commercial reasonableness of a security procedure is a question of law to be determined by considering the wishes of the customer expressed to

271. U.C.C. §4A-203, Official Comment 2.

272. "Prove" with respect to a fact means to meet the burden of establishing the fact (U.C.C. §1-201(8)). U.C.C. §4A-105(a)(7).

273. U.C.C. §4A-202(b); U.C.C.§4A-202(b)(i); U.C.C. §4A-202(b)(ii) respectively. Under §4A-105(a)(6), "good faith" means honesty in fact and the observance of reasonable commercial standards of fair dealing.

274. U.C.C. §4A-203, Official Comment 3.

275. U.C.C. §4A-203, Official Comment 4.

the bank, the circumstances of the customer known to the bank, including the size, type, and frequency of payment orders normally issued by the customer to the bank, alternative security procedures offered to the customer, and the security procedures in general use by customers and receiving banks similarly situated.[276]

In determining what is commercially reasonable, the costs generated by labor and equipment must be weighed against the degree of security sought.[277] State of the art equipment and procedures may be the only things that are commercially reasonable for customers who send many large orders, while such procedures and equipment may not be cost effective for customers who send fewer and smaller orders. Because of the volume they generate, large banks may be able to utilize state of the art equipment, while small rural banks may find such equipment to be too expensive. Because security procedures will tend to be standardized in the banking industry, making the determination of their reasonableness a matter of law leads to greater predictability. A procedure is not commercially reasonable if it fails to meet the prevailing banking standards applicable to a particular bank.

There may be situations in which a customer insists upon a less expensive or more convenient but higher risk procedure. The procedure chosen by the customer will be deemed as a matter of law to be commercially reasonable if (1) the bank offered, and the customer refused, a security procedure that was commercially reasonable for that customer and (2) the customer expressly agreed in writing to be bound by any payment order, whether or not authorized, issued in its name and accepted by the bank in compliance with the security procedure chosen.[278]

If the bank fails to offer a commercially reasonable security procedure or fails to comply with the security procedure adopted, the bank suffers the loss and must try to recover from the beneficiary.[279] The theory behind this allocation of loss scheme is that the use of a commercially reasonable security procedure is the best way of preventing loss.[280] The procedure allows the receiving bank to be able to rely upon objective criteria. The bank's employees should be properly trained to test payment orders. The bank takes responsibility for the proper conduct of its employees in testing the orders. If the fraud is not detected because the employee did not follow the proper steps, the bank suffers the loss.

276. U.C.C. §4A-202(c).
277. U.C.C. §4A-203, Official Comment 4.
278. U.C.C. §4A-202(c).
279. U.C.C. §4A-203, Official Comment 2.
280. U.C.C. §4A-203, Official Comment 3.

8. *Burden on Customer to Prove Not Responsible for Loss*

If the bank bears its burden of proof, the order is a verified payment order.[281] As such, the order is effective as the order of the customer whether or not it was authorized by the customer.[282] The customer is therefore liable to the receiving bank for the amount of the order.[283] The loss is thrust on the customer because it is the customer's burden to supervise its own employees and to ensure that confidential information and access to transmitting facilities are kept secure.[284] To breach a commercially reasonable security procedure, the wrongdoer must have knowledge of the procedure, codes, or devices.[285] The person also may need access to the transmitting facility. The odds are that the source of this leak was the customer.

There will be times, however, in which the leak came from the bank instead of from the customer. When this occurs, it would be unfair to make the customer suffer the loss. For this reason, if the customer can prove that the information was not obtained from an agent or former agent of the customer or from a source controlled by the customer, the bank should suffer the loss.

What must the customer prove to avoid liability? The customer must prove that the order was not caused, directly or indirectly, by a person who falls into one of two categories. The first category includes any person who was entrusted at any time with duties to act for the customer with respect to payment orders or the security procedure.[286] The second category comprises any person who (1) obtained access to the customer's transmitting facilities or (2) obtained, from a source controlled by the customer and without authority of the receiving bank, information facilitating breach of the security procedure, regardless of how the information was obtained or whether the customer was at fault.[287] Information includes any access device, computer software, or the like.[288]

The customer must, in other words, prove a negative—that the leak did not come from any source controlled by the customer. It will be extremely difficult for the customer to bear this burden of proof unless the customer can

---

281. U.C.C. §4A-202(b).

282. U.C.C. §4A-202(b).

283. U.C.C. §4A-202(b). In addition, the customer becomes the sender of any order effective under U.C.C. §4A-202(b). U.C.C. §4A-202(d).

284. U.C.C. §4A-203, Official Comment 3.

285. U.C.C. §4A-203, Official Comment 5.

286. U.C.C. §4A-203 (a)(2)(i).

287. U.C.C. §4A-203 (a)(2)(ii).

288. U.C.C. §4A-203 (a)(2).

affirmatively show that the leak came from a source controlled by the bank. It will be easier for the customer to bear this burden where, for example, a criminal investigation or the bank's internal investigation discloses that a bank employee had perpetrated the fraud.[289]

9. Summary of When Loss Falls upon Bank

There are, thus, four situations in which the loss caused by an unauthorized payment order falls upon the bank and not the customer:[290]

1. no commercially reasonable procedure was in effect;
2. the bank did not comply with the security procedure in place;
3. the customer can prove that the wrongdoer did not obtain the information from it; or
4. the bank agreed to assume all or part of the loss.

10. Damages

A receiving bank must refund any payment of an order to the extent the bank is not entitled to enforce payment of the order.[291] In addition, the bank must pay interest on the refundable amount calculated from the date the bank received payment to the date of refund.

The customer is not entitled to interest on the refund if the customer fails to exercise ordinary care in determining that the order was not authorized and in notifying the bank of the relevant facts within a reasonable time (not exceeding 90 days) after the date the customer received notification from the bank that the order was accepted or that the customer's account was debited for the order.[292] Whether the time is reasonable depends, to some extent, upon what fraud was committed. For example, a change in the name of the beneficiary may take longer to discover than the sending of a wholly unauthorized order.[293]

The penalty of the loss of interest is designed to encourage the customer

---

289. U.C.C. §4A-203, Official Comment 5.
290. U.C.C. §4A-204, Official Comment 1.
291. U.C.C. §4A-204(a).
292. U.C.C. §4A-204(a). Under Regulation J, a sender has only 30 calendar days to notify a Federal Reserve Bank of an unauthorized payment order. 12 C.F.R. §210.28(c).
293. U.C.C. §4A-204, Official Comment 2.

to act promptly. The customer's loss of interest is the only remedy that the receiving bank has against the customer for breach of his duty to notify the bank of the unauthorized nature of the order.[294] The bank's remedy is to recover from the beneficiary if the beneficiary was a party to the fraud.[295] Considering that the wrongdoing beneficiary probably either could not be located or, if located, would be insolvent, the bank more than likely would not have been able to recover from the beneficiary even if it had received prompt notice from the customer. Because of the likelihood that the bank did not suffer any loss on account of the customer's delay, the penalty for the customer's breach does not include shifting of the loss from the bank to the customer. Although what constitutes a reasonable time within which notice must be given to the bank may be fixed by agreement, the obligation of a receiving bank to refund payment may not otherwise be varied by agreement.[296]

Article 4A does contain a statute of repose for objecting to debits made to the customer's account in any case in which the receiving bank has improperly debited the customer's account or otherwise received payment from the customer after paying an order purportedly sent by the customer.[297] The customer is precluded from objecting to the bank's retention of his payment for the order if the customer does not notify the bank of his objection within one year after he received the notification reasonably identifying the order.[298]

G.   ERRONEOUS PAYMENT ORDERS AND MISDESCRIPTIONS

1.   Erroneous Payment Orders

What happens if GM makes a mistake in the payment order it sends and Bank of America accepts the order without noticing the error? GM may have mistakenly instructed that payment be made to Xerox instead of to IBM, or GM may have sent an order duplicative of an order previously sent to IBM or in an amount greater than it had intended. Without an established security procedure, Bank of America could have no way of determining that an error had

---

294. U.C.C. §4A-204(a).
295. U.C.C. §4A-204, Official Comment 2.
296. U.C.C. §4A-204(b).
297. U.C.C. §4A-505, Official Comment.
298. U.C.C. §4A-505; U.C.C. §4A-505, Official Comment.

been made. Because only GM could have prevented the error, where no security procedure for detecting error has been adopted, the loss falls on GM.[299] GM's remedy is to recover from Xerox, in the first case, and from IBM in the last two cases.

But when a security procedure to detect such errors is in place, Bank of America may be able to detect the error by verifying orders in compliance with the procedure. Security procedures can be devised to reduce greatly the chance of error. A procedure can require special verification that payment is to be made to a specific account. The procedure can provide for a special code for different size orders. The procedure may also provide a separate number for each order so that duplicate orders can be detected. When there is a security procedure in place to detect such errors, the loss from an erroneous payment may be shifted, under certain circumstances, to Bank of America.

a.   When Does Loss Shift to Receiving Bank?

The loss shifts to Bank of America only if GM proves that GM had complied with the security procedure and that the error would have been detected if Bank of America had also complied with the security procedure.[300] If GM sustains this burden of proof, it is relieved from the obligation to reimburse Bank of America if the error occurred in sending the order to the wrong beneficiary or in sending a duplicate order.[301] Thus, the burden of recovering from Xerox or IBM shifts to Bank of America. Bank of America has the right to recover from Xerox or IBM to the extent permitted by the law of mistake and restitution.[302]

If GM's error is in the amount of the order, it will only be obliged to pay the amount that GM had intended the order to be.[303] If GM had intended to send an order for $5 million but had erroneously sent an order for $7 million, GM would be obligated to pay Bank of America only $5 million. Bank of America could recover the remaining $2 million from IBM (the beneficiary of the order) to the extent allowed by the law governing mistake and restitution.[304] To the extent that IBM could retain the entire payment, Bank of America would be subrogated to IBM's rights against GM.

299. U.C.C. §4A-205, Official Comment 1.
300. U.C.C. §4A-205(a)(1); U.C.C. §4A-205, Official Comments 1, 2. The bank and the customer can agree to allocate the loss to the customer or in any other manner. U.C.C. §4A-205, Official Comment 3. Section 4A-205 applies to amendments as well as to the original payment order. U.C.C. §4A-205(c).
301. U.C.C. §4A-205(a)(2); U.C.C. §4A-205, Official Comment 1.
302. U.C.C. §4A-205(a)(2); U.C.C. §4A-205, Official Comment 1.
303. U.C.C. §4A-205(a)(3); U.C.C. §4A-205, Official Comment 1.
304. U.C.C. §4A-205(a)(3); U.C.C. §4A-205, Official Comment 1.

b. Sender's Duty upon Receipt of Notice of Acceptance

Once GM receives notification from Bank of America that the order has been accepted by Bank of America or that GM's account has been debited in the amount of the order, GM has a duty of ordinary care to discover (on the basis of the information that it has) any error concerning the order and to advise Bank of America of the relevant facts within a reasonable time (not exceeding 90 days) after notification is received by GM.[305] If Bank of America proves that GM failed to perform this duty, GM is liable to Bank of America for any loss, not exceeding the amount of the order, that Bank of America proves it incurred as a result of the failure.[306] For the loss to shift back to GM, Bank of America must prove that timely notice would have prevented the loss.[307] Bank of America will not be able to prove a loss when, for example, because of the beneficiary's intervening insolvency, Bank of America could not have recovered from the beneficiary even had timely notice been given.

c. Error by Intermediary Funds-Transfer or Communication System

Sometimes a sender will use a funds-transfer or communication system to transmit its order to the receiving bank.[308] For example, Bank of America may use CHIPS to transmit its order to Bank of Missouri. When CHIPS or other funds-transfer or communication system makes an error, is Bank of America liable for the error? Assume, as an example, that GM instructs Bank of America to send orders to several of its suppliers. Bank of America chooses to transmit the orders by an ACH.[309] GM sends the orders in an electronic device to Bank of America, which sends the device to the ACH for processing to the various beneficiary's banks. The ACH erroneously sends an order to Chase Manhattan Bank to pay Vincent's Vinyl in the amount of $100,000 instead of in the intended amount of $10,000. Is Bank of America obligated as sender to pay Chase Manhattan Bank $100,000 or is it only liable for the amount of the order it sent to the ACH? The answer depends on whether the ACH is operated by a Federal Reserve Bank. When a funds-transfer system is not operated by a Federal Reserve Bank, the funds-transfer system or other third-party communication system is deemed to be the agent of the sender for purposes of

---

305. U.C.C. §4A-205(b); U.C.C. §4A-205, Official Comment 2.
306. U.C.C. §4A-205(b); U.C.C. §4A-205, Official Comment 2.
307. U.C.C. §4A-205, Official Comment 2.
308. U.C.C. §4A-206, Official Comment 1.
309. U.C.C. §4A-206, Official Comment 2.

transmitting the order.[310] If the system transmits an order that differs from the sender's original order, the sender is bound by the order that the system transmits to the receiving bank.[311] Having chosen the ACH to transmit the order, Bank of America is obligated to pay the entire $100,000 order to the beneficiary's bank. The ACH's potential liability to Bank of America is not governed by Article 4A.

The result would be different if the ACH is operated by a Federal Reserve Bank. A funds-transfer system operated by a Federal Reserve Bank is deemed to be an intermediary bank and not the sending bank's agent.[312] As a result, Bank of America will be obligated to reimburse the Federal Reserve Bank only for $10,000, the amount of its order. The Federal Reserve Bank, however, must pay the beneficiary's bank the entire $100,000.

2.   *Misdescriptions*

a.   **Nonexistent or Unidentifiable Person or Account**

What happens if GM's payment order misdescribes the beneficiary. For example, assume that one of GM's creditors is Ace Welding Company. In sending a payment order to Bank of America, GM misdescribes the beneficiary as "Acme Welding Company." Unfortunately, accounts exist at Chase Manhattan Bank not only under the name of "Ace Welding Company" but also under the name of "Acme Hardware Company." What does Chase Manhattan Bank do? Clearly, Chase Manhattan Bank has no way of knowing whose account should be credited. Because of the ambiguous nature of the beneficiary's description, Chase Manhattan Bank cannot identify which of its customers is the beneficiary. In this situation, it would make little sense to allow Chase Manhattan Bank to guess at which customer was the intended beneficiary. Rather, Chase Manhattan Bank should just reject the order. In fact, this is the rule.

Subject to the exception below, if the name, bank account number, or other identification of the beneficiary refers to a nonexistent or unidentifiable person or account, no person has rights as the beneficiary of the order.[313] As a result, Chase Manhattan Bank cannot accept the order and the funds trans-

---

310. U.C.C. §4A-206(a); U.C.C. §4A-206, Official Comment 1. Section 4A-206 applies to cancellations and amendments of payment orders to the same extent as it does to payment orders. U.C.C. §4A-206(b).

311. U.C.C. §4A-206(a).

312. U.C.C. §4A-206(a); U.C.C. §4A-206, Official Comment 2.

313. U.C.C. §4A-207(a).

fer cannot be completed.[314] Each sender in the funds transfer is relieved of liability and is entitled to a refund to the extent of any payment. Thus, if Bank of America sent a payment order to Bank of Missouri, which sent a payment order to Chase Manhattan Bank, neither Bank of America nor Bank or Missouri would be liable on their payment orders. Similarly, GM would have no obligation to pay Bank of America.[315]

b. Where Beneficiary Identified by Both Name and Number

Different rules apply, however, when a payment order identifies the beneficiary both by name and by an identifying number or bank account number and the name and number identify different persons.[316] Assume that GM's order identified the supplier as "Ace Welding Company, Acct. No. 1234." Payment orders received by Chase Manhattan Bank (like other beneficiary's banks) from another bank are processed by an automated device that processes the order by reading the identifying number or the bank account number. The device does not read the name of the beneficiary. Chase Manhattan Bank processes orders in this manner because processing orders manually is substantially more expensive. Thus, Chase Manhattan Bank credits the order to account number 1234. Although GM has identified properly the beneficiary by name, the account number is the number of Avis Rent-a-Car. As a result, the money is paid to Avis and not to Ace.

Is Bank of America obligated to pay Chase Manhattan Bank? The answer is "yes." Chase Manhattan Bank may rely on the number as the proper identification of the beneficiary[317] and credit account number 1234. It has no duty to determine whether the account number is truly that of Ace Welding Company. Chase Manhattan Bank, therefore, would be entitled to payment from Bank of America.[318] If the order had been sent by Bank of Missouri, Chase Manhattan Bank would be entitled to payment from Bank of Missouri. Bank of Missouri would then be entitled to payment from Bank of America.[319] A bank is expected to be aware of the risk in using an identifying number or bank account number that may differ from the name of the beneficiary.[320]

Where Chase Manhattan Bank knows that the name and number refer to

314. U.C.C. §4A-207; U.C.C. §4A-207, Official Comment 1.
315. U.C.C. §4A-402(c); U.C.C. §4A-207, Official Comment 1.
316. U.C.C. §4A-207, Official Comment 2.
317. U.C.C. §4A-207(b)(1).
318. U.C.C. §4A-207, Official Comment 2.
319. U.C.C. §4A-207(c)(1).
320. U.C.C. §4A-207, Official Comment 3.

different persons, no acceptance can occur and therefore Bank of America would have no obligation to pay Chase Manhattan Bank.[321] Ironically, the allocation of loss is the same even if Chase Manhattan Bank processes the order manually.[322] Of course, in this situation, it is more likely that Chase Manhattan Bank will know that the name and number refer to different persons.

Returning to our assumption that Chase Manhattan Bank did not know that the name and number refer to different persons, is GM liable to Bank of America? GM is not obligated to pay the order unless Bank of America proves that before acceptance of GM's order GM received notice from Bank of America that payment might be made on the basis of the identifying number or bank account number even if it identifies a different person.[323] What is the easiest way for Bank of America to prove that GM had notice that payment may be made on the basis of an identifying number or a bank account number? The easiest way is for Bank of America to have GM sign, before the payment order was accepted, a writing indicating GM's awareness that payment may be made on the basis of an identifying number or bank account number even if it identifies a different person.[324] If GM had signed such a statement GM would bear the loss because it made the mistake and knew of the beneficiary's bank's reliance on the bank account number.[325] GM could have prevented the loss by refraining from using an account number of which it was not certain. Whichever party (GM or Bank of America) is ultimately liable may recover the payment from Avis Rent-a-Car to the extent permitted by the law governing mistake and restitution.[326]

The result is different when Chase Manhattan Bank either pays the person identified by name or knows that the name and the number identify different persons. Under these circumstances, Chase Manhattan Bank assumes the risk that it paid the person intended by GM. If Chase Manhattan Bank pays the person intended by GM, Bank of America must reimburse Chase Manhattan Bank, and GM must reimburse Bank of America.[327] The funds transfer went as planned and each sender must reimburse its receiving bank. If, however, Chase Manhattan Bank does not pay the person intended by GM, the order is deemed not to have been accepted.[328] Thus, if Chase Manhattan

---

321. U.C.C. §4A-107(b)(2).

322. U.C.C. §4A-207, Official Comment 2.

323. U.C.C. §4A-207(c)(2).

324. U.C.C. §4A-207(c)(2). Because the information need only be supplied once, this writing would apply to all subsequent orders. U.C.C. §4A-207, Official Comment 3.

325. U.C.C. §4A-207, Official Comment 3.

326. U.C.C. §4A-207(d)(1) and (2).

327. U.C.C. §4A-207(b)(2).

328. U.C.C. §4A-207(b)(2).

Bank recognizes the mistake and pays Ace Welding Company, the bank has made a proper payment because Ace Welding Company in fact was entitled to the payment. If, however, Avis Rent-a-Car and not Ace Welding Company was paid, no person has any rights as the beneficiary and the order cannot be accepted.

Similarly, if Chase Manhattan Bank recognizes the discrepancy, it bears the risk of paying the wrong beneficiary even when it pays according to the account number.[329] The order cannot be accepted.[330] Bank of America is not obligated to pay Chase Manhattan Bank and GM is not obligated to pay Bank of America.[331] Chase Manhattan Bank suffers the loss whether or not GM was negligent.

c. Misdescription of Intermediary Bank or Beneficiary's Bank

Similar problems and solutions are found where an order misdescribes the intermediary bank or the beneficiary's bank. Because receiving banks process orders by automated means whenever possible, when a payment order identifies an intermediary bank or the beneficiary's bank by an identifying number only, the receiving bank will rely on the number and will not determine whether the number identifies a bank.[332] As with identification of the beneficiary by number, the bank sending the order will suffer any loss caused by the order being accepted by the wrong bank.[333]

Assume that GM issues a payment order to Bank of America identifying the beneficiary's bank as Chase Manhattan Bank. Bank of America issues a payment order to Bank of Missouri (the intermediary bank) describing the beneficiary's bank as "Bank No. 156234." However, the number actually describes Bank of Connecticut. Bank of Missouri sends the order to Bank of Connecticut, which accepts the order. Bank of Missouri is entitled to reimbursement from Bank of America.[334] Not only is Bank of America not entitled to reimbursement from GM, but it is liable for damages to GM as provided for under §4A-305(b). The damages available under §4-305(b) are discussed in Chapter 7C.

If the number does not indicate a bank, the funds transfer cannot be com-

329. U.C.C. §4A-207, Official Comment 2.
330. U.C.C. §4A-207(b)(2).
331. U.C.C. §4A-207, Official Comment 2.
332. U.C.C. §4A-208, Official Comment 1.
333. U.C.C. §4A-208(a)(1).
334. U.C.C. §4A-208, Official Comment 1, Case #1.

pleted.[335] Bank of America is not obligated to pay Bank of Missouri for the amount of the order but is liable to Bank of Missouri for any loss and expenses incurred by Bank of Missouri as a result of its reliance on the number in executing or attempting to execute the order.[336] Bank of America is also liable for damages to GM. Of course, if GM supplied only the number and not the name of the beneficiary's bank, GM would be obligated to reimburse Bank of America.[337]

Similarly, when there is a conflict between the name of the beneficiary's bank (or intermediary bank) and the identifying number and the receiving bank relies upon the number, the loss generally falls on the sending bank.[338] Assume that Bank of America, in its order to Bank of Missouri, describes the beneficiary's bank as "Chase Manhattan Bank, No. 156234." Unfortunately, No. 156234 describes Bank of Connecticut. Because Bank of America is a bank, Bank of Missouri may rely on the number as the proper identification of the beneficiary's bank if it does not know at the time it executes the order that the name and number identify different persons.[339] Bank of Missouri has no duty to determine whether the name and number identify different banks or whether the number refers to a bank at all. Bank of America must compensate Bank of Missouri for any loss and expenses incurred by it as a result of its reliance on the number in executing or attempting to execute the order.[340] Bank of America is not entitled to reimbursement from GM.

If GM, a non-bank sender, had included the conflicting description of the beneficiary's bank in its order to Bank of America, it would be obligated to reimburse Bank of America for any losses or expenses incurred in executing or attempting to execute the order if GM received notice that Bank of America might rely on the identifying number only before its order was accepted by Bank of America.[341] If GM did not receive the requisite notice, GM would not be liable to Bank of America and would be able to recover whatever damages it suffered from Bank of America.[342]

335. U.C.C. §4A-208, Official Comment 1, Case #2.

336. U.C.C. §4A-208(a)(2); U.C.C. §4A-208, Official Comment 1, Case #2.

337. U.C.C. §4A-208(a)(2).

338. U.C.C. §4A-208, Official Comment 1. The allocation of loss does not change when the processing is done manually. U.C.C. §4A-208, Official Comment 3.

339. U.C.C. §4A-208(b)(1).

340. U.C.C. §4A-208(b)(1); U.C.C. §4A-208, Official Comment 1.

341. U.C.C. §4A-208(b)(2). The burden of proof is satisfied by proof that the originator, before the payment order was accepted, signed a writing stating the information to which the notice relates. U.C.C. §4A-208(b)(2). Bank of America's proof of the required notice exonerates it from liability to GM for breach of §4A-302(a)(1) and entitles it to compensation from GM for any losses or expenses caused by the error. U.C.C. §4A-208, Official Comment 2.

342. U.C.C. §4A-208, Official Comment 2.

Assume that in the previous example the named beneficiary, Vincent's Vinyl, had no account at Bank of Connecticut. Under these circumstances, because there is no beneficiary, the order cannot be accepted.[343] Bank of America is then not liable to Bank of Missouri for the amount of the order, Bank of Missouri is not liable to Bank of Connecticut, and GM is not liable to Bank of America. Bank of America, however, may be liable to GM for damages for improperly executing the order. In addition, Bank of America must compensate Bank of Missouri for any losses suffered in its attempt to execute the order.

The results are somewhat different if the receiving bank relies upon the name, rather than the number, of the intermediary bank or of the beneficiary's bank. Whether or not the sender is a bank, the receiving bank may rely on the name as the proper identification of the intermediary bank (or the beneficiary's bank) if the receiving bank at the time it executes the sender's order does not know that the name and the number refer to different persons.[344] If the receiving bank knows that the name and the number identify different banks, reliance on either the name or the number, if incorrect, is a breach of its duties in executing the sender's payment order.[345]

H.   CREDITOR'S PROCESS AND INJUNCTION AGAINST PAYMENT

Can the funds represented by the payment order be attached or garnished by the originator's creditors? By the beneficiary's creditors? Can a receiving bank send a payment order after the originator's creditor has garnished the bank account out of which the bank intends to reimburse itself? Can the creditor of the beneficiary enjoin payment of the payment order? These are the questions that we will cover in this section.

As used in Article 4A, the term "creditor process" is a generic term encompassing any means by which a creditor or claimant may seize a bank account.[346] These means may include levy, attachment, garnishment, notice of

---

343. U.C.C. §4A-208, Official Comment 1, Case #1. The result would be the same if Vincent's Vinyl is described in the order only by account number and no such account exists at the bank.

344. U.C.C. §4A-208(b)(3); U.C.C. §4A-208, Official Comment 2. The receiving bank has no duty to determine whether the number and the name refer to the same bank. U.C.C. §4A-208(b)(3).

345. U.C.C. §4A-208(b)(4).

346. U.C.C. §4A-502, Official Comment 5.

lien, sequestration, or similar process issued by or on behalf of a creditor or other claimant with respect to an account.[347]

1. *Originator's Creditor*

An originator has no ownership interest in the payment order that it sends to the receiving bank. The payment order is simply an order given by it to the bank. The only relevance of the payment order to the originator's creditor is that the receiving bank may, on acceptance, debit the originator's bank account. Thus, if one of GM's creditors wants to levy a creditor process on GM's assets, the creditor will levy the process on GM's bank account and not on the payment order. The question that arises is whether Bank of America's right to reimbursement for the payment order that it issued on behalf of GM has priority over the creditor process.

If a judgment creditor of GM executes upon its account at Bank of America after GM has sent a payment order to Bank of America, the writ of garnishment or execution has priority over Bank of America's right to reimbursement if the writ is served at a time and in a manner affording Bank of America a reasonable opportunity to act on the process before it accepts the payment order.[348] Once Bank of America accepts the payment order by executing it, GM's account will be deemed to be reduced by the amount of the payment order to the extent that GM has not already paid Bank of America through other means.[349]

2. *Beneficiary's Creditor*

When Bank of America sends a payment order to Chase Manhattan Bank for IBM's account, the payment order represents an asset of IBM. After Chase Manhattan Bank accepts the order, IBM's account will be credited with the amount of the funds represented by the order. Once Chase Manhattan Bank accepts the order, a creditor of IBM may seize the funds represented by the payment order by levying upon the bank account.[350] If the creditor process is served after Chase Manhattan Bank has accepted the order, Chase Manhattan Bank must honor the process if it was served at a time and in a manner giving

347. U.C.C. §4A-502(a).
348. U.C.C. §4A-502(b).
349. U.C.C. §4A-502(b).
350. U.C.C. §4A-502(c)(1).

Chase Manhattan Bank a reasonable opportunity to prevent IBM's withdrawal of the funds represented by the payment order.[351]

If the creditor process is served before Chase Manhattan Bank accepts the order, can Chase Manhattan Bank reject the payment order so as to deprive the creditor of the funds represented by the order? The answer is "no."[352] If Chase Manhattan Bank has had a reasonable opportunity to act upon service of the creditor process, the bank may not reject the payment order if its sole reason is that the creditor process has been served.[353] The bank must have some other legitimate reason for the rejection.

If the creditor is attempting to attach the payment order from GM to IBM, the creditor process must be served on Chase Manhattan Bank (the beneficiary's bank) with respect to the debt that arises from that bank to IBM upon acceptance of the payment order.[354] Any other bank may ignore the process. If served with a writ attempting to attach the payment from GM to IBM, Bank of America (the originator's bank) may ignore the writ and pay Chase Manhattan Bank.

3.   Obtaining an Injunction

If a creditor of IBM knows that GM is intending to transfer funds to IBM, can the creditor prevent the transfer? The answer is "yes." The creditor can stop the transfer at several different points. The creditor can obtain an injunction preventing GM from issuing a payment order initiating a funds transfer to IBM.[355] The creditor can also enjoin Bank of America from executing GM's payment order. Finally, the creditor can enjoin Chase Manhattan Bank from releasing funds to IBM or IBM from withdrawing the funds.

However, a court may not otherwise restrain a person from issuing a payment order, or receiving payment of an order, or otherwise acting with respect to a funds transfer. In sum, the funds transfer can be stopped before it is begun by enjoining GM or Bank of America.[356] But, no intermediary bank can be enjoined from executing a payment order or a receiving bank from accepting the order or receiving payment from the sender.

---

351. U.C.C. §4A-502(c)(2); U.C.C. §4A-502, Official Comment 3.
352. U.C.C. §4A-502, Official Comment 2.
353. U.C.C. §4A-502(c)(3).
354. U.C.C. §4A-502(d).
355. U.C.C. §4A-503.
356. U.C.C. §4A-503, Official Comment.

CHAPTER 8

Consumer Electronic Fund Transfers

A. ELECTRONIC FUND TRANSFER ACT ("EFTA")

On your way home from work, you realize that you have no food in the house. You decide to stop by Ralph's Supermarket ("Ralph's") to do your weekly shopping. After the checker rings up the bill for your cartload of groceries, you realize that you do not have sufficient cash to pay for the groceries. In addition, you have left your checkbook at home. The checker notices that you have your Versateller Card ("ATM card"), which you use to withdraw cash at Bank of America, the bank at which you keep your account. The checker tells you that you can pay for the groceries by use of your ATM card. You are a little hesitant at first since you have never done this before.

The checker tells you that the process is very simple and that she will guide you through it. She first shows you the point of sale ("POS") terminal and tells you to press the button reading "debit." You ask why you are pressing this button instead of the one reading "credit." She tells you that you are using your debit card instead of a credit card. By using a debit card, you are asking that your bank debit your account just as if you had written a check. Unless you have adequate funds in the account (or overdraft protection), your bank will not approve your purchase. Had you used a credit card, you would be asking your bank to extend you credit. Rather than debiting your bank account, your bank would be placing the charge on your credit card bill.

The checker then tells you to enter your personal identification number ("PIN") so that the computer can verify whether you are the person who has the right to use the debit card. After entering your PIN, you are instructed to enter the amount of the purchase. You ask the checker what happens now. She tells you that the machine is now determining through a computer network whether you have sufficient funds in your account to cover the debit.

The type of POS terminal that Ralph's uses functions by sending to a computer switch[1] ("switch") the following information: (1) your PIN; (2) your bank account number; (3) the identity of the bank at which you maintain your account; (4) the amount of your purchase; (5) Ralph's bank account number; and (6) the identity of the bank at which it maintains its account. The switch sends the information to Bank of America (your bank). If the PIN you imputed is the proper one to access your acount and you have adequate funds in your account, Bank of America's computer will inform the switch that your purchase is authorized. By authorizing the purchase, Bank of America becomes obligated to pay Wells Bank (Ralph's bank). Bank of America's computer will, at the same time, debit your account for the amount of the purchase. The switch will notify Wells Bank's computer of the transaction. Wells Bank's computer may or may not be programmed to immediately credit Ralph's account. Whether Ralph's account is immediately credited depends, to a large extent, upon whether Bank of America immediately makes payment to (or "settles with") Wells Bank. Although Bank of America is obligated to pay for the purchase, it may not immediately pay Wells Bank, depending upon the agreement between Bank of America and Wells Bank. If both Bank of America and Wells Bank have accounts at the same Federal Reserve Bank, the agreement between the parties may be that the switch will send authorization to the Federal Reserve Bank to immediately debit Bank of America's account and credit Wells Bank's account. (See Figure 8.1.)

Another possibility is that rather than settling for each individual purchase, Bank of America and Wells Bank may settle daily on a net basis for all of the purchases made during the day by any of their customers upon customers of the other bank.[2] Whether or not Bank of America immediately settles with Wells Bank for the purchase, the purchase transaction is deemed complete the moment that it is authorized by Bank of America. The entire duration of this authorization process usually takes only a few seconds.

---

1. In another type of system, the information is first sent to Wells Bank (Ralph's bank), which forwards the information to Bank of America (your bank).

2. For example, assume that three customers of Bank of America made purchases in the total amount of $2,000 at POS terminals operated by customers of Wells Bank. Assume also that five customers of Wells Bank made purchases in the total amount of $3,000 at POS terminals operated by Bank of America customers. At the end of the day, Wells Bank would owe Bank of America $1,000. Wells Bank would settle this obligation by having the Federal Reserve Bank debit Wells Bank in that amount and credit Bank of America's account in the same amount.

A. Electronic Fund Transfer Act ("EFTA")

FIGURE 8.1

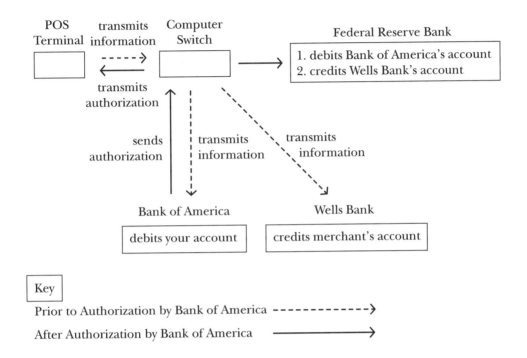

You have just paid by an electronic fund transfer. You like this idea but have some worries. What happens if you lose your ATM card? Will you be liable for any purchases made by the finder of the card? What if your account is debited in a greater amount than you had authorized? Must your bank recredit your account for the difference? May you refuse to pay your bank if the groceries or other goods you purchased are defective?

Congress had these same concerns. Although Congress saw the benefits of having an electronic system by which consumers could make all types of payments, it also saw the need to make the system safe for consumers to use. Therefore, Congress enacted the Electronic Fund Transfer Act ("EFTA")[3] for the express purpose of protecting consumers against some of these risks.[4] Although the EFTA contains the basic framework for governing consumer

3. 15 U.S.C. §1693.
4. 15 U.S.C. §1693 (b).

electronic fund transfers, the specific rules are contained in Regulation E, which was adopted by the Board of Governors of the Federal Reserve Board. Regulation E is accompanied by an Official Staff Commentary prepared by the staff of the Federal Reserve Board. The Official Staff Commentary provides guidance to financial institutions and practitioners as to many specific issues. It also provides examples of many of the rules. A financial institution is given an incentive to comply with Regulation E and its Official Staff Commentary in that a financial institution that in good faith complies with Regulation E or its Official Staff Commentary is shielded from liability under the EFTA even if a court subsequently finds the regulation or commentary to be invalid.[5]

The EFTA preempts state law to the extent that the state law is inconsistent with the EFTA.[6] State laws that provide greater protection for consumers than the protection afforded by the EFTA are consistent with the purposes of the EFTA and are therefore not preempted.

1. What Is an Electronic Fund Transfer?

An "electronic fund transfer" is "any transfer of funds that is initiated through an electronic terminal, telephone, or computer or magnetic tape for the purpose of ordering, instructing, or authorizing a financial institution to debit or credit an account. The term includes, but is not limited to:

1. point-of-sale transfers;
2. automated teller machine transfers;
3. direct deposits or withdrawals of funds;
4. transfers initiated by telephone; and
5. transfers resulting from debit card transactions, whether or not initiated through an electronic terminal."[7]

What are some of the more typical types of electronic fund transfers? We have already examined a POS transaction. You have probably used an automated teller machine ("ATM"). You may have made a cash withdrawal from an ATM or you may have transferred funds from your savings account to your checking account. You may have even had your paycheck deposited directly by your employer into your bank account. This is a type of preauthorized electronic fund transfer. As we will discuss later, direct deposit of paychecks or gov-

5. EFTA §1693m(d).
6. 15 U.S.C. §1693q; 12 C.F.R. §205.12(b).
7. 15 U.S.C. §1693a(6); 12 C.F.R. §205.3(b).

A. Electronic Fund Transfer Act ("EFTA")

ernmental benefits are considered electronic fund transfers because the employer or the government agency sends the payment instruction to your bank through a computer or magnetic tape. You may have preauthorized payment of your bills (another type of preauthorized electronic fund transfer) by having your bank automatically debit your account for certain recurring bills. A less common type of electronic fund transfer is a pay-by-phone service by which you give a telephone order to your bank to pay your bills by directing funds to your creditor's account.

New types of electronic payment systems are being developed. Currently under testing are smart cards[8] and value-added cards. A "smart card" is a plastic card in which is imbedded a computer chip. The computer chip can contain various types of information and perform various types of functions. For payment purposes, one function of a smart card would be to function as a value-added card (also called a "stored-in value" or "pre-paid" card). A "value-added card" is a card that itself contains funds (as described below).[9]

Let us look at how a smart card can function as a value-added card. You insert your smart card into an ATM, which enables you to transfer funds from your bank account to the smart card. When you want to make a purchase, you hand the merchant your smart card. The merchant runs the card through a terminal, which reads the card. The computer chip in the card contains your PIN. You punch your PIN into keyboard of the terminal. If your PIN matches the one contained on the smart card and if you have adequate funds left on the smart card, the terminal will debit your smart card for the amount of the purchase and credit the amount owed to the merchant in the terminal. When you have exhausted the funds on your card, you can go back to an ATM and transfer more funds to the card.

Although experimentation is continuing with smart cards, it appears that, for at least two reasons, widespread use of these cards is still several years away.[10] In the first place, smart cards are expensive to manufacture. Secondly, the present POS terminals that read the magnetic strips contained on ATM cards cannot read the computer chip found in smart cards. As a result, new terminals would have to be purchased by merchants. At present, the advantages of smart cards do not outweigh these added costs.

As you can tell, the definition of an electronic fund transfer is not very illuminating. Let us now break down the definition into its elements so that we

8. For a discussion of smart cards, see Donald I. Baker and Roland E. Brandel, The Law of Electronic Fund Transfer Systems 9-1 to 9-31 (Rev. Ed. 1996).

9. Not all value-added cards are smart cards. Another simpler form of value-added or pre-paid cards are telephone cards by which you purchase a certain amount of calling minutes. You insert this card into the telephone and it subtracts those minutes.

10. See Benjamin Geva, The Law of Electronic Funds Transfers 6-14 (1994).

can understand what an electronic fund transfer really is. First, of course, there must be a transfer of funds.

Second, the transfer of funds must involve a debit or a credit to a consumer asset account. Although the term "consumer asset account" is not used in the operative provisions of EFTA, the definition of "account" makes it clear that the transfer must be to or from an account containing a consumer's assets. "Account" is defined as including a "demand deposit (checking), savings, or other consumer asset account (other than an occasional or incidental credit balance in a credit plan) held either directly or indirectly by a financial institution and established primarily for personal, family, or household purposes."[11] We know that the account must be a *consumer* account because the account must be "established primarily for personal, family, or household purposes."[12] It is also clear that the account must be an *asset* account.[13] In other words, the consumer must own the funds in the account. Thus, electronic fund transfers resulting in an extension of credit on a credit line are not covered by the EFTA.

To be a consumer asset account, the account must also be held either directly or indirectly at a financial institution. Financial institutions include not only typical bank-like entities such as a bank, a savings association, a credit union, or any other person who, directly or indirectly, holds an account belonging to a consumer,[14] but also anyone, like a retail store and an oil company, who issues access devices (for example, cards permitting access to an ATM) and agrees with a consumer to provide electronic fund transfer services.[15]

The fund transfer must involve a credit or a debit to a consumer asset account. Therefore, transfers entirely between commercial accounts are not covered. Similarly, the EFTA does not govern a transfer when there is no actual credit or debit to the consumer's account. For example, when you deposit a check or cash at an ATM for the purpose of paying a credit card bill owed to your bank, the EFTA does not apply.[16] There has been no debit or credit to a consumer asset account. Because you are paying by cash or check, your account has not been debited. There is also no credit to a consumer asset account because the funds are credited to the bank's account (the bank, of course, is not a consumer).

---

11. 12 C.F.R. §205.2(b)(1).
12. "Consumer" is defined as a natural person. 15 U.S.C. §1693a(5); 12 C.F.R. §205.2(e).
13. 15 U.S.C. §1693a(2); 12 C.F.R. §205.2(b)(1).
14. 15 U.S.C. §1693a(8).
15. 12 C.F.R. §205.2(g).
16. 12 C.F.R. §205.3(b)(2), Official Staff Commentary.

A. Electronic Fund Transfer Act ("EFTA")

Similarly, the pivotal issue in determining whether smart or value-added cards are electronic fund transfers for purposes of the EFTA and Regulation E is whether there has been a transfer to or from a consumer asset account.[17] The problem is that a smart or value-added card itself is not an account. Thus, the consumer's payment to the merchant by use of the smart card would not be covered. Because the smart card itself is not a consumer asset account, there has been no debit to a consumer asset account. Conversely, because the merchant's account is not a consumer asset account, there has been no credit to a consumer asset account. The only transaction in which there has been a credit or debit to a consumer asset account is the one in which the consumer transfers, through the ATM, funds from his account to the card. Because the consumer's asset account is being debited, this transfer is covered.

Likewise, when an account is not established by or under the control of a consumer, a transfer of funds to or from the account is not covered by the EFTA. For example, when your mortgage company requires you to set up an escrow account into which you are to deposit funds to cover real estate taxes, transfers into and out of the escrow account are not covered by the EFTA because the use of the funds is not under your control.[18]

Third, with one exception, the transfer must be initiated through an electronic terminal, telephone, or computer or magnetic tape for purpose of ordering, instructing, or authorizing a financial institution to debit or credit an account. An "electronic terminal" is "an electronic device, other than a telephone operated by a consumer, through which a consumer may initiate an electronic fund transfer."[19]

Electronic terminals include POS terminals, ATMs, and cash dispensing machines. A POS payment is covered because it is initiated through an electronic terminal. Transfers through an automated clearing house (ACH), as discussed in Chapter 7, are covered because they are conducted through computer or magnetic tape. When a consumer preauthorizes a creditor to initiate a debit to the consumer's account, the transaction is governed by the EFTA if the bank debits the consumer's account according to information provided to the bank by the creditor on computer or magnetic tape.[20] The EFTA also covers home banking services in which a consumer initiates transfers to or from an account (1) by a computer or a television set linked to the financial institution's computer system, or (2) under a pay-by-phone plan by which the consumer telephonically instructs his financial institution to make a payment to a creditor.

17. See 59 Fed. Reg. 10684, 10685 (March 7, 1994).
18. 12 C.F.R. §205.2(b)(1), Official Staff Commentary.
19. 12 C.F.R. §205.2(h).
20. 12 C.F.R. §205.3(b)(1), Official Staff Commentary.

The one exception to the requirement of the use of an electronic terminal is a transfer from a consumer account initiated through use of a debit card.[21] A consumer may be able to use a debit card almost like a check to purchase goods or services. In this type of transaction, the merchant makes a copy of the information contained on the card and asks the consumer to sign the debit slip. The debit slip is then forwarded for payment through the merchant's bank to the consumer's bank. Although no electronic terminal is used, the transaction is nonetheless governed by the EFTA as long as a consumer's asset account is subsequently debited for the amount of the transfer.[22] Transactions involving debit slips are included under the coverage of the EFTA to protect consumers who may naturally assume that because the transaction is initiated by a debit card, they have the same protections whether the merchant makes a copy of the debit card or has the consumer run the debit card through an electronic terminal.

Welfare and food stamp payments in which the recipient receives the payment through an ATM or an electronic terminal are not currently subject to the EFTA because they do not involve a debit or credit to a consumer account. The funds are paid in cash directly to the consumer rather than deposited in the consumer's account. Effective March 1, 1997, however, a new part of Regulation E will go into effect that , with some modifications, will bring these types of payments within the scope of Regulation E.[23] This means that the federal, state, and local governmental agencies making the transfer payments will be bound to some extent by Regulation E.

2.   *What Transactions Are Not Covered by the EFTA?*

a.   Transfers Initiated by Check, Draft, or Similar Instrument

In order to distinguish between negotiable instruments governed by Articles 3 and 4 and electronic fund transfers, the transfer cannot have been originated by a check, draft, or similar paper instrument. Thus, (1) a transfer of funds originated by check, draft, or similar paper instrument or (2) any payments made by check, draft, or similar paper instrument at an electronic ter-

21. 12 C.F.R. §205.3(b)(5).
22. 12 C.F.R. §205.3(b)(1), Official Staff Commentary.
23. 59 Fed. Reg. 10684-01 (1994).

minal are excluded from coverage under the EFTA.[24] Fund transfers involving checks presented electronically through a check truncation system are not covered by the EFTA. Under a check truncation system, the consumer writes a check, which the merchant deposits in its bank account. The merchant's bank, rather than sending the check itself for collection, transmits electronic instructions to the consumer's bank to debit the consumer's account. Because the transfer is initiated by a check, the transaction is not governed by the EFTA. Similarly, use of a check guarantee card by which your bank guarantees to the merchant that your check will be paid is not covered by the EFTA because the ultimate transfer of funds is initiated through the use of a check.[25]

b.   Commercial Wire Transfers

A wire transfer of funds transmitted solely through Fedwire or a similar network (such as CHIPS), which is used primarily for transfers between financial institutions or between businesses, is exempt even if the transfer is to or from a consumer.[26] However, where only a portion of a fund transfer takes place over Fedwire or a similar network, the part of the transfer that is not transmitted over Fedwire (or the similar network) may be governed by the EFTA. For example, assume that funds are transferred over Fedwire to a bank that thereafter transfers the funds into a consumer account through an ACH. The transfer to the bank over Fedwire is not governed by the EFTA. However, the transfer by the bank to the consumer's account through the ACH is covered.[27]

c.   Transfers for Purchase and Sale of Securities

A fund transfer primarily for the purchase or sale of securities or commodities is exempt from the coverage of the EFTA if neither the securities or commodities themselves, or the broker, dealer, or merchant from whom they were bought are regulated by the Securities and Exchange Commission or the Commodity Futures Trading Commission.[28] The rationale for this exemption is that the interests of the consumer are already adequately protected by these commissions. The purpose of the fund transfer must be primarily for the sale

---

24. 12 C.F.R. §205.3(c)(1).
25. 15 U.S.C. §1693a(6)(A); 12 C.F.R. §205.3(c)(2).
26. 15 U.S.C. §1693a(6)(B); 12 C.F.R. §205.3(c)(3).
27. 12 C.F.R. §205.3(c)(3)-1, Official Staff Commentary.
28. 15 U.S.C. §1693a(6)(C); 12 C.F.R. §205.3(c)(4).

or purchase of securities. Such a fund transfer is to be distinguished from a fund transfer from a money market account maintained at a brokerage house. Many consumers have money market accounts at brokerage houses, which accounts function like checking accounts. When a consumer uses a debit card to debit a money market account in order to purchase goods and services, the transfer is covered by the EFTA[29] because the transfer is not for the purpose of purchasing or selling securities. Similarly, when the brokerage house electronically transfers funds into the consumer's account for the payment of interest or dividends on securities, the transfer is covered by the EFTA.

d. Preauthorized Intra-Institutional Automatic Transfers

The following transfers between a consumer and his financial institution pursuant to a pre-existing agreement by which the financial institution initiates individual transfers of funds without a specific request from the consumer are exempt from the EFTA. First, a transfer from one of the consumer's accounts (like a savings account) at the financial institution to another of the consumer's accounts at the same institution (like a checking account) is exempt from the EFTA.[30] Such a transfer may be, for example, for the purpose of covering overdrafts or maintaining a minimum balance. Second, transfers to an account of a member of the transferor's family who is also a customer at the same financial institution are also excluded from the EFTA.[31] Third, a transfer by the financial institution to the consumer's account, for example, the crediting of interest to a savings account, is excluded.[32] Finally, a transfer from a consumer's account to the account of the financial institution, for example, to make a loan payment, is exempt from coverage under the EFTA.[33]

e. Transfers Initiated by Telephone

A transfer of funds initiated through a telephone conversation between a consumer and an employee or officer of a financial institution is only subject to the EFTA if it is pursuant to a prearranged plan under which periodic transfers are contemplated.[34] For example, when a bank and a consumer agree that

29. 12 C.F.R. §205.3(c)(4)-2, Official Staff Commentary.
30. 15 U.S.C. §1693a(6)(D);12 C.F.R. §205.3(c)(5)(i).
31. 15 U.S.C. §1693a(6)(D); 12 C.F.R. §205.3(c)(5)(ii).
32. 15 U.S.C. §1693a(6)(D);12 C.F.R. §205.3(c)(5)(iii).
33. 15 U.S.C. §1693a(6)(D); 12 C.F.R. §205.3(c)(5)(iii).
34. 15 U.S.C. §1693a(6)(E); 12 C.F.R. §205.3(c)(6).

the bank will transfer funds to pay the consumer's creditors upon telephonic instruction from the consumer, the transfer is covered by the EFTA because the transfer is pursuant to a pre-existing plan. However, the plan must be a true one. A signature card opening up a bank account that merely authorizes the bank to honor the consumer's telephone request is not a pre-existing plan to transfer funds upon the consumer's telephonic instruction.[35] It is, by itself, only an agreement holding the bank harmless in the event that the bank agrees to honor a telephone transfer request. In contrast, when there is a pre-existing telephone transfer plan, transfers are covered by the EFTA even if the consumer is required by the plan to make a separate request for each transfer and even if the requests are made infrequently.[36]

f. Transfers to or from Trust Accounts

A transfer to or from a trust account held under a bona fide trust agreement is exempt from the EFTA.[37] For example, transfers to and from Individual Retirement Accounts[38] or accounts held by financial institutions for depositors under custodial agreements such as profit sharing and pension accounts[39] are all exempt as long as the custodial agreement is the equivalent of a trust agreement.

g. Small Institution Exemption

Preauthorized electronic fund transfers to or from an account at a financial institution with assets of $100 million or less are exempt from the EFTA.[40] "Preauthorized electronic fund transfer" is defined as "an electronic fund transfer authorized in advance to recur at substantially regular intervals."[41] The purpose of the small institutions exclusion is so that such institutions will not be burdened with all of the requirements of the EFTA.

The institution is not given a complete exemption from the EFTA. The institution is only exempt from the requirements governing preauthorized electronic fund transfers and is still governed by other requirements of the

---

35. 12 C.F.R. §205.3(c)(6)-1, Official Staff Commentary.
36. 12 C.F.R. §205.3(c)(6)-2, Official Staff Commentary.
37. This is because the definition of "account" found in 12 C.F.R. §205.2(b)(2) excludes an "account held by a financial institution under a bona fide trust agreement."
38. 12 C.F.R. §205.2(b)(2)-2, Official Staff Commentary.
39. 12 C.F.R. §205.2(2)(i), Official Staff Commentary.
40. 12 C.F.R. §205.3(c)(7).
41. 12 C.F.R. §205.2(k).

EFTA.[42] For example, the institution may not force use of electronic fund transfers upon its borrowers. (See section C.) Similarly, the institution is subject to the civil and criminal liability provisions of the EFTA.

B.   CONSUMER'S LIABILITY FOR UNAUTHORIZED TRANSFERS

On March 1st, you lose your ATM card. You had written your personal identification number (PIN) on the card. You do not realize that the card is gone until March 15th. On March 20th, you notify your bank of the loss. It turns out that on March 10th, the finder withdrew $400 in cash from your account. The finder had withdrawn another $600 on March 19th. In this section we explore the question of for how much of the loss you will be liable.

1.   What Is an Unauthorized Fund Transfer?

Fortunately, you have only limited liability for unauthorized electronic fund transfers. An electronic fund transfer is unauthorized if two conditions are met. First, the transfer is initiated by a person without actual authority to initiate the transfer. A person does not have actual authority to initiate a transfer unless he is expressly or impliedly authorized to make the transfer. It is not good enough that the person has apparent authority to make the transfer. For example, assume that although your grandfather had authorized his nurse to write checks on his account, he did not authorize her to initiate electronic fund transfers. However, because of the frequency with which she has been writing checks, your grandfather's bank reasonably believes that she has full authority to conduct financial transactions for him. Although the nurse may have apparent authority to initiate electronic fund transfers, any transfer initiated by her is nonetheless unauthorized because she has no actual authority to do so. Actual and apparent authority are discussed more fully in Chapter 3.

Second, the consumer has not received a benefit from the transfer.[43] For example, assume that the nurse, without your grandfather's authority, secretly

---

42. Automatic repayment of credit that is extended under an overdraft credit plan or that is extended to maintain a specified minimum balance in the consumer's account may be required. 12 C.F.R. §205.3(c)(7); 12 C.F.R. §205.10(e)(1).

43. 15 U.S.C. §1693a(11); 12 C.F.R. §205.2(m).

learns his PIN and makes his mortgage payment by an electronic fund transfer. Although she did not have actual authority to make the transfer, the transfer is not unauthorized because your grandfather received a benefit from it.

There is an important exception to the rule that unless the nurse is actually authorized to initiate the electronic fund transfer for your grandfather, the transfer is unauthorized. An electronic fund transfer is not unauthorized if the consumer (your grandfather) gave to the person initiating the transfer (the nurse) an access device unless the consumer (your grandfather) has notified the financial institution involved that transfers by that person (the nurse) are no longer authorized.[44]

An "access device" is a "card, code, or other means of access to a consumer's account, or any combination thereof, that may be used by the consumer for the purpose of initiating electronic fund transfers."[45] For example, your grandfather's ATM card is an access device. A debit card, a PIN, and a code used to make telephonic fund transfers are also access devices. Thus, if your grandfather gave his ATM card and his PIN to his nurse, the nurse's withdrawal of funds through the use of the card is not regarded as unauthorized even though he told the nurse not to use the card until he authorized her to do so.

The rationale for this exception should be obvious. By giving the nurse his ATM card and his PIN, your grandfather gave the nurse the means to make the transfer without the financial institution or a merchant (if the transfer is at a POS terminal) knowing that her use was unauthorized. The fault lies with your grandfather and not with the financial institution or the merchant.

However, any transfer by the nurse is an unauthorized transfer once your grandfather notifies the card-issuing financial institution that the nurse is no longer authorized to use the access device. After being notified, the financial institution can prevent any further transfers by blocking the ability of the device to access the account.

In contrast to the foregoing situation in which your grandfather voluntarily gave the access device to his nurse, any transfer is an unauthorized electronic fund transfer if it is made with an access device that was obtained either through robbery or through fraudulent inducement.[46] For example, assume that your grandfather's wallet, which contained his ATM card, is stolen. A subsequent transfer initiated by the thief's use of the card would be unauthorized. The same would be true if the nurse, without your grandfather's consent, took the card out of his wallet. For policy reasons, if your grandfather was forced at

---

44. 15 U.S.C. §1693a(11); 12 C.F.R. §205.2(m)(1).
45. 12 C.F.R. §205.2(a)(1).
46. 12 C.F.R. §205.2(m)(3), Official Staff Commentary.

gunpoint to withdraw funds from an ATM, his withdrawal also would be treated as an unauthorized transfer.[47]

There are two remaining situations in which a fund transfer is not regarded as being unauthorized. First, a fund transfer is not unauthorized where it is initiated with fraudulent intent by the consumer or any person acting in concert with the consumer.[48] Second, a fund transfer initiated by the financial institution or its employee is not, for technical reasons, treated as being an unauthorized fund transfer.[49] However, the consumer is not liable for transfers initiated, without the consumer's actual authority, by the financial institution itself or its employee.

2. Consumer's Liability for Unauthorized Fund Transfers

As a general rule, you are not liable for an unauthorized fund transfer. However, there are certain situations in which you may have limited liability for the transfer. Before you can be liable for an unauthorized fund transfer, three conditions must be met.[50]

The first condition is that the unauthorized transfer must have been made by an accepted access device. If a transfer is made from your account without the use of an access device, you incur no liability for the transfer. For example, if a computer expert rigs an ATM to debit accounts at random for the computer expert's cash withdrawals, you are not liable for the transfer even if one of the accounts debited was your account.

Even if an access device is used by the computer expert to debit your account, you cannot be liable for the transfer unless you had accepted the access device. There are several ways in which an access device can be accepted. An access device is accepted by your mere receipt of the device if you requested the financial institution to issue the device to you.[51] Thus, for example, if your access device is stolen from the post office before it is received by

47. 12 C.F.R. §205.2(m)(4), Official Staff Commentary.
48. 15 U.S.C. §1693a(11); 12 C.F.R. §205.2(m)(2).
49. 15 U.S.C. §1693a(11); 12 C.F.R. §205.2(m)(3).
50. 15 U.S.C. §1693g(a); 12 C.F.R. §205.6(a). Some state laws provide greater protection for consumers than does the EFTA and therefore are not preempted by the EFTA. Colorado, Massachusetts, and Iowa limit customer liability to $50 for unauthorized transfers if an access device is lost or stolen. Colo. Rev. Stat. §§11-6.5-109(2), 11-48-106(2); Mass. Gen. Laws Ann. ch. 167B, §18; Iowa Code Ann. §527.8.1. There is no liability in Colorado if the consumer was not at fault. Colo. Rev. Stat. §§11-6.5-109(2), 11-48-106(2).
51. 12 C.F.R. §205.2(a)(2)(i).

you, you will not be liable for any transfers made by the thief's use of the device. However, if it is stolen from you after you received the device, the access device would fulfill the requirement of being accepted.

If you have not requested that the access device be issued to you, you accept the device if you[52] (1) sign the access device, (2) use or authorize another person to use the device for the purpose of transferring funds or obtaining money, property, or services, or (3) request validation of the device. An unsolicited access device may be validated only upon your request and only after your identity has been verified by reasonable means.[53] Validation occurs when the financial institution has taken all steps necessary to enable you to use the access device to initiate an electronic fund transfer.

In addition, an access device is accepted if it is issued in substitution for or in renewal of a previously accepted access device.[54] The substitute or renewed access device may not make additional accounts accessible without your request.[55]

The second condition is that the financial institution must have provided some means by which you can be identified when you use the device.[56] The means will often be a PIN, but it may also be a signature, photograph, or fingerprint.

The third condition is that the financial institution must have provided you with certain written disclosures as to your liability for unauthorized transfers.[57]

3. *Limitation of Consumer Liability*

You may incur liability for an unauthorized electronic fund transfer if these three conditions are met. However, if you promptly report the loss of your access device and promptly inform the financial institution of any unauthorized fund transfers, your liability will be very limited.

---

52. 12 C.F.R. §205.2(a)(2)(i)–(ii).

53. 12 C.F.R. §205.5(b)(4). The regulation suggests that identification be by photograph, fingerprint, personal visit, or signature comparison.

54. 12 C.F.R. §205.2(a)(2)(iii).

55. 12 C.F.R. §205.5(1), Official Staff Commentary.

56. 12 C.F.R. §205.6(a).

57. 12 C.F.R. §205.6(a). The written disclosure must provide, among other items, a summary of the consumer's liability, the telephone number and address of the person or office to be notified in the event the consumer believes that an unauthorized electronic fund transfer has been or may be made, and the financial institution's business days. 12 C.F.R. §205.7.

If the three conditions are met, you are liable for the lesser of (1) the amount of any unauthorized fund transfers or (2) $50.[58] You are not liable for any unauthorized fund transfers that occur after you have given notice to the financial institution that an unauthorized electronic fund transfer involving your account has been or may be made. Recall our example at the beginning of this chapter when you lost your ATM card on March 1st. Assume that you had reported the loss to your bank on March 2d. Assume also that the finder makes an ATM withdrawal of $20 on March 1st. He makes an additional ATM withdrawal of $200 on March 3d. Your liability in this example would be limited to $20. Because the $200 withdrawal was made after you gave notice to the bank of the loss of your access device, you are not liable for any part of that withdrawal. If, instead, the finder had made a $200 withdrawal on March 1st, your liability would have been in the amount of $50 because you are only liable for the lesser of the amount of the unauthorized electronic fund transfer or $50.

You may wonder whether your liability will be increased because you wrote your PIN on the card, thus enabling the thief to access your account. The answer is "no."[59] The limitations on liability apply whether or not you are negligent.

4. Failure to Report Loss of Device

However, your liability may be increased if you do not promptly notify the financial institution once you learn that your access device has been lost or stolen. If you do not notify your financial institution of the loss or theft of the access device within two business days after learning of the loss or theft, your liability increases to the lesser of

1. $500 or
2. the sum of (a) $50 or the amount of unauthorized electronic fund transfers that occur before the close of the 2 business days, whichever is less, and (b) the amount of unauthorized electronic fund transfers that the financial institution establishes would not have occurred but for your failure to notify the institution within two business days after

---

58. 15 U.S.C. §1693g(a); 12 C.F.R. §205.6(b). The liability limits can be less if applicable state law or an agreement between the consumer and financial institution imposes lesser liability. 12 C.F.R. §205.6(b)(6).

59. 12 C.F.R. §205.6(b)-2, Official Staff Commentary.

B. Liability for Unauthorized Transfers

you learn[60] of the loss or theft of the access device, and that occur after the close of the two business days and before notice[61] to the financial institution.[62]

Recall again our example in which you lost your ATM card on March 1st. Assume now that you did not realize that your ATM card was gone until March 15th. On March 20th, you notified your bank of the loss. It turns out that on March 10th the finder withdrew $400 in cash from your account. The finder withdrew another $600 on March 19th. Under the second alternative in (2)(a), the amount of loss that occurred *before* two days after you learned of the loss is $400. Since that amount is larger than $50, you are only liable under (2)(a) for $50 of the original $400 loss. The $600 withdrawal, however, occurred *more* than two days after you learned of the loss of your ATM card. Had your financial institution known of the loss of your ATM card, it could have deactivated the card. Your failure to report the loss of the card caused the entire $600 loss. Therefore, your total liability under (2)(a) and (2)(b) is $650. However, under (1), your liability is only $500. Since you are liable only for the lesser of (1) and (2), your liability is in the amount of $500.

---

60. Receipt of a periodic statement showing unauthorized electronic fund transfers may provide some proof of the consumer's knowledge of loss or theft of the access device but is not conclusive on the question of the consumer's knowledge. 12 C.F.R. §205.6(b)(1)-2, Official Staff Commentary.

61. Notice may be given in any manner reasonably designed to provide the institution with pertinent information. Notice can be given personally, by telephone, or in writing. Notice in writing is deemed given at the time the consumer deposits the notice in the mail or delivers the notice for transmission by any other usual means to the financial institution. Notice is also given when the financial institution becomes aware of circumstances that lead to the reasonable belief that an unauthorized transfer involving the consumer's account has been or may be made. 12 C.F.R. §205.6(b)(5).

The time periods for giving notice may be extended if the delay was due to extenuating circumstances, such as extended travel or hospitalization. 12 C.F.R. §205.6(b)(4), Official Staff Commentary.

It is not necessary that the notice be sent to an address or made by phone at a number provided by the institution for the purpose of reporting card losses or unauthorized transfers. 12 C.F.R. §205.6(b)(5)-1, Official Staff Commentary. It is not necessary for the consumer to furnish the institution with a card or account number. 12 C.F.R. §205.6(b)(5)-3, Official Staff Commentary. All that is required is for the consumer to take reasonable steps to notify the financial institution and to provide enough information for the institution to be able to identify the affected account. Id.

62. 12 C.F.R. §205.6(b)(2).

5.   Periodic Statement

So far you may feel very complacent about any liability you may face from the loss of your ATM card. You figure "what the heck! I cannot be liable for more than $500." Well, don't feel too complacent. Your liability may increase dramatically if you fail to review the periodic statements that you receive from your bank listing electronic fund transfers and to report any unauthorized electronic fund transfer shown on a statement.

In the event that you fail to report within 60 days of a statement's transmittal any unauthorized electronic fund transfer that appears on the periodic statement, you are liable to the financial institution for:

1. up to $50 of any unauthorized transfer or transfers that appear on the statement; plus
2   the full amount of any unauthorized transfers that occur after the close of the 60 days after transmittal of the statement and before you give notice to the financial institution.[63]

Assume in our original example that you did not notice and therefore did not report to your bank the unauthorized transfers appearing on your periodic statement arriving on April 1st. In April, $2,000 in additional unauthorized transfers took place. In May, $3,000 in additional unauthorized transfers took place. In June $4,000 in additional unauthorized transfers took place. You finally notify your bank of these unauthorized transfers on July 1st.

We have here a combination of a failure to report a lost or stolen access device and a failure to report the loss after the receipt of a periodic statement. In this situation, the provisions that impose liability for the failure to report the lost or stolen access device govern the amount of liability for transfers that appear on the periodic statement and before the close of 60 days after you first received a periodic statement showing an unauthorized transfer. The provisions imposing liability for the failure to report the losses that appear on a periodic statement govern thereafter.[64]

The provisions governing the failure to report a lost or stolen access device determine your liability for unauthorized transfers up to June 1st, which is 60 days after transmittal of the statement showing an unauthorized transfer. Your liability is limited to $500 for the transfers up until June 1st even

---

63. 12 C.F.R. §205.6(b)(3). See Kruser v. Bank of America, 230 Cal. App. 3d 741, 281 Cal. Rptr. 463 (1991) (failure of consumer to report a $20 unauthorized transfer shown on his periodic statement made the consumer liable for $9,020 of unauthorized transfers occurring nine months later even though he promptly reported these later transfers).

64. 12 C.F.R. §205.6(b)(3).

though the total of these unauthorized transfers was $6,000. However, there is no such limit to your liability for unauthorized transfers occurring after June 1st and before the time you notify your bank. You are therefore liable for the entire $4,000 of unauthorized transfers thereafter occurring. Your total liability is therefore $4,500 ($500 up to June 1st and $4,000 thereafter).

Liability for failure to report an unauthorized transfer contained in your periodic statement applies even though the unauthorized transfer did not involve the use of an access device.[65] However, you are only liable for losses resulting from transfers that do not involve an access device if they occur more than 60 days after the periodic statement containing an unauthorized transfer was transmitted by the finanancial institution to you.[66] For example, if an unauthorized transfer not involving an access device occurred before June 1st, you would not be liable for that transfer. If a subsequent transfer, whether or not involving an access device, occurs after June 1st, you would be fully liable for that subsequent transfer.

6. *Relation to Truth in Lending Liability Rules*

As we will cover in the next chapter, a consumer's liability for an unauthorized use of a credit card is governed by Regulation Z promulgated pursuant to the Truth in Lending Act. What happens if your access device is also your credit card? Do the liability rules found in Regulation Z or Regulation E apply when you lose your credit card? The answer depends upon whether the unauthorized activity was a transfer of funds from a consumer asset account or from a line of credit.

The liability rules in Regulation E apply if an electronic fund transfer was initiated by a credit card used as an access device.[67] Therefore, if the use of your credit card results in a draw on a consumer asset account, Regulation E governs.[68] Furthermore, if the transfer involves an extension of credit under an agreement between you and your bank to extend credit in the event that your asset account is overdrawn or in order to maintain a specified minimum balance in your asset account, the liability rules in Regulation E apply.[69]

However, if a credit card, which happens also to be an access device, is

---

65. 59 Fed. Reg. 10687 (Mar. 7, 1994). 12 C.F.R. §205.6(b)(3)-2, Official Staff Commentary.
66. 12 C.F.R. §205.6(b)(3)-2, Official Staff Commentary.
67. 12 C.F.R. §205.12 (a)(1), Official Staff Commentary.
68. 12 C.F.R. §205.12 (a)(1), Official Staff Commentary.
69. 12 C.F.R. §205.12(a)(ii).

used in any way other than to effectuate an electronic fund transfer, the Regulation Z rules apply.[70] This includes the use of a credit card to draw upon a credit line rather than on a bank account.[71] Where a stolen credit card is used to both make unauthorized withdrawals from a checking account and to draw upon a credit line, Regulation E would apply to the unauthorized withdrawals involving the checking account, while Regulation Z would apply to the transfers involving the credit line.

C. LIMITATIONS ON ISSUANCE OF ACCESS DEVICES, DISCLOSURE, AND DOCUMENTATION REQUIREMENTS

There are strong economic reasons why financial institutions, employers, and others may want to encourage the use of electronic fund transfers. Both operational costs and losses from forgeries and alterations can be reduced if payment is made by electronic fund transfer rather than by check. Because of these advantages, employers or government agencies may attempt to condition employment or receipt of governmental benefits upon the consumer's agreement to receive payment through an electronic fund transfer. Congress believed that employers' and government agencies' ability to impose receipt of payment by electronic fund transfer should be subject to some limitations. Thus, the EFTA prohibits the conditioning of employment or the receipt of government benefits on a consumer's establishment of an account for receipt of electronic fund transfers at a particular financial institution.[72] Although the employer or governmental agency can require that the consumer receive payment by electronic fund transfer, the employer or governmental agency cannot require that the account be established at any particular institution. The EFTA also prohibits the conditioning of the extension of credit on the consumer's repayment by means of a preauthorized electronic fund transfer.[73]

The protections given to consumers by the EFTA may not be waived.[74] Of course, consumers may be given more extensive rights or remedies by the financial institution than is required by the EFTA.

70. 12 C.F.R. §205.12(a)(2)(ii).
71. 12 C.F.R. §205.12 (a)(1), Official Staff Commentary.
72. 15 U.S.C. §1693k(2).
73. 15 U.S.C. §1693k(1).
74. 15 U.S.C. §1693l.

C. Limitations on Issuance of Access Devices

1. Restrictions on Issuance of Access Devices

In order to protect consumers against unexpected liabilities, the EFTA places restrictions on the ability of financial institutions to issue access devices to consumers who have not requested the device.[75] An access device not requested by the consumer may be issued only if it is not validated.[76] An access device is not validated when the institution has not yet performed all the procedures that would enable a consumer to initiate an electronic fund transfer.[77] For example, because a debit card cannot access a consumer's account without a PIN, an access device is not validated unless a PIN has been assigned to it. Thus, a financial institution cannot send an unsolicited debit card to a consumer if a PIN has been assigned to the card. The reason for this is simple. If it were to send a debit card that already had the capability of accessing the consumer's account, the consumer, without his consent, would be exposed to the risk that the unwelcomed card could be stolen and his account could be wrongfully debited by an improper use of the card before he has had a chance to return the card to the institution. Because the consumer would not have accepted the access device, although he would not be liable for any such transfers, he would have to go through the trouble of having his account recredited. For this reason, the unsolicited access device may not be validated unless requested by the consumer and then only after the institution has verified the consumer's identity.[78]

In addition, issuance by the financial institution of an unrequested access device must be accompanied by a complete disclosure (1) as to the consumer's rights and liabilities once the device is validated;[79] (2) clearly explaining that the access device is not validated; and (3) instructing the consumer on how to dispose of the device in the event that the consumer does not wish to use the device.[80]

Once the consumer accepts a debit card (thereby making it an accepted access device), the bank may send a PIN without the consumer's consent. Because the debit card is now coupled with a PIN, the debit card can be used to access the consumer's account through an ATM, POS terminal, or other electronic terminal. This exposes the consumer to the risk that the debit card and the PIN will be used to wrongfully debit his account. To protect a con-

---

75. 15 U.S.C. §1693i(a); 12 C.F.R. §205.5(b). An access device may also be sent unsolicited in renewal or in substitution for an accepted access device.

76. 15 U.S.C. §1693i(b); 12 C.F.R. §205.5(b)(1).

77. 15 U.S.C. §1693i(c); 12 C.F.R. §205.5(b)(1).

78. 12 C.F.R. §205.5(b)(4).

79. 12 C.F.R. §205.5(b)(3).

80. 12 C.F.R. §205.5(b)(2).

sumer against this risk, the consumer is not liable for any unauthorized transfer until the combination PIN and debit card become an *accepted* access device.[81] This may occur by the consumer using the PIN and access device together.

When a credit card also qualifies as an access device because it allows a consumer to initiate an electronic fund transfer, both the EFTA and the Truth in Lending Act apply.

The EFTA and Regulation E govern:

1. issuance of the access device,
2. addition to a credit card of the capability to initiate electronic fund transfers, and
3. issuance of an access device that permits credit extensions only to cover overdrafts or maintain minimum balances on consumer accounts.[82]

The Truth in Lending Act and Regulation Z govern:

1. the issuance of a credit card,
2. the addition of credit features to an accepted access device, and
3. the issuance of credit cards that are also access devices unless the only credit feature is that the device permits credit extensions to cover overdrafts or maintain minimum balances on consumer accounts.[83]

2. Disclosure Requirements

Before a consumer can decide whether she wants to use an electronic fund transfer service, she must know not only the costs and risks involved in use of such a service, but also her rights. The EFTA and Regulation E require that the financial institution make certain disclosures to the consumer regarding electronic fund transfer services both before the consumer employs such services[84] and whenever the terms of the relationship between the financial institution and the consumer are changed.[85]

---

81. 12 C.F.R. §205.5(b)-2, Official Staff Commentary.
82. 12 C.F.R. §205.12(a)(ii).
83. 12 C.F.R. §205.12(a)(2).
84. 15 U.S.C. §1693c(a); 12 C.F.R. §205.7.
85. 15 U.S.C. §1693c(b); 12 C.F.R. §205.8.

C. Limitations on Issuance of Access Devices

a. Initial Disclosures

At the time a consumer contracts for electronic fund transfer services or before the first electronic fund transfer is made involving the consumer's account, the financial institution must supply to the consumer the following information:[86]

1. a summary of the consumer's liability for unauthorized electronic fund transfers,
2. the telephone number and address of the person or office for the consumer to notify if the consumer believes that an unauthorized electronic fund transfer has been or may be made,
3. the financial institution's business days,[87]
4. the types of electronic fund transfers that the consumer may make and any limitations on the frequency and dollar amount of the transfers;[88]
5. any charges for electronic fund transfers or for the right to make transfers,
6. a summary of the consumer's rights under Regulation E to receive documentation of electronic fund transfers,
7. a summary of Regulation E as to a consumer's right to stop payment of preauthorized electronic fund transfers and the procedure for stopping payment,
8. a summary of the financial institution's liability under Regulation E for failure to make or to stop transfers as required by law,
9. the circumstances under which the financial institution in the ordinary course of business will disclose information about the consumer's account to third parties, and
10. a notice regarding error resolution procedures.[89]

---

86. 15 U.S.C. §1693c(a); 12 C.F.R. §205.7(b).

87. 12 C.F.R. §205.7(b)(3). A business day is any day other than a Saturday, a Sunday, or any of the legal public holidays specified in 5 U.S.C. §6103(a). 12 C.F.R. §205.2(d).

88. 15 U.S.C. §1693c(a)(3); 12 C.F.R. §205.7(b)(4). The institution is not required to provide details of the limitations if the confidentiality of such limitations is essential to the security of the system. Id.

89. 12 C.F.R. §205.7(b)(10). The financial institution is required to provide the consumer with the prescribed error resolution notice at least once each calendar year or is required to send a notice with each periodic statement in the form prescribed. 12 C.F.R. §205.8(b).

b. Disclosures after Changes in Terms

A financial institution must generally give notice to the consumer before making material changes in the terms governing electronic fund transfer services. The financial institution must mail or deliver a written notice to the consumer at least 21 days before the effective date of any of the following changes:[90]

1 an increase in fees or charges,
2. an increase in the consumer's liability,
3. a decrease in the types of available electronic fund transfers, or
4. stricter limitations on the frequency or dollar amounts of transfers.

c. Special Rules for Preauthorized Transfers

One type of electronic fund transfer is a "preauthorized electronic fund transfer," which is any transfer that is authorized in advance and that recurs at substantially regular intervals.[91] A preauthorized transfer can either be a transfer from your account or to your account. For very good reasons, as we will see, special rules apply to preauthorized electronic fund transfers.

Let us first examine a preauthorized transfer to your account. For example, you may have your paycheck automatically deposited by your employer into your bank account. To do so, you authorize your employer to pay you through automatic deposit of your paycheck. Your employer prepares a magnetic tape containing each employee's name, account number, and the bank at which the account is maintained. It sends the tape to your bank. Your employer's bank credits the account of any employee who also maintains an account with it ("on-us" transfers). It then prepares a new tape containing information as to the employees not having accounts with it and forwards the tape to an Automated Clearing House ("ACH"). The ACH electronically sends the information as to the remaining employees to each of their respective banks. (See Figure 8.2.)

---

90. 15 U.S.C. §1693c(b); 12 C.F.R. §205.8(a). If the security of the system depends on secrecy of withdrawal limits, it is not necessary to disclose changes in those limits. 12 C.F.R. §205.8(a)-3, Official Staff Commentary. Prior notice is not required if the change is necessary to restore or maintain the security of the fund-transfer system or the account. 12 C.F.R. §205.8(a)(2).

91. 15 U.S.C. §1693a(9); 12 C.F.R. §205.2(k).

C. Limitations on Issuance of Access Devices

FIGURE 8.2

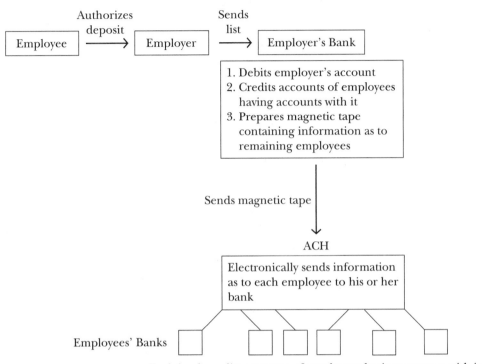

Each bank credits accounts of employees having accounts with it.

How do you know that your paycheck has in fact been deposited into your account? You need to know promptly whether your paycheck has been properly credited. Otherwise how can you safely write checks on the account? Unless you quickly learn that your account has not been properly credited, checks you have subsequently written may be dishonored for insufficient funds. On the other hand, it would be a large imposition on the bank to immediately inform each of its depositors as to whether their paycheck has been deposited. EFTA and Regulation E have attempted to reach a balance between the needs of the depositor to learn quickly whether the deposit has been made and of the financial institution to reduce the costs of communicating this information to each depositor.

If your account is to be credited by a preauthorized electronic fund transfer from the same payor at least once every 60 days, your bank must give you notice of the deposit.[92] There are several ways in which your bank can comply with the notice requirement. First, your bank may give you oral or written notice within two business days after the transfer that the transfer has occurred.[93] Your bank does not have to give you notice if your employer or other payor gives you notice that the transfer has been initiated.[94] This is why you will often receive from your employer something that looks very much like a paycheck, but is, in fact, an acknowledgment that the electronic deposit of your paycheck was initiated by your employer.

Second, your bank may instead decide to give notice within two business days after a scheduled funds transfer that the transfer has *not* occurred.[95] Third, your bank may instead provide a readily available telephone line that you may call to ascertain whether or not the preauthorized transfer occurred.[96] If the bank exercises this option, it must disclose the telephone number on the required initial disclosures and on each periodic statement.

Let us now examine preauthorized debits to your account. You may have your gas or other utility bill automatically deducted from your bank account. Assume that you pay your gas bill through a preauthorized debit. You would first sign a form authorizing the Gas Company to initiate every month a transfer of funds in the amount of that month's gas bill from your account to the Gas Company's account. The form would also authorize your bank to debit your account in the amount specified by the Gas Company. A preauthorized electronic fund transfer can be authorized by the consumer only in a signed writing or similar authentication[97] and only if a copy of the authorization is provided to the consumer by the party obtaining the authorization (the Gas Company).[98]

Each month the Gas Company prepares a list indicating the identity of each customer, the amount of the debit, the customer's account number, and the identity of the bank at which the customer's account is maintained. The Gas Company sends this list to its bank. The Gas Company's bank prepares the list in the form of a magnetic tape, which it forwards to an ACH. The ACH then transmits to each bank at which a customer maintains an account the portion of the list relating to that particular bank's customers. Your bank, upon receipt of this list, debits your account in the amount specified in the list. (See Figure 8.3.)

92. 12 C.F.R. §205.10(a)(1).
93. 12 C.F.R. §205.10(a)(i).
94. 12 C.F.R. §205.10(a)(2).
95. 12 C.F.R. §205.10(a)(ii).
96. 12 C.F.R. §205.10(a)(iii).
97. 12 C.F.R. §205.10(b).
98. 12 C.F.R. §205.10(b).

C. Limitations on Issuance of Access Devices

Figure 8.3

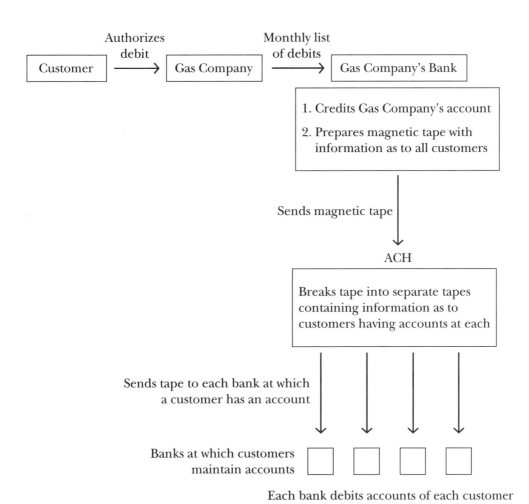

Where the debit is in the same amount each month, no notification is required. Because you know that the debit will occur, any notification would be superfluous. In contrast, if debits are in a varying amount, it is important that you are informed of the amount of the debit. Otherwise, your account may not contain sufficient funds to cover the debit. For this reason, you have the right to receive notice if a transfer varies in amount from the previous transfer or from the preauthorized amount.[99] Notice must be given either by your bank or by the payee at least ten days before the scheduled transfer date. This enables you not only to verify whether the amount is correct, but also to deposit funds in the account to cover any deficit.

3.   Documentation Requirements

One of the disadvantages of making payment or withdrawing funds by electronic fund transfer rather than by check is the absence of a returned check to evidence the payment or the withdrawal. To remedy this deficiency, the EFTA and Regulation E contain various documentation requirements for electronic fund transfers.

a.   Receipts at Electronic Terminals

When you initiate an electronic fund transfer at an electronic terminal, the financial institution itself, or through another party (like the merchant at a POS terminal) must provide you with a written receipt containing the following information:[100]

1. the amount of the transfer;
2. the calendar date you initiated the transfer;
3. the type of transfer and type of your account to or from which the transfer is made (for example, withdrawal from savings account);
4. a number or code identifying you, your account(s), or the access device used to initiate the transfer;
5. the location of the terminal at which the transfer was initiated or an identification (such as a code or terminal number); and
6. the name of any third party to or from whom funds are transferred, unless the name is provided by you in a form that the terminal cannot duplicate on the receipt.[101]

---

99. 12 C.F.R. §205.10(d). The payee or financial institution can give the consumer the option to receive notice only when the transfer falls outside of a specified range of amounts. Id.

100. 15 U.S.C. §1693d (a); 12 C.F.R. §205.9 (a). Because "electronic terminal" does not include a telephone, the receipt requirement does not apply to transfers made over the telephone. 15 U.S.C. §1693a(7); 12 C.F.R. §205.2(h). The terminal may provide the option to the consumer as to whether to receive the receipt. 12 C.F.R. §205.9(a)(1).

101. 12 C.F.R. §205.9(a)(6), Official Staff Commentary.

C. Limitations on Issuance of Access Devices

In order to provide you with some of the evidentiary protections provided by a returned check, the receipt is deemed prima facie proof of the transfer of funds to the third person.[102]

b. Periodic Statements

Your bank or other financial institution must provide periodic statements to you for each account[103] to or from which electronic fund transfers can be made.[104] The statement must provide the following information for each transfer occurring during the period covered:

1. the amount of the transfer, including any charge[105] added by the owner or operator of the electronic terminal;
2. the date the transfer was credited or debited to your account;
3. the type of transfer and the type of your account to or from which the funds were transferred;
4. the location of the electronic terminal at which the transfer was initiated;
5. the name of any person to or from whom funds were transferred;
6. the number(s) of your accounts for which the statement is issued;
7. the amount of any fees or charges, other than a finance charge, assessed against the account during the statement period for electronic fund transfers or for the right to make such transfers, or for account maintenance;
8. the balance(s) in your account(s) at the beginning and close of the statement period; and

---

102. 15 U.S.C. §1693d(f).

103. In the case of a passbook account that may not be accessed by an electronic fund transfer other than a preauthorized transfer to the account, the financial institution is not required to provide the periodic statement and may instead provide the consumer with documentation upon presentation of the passbook by entering in the passbook or on a separate document the amount and date of each electronic fund transfer made since the passbook was last presented. 12 C.F.R. §205.9(c)(i). If the account is not represented by a passbook and may be accessed electronically only through a preauthorized transfer to the account, the institution need only provide quarterly statements. 12 C.F.R. §205.9(c)(ii).

104. 15 U.S.C. §1693d(e); 12 C.F.R. §205.9(b). Such statements must be provided for each monthly or shorter cycle in which an electronic fund transfer has occurred and must be provided at least quarterly if no transfer has occurred. 15 U.S.C. §1693d(d); 12 C.F.R. §205.9(b).

105. Notice must be given of the fee charged for the transaction. The notice may be disclosed on the receipt and displayed on the screen of the terminal or at the terminal itself. 12 C.F.R. §205.9(a)(1). 12 C.F.R. §205.9(a)(1), Official Staff Commentary.

9. the address and telephone number to be used for inquiry or notice of error unless the address and telephone number were included on the notice of error resolution procedures.

It is essential that you examine your periodic statements. As we discussed in section B, you may be liable for subsequent unauthorized fund transfers if you do not report within 60 days an unauthorized fund transfer shown on a periodic statement.

D. STOPPING PAYMENT OF ELECTRONIC FUND TRANSFERS AND LIABILITY FOR SYSTEM MALFUNCTION

1. No Right to Reverse Ordinary Fund Transfer

You just purchased a television set from Radio Shack. You paid for the set by an electronic fund transfer through the POS terminal located at the store. You took the television set home and discovered that it did not work. Radio Shack refuses to take the set back. May you prevent your bank from paying Radio Shack?

Your question is really two separate questions. The first question is a practical question. Can you, as a practical matter, prevent your bank from paying Radio Shack? The answer to this question is clearly "no." As discussed in section A, a POS transfer is usually an instanteous transfer of funds from your account to Radio Shack's account. By the time that the POS terminal indicates that the transfer is authorized, your account has been debited and Radio Shack's account credited. Even when the arrangement between your bank and Radio Shack's bank is that the settlement between them will be made at the end of the day, once your bank has authorized the transfer, it is absolutely liable to pay Radio Shack's bank. Your breach of warranty claim against Radio Shack that the set was defective would not provide your bank a defense to its obligation to pay Radio Shack's bank.

The second question is a legal one. Do you have the right to order your bank to reverse the transfer? In other words, can your bank notify Radio Shack's bank that the transfer has been reversed and demand that Radio Shack's bank return the money? Congress in enacting the EFTA determined that a consumer should have no right to reverse an electronic fund transfer

D. Stopping Payment of Electronic Fund Transfers

(other than preauthorized electronic fund transfers discussed below). Payment by electronic fund transfer should be the equivalent of payment in cash. If you want to retain the ability to prevent Radio Shack from receiving payment for the set, you could always pay by check rather than by electronic fund transfer. Once the electronic fund transfer is completed, your only recourse is to attempt to recover the payment from Radio Shack.

A few state legislatures reached a determination contrary to that of Congress. These state legislatures were of the opinion that the need to protect consumers against unscrupulous merchants outweighed the need to preserve the cash-like nature of electronic fund transfers. In these states an electronic fund transfer initiated by a consumer may be reversed under certain conditions. Under Michigan law,[106] for example, a consumer may reverse a fund transfer if the following conditions are met:

1. The consumer makes a good faith effort to seek redress from the merchant and return the goods or services;
2. The transaction is for more than $50; and
3. The request for reversal is made within four calendar days of the transaction.

2. *Stopping Payment on Preauthorized Electronic Fund Transfers*

You do, however, have the right to stop payment of any preauthorized electronic fund transfer from your account. We discussed the operation of preauthorized electronic fund transfers in section C. Preauthorized electronic fund transfers serve a very different purpose than do POS or other similar transfers. The primary purpose of a POS transfer is as a substitute for payment in cash. Allowing reversibility would defeat this purpose. In contrast, the primary purpose of a preauthorized electronic fund transfer is to eliminate the expense and inconvenience of paying by check. The consumer is relieved of the burden and expense of writing out and mailing checks. The creditor is saved the time and expense of opening the mail containing the checks and of depositing the checks into its account. Allowing the consumer the right to stop payment of a preauthorized debit does not undercut the advantages either party has already obtained through the arrangement. Furthermore, consumers

---

106. Mich. Comp. Laws §488.16.

would not agree to payment by preauthorized electronic fund transfer if it meant waiving their right to refuse payment in an appropriate case.

You can stop payment of a preauthorized electronic fund transfer by giving oral or written notice to your financial institution at any time up to three business days before the scheduled date of the transfer.[107] Thus, if the preauthorized transfer is scheduled to take place on Monday, February 1st, you can stop payment of the transfer by giving notice any time up to Wednesday, January 27th. (Remember that Saturday and Sunday do not count because they are not business days.) If your notice is oral, your financial institution may require that written confirmation of the stop payment order be given within 14 days of the oral notification. In order to require written confirmation, the financial institution must inform you of this requirement and give you the address to which the confirmation should be sent at the time the oral notification is given. If, upon request, you fail to confirm the stop payment order in writing, the oral stop-payment order ceases to be binding 14 days after it has been made.

Reconfirmation in writing is a practical necessity. For example, assume that on September 5th, you order your bank to stop payment on your gas bill payable on September 11th. You confirm the order in writing on September 17th. If the Gas Company resubmits the bill on September 29th, your bank must stop payment of the bill.[108] Had you not reconfirmed the order in writing, your bank could have paid the bill.

You also have the right to instruct your bank to block all subsequent payments of your gas bills. Your bank has the right to confirm that you have informed the Gas Company of the revocation and to require receipt of a copy of your revocation.

3.   Consumer Liability to Third Parties in the Event of System Malfunction

What happens if there is a malfunction in the fund transfer system that prevents your preauthorized payment to the Gas Company to be made. Can the Gas Company turn off your gas? The answer is "no." If the Gas Company has agreed to accept payment through an electronic fund transfer, your obligation to make the payment is suspended until the system malfunction is corrected and the electronic fund transfer may be completed.[109] However, you must pay

---

107. 12 C.F.R. §205.10(c).
108. 12 C.F.R. §205.10(c)-1, Official Staff Commentary.
109. 15 U.S.C. §1693j.

the bill if any time before the malfunction is corrected, the Gas Company demands in writing that payment be made by means other than an electronic fund transfer.

E.   ERROR RESOLUTION PROCEDURES

You notice on your bank statement that your account was debited in the amount of $1,000 for a purchase of a $100 telephone at Radio Shack made through a POS terminal. What do you do? How quickly must your bank rectify the error? Must the bank recredit your account during the investigation? We will explore these questions in this section.

1.   What Is an Error?

The EFTA and Regulation E establish precise procedures that your bank must follow when you claim that an error has occurred involving an electronic fund transfer. The procedure only applies if your claim is an "error."

Regulation E lists seven types of errors. The first type of error is an unauthorized electronic fund transfer.[110] We discussed unauthorized electronic fund transfers in section B. Because the loss or theft of an access device is not an unauthorized transfer, it is not an error and therefore does not trigger the error resolution procedure discussed below. However, if the consumer also alleges possible unauthorized use as a consequence of the loss or theft, the error resolution procedure will apply.[111]

The second type of error is an incorrect electronic fund transfer to or from the consumer's account.[112] For example, you would be asserting an error if you claimed that a transfer was in the wrong amount or made to the wrong beneficiary. The bank's debiting of your account for $1,000 is an error because it was an incorrect transfer from your account.

The third type of error is the omission from a periodic statement of an electronic fund transfer.[113] This type of error includes both completed elec-

---

110. 15 U.S.C. §1693f(f)(1); 12 C.F.R. §205.11(a)(1)(i).
111. 12 C.F.R. §205.11(a)-3, Official Staff Commentary.
112. 15 U.S.C. §1693f(f)(2); 12 C.F.R. §205.11(a)(1)(ii).
113. 15 U.S.C. §1693f(f)(3); 12 C.F.R. §205.11(a)(1)(iii).

tronic fund transfers that do not appear on the periodic statement and transfers that were never completed despite proper instructions. The fourth type of error is a computational or bookkeeping error made by the financial institution relating to an electronic fund transfer.[114]

The fifth type of error is the consumer's receipt of an incorrect amount of money from an electronic terminal.[115] For example, assume that you have instructed an ATM to dispense $200 in cash. Despite the fact that you received only $100 from the ATM, the receipt indicates that your account has been debited for the entire $200. You may wonder how the bank can determine whether an error has really occurred. Sometimes, it is easy. If the bank's records show that the ATM has a surplus of $100 over the amount that should have been dispensed according to the total amount of withdrawals recorded that day, the bank knows that your claim is correct (unless someone else also claimed a $100 shortage). However, where the bank's records do not corroborate your claim, resolution of this matter will depend, to a large extent, upon your credibility. If you are a good customer who has never before made a similar claim, the bank (or if the case is litigated, the trier of fact) will very likely believe you.

The sixth type of error is an electronic fund transfer that is not identified as required by the provisions in Regulation E dealing with documentation and preauthorized transfers to the consumer's account.[116] For example, it would be an error if the date of the transfer was omitted from the receipt you received at an ATM.

The final type of error is a consumer's request for any documentation required by Regulation E or for additional information or clarification regarding an electronic fund transfer.[117] The documentation, additional information, or clarification must relate to the assertion of an error. This type of error does not include routine inquiries as to the balance in your account or a request for documentation for tax or other recordkeeping purposes.[118]

---

114. 15 U.S.C. §1693f(f)(4); 12 C.F.R. §205.11(a)(1)(iv).
115. 15 U.S.C. §1693f(f)(5); 12 C.F.R. §205.11(a)(1)(v).
116. 12 C.F.R. §205.11(a)(1)(vi).
117. 15 U.S.C. §1693f(f)(6); 12 C.F.R. §205.11(a)(1)(vii).
118. 12 C.F.R. §205.11(a)(2).

E. Error Resolution Procedures

2. *Notice of Error*

If you want your bank to investigate an error, you must give oral or written notice of error to your bank. Your notice must be given no later than 60 days after the bank provided you with the periodic statement indicating the error.[119] If you fail to give notice within the 60-day period, you have no right to require that your bank go through the error resolution procedure. Neither the EFTA nor Regulation E indicate whether there is any other consequence of your failure to promptly report the error. Nothing in the EFTA nor Regulation E would seem to prevent you from bringing an action against the bank to recredit your account because of the error.

If an error is not reflected in a periodic statement, but appears only in documents thereafter requested by you from the bank, the 60-day period begins to run when these documents are transmitted to you by your bank.[120] The notice[121] of error must[122] (1) enable your bank to identify you and your account number, (2) indicate the reasons why you believe that an error exists, and (3) to the extent possible, indicate the type, the date, and the amount of the error.

3. *Bank's Duty to Investigate*

Upon receipt of your notice of error, your bank has the duty to promptly investigate and determine whether an error has occurred.[123] Your bank has a choice as to when it must complete its investigation. If your bank does not want to provisionally recredit your account during the investigation, it must transmit the result of its investigation to you within ten business days.[124] If,

---

119. 15 U.S.C. §1693f(a); 12 C.F.R. §205.11(b)(1)(i). In the case of a passbook account, the notice must be given within 60 days after transmittal of documentation on which the alleged error was reflected. Id. If the institution fails to provide a statement as required, the consumer has 60 days from the date that the statement should have been transmitted to notify the institution of its error in failing to send the statement. 12 C.F.R. §205.11(b)(1)-4, Official Staff Commentary.

120. 12 C.F.R. §205.11(b)(3).

121. If an oral notice is given, the financial institution may require a written confirmation to be received within ten business days of an oral notice if, when the oral notice is given, the consumer is advised of the requirement and of the address to which the confirmation must be sent. 12 C.F.R. §205.11(b)(2).

122. 12 C.F.R. §205.11(b)(1)(ii)–(iii).

123. 15 U.S.C. §1693f(a); 12 C.F.R. §205.11(c).

124. 15 U.S.C. §1693f(a); 12 C.F.R. §205.11(c)(1) and (2)(i).

instead, your bank does not mind provisionally recrediting your account in the amount of the alleged error (including any applicable interest) within ten business days after receipt of your notice of error, your bank may, as long as it acts promptly, take up to 45 calendar days to transmit the results of its investigation.[125] Your bank must also within two business days after recrediting your account, orally report or mail (or otherwise deliver) notice to you of the amount and date of the recrediting and give you full use of the funds pending the investigation.[126] However, if your bank has reasonable grounds to believe that an unauthorized electronic fund transfer has occurred for which you may be liable, your bank may withhold up to $50 from the amount recredited.[127]

The time periods for determining whether an error has occurred are extended if the transfer was initiated outside the United States or resulted from a point-of-sale debit card transaction. In these cases, the ten-business-day limit increases to 20 business days and the 45 calendar day limit increases to 90 calendar days.[128]

4. What Happens after the Bank Makes Its Determination?

If your bank determines that an error has occurred, it must promptly, and no later than one business day after this determination, correct the error.[129] Whether or not your bank determines that an error has occurred, it must mail or deliver to you a written explanation of its findings within three business days after concluding its investigation.[130]

If your bank had provisionally recredited your account pending its investigation, you may have written checks in reliance upon your account containing these funds. In order to inform you that you no longer have the right to draw upon these funds, your bank must orally report, mail, or otherwise deliver notice to you of the date and the amount of the debiting. However, you may have already written checks or other instruments in reliance upon the presence of these funds prior to receiving this notice. To protect you from an

---

125. 15 U.S.C. §1693f(c); 12 C.F.R. §205.11(c)(2). Your bank does not have to provisionally recredit your account if it had requested but did not receive timely written confirmation or oral notice of an error. 12 C.F.R. §205.11(c)(2)(i)(A).

126. 12 C.F.R. §205.11(c)(2)(ii).

127. 12 C.F.R. §205.11(c)(2)(i).

128. 12 C.F.R. §205.11(c)(3).

129. 15 U.S.C. §1693f(b); 12 C.F.R. §205.11(c)(2)(iii).

130. 15 U.S.C. §1693f(d); 12 C.F.R. §205.11(c)(2)(iv).

embarrassing dishonor of these checks or other instruments, your bank must honor checks, drafts, or other instruments payable to third parties or preauthorized transfers drawn on the provisionally recredited funds for five business days after transmittal of the notice. In order to ensure that you are aware of this right, the notice must inform you of this right.[131]

5. Relation to Truth in Lending Dispute Resolution Procedures

If an access device can access both your credit line and your asset account, the determination of whether the error resolution procedure in Regulation E or Regulation Z applies depends upon from which account the alleged erroneous transfer occurred. Where the transfer is out of an asset account, Regulation E's procedure is applicable. Where the transfer is out of a credit line, Regulation Z's procedure is applicable. The one exception involves a transfer to cover amounts overdrawn or to maintain a specified minimum balance in which case Regulation E applies.[132]

F. CIVIL AND CRIMINAL LIABILITY

The EFTA has three provisions governing liability for the failure to comply with its provisions: [133]

1. a provision specifically governing the financial institution's liability to its customer for failing to conduct a funds transfer or to stop payment of a pre-authorized transfer;
2. a general provision providing for civil liability for any person's failure to comply with any provision of the EFTA except for an error resolved in accordance with the error-resolution procedures; and
3. a provision providing for criminal liability for knowingly and willfully failing to comply with the EFTA or for knowingly misusing a forged or stolen access device in interstate or foreign commerce.

131. 12 C.F.R. §205.11(d)(2). Of course, your bank is only required to honor checks that would have been honored if the debit had not occurred. 12 C.F.R. §205.11(d)(2)(ii).
132. 12 C.F.R. §205.12(a)(1)(iii).
133. 15 U.S.C. §1693h; 15 U.S.C. §1693m; 15 U.S.C. §1693n respectively.

1. *Financial Institution's Liability to Customer for Failure to Conduct Fund Transfer or Stop Payment of Preauthorized Transfer*

You instruct your bank to transfer funds by August 1st to the seller of the house you want to purchase. The bank fails to do so. Because of the bank's failure, you lose the right to purchase the house. The house appreciates in value. Is the bank liable to you for your lost profit on the purchase? You stop payment on a preauthorized electronic fund transfer to your cable television supplier because you are not satisfied with the service. Your bank ignores your stop payment order. You are required to file a lawsuit to recover the funds. Is the bank liable for your expenses in recovering from the cable television supplier? As we will examine, the truth is that although you have a right to damages from your bank for breach of these duties, it is not at all clear to what type of damages you are entitled.

a.   When a Financial Institution Is Liable to Customer for Damages

The EFTA specifically provides that a financial institution is liable to its customer for damages in two situations. First, a financial institution is liable to its customer for damages if, upon a proper stop-payment order being given, the institution fails to stop payment of a preauthorized fund transfer.[134] Thus, absent a defense, your bank would be liable to you for failing to stop payment of your preauthorized fund transfer to your cable television supplier.

Second, a financial institution is liable to its customer if it fails to make a fund transfer in the correct amount and in a timely manner.[135] Thus, absent a defense, your bank would be liable to you for failing to make the fund transfer to the seller of the house by August 1st. The bank would likewise be liable if it had transferred the incorrect amount of funds, whether greater or lesser than authorized.

Of course, the financial institution is only liable if the customer has sufficient funds in his account to cover the transfer. There is one exception to this requirement. The existence of insufficient funds in a customer's account is not an excuse for the institution's failure to make a transfer if the insufficiency is caused by the failure of the institution to properly credit the consumer's account with a deposit.[136]

134. 15 U.S.C. §1693h(a)(3).
135. 15 U.S.C. §1693h(a)(1).
136. 15 U.S.C. §1693h(a)(2).

F. Civil and Criminal Liability

The financial institution is not liable if the failure of the account to contain sufficient funds to cover the transfer resulted from the institution's improper charging of its customer's account for an unauthorized electronic fund transfer which error has subsequently been properly resolved under the error resolution process. For example, assume that the financial institution had previously debited its customer's account for an unauthorized electronic fund transfer for which the customer was not liable. Prior to the customer's noticing that his account had been debited for an unauthorized electronic fund transfer, the financial institution fails to make a subsequent electronic fund transfer. Had the account not been improperly debited, the customer would have had sufficient funds to cover this subsequent electronic fund transfer. The financial institution is not liable to the customer for failing to make this subsequent transfer.

The reason for this is that an unauthorized electronic fund transfer constitutes an error under the EFTA. A financial institution is not liable if its noncompliance with the EFTA resulted in an error that was properly resolved pursuant to the EFTA error resolution procedure.[137] Under the error resolution procedure contained in the EFTA and Regulation E, the financial institution has no obligation to immediately recredit an account if the institution intends to determine within ten days whether an error has occurred. Therefore, the customer's account does not contain sufficient funds to cover the subsequent transfer until the financial institution has the duty to recredit the account. As a result, the financial institution has acted properly in failing to make the subsequent fund transfer.

If, however, the customer gives notice of the error and the financial institution fails to comply with the error resolution procedure, the financial institution would be liable if it subsequently fails to make an electronic fund transfer (assuming had the institution complied with the procedure, it would have been obligated to have recredited its customer's account).

Even when there are sufficient funds in the consumer's account to cover a transfer, the bank has no obligation to make the transfer if the funds are subject to legal process or other encumbrances restricting the transfer.[138] Where the consumer has a credit line with the financial institution, the institution has no obligation to make the transfer if the transfer would exceed the customer's credit limit.[139] If the transfer is a withdrawal of cash from an electronic terminal (usually an ATM), the institution is not liable to its customer if the electronic terminal does not have sufficient cash to complete the transaction.[140]

---

137. 15 U.S.C. §1693m(a).
138. 15 U.S.C. §1693h(a)(1).
139. 15 U.S.C. §1693h(a)(1).
140. 15 U.S.C. §1693h(a)(1).

There are certain other defenses available to the institution. When the failure is caused by an act of God or other circumstance beyond the institution's control, the institution is not liable as long as it exercises reasonable care to prevent the occurrence and exercises reasonable diligence after the occurrence has happened.[141] If the customer knows, when he attempts to initiate a transfer, that the transfer cannot be completed because of a technical malfunction, the financial institution is not liable to the customer.[142] Similarly, the institution is not liable for failing to make a preauthorized electronic fund transfer if the consumer was aware of a technical malfunction at the time the transfer should have occurred.

b.   Damages

Although your bank is liable to you for all damages proximately caused by virtue of its failure to properly and timely make a fund transfer or to stop payment of a preauthorized fund transfer, if the bank's failure was unintentional and occurred despite reasonable precautions established by the institution to guard against such failures, you are limited to actual damages proved.[143]

No guidance is given in the commentary nor in case law for what constitutes "actual damages proved" as distinguished from "damages proximately caused." Read literally, nothing would prevent a court from interpreting "actual damages" to include consequential damages. However, most commentators in the field believe that the phrase was intended to cover direct but not consequential damages.[144] Assuming that these commentators are correct, you would not be allowed to recover your lost profits on the purchase of the house if your bank's failure was unintentional and your bank employed reasonable precautions to avoid such a failure. You would be limited to your costs

---

141. 15 U.S.C. §1693h(b)(1).

142. 15 U.S.C. §1693h(b)(2).

143. 15 U.S.C. §1693h(c).

144. It appears that the phrase "actual damages proved" was taken from the pre-1990 version of U.C.C. §4-402. In §4-402, the phrase was intended to eliminate the presumption of trade libel in cases of a wrongful dishonor of a check drawn by a merchant. In cases of trade libel, there was a presumption that a merchant's reputation and thus the profitability of his business were harmed by a libelous statement. The trier of fact could award damages to the merchant even if the merchant failed to introduce any evidence of actual loss. Since the EFTA covers consumer asset accounts and thus would rarely apply to a merchant, the phrase "actual damages proved" must serve a different purpose. From all that anyone can discern, it appears that its purpose is to exclude damages proximately caused by the failure. Donald I. Baker and Roland E. Brandel, The Law of Electronic Fund Transfer Systems 17-20, n. 80 (Rev. Ed. 1996). See also Benjamin Geva, The Law of Electronic Funds Transfers 6-190 (1994).

in making the transfer and any loss of interest. If your bank's failure was intentional or your bank did not employ reasonable precautions, you would then be entitled to your lost profits.

The issue becomes more difficult when the bank fails to honor your stop payment order. It is likely that when the bank's failure was not intentional, a court would adopt the measure of recovery found in Article 4 governing the failure of a bank to honor a stop payment order on a check. As we discussed in Chapter 6, in such a case your bank would be liable for the loss you suffered by virtue of the bank's failure to honor the stop payment order. Assume that you owed your cable television supplier $200, but that you would be able to assert against the cable television supplier a claim for damages in the amount of $50. If the cable television supplier is solvent, you will not suffer any loss except for interest for the loss of the use of the funds. Had payment been stopped, the cable television supplier would have sued you for the $200. After offsetting your claim for damages, the court would have awarded the cable television supplier $150. Had payment not been stopped, you could have recovered from your cable television supplier your $50 damages. You would have ultimately paid the same $150. However, if the cable television supplier is insolvent, you are not able to recover the $50 from it and therefore the bank's failure to honor the stop payment order has cost you $50. If the bank's failure was intentional, even if the cable television supplier is solvent, the bank should be obligated to pay as consequential damages your legal expenses in recovering the $50 from the cable television supplier together with interest for the loss of the use of the funds.

2. Civil Liability for Failure to Comply with the EFTA

The provisions of the EFTA may be enforced by administrative action. The EFTA delegates administrative enforcement to various agencies, depending on the type of institution involved.[145] Besides administrative enforcement, the

---

145. For example, if the financial institution is a national bank, administrative enforcement is delegated to the Comptroller of the Currency. 15 U.S.C. §1693o. If the financial institution is a member of the Federal Reserve System but not a national bank, enforcement is delegated to the Federal Reserve Board. 15 U.S.C. §1693o. Other agencies that may be involved in enforcing the EFTA are the Federal Deposit Insurance Corporation, the Office of Thrift Supervision, the National Credit Union Administration Board, the Department of Transportation, and the Securities and Exchange Commission. 12 C.F.R. §205, Appendix B. Unless administrative enforcement is delegated to another specific agency, the Federal Trade Commission is charged with enforcing the EFTA.

EFTA also provides for civil actions by consumers and for limited criminal actions.[146]

An institution that fails to comply with the provisions of the EFTA is liable to the injured consumer in an amount equal to any actual damage sustained by the consumer because of the noncompliance together with an amount not less than $100 nor greater than $1,000 plus the costs of a successful action to enforce the liability, including reasonable attorney's fees.[147]

In the event of a class action, instead of the $100 and $1,000 limitations, the total recovery for the class arising out of the same failure to comply is limited to the lesser of $500,000 or 1 percent of the net worth of the defendant plus actual damages, costs, and reasonable attorney's fees.[148]

In making its award, the court is required to take into account the frequency and persistence of noncompliance, the nature of noncompliance, and the extent to which noncompliance was intentional.[149] In a class action, the court is also required to take into account the resources of the defendant and the number of persons adversely affected.[150]

Under certain conditions, damages may be trebled where the noncompliance is a failure to comply with the error resolution rules. Damages may be trebled if the financial institution failed to provisionally recredit the consumer's account within ten days after receiving notice of error and either did not make a good faith investigation or unreasonably believed that the consumer's account was not in error.[151] Damages may also be trebled if the financial institution knowingly and willfully concluded that the consumer's account was not in error when such a conclusion could not reasonably have been drawn from the evidence available to the financial institution at the time of its investigation.

a.   Defenses to Liability

A financial institution is not liable if its noncompliance resulted in an error that was properly resolved pursuant to the EFTA error resolution procedures.[152] For example, if your bank improperly charged your account for an electronic fund transfer that did not take place, your bank is not liable to you if it, in a timely manner, investigated your claim and recredited your account.

146. 15 U.S.C. §§1693m & 1693n.
147. 15 U.S.C. §1693m(a).
148. 15 U.S.C. §1693m(a)(2)(B).
149. 15 U.S.C. §1693m(b)(1).
150. 15 U.S.C. §1693m(b)(2).
151. 15 U.S.C. §1693f(e).
152. 15 U.S.C. §1693m(a).

F. Civil and Criminal Liability

A financial institution is also not liable if it proves by a preponderance of the evidence that the noncompliance was not intentional and resulted from a bona fide error notwithstanding the maintenance of procedures reasonably adapted to avoid such noncompliance.[153] A financial institution is likewise not liable if it both notifies the consumer of the noncompliance prior to the consumer bringing an action and pays to the consumer his actual damages.[154]

b. Statute of Limitations

The consumer must bring his action within one year from the date of the occurrence of the violation.[155] If a consumer's unsuccessful action is determined to have been brought in bad faith or for purposes of harassment, the court is required to award the institution's costs, including reasonable attorney's fees.[156]

3. Criminal Liability for Failure to Comply with the EFTA

Any financial institution or other person who knowingly and willfully fails to comply with any provision of the EFTA is liable for up to a $5,000 fine or imprisonment for one year or both.[157] This includes, among other acts of noncompliance, the giving of false or inaccurate information or the failure to provide information required to be disclosed under the EFTA or Regulation E.

As is to be expected, a person commits a criminal offense if the person knowingly (1) uses a lost, stolen, or counterfeit access device, (2) transports or sells in interstate or foreign commerce counterfeit, lost, or stolen access devices; or (3) receives or transports goods and services obtained through use of a lost, stolen, or counterfeit access device.[158] The penalty for committing any of the above offenses is a fine of not more than $10,000 or imprisonment for not more than ten years or both.

153. 15 U.S.C. §1693m(c).
154. 15 U.S.C. §1693m(e).
155. 15 U.S.C. §1693m(g).
156. 15 U.S.C. §1693m(f).
157. 15 U.S.C. §1693n(a).
158. 15 U.S.C. §1693n(b).

CHAPTER 9

Lender Credit Cards

A. NATURE OF TRANSACTION AND APPLICABLE LAW

1. The Nature of a Credit Card Transaction

You want to purchase a television set from Radio Shack. However, you cannot afford it yet. Your birthday is coming soon and you know that you will receive enough gifts in money to cover the cost of the set. You ask the clerk at Radio Shack whether the store sells goods on credit. He tells you that you can sign a promissory note agreeing to repay, over a two-year period, the purchase price, together with interest at the rate of 18 percent per annum. You do not like the idea of paying such a high rate of interest.

In light of this, you decide to put the purchase on your MasterCard. Your MasterCard was issued to you (the "cardholder") by your bank, Bank of America (the "issuing bank" or the "card issuer"). Bank of America has acquired the right to issue you a MasterCard by agreement with MasterCard International, the organization that sponsors MasterCard. Bank of America pays a fee to MasterCard International for the right to issue MasterCards. Under the agreement, Bank of America is bound by the rules and regulations of Master-Card International. Likewise, Wells Bank (the "merchant's bank"), the bank at which Radio Shack (the "merchant") maintains its account, is also a member of MasterCard International. Wells Bank and Radio Shack have an agreement under which Radio Shack agrees to honor MasterCards in payment for purchases and Wells Bank agrees to reimburse Radio Shack, minus a small discount, for any purchases made by the use of a MasterCard.

You hand your MasterCard to the clerk who begins to prepare a multiple copy receipt (called a "sales slip") by running a blank sales slip form and your MasterCard through an imprinting machine. The machine imprints upon the form not only your name, a number identifying Bank of America as the issuing bank, and your credit card account number, but also Radio Shack's name, address, and its merchant number at Wells Bank. The clerk completes the sales slip by adding the date, description, and amount of the transaction (including taxes).

Before it will accept payment by MasterCard for such a large purchase, Radio Shack, for its own protection, will seek authority from Bank of America for the charge. To do so, Radio Shack will either telephone the authorization center or use an electronic terminal connected to a computer containing the necessary information. The computer will check to determine whether your account is still active, whether the purchase amount is within your credit limit, and whether your card has been lost or stolen. By authorizing the charge, Bank of America is obligated under its agreement with MasterCard International to pay the amount of the charge. If Radio Shack fails to obtain this authorization, Radio Shack has no assurance that it will receive payment. However, for charges below a certain amount, Radio Shack may have the right to payment from Bank of America even without obtaining authorization. As to these charges, Radio Shack may still have the obligation to check a periodic list that it receives from MasterCard International to see if your card has been lost or stolen or your account closed.

The clerk now hands you the sales slip for your signature. The sales slip itself does not impose any additional obligation upon you. It is simply proof that you authorized the charge. When you use your MasterCard over the telephone or by mail, there is, of course, no sales slip to sign. The absence of your signature does impose a risk upon the merchant. You are liable only if you, in fact, authorized the purchase. Therefore, merchants must adopt means other than signature verification to guard against the risk that the charge was unauthorized. For example, when you purchase airline tickets over the telephone, the airline protects itself by mailing the tickets to your credit card billing address.

At the end of each day, Radio Shack retains one copy of each of the sales slips from purchases made that day and sends the original sales slips, together with a letter indicating the total amount of the slips, to Wells Bank. Wells Bank gives Radio Shack credit for the total amount of the sales slips less a discount. Wells Bank retains the original slip and electronically transmits the information contained on your sales slip to Bank of America which pays Wells Bank.

A. Nature of Transaction and Applicable Law

Bank of America then charges your account for the amount of the purchase and bills you periodically (for example, every 30 days) for the total charges made on your card the preceding month. (See Figure 9.1.)

FIGURE 9.1

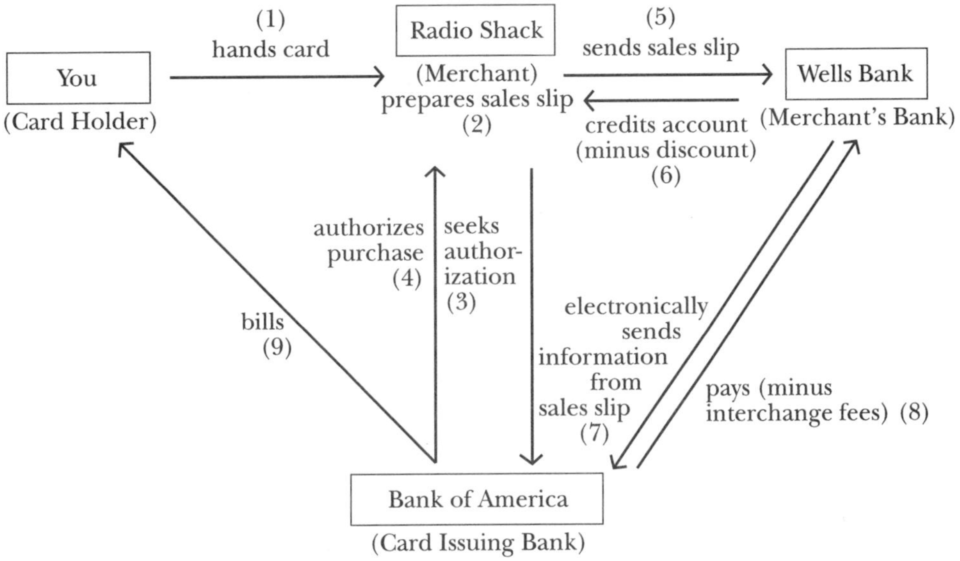

Bank of America earns the bulk of its money from the annual fee that it charges together with the finance charges assessed to you if you do not pay your bill within a certain number of days. In addition, Wells Bank pays to Bank of America a portion of the discount subtracted from the amount charged.

As we will later explore, there are several reasons why Bank of America (the issuing bank) may have the right not to pay the obligation evidenced by the sales slip. For example, the charge may have been unauthorized or you may have asserted a claim in recoupment or a defense to your obligation to pay the charge. Allocation of the loss between Bank of America and Wells Bank or between Wells Bank and Radio Shack is not governed by any statutory or regulatory law. Rather, the allocation of loss is governed by the contract between the parties. Bank of America will usually have the right, under the rules of MasterCard International (of which both banks are members) to return (called "charge back") the sales slip to Wells Bank, which will recredit Bank of America's account for the amount of the payment.

Wells Bank will then charge back Radio Shack's account for the amount of the payment. The agreement between Radio Shack and Wells Bank will, more than likely, permit Wells Bank to charge back Radio Shack's account when: (1) the goods or services are returned or not delivered or the purchaser otherwise has a defense or set-off; (2) no authorization was obtained; (3) the credit card expired prior to the date of sale; (4) the sales slip is fraudulent; or (5) the cardholder denies making the purchase or the merchandise was sent to an address other than that of the cardholder. Unlike the swiftness of the check collection process, the charge back may, more than likely, not occur until 30 to 180 days after the initial sale.

You may have a Visa Card instead of a MasterCard. Visa Cards operate similarly to MasterCards except that they are issued by VISA International. Both MasterCards and Visa Cards are not only payment mechanisms, but also include a revolving credit feature by which the cardholder, instead of paying the card, may make the minimum payment and pay the remainder over time together with the accruing finance charges.

American Express and Diner's Club cards are similar to Visa Cards and MasterCards except that they do not have the revolving credit feature. American Express, however, does allow you to transfer your unpaid balance to a credit line if you desire. In contrast to these credit cards, "charge cards" issued by sellers of goods (for example, Sears, Saks Fifth Avenue, Bloomingdale's) are pure extensions of credit by the merchant to the buyer and are not a means of payment. In other words, when you charge a purchase on your Sears card, you are simply promising to pay the amount charged under the terms of your cardholder agreement. Your charge alone does not result in the transfer of any funds to Sears.

2.   Law Governing Credit Card Transactions

Unlike in the case of negotiable instruments, credit cards are not governed by a comprehensive set of statutes or regulations. As a matter of fact, with two exceptions,[1] credit cards issued for business purposes are not governed by any statute or regulation. The relationship between a holder of a credit card issued for business purposes and the card issuer is governed by their agreement.

The focus of state and federal credit card legislation has been on consumer protection. The federal law of credit cards can be found in The Truth in Lending Act,[2] as amended both by the Fair Credit and Charge Card Dis-

---

1. Business credit cards are subject to the same rules governing liability for unauthorized use and the right of the card issuer to issue unrequested cards as are consumer credit cards. We discuss these exceptions later in this chapter.

2. 15 U.S.C. §1601 et seq.

closure Act and the Fair Credit Billing Act, and Regulation Z[3] promulgated pursuant to the Truth in Lending Act. Federal law covers only the card issuer/ cardholder relationship. Even as to this relationship, it covers only certain issues: disclosure requirements, error resolution, the right of a cardholder to raise defenses, and the liability of a cardholder for unauthorized transactions. State law may affect the rights of consumers either where the state law provides greater protection than do the federal rules or where the issue is not covered by the federal rules. We will mention some of these state laws as they are relevant. Much of the cardholder/card issuer relationship is left to the cardholder agreement. The remaining relationships, that is merchant/merchant bank and card issuer/merchant bank, are governed by the agreements establishing their respective relationships. The law governing the agreements between the various parties to a credit card transaction is ordinary contract law. Neither the U.C.C. nor any other special rules of law (other than as mentioned above) apply to credit card agreements.

B. LIABILITY FOR UNAUTHORIZED TRANSFERS

You lose your MasterCard on March 1st. You do not notice that the Mas-terCard is gone until April 10th when you get your MasterCard bill showing charges in the amount of $5,000. You immediately notify Bank of America. Are you liable for the entire $5,000? For none of it?

The answer is "almost none." Congress made a decision that rather than having you, the unlucky and probably innocent cardholder, suffer the loss, the loss should be imposed initially upon the card issuer who can spread the cost to all cardholders in the form of an increased rate of interest. However, in order to encourage you to be careful with your card and to promptly report its loss or theft, you are liable for up to $50 of the unauthorized charges incurred before you give notice to Bank of America of the loss.[4] You have no liability for any unauthorized charges incurred after giving notice.[5] The rule is that when there is an unauthorized use of your card, you are liable for the lesser of (1) $50 or (2) the amount of money, property, labor, or services obtained by the

---

3. 12 C.F.R. part 226.
4. 15 U.S.C. §1643(a)(1)(B); 12 C.F.R. §226.12(b).
5. 15 U.S.C. §1643(a)(1)(E); 12 C.F.R. §226.12(b).

unauthorized use.[6] These limits remain the same even if you were negligent in losing your card or in failing to promptly notify Bank of America of the loss or theft.

The cardholder has no liability for an unauthorized use of his card unless three conditions are met. First, your MasterCard must be an *accepted* credit card.[7] An "accepted credit card" is any credit card that a cardholder has (1) requested or applied for and received, (2) has signed, or (3) used or authorized another person to use to obtain credit.[8] Any credit card issued as a renewal or substitute becomes an accepted credit card when received by the cardholder.

Second, Bank of America must have provided you with adequate notice of your maximum potential liability and of the means by which you can notify Bank of America of the loss or theft of your card.[9] The notice must: (1) state that your liability cannot exceed $50 (or any lesser amount), (2) state that the notice you give to Bank of America as to the loss or theft of the card or as to an unauthorized transaction may be given either orally or in writing, and (3) describe a means of notification (for example, a telephone number, an address, or both).

Third, Bank of America must have provided a means by which the merchant could have identified you as the authorized user of the card.[10] Two of the more common ways for a card issuer to provide a means of identification are by (1) including tape on the back of the credit card where the cardholder may provide a sample of his signature and (2) including a photograph of the cardholder on the face of the credit card.[11] Identification can also be by means of fingerprint or electronic or mechanical confirmation.

---

6. 15 U.S.C. §1643(a)(1); 12 C.F.R. §226.12(b). State law will govern if it provides for lesser liability than does the federal law. 12 C.F.R. §226.12(b)(4). There are some states that provide for either more conditions to the cardholder's liability or a lower limit. Alaska Stat. §06.05.209(a) (Credit card not considered accepted until customer executes written statement of acceptance); 815 I.L.C.S. §145/2(cardholder not liable in excess of $25 for a card without a signature panel); Kan. Stat. Ann. §16-842 (no liability unless telephone number provided so that the cardholder can call in the event of loss or theft of the credit card).

Where a credit card is used to effectuate an electronic fund transfer, Regulation E applies. 12 C.F.R. §226.12(g).

7. 12 C.F.R. §226.12(b)(2)(i).

8. 12 C.F.R. §226.12(a)(2), n.21.

9. 12 C.F.R. §226.12(b)(2)(ii). Notice is adequate when it is given by any means that reasonably assures that you will receive the notice. 12 C.F.R. §226.12(b)(2)(ii), n.23. The notice must be a printed notice setting forth clearly the pertinent facts so that you may reasonably be expected to have noticed it and understood its meaning. 12 C.F.R. §226.12(b)(2)(ii), n.23.

10. 12 C.F.R. §226.12(b)(2)(iii).

11. 12 C.F.R. §226.12, Official Staff Commentary, comment 12(b)(2)(iii).

B. Liability for Unauthorized Transfers

You have no liability at all for any charges incurred after you have given notice to Bank of America. Notice is deemed to have been given when you have taken all steps reasonably required in the ordinary course of business to provide Bank of America with the relevant information about the loss, theft, or unauthorized use of the credit card.[12] Notice is effective even if no particular officer, employee, or agent of Bank of America does, in fact, receive the information. Notice may be given, at your option, in person, by telephone, or in writing. Written notice is considered given at the expiration of the time ordinarily required for the transmission to be received, whether or not it is actually received, or at the time received, if earlier. For example, if you mailed the notice on November 1st and it would ordinarily take two days for the letter to be delivered, notice is deemed to have been given on November 3d even if the notice is received on a later date or not received at all. If, in fact, the notice arrives on November 2d, the notice is deemed to have been received on that date.

1. Unauthorized Use

After learning about your very limited liability for the unauthorized use of your card, you may be feeling pretty smug. You may be thinking, "I have nothing to worry about. As long as I do not give anyone the authority to use my MasterCard, I can never be liable for more than $50." Unfortunately, there are some potential traps for the unwary in how liberally courts have found use of a credit card to be authorized.

"Unauthorized use" is defined as the use of a credit card by a person, other than the cardholder, who does not have actual, implied, or apparent authority for such use, and from which the cardholder receives no benefit.[13] The card issuer has the burden of proving that use of a card was authorized.[14] Whether the user had authority is determined by the state's law of agency.[15]

There are two ways in which a use can be authorized: (1) where the user has actual authority to use the card or (2) where the user has apparent authority to use the card. The user has actual authority to use a credit card when the cardholder either expressly, or by implication, gives the user authority to use the card. For example, assume that your brother asks you for money to fill his car with gas. Without saying a word, you hand him your credit card. You have

---

12. 12 C.F.R. §226.12(b)(3).
13. 12 C.F.R. §226.12(b), n.22.
14. 15 U.S.C. §1643(b).
15. 12 C.F.R. §226.12, Official Staff Commentary, comment 12(b)(1)-1.

impliedly authorized him to use the card to purchase gas. (Had you told your brother that he could use your card to purchase gas, he would have express actual authority.) However, you did not give him actual authority to use the card to purchase a television set when you loaned him the card to buy gas.

However, even when the user does not have actual authority, a use is not unauthorized if the user has apparent authority for such use. A user has apparent authority when the cardholder gives the impression to third parties that the user is authorized to use the card. The specific characteristics of a credit card transaction have encouraged courts to adopt a very expansive definition of what constitutes apparent authority.

The clearest example of apparent authority would be if the gas station owner called you to ask whether your brother was authorized to use your card and you told him that your brother could charge the purchase of gas on your card. You forget to get the card back from your brother. The next week, your brother charges another purchase of gas on your credit card. Your telephone confirmation of your brother's authority to use your card gave the gas station owner the impression that your brother was authorized to use the card. Even though your brother was not, in fact, authorized to make the second purchase of gas, your brother had apparent authority to do so. Therefore, his use of the card was authorized and you are liable for the second purchase as well as for the first.

If your brother went to Radio Shack and purchased a television set against your orders, would the fact that you gave him the card to purchase gas give him apparent authority to purchase the television set? On the one hand, you gave no indication to Radio Shack that your brother was authorized to use your card. On the other hand, you did voluntarily and knowingly give your brother the card. You knew that he could use the card for other purchases. In giving him the card, you were trusting him to use the card only as agreed. It could be said that by voluntarily giving your brother the card, you had given Radio Shack the impression that he had the right to use the card.

In fact, it is very possible that a court may accept this argument and find your brother to be apparently authorized to use the card to purchase the television set. In one case[16] a cardholder gave his business associate his American Express Card with express authority to charge up to $500. The cardholder instructed American Express not to allow the total charges on his American Express Card to exceed $1,000. The business associate charged $5,300 on the card. The court found that the business associate had apparent authority to charge the entire $5,300 on the card and therefore held that the cardholder was liable for the entire amount.

16. See Martin v. American Express, 361 So. 2d 597 (Ala. Ct. App. 1978).

B. Liability for Unauthorized Transfers

Some courts have held that the cardholder is no longer liable for purchases made by the user as soon as the cardholder informs the card issuer that the user no longer has actual authority to use the card.[17] Some other courts have held that, even if the user remains apparently authorized to use the card after notice is given, the card issuer is prevented from claiming that the user was apparently authorized if the card issuer could have prevented the loss by the use of reasonable care. In one case,[18] the office manager of the cardholder, without authority, applied for a credit card on behalf of the cardholder. The card issuer failed to use reasonable care to determine whether the office manager had authority to do so. The office manager made thousands of dollars of purchases on the card over a period of many months. The card issuer was precluded from asserting that the office manager had apparent authority to use the card for purchases made before the cardholder received its first periodic statement. However, once the cardholder received the periodic statement showing the unauthorized purchases, the cardholder was found to have the duty to report the unauthorized transactions. By failing to do so, the cardholder was deemed to have given the office manager apparent authority to make subsequent purchases.

However, some courts have held that a user had apparent authority even after the cardholder informed the card issuer that the user was no longer authorized. In one case,[19] a court held that use of a credit card by a spouse was apparently authorized even though the cardholder had notified the card issuer that the spouse's use of the card was no longer authorized. The court based its finding of apparent authority on the failure of the cardholder to return the card to the card issuer. The failure to return the card enabled the spouse to continue to charge on the card without the merchant knowing that the spouse was no longer authorized to use the card. The court's decision in this case may have been influenced by the fact that, although the account was in the cardholder's name, the spouse was issued a card in his own name. Had the card not been in the spouse's name, the merchant may have had reason to question his use of the card.

2. Liability for Business Use of Card

Most of the rules in the Truth in Lending Act apply only to consumer use of a credit card. However, some of the rules also apply to business use. With one

---

17. See Standard Oil Co v. Steele, 489 N.E.2d 842 (Ohio Mun. Ct. 1985).
18. See Transamerica Insurance Co. v. Standard Oil Co., 325 N.W.2d 210 (N.D. 1982).
19. See Walker Bank & Trust v. Jones, 672 P.2d 73 (Utah 1983).

exception, the rules governing liability for unauthorized use of a credit card apply to credit cards used for business purposes as well as for consumer purposes.[20]

The one exception involves issuance by a card issuer of ten or more credit cards for use by the employees of an organization. In this situation the card issuer and the organization may contractually set liability for unauthorized use at an amount greater than otherwise permitted by law.[21] However, an employee of the organization has the same limited liability as does a consumer as to both his employer and the card issuer. For example, if Bank of America issues to IBM 1,000 cards to be used by its employees, the limitations on liability applicable to consumers is applicable to IBM's and its employees' liability on these credit cards absent an agreement to the contrary. However, Bank of America and IBM may agree that IBM will be liable, for example, for up to $1,000 of any unauthorized charges. Despite this agreement, the employee cardholder is not liable to either Bank of America or IBM beyond the $50 limit imposed by the Truth in Lending Act.

C.   RIGHT TO REFUSE PAYMENT

Let us return to our hypothethical in which you place the purchase of a television set from Radio Shack on your MasterCard. It turns out that the set is defective. You go back to Radio Shack and demand that it either fix the television set or give back your money. Radio Shack refuses to do either. Your MasterCard bill comes. Do you have to pay the charge for the television set? The answer may be "no."

The fact that Radio Shack failed to satisfactorily resolve a dispute as to a product (the television set) purchased with your MasterCard allows you (a consumer) to assert against Bank of America (the card issuer) all claims (other than tort claims) and defenses arising out of the transaction and relating to the failure to resolve the dispute.[22] In this case, you would have the right to

---

20. 15 U.S.C. §1645. A consumer is a natural person. 12 C.F.R. §226.2(a)(11). Consumer credit means credit offered or extended to a consumer primarily for personal, family, or household purposes. 12 C.F.R. §226.2(a)(12).

21. 15 U.S.C. §1645; 12 C.F.R. §226.12(b)(5).

22. 15 U.S.C. §1666i; 12 C.F.R. §226.12(c)(1). A state law that is more protective of the cardholder's rights to assert claims or defenses against the card issuer arising out of the underlying transaction is not preempted by the federal legislation and regulations. 15 U.S.C. §1666j. For example, a cardholder in Vermont may assert all defenses available on the contract that

C. Right to Refuse Payment

assert Radio Shack's breach of the warranty of merchantability as a defense to your obligation to pay Bank of America for the amount charged. If Bank of America recredits your account, Bank of America would pass the loss back down the line to Wells Bank (the merchant's bank) and Wells Bank would charge back Radio Shack's account. If Radio Shack believes that your claim is not well founded, it would then have to attempt to recover the payment from you.

There are three conditions to your right to withhold payment of your credit card bill for this purchase. First, you must make a good faith attempt to resolve the dispute with Radio Shack.[23] There is no clear standard for determining whether you have a made good faith attempt to resolve a dispute. The fact that you went to Radio Shack and asked it to fix the set or return your money is probably sufficient.[24] Second, you must have charged more than $50 for the purchase of the television set.[25]

Third, your purchase must have occurred in the same state as your current designated address or, if not within the same state, within 100 miles of that address.[26] For example, if you live in New York City, you may withhold payment on a purchase made in any location in the state of New York as well as on any purchase made within 100 miles of your residence. This means that if you purchase a television set at the Radio Shack store in Newark, New Jersey (which is within 100 miles of New York City), you may refuse to pay the charge for the television set to the extent that the set was defective. However, you may not refuse payment on a charge made in Los Angeles. By issuing a credit card to you, the card issuer undertakes the obligation of monitoring merchants in your area, but not in areas outside your state or more than 100 miles from your residence. If no geographical limitation was placed on your right to refuse payment, merchants distant from your residence may be leery of allowing you to pay by credit card. If you refuse to pay the credit card charge, the merchant would have to undertake the costly task of attempting to recover from you in your state of residence.[27]

The question as to where a transaction occurs is easy when the transaction is face-to-face. What happens, however, if you, a New York resident, purchase

---

gave rise to the credit card transaction if the transaction occurred in Vermont and was charged to a bank credit card account established by a Vermont bank. Eliminating the conditions precedent to the cardholder's right to raise these defenses gives the cardholder more rights than are available under Regulation Z. Vt. Stat. Ann., Tit. 8, §1305.

23. 12 C.F.R. §226.12(c)(3)(i).

24. 12 C.F.R. §226.12, Official Staff Commentary, comment 12(c)(3)(i).

25. 12 C.F.R. §226.12(c)(3)(ii).

26. 12 C.F.R. §226.12(c)(3)(ii).

27. S. Rep. No. 278, 93d Cong., 1st Sess. 10-11 (1973).

goods by mail or over the telephone from a company located in Los Angeles? Does the purchase occur in New York or in Los Angeles? You would think that Regulation Z would provide an answer to this seemingly everyday question. Unfortunately, no answer is given. Rather, the Official Staff Commentary to Regulation Z simply states that "[T]he question of where a transaction occurs (as in the case of mail or telephone orders, for example) is to be determined under state or other applicable law."[28]

To add to the uncertainty, not only have no reported cases as of yet discussed this issue, but there does not appear to be any appropriate state or other law that can be looked to for guidance. There is law on the question as to where a transaction occurs. However, the case or statutory laws that exist go to the question as to where a transaction occurs for purposes that are not analogous to the issue presented here. For example, a state law may determine where a sale of goods has occurred for purposes of determining whether the state's sales tax applies to the purchase. But this law cannot be looked to for guidance. The factors that may be relevant in deciding whether a state has a right to tax a particular transaction have little to do with the determination as to whether a cardholder in New York should have the right to assert his defense when the purchase is made over the telephone from a merchant in Los Angeles.[29]

A strong argument can be made that if the California merchant advertises or otherwise solicits in the buyer's state of residence (in our case New York), whether directly or indirectly (for example, through magazines, television, or radio), the transaction should be deemed to occur in the buyer's state of residence. By doing so, the merchant is competing with New York merchants for the buyer's business and should be subject to the same limitations. Furthermore, unlike a New York cardholder who makes his purchase from a local merchant during a visit to Los Angeles, a New York cardholder who makes his purchase from his own home by telephone or by mail may reasonably expect that the merchant by reaching out to make a sale in New York has exposed himself to the risk of bringing an action in New York if the cardholder refuses to pay the credit card charge.

The second and third limitations discussed above do not apply when the merchant: (1) and the card issuer are the same person; (2) is directly or indirectly controlled by or controls the card issuer;[30] (3) is a franchised dealer of the card issuer's products or services; or (4) has obtained the order for the dis-

28. 12 C.F.R. §226.12, Official Staff Commentary, comment 12(c)(3)(ii)(1).
29. See Ralph J. Rohner, The Law of Truth in Lending 10-29 (1984).
30. This also includes being under the direct or indirect control of a third person that also directly or indirectly controls the card issuer.

C. Right to Refuse Payment

puted transaction through a mail solicitation made or participated in by the card issuer.[31]

You can only raise claims or defense that would be effective against the merchant. For example, assume that Radio Shack sold you the television set "as is." Because you have no right to have Radio Shack repair the set or return your money, you have no right to refuse to pay Bank of America the amount charged for the set.[32]

Your right to assert the claim or defense against the card issuer may be used only as a shield and not as a sword. The amount of the claim or defense that you may assert cannot exceed the amount of credit outstanding for the disputed transaction at the time you first notified Bank of America or Radio Shack of the existence of the claim or defense.[33] In order to dispel any fear of yours that your credit standing will be impaired as a result of withholding payment, Bank of America has no right to report that amount as delinquent until the dispute is settled or judgment is rendered.[34]

You have no right to withhold payment on a purchase that is not made on the credit card itself. [35] For example, if you paid for the television set by writing a check, you have no right to withhold payment even if your MasterCard guaranteed payment of the check or your check was a cash advance check drawn on your MasterCard account. Similarly, assume that your MasterCard doubles as your debit card and as your credit card. Your MasterCard includes an overdraft credit plan that advances you funds in the event that you overdraw your checking account. Despite these features, if you use your debit card to pay for the television set through an electronic fund transfer, you do not have the right to withhold payment. Unlike a credit transaction, Radio Shack accepts these types of payment as the equivalent of cash.

What would have happened if Radio Shack had agreed to fully credit you for the purchase price in exchange for your return of the television set. Assuming that Radio Shack tells you that it will give you a credit on your MasterCard for the amount of the purchase, how soon will your account be recredited?

---

31. 12 C.F.R. §226.12(c)(3), n.26.

32. See Izraelewitz v. Manufacturers Hanover Trust Co, 465 N.Y.S.2d 486, 120 Misc. 2d 125 (N.Y. Civ. Ct. 1983).

33. 12 C.F.R. §226.12(c)(1); 12 C.F.R. §226.12(c)(1), n.25. To determine the amount of credit outstanding, payments and other credits are applied to: (1) late charges in the order of entry to the account; then to (2) finance charges in the order of entry to the account; and then to (3) any other debits in the order of entry to the account. If more than one item is included in a single extension of credit, credits are to be distributed pro rata according to prices and applicable taxes. 12 C.F.R. §226.12(c)(1), n.25.

34. 12 C.F.R. §226.12(c)(2).

35. 12 C.F.R. §226.12(c)(1), n.24.

If Radio Shack (assuming that it is not itself the card issuer) accepts return of the television set (or forgives a debt for services), Radio Shack must, within seven business days from accepting the return (or forgiving the debt), transmit a credit statement to Bank of America through Bank of America's normal channels for credit statements.[36] Within three business days from the time Bank of America receives this credit statement, Bank of America must credit your account with the amount of the refund.[37]

Can you demand that Radio Shack give you a refund in cash? Possibly. If Radio Shack routinely gives cash refunds to consumers paying in cash, Radio Shack is required to give credit or a cash refund to you even though you used a credit card, unless Radio Shack disclosed at the time the transaction was consummated that credit or cash refunds for returns are not given.[38]

D. ERROR RESOLUTION PROCEDURES

You receive your credit card statement and notice that you were charged not only for the television set that you in fact purchased from Radio Shack, but also for a VCR that you looked at but did not purchase. You want the charge for the VCR taken off your bill. What must you do? What obligation does Bank of America have to respond to this billing error?

1. What Is a Billing Error?

Bank of America has certain obligations once you notify it of a billing error. "Billing errors" are basically mistakes found in your periodic credit card statement that Bank of America sends to you. A billing error occurs when Bank of America does one of the following:[39]

---

36. 15 U.S.C. §1666e; 12 C.F.R. §226.12(e)(1).

37. 12 C.F.R. §226.12(e)(2).

38. 12 C.F.R. §226.12(e)(3). The rule does not require refunds for returns nor does it prohibit refunds in kind.

39. 12 C.F.R. §226.13(a)(1); 12 C.F.R. §226.13(a)(3); 12 C.F.R. §226.13(a)(2); 12 C.F.R. §226.13(a)(4); 12 C.F.R. §226.13(a)(5); 12 C.F.R. §226.13(a)(7) respectively. In addition, your request for additional clarification or documentary evidence is treated as a billing error. 12 C.F.R. §226.13(a)(6). As a result, such a request imposes the same obligations upon the card issuer to respond as does notice of any normal billing error.

D. Error Resolution Procedures

1. bills you for an extension of credit that was not made to you (or to a person who has actual or apparent authority to charge on the card);
2. bills you for property or services that were neither accepted by you nor delivered to you;[40]
3. did not properly identify an extension of credit;
4. failed to properly credit a payment or other credit issued to your account;
5. made a computational or accounting error; or
6. failed to mail or deliver a periodic statement to your last known address.[41]

The charge for a VCR that you never purchased would be a billing error because you were billed for an extension of credit that was not made to you.

2. What the Cardholder Must Do upon Notice of Billing Error

You have just received your credit card statement and you notice the error. What must you do? You must send a written notice of the billing error.[42] The notice must be sent to the address designated for receipt of billing error notices so that it is received by Bank of America no later than 60 days after Bank of America transmitted the statement that reflected the billing error. For example, if the statement reflecting Radio Shack's erroneous billing of the VCR to your account was transmitted to you on March 1st, Bank of America would have to receive your billing error notice by May 1st. If Bank of America does not receive your billing error notice by May 1st, you lose your right to the protections accorded you under the error resolution procedure. However, you are not prevented from bringing a breach of contract or other action against Bank of America for recrediting of your account.[43]

The notice must (1) state your name and account number[44] and (2) to the extent possible, indicate the reasons why you believe that a billing error

---

40. This would include goods you rejected because they are nonconforming, delivery of property or services different than agreed upon, delivery of the wrong quantity, late delivery, and delivery to the wrong location. 12 CFR §226.13(a)(3), Official Staff Commentary.

41. The address must have been received by the creditor, in writing, at least 20 days before the end of the billing cycle for which the statement was required.

42. 12 C.F.R. §226.13(b)(1).

43. See Ralph J. Rohner, The Law of Truth in Lending 9-18 (1984).

44. 12 C.F.R. §226.13(b)(2).

exists, and the type, date, and amount of the error.[45] You may use the payment stub attached to your periodic statement as a means of indicating the error unless Bank of America has made it clear that you must send a separate statement.[46]

3.   What the Card Issuer Must Do upon Receipt of Billing Error Notice

Within 30 days after receiving your billing error notice, Bank of America must either (1) mail or deliver to you a written acknowledgment of receipt of the notice or (2) comply with the appropriate resolution procedures.[47]

If Bank of America determines that the billing error mentioned in the notice has occurred, Bank of America must, within two complete billing cycles (but in no event later than 90 days) after receiving the billing error notice, correct the billing error and credit your account with any disputed amount and related finance or other charges, if any.[48] Bank of America must also, during this period, mail or deliver to you a correction notice.[49]

Before Bank of America may determine that no billing error has occurred, it must conduct a reasonable investigation.[50] If you claim that the error was in the nondelivery of property or services or that information appearing on a periodic statement is incorrect because Radio Shack has made an incorrect report to Bank of America, the bank must conduct a reasonable

---

45. 12 C.F.R. §226.13(b)(3).

46. 12 C.F.R. §226.13(b), n. 29.

47. 12 C.F.R. §226.13(c)(1). A creditor that has fully complied with the requirements of the billing error resolution procedure has no further responsibility under those procedures if a consumer reasserts substantially the same billing error. 12 C.F.R. §226.14(h).

A state law may adopt its own billing error procedure if such law gives greater protection to the consumer. 15 U.S.C. §1666j(a). However, the Federal Reserve Board has determined that state law requirements are preempted if they provide rights, responsibilities, or procedures for consumers or creditors that are different from those required by the federal law. 12 C.F.R. §226.28(a)(2)(i).

A state law that allows a consumer to inquire about an open-end credit account and imposes on the creditor an obligation to respond to such inquiry after the time allowed in the federal law for the consumer to submit written notice of a billing error is not preempted in any situation where the time period for making the written notice under Regulation Z has expired. 12 C.F.R. §226.28(a)(2)(i).

48. 12 C.F.R. §226.13(e)(1).

49. 12 C.F.R. §226.13(e)(2).

50. 12 C.F.R. §226.13(f).

investigation to determine whether the property or services were actually delivered, mailed, or sent as agreed or that the information was correct.[51]

If, after conducting a reasonable investigation, Bank of America determines that no billing error occurred, it must, within two complete billing cycles (but in no event later than 90 days) after receiving the billing error notice, mail or deliver to you an explanation that sets forth the reasons for Bank of America's belief that your alleged billing error is incorrect in whole or in part.[52] You may request that Bank of America furnish copies of documentary evidence of your indebtedness.[53] If you still disagree with Bank of America's determination, you still have your right to have a court determine whether you or Bank of America is correct.[54]

If Bank of America determines that a different billing error occurred, Bank of America must correct the billing error and credit your account with any disputed amount and related finance or other charges, as applicable, within two complete billing cycles (but in no event later than 90 days) after Bank of America receives the billing error notice.[55]

Failure to comply with the requirements of the billing error resolution procedure results in Bank of America forfeiting the right to collect from you the amount of the alleged error together with any finance charges on that amount. The amount of the forfeiture, however, cannot exceed $50.[56]

4. *What the Card Issuer Must Do If It Determines that You Owe Some or All of Amount*

If Bank of America, after complying with the billing error resolution procedure, determines that you owe all or part of the disputed amount and related finance or other charges, it must promptly notify you in writing of the time when payment is due and the portion of the disputed amount and related finance or other charges that you still owe.[57] You have, however, the same grace period within which to pay the amount due without incurring additional finance or other charges that you would have had had you just received the periodic statement showing the charge.[58] For example, assume that Bank of

---

51. 12 C.F.R. §226.13(f), n.31.
52. 12 C.F.R. §226.13(f)(1).
53. 12 C.F.R. §226.13(f)(2).
54. See Ralph J. Rohner, The Law of Truth in Lending 9-18 (1984).
55. 12 C.F.R. §226.13(f)(3).
56. 15 U.S.C. §1666(e).
57. 12 C.F.R. §226.13(g)(1).
58. 12 C.F.R. §226.13(g)(2).

America allows a 21-day grace period to make payment without incurring a finance charge. If on March 1st Bank of America notifies you that you owe the charge for the VCR, you have until March 22d to pay, without a finance charge, the amount found not to be in error.

5. What the Card Issuer Is Prohibited from Doing until Billing Error Is Resolved

While you and Bank of America are engaged in the billing error resolution process, you are not required to pay (and Bank of America may not try to collect) any portion of the disputed amount (including related finance or other charges).[59] Bank of America, however, may attempt to collect any undisputed portion of the item or bill.[60] Bank of America also retains the right to deduct the disputed amount (and related finance or other charges) from your credit limit on the account and may reflect these amounts on the periodic statement. For example, assume that you dispute $200 of your $600 bill and that your credit limit is $1,500. Bank of America may not attempt to collect the $200 in dispute. Bank of America may attempt to collect the $400 that is undisputed and may continue to list the entire $600 on your periodic statement as being unpaid. In addition, Bank of America may deduct the entire $600 from your credit limit, thus leaving you with a remaining limit of $900.

Bank of America may not itself, or through a collection agent, directly or indirectly, make or threaten to make an adverse report to any person about your credit standing or report that an amount or account is delinquent simply because you failed to pay the disputed amount or related finance or other charges.[61]

However, once Bank of America has properly complied with the billing error resolution procedure and determined that no error has occurred, and has given you the proper notice, Bank of America may report your account or the amount as delinquent if, after the required grace period, you fail to make payment.[62]

59. 12 C.F.R. §226.13(d)(1). Similarly, if you have a deposit account with Bank of America and have agreed to pay the credit card debt by periodic deductions from this account, Bank of America may not deduct any part of the disputed amount or related finance or other charges if a billing error notice is received any time up to three business days before the scheduled payment date. Id.

60. 12 C.F.R. §226.13(d)(1), n. 30. If the disputed amount is reflected on the periodic statement, the creditor must indicate on or with the periodic statement that payment of any disputed amount and related finance or other charges is not required pending the creditor's compliance with the error resolution procedures. Id.

61. 12 C.F.R. §226.13(d)(2).

62. 12 C.F.R. §226.13(g)(3).

D. Error Resolution Procedures

What happens if, after Bank of America has made its determination, you still believe that a billing error has occurred? Can Bank of America discourage you from asserting your rights by reporting your account as delinquent? Bank of America is limited in reporting your account as delinquent if it receives within the time allowed for payment further written notice from you that any portion of the same alleged billing error is still in dispute.[63] Under these circumstances, Bank of America may only report your account delinquent if it (1) promptly reports that the amount or account is in dispute, (2) mails or delivers to you (at the same time the report is made) a written notice of the name and address of each person to whom the report is sent, and (3) promptly reports any subsequent resolution of the reported delinquency to all persons to whom Bank of America sent the report.

6. Prohibition on Cancellation

Bank of America may not accelerate any part of your debt or restrict or close your account solely because you have exercised in good faith your billing error rights under the billing error resolution procedure.[64] Despite any provision in the credit card agreement to the contrary, Bank of America must have an independent justification for cancelling your card if it intends to do so and should give you notice of the cancellation.[65]

7. Relationship to the EFTA and Regulation E

If an extension of credit is incident to an electronic fund transfer under an agreement between a consumer and a financial institution to extend credit when the consumer's account is overdrawn or to maintain a specified minimum balance in the consumer's account, the creditor must comply with the requirements of Regulation E, which govern electronic fund transfers.[66] The only provisions of Regulation Z that are applicable are the rules found in §226.13(d) and (g) governing what the card issuer is prohibited from doing until the billing error is resolved and what the card issuer may do after the error is resolved.

---

63. 12 C.F.R. §226.13(g)(4).
64. 12 C.F.R. §226.13, n.27.
65. See Gray v. American Express Co., 743 F.2d 10 (D.C. Cir. 1984).
66. 12 C.F.R. §226.13(i).

E.   CONSUMER PROTECTIONS AS TO
CREDIT ASPECTS

You have just graduated from college. Because of your earning (and therefore spending) potential, you receive numerous offers to apply for a credit card. You are in heaven! You can purchase that new stereo system that you have been dying for. You fill out the application and receive your card in the mail. The next day you go to Radio Shack and charge the $1,000 purchase price of the stereo system on your new MasterCard. In 30 days the bill comes. You notice that there is a $25 annual fee included on the bill in addition to your $1,000 charge. You figure, "What's $25 for the right to buy now and pay later!" Because you are a little cash short, you do not pay any of your bill. The next month, you use your MasterCard to obtain a cash advance of $100. When your next bill comes, you notice that you were charged a fee of $5 for your cash advance, a late charge for failing to make the minimum payment on your bill and an interest charge of $25 (interest for one month on the $1,000 purchase at 30 percent per annum). Now you feel a little sick. What have you gotten yourself into? Had you known of all these additional charges prior to applying for the MasterCard, you would not have applied for it. Had you known of the charges prior to using it, you would not have used it.

You are not alone. Before federal and state consumer protection laws and regulations were enacted, many consumers were taken advantage of by credit card companies that held out the lure of instant gratification without clearly disclosing the costs of using the card. Federal and state consumer protection laws attempt to remedy this situation. As we will discuss shortly, the principal protection granted by these laws is a comprehensive disclosure requirement, which mandates that the card issuer furnish all relevant information to the consumer in enough time for the consumer to either not apply for or not use the card.

However, disclosure laws were not considered to be sufficient to fully protect consumers. As a result, some substantive laws were also enacted. Some of these laws limit the rate of interest that can be charged on a loan (called "usury laws"). Other laws limit the way in which the finance charge can be computed or the ability of a credit card issuer to charge annual fees or delinquency fees. Even absent legislation, courts have struck down excessive fees as unconscionable or as constituting unfair business practices.

Other legislation limits the rights of card issuers in other ways. In California (with some exceptions), a card issuer cannot cancel a credit card without first giving the cardholder 30 days written notice of its intention to do so.[67]

_____

67. Cal. Civil Code §1747.85. Exceptions to the notice requirement exist when the card-

E. Consumer Protections as to Credit Aspects

Other states prohibit merchants from asking for personal identification information from the cardholder, such as the cardholder's address and phone number, and noting the information on the credit card slip.[68] Regulation Z denies the card issuer the right to prohibit a merchant from offering a discount to a consumer to induce the consumer to pay by cash, check, or similar means rather than by use of a credit card for the purchase of property or services.[69] Regulation Z also denies the card issuer the right to offset a cardholder's indebtedness arising from a consumer credit transaction against funds of the cardholder held on deposit with the card issuer.[70]

Much of this legislation is not directly related to the law of payment systems. For that reason we will leave these laws to your consumer protection class. In this section we will deal primarily with the limitations imposed on a card issuer in issuing unrequested cards and with disclosure requirements.

1. Rules Governing Issuance of Credit Cards

As with your purchase of the stereo system, once a consumer obtains possession of a credit card, the temptation to use the card is great. Sometimes out of necessity, other times out of impulse, a consumer may make a purchase without first learning what obligations are incurred upon use of the card. For this reason, it is important that a consumer be told of the credit and other essential terms of the cardholder/card issuer agreement before the consumer obtains possession of the card. For example, you may not have applied for that

---

holder has been in default within the last 90 days or has otherwise been in violation of the credit card agreement, or if the card issuer has evidence or the reasonable belief that the cardholder is unable or unwilling to repay obligations incurred under the agreement or that an unauthorized use of the card may be made. The card issuer may also place the account on inactive status if the cardholder has not used the card for more than 18 months.

68. See, e.g., Cal. Civ. Code §1747.8; Del. Code Ann. tit. 11, §915; D.C. Code Ann. §47-3153; Ga. Code Ann. §10-1-393.3; Mass. Gen. Laws, Ch. 93, §105; Minn. Stat. §325 F. 982; Nev. Rev. Stat. §598.088; N.J. Stat. Ann. §56:11-17; N.Y. Gen. Bus. Law, Ch. 20, Art. 20-A, §520-a; Ohio Rev. Stat. §1349.17; Or. Rev. Stat. §646.892; Pa. Stat. 69 P.S. §2602.

69. 15 U.S.C. §1666f; 12 C.F.R. §226.12(f)(1).

70. 15 U.S.C. §1666h; 12 C.F.R. §226.12(d)(1). This rule does not affect any right of a card issuer acting under state or federal law to obtain or enforce a consensual security interest in the funds, attach or otherwise levy upon the funds or obtain or enforce a court order relating to the funds. 12 C.F.R. §226.12(d)(2).

The rule against offset does not prohibit a plan, if authorized in writing by the cardholder, under which the card issuer may periodically deduct all or part of the cardholder's credit card debt from a deposit account held with the card issuer. The ability of the card issuer to deduct amounts owing is subject to the cardholder's right to withhold funds in the event of a billing dispute. 12 C.F.R. §226.12(d)(3).

particular MasterCard if you knew that the interest rate was 30 percent per annum.

Federal law protects you by ensuring that you will obtain the essential information before you acquire the credit card. The first step in this protection is that a card issuer is prohibited from issuing a credit card except in response to a request or application for a card.[71] Because the same risk exists in the case of small businesses, this prohibition also applies to the issuance of business credit cards. A card issuer, however, may issue a credit card in renewal of, or in substitution for, an *accepted* credit card without a request or application by the cardholder.

2. *Terminology Used in Disclosure Requirements*

Before we examine specific disclosure requirements, it is necessary to understand the terminology involved. Many terms are defined very specifically in Regulation Z. The first term is "finance charge." A finance charge is the true cost of consumer credit expressed in a dollar amount.[72] Interest, of course, is the primary component of a finance charge, but finance charges also include any charge payable directly or indirectly by the consumer and imposed directly or indirectly by the creditor as a condition of the extension of credit. For example, a service or transaction cost that would not be incurred if payment was made in cash is a finance charge. This would include, among others, a time-price differential,[73] loan fees, appraisal fees, points,[74] and credit insurance premiums.[75] On the other hand, finance charges do not include payment for the right to have a credit line, like an application or annual fee, or a fee for breaching your obligations, like a late fee or an over-limit fee.[76] Thus, for example, if you paid $100 in interest, $2 charge on a cash advance of $100 (2 percent of $100), $4 in credit insurance premiums, and a late fee of $10, you would have paid a total finance charge of $106. The $10 late fee would not be included as part of the finance charge. "Annual percentage rate" is a measure of the cost of credit, expressed as a yearly rate.[77] If the interest rate is 2 percent per month, the annual percentage rate is 24 percent (2 percent × 12 months).

71. 15 U.S.C. §1642; 12 C.F.R. §226.12(a).

72. 12 C.F.R. §226.4(a).

73. The difference between the purchase price a cash buyer must pay and the purchase price a buyer on credit must pay.

74. A percentage of the loan that is charged up front as a fee for being given the loan.

75. 12 C.F.R. §226.4(b).

76. 12 C.F.R. §226.4(c).

77. 12 C.F.R. §226.14(a).

"Grace period" is the period within which any credit extended for purchases may be repaid without incurring a finance charge.[78] For example, if Bank of America does not assess interest on a charge until 15 days after transmission of the statement showing the charge, the grace period is the period from the time you charged the purchase to 15 days after the transmission of the statement.

"Billing cycle" is the interval between the dates of the regular periodic statements.[79] The interval must be equal (meaning not varying by more than four days) and no longer than three months. Most credit card issuers use a billing cycle of either 30 days or a month.[80]

"Balance computation method" is the method used to calculate the balance upon which the finance charge is imposed.[81] There are several different types of balance computation methods. The "average daily balance method" is determined by adding the total outstanding balance for each day of the period and dividing the total by the number of days.[82] For example, if $100 was owed for 15 days ($1,500) and $200 owed for 15 days ($3,000), the total of $4,500 is divided by 30 to give an average daily balance of $150. Another method is the "two-cycle average daily balance method" in which the balance is the sum of the average daily balances for two billing cycles.[83] The two cycles are the current billing cycle and the previous billing cycle. If the periodic statement sent covers the month of March, the two billing cycles would be February and March.

3.   Disclosures in Connection with Solicitations or Applications

The prohibition against issuance of unrequested credit cards would do little good if there was not a mechanism for ensuring that the potential cardholder obtain the relevant information before requesting or applying for the card. If the issuer of your MasterCard did not have to furnish you with the relevant information before you obtained possession of your card, you might use your card before you realized the consequences. To prevent this from occuring, the card issuer has certain pre-issuance obligations. First, any advertising must

78. 12 C.F.R. §226.5a(b)(5).
79. 12 C.F.R. §226.2(a)(4).
80. 12 C.F.R. §226.2(a)(4), Official Staff Commentary.
81. 12 C.F.R. §226.5a(g).
82. 12 C.F.R. §226.5a(g)(1)(i) and (ii).
83. 12 C.F.R. §226.5a(g)(2)(i) and (ii).

accurately reflect the credit terms.[84] Secondly, the card issuer must disclose the following information at the time that it solicits you to open or to apply for a credit or charge card account:[85]

1. The interest rate used to compute the finance charge on an outstanding balance must be expressed as an annual percentage rate. When more than one rate applies, the range of balances to which each rate is applicable shall also be disclosed;[86]
2. Any fee imposed for issuance or availability of the card, for a cash advance, for late payments or for exceeding a credit limit;[87]
3. Any minimum or fixed finance charge that could be imposed during a billing cycle or any transaction charge imposed for use of the card;[88]
4. Whether there is a grace period;[89] and
5. The balance computation method used to determine the amount on which the finance charge is imposed.[90]

---

84. 12 C.F.R. §226.16.

85. 15 U.S.C. §1637(c); 12 C.F.R. §226.5a. These disclosure requirements do not apply to certain home equity plans accessible by credit or charge card, overdraft lines of credit tied to asset accounts accessed by check guarantee cards or by debit cards, or lines of credit accessed by check guarantee cards or by debit cards that can be used only at automated teller machines. 12 C.F.R. §226.5a(a)(3).

86. 12 C.F.R. §226.5a(b)(1). If a variable rate may be charged, the card issuer must also disclose that the rate may vary and how the rate is determined. 12 C.F.R. §226.5a(b)(1)(i).

87. 12 C.F.R. §226.5a(b)(2). If the fee is based on a percentage of some amount, the percentage used and the identification of the amount against which the percentage is applied may be disclosed instead of the amount of the fee. 12 C.F.R. §226.5a(a)(4). 12 C.F.R. §226.5a(b)(8). If the amount of the fee is based on a percentage of another amount, for example, the amount of cash obtained, the percentage used and the identification of the amount against which the percentage is applied may be disclosed instead of the amount of the fee. 12 C.F.R. §226.5a(a)(4). 12 C.F.R. §226.5a(b)(9). If the fee is based on a percentage of another amount, for example, the amount of the delinquency, the percentage used and the identification of the amount against which the percentage is applied may be disclosed instead of the amount of the fee. 12 C.F.R. §226.5a(a)(4). 12 C.F.R. §226.5a(b)(10). If the fee is based on a percentage of another amount, for example, the amount in excess of the limit, the percentage used and the identification of the amount against which the percentage is applied may be disclosed instead of the amount of the fee. 12 C.F.R. §226.5a(a)(4).

88. 12 C.F.R. §226.5a(b)(3); 12 C.F.R. §226.5a(b)(4). If the fee is determined on the basis of a percentage of another amount, for example, the amount of the transaction for which the charge is made, the percentage used and the identification of the amount against which the percentage is applied may be disclosed instead of the amount of the fee. 12 C.F.R. §226.5a(a)(4).

89. 12 C.F.R. §226.5a(b)(5).

90. 12 C.F.R. §226.5a(b)(6).

4.   Manner of Making Disclosures

If the card issuer mails to a consumer any application or solicitation for a credit card, the card issuer must include the required disclosures with the application or solicitation.[91] To ensure that the potential cardholder sees the disclosures, the disclosures are to be provided in a prominent location on or with the application or solicitation.[92]

If the card issuer solicits the consumer by telephone to open or apply for a credit card account, the card issuer must orally disclose the annual percentage rate, fees for issuance or availability, minimum finance charges, transaction charges, grace period, balance computation method and, if a charge card, the fact that payments are due upon receipt of the periodic statement.[93]

Three methods of disclosure are acceptable where the application or solicitation is made available to the general public as, for example, where it is contained in a catalog or magazine.[94] First, the card issuer may disclose in a prominent location on the application or solicitation all of the required information.[95] Second, the card issuer may provide a description of the various charges that might be imposed, including the finance charge and the method of its computation.[96] Third, the card issuer may state in a prominent location on the application or solicitation that there are costs associated with the use of the card and that the consumer may contact the card issuer to request specific information about the costs, along with a toll-free telephone number and a mailing address for that purpose.[97]

---

91. 12 C.F.R. §226.5a(c).

92. 12 C.F.R. §226.5a(2)(i). The disclosure is to be in the form of a table with headings substantially similar to any of the applicable tables found in Appendix G to Regulation Z. Id.

93. 12 C.F.R. §226.5a(d)(1). The oral disclosure need not be given if the alternative disclosure is provided as discussed below. The alternative disclosure method is available if no charge is imposed for issuance of the card or for its availability or if the charge is imposed only if the recipient of the card uses it. 12 C.F.R. §226.5a(d)(2). The card issuer must provide all applicable disclosures in writing within thirty days after the consumer requests the card, but in no event later than the delivery of the card. 12 C.F.R. §226.5a(d)(2). The card issuer must also disclose in writing that the consumer need not accept the card or pay any fee unless the consumer uses the card. 12 C.F.R. §226.5a(d)(2)(ii).

94. 12 C.F.R. §226.5a(e).

95. 12 C.F.R. §226.5a(e)(1).

96. 12 C.F.R. §226.5a(e)(2).

97. 12 C.F.R. §226.5a(e)(3). Upon receiving a request for any of the information that is required to be disclosed, the card issuer must promptly disclose the information requested. 12 C.F.R. §226.5a(e)(4).

5. Required Disclosures before First Credit
Transaction

The card issuer must make certain disclosures to the cardholder before the first credit transaction is conducted.[98] These initial disclosures may be combined with disclosures made in solicitations and applications as long as the information, as well as the format and timing, required for each is met.[99] The required initial disclosures include:[100]

1. a description of when a finance charge will be imposed, including any grace period, the periodic rates that may be used to compute the finance charge, and the method of calculating the balance upon which the finance charge will be imposed;
2. the amount of other charges that may be imposed as part of the plan and an explanation as to how the charge will be determined;
3. whether the card issuer will acquire a security interest in the property purchased;
4. a statement of the cardholder's right to assert defenses; and
5. a statement as to the billing error resolution procedure.

6. Periodic Statements

The card issuer must also mail or deliver a periodic statement for each billing cycle.[101] The periodic statement is required to contain the following information: [102]

---

98. 15 U.S.C. §1637(a); 12 C.F.R. §226.5(b)(1).

99. 12 C.F.R. §226.5a, Official Staff Commentary, comment 2.

100. 12 C.F.R. §226.6(a)–(d) respectively.

101. 15 U.S.C. §1637(b); 12 C.F.R. §226.5(b)(2)(i). The card issuer has no duty to deliver a statement if the account has a debit or credit balance of less than $1 and where no finance charge has been imposed. Also no periodic statement need be sent if the creditor deems the account uncollectible, or if delinquency collection proceedings have been instituted or if furnishing the statement would violate federal law.

The card issuer must mail or deliver the periodic statement at least 14 days prior to any date or the end of any time period required to be disclosed in order for the consumer to avoid an additional finance or other charge. A card issuer that does not meet this requirement shall not collect any finance or other charge imposed as a result of such failure. 12 C.F.R. §226.5(b)(2)(ii).

102. 12 C.F.R. §226.7(a); 12 C.F.R. §226.8(a); 12 C.F.R. §226.7(c); 12 C.F.R. §226.7(d); 12 C.F.R. §226.7(e); 12 C.F.R. §226.7(f); 12 C.F.R. §226.7(g); and 12 C.F.R. §226.14(a); 12 C.F.R.

1. the account balance outstanding at the beginning of the billing cycle;
2. identification of each credit transaction. Basically, the information that must be disclosed is the amount of the transaction, either the date of the transaction or the date of the debiting of the transaction to the consumer's account, a brief identification of any property or services purchased, and the seller's name and location of the transaction;
3. any credits to the account, including the amount and the date of the crediting;
4. each periodic rate that may be used to compute the finance charge together with the range of balances to which the rate is applicable as well as the corresponding annual rate;
5. the amount of the balance to which a periodic rate was applied and an explanation of how that balance was determined;
6. the amount of any finance charge added to the account during the billing cycle. The finance charge must be itemized and show the amounts due to the application of any periodic rates and the amounts of any other type of finance charge;
7. the finance charge expressed as an annual percentage rate;
8. any charges other than finance charges, itemized by type, that were added to the account during the billing cycle;
9. the account balance owing on the closing date of the billing cycle;
10. the date by which the new balance or any portion of the new balance must be paid to avoid additional finance charges; and
11. the address to be used to give notice of billing errors.

7. Additional Disclosure Requirements

Three other disclosures requirements are worth mentioning. In order to ensure that the cardholder is aware of her rights upon discovering a billing error or an unauthorized transaction, the card issuer must mail or deliver, at least once per calendar year, a statement outlining the billing error resolution procedure and the allocation of liability for unauthorized use.[103]

If there is a change in any of the originally disclosed terms, the cardholder may prefer to terminate use of the card and apply for a different credit

---

§226.7(h); 12 C.F.R. §226.7(i); 12 C.F.R. §226.7(j); 12 C.F.R. §226.7(k); respectively. As an alternative, the creditor may provide the address on the billing rights statement permitted by 12 C.F.R. §226.9(a)(2).

103. 12 C.F.R. §226.9(a)(1).

card. For example, the card issuer may decide to impose an annual fee or to increase the interest rate. Because the cardholder may need time to obtain another credit card, the creditor must mail or deliver written notice of any such change at least 15 days prior to the effective date of the change.[104]

Finally, where the card issuer imposes an annual or other periodic fee to renew a credit or charge card account (including any fee based on account activity or inactivity), the card issuer must mail or deliver written notice of the renewal to the cardholder at least 30 days or one billing cycle, whichever is less, before the mailing or the delivery of the periodic statement on which the renewal fee is initially charged to the account.[105] The notice must contain (1) the basic disclosures required for the original solicitation for the card and (2) how and when the cardholder may terminate credit availability under the account to avoid paying the renewal fee.[106]

8. *Effect of State Law Disclosure Requirements*

The provisions in the Truth in Lending Act and Regulation Z regarding (1) disclosure in credit and charge card applications and solicitations and (2) disclosure for renewal supersede any provision of the law of any state relating to the same subject.[107] Thus, any state law relating to these subjects, whether more or less protective than the federal rules, is completely preempted.

As to the initial disclosures, disclosures in the periodic statement, or disclosure upon changes being made, the federal rules supersede only inconsistent state law, and then only to the extent of the inconsistency. A state law is

---

104. 12 C.F.R. §226.9(c)(1). No notice is required when any of the following terms are changed: late payment charges, charges for documentary evidence, over-the-limit charges, a reduction of any component of a finance or other charge, suspension of future credit privileges, termination of an account or plan, changes resulting from an agreement involving a court proceeding, or from the consumer's default or delinquency (other than an increase in the periodic rate or other finance charge). 12 C.F.R. §226.9(c)(2); see Litwin v. American Express Co, 838 F. Supp. 855 (S.D.N.Y. 1993).

105. 12 C.F.R. §226.9(e)(1). The disclosures may be provided later than the time stated above, but no later than the mailing or the delivery of the periodic statement on which the renewal fee is initially charged to the account, if the card issuer also discloses at that time that:

1. The cardholder has 30 days from the time the periodic statement is mailed or delivered to avoid paying the fee or to have the fee recredited if the cardholder terminates credit availability under the account; and
2. The cardholder may use the card during the interim period without having to pay the fee. 12 C.F.R. §226.9(e)(2).

106. 12 C.F.R. §226.9(e)(1).
107. 15 U.S.C. §1610(e).

considered inconsistent if it requires the creditor to make disclosures or take actions that contradict the requirements of the Truth in Lending Act and Regulation Z. A state law is considered contradictory if, for instance, it requires the use of the same term to represent a different amount or a different meaning than the federal requirements or if it requires the use of a term different from the federal law to describe the same item.[108] For example, a state law that defines the term "finance charges" to include fees that the federal law excludes, or to exclude fees the federal law includes, would be preempted.[109] Laws that require more detailed disclosures, for example, are not preempted.[110]

As to billing error rules and regulation of credit reports, state law is preempted if the rules are different from the federal rules.[111] Thus, any state law that provides for different timing or different steps for the billing error resolution process is preempted.[112]

The Board of Governors of the Federal Reserve System (the Board) has the authority to exempt from the Truth in Lending Act's disclosure requirements any class of credit transaction within any state if the Board determines that the class of transaction is subject to state law requirements substantially similar to those imposed by the Truth in Lending Act and Regulation Z, and that there is adequate provision for enforcement.[113] The exemption does not extend to the civil liability provisions so as to assure that consumers have access to both Federal and state courts in seeking damages or civil penalties for violations.[114]

F. CIVIL LIABILITY

Both administrative enforcement and private civil remedies are available for violation of the rules found in the Truth in Lending Act and in Regulation

108. 12 C.F.R. §226.28(a).

109. 12 C.F.R. §226.28, Official Staff Commentary, comment 28(a)(2).

110. 12 C.F.R. §226.28, Official Staff Commentary, comment 28(a)(3).

111. 12 C.F.R. §226.28(a)(2)(i); 12 C.F.R. §226.28, Official Staff Commentary, comment 28(a)(5).

112. 12 C.F.R. §226.28, Official Staff Commentary, comment 28(a)(5).

113. 12 C.F.R. §226.29(a). Exemptions from the disclosure requirements have been granted to Maine, Connecticut, Massachusetts, Oklahoma, and Wyoming. 12 C.F.R. §226.29, Official Staff Commentary, comment 29(a).

114. 12 C.F.R. §226.29(b); 12 C.F.R. §226.29(b), Official Staff Commentary.

Z. The provisions of the Truth in Lending Act and Regulation Z may be enforced by whichever administrative agency has responsibility over the card issuer.[115] If, for example, the card issuer is a national bank, the Comptroller of the Currency would be the agency charged with enforcing the rules.[116]

There are many remedies that the agency can seek. For example, the agency may require the card issuer to recredit individual account balances in the event that the card issuer's calculations were not in accord with its disclosure of the annual percentage rate or finance charge.[117]

1. Civil Liability

When a card issuer fails to comply with a Truth in Lending rule pertaining to issuance of a credit card, disclosure,[118] or billing error resolution, the card issuer is liable to the injured cardholder for any actual damage sustained by such person as a result of the failure.[119]

The usual type of violation is in the disclosure requirements. The purpose of the disclosures required by the Truth in Lending Act and Regulation Z is to permit the cardholder to make an informed choice as to (1) whether to enter into a credit transaction and (2) from which lender to borrow. Because of this purpose, the standard for determining the actual damages to which a cardholder is entitled when the creditor has failed to comply with a disclosure requirement is whether the cardholder could have obtained credit on more favorable terms but for the alleged violation.[120] Considering that credit terms and rates are fairly uniform for similar credit risks, the cardholder will usually have a difficult time establishing any damages.[121] Even if the cardholder

115. 15 U.S.C. §1607.
116. 15 U.S.C. §1607(a)(1)(A).
117. 15 U.S.C. §1607(e)(1).
118. In connection with the required periodic disclosures, a creditor has liability for damages in addition to actual damages discussed above only for failing to properly calculate and disclose the applicable finance charge, for failure to provide the outstanding balance in the account at the end of the billing period, for failing to give the date or period within which payment must be made to avoid additional finance charges and for failing to give the address to be used for purpose of sending billing inquiries. 15 U.S.C. §1640(a).
119. 15 U.S.C. §1640(a)(1). Additional liability may also be imposed for failing to comply with disclosure requirements under state law for any term or item that the Board of Governors of the Federal Reserve System has determined to be substantially the same in meaning as the initial and periodic disclosures required under federal law. 15 U.S.C. §1640(a).
120. See Adiel v. Chase Fed. Sav. & Loan Assn., 630 F. Supp. 131, 133 (S.D. Fla. 1986), aff'd, 810 F.2d 1051 (11th Cir. 1987). See also Ralph J. Rohner, The Law of Truth in Lending S12-11 (1984, 1989 Cum. Supp.).
121. See Ralph J. Rohner, The Law of Truth in Lending 12-21–12-23 (1984).

proves that it could have obtained more favorable terms elsewhere, the actual monetary difference will usually be quite small.

If the violation is in some other requirement, actual damages may be easier to prove. For example, if the creditor improperly set off a credit card debt against the cardholder's deposit account, the cardholder may have substantial losses. The wrongful setoff may result in the cardholder being unable to make his car payment or pay his mortgage, resulting in the repossession of his car or foreclosure of his mortgage.

However, usually a cardholder's only damages will be the statutory damages to which he is entitled in addition to his actual damages. The injured cardholder can recover (in statutory damages) twice the finance charge in connection with the transaction in an amount no less than $100 nor greater than $1,000.[122]

The cardholder may also recover the costs of bringing the action, together with a reasonable attorney's fee.[123] The minimum damage award, together with the right to recover costs and attorney's fees, makes it possible for an injured cardholder to enforce compliance despite the absence of any significant amount of damages.

If the failure was in connection with (1) the required disclosures in credit and charge card applications and solicitations or (2) the required disclosures upon renewal, the card issuer is liable only to a cardholder who pays an annual membership or account maintenance fee or who uses the credit or charge card.[124]

What happens if the card issuer repeatedly fails to disclose the same required information in each periodic statement? For example, the card issuer may have failed to disclose the finance charge in the form of an annual percentage rate. Is the cardholder entitled to the $100 minimum recovery for each periodic statement? The answer is "no." Multiple failures to disclose required information to any cardholder result in only a single recovery under the Truth in Lending Act civil liability section.[125] However, if after the cardholder recovers, the card issuer again fails to disclose the information, the cardholder may recover for the new failure.

---

122. 15 U.S.C. §1640(a)(2)(A)(i).
123. 15 U.S.C. §1640(a)(3).
124. 15 U.S.C. §1640(a).
125. 15 U.S.C. §1640(g).

2.   *Class Actions*

The court in a class action has the discretion as to what recovery to allow in addition to actual damages.[126] However, there is no minimum recovery required as to each member of the class, as there is in the case of individual plaintiffs bringing separate actions. The rationale for imposing a minimum recovery in the case of individual plaintiffs is that, absent such a minimum, the amount of a cardholder's actual damages would usually be too small to justify the cardholder in bringing the action. The minimum gives the cardholder an incentive to bring the action. Because of the multitude of plaintiffs involved in a class action, no incentive is necessary.

The total amount allowed in addition to actual damages in any class action or series of class actions arising out of the same failure to comply by the same card issuer cannot be more than the lesser of (1) $500,000 or (2) 1 per centum of the net worth of the creditor. Because damages are intended to have a deterrent effect, they are limited by the card issuer's ability to pay them. Thus, if the card issuer had a net worth of $100 million, the maximum amount of damages, other than actual damages suffered by the members of the class, is $500,000. This is because 1 percent of the card issuer's net worth is $1 million, which is greater than $500,000. If, however, the card issuer has a net worth of $2 million, the maximum amount of damages, other than actual damages, is $20,000 ($2 million $\times.01 = \$20,000$).

To determine the amount of the award in any class action, the court must consider, among other relevant factors, the amount of any actual damages awarded, the frequency and persistence of failures of compliance by the creditor, the resources of the creditor, the number of persons adversely affected, and the extent to which the creditor's failure of compliance was intentional.[127]

3.   *Defenses to Liability*

One of the major purposes of allowing the cardholder to recover statutory damages in addition to the actual damages suffered by the failure is to give the cardholder an incentive to act as a private attorney general in forcing compliance by the card issuer. There is no reason to encourage a cardholder to pursue a claim for what would more than likely be a nominal amount of damages if the card issuer's violation was totally innocent. The cardholder's interest in

126. 15 U.S.C. §1640(a)(2)(B).
127. 15 U.S.C. §1640(a).

being compensated for his nominal loss is outweighed by the risk that the attorney's fee and statutory damages provisions will encourage some cardholders to bring actions solely to harass card issuers. To eliminate this possibility, a card issuer is not liable for violating the Truth in Lending Act if its violation was not intentional and resulted from a bona fide error notwithstanding the maintenance of procedures reasonably adapted to avoid any such error.[128] For example, a card issuer is not liable where the error is due to a clerical, calculation, computer malfunction and programming, or printing error. However, an error of legal judgment with respect to the card issuer's obligations is not a bona fide error.

For similar reasons, a card issuer is not liable under the Truth in Lending Act if within 60 days after discovering an error, and prior to the institution of an action by, or the receipt of written notice of the error from the cardholder, the creditor or assignee notifies the cardholder of the error.[129] Within the 60-day time period, the card issuer must also make whatever adjustments are necessary to assure that the person will not be required to pay an amount in excess of the charge actually disclosed, or the dollar equivalent of the annual percentage rate actually disclosed, whichever is lower.

128. 15 U.S.C. §1640(c).
129. 15 U.S.C. §1640(b).

Table of Cases

Table of Cases

Table of U.C.C. Section References

Table of U.C.C. Section References

3-113(a)	41 n.86; 45 n.110
3-113(b)	41 n.87
3-114	40 n.81; 254 n.104
3-115(a)	258 nn.124, 125
3-115(b)	33 n.56; 258 nn.126, 127; 259 nn.132-134
3-115(c)	259 n.136
3-115, Comment 1	258 nn.124-126; 259 n.132
3-115, Comment 2	259 n.133
3-115, Comment 3	258 n.127; 259 n.136
3-116	178
3-116(a)	183 n.119; 205 n.192; 206 nn.197, 198
3-116(b)	183 n.120; 205 n.194
3-116(c)	206 n.196
3-116, Comment 1	n.196
3-116, Comment 2	206 nn.197, 198
3-117	108 n.190; 128 nn.239-242; 129 n.247
3-117, Comment 1	128 n.242
3-118	378 n.17
3-118(a)	217 n.247
3-118(b)	217 nn.248, 249
3-118(c)	217 n.250
3-118(d)	221 n.262
3-118(g)	242 n.52
3-118, Comment 1	217 n.246
3-118, Comment 3	217 n.250; 221 n.262
3-121	404 n.105
3-201(a)	57 n.9
3-201(b)	59 nn.15, 16; 227 n.5
3-201, Comment 1	56 n.7; 57 n.11; 58 n.12
3-201, Comment 3	59 n.19
3-202(b)	113 n.206
3-203(a)	132 n.264
3-203(b)	132 n.263; 134 n.268; 136 n.272; 257 n.118
3-203(c)	134 n.266
3-203, Comment 1	132 nn.263, 264; 133 n.265
3-203, Comment 3	134 nn.266, 267
3-204(a)	59 n.16; 60 n.20; 61 n.26; 155 n.19
3-204(c)	60 n.20
3-204(d)	63 n.35; 64 nn.37, 38
3-204, Comment 3	63 n.35; 64 nn.36-38
3-205	62 n.28
3-205(a)	60 n.22
3-205(b)	60 n.23
3-205(c)	61 n.25
3-205(d)	60 n.21; 170 n.86
3-205, Comment 2	60 n.24; 61 n.25
3-205, Comment 3	60 n.21
3-206(a)	60 n.21; 290 n.234
3-206(c)	289 n.230
3-206(c)(1)	293 nn.245, 246
3-206(c)(2)	292 n.243
3-206(c)(4)	292 nn.239, 242
3-206(d)	289 n.231; 293 n.248
3-206(e)	60 n.21; 289 n.232; 292 nn.240, 244; 293 n.246
3-206(f)	290 n.235
3-206, Comment 3	292 nn.239, 242, 243; 293 n.245
3-206, Comment 4	294 nn.249, 253
3-206, Comment 5	290 n.235
3-206, Comment 6(1989)	293 n.247
3-207	136 n.273; 137 nn.274, 275; 138 n.276
3-207, Comment 136	n.273; 138 n.276
3-207, Comment, Case #1	137 n.275
3-208(e), Comment 6, Case #6	75 n.86
3-301	150 n.2; 214 n.230
3-301, Comment	214 n.231
3-302	73 n.77; 141 n.289
3-302(a)	54 n.3; 96
3-302(a)(1)	90 n.117
3-302(a)(2)	90 n.119
3-302(a)(2)(i)	54 n.3
3-302(a)(2)(ii)	54 n.3
3-302(a)(2)(iii)	90 n.118
3-302(a)(2)(vi)	84 n.104

3-302(a)(3)	90 n.121
3-302(b)	87 n.110; 96 n.141
3-302(c)	97 n.145
3-302(c)(ii)	98 n.146; 135 n.270
3-302(c)(iii)	97 n.144
3-302(d)	73 n.73; 74 n.79
3-302(e)	75 nn.85, 87
3-302(f)	84 n.105
3-302, Comment 3	96 nn.141, 142
3-302, Comment 5	97 nn.143-145; 98 n.146; 99 nn.147, 149
3-303	78; 184 n.123
3-303(a)(1)	72 nn.75, 76
3-303(a)(2)	72 n.75; 74 n.81; 75 nn.83, 84
3-303(a)(3)	72 n.75; 76 n.88; 109 n.196; 110 n.197
3-303(a)(4)	72 n.75; 77 n.91
3-303(a)(5)	72 n.75; 77 n.91
3-303(b)	110 n.198
3-303, Comment 1	110 n.198
3-303, Comment 2	74 n.78
3-303, Comment 3	74 n.81; 75 nn.82-84
3-303, Comment 4	76 n.89; 109 n.196
3-303, Comment 5	77 n.92
3-303, Comment 6	74 n.80
3-303, Comment 6, Case #5	74 n.79
3-304(a)(1)	90 nn.119, 120
3-304(b)(1)	92 n.123
3-304(b)(2)	92 n.124
3-304(b)(3)	92 n.122
3-304(c)	92 n.125
3-304, Comment 1	90 n.121
3-304, Comment 2	92 nn.123, 125
3-305	178; 217
3-305(a)	84; 391 n.68
3-305(a)(1)	186 n.127
3-305(a)(1)(i)	105 n.175
3-305(a)(1)(ii)	106 n.177
3-305(a)(1)(iii)	107 nn.179, 181
3-305(a)(1)(iv)	108 n.183
3-305(a)(2)	58 n.13; 108 nn.186, 187; 109 nn.194,
	195; 131 n.254
3-305(a)(3)	112 nn.200, 202; 185 n.125
3-305(b)	53 n.1; 103 n.166; 105 n.173; 108 nn.185, 188; 112 n.201; 134 n.269; 136 n.271; 176 n.100; 186 n.129; 217 n.245; 391 nn.68, 69
3-305(c)	113 n.204; 115 n.212
3-305(d)	184 n.124; 185 n.126; 188 n.139
3-305, Comment 1	105 nn.174-176; 106 n.178; 107 nn.179-182; 108 nn.183, 184
3-305, Comment 2	104 n.172; 108 nn.187-190; 109 nn.191-193
3-305, Comment 3	103 n.171; 112 nn.202, 203
3-305, Comment 4	113 n.204; 115 n.212
3-306	56 n.6; 84; 113 nn.205, 207; 120 n.224; 134 n.269; 141 n.290; 294 n.251
3-306(a)	346 n.169
3-306(b)	346 n.169
3-306(d)(2)	294 n.252
3-306, Comment	114 n.208; 115 n.211
3-307(a)(1)	93 n.128
3-307(a)(2)	93 n.127
3-307(b)(1)	94 n.132
3-307(b)(2)	94 n.133; 95 n.137; 294 n.250
3-307(b)(2)(i)	95 n.135
3-307(b)(3)	95 n.140
3-307(b)(4)	95 n.136
3-307(b)(i)	93 n.130
3-307(b)(ii)	93 n.130
3-307(b)(iii)	93 n.126
3-307, Comment 2	93 nn.129-131; 94 n.134
3-307, Comment 3	95 n.135

Table of U.C.C. Section References

Table of U.C.C. Section References

Table of U.C.C. Section References

Index

Index

Index

Index